T0291164

Is the Bangladesh Paradox Sustainable?

Bangladesh is widely seen as a 'paradox'. Over the last quarter of a century, it has maintained economic growth and has outperformed many countries on social indicators while scoring very low on the quality of governance. Moreover, its economic progress does not seem to indicate significant improvement in comparative institutional indicators. *Is the Bangladesh Paradox Sustainable?* thus examines whether such a paradoxical combination can be sustained in the long run if growth continues with no improvement in the quality of institutions. It argues that although Bangladesh has become the second largest world exporter in the garments, export diversification is needed, both within and outside the garment sector, if it is to maintain its development pace. Based on a thorough account of the country's economic, social, and political development, this companion volume analyses Bangladesh's critical institutional issues in relation with development-sensitive areas such as the garment sector, banking, taxation, land management, the judiciary, and education. This title is also available as Open Access on Cambridge Core.

Selim Raihan is Professor at the Department of Economics, University of Dhaka, Bangladesh, and the Executive Director of the South Asian Network on Economic Modeling (SANEM). He is Honorary Senior Research Fellow at the University of Manchester, UK, and Member of the Board of Directors, Global Development Network. His publications include more than 100 articles and 10 books.

François Bourguignon is Emeritus Professor of Economics, the Paris School of Economics and EHESS, Paris. He is Former Chief Economist and Senior Vice President of the World Bank and the Co-founder of the European Development Network. His awards include Dan David Prize and CNRS silver medal.

Umar Salam is Principal Economist, Oxford Policy Management, and a Scientific Committee Member of the Economic Development and Institutions (EDI) Programme.

The Institutional Diagnostic Project

A suite of case-study monographs emerging from a large research program on the role of institutions in the economics, and the political economy of development in low-income countries, supported by a synthesis volume of the original case studies. This program was funded by the United Kingdom's Foreign and Commonwealth Development Office during a period of six years, during which program researchers had regular interactions with its staff, either directly or through Oxford Policy Management (the lead managing organisation).

Is the Bangladesh Paradox Sustainable?

The Institutional Diagnostic Project

Edited by

SELIM RAIHAN
University of Dhaka and SANEM

FRANÇOIS BOURGUIGNON
Paris School of Economics and EHESS, Paris

UMAR SALAM
Oxford Policy Management

CAMBRIDGE
UNIVERSITY PRESS

Shaftesbury Road, Cambridge CB2 8EA, United Kingdom

One Liberty Plaza, 20th Floor, New York, NY 10006, USA

477 Williamstown Road, Port Melbourne, VIC 3207, Australia

314–321, 3rd Floor, Plot 3, Splendor Forum, Jasola District Centre, New Delhi – 110025, India

103 Penang Road, #05–06/07, Visioncrest Commercial, Singapore 238467

Cambridge University Press is part of Cambridge University Press & Assessment, a department of the University of Cambridge.

We share the University's mission to contribute to society through the pursuit of education, learning and research at the highest international levels of excellence.

www.cambridge.org
Information on this title: www.cambridge.org/9781009284691

DOI: 10.1017/9781009284677

First published 2023

A catalogue record for this publication is available from the British Library

A Cataloging-in-Publication data record for this book is available from the Library of Congress

ISBN 978-1-009-28469-1 Hardback

Contents

Figures

Tables

Boxes

Notes on Contributors

M. Abu Eusuf is holding the position of Professor & Former Chair in the Department of Development Studies at the University of Dhaka. He is the Director of 'Centre on Budget and Policy' at the University of Dhaka. He is also the Executive Director of a national think-tank Research and Policy Integration for Development (RAPID). He is an economist by training. He was awarded PhD in Development Policy and Management (Development Economics Cluster) from the University of Manchester as a Commonwealth Scholar. He also completed his MA in Development Studies at the Institute of Social Studies (ISS), Netherlands, under the UN fellowship program.

Md. Jahid Ebn Jalal is a senior research associate at South Asian Network on Economic Modeling (SANEM). As part of a study project supported by The Belt & Road Initiative and Zhongnan University of Economics and Law (ZUEL), he is employed as 'Research Fellow' at the Bureau of Socioeconomic Research & Training. At ZUEL, he is presently pursuing his PhD in World Economy. He formerly held positions as a 'MEL Officer' for WaterAid. In addition to earning his MSc in Economics from Indira Gandhi Institute of Development Research, he also earned his BSc and MS in Agricultural Economics from Bangladesh Agricultural University.

Sadiq Ahmed is Vice Chairman of the Policy Research Institute of Bangladesh. He did his MSc from London School of Economics and PhD from Boston University. He held several key positions at the World Bank: Country Economist, Egypt, the Middle East and North Africa Region; Principal Economist, Indonesia, PNG and Pacific Islands, East Asia and Pacific Region; Lead Economist, Pakistan, Sri Lanka and Afghanistan; Country Director, Pakistan and Afghanistan Program; Chief Economist, South Asia Region; Sector Director, Poverty Reduction and Economic Management, Finance and Private Sector, South Asia Region; and Senior Manager,

Regional Programs, South Asia Region. He published several books and 30 plus articles in national and international journals, as well as in World Bank publications.

Thorsten Beck is Director of the Florence School of Banking and Finance and Professor at the European University Institute. He is a research fellow of the Centre for Economic Policy Research (CEPR) and the CESifo. Earlier, he was professor at Bayes Business School (formerly Cass) in London between and professor and the founding chair of the European Banking Center at Tilburg University. Previously, he worked for the World Bank, the European Central Bank, the Bank of England, the BIS, the IMF, the Inter-American Development Bank, the Asian Development Bank, the European Commission, and the German Development Corporation. He is also Co-editor of the Journal of Banking and Finance and member of the Advisory Scientific Committee of the European Systemic Risk Board.

Sayema Haque Bidisha is Professor at the Department of Economics, University of Dhaka, Bangladesh, and Research Director of the South Asian Network on Economic Modeling (SANEM). She obtained PhD from the University of Nottingham. Her broad areas of research are labour economics and development economics. She worked on several research projects on labour market, poverty and vulnerability, skill and education, youth population, gender and women empowerment, financial inclusion, migration and remittance, credit and food security, child marriage, etc. She also worked closely with the Government of Bangladesh in preparing various policy documents, for example Sixth Five Year Plan and Perspective Plan 2041 of Bangladesh. She published several articles/book chapters in peer-reviewed international publications.

François Bourguignon is Director of Studies at the Ecole des Hautes Etudes en Sciences Sociales (EHESS) and Emeritus Professor at the Paris School of Economics, where he previously held the position of director. From 2003 to 2007, he was Chief Economist and Vice President of the World Bank. He was also Chairman of the Institutional Diagnostic Project. He has vast experience in advising governments and international organisations. In addition, he is the author/editor of numerous books and articles in international economic journals: his work, theoretical and empirical, focuses mainly on the distribution and redistribution of income in developing and developed countries. During his career, he has received several scientific distinctions, such as the Dan David Prize in 2016.

Rafiqua Ferdousi is a PhD student at the UBC Political Science Department. She is passionate about using causal inference and insights to drive peace, justice, and social progress. She has published extensively in leading platforms. She has also been the recipient of the UBC President's Academic Excellence and the Erasmus Mundus Awards. With her focus located at the intersection of Comparative Politics and International Relations, her research interest includes Political Institutions, Political Economy, Politics of Development, Culture and Identity, Behavioural Economics, and Quantitative and Multi-method Design.

Bazlul Haque Khondker is former Professor at the Department of Economics, University of Dhaka and Chairman of the South Asian Network on Economic Modeling (SANEM). He holds a PhD degree in Economics from the University of Warwick, England. His areas of expertise include analysis of poverty and social protection; micro-, meso-, and macrodata analyses for impact assessment and policy formulation; and assessing the trends in inter-generation equity using the National Transfer Account (NTA) methodology. He has also formulated the technical framework for the Five-Year Plans for Bangladesh. He has produced several reports and published articles, books on social issues including poverty and social protection, regional disparity, and economic and welfare impacts of public policy reforms.

Mirza M. Hassan is a political economist and Head of the Governance and Politics Cluster of BIGD, BRAC University. His research largely focuses on political development, state–business relations, urban governance and local governance, justice sector and human rights, and related issues in South Asia, Pacific region, and North Africa. He has more than 20 years of consulting experience on these issues for several national and international agencies. He is well versed in conducting political economy analysis, institutional and stakeholder analysis, and using mixed methods. He completed his PhD in Development Studies from the University of London, UK, and MA from the Massachusetts Institute of Technology (MIT), Cambridge, USA.

Christopher Heady is Emeritus Professor of Economics at the University of Kent. He obtained his PhD at Yale University. He held academic positions at Yale, University College London, University of Bath, the Universities of Aarhus (Denmark), Queens (Canada), and Warwick. In June 2000, he joined the OECD and was Head of its Tax Policy and Statistics division until March 2009. He also worked for the IMF, the World Bank, the National Radiological Protection Board, the Asian Development Bank, the Department for International Development, and PricewaterhouseCoopers. His research interests are all related to the microeconomic analysis of public policy issues in both developed and developing countries, using both theoretical and empirical analysis.

Zubayer Hossen holds degrees in Economics from the University of Dhaka. His experiences as a professional are in the field of research and policy advocacy. Thus far, he has carried out analytical research on diverse issues including poverty, inequality, climate change, ocean economy, employment, sectoral productivity, RMG, governance, unpaid domestic works, social protection, innovative financing solutions for SDGs, green growth, etc. He is currently working as an economist at UNDP Bangladesh. Before joining UNDP, he worked for South Asian Network on Economic Modeling (SANEM) and Nielsen Company (Bangladesh) Ltd., where he received training in economic and market research.

Elizabeth M. King is Non-resident Senior Fellow at the Brookings Institution, Managing Editor of the Journal of Development Effectiveness, and Adjunct Professor at Georgetown University School of Foreign Service. She serves on the boards of the International Initiative for Impact Evaluation (3ie), Room to Read, and Education Commission-Asia; is technical adviser to Echidna Giving and the World Bank's Africa Gender Innovation Lab, and a judge of the Yidan Prize Foundation. She was the World Bank's global director for policy and strategic issues in education and acting vice president for human development sectors. She has published on human capital, labour markets, and gender. She received her PhD in Economics from Yale University.

Towhid I. Mahmood is a PhD candidate in the Department of Agricultural and Applied Economics in the Gordon W. Davis College of Agricultural Sciences & Natural Resources at Texas Tech University. Towhid earned his BSS in Economics from University of Dhaka in Bangladesh and a Masters in Applied Economics from Western Kentucky University. Prior to joining Texas Tech University, he served as a research economist on issues in Bangladesh at South Asian Network on Economic Modeling (SANEM). His research interests include economic development, new institutional thought, and corruption.

Kazi Maruful Islam is Professor at the Department of Development Studies, University of Dhaka, Bangladesh. Earlier, he served as faculty member of the Department of Public Administration, University of Rajshahi. He currently teaches Politics of Development, Qualitative Research Methodology, Public Policy Analysis, and Civil Society and Development. He has Masters of Philosophy from the University of Bergen, Norway, and Doctorate from the University of Heidelberg, Germany. With thematic interest in Local Governance, Urban Governance, and Climate Change Governance, he has worked as a governance specialist for various research projects within and outside Bangladesh.

Jaime de Melo joined the faculty of the University of Geneva in 1993 and emeritus since 2013. He is CEPR fellow and Senior Fellow at FERDI (Fondation pour les études et recherches dans le développement international). He was an economist in the World Bank research department (1980–2013), where he served as Division Chief and Manager (1990–2013). He served on editorial boards and was Editor of the World Bank Economic Review, 2005–2010. He has advised, inter alia, the Africa Development Bank, the European Commission, the IMF, USAID, and the Swiss government.

Dilip Mookherjee studied economics at Presidency College, Calcutta, and Delhi School of Economics and received his PhD in 1982 from London School of Economics. He taught at Stanford University from 1982 to 1989 and at Indian Statistical Institute in New Delhi from 1989 till 1995. Since 1995, he has been teaching at Boston University in the Department of Economics, besides directing the Institute for Economic Development since 1998. His main research interests are development, inequality, organisations, and political economy. He is a fellow of the Econometric Society and a fellow/ affiliate of NBER, CEPR, and BREAD.

Jean-Philippe Platteau is Co-director of the Institutional Diagnostic Project. He is Emeritus Professor at the University of Namur (Belgium) and active member of the Center for Research in Development Economics (CRED). Jean-Philippe Platteau is the author of numerous journal articles and several books. Most of his work has been devoted to the study of the role of institutions in economic development and the processes of institutional change. He has always paid particular attention to informal institutions such as social norms, informal markets, and the rules of village societies, leading him to take an interest in the influence of non-economic factors and in problems located at the frontier of economics and other social sciences. His latest work focuses more specifically on the role of culture and religion.

Selim Raihan is Professor at the Department of Economics, University of Dhaka, Bangladesh, and the Executive Director of the South Asian Network on Economic Modeling (SANEM). He received his PhD from the University of Manchester, UK. He is Honorary Senior Research Fellow at the University of Manchester, UK, and Member of the Board of Directors, Global Development Network. His publications include more than 100 articles and 10 books. He is in the editorial boards of the Indian Journal of Labour Economics, Journal of Asian Economic Integration, International Studies, and Journal of South Asian Development. He possesses vast expertise in empirical research on international trade, economic growth, poverty, labour market, macroeconomic policies, political economy, and climate change issues. He has worked for several national and international organisations.

Umar Salam is Principal Economist at Oxford Policy Management, based in Oxford, UK. Within the Economic Development and Institutions (EDI) programme, he served as a member of the Scientific Committee for the development of the Institutional Diagnostic. His research interests include economic growth, institutional economics, and science and technology policy in developing countries. He studied at the Universities of Oxford, where he received a DPhil in development economics, and Cambridge, where he was a researcher in algebraic geometry and string theory.

Eshrat Sharmin is a senior research associate at South Asian Network on Economic Modeling (SANEM). She has been working as a researcher in SANEM for five years. She has completed her master's in Economics from Jahangirnagar University. Her area of research interest includes inequality, political economy, development economics, and labour economics, among others.

Preface

The vital importance of institutions for economic development is widely acknowledged in both the theoretical and empirical literature. Yet, the precise nature of the relationship between the two is unclear: do 'good' institutions produce development, or does development lead to 'good' institutions? The Economic Development and Institutions (EDI) research programme, funded by the UK Foreign, Commonwealth, Development Office (FCDO), formerly Department for International Development (DFID), aims to investigate that relationship and to develop an 'institutional diagnostic' framework that can help us understand better the nature of institutional impediments to development, and identify ways of attenuating them. In this study under the EDI research programme, the South Asian Network on Economic Modeling (SANEM), a Dhaka-based research organisation and think-tank, in collaboration with Oxford Policy Management, has carried out such a diagnostic of Bangladesh institutions, which aims to identify weak institutional areas that restrict development and suggest appropriate directions for reform.

Bangladesh's economic growth and development performance over the past five decades have been impressive. With the poor quality of institutions, such performance has often been termed a 'development surprise' or the 'Bangladesh paradox'. But is it actually a 'surprise' or a 'paradox'? This Bangladesh institutional diagnostic provides an elaborated and convincing answer to this question by analysing the characteristics of the country's growth and development processes, exploring the key institutional features in these processes, unearthing major institutional weaknesses, and proposing associated reforms for future sustained and inclusive development.

The diagnostic of institutions in Bangladesh suggests that the secret to understanding the importance of critical institutional reforms for growth and development is to consider the factors that connect economic and social outcomes to structural characteristics of the economy and the underlying political economy dynamics. The diagnostic proceeds in several stages. After a thorough study of Bangladesh's development challenges, along with qualitative research into the opinions of the main stakeholders, a number of critical areas were identified: the ready-made garments sector and, most importantly, the lack of progress in export diversification; regulation of the banking sector and the problem of non-performing loans; the tax system and the exceedingly low capacity for revenue mobilisation; primary education as an important component of public expenditure but also as a key part of human capital accumulation; the management of land issues, in particular, the administration of special economic zones; and the judiciary, especially its limited capacity to handle cases of land-grabbing. Each of these areas is the subject of a 'deep-dive' thematic analysis undertaken by Bangladeshi academics, along with discussions of these analyses by international experts. In each of these areas, interrelated proximate causes for identified institutional weaknesses were sought for and their deep factors were scrutinised. The concluding 'synthesis' chapter combines these findings to examine the causal connections that determine how institutions work in Bangladesh, and how they impact development, and, finally, what this means for reform.

Acknowledgements

We wish to acknowledge the precious help the editors and authors of this study received from many friends and colleagues. In the first place, we would like to thank Umar Salam, who has chiefly managed this project at Oxford Policy Management. We are also deeply grateful to the thematic study discussants, Thorsten Beck, Jaime de Melo, Chris Heady, Beth King, Dilip Mookherjee, and Jean-Philippe Platteau, for the crucial role they have played in providing critical remarks and advice. Deep thanks also go to Jean-Philippe Platteau, co-research directors of the EDI research programme, and Ravi Kanbur, member of the scientific committee of the institutional diagnostic research activity, for most valuable advice and comments. Their constant challenging of the arguments and conclusions of the study pushed the authors to produce higher-quality research. We also wish to thank the adviser of the project, Wahiduddin Mahmud, whose guardianship and advisory role on this work ensured it was of a high quality, informed by a diverse set of viewpoints, and situated in the reality of the Bangladeshi context.

We are also grateful to the enumerators and supervisors who helped during the institutional survey. We must acknowledge the decision makers (from the private and public sectors, representatives from international organisations and donors in Bangladesh, as well as from the civil society) who participated in the institutional survey in 2018/2019 and also in the policy engagement workshop in September 2018.

We also acknowledge the EDI team members at Oxford Policy Management, who contributed valuable insights and provided a management assistance to the process, including Stevan Lee, Mark Henstridge, Benjamin Klooss, Rachel Smith-Phiri, and Umar Salam. We also acknowledge Ashibur Rahman and Shoaib Ahmed from SANEM, for their coordination support in relation to the organisation of key events in Dhaka. We also wish to thank the academics and government officials who participated in the workshops and provided insights that helped us to understand a number of issues related to the development challenges in Bangladesh.

This project was funded with UK aid from the UK Government.

Institutional Diagnostic Project

Preamble

François Bourguignon and Jean-Philippe Platteau

Institutions matter for growth and inclusive development. But despite increasing awareness of the importance of institutions on economic outcomes, there is little evidence on how positive institutional change can be achieved. The Economic Development and Institutions – EDI – research programme aims to fill this knowledge gap by working with some of the finest economic thinkers and social scientists across the globe.

The programme was launched in 2015 and concluded in 2022. It is made up of four parallel research activities: path-finding papers, institutional diagnostic, coordinated randomised control trials (RCTs), and case studies. The programme is funded by the UK Foreign and Commonwealth Development Office (FCDO). For more information, see http://edi.opml.co.uk.

This study of Bangladesh is one of four case studies in a research project whose final aim is to devise a methodology that would establish an 'institutional diagnostic' of economic development in a particular country. The objective of such a diagnostic is to identify the institutional factors that may slow down development or reduce its inclusiveness or sustainability, the reforms likely to overcome these weaknesses, but also the political economy that may prevent or facilitate such reforms. These diagnostics must thus rely on a thorough review of economic development and institutional features of countries under analysis, which is the content of this volume on Bangladesh. As a preamble, the following pages offer a general description of the whole diagnostic project.

I 'INSTITUTIONS MATTER'

'Institutions matter' became a motto among international development agencies in the late 1990s, when it became clear that structural adjustment policies themselves based upon the so-called 'Washington Consensus' and their emphasis on markets were not delivering the growth and development that was expected. The slogan sounded a note of disappointment for those liberalist reformers, sometimes jokingly called the 'marketeers', who promoted the reliance on market mechanisms and the pre-eminence of private actors in order for developing countries to get out of the crises of the 1980s and restore long-run growth. Giving more space to the market was probably justified from a theoretical point of view. Practically, however, it was another story. What the 'marketeers' had not fully realised was that a well-functioning market economy requires regulating institutions, public goods, and non-market services which most often were missing or deficient in the economies being considered. Under these conditions, liberalising, privatising, and deregulating might in effect prove counterproductive without concomitant institutional changes.

Nowadays, the 'institutions matter' slogan appears as a fundamental truth about development, and it is indeed widely shared by the development community, including international organisations. Equally obvious to all is the complementarity between the market and the state: the economic efficiency expected from the former requires some intervention by the latter through adequate policies, the provision of public services, and, more fundamentally, institutions able to impose rules constraining the activity of various economic actors, whether public and private. Practically, however, the institutions of a country are the outcome of history and specific events or circumstances. Therefore, they are not necessarily well adapted to the current economic context and to the modern development challenge. This raises the issue as to how existing institutions can be reformed.

That 'institutions matter' has also long been evident for those academic economists and political scientists who kept stressing that development is the outcome of the joint and interactive evolution of the economy and its institutional setup, with the latter encompassing not only state and political agencies but also cultural and social norms. As a matter of fact, the study of the role of institutions has a long history in the development economics literature, from the very fathers of the discipline in the post-WWII years and their emphasis on development as a structural and cultural transformation, as for instance in the writings of Peter Bauer, Albert Hirschman, Arthur Lewis, or Hla Myint, to the New Institutional Economics as applied to development issues, in particular with the work of Douglass North, to the Institutional Political Economy approach put forward nowadays by social scientists like Mushtaq Khan, and to the more formalised school of Political Economics pioneered by Daron Acemoglu and James Robinson.

II HOW INSTITUTIONS MATTER IN DEVELOPMENT POLICY TODAY: THE ROLE OF 'GOVERNANCE'

Faced with the disappointing performances of the so-called 'Washington Consensus', which governed the market-oriented 'structural adjustment' policies put to work in developing countries at the time of the macroeconomic crisis of the early 1980s, international organisations and bilateral development agencies switched to what was called the 'post-Washington consensus'. This extended set of principles were seen as a way of compensating for the neglect of institutional considerations in the original set of policies. Market-oriented reforms had thus to be accompanied by other reforms, including the regulation of various sectors, making government more efficient, and improving human capital formation. Most importantly, however, emphasis was put on good governance as a necessary adjuvant to market-led development, especially in its capacity to protect property rights and guarantee contract enforcement. With time, governance then became a key criterion among donors for allocating aid across low-income countries and monitor its use.

It is fair to say that, practically, governance is defined and evaluated in a rather ad hoc way, based on some expert opinion, firm surveys, and some simple economic parameters like the rate of inflation or the size of budget deficit. The relationship with the actual nature and quality of institutions is thus very indirect. This still seems the case today, even though the recent World Development Report by the World Bank, entitled 'Governance and the Law', intends to go deeper by showing how governance, or policymaking in general including institutional reforms, depends on the functioning of institutions, the role of stakeholders and their relative political power. Practically, however, there remains something rather mechanical and schematic in the way institutions are represented in this report, which is actually more about effective policymaking than on the diagnosis of institutional weaknesses and possible avenues for reform.

If there is no doubt that institutions matter for development, the crucial issue is to know how they matter. After all, impressive economic development achievements have been observed despite clear failures in particular institutional areas. In other words, not all dimensions of governance may be relevant at a given point of time in a given country. Likewise, institutional dimensions that are not included in governance criteria may play a decisive role.

There is admittedly limited knowledge about how institutions affect development, how they form, and how they can be reformed in specific contexts. Despite intensive and increasing efforts over the last few decades, the challenge remains daunting. The difficulty comes from the tight imbrication of the way the quality of existing institutions affects the development process, including policies, the political economy context which conditions possible institutional reforms, and the influence that the pace and structure of development exerts, directly or indirectly, on the dynamics of institutions.

III SEARCHING FOR EVIDENCE ON THE RELATIONSHIP
BETWEEN THE QUALITY OF INSTITUTIONS
AND DEVELOPMENT

Three approaches have been followed to help in the identification of development-hindering or promoting institutional features, and of their evolution over time, whether autonomously or through discretionary reforms. All three approaches have their own drawbacks.

The first approach consists of historical case studies. These are in-depth studies of successful, or unsuccessful, development experiences, and their causes and processes as they unfolded in the historical past or in the contemporary world. The formation and success of the Maghribi trading networks in the eleventh-century Mediterranean basin, the effects of the Glorious Revolution in Britain, the enactment of effective land reforms in Korea and Taiwan after the demise of the Japanese colonial rule, and the implementation of the Household Responsibility System in rural China are all examples of institutional changes that led to vigorous development, whether state-led or resulting from decentralised initiatives triggered off by external factors. On the other hand, violent fights for the appropriation of natural resource rents in several post-independence African states illustrate the opposite course of blocked development under essentially predatory states. Studying such events is of utmost interest insofar as they highlight rather precise mechanisms susceptible of governing the transformation of institutions, often under the pressure of economic and other circumstances, sometimes prompting sometimes hampering development. In their best-selling book *Why Nations Fail*, for instance, Acemoglu and Robinson (2012) masterfully show the role of institutions in several historical and contemporaneous experiences of sustained or failed development. In particular, they stress the critical role of inclusive institutions as compared with predatory ones, and most importantly the role of favourable political conditions in changing institutions and sparking off development. The most serious problem with this approach, however, is that the experiences thoroughly analysed in the history-based empirical literature are rarely transferable in time or in space and are not necessarily relevant for developing countries today.

Under the second approach are cross-country studies pertaining to the contemporaneous era. It relies on indicators that describe the strength of a particular set of institutions or a specific aspect of governance in a country, for example protection of property rights, nature of legal regimes, extent of democracy, strength and type of controls on the executive, extent of corruption etc., the issue being whether there is a correlation between these indicators and GDP growth or other development outcomes. These institutional and governance indicators are generally based on the opinion of experts in various areas evaluating, on a comparative basis, countries on which they have specialised knowledge. They are thus based on largely subjective grounds and lack the precision needed for statistical analysis. If correlation with development outcomes is sometimes significant and often fit intuition, the use that can be made of them is problematic as they essentially refer, by construction, to an abstract 'average country' and may be of little use when focusing on a particular country. Most importantly, they say nothing about causality and still less about the policy instruments that could improve institutions under consideration. Corruption is generally found to be bad for development, but in what direction does the causality go? Is it true in all countries and all circumstances? What about the cases where corruption 'greases the wheels' and reintroduces economic efficiency in the presence of too stringent administrative constraints? And, if it is to be curbed, what kind of reform is likely to work?

Cross-country studies are a useful approach provided that it is considered as essentially exploratory. They need to be complemented by more country-specific analyses that can detect causal relationships, shed light on dynamic processes at play in key sectors of the economy as well as on their interactions with institutions and the political arena, and inform on potential ways of conducting reforms.

The third approach exploits the fact that some sorts of institutional weaknesses or strengths are readily observable, such as the delivery of public services like education or health care. For instance, the absenteeism of teachers in public schools reveals a breach of contract between civil servants and their employers and/or a monitoring failure by supervisors. There are ways of incentivising teachers so that they show up in school, and numerous experimentations, rigorously evaluated through randomised control trial (RCT) techniques in various community settings, have successfully explored the impact of such schemes in various countries over the last two decades or more. Identification of similar institutional weaknesses at the micro level and experimentation of ways to remedy them have sprouted up in the recent past, so much so that the field has become the dominant subject among researchers in development economics. Inspired by the RCT methodology and its concern with causality, a new economic approach to history has also blossomed in the last decades. This literature exploits so-called 'natural experiments' and intends to assess the impact of institutional changes that exogenously emerged in particular geographic areas in the past, the outcomes of which can still be observed and compared to otherwise similar neighbouring regions today. These outcomes can be of an economic, social, or political nature.

A major limitation of the third approach is that it generally addresses simple cases that are suitable for experimentation. Identifying more macro-level institutional failures and testing appropriate remedies through the RCT method is much less easy, if not impossible. In addition, successful testing of reforms susceptible of correcting well-identified micro-level institutional failures does not mean that the political will exists, or an effective coalition of interest groups can be formed, to fully correct the detected inefficiency. Thus, in the above example of teachers' absenteeism, there is no guarantee that the state will systematically implement the incentive scheme whose impact has been shown to be the best way to improve school performances. The institutional weakness may thus not be so much in the breach of contract between teachers and their public employer as in the incapacity of the latter to design and implement the right policy. As this example shows, an in-depth understanding of macro-political factors is needed to reach a proper assessment of the feasibility of reforms and the conditions required for their successful implementation.

The above empirical approaches leave a gap between an essentially macro-view of the relationship between institutions and development, whether it consists of stylised historical facts or cross-country correlations between GDP growth and governance or institutional indicators, on the one hand, and a micro-perspective on institutional dysfunction (e.g. the observation of absenteeism of civil servants or corrupt tax inspectors) and possible remedies, on the other hand. Also note that, in most cases, these approaches permit to identify relationships between institutional factor and development outcomes but not the mechanisms responsible for them. In economic modelling parlance, they give 'reduced form' rather than 'structural' evidence about the institution–development nexus. Filling this twofold gap requires a meso-approach based, as much as possible, on structural analysis conducted at intermediate levels of the social and economic structure of a country, including economic or social sectors as well as key groups of actors and official decision-making or monitoring entities.

Awareness of these drawbacks of the standard analysis of the relationship between institutions and development and, therefore, of the need for a more structural, sectoral, and political economy approach to that relationship has motivated the exploratory research undertaken within the present Institutional Diagnostic Project.

IV INSTITUTIONAL DIAGNOSTIC AS A NEW APPROACH TO INSTITUTIONS AND DEVELOPMENT

The Institutional Diagnostic Project research programme aims at developing a methodology or, better said, a framework that allows the identification of major institutional weaknesses or dysfunctions that block or slow down economic growth and structural transformation, and/or make them non-inclusive and non-sustainable, in a given country at a given stage of its development process. The diagnostic is also intended to formulate a reform programme and point to the political stakes involved in its implementation. In other words, it should contribute simultaneously to a better understanding of the specific relationship between institutions and development in the country under consideration, to a more complete stocktaking of policies and reforms likely to improve the development context, and to characterising the political barriers that might obstruct these reforms. It is a country-centred approach that differs from historical case studies, in the sense that the focus is not on a particular event, circumstance, or episode in a country but on the overall functioning of its economy and society. It also goes beyond the mere use of governance or institutional indicators that appear much too rough when dealing with a specific economy. On the other hand, it makes use of micro-economic evidence on institutional weaknesses and dysfunction in a country and, when available, on whatever lesson can be learned from experimental works that may have been conducted in the area concerned. It thus makes use of the various methodological approaches to the study of the institution–development relationship but goes beyond them by embedding them in essentially a structural approach adapted to the particulars of a country.

A priori, it would seem that institutional diagnostics should resemble the 'growth diagnostics' approach developed by Hausmann, Rodrik, and Velasco some 15 years ago to identify the binding economic constraints to economic growth. The resemblance can only be semantic, however. Practically, if the objective is similar, the difference is huge. Most fundamentally, the growth diagnostics approach relies explicitly on a full theoretical model of economic growth based on the accumulation of means of production and innovation in the private sector, the availability of infrastructure, financial facilities, the control of risk through appropriate insurance mechanisms, and the development of human capital. Constraints in one of these dimensions should logically translate into a high relative (so called) 'shadow' price paid for that resource or that facility, that is the actual cost paid by the user of that resource which may differ from its posted price. The observation of those prices should then allow the analyst to identify the constraints most likely to be binding. No such model is available, even implicitly, in the case of the relationship between institutions and development: there is no shadow price easily observable for the availability of a fair and efficient judiciary, an uncorrupted civil service, an effective regulatory agency, or a transparent budget. Another, more heuristic approach needed to be developed.

In the exploratory attempt of the Institutional Diagnostic research programme, we decided to avoid designing a diagnostic framework a priori, testing it through application to various countries, and then revising it progressively in the light of accumulated experience. Instead, our preference went to a more inductive approach consisting of exploring the relationship between existing institutions and the development process in a limited number of countries. On the basis of these in-depth country case studies, the idea is to draw the contours of an institutional diagnostic framework destined to be applied to other countries. The purpose of this framework is to identify pivotal and dysfunctional institutions, understand the causes of the dysfunction, and suggest feasible ways of correcting them in the particular social and political context of a country. In short, the elaboration of the diagnostic methodology has proceeded quasi-heuristically, from a few exploratory yet detailed attempts to understand the role and the dynamic of major institutions in a country, as well as their interactions with the local environment, including the society, the polity, and the geography.

A requirement of the UK Department for International Development, now the FCDO, that funded this research project, was to focus on low-income and lower middle-income countries. Accordingly, and in view of available resources, the four following countries were selected: Bangladesh, Benin, Mozambique, and Tanzania. The rationale for this choice will be provided in the individual case studies. At this stage, it will be sufficient to emphasise that, taken together, these four countries exhibit the diversity that is needed in such an exploratory exercise, diversity being understood in terms of geography, population size, economic endowments, historical and cultural legacy, or development strategy. Despite that diversity, however, the fact that they often face similar economic and institutional challenges in their development suggests there may be common lessons to be drawn from the in-depth study of these challenges.

V STRUCTURE OF CASE STUDIES

Before presenting the structure of the case studies, it is worth defining more precisely what is meant by 'institutions'. In the present research programme, we use a definition derived from North (1990), proposed by Baland *et al.* (2020, p. 3) in the recently published Handbook of Institutions and Development:

(Institutions are defined) as rules, procedures or other human devices that constrain individual behaviour, either explicitly or implicitly, with a view to making individual expectations about others' behaviour converge and allowing individual actions to become coordinated.

According to that definition, laws and all that they stipulate are institutions, insofar as they are commonly obeyed. Even though often appearing under the label of governance, democratic elections, the control of the executive or the functioning of public agencies are institutions too. But this is also the case of customary law, even unwritten, or common cultural habits. Institutional failures correspond to situations where a law or a rule is inoperant and contraveners are not punished. Actually, this situation may concern large groups of people such as when, for instance, several laws coexist, or a law cannot be enforced on the whole population for lack of resources. The formal production relationship between employers and employees or between firm managers and the state through tax laws are institutions that govern modern companies in developing countries, but the existence of informal production sectors results from the inability of the state to have labour and tax laws enforced throughout the whole production fabric, especially among micro and small enterprises. Yet, implicit rules govern the relationship between informal managers, their clients and people who work for them. As such, production informality may thus be considered as an institution in itself, which coexists with formal labour laws. The concept of institution also applies to laws and customs that rule social and family life. Here too, informal institutions as when religion or tribal tradition dictate behavioural rules that differ from secular laws, for instance in areas like marriage, divorce, or inheritance. However, note that, because the focus is on economic development, most institutions or institutional weaknesses considered in the Institutional Diagnostic Project generally refer to those likely to have a significant impact on the economy.

Equipped with this definition, the in-depth study of the relationship between institutions and development in a country and the identification of institutional impediments to long-term inclusive and sustainable development will proceed in three steps. The first one is 'mechanical'. It consists of reviewing the economic, social, and political development of a country, surveying the existing literature, and querying various types of decision makers, top policymakers, and experts about their views on the functioning of institutions in their country. The latter can be done through questionnaire surveys or through focused qualitative interviews. Based on this material, some binding 'institutional weaknesses' on economic development, may be identified and hypotheses elaborated regarding their economic consequences and, most importantly, their causes.

This direct but preliminary approach to the institutional diagnostic of a particular country is also expected to point to several thematic areas where critical institutions seem to be at play. Depending on the country considered, some of the areas obviously deserving scrutiny are the following: modalities of state functioning, that is the bureaucracy and the delivery of basic public goods like education; tax collection; economic regulation and the relationship between private business and political power; land allocation system and property rights; decentralisation, etc.

The second step consists of a thorough analysis of these critical areas in order to precise the modus operandi of relevant institutions and the sources of their inefficiencies, the ways of remedying the situation, and the most important challenges posed by the required reforms. Are the observed institutional inefficiencies caused by a lack of competent civil servants, their tendency to shirk or get involved in corrupt deals, the excessively intricate nature of the law or administrative rules or their undue multiplication and their mutual inconsistency, or else the bad organisation of the administration? Moreover, why is it that reforms that seem adequate to correct major institutional inefficiencies have not been undertaken or why important reforms voted in the parliament have not been effectively implemented? Who would be the gainers and the losers of particular reforms and, therefore, who is likely to promote or oppose them?

Based on these detailed analyses of key thematic areas, the third step of the case studies, and the most challenging task, is to synthesise what has been learned into an articulated view of the main institutional problems hindering progress in various areas, their negative consequences for development, and, most importantly, their causes, proximate or more distant, as well as their susceptibility to reforms. This is the essence of the 'diagnostic' that each case study is expected to deliver.

It bears emphasis that the above exercise is a diagnostic, not a reform agenda. Because there are gainers and losers from most reforms, political and economic circumstances will determine whether they can be undertaken or not. This needs to be thoroughly discussed, but it must be clear that no firm conclusion about the political feasibility can be reached without a precise evaluation of the distribution of political power in the society, something that goes beyond the contemplated diagnostic. From the strict standpoint of the diagnosis, however, its critical contribution is to expose the nature of the institutional dysfunction, highlight possible reforms and the stakes involved. In other words, the diagnostic must eventually make all key actors aware of the implications of the needed reforms and of the expected collective gains and the possible losses they would entail for some groups of the population or some categories of key economic and political actors.

I

An Institutional Diagnostic of Bangladesh

An Introduction

Selim Raihan and François Bourguignon

1 WHY AN INSTITUTIONAL DIAGNOSTIC?

Economic development literature has long emphasised the importance of institutions – that is, the explicit or implicit set of rules that govern the functioning of a society – for the development of a country. Numerous authors have reflected on the various channels through which political, judiciary, economic, and social institutions may affect the pace and the structure of economic growth, as well as, in turn, the way economic development itself modifies the nature and working of institutions. However, evidence relating to these complex circular relationships is limited. This is in large part due to the difficulty in precisely describing the way institutions, in their many dimensions, do or do not work in a specific context. Unlike in many areas of economics, quantification is problematic. Indicators of the quality of institutions, especially of the many aspects of governance, are increasingly available on a comparative basis across countries – but what they cover is not totally clear, as they often describe more the consequences of the way a set of institutions taken together work, rather than the quality of individual institutions themselves. Even when they point to obvious institutional failures, they are too general to give any indication about where the root cause of the problem is, and where to seek a possible remedy. These indicators have been repeatedly put to work in cross-country statistical exercises to explore the relationship between institutions and various features of development. The results of such exercises often are of little significance and, when they are, they are of little help in understanding the institutional weaknesses and strengths of a given country.

The idea of establishing an 'institutional diagnostic' of a country is a way to address these difficulties. The diagnostic exercise consists of a deep dive into the way institutions that are *a priori* most likely to affect economic development do actually function and shape the evolution of the economy of a specific country. Through such exploration, one may hope to identify, more precisely than through general indicators, what the most likely institutional obstacles to development are, the deep factors behind them, directions for reforms, and, possibly, the probable political economy sources of resistance to, or support for, such reforms.

The analogy with the 'growth diagnostics' methodology proposed several years ago by Hausmann *et al.* (2005) comes immediately to mind. The methodology proposed by these authors consists of identifying in an economy those constraints that seem the most binding for economic growth. This is done following the lines of a model that provides a rather general representation of the determinants of economic growth and various types of economic behaviour that drives growth. The key difficulty in applying this methodology to institutions is to identify the institutional origin of the 'binding' constraint. One may indeed find that the lack of infrastructure, or their quality, is a major hindrance to development – but it is much less easy to identify the causes of such a situation. Is it insufficient resources or resource misallocation, lack of interest on the part of the political and economic elites, inefficient public administration, corrupted contractors, or some combination of all of these factors? And what institutional weakness is behind those factors?

What makes the growth diagnostic approach problematic in the case of institutions is that, unlike with economic growth, there is no widely agreed view on the way institutions do affect development, not to mention the reciprocal relationship between development and institutions. Existing economic models in the line of Acemoglu *et al.* (2005) or Acemoglu and Robinson (2008) are illuminating in showing that the relationship between institutions and development goes beyond economics *stricto sensu*, as it necessarily includes political and sociological factors. But these models are too general to be of practical relevance in a particular country, and to identify the role played by specific institutions in raising obstacles to – or, on the contrary, helping – development. What institution does matter? Is it state capacity, the judiciary system, the vested interest of an economic elite, ethnic confrontation, and social norms?

The objective of an institutional diagnostic is not only to understand the role that the nature of institutions and the way they work plays in hindering or helping development in a country: it is also to understand how institutions may be reformed to make them better adapted to the pursuit of development, keeping in mind that the feasibility of reforms depends in turn on the political economy context, and, in some way, on the distribution of political power within the society.

The present volume is part of a research project within the Economic Development and Institution programme, funded by the British Department for International Development (DFID).[1] The project aims to design a methodology

---

[1] In 2020, DFID was merged with the Foreign and Commonwealth Office to form the Foreign, Commonwealth and Development Office (FCDO).

that makes it possible to both identify the main institutional features that may detain faster development and poverty reduction in low-income or lower middle-income countries or threaten their sustainability over time and explore directions of reform. Assessing whether these reforms will be undertaken clearly goes beyond the diagnostic exercise. However, it is presumed that the diagnostic itself, and the reforms envisaged therein, will feed into the public debate in the country being analysed, and will ultimately influence the evolution of institutions.

Without a clear and solid theoretical basis on which to design *a priori* a methodological framework suited for such a diagnostic, it was decided to launch in-depth case studies on the relationship between institutions and development in a few developing countries and to identify areas for improvement. The idea is then to see whether some common lessons can be learned from these experiences to help to build such a framework.

Although it has recently graduated from low-income to lower middle-income country status according to the World Bank classification, Bangladesh demanded to be included in the list of case studies because of the enigma it poses as regards considering the relationship between development performance and the quality of institutions. From independence in 1972 until now, Bangladesh has been able to increase its per capita gross domestic product (GDP) almost fourfold, cut its poverty rate from as much as 70% to the 20% figure today, and become the second largest exporter of ready-made garments (RMG) in the world. However, while the country ranks among the top 15 countries in the world in terms of growth of GDP per capita over the last 15 years, it ranks in the bottom 20% in most international rankings of governance and institutional quality indicators, be it Transparency International for the control of corruption, the Worldwide Governance Indicators for government effectiveness, political stability or regulatory quality, or the institution index of the Global Competitiveness Index. There is thus a 'Bangladesh paradox' when it comes to the commonly held view that good institutions and vigorous development go together. Analysing that paradox should help us to better understand the relationship between institutions and development and to design an institutional diagnostic framework that goes beyond mere governance indicators.

One may wonder whether, beyond analysing the aforementioned paradox, there is much to be learned from a country that apparently does not face strong obstacles to its economic development. Despite its seemingly robust economic performance, however, it turns out that Bangladesh faces serious challenges in relation to inclusiveness and sustainability. The recent past has shown some increase in economic inequality, which suggests that growth benefits more an elite than the mass of workers and farmers, and that poverty reduction could occur much faster than it actually is. On the other hand, there are concerns about how long RMG exports can continue to drive economic growth if they are not complemented by the development of other manufacturing exports, which, in turn, requires adequate policies and public investments. The question then arises why institutions in Bangladesh have not yet satisfactorily addressed these two major concerns, at the risk of missing the stated goal of Bangladesh becoming an upper middle-income country – according to the World Bank classification – by 2031.

The rest of this introductory chapter is organised as follows. The first section will describe the general approach pursued in this volume to identify institutional weaknesses that may be preventing growth in Bangladesh from being faster and more inclusive today, and that may cause it to slow down in the future. The next section will give a brief overview of the political history of the country, without which it is difficult to understand its development achievement, as well as the present political economy context. Finally, in the light of that historical sketch, some reflections will be offered on the specificity of the institutional link between business and politics in Bangladesh, a link that very much frames its development and that will often be referred to throughout this volume.

II METHODOLOGICAL APPROACH TO THE BANGLADESH INSTITUTIONAL DIAGNOSTIC AND THE ORGANISATION OF THIS VOLUME

In the absence of a precise methodological framework for diagnosing institutional obstacles to development in Bangladesh, a simple heuristic approach will be followed. It comprises two parts. The first part might be characterised as 'mechanical'. It consists of three exercises. First, in Chapter 2, a 'growth diagnostic' of Bangladesh is performed, based on the existing literature and the research work carried out by the editors of this volume. The goal of this first exercise is to identify economic and social areas where development limitations are present today or likely to appear in the future. The institutional aspects of these potential obstacles are then explored in more depth later in this volume. Second, in the first part of Chapter 3, a systematic comparison of Bangladesh with benchmark countries within the South Asian region and outside the region is pursued, based on available cross-country governance and institutional quality indicators. The goal of this analysis is to identify institutional areas where Bangladesh may significantly differ from comparable countries, thus indicating possible institutional causes of economic constraints. Third, in the second part of Chapter 3, the opinions of local experts and people with direct experience of Bangladeshi institutions are summarised and synthesised, regarding what they see as possible obstacles to economic development. Most of them were consulted through means of a questionnaire survey, but a few of them – top policymakers and decision makers – were consulted through open-ended interviews.

Putting together the conclusions of these approaches to economic constraints and perceived institutional obstacles to development, the second step in our approach to diagnosing institutional obstacles to development in Bangladesh consists of selecting thematic areas where critical institutional factors seem to play a predominant role with major negative economic consequences for development or for its sustainability. This thematic choice, motivated by the conclusion to the first part of the study, led to a focus in the second part of the study on six areas: the RMG sector and the lack of export diversification; the governance of the banking sector; the low overall tax rate and the inefficient tax system; the low-quality primary education; the complex land management and the Special Economic Zones initiative; and finally, the judiciary, with an accent put on land-dispossession cases. The second part of the volume thus consists of a thorough analysis of these six critical areas, each given its own chapter, in order to understand what is not functioning on the institutional side, why and how things could be fixed, and what would be at stake in such reforms. Each of these six chapters thus addresses the following questions. Are the observed institutional weaknesses due to a lack of skills among civil servants, the fact that they shirk or are corrupt, that the law or administrative rules are too complicated and possibly inconsistent, that the administration is badly organised, or that the political elite imposes its view and personal interest? What reforms would be adequate to remedy these weaknesses, and why aren't they undertaken? What is the political economy behind this status quo?

Based on these detailed analyses of key thematic areas, the tentative diagnostic provided at the end of the volume synthesises what has been learned from them into a list of basic institutional weaknesses common to various areas, their negative consequences for development, and, most importantly, their causes, proximate or more distant, and the potential for remedies and reforms. Finally, the volume also provides a list of the potential reforms suggested in the six thematic studies.

III A BRIEF OVERVIEW OF BANGLADESH'S POLITICAL HISTORY

Bangladesh emerged as an independent country on 16 December 1971, after a nine-month-long War of Independence that cost more than 3 million lives. Long before the war, there had been a fundamental polarisation of politics and political parties on the question of the country's independence. In 1947, with the departure of the British colonial power, two independent states – India and Pakistan – emerged. Pakistan had two wings: East Pakistan (now Bangladesh) and West Pakistan (now Pakistan). From 1947 to 1971, the Awami League led the political movement for the rights of the Bengalese, which eventually, and especially after the six-point demands in 1966,[2] turned

---

[2] On 7 June 1966, the Awami League announced its six-point demands. The six-point demands envisaged a federal form of government based on the 1940 Lahore Resolution, a parliamentary system of government directly elected by the people on the basis of adult franchise, two separate currencies or two reserve banks for the two wings of Pakistan, and a paramilitary force for East Pakistan (see www.thedailystar.net/news-detail-40021).

into a political movement for the autonomy of East Pakistan. After the 1970
Pakistan election, in which the Awami League won the majority of the seats
(in all of Pakistan, not just in East Pakistan[3]), the ruling political elites and
the military refused to transfer power. The Awami League then campaigned
for secession from (West) Pakistan and became the main actor in the War of
Independence in 1971 (Lewis, 2011). Most of the left-leaning parties supported the movement for independence and joined the war. By contrast, most
of the right-leaning religion-based parties were against independence and collaborated with the Pakistani forces, and actively participated in a variety
of criminal activities which fall under the purview of war crimes (Bertocci,
1981). Against this backdrop, just after independence, the political parties
that collaborated with the Pakistanis were banned and their leaders were
brought to trial for committing crimes against humanity during the war
(Jahan, 1997).

From then on, the political history of East Pakistan, the newly named
Bangladesh, can be divided into three distinct phases that can be distinguished
from each other by the degree of democratic features within the regimes.[4]

A The Difficult Installation of Democracy

The 1972 Constitution, adopted on 4 November 1972, was based on four
important fundamental State Principles: nationalism, socialism, democracy,
and secularism. The Constitution established a multi-party parliamentary
democracy. The first election was held in 1973 and the Awami League won
293 out of 300 seats in the national parliament. However, the political history
of Bangladesh for the next 17 years was one of extreme instability, with a succession of coups, short-lived dictatorships, and rigged elections.

Against the incumbent Awami League, the political opposition comprised ultra-left political parties and a newly formed party named Jatiya
Samajtantrik Dal, initially a faction within the Awami League but with
a more radical left-leaning political agenda (Maniruzzaman, 1975).
Throughout 1972–1975, there was considerable conflict between the main
political parties. Amid the political turbulence, through a Constitutional
amendment in January 1975, the Awami League imposed a one-party system
and a presidential regime. Under the presidency of Sheikh Mujibur Rahman,
the Bangladesh Krishak Sramik Awami League (BAKSAL), which advocated

---

[3] In East Pakistan, the Awami League won 160 out of 162 seats plus all 7 of the seats reserved
for women, in West Pakistan, Zulfikar Ali Bhutto's Pakistan People's Party (PPP) won only 81
out of 138 seats plus 5 of the 6 seats reserved for women. The remaining seats in West Pakistan
were won either by Islamist parties, the various factions of the Muslim League (Jinnah's party),
smaller left-wing parties or independents. Overall, the Awami League won 167 of 313 seats and
polled 12.9 m votes against the PPP's 6.1m.
[4] The successive governments and their type are listed in Annex 1.1.

'state socialism' and comprised the Awami League and its left allies, was the sole party in power. All other political parties were banned from participating in politics (Rashiduzzaman, 1977).

The BAKSAL was dissolved after the assassination of Sheikh Mujibur Rahman a few months later by a group of military personnel. Between August and November 1975, there were several military coups and countercoups, until General Ziaur Rahman, known as General Zia, became the Chief Administrator of Martial Law. Martial law imposed major changes on the Constitution. The one-party system of BAKSAL was replaced by a multi-party system. In 1977, General Zia Rahman declared himself the president, and he arranged a referendum that same year to legitimise his position. There was a presidential election in 1978, which he won, and he then established the Bangladesh Nationalist Party (BNP). Zia then arranged a parliamentary election, still under martial law, in 1979, which was won by the BNP, with a two-thirds majority. In April 1979, all ordinances decreed since 1975 were legalised through an amendment to the Constitution.[5]

Under General Zia, the ideology of the state drastically changed, from 'state socialism' to private sector-led capitalist development. Also, 'secularism' was replaced by Islamic principles (Uddin, 2015). The banned Islamic fundamentalist parties, especially Jamaat-e-Islami, which had collaborated with the Pakistani forces during the 1971 War of Independence, and which was seriously suspected of being involved in war crimes (Jahan, 1997),[6] were re-instated in politics. Furthermore, all of the leaders and members of these political parties who had been charged with war crimes and subject to trial were given immunity and freed (Jahan, 1997).

General Zia was killed in a failed military coup on 30 May 1981, but his party stayed in power until 24 April 1982, when General Ershad took power in a bloodless military coup and again imposed martial law. Ershad declared himself the president in 1983. However, from the moment he took power, Ershad faced regular and violent protests from most leading political parties, including BNP, the Awami League, and the left-leaning parties. Strong protests were also carried out by university students, workers of state-owned enterprises, and civil society.

---

[5] General Ziaur Rahman, as the Chief Administrator of Martial Law, issued a series of Proclamation Orders between 1975 and 1979. The most significant were those defining Bangladeshi citizenship, those that inserted religious references into the Constitution, and the controversial Indemnity Ordinance which gave indemnity to the killers of Sheikh Mujibur Rahman. The Fifth Amendment in 1979 validated all Proclamation Orders of the martial law authorities (Ghosh, 1986).

[6] Jamaat-e-Islami opened several fronts during the 1971 war to collaborate with the Pakistani military operation. Their prominent fronts were rajakars (armed volunteers) who were raised and given and arms to counter the freedom fighters, and Al Badr and Al-Shams, who were trained and took the lead in the arrest and killing of the intellectuals during 12–14 December 1971 (Jahan, 1997).

In January 1986, General Ershad established his own political party, the Jatiya Party. In May 1986, a parliamentary election was held, with the participation of the Awami League, some small left-parties, and some Islamic parties, especially the Jamaat-e-Islami; the BNP boycotted the election. The election was won by the Jatiya Party amidst allegations of election rigging and manipulation. General Ershad was then elected as the president in the presidential election that took place in October 1986. That election was boycotted by all the major political parties but was nevertheless reported as being marred with widespread irregularities. Facing continuous protests, General Ershad dissolved the parliament in December 1987. Another election was held in March 1988, which was again boycotted by all major political parties and was consequently won by the Jatiya Party. In 1989, General Ershad passed through the parliament an amendment to the Constitution which declared Islam as the 'state religion'.

Protests increased throughout the later months of 1990 and eventually the military also withdrew their support for General Ershad. He resigned and handed over power to a neutral interim non-partisan government, named the caretaker government (CTG) (see Box 1.1), which was mandated to hold free and fair national parliamentary elections within the next three months. Holding elections under a CTG had been a popular political demand among the opposition parties during the late 1980s, when all the elections were alleged to be fixed by the state machinery. After several episodes of dictatorship, accompanied by rigged elections, it seemed that democracy was finally installed in Bangladesh. Also, a fundamental component of the Bangladeshi political system had appeared: the CTG, which was in charge of organising neutral and honest elections. This facility was used repeatedly until the late 2000s, when it was demolished.

B The Era of Competitive Democracy (1990–2011)

The CTG held the election for the fifth national parliament on 27 February 1991. The BNP won 140 out of 300 seats, 11 seats short of a parliamentary majority. It then formed a coalition government with the support of the Islamist party Jamaat-e-Islami, which won 18 seats. Khaleda Zia (wife of the late General Zia) became the prime minister.

It should be noted here that on 6 August 1991, the Twelfth Amendment of the Constitution restored a parliamentary system of government. Under this system, the prime minister is the executive head of the government and the president, elected by the members of parliament, is the ceremonial head and acts under the advice of the prime minister. A nationwide referendum held on 15 September 1991 overwhelmingly endorsed this shift back to parliamentary democracy, which had been transformed into a presidential regime at the time of General Zia.

Box 1.1 The institution of the CTG: 1991–2011

The CTG was essentially an interim government, headed by selected non-partisan personalities, in charge of managing the transition from one elected government to another. Appointed for three months, the CTG was responsible for organising a general election, as the public did not trust the party in power to run election in a neutral and transparent way. Thus, the outgoing government handed over power to the non-elected and non-partisan CTG, and the latter handed over power to the newly elected government after the election three months later. The main function of the CTG was to create a level playing field in which an election could be held in a free and fair manner without any political interference by the outgoing government. The CTG was not empowered to take any policy decisions unless it was necessary but dealt with current affairs. The head of the CTG, called the Chief Adviser, was appointed by the president of Bangladesh. The Chief Adviser selected the other members. The CTG reported solely to the president of Bangladesh.

The CTG functioned satisfactorily for the 1991, 1996 and 2001 elections but the situation became more difficult in relation to the 2006 elections. The political climate was extremely tense. Conflicts arose over the appointment of the Chief Adviser, and rivalry intensified between the two main parties, the Awami League and the BNP. With the Awami League threatening to boycott the election, and in the midst of violent protests led by the League (40 people were killed during one protest), the date was postponed. This did not reduce the tension, however. After one year of trouble, the military came out in support of the CTG. The Chief Adviser had to resign to reduce the tension. The new CTG then prohibited all political activities for a while and took action against those party leaders who were accused of feeding political violence. Things calmed down after another year and the elections finally took place at the end of 2008, that is, after a two-year delay.

Possibly because of this episode and the prominent role played in this occasion by the CTG, this procedure for dealing with elections was declared unconstitutional by the Supreme court in 2011.

Source: Authors' compilation and analysis from various sources.

In March 1994, controversy over a parliamentary by-election, which the Awami League–led opposition claimed the BNP government had rigged, led to an indefinite boycott of parliament by the entire opposition. Amid a series of violent political events, the sixth national parliamentary elections were held on 15 February 1996. They were boycotted by most opposition parties. The BNP won all 300 parliamentary seats. This administration was short-lived, however. Strikes and civil disobedience movements struck quickly, forcing the government to pass a law that allowed a new national election to be held under a non-partisan CTG. That election was held on 12 June 1996. The Awami League won 146 out of 300 seats and came to power with the support of the Jatiya Party – the party created by General Ershad. Sheikh Hasina (daughter of the late Sheikh Mujibur Rahman) became the prime minister.

The economy of Bangladesh grew steadily during Sheikh Hasina's tenure as the prime minister, yet politics remained very tense, with several protests and strikes led by the BNP, political violence in the streets, and boycotts of parliamentary proceedings. Within this adverse context, Hasina stood firm and, by 2001, became the first prime minister since independence to serve a full mandate.

'Alternating in power' continued in the 2001 election. Held again under a CTG, this was won by the BNP, who obtained 193 out of the 300 seats. Khaleda Zia returned as the prime minister and the BNP ruled until 2006. Her main concern was governance issues, particularly the deteriorating law and order situation. Corruption was seen by her administration to be more prominent than any other economic issue, although this policy focus may have been partly political, as it was used to jail Sheikh Hasina for a few months on corruption charges. Towards the end of 2006, as the election date was approaching, the country again witnessed serious political unrest, with a demand for a 'free and neutral' general election under a neutral CTG. This led to the formation of a 'civil' CTG backed by the military in January 2007, which ruled for the next two years (see Box 1.1 on the CTG).

In the December 2008 national election, the Awami League returned to power with 230 out of 300 parliamentary seats and Sheikh Hasina returned as the prime minister. In May 2011, the Supreme Court ruled that the system of the interim CTG was unconstitutional. This decision was most likely taken with the view that the experience of a two-year period during which a CTG practically abolished political parties and launched policy reforms, which formally was not in its mandate, should not be repeated. This decision *de facto* reinforced the party in power. The Awami League, headed by Sheikh Hasina, has been at the helm of the country ever since.

C The Era of the Dominant Party (2012–Present)

The 2008–2013 term of the Awami League administration was almost as eventful as previous periods in Bangladesh's history, yet the party in power was able to reinforce its control over the political game by considerably weakening the opposition. A new general election was held in line with the Constitution in January 2014. It was as controversial as preceding editions, with almost all major opposition parties boycotting and 153 of the total 300 seats being uncontested. Unsurprisingly, the Awami League won with 234 seats in the national parliament and Sheikh Hasina became the prime minister once more. Five years later, the supremacy of the Awami League seemed well established. Although the main opposition party, the BNP, participated in the December

2018 election, the Awami League and its allies won 292 out of 300 seats in the national parliament. Sheikh Hasina remained the prime minister, her fourth mandate in 22 years.

Two political parties (the Awami League and the BNP) have been the main political actors since the democratic transition, as is the case in many democracies. However, what is somewhat remarkable in the case of Bangladesh is their dynastic aspect and the fully centralised structure of power that this implies. Both Khaleda Zia and Sheikh Hasina have had full control of their parties over the last 30 years. They maintained this control even while they were at the same time fiercely fighting their opponents using all existing legal and illegal instruments of the political game. Cronyism, the politicising of the civil service, the control of local government, violence, jailing the opposition etc. have been common features under all political regimes in Bangladesh, in varying degrees, with the clear goal of reinforcing the power of the party in government rather than allowing democracy to function.

The political regime in place over the last 10 years or so can clearly be termed a 'dominant party regime'. Over time, it has evolved to become a nexus of five main actors: the ruling political elites, powerful economic elites, the military bureaucracy, the civil bureaucracy, and law-enforcement agencies. The 'shaping' and 'sustaining' of this regime is the result of Sheikh Hasina's firm and shrewd governing strategy. There is an apparently stable political settlement among these five actors as regards the generation, distribution, and management of rents from critical economic domains, such as the RMG sector, the power sector, and big infrastructure projects. Within the Awami League, Sheikh Hasina's leadership is unchallenged. She has announced that she will retire in the coming years, but observers believe she will probably only be willing and able to pass the baton to someone in her own family, that is her son, her daughter, or someone else close to her. At the same time, the politics of the main opposition party, the BNP, suffers from a serious lack of direction as its top leaders are either in jail (Khaleda Zia was jailed for corruption in 2018[7]) or in exile (Tareq Zia, son of Khaleda Zia and the second top leader of the BNP, has been in exile since 2008[8]), or facing criminal charges (most of the other top leaders of the BNP are charged with numerous criminal offences). During this regime, a special tribunal has been set up to try the war criminals of the 1971 War of Independence. The top leaders of Jamaat-e-Islami were tried for their

---

[7] In 2018, Khaleda Zia was jailed for a total of 17 years for the 'Zia Orphanage Trust' corruption case and 'Zia Charitable Trust' corruption case. She was found guilty of embezzling funds destined for orphanage trusts set up while she was the prime minister (see www.dhakatribune.com/bangladesh/court/2018/10/30/zia-orphanage-trust-graft-case-hc-raises-khaleda-s-jail-term-to-10yrs).

[8] Tareq Zia has been in exile in London since he left Bangladesh in September 2008. In absentia, in October 2018, he was sentenced to life imprisonment for his role in the 2004 Dhaka grenade attack, as well as another 10 years for the Zia Charitable Trust corruption case in February 2018, and seven more years for a money laundering case in July 2016 (see www.dw.com/en/bangladesh-court-sentences-opposition-bnp-leader-rahman-to-jail/a-19415933).

war crimes, and many were executed in 2016. Opponents of these trials raised concerns that there were political intentions behind them.[9]

Compared to the tumultuous past, the present dominant party regime has over the last 15 years or so provided a stability in the political system in Bangladesh never seen since independence. This undoubtedly represents huge progress and has probably had a favourable impact on economic development. However, there are big question marks about whether this political stability represents a major step towards a truly democratic functioning of society. The 2014 and 2018 national elections, and many of the local-level elections in recent years, aroused allegations of irregularities, and at the same time there, has been a decline in participation in elections. There are concerns that the national parliament is dysfunctional when it comes to having meaningful debates on development issues, democratic rights, and freedom of expression. There are also concerns among the civil society on the squeezing of the democratic space.

This is not the place to make predictions about the future of politics in Bangladesh. However, it is probable that having been at the helm of the country for 15 successive years, the dominant party has acquired considerable political strength. Unless some adverse event discredits it, challenging it will be difficult in the years to come. Thus, the political context in which the 'institutional diagnostic' undertaken in this volume must be conducted is this dominant party regime and the way politics have been observed to function in the last decade or so, rather than the troubled years of 'competitive democracy'.

IV BUSINESS AND POLITICS IN BANGLADESH: THE KEY ROLE OF 'DEALS'

Hassan and Raihan (2018) use the 'deals environment' framework, as developed by Pritchett *et al.* (2018), to understand the politics of development in Bangladesh. As this approach deviates somewhat from the standard institutional framework, and because it will be referred to on several instances in this volume, it seems necessary to present it in some detail and to briefly show its relevance in the Bangladeshi context.

A deals environment may be defined in opposition to a 'rules' environment, whether the latter refers to formal institutions (i.e. formal law–based governance whereby state–business interactions are governed by impersonal transactions and universal enforcement), or to informal institutions (i.e. 'unwritten rules applying to a restricted social group or community and enforceable through non-legal mechanisms at work inside that group or community'[10]). By contrast, a 'deals' environment is characterised by individual

---

[9] See Jalil (2010) and Mollah (2019).
[10] This is the definition given by Baland *et al.* (2020).

contracts between two parties with selective enforcement (although it is difficult to think of a stable environment where contracts are systematically unenforced).

An effective 'deals' environment where major economic initiatives are based upon the agreement between two individual actors to behave in some coordinated way, irrespectively of what the formal or informal rules may be, and possibly sometimes in violation of them, is essentially the sign of institutions not working. Deals may be detrimental to development, as in a typical 'corruption' deal, where an agent endowed with some formal power uses it to create undue and development-unfriendly advantages accruing to another agent and sharing the proceeds with that agent; but they may also be favourable to development, when they make it possible to exploit development-friendly opportunities that formal or informal rules might impede being taken advantage of. A manager obtaining a loan at a zero rate of interest from a bank and sharing part of the profits of his/her investment with the banker is a deal that violates formal rules (preferential treatment, profit shared with an agent rather than the bank itself). However, it may contribute to development if the investment had not been undertaken otherwise. It may also be pure corruption or embezzlement if the loan is for personal consumption or is never repaid.

The point is that the relationship between business and politics, which to a large extent shapes the development process in Bangladesh, is very much based on deals made outside formal rules, sometimes with a positive impact on development but more often with negative consequences. Because of their ubiquity in Bangladesh's economic functioning, it will be helpful to make use in this volume of the taxonomy of deals that has been proposed by Pritchett *et al.* (2018) and used by Hassan and Raihan (2018) to analyse the country's historical development.

Referring to the relationship between business and the political elite, a deals environment can be divided into several dimensions. Deals may be restricted to an elite or widely available. In the former case, they are said to be 'closed'; in the latter, they are said to be 'open'. Likewise, they are said to be 'ordered' if they are honoured by the two parties, particularly the government side; and in the opposite case, they are said to be 'disordered'.

Of course, the two dimensions can be combined so that it is possible to refer to contexts of 'closed and ordered' or 'open and disordered' deals. For instance, Hassan and Raihan (2018) describe the time the government was trying to bolster the private sector in the late 1970s as an 'increasingly open and ordered deals environment'. By contrast, they describe the rise of monopolistic situations during the competitive democratic phase as closed and ordered.

These concepts will prove useful when analysing some critical areas of Bangladesh's economy, particularly the RMG manufacturing sector or the banking sector, and when characterising the contemporaneous institutional context of Bangladesh's development.

(1) The installation of democracy

Period	Type of access to power	Type of regime	Party in power	State leader, title
Apr. 1971–Mar. 1973	War of Independence in 1971, formation of a provisional government-in-exile in April 1971, which continued until the general election in 1973	Pres.	Awami League	Sheikh Mujibur Rahman, President until Jan. 1972 and then Prime Minister
Mar. 1973–Jan. 1975	General election in 1973	Parl.	Awami League	Sheikh Mujibur Rahman, Prime Minister
Jan. 1975–Aug. 1975	Constitutional amendment	Pres.	Bangladesh Krishak Sramik Awami League (BAKSAL)	Sheikh Mujibur Rahman, President
Nov. 1975–May 1981	Coup and then presidential and general election	Dict.	Bangladesh National Party (BNP, 1978)	General Ziaur Rahman ('Zia'), Chief Administrator of Martial Law and then President
May 1981–Apr. 1982	Failed coup and then presidential election	Pres.	BNP	Justice Abdus Sattar, President
Apr. 1982–Dec. 1990	Coup and then presidential and general election	Dict.	Jatiya Party (1986)	General Ershad, Chief Administrator of Martial Law and then President

(2) The competitive democracy

Feb. 1991–Feb. 1996	General election under the CTG	Parl.	BNP	Khaleda Zia (widow of General Zia), Prime Minister
June 1996–Oct. 2001	General election under the CTG	Parl.	Awami League	Sheikh Hasina (daughter of Sheikh Mujibur Rahman), Prime Minister
Oct. 2001–Oct. 2006	General election under the CTG	Parl.	BNP	Khaleda Zia, Prime Minister
Oct. 2006–Jan. 2007	CTG			President Iajuddin Ahmed, as the head of CTG
Jan. 2007–Dec. 2008	Military-backed CTG			Fakhruddin Ahmed, as the head of CTG, backed by the Military Chief General Moeen Uddin Ahmed

(3) The dominant party era

Dec. 2008–Jan. 2014	General election under the CTG	Parl.	Awami League	Sheikh Hasina, Prime Minister
Jan. 2014–Dec. 2018	General election under Awami League	Parl.	Awami League	Sheikh Hasina, Prime Minister
Dec. 2018–	General election under Awami League	Parl.	Awami League	Sheikh Hasina, Prime Minister

PART I

THE ECONOMIC AND INSTITUTIONAL BACKGROUND OF BANGLADESH'S DEVELOPMENT

2

Bangladesh's Development

Achievements and Challenges

Selim Raihan and François Bourguignon

I INTRODUCTION

Bangladesh's economic growth and development experiences over the past five decades, since independence in 1971, have generated much interest among academics and development practitioners both home and abroad. From its war-torn economy of 1972 until now, Bangladesh has been able to increase its per capita GDP in real terms[1] by 3.7 times (from US$ 460 in 1972 to US $1,700 in 2018), cut down the poverty rate from as much as 71% in the 1970s to 20.5% in 2019, become the second largest exporter of ready-made garments (RMG) in the world, and registered some notable progress in social sectors. In 2015, Bangladesh graduated from the World Bank's classification of low-income country to the lower middle-income country category. Also, in 2018, the country met the first review of the three criteria required to graduate from the least developed country (LDC) status and is on track to meet the criteria under the second review in 2021 to finally graduate out of LDC status by 2024. At the same time, Bangladesh's aforementioned development has happened in a context of a widely recognised weak institutional capacity. Bangladesh has almost always been ranked in the bottom part of most international rankings of governance indicators, as summarised in the Worldwide Governance Indicators database. Also, up to the late 2000s, its political climate was extremely tense, unstable, and often violent. All these factors have prompted some to term Bangladesh's development the 'Bangladesh paradox' or the 'Bangladesh surprise'.[2]

Over the past five decades, the major factors behind Bangladesh's growth and development achievements have been both internal and external. The

---

[1] At constant domestic prices in 2018 US$.
[2] See World Bank (2007a), World Bank (2010), and Mahmud *et al.* (2008).

major internal factors include an overall stable macroeconomy, large expansion of the private sector, robust growth in exports driven by the performance of the RMG sector, robust growth in remittances, resilient growth in the agricultural sector, a reasonably 'working' political climate over the last 12 years, some expansion of social protection programmes, and a wide coverage of social needs by non-governmental organisations (NGOs). The major external factors include favourable market access in major export destinations, reasonably stable economic conditions in Bangladesh's major trading partner countries, Bangladesh's stable political relations with neighbouring countries, some degree of regional cooperation in South Asia (especially with India), and Bangladesh's 'weak' financial linkages with the global economy, which cushioned Bangladesh from the Global Financial Crisis. In 1990, Bangladesh was the 50th largest economy in the world (in international dollars). Impressively, by 2018, Bangladesh improved its position in this ranking to 33rd. According to PricewaterhouseCoopers (2019), it should become the 28th largest economy by 2030 and close to the 20th by 2050. The main question addressed in this chapter is whether the internal and external factors just mentioned will indeed keep pushing Bangladesh's economy up at the same speed, or possibly even faster. More precisely, the issue considered is what constraints the economy may face in the future and whether further development can be achieved without a significant new direction in policy.

There are concerns that the weak institutional capacity of the country may work as a binding constraint as Bangladesh attempts to meet the stiff targets of the Sustainable Development Goals (SDGs) by 2030, and as it aspires to become an upper middle-income country by 2031. Moreover, the dividends from the so-called 'Bangladesh surprise' are likely to be on a decline as the country is confronted by several serious economic challenges. These include the slow progress in the structural transformation of the economy, the lack of export diversification, the high degree of informality in the labour market, the slow pace of formal job creation, the poor status of physical and social (i.e. education, healthcare) infrastructure, the slow reduction in poverty and rising inequality, and the consequences of the COVID-19 pandemic.

Against this backdrop and keeping in mind the ambitious development targets the country wants to meet in the next two to three decades, this chapter analyses the major development achievements of the Bangladeshi economy until today and seeks to identify the major challenges it will have to address in the future. Whether these challenges can be overcome, and which reforms can be undertaken for this to happen, depends in turn on the institutional context of the country. This particular aspect will be considered in the institutional diagnostic chapter at the end of the volume, after a deeper reflection on Bangladesh's politico-economic institutions, through the analysis of key economic sectors and major socio-economic issues.

Focusing exclusively on economic and social issues, this chapter first analyses the sources of growth and possible limitations of the present development regime (Section II). It then evaluates the financing constraints faced by the economy in general, and by the public sector in particular (Section III). The next sections (Sections IV–VI) focus on sources of concern in social and environmental areas and the COVID-19 crisis. The conclusion summarises the main results of this chapter.

II SOURCES OF GROWTH AND POSSIBLE LIMITATIONS OF THE PRESENT DEVELOPMENT REGIME

In this section, economic growth in Bangladesh is first analysed at the aggregate level, before considering the structural evolution of the economy, the key role played by trade, and the constraints arising from lagging infrastructure and progress in the business environment.

A Aggregate Growth

The long-term trend in the GDP growth rate shows that Bangladesh has steadily increased its rate of growth over the past 47 years, since independence in 1971 (Figure 2.1). Starting from a highly volatile growth rate in the 1970s, growth became more stable and slightly faster in the 1990s and has accelerated since the turn of the millennium. From an average rate equal to or below 4% per annum in the 1970s and 1980s, growth accelerated and shot up to over 5% in the 2000s, then exceeded 6% for several years during the 2000s, and has crossed the 7% mark in recent years. Bangladesh has been able to increase the average GDP growth rate by 1 percentage point in each decade since the 1990s. In 2018, the country achieved its highest growth rate in the past four decades: 7.9%.[3] In Figure 2.1, the steps indicate the average growth rates of the decades, and the highlighted years indicate the years of political transition in Bangladesh.[4]

GDP per capita has grown less rapidly because of population growth, but because the latter has significantly slowed down over the last 40 years, the growth acceleration is even more noticeable for GDP per capita. The 10-year average growth rate increased from 1.5% in the 1980s to more than 5% over today.

---

[3] However, doubts have been expressed about this figure – see the subsequent discussion.

[4] 1975 – assassination of President Sheikh Mujibur Rahman and a subsequent military coup; 1981 – assassination of President Ziaur Rahman and a subsequent military coup; 1991 – Bangladesh Nationalist Party came to power through a general election; 1996 – repeated political violence, and Bangladesh Awami League won the election and came to power; 2001 – Bangladesh Nationalist Party won the election; 2006 – repeated political violence leading to a 'civil' caretaker government backed by the military in early 2007; 2008 – Bangladesh Awami League came to power through the election under the caretaker government; 2014 – Bangladesh Awami League won an election that was boycotted by all major political parties; 2018 – Bangladesh Awami League won the election and remains in power.

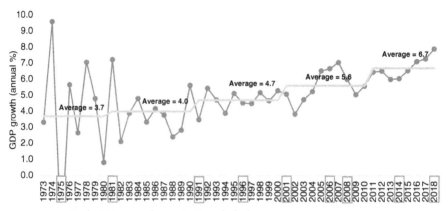

FIGURE 2.1 Real GDP growth rate in Bangladesh
Source: World Development Indicators (WDI).

Compared to other developing countries, in international purchasing power (purchasing power parity 2011 US$), Bangladesh's per capita GDP was US$ 3,880 in 2018, around 1.5 times the average for LDCs, 57% of the average for lower middle-income countries, 50% of the South Asian average, and 23% of the average for upper middle-income countries. In terms of growth, however, Bangladesh has done substantially better than the average country in all of these groupings.

Interestingly enough, the vigorous acceleration of GDP growth since 1990, from 4% to 6.6%, is in line with the increase in the share of investment in GDP. The investment to GDP ratio was 17.5% around 1990. It increased regularly since then and reached 31% in 2018. However, two remarks are in order here. First, further growth acceleration, as targeted by the present government, may require a substantial increase of the investment to GDP ratio. The Perspective Plan 2041 targets an 8.5% real GDP growth rate by 2025. Given an average incremental capital output ratio of 4.3 for the period 2014–2018, the investment to GDP ratio should be more than 36% by 2025, which represents a growth rate for investment that is much faster than what has been observed in the recent past. Second, an important aspect of Bangladesh's investment regimes in the 1990s and 2000s is that the major contribution to the growth of the investment to GDP ratio came from the rise in private investment and its share in total investment. However, the GDP share of private investment has remained stagnant in recent years, so the growth of the overall GDP share of investment has been mainly due to its public component.[5] The stability of the

[5] The ratio of public investment to GDP increased from 5.3% in 2011 to 7.9% in 2018, while the share of private investment increased from 22.2% to 23.3% during the same period (Source: World Bank, World Development Indicator).

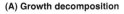

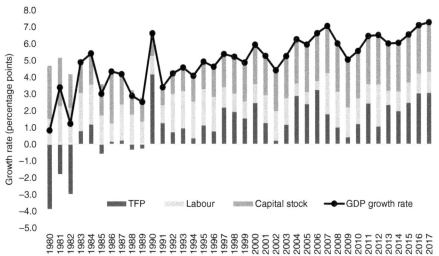

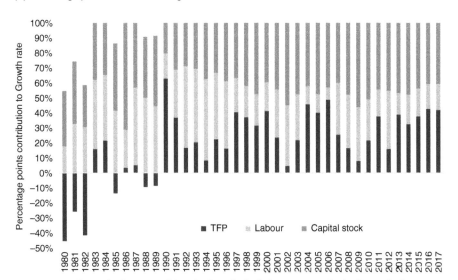

FIGURE 2.2 Growth decomposition in Bangladesh (1980–2017). A. Growth decomposition. B. Percentage points contribution to growth rate
Source: Authors' calculation using the Penn (World Table 9.1) database.

ratio of private investment to GDP might make it possible to sustain present growth rates but may be a concern for further acceleration.

Conventional growth accounting[6] is helpful in regard to obtaining insights into the aggregate sources of GDP growth, that is what portion is derived from capital accumulation, the growth of the labour force, and total factor productivity (TFP) in general. Figure 2.2 shows the result of that decomposition on an annual basis since 1980, although the 1980s may not be relevant given that this was a very tumultuous period from both a political and an economic point of view.

Over the next three decades, capital accumulation was, on average, the most important factor of growth. This dominance increased over time, in line with the acceleration of investment just mentioned. The contribution of labour steadily declined over time, in part because of slowing population growth, but above all because capital grew much faster. TFP growth is the residual: it represents the productivity gains that were independent of the accumulation of capital, making up a little less than one-third of total GDP growth.

Subtracting the contribution of labour to GDP growth in the preceding decomposition is equivalent to considering the growth of the average productivity of labour: that is, GDP per worker. It has steadily increased over time.

B Structural Transformation

Part of the TFP growth in the preceding decomposition is caused by structural changes taking place in the economy. Over time, the allocation of production factors changes with net movements across sectors of activity. If productivity is not the same in the sectors of origin and in the sectors of destination, these movements affect the overall level of productivity in the economy. This mechanism has been seen as a major driver of development ever since the work of Lewis (1954). However, it has recently been found that, since the 1990s, this process has worked in the opposite way. Working on sub-Saharan African and Asian countries, McMillan and Rodrik (2011) found that structural change in those countries had a negative impact on overall labour productivity. However, Bangladesh did not follow such a pattern in the past, and this remains the case today.

Table 2.1 shows the evolution of the GDP and employment structure by sector of activity between 1991 and 2018. The contribution of agriculture, both to GDP and employment, sharply declined during 1991 and 2018, and those of non-agricultural sectors, especially the services sector, increased. Comparing the structure of GDP and that of employment, it is readily apparent that in 1991, productivity was the lowest in agriculture and the highest in 'other industry', followed by services. This means that net labour movements have

---

[6] See Annex 2.1.

TABLE 2.1 *Structural change in the economy (percentage share of total)*

Broad sectors	GDP		Employment	
	1991	2018	1991	2018
Agriculture	31.7	13.1	69.5	40.1
Manufacturing	13.9	17.9	12.4	14.2
Other industry	7.2	10.6	1.2	6.3
Services	47.2	58.4	16.9	39.4

Source: World Bank, WDI.

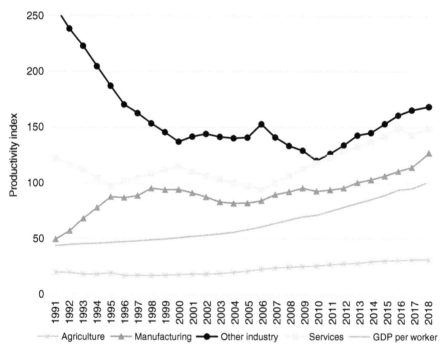

FIGURE 2.3 Bangladesh's labour productivity by sector and for the whole economy (GDP per worker 2018 = 100)
Source: Authors' calculation, from World Bank, WDI.

been from low-productivity to high-productivity sectors, that is mostly from agriculture to services and 'other industry'. Structural change has thus had a positive effect on the overall labour productivity in the economy, in line with Lewis (1954).

At the same time, Figure 2.3 shows that in the 1990s, labour productivity increased overall in all sectors of activity except 'other industry', possibly because of structural changes within that sector. These sectoral productivity

TABLE 2.2 *Decomposition of labour productivity growth in Bangladesh*

	1991–2000			2001–2010			2011–2018		
	Total	WSE	SRE	DRE	Total	WSE	SRE	DRE	Total	WSE	SRE	DRE
GDP per worker	0.166	0.031	0.246	–0.110	0.356	0.111	0.261	–0.016	0.338	0.240	0.077	0.020

Note: GDP per worker is in purchasing power parity constant 2011 international $.
Source: Authors' calculation, from World Bank, WDI.

increases thus provided a second source of overall productivity gain, in addition to structural change.

Figure 2.3 also shows some interesting short-run variations in productivity gains. For instance, the 1991–1995 period exhibited a huge increase in manufacturing productivity – a doubling in four years – apparently precisely at the time the RMG sector was taking off. It is also striking that productivity did not change in the four sectors of activity between 1995 and 2005, but overall productivity increased because of net labour movements from agriculture to other sectors, that is structural change.

Avillez (2012) provides an interesting method for decomposing aggregate labour productivity gains[7] into structural change and within-sector productivity growth. This distinguishes three components: (1) the within-sector effect (WSE) reflects the overall impact of productivity growth within individual sectors on aggregate productivity; (2) the static reallocation effect (SRE, Denison effect) captures the impact of the reallocation of employment from less productive to more productive sectors (i.e. it arises from sectoral differences in initial productivity levels); and (3) the dynamic reallocation effect (DRE, Baumol effect) describes the impact of reallocating employment to sectors with fast- or slow-growing productivity (i.e. this results from asymmetric productivity growth rates across sectors).[8] The last two effects correspond to the impact of structural change on growth.

Table 2.2 presents the decomposition of labour productivity growth in Bangladesh into WSE, SRE, and DRE using data for the four sectors appearing in Table 2.1 and three approximately 10-year periods. It appears that while

---

[7] See Annex 2.2 for technical details.

[8] The Baumol effect reduces aggregate productivity growth when labour moves towards (away from) a sector with negative (positive) labour productivity growth. Note that the magnitude of this effect depends not only on the sectoral productivity rates of growth and sectoral employment shifts but also on the ratio between the sectors' productivity levels and the aggregate productivity level. This dynamic effect does not appear in more conventional structural change analysis, such as Mcmillan and Rodrik (2011), which focus on absolute rather than relative productivity changes.

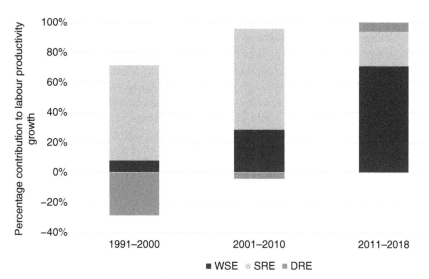

FIGURE 2.4 Percentage contribution to labour productivity growth in Bangladesh
Source: Authors' calculation from World Bank, WDI.

total labour productivity growth doubled after 2000 compared to what it was in 1991–2000, the contributions of WSE, SRE, and DRE changed quite dramatically across the periods. WSE increased by more than 10-fold between the first and the last sub-periods, while structural change, that is the sum of SRE and DRE, which was strong and approximately constant in the first two sub-periods, declined significantly in the last decade. Interestingly, the dynamic productivity effect, DRE, was strongly negative in the 1990s, suggesting that labour shifts during that period were towards sectors with higher but slow-growing productivity. That effect then practically vanished.

Figure 2.4 suggests that in the recent decade, the major contribution to labour productivity comes from WSE (71%), followed by SRE (23%) and DRE (6%). This suggests that productivity growth within individual sectors, rather than the reallocation of employment from less productive to more productive sectors and reallocating employment to sectors with growing productivity, has been the driving factor behind labour productivity growth during the 2011–2018 period. What is surprising in that evolution, and in the difference compared to the previous period, is that with agriculture still accounting for 40% of the labour force and having a substantial productivity gap, there would seem to still be a huge potential for structural change. Productivity has increased very quickly in the service sector during the last decade, with that sector being responsible for the high WSE effect in that sub-period. But it follows that it created less jobs than in the previous sub-periods, thus weakening labour movements and the structural change effect on GDP per worker, or closely related GDP per capita.

To understand better the reason for this slowing down in structural change requires disaggregating the services sector, which comprises very different types of activity, ranging from financial services to informal retail trade or ancillary jobs. It cannot be excluded that what is being observed is a mounting productivity gap within that sector that hides a falling gap between agriculture and low-productivity service activities, and thus a weakening of incentives to move away from agriculture, while huge productivity gains and faster growth take place in high-productivity services like finance. Unfortunately, employment data do not allow for a more detailed analysis that would make it possible to test that hypothesis.

C Trade

After independence in 1971, Bangladesh adopted a highly restricted trade regime that was characterised by high tariffs and non-tariff barriers and an overvalued exchange rate system, in support of the Government's import-substitution industrialisation strategy. This policy was pursued with the aim of improving the country's balance of payment position and creating a protected domestic market for manufacturing industries (Bhuyan and Rashid, 1993). Then, in the mid-1980s, the trade regime registered a major shift, when a moderate liberalisation reform was initiated. Yet the boldest transition from a protectionist stance to a freer trade regime took place in the early 1990s, which led to a drastic reduction in the average tariff rate, from as high as 105% in 1990 to 13% in 2016 (Raihan, 2018a).

The liberal import policies during the 1990s and onwards led to a fast growth of imports. Figure 2.5 shows that the import to GDP ratio increased from 13% in the early 1990s to 23.5% today. The export to GDP ratio had started to rise by 1990, from a very low level of slightly above 5% of GDP in the 1980s, but it then closely followed imports, reaching an all-time peak of 20% in 2010. The trade deficit is endemic to the Bangladesh economy, even though it has been rather stable over time, fluctuating at around 5%, with some widening since the mid-2000s. In this long-run ascending trade perspective, there may be some concern with respect to the substantial decline in the GDP share of both imports and exports over the last five years. Is this the result of temporary shocks or the sign of deeper structural changes?

Over the years, the composition of imports has also changed in Bangladesh. There has been a move away from the heavy dominance of food imports in the early 1970s to industrial raw materials and machinery today. The change in favour of industrial raw materials and capital machinery is partly linked to the rapid expansion of the manufacturing sector, particularly RMG exports, which is the dominant feature of the Bangladeshi economy over the last four decades.

Bangladesh's fast export growth since the late 1980s has indeed been overwhelmingly driven by the dynamism of the RMG sector alone. While the

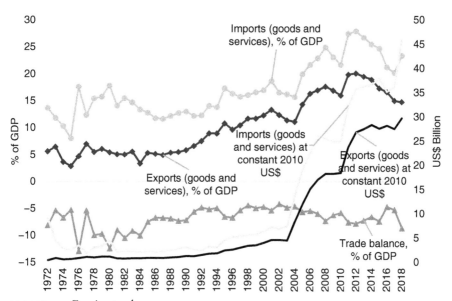

FIGURE 2.5 Foreign trade
Source: World Bank, WDI.

export basket was heavily dominated by jute and jute products in the early 1970s, the composition of exports in Bangladesh has evolved steadily in favour of RMG products. Today, they constitute more than 80% of export earnings. The drastic change in the import mix, as well as the spectacular surge of RMG manufacturing exports, bear witness to the structural transformation of Bangladesh's economy and the role played by foreign trade.

The growth of Bangladesh's RMG exports had its origins in the international trade regime in textiles and clothing, which, until 2004, was governed by Multi-Fibre Arrangement (MFA) quotas. This quota system restricted competition in the global market by providing reserved markets for numerous developing countries, including Bangladesh, where textiles and clothing items were not traditional exports. The duty-free access of Bangladesh's RMG products to the European Union (EU) has also greatly supported the growth of the sector. Yet the surge in RMG exports from Bangladesh took place precisely at the time of the extinction of the MFA regime and its successor Agreement on Textile and Clothing: that is, at the time the international market was liberalised and the RMG Bangladeshi sector appeared as particularly competitive relative to other providers in developing countries (outside China).

The growth of RMG exports has been one of the main growth drivers of Bangladesh's economy over the past three decades. Although the sector directly contributes to only a little more than 6% of GDP, its indirect contribution is much larger: accounting for both backward and forward linkages, it accounts for at least twice as much. With exports increasing at an average annual rate of

12% over the last two decades, and probably more for its RMG component, the sector may have directly contributed to close to 1.4% GDP growth during that period. Yet such an estimate does not include the indirect effects on aggregate demand, on easing the foreign currency constraint, and on investment incentives. The econometric exercise reported in Annex 2.3 suggests an even larger contribution when all these effects are accounted for. With an estimated elasticity of GDP to the volume of exports of 0.22, a 12% growth of exports generates a 2.6% increase in GDP – a little less than half the average growth rate since 2000.

Despite this impressive growth record, it bears emphasis that the export base and export markets have remained rather narrow in Bangladesh, which is a matter of great concern. Undiversified exports, both in terms of market and product range, are likely to be much more vulnerable to external and internal shocks than well-diversified exports. Despite various incentives provided by trade policy reforms, Bangladesh's manufacturing sector seems to have failed until now to develop a diversified export structure. Bangladesh's export markets have been highly concentrated – North America and the EU being its major clients. Bangladesh's growth is thus heavily dependent on economic activity in these two parts of the world. As far as the export product range is concerned, UNCTAD's export concentration index suggests that Bangladesh's export concentration has increased over the last two decades. In fact, it is much higher today than the averages for LDCs, lower middle-income countries, upper middle-income countries, and South Asian countries.[9]

Despite a very high share of manufacturing exports in total merchandise exports, the export basket of Bangladesh thus remains highly concentrated around low-complexity products with lower growth prospects in world markets. A measure of the complexity of the economy is the Economic Complexity Index (ECI) of the Centre for International Development at Harvard University, which measures the knowledge intensity of an economy by considering the technical knowledge that is incorporated into the products it exports. In this respect, Bangladesh performs very poorly, with an ECI that has deteriorated over time. Following the current view on the relationship between economic complexity and the level of income, Bangladesh's growth prospects would not seem favourable, as a low ECI would be compatible with a relatively low level of GDP per capita.[10]

On the import side, it must be stressed that, despite the liberalisation of tariffs, Bangladesh's average applied tariff rate in 2016 was the highest in South Asia, and much higher than those of the countries in Southeast Asia. Also, in 2016, the share of tariff lines with international peaks (rates that exceed 15%) in total tariff lines was as high as 39%, which was much higher than most of the South Asian (except Nepal and Pakistan) and Southeast Asian countries.[11]

---

[9] https://unctadstat.unctad.org/EN/
[10] See Hidalgo and Hausmann (2009).
[11] Data from the World Bank, WDI.

Given this scenario, there seems to be room for further tariff liberalisation in Bangladesh as part of a broader trade policy reform aimed at accelerating export growth and export diversification (Raihan, 2018a; Sattar, 2019).

The need to diversify exports thus appears as a key policy agenda in Bangladesh. It is essential to sustain long-term growth and employment creation, as it is far from clear that Bangladesh will be able to keep increasing its global market share in low value–added RMG products as fast as it has done in the past. Low-wage competitors are appearing in sub-Saharan Africa, for example, Ethiopia, and the whole industry is mechanising so that low labour costs may not be as strong a comparative advantage as before, and, domestically, the sector will provide less jobs. Foreign clients of Bangladeshi RMG firms are also more and more attentive to the labour conditions among their suppliers, particularly after the 2013 Rana Plaza accident that cost the life of a thousand employees. At the same time, the pressure for higher wages and better labour conditions is increasing in the country, making the RMG sector less competitive internationally.

D Remittances and Foreign Direct Investment

Remittances can be considered the second major driver of growth in Bangladesh. Figure 2.6 shows the evolution of remittances sent back home by Bangladeshi workers employed abroad since the mid-1970s. Starting from a low base, remittances increased at slow rates until the turn of the millennium. Since then, however, they have increased at very sharp rates, reaching US\$ 14 billion around 2013 but then remaining roughly constant. In terms of GDP, they went up from 1% around 1995 to 10% in 2008–2012, falling back to 6% today. A reduction of transaction costs and remitting delays, but above all the fast-growing demand of foreign workers in the Gulf, where the net inflow of migrants multiplied by 5 between 2000 and 2010, made a major contribution to the increase in the flow of remittances.

Remittances contribute to domestic growth essentially by increasing aggregate demand, that is domestic spending, while at the same time eliminating foreign currency bottlenecks that could constrain an increase in production. Other things being equal, the same increase in spending would not have resulted in more production if it had a purely domestic origin, because of the constraint arising from the financing of imported raw materials and equipment required by any increase in domestic output. Thus, one may estimate that, with an average annual growth rate of 11% between 2000 and 2018, remittances have contributed to roughly 1 percentage point of annual GDP growth.[12] The econometric exercise reported in Annex 2.3 suggests a long-run elasticity of GDP to real remittances of 0.14. When all indirect effects are accounted for,

---

[12] During that period, remittances grew in real terms, that is measured in domestic purchasing power, at 14% a year, while representing on average 7% of GDP.

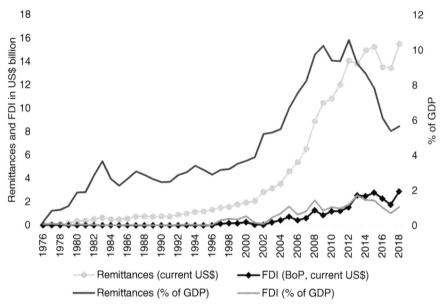

FIGURE 2.6 Remittances and foreign direct investment
Source: World Bank, WDI.

the contribution of remittances to GDP growth is thus 1.5% per annum on average. Together with export growth, they thus generate roughly two-thirds, that is 4.1% annually, of overall growth.

Foreign direct investment represents another regular inflow of foreign currency that has the potential to accelerate domestic growth. In the case of Bangladesh, however, that contribution has been only marginal. If the amount of foreign direct investment has increased since the mid-1990s, it has represented only around 1% of GDP after the mid-2000s, and a little more than that over recent years. This does not compare well with what is observed in LDCs (3.3% on average), or in Southeast Asian manufacturing exporters such as Cambodia, Laos, and Vietnam – all RMG competitors of Bangladesh – where the foreign direct investment to GDP ratio is above 6%. At the same time, Bangladesh's domestic investment effort is larger and more dynamic.

E Infrastructure and Megaprojects

If Bangladesh does not rank high either in the availability or quality of its infrastructure according to the World Economic Forum 2019 Global Competitiveness Index, its overall score is nevertheless comparable to those of African countries at a comparable level of GDP per capita (Ghana, Kenya) and not much below dynamic middle-income industrialising Asian countries except Vietnam. However, the situation differs depending on the kind of infrastructure being

considered. If Bangladesh compares well with other lower-middle income countries in transport infrastructure, the gap is more pronounced with respect to
power and water. True, 80% of the population now has access to electricity, a
spectacular progress mostly achieved over the last 10 years. But with an average
consumption of 330 kWh per person and per year, Bangladesh keeps lying well
below the rest of South Asia – except Nepal –, industrialising Asia, and even
some African country like Ghana. Moreover, outages in urban areas are still
frequent, which entails substantial costs. As far as access to safe drinkable water
is concerned, on the other hand, the situation is definitely worse in Bangladesh
than in most countries at a comparable level of development.

As in other developing countries, considerable efforts are still to be made
to provide to economic agents the infrastructure that development, especially
industrialisation, imperatively requires. Lately, these efforts have taken the
form of a few 'mega-projects' meant to accelerate the pace of development
and make it more transformative. These essentially are major infrastructure
projects, with complex logistics, high technological requirements, and very
substantial funding needs. Undertaken in key sectors such as transportation,
energy, seaport, airport, mining, etc.,[13] they are intended to have a significant
impact on the country's development through job creation, enhanced connectivity, regional trade facilitation, geographic integration, and energy provision.

These mega-projects also raise several concerns, which relate to: (i) their
financing; (ii) their implementation, including construction delays and their
final cost; and (iii) their political significance within the context of Bangladesh's
political economy.

The total cost of the seven largest mega-projects has been estimated at
USD 31.2 billion,[14] of which only 9.9 billion was funded on government funds.
The rest was mostly funded by loans, part of which from foreign donors.
The foreign debt of Bangladesh was significantly affected by these projects,
and the issue arises of whether their return will cover reimbursement. In this
regard, the systematic over-running of both construction delays and costs may
be a worry. They stem from a general lack of experience in dealing with such
large-scale projects but also to a lack of transparency and political pressure
in selecting the implementing agency, and in procurement. In effect, many of

---

[13] The largest of these megaprojects include the 6.1-kilometre-long double-deck Padma Multi-
purpose Bridge (connecting the southern part of Bangladesh with the capital city as well as
the eastern part of the country); Matarbari Deep Sea Port; Dhaka Metrorail Project; Dhaka
Elevated Expressway; Rooppur Nuclear Power Plant (a 2.4-GW nuclear power plant for a cost
of US$12.6 billion); Karnaphuli Underwater Tunnel to transform the port city of Chattogram
in 'One City Two Towns'; Chattogram-Cox's Bazar Rail Link (a 120-kilometre dual-gauge
passenger line to Cox's Bazar), one of the most popular tourist destinations in the country;
The Coal-Fired Power Plant of Matarbari; The Coal-Fired Power Plant of Rampal (will be the
country's largest power plant).
[14] https://m.theindependentbd.com/post/265537

implementation issues reflect complex dynamics of rent generation and sharing which are typical of large economic projects (Hassan and Raihan 2018).

Even though their economic utility is not in doubt, the multiplication of these mega-projects owes much to political factors. These include vested interests created by a range of stakeholders benefiting from these projects, their multiplier effects, the clout and image associated in public opinion with such prestigious project but also the relative ease in spending money quickly, including the rent-sharing opportunities that it creates. In this respect, the key role that the Bangladesh Army has played in some of the projects may be underscored, as it may have been a way of distracting it from politics.

In summary, the recent and spectacular expansion in infrastructure projects has the potential to deliver significant economic development impacts, alleviating some key binding constraints, in terms of power, transport, and connectivity. Yet, management flaws and rent-seeking behaviour made those projects notably more costly than they should have been.

F Bangladesh's Growth Engines and the Possible Limitations of Its Present Development Regime

Such are Bangladesh's achievements and challenges on the economic growth front, as they appear from a thorough review of the pace of the accumulation of essential production factors, their allocation, and productivity gains. The main lesson to retain from this review is the major role of RMG exports and remittances in explaining the overall satisfactory growth performance over the last two or three decades. Exports and the RMG sector have been particularly important in making the economy more dynamic, accelerating structural change, increasing productivity, and incentivising investment. Remittances have contributed to the growth of aggregate demand and the response of the domestic production machinery. Both exports and remittances have eased the foreign currency constraint that most developing countries at Bangladesh's development stage are confronted with. Together, RMG exports and remittances may have been responsible for two-thirds of the overall growth in GDP per capita over the last 20 years or so, the remaining third consisting of productivity gains in other sectors and the net movement of workers away from low-productivity agriculture.

The role played by manufacturing RMG exports in Bangladesh is in many respects remarkable. At the same time, the present situation hides weaknesses. On the one hand, there seems to be some anomaly in observing such a high concentration of exports in a country where apparel manufacturing export is already a mature although still growing activity. On the other hand, the international context, which has been favourable to Bangladesh RMG exports until now might become less so in the years to come.

On the first point, a common observation among countries whose development is based on manufacturing exports is precisely the fast diversifying array of products they offer. The rationale behind this diversification is the inherent complexity of manufacturing products in comparison with raw materials or commodities, which leads to progress taking place at both the intensive and the extensive margin that is exporting more of the same but also closely related products upstream or downstream as well as integrating into global value chains related to initial exports.[15] Such an evolution does not seem to take place in Bangladesh, and it will be important to understand why.

On the future of RMG exports, several obstacles were already mentioned: the appearance of low-labour cost competitors in both East Asia and sub-Saharan Africa, the pressure to improve labour conditions and its impact on cost-competitiveness or the automation of production which also reduces Bangladesh's comparative advantage. To these, should be added the forthcoming graduation of the country from the LDC status, which granted to it some trade preferences in both the EU and the United States.

If not able to increase its global market share, the RMG sector will be, at best, growing as foreign demand, the same being true of migrant remittances. This means that, if Bangladesh wants to maintain its fast pace of development, it has to substantially diversify its economy, and its exports in the first place.

Another limitation that needs to be mentioned, which has been absent from this review: land. It indeed bears emphasis that, except for a handful of tiny countries, Bangladesh is the country with the highest population density on earth: Singapore and Hong Kong have a higher population density, but Bangladesh has 20 or 30 times more inhabitants. Even though it is difficult to quantify the impact of this on growth, it is difficult to imagine that the (un) availability of land is not exerting a severe constraint on Bangladesh's development. This makes especially important the procedures for the allocation of land among its various economic uses. This point will be dealt with in some detail in the chapter on land in this volume.

III THE STATE AND THE FINANCING OF THE ECONOMY

State capacity is not a factor of production, properly speaking, and it would be difficult to provide a quantitative measure of it. Yet the ability of the state to coordinate the activity of private economic actors and, most importantly, to provide the public goods that are needed for the smooth working of the private sector is essential. This section reviews the financial aspects of the public sector in Bangladesh: that is, both its capacity to cover the public expenditures necessary for the development of the country and its ability to finance state-owned and private enterprises through public financial entities or the supervision of the private banking sector. It will be seen that, in both cases, the diagnostic is

---

[15] See the analysis by Hidalgo *et al.* (2007).

rather unfavourable. When considering the overall financing of the economy, however, a rather favourable feature is Bangladesh's autonomy with respect to foreign financing.

A Public Finance and State Capacity

The key function of the government sector is public revenue and expenditure management, with the aim of providing the public goods needed by the population and required for accelerating economic growth, reducing infrastructure gaps, promoting investment, and ensuring an efficient redistribution of resources to alleviate poverty and reduce inequality.

Table 2.3 presents the performance of key fiscal indicators in Bangladesh between fiscal years 2013/14 and 2017/18. Focusing first on the revenue side at the top of the table, two features are striking. First, government revenues are extremely low. Second, they show no sign of growth, relative to GDP. With a 10% tax to GDP ratio, Bangladesh is among the countries with the lowest taxes in the world. Unlike some countries that can count on other sources of public revenues, for instance through royalties on exports of natural resources, non-tax revenues add only marginally to the fiscal space in Bangladesh. On several instances, the Government announced major tax reforms that would drastically increase the tax/GDP ratio. Until now, however, such reforms have failed to materialise.

The tax system generates little revenue and, on top of that, it is highly distortive and regressive. Less than a third of government revenue comes from direct taxes and only half of that is from personal income tax. As far as the latter is concerned, a large number of potential taxpayers, including many ultra-rich people, remain outside of the tax net or pay a small amount of taxes. Also, several economic sectors that are capable of paying taxes are either fully exempted or enjoy substantial tax rebates. By contrast, indirect taxes (value-added tax, excise taxes, and import duties) that fall on the whole population and are on balance regressive account for the bulk of government revenues.[16] Overall, these features result in a tax system that is unable to raise enough revenue to finance the country's development, as non-tax revenues are marginal; that is inefficient and distortive of economic activity because tax privileges are granted to specific sectors or firms; and that is inequality enhancing.

The situation is not different on the expenditure side of the general government account. Even though the total spent is substantially higher than the revenue figure, Bangladesh's government expenditures are lower, in relation to GDP, than in many countries. Recurrent expenditures, for instance, amount on average to 9% of GDP, approximately the same level as revenues. Over the recent period, only 10 countries in the world have exhibited such a low level.

---

[16] A discussion of the structure of taxation can be found in Chapter 6.

TABLE 2.3 *Government revenue and expenditure in Bangladesh*

Fiscal year	2013/14	2014/15	2015/16	2016/17	2017/18
	(as % of GDP)				
Revenue and grants	10.92	9.77	10.09	10.22	9.66
Total revenue	10.45	9.62	9.98	10.18	9.62
Tax revenue	8.64	8.48	8.76	9.01	8.64
National Board of Revenue (NBR) tax revenue	8.29	8.17	8.44	8.69	8.31
Non-NBR tax revenue	0.34	0.32	0.33	0.33	0.32
Non-tax revenue	1.81	1.13	1.22	1.17	0.99
Grants	0.47	0.15	0.11	0.04	0.04
	(as % of GDP)				
Total expenditure	14.01	13.46	13.76	13.64	14.30
Non-development expenditure including net lending	9.60	9.27	9.06	9.18	8.87
Non-development expenditure	9.01	8.53	9.05	8.90	8.51
Revenue expenditure	8.23	7.84	8.33	8.33	7.95
Capital expenditure	0.78	0.69	0.71	0.58	0.56
	(as % of GDP)				
Net lending	0.60	0.74	0.01	0.28	0.37
Development expenditure	4.40	4.19	4.70	4.45	5.43
Annual Development Programme (ADP) expenditure	4.12	3.98	4.58	4.26	5.31
Non-ADP development spending	0.28	0.22	0.12	0.20	0.12
	(as % of GDP)				
Overall balance (excl. grants)	−3.56	−3.85	−3.78	−3.45	−4.68
Overall balance (incl. grants)	−3.09	−3.69	−3.67	−3.42	−4.64
Primary balance	−0.99	−1.65	−1.76	−1.62	−2.78
	(as % of GDP)				
Financing	3.09	3.69	3.67	3.42	4.64
External(net) (including market borrowing)	0.25	0.32	0.74	0.59	1.14
Loans	0.89	0.79	1.13	0.95	1.47
Amortisation	−0.64	−0.47	−0.39	−0.36	−0.33
Domestic	2.84	3.37	2.93	2.83	3.50
Bank	1.35	0.03	0.29	−0.42	0.52
Non-bank	1.49	3.34	2.64	3.25	2.98

Note: Net financing includes market borrowing. Bank includes secondary market.
Source: Ministry of Finance.

Combined with the level of GDP per capita, this suggests that the provision of public services, as measured by spending per capita, is most likely to be of worse absolute and relative quality in Bangladesh than in most countries in the world. Such a state of affairs can only have negative implications for both current economic growth and poverty reduction but also for future growth and economic welfare, as human capital formation is necessarily affected by this lack of resources.

It is difficult to make a judgement about the size of development expenditures in Bangladesh in comparison to other countries, and similarly about public investment, as no recent dataset with comparable international data is available. From what can be gathered from work referring to the mid-2000s, Bangladesh would seem close to the international norm, but somewhat below it.[17] Yet what is most striking is the fact that the financing of the investments scheduled in the Annual Development Programme, a multi-year development plan, is almost fully funded by government debt. Indeed, over the last five years, development expenditures represent on average 4.7% of GDP, whereas the deficit of the general government is slightly below 4%.

This deficit remains in relatively reasonable territory, yet it contributes in normal times to an increase in the public debt relative to GDP: as Table 2.3 shows, the Bangladesh Government exhibits a primary deficit, that is after taking into account the payment of interest on the outstanding debt, which is above 2% of GDP and has been clearly increasing over recent years. It is also interesting to note that one-quarter of the loans to the Government originate abroad and three-quarters originate domestically. Because of this heavy reliance on domestic lending, it cannot be discarded that public investment and the lack of fiscal space due to a low tax to GDP ratio is crowding out private investment.

To conclude this brief review of the government sector, it is worth mentioning that a recent study by the General Economics Division of the Planning Commission of Bangladesh (2017), estimated that the tax to GDP ratio in Bangladesh needs to be progressively increased to 16–17% by 2030 in order to achieve the major SDGs. This figure shows the huge revenue increase that the country needs to reach its announced development goals. The comparison with today's resources shows that such a target is ambitious but not unachievable if growth continues at the current pace. However, three years after this statement of goals, no real change is observed.

---

[17] See Cavallo and Daude (2008), who rely on World Economic Outlook (International Monetary Fund (IMF)) data on gross public and private capital formation. The IMF stopped publishing this breakdown of investment in 2006. In connection with public investment, an interesting result is found in Haque (2013), who shows that public investment positively influences GDP growth in Bangladesh, but much less than private investment. The problem is that the time-series analysis covers the period 1973–2010, which seems too heterogeneous for the estimation of this type of econometric model.

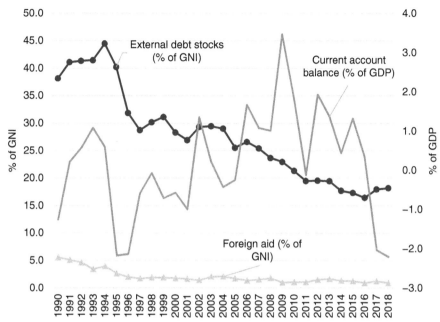

FIGURE 2.7 Current account, foreign debt, and foreign aid as a share of GDP, 1990–2018
Source: World Bank, WDI.

B External Financing of the Economy

The evolution of the external financing of the Bangladeshi economy is summarised in Figure 2.7. Since 1990, the balance of the current account has fluctuated over time in a rather narrow interval around equilibrium. Over the last two decades, it has been mostly on the positive side, except for the last two years, where it shows a more pronounced deficit. Overall, it is thus fair to say that the financing of the Bangladesh economy has been mostly domestic. This is well reflected in a debt to GDP ratio which is today around 20%, after peaking at close to 50% in the tumultuous 1980s and early 1990s.

This does not mean that the economy is free from financing from the rest of the world. Actually, it can be seen in Figure 2.7 that the trade balance has systematically been negative ever since independence, with a deficit ranging from 5% to 10% of GDP. Historically, the financing of that deficit has been covered by the remittances of Bangladeshi workers abroad and foreign aid. Over time, foreign aid dwindled, and current grants are today almost negligible – although the country still benefits from concessional loans from donors. Aid grants became unnecessary when remittances surged after the turn of the millennium, as was seen earlier, whereas concessional loans mattered more for technical assistance than for financing. At the same time, however, Bangladesh has become extremely dependent on the economy of those countries that host its migrant workers, led by the Gulf countries. However, as remittances started to fall rather drastically around 2015, precisely at the time oil prices plummeted and the Gulf countries cut down on their public spending. Two years later, this entailed a higher than normal deficit of the current account.

The rather balanced external position of Bangladesh's economy does not mean that the country did not have to request the help of the IMF on a few occasions over the past two decades. The first time was in 2001 after several years of a negative balance of the current account that had led the country to run down its reserves of foreign exchange. A stabilisation programme was then signed with the IMF for the 2003–2006 period, which came with some conditionalities relating to the management of state-owned companies and state-owned banks, tax revenues, and more general governance issues.[18] In 2011, an 'extended credit facility' was requested due to the impact of the European crisis on Bangladesh's balance of payment. It is thus not the case that the country is fully autonomous with respect to foreign financing. If they are strong and persistent, external shocks require payment facilities of the type provided by the IMF.

C Domestic Financing: The Banking Sector and the Weak Regulation of the Financial Sector

Two indicators can be used to evaluate the degree of development of the financial sector of a country: the broad money (M2) to GDP ratio, which measures the depth of the financial sector; and the domestic credit to the private sector by banks as a share of GDP, which measures the lending activity of the banking sector. These indicators were, respectively, 65% and 47% in Bangladesh in 2018. They doubled over the last two decades and have now reached the same level as other South Asian and lower middle-income countries. Yet they are substantially below levels observed among emerging manufacturing exporters in Southeast Asia (e.g. Cambodia or Vietnam), which were at comparable levels of financial development around 2000. The past two decades have also seen efforts to increase the quantity and the quality of banking services in Bangladesh. A broad-spectrum digitalisation, including electronic, has enabled the country to expand the coverage of its banking sector and the range of banking products not only in urban areas but also in rural areas. Yet, despite notable success, the banking sector in Bangladesh has some inherent weakness. One of its major weaknesses is the recurrent high level of non-performing loans (NPLs). The situation had become unsustainable at the end of the 1990s when NPLs reached the level of 40% of all outstanding loans. Some reforms in the regulation of the financial sector, as part of the 2003–2006 IMF stabilisation programme, were able to bring NPLs down

---

[18] An analysis of this stabilisation programme can be found in Hossain (2005).

during the 2000s. The share of NPLs in outstanding loans even reached 6% in 2011. In recent years, however, this share has started increasing again and is now above 10% – much higher than most comparable countries in South Asia and Southeast Asia, and undoubtedly damaging for the efficient functioning of the banking sector.

Even at 10%, the NPL rate is a real drain on the development capacity of the country and a powerful factor in relation to inequality. To measure its effect, the following rough calculation is instructive. It is estimated that approximately two-thirds of the NPLs can be recovered at the end of a long and costly litigation procedure. The other third must be recapitalised by the Government through drawing on fiscal resources. As NPLs are unlikely to finance the enlargement of the production capacity of the economy and are more likely to increase the wealth of defaulters, they may be considered as a sizeable net transfer – that is 3.3% of GDP – from investible resources paid by taxpayers to top income scammers.[19]

A lax regulation of the banking sector plays an important role in creating and piling up NPLs, particularly in state-owned banks and other public financial institutions. Cases of loans approved due to political considerations or family connections are frequent. Loans are then often disbursed without a proper or adequate credit assessment or sanction procedure, either in terms of the viability of the project they are supposed to fund or proper valuation of collateral. When default occurs, nepotism in the sanctioning procedure in favour of politically connected people makes recovering the lost money difficult.[20]

The lack of independence of the central bank, the Bangladesh Bank, and the fact that it has no control over the sizeable state-operated financial sector, are responsible for the weak regulation of the overall banking sector, that is private and state-owned. As an example of the limited regulating power of the central bank, an amendment to the Bank Company Act was recently passed that clearly facilitates the control of private banks by family or political interests.[21]

Beyond increasing the frequency of NPLs, the weak regulation of the financial sector has two major consequences for the real economy. On the one hand, it allows the financial sector not to strictly obey capital adequacy requirements. This increases the probability of crises and the periodic refinancing of some

---

[19] This argument assumes that the NPL share of outstanding loans is at a steady state, so that actual defaults and loans leaving the stock of NPLs are replaced by new ones.

[20] On the role of politicians, see Khanam *et al.* (2013). See also Chapter 6 in this volume for a thorough account of current fraudulent practices in the Bangladeshi banking sector.

[21] On 7 May 2018, the Government approved amendments to the Bank Company Act 1991. The changes extended the grip families can hold over a bank, allowing four members of a family to sit on the bank board at a time (the number had previously been two). The changes also paved the way for directors to stay on the board for nine years in a row, up from the previous six years (see https://tbsnews.net/analysis/will-give-more-leeway-loan-defaulters).

banks by the state. This is especially the case for state-owned banks, where the NPL rate is the highest, as is well documented in the press.[22] On the other hand, weak control of the lending activity of banks is responsible for an inefficient allocation of investment funds. It is certainly the case that valuable projects are being financed, and the past industrial growth of Bangladesh is testimony to this, but it is also the case that weak projects are being financed, thus depriving much better projects of funding. Evidence of this is provided by the causal effect of NPLs on banks' availability of funds, their cost, and the interest rate being charged.[23] Unfortunately, measuring the consequences of this inefficient use of those funds which have not leaked through fraudulent NPLs is extremely difficult and does not seem to have been attempted in the academic literature on Bangladesh.

Summarising, this section on the financing of the economy suggests two different views. The favourable one is that Bangladesh has been able to finance a successful industrial development in the RMG sector and is not excessively relying on foreign financing, except perhaps through the remittances of its migrant workers, which raises different issues. The less favourable one is that the exceedingly low revenue raised by the state through taxes and other means, as well as the very lax regulation of the financial sector, especially in regard to the state-owned institutions, leads to a sizeable waste of resources, and most likely to an inefficient allocation of investment.

IV SOCIAL MATTERS

Even though analysis of employment and the labour market would seem to belong to an analysis of output growth, it will be handled under the heading 'social matters' because of the deep consequences for the whole society of the pace of decent job creation in the economy, and, by contrast, the evolution of informal and often precarious employment. In particular, the state of the labour market and its evolution has direct implications for the distribution of economic welfare within the population and for the pace of poverty reduction. Human capital policies, that is education and healthcare, also affect the future level of employment and earnings, and present welfare, respectively.

A The Labour Market

The major labour market and employment challenge in Bangladesh, notably in the context of achieving the SDGs by 2030, is to provide enough jobs to the population of working age, particularly to women and youth.

---

[22] See, for instance, Lata (2015) and Dey (2019). See also the views expressed in the press, such as in www.dhakatribune.com/business/banks/2018/05/30/recapitalization-of-state-owned-banks-to-continue.

[23] See Islam (2019).

A difficulty common to most emerging and developing countries is the measurement of employment and what is actually meant by a 'job'. Without an unemployment insurance system, the notion of being unemployed is ambiguous, and in many cases irrelevant. A person without resources will always 'do something' to try to survive and will be recorded as 'employed' by enumerators. In fact, only people with some resources can afford to be truly unemployed. To a large extent, the level of employment is thus practically determined by the size of the labour force.

However, it is not the case that if most people report themselves as employed then there is no employment problem. If almost all people 'have a job', then Raihan (2015) is right to make a distinction in Bangladesh between 'good enough', 'good', and 'decent' jobs, where the first category corresponds roughly to jobs in the informal sector – self-employment or wage work without a formal labour contract – and the last two categories to the formal sector. In the latter, however, a distinction must be made between 'good' jobs, with a labour contract and possibly some social insurance – healthcare, pensions – and 'decent jobs' that would fit the International Labour Organization definition. In the case of Bangladesh, that distinction is important. The Rana Plaza collapse on thousands of workers in 2013 showed that RMG jobs are not always 'decent' jobs, given the lack of security of workplaces. Other features defining a decent job are also often missing in the RMG sector and in other formal firms.[24]

Based on that distinction, a good measure of the employment performances of a country is the creation of jobs in the formal sector, and within them the proportion of decent jobs. Based on labour force surveys over the last two decades, Rahman *et al.* (2019) found that the share of informal jobs in total employment probably increased a bit between 2000 and 2006 – from 75.2% to 78.5% – and very slightly declined between 2010 and 2016: the problem being that no direct comparison is possible between 2006 and 2010 because the nature of the survey questions used to decide whether a job is formal or informal changed. According to the post-2006 surveys, the degree of informality was 87% in 2010 – indeed a big difference compared to previous estimates – and 86% in 2016. Overall, it would thus seem that: (a) the degree of informality is extremely high in Bangladesh; (b) it has varied only marginally over time. This means that formal employment grew approximately alongside the labour force, at an annual rate around 1% over the last two decades, but substantially faster since 2010, with a rate slightly above 2%. Over the recent past, Raihan and Uddin (2018) find similar results for 'decent' jobs, the employment share of which increased from 10% in 2010 to 12% in 2018: that is, an annual growth rate of 3.3%. However, two or three times the rate of growth of the labour

---

[24] On the International Labour Organization definition of 'decent' jobs, see www.ilo.org/global/topics/decent-work/lang--en/index.htm?

force does not make a big difference in terms of the degree of informality, given the overwhelming weight of the informal sector in total employment. It is interesting that formal or decent jobs have tended to increase at a faster pace lately, but, at that pace, it will take many years for the growth of the formal sector to make a dent in informality. This is a major challenge for Bangladesh: formal and decent job creation needs to proceed much faster.

There are bad and good signs with respect to this challenge. On the bad side, it may be stressed that between 2013 and 2016/17, and despite average annual manufacturing growth being above GDP growth, at 6.6%, the number of manufacturing jobs declined by 0.77 million, and by 0.92 million for women. This represents a 10% drop in total employment and a strong substitution of female by male jobs.

This drop in the level of employment in the manufacturing sector despite RMG exports still increasing in volume is the result of a strong automation drive that has started to displace jobs. It is a sign that the manufacturing sector might not contribute to employment growth in the future as much as it has done in the past, and that Bangladesh's low-wage low-skill labour comparative advantage may be weakening. Even though the country may succeed in keeping, and even possibly increasing, its share of the global RMG market, the favourable social consequences of that development through the labour market will probably decline.

However, there is also a good sign in the fact that the share of the formal sector in total employment has not fallen despite an adverse evolution in manufacturing. Other formal sectors have created jobs, and presumably decent jobs, thus compensating for the loss in manufacturing. One may expect a large part of these jobs to be in the service sector, including transport and information and communication technology, and to concern workers with higher skill levels. If so, this points to the need to equip the labour force with more human capital and to invest more in education than has been done in the past.

Female employment may also be an issue. Over the past three decades, female labour force participation has increased, possibly in part as a response to the growth in RMG-based demand. Nevertheless, female labour supply has remained stagnant since 2010. Raihan and Bidisha (2018) explored both labour supply- and demand-side factors affecting female labour force participation in Bangladesh. Their analysis suggests that custom factors like child marriage, early pregnancy, or reproductive and domestic responsibilities have not changed much with the economic progress of the country and continue to constrain female work. But the demand side also plays a role, including the stagnation, and then the recent drop, in female employment intensity. Firm-level data from the World Bank's Enterprise Survey of 2007 and 2013 suggest that the ratio of female to male employment declined in major manufacturing and service sectors during that period, mostly due to the impact of innovation and technological upgradation.

Youth employment may also suffer from these changes. The share of youth not in education, economic activities and training (NEET) significantly increased from 25% in 2013 to 30% in 2016/17, with 87% of the youth NEET being female, possibly affected by the loss of jobs in the RMG sector.

Migrant work might be taken as a possible equilibrating mechanism of the labour market, lack of dynamism at home being compensated by more migrants. However, the driver of migration is unclear. Is it the domestic labour market pushing Bangladeshis abroad, or the labour demand pulling them towards destination countries? The recent drop in remittances, apparently linked to the slowdown in economic activity in the Gulf countries, would suggest that foreign demand matters most. Having said this, outmigration has undoubtedly had a huge impact on the domestic labour market, by reducing the supply of predominantly young, unskilled male workers, although a non-negligible share of migrants is skilled. According to World Bank statistics, some 7.7 million Bangladeshi work abroad,[25] which represents a little more than 10% of the domestic labour force.

B Poverty and Inequality

Bangladesh has made important progress in reducing poverty over the past one and half decades. According to the national estimates, the overall poverty headcount was halved between 2000 and 2016, from as high as 49% to 24%. Extreme poverty, defined by the international poverty line of 1.90 2011 international US$ per person and per day, fell still more drastically from 34% to 13% during the same period.

According to the United Nations Development Programme (UNDP) multidimensional poverty index, based not on income or consumption expenditure per capita but on various types of deprivation (nutrition, child mortality, school attendance, sanitation access to drinking water, etc.), Bangladesh has also made significant progress. The poverty headcount fell from 66% in 2004 to 47% in 2014, with particularly strong progress in child mortality, school attendance, and access to electricity, and more modest gains in access to drinking water and housing.[26] Overall, however, Bangladesh remains in the bottom third of emerging and developing countries. As this rank is somewhat below its rank in GDP per capita ranking, this suggests that Bangladesh does not do as well as other countries in the social area.

One area of concern relating to the poverty headcount is that its rate of decline seems to be slowing down. The average annual (monetary) poverty reduction has declined gradually over the past one and half decades, the same being true of the growth elasticity of poverty, which measures the capacity

[25] This figure is drawn from the Bilateral Migration Matrix on the World Bank site: www.worldbank.org/en/topic/migrationremittancesdiasporaissues/brief/migration-remittances-data.
[26] See UNDP (2019).

of economic growth to reduce poverty.[27] There are good reasons to expect such a slowdown in the reduction of poverty when poverty is already very low, as the average poor person is further and further away from the poverty line. But poverty in Bangladesh is not yet at this stage, which suggests that growth is not as inclusive today as it was in the past, and not as inclusive as it could be.

A possible explanation for the decline in the pace of poverty reduction may be the steady increase in income inequality that has been observed over time in Bangladesh. Such an increase means that better-off households benefited more, and/or worse-off households less, from economic growth. Inequality markedly increased during the 1990s. It then increased again, especially since 2010, as growth was accelerating. According to the Bangladesh Bureau of Statistics, based on its Household Income and Expenditure Survey, the Gini coefficient of income rose from 0.458 in 2010 to 0.482 in 2016. The poorest 10% of the household population saw its share of the total household income fall from 2% in 2010 to 1% in 2016. By contrast, the share of the richest 10% increased from 35.8% to 38.2%.

While the preceding figures refer to household income, it is worth emphasising that a different conclusion is reached when considering the inequality of consumption expenditures per capita, as is done in the Povcalnet database maintained by the World Bank, which relies on the same household surveys as the BBS. There, no noticeable change in inequality, as measured by the Gini coefficient, seems to have taken place since 2000, and particularly between 2010 and 2016. A possible explanation could be that top incomes saved a higher fraction of their income in 2016 than was the case in 2010, but the reason for such a behavioural change is unclear. On the other hand, this hypothesis is consistent with the sizeable drop in the share of aggregate consumption expenditures in GDP since 2010. It is indeed little likely that low- and middle-income households, whose saving rates are very low, were responsible for such a fall in the aggregate propensity to consume.[28]

The inequality issue also involves regional disparity in development. While Dhaka and a few metropolitan cities have been the major beneficiaries of development so far, many regions in the country are lagging behind. There also are genuine concerns that large discrimination prevails when it comes to budgetary allocation for social sectors and physical infrastructure, with Dhaka

---

[27] Between 2000 and 2005, on average, annually overall poverty rate declined by 1.8 percentage points, whereas between 2010 and 2016, annually the poverty rate declined by 1.2 percentage points. Also, between 2000 and 2005, the poverty elasticity of growth was a negative of 0.32 which declined to a negative of 0.16 during 2010 and 2016.

[28] Osmani and Sen (2011) suggested that the discrepancy between the evolution of inequality measured with income or consumption expenditure in rural areas in the 2000s could be due to the expansion of micro-credit, allowing people to smooth consumption in the presence of income fluctuations.

and a few other metropolitan cities benefitting as against many other regions in the country.[29] With two to seven times more development spending per capita in the Dhaka region in comparison with other regions, it is predicted that the country's inequality situation will worsen in the future, despite the small improvement observed in the 2000s in the east–west gap.[30]

C Education

As measured by the number of years of schooling, the level of education in Bangladesh's population above 25 years old was 5.8 years in 2017. Among South Asian countries, this was higher than Pakistan (5.2) but lower than India (6.4), and far behind Sri Lanka (10.9) and leading Southeast Asian countries like Malaysia (10.2), Thailand (7.6), and Vietnam (8.2). In the recent past, however, Bangladesh has made remarkable progress in primary school enrolment, with near universal enrolment attained by 2010, as well as in secondary enrolment, with a rate now reaching 63%. It is thus to be expected that the average years of schooling of the Bangladeshi adult population and labour force will increase at a fast rate in the one or two decades to come.

Despite considerable progress in primary school enrolment, however, the country is seriously lagging in terms of the quality of education. Numerous studies point to low learning achievement of children who have gone through primary education. According to a recent evaluation, 59% of Grade 3 students and 90% of Grade 5 students were below the required level in mathematics at the end of the respective grades.[31] It is thus not clear that the recent increase in years of schooling will soon entail a higher productivity of the labour force. Serious efforts are now needed to improve the education system.

Regrettably, Bangladesh is among the countries in the world with the lowest ratio of public expenditure on education to GDP. This ratio has fluctuated around 2% over recent years,[32] a level that is much lower than most sub-Saharan countries, although these countries generally are poorer than Bangladesh. The contrast with the recommendation by the United Nations Educational, Scientific and Cultural Organization that countries should target educational expenditures amounting to 6% of GDP cannot be starker.

It is important to mention that Bangladesh's education sector also suffers from huge disparities. There is a high degree of inequality with respect to access to quality education, depending on where people live. Consequently, major spatial differences are observed in educational performances among primary schools, with schools closer to metropolitan areas performing much better than others (Raihan and Ahmed, 2016).

---

[29] https://tbsnews.net/bangladesh/infrastructure/pie-not-divided-fairly-45607
[30] See Sen *et al.* (2014).
[31] See Chapter 7.
[32] World Bank, World Development Indicator figure.

D Healthcare

Bangladesh has made considerable progress in basic health indicators over the last decades. Advances in life expectancy, infant mortality, and maternal mortality are noteworthy. Over the last 20 years, life expectancy has risen by eight years, to reach 72 by 2016, higher than the average for lower middle-income countries and for South Asia. Infant mortality was reduced by a factor of almost 3, being today 30 per 1,000, lower again than lower middle-income and South Asian countries. Finally, maternal mortality was brought down from more than 300 to 170 for 100,000 live births. However, to achieve the targets under SDG Goal 3 by 2030, Bangladesh still has to make significant efforts: both infant and maternal mortality must still be divided by 2.5.

There are numerous challenges for Bangladesh in achieving these targets. In particular, the public health budget is only 0.39% of GDP, which is one of the lowest in the world. For this reason, the share of out-of-pocket health expenditure in total health expenditure is much higher than in other countries, reaching 71.8%. Overall, including NGOs, it is estimated that total health expenditures amount to around 3% of GDP. In other words, the public sector covers only 13% of the cost of healthcare.

With such a low level of health expenditure compared to GDP, especially in the public sector, how has Bangladesh achieved so much in terms of the health indicators mentioned above? There is evidence that over the past few decades, Bangladesh has successfully opted for low-cost solutions to some vital health-related problems. Also, widespread activities of NGOs created a deeper awareness of health issues among the population (Sarwar, 2015). A study of the use of remittances also showed that they played an important role in increasing the capacity of households to pay for health expenditure (Raihan *et al.*, 2017a).

However, in the future, such options are likely to be limited as the health system in Bangladesh is increasingly facing hard and multifaceted challenges. These result from new pressures originating from an ageing population, the rising prevalence of chronic diseases, and the growing need for more intensive use of expensive and still critical health-related equipment (like advanced scanners, MRI machines, etc.). On the other hand, financing health-related problems through out-of-pocket expenditures increases inequality, as this places a huge cost burden on poorer people and feeds the vicious disease–poverty cycle (World Health Organization and World Bank, 2019). More investment in healthcare is thus not only a desirable but also an essential policy priority. It is hard to imagine that this could be done without a substantial increase in government revenues.

E NGOs and Microcredit

Bangladesh is famous around in the world for the number and the dynamism of its NGOs. It is said they have their roots in the intense solidarity movements that developed after a deadly cyclone and the war of independence that left the country devastated and during the terrible famine that killed more than a million people during 1974–1975.[33] Thanks to them, Bangladesh has shown strong progress on several social indicators, mostly due to a multifaceted service provision regime. The expansion and multiplication of NGOs made it possible to scale up innovative anti-poverty experiments into nationwide programmes. Some notable programmes include innovations in providing access to credit to previously 'unbanked' poor; the development of a non-formal education system for poor children (particularly girls); and the provision of door-to-door health services through thousands of village-based community health workers. On a different level, it must also be stressed that NGOs have notably contributed to the empowerment of women within a strongly patriarchal society. The large portion of NGO beneficiaries who are poor women is evidence that a cultural change that is taking place in regard to the position of women in society.

The delivery of social services and pro-poor advocacy are not NGOs' only activities. They have also developed commercial ventures aimed at creating a bridge between poor subsistence farmers and markets, as well as an internal revenue generation model for the NGOs themselves. Their largely self-financed pro-poor services have become an integral part of achieving national poverty reduction targets.

NGOs differ in their size and coverage. There are about 2,000 development NGOs, some of which are among the largest of such organisations in the world. NGOs such as BRAC, Grameen Bank, ASA, and PROSIKA have tens of thousands of employees and multi-million-dollar budgets, with their operations spreading throughout the nation. Other NGOs are smaller in scale and function with limited managerial and staff capacity.

Microfinance is a key factor behind the growth of NGO programmes. Some 55% of rural households have resorted to microfinance at some stage in their lives, and almost 46% hold the status of current borrowers (Raihan *et al.*, 2017b). The sector is dominated by the Grameen Bank, BRAC, ASA, and PROSHIKA, which between them cover around 90% of microfinance operations. Even though there is some ambiguity regarding whether micro lending has a long-run transformative impact on household income,[34] it reduces current poverty and provides insurance against weather shocks or other accidents. Improvements in social indicators like female empowerment, children's schooling, and health status in part reflect the complementary social mobilisation, training, and awareness building activities developed by NGOs alongside microcredit.

---

[33] Along the major NGOs in Bangladesh, it is noteworthy that BRAC was founded in 1972 just after independence, PROSHIKA in 1975 as a sequel of the famine and Muhammad Yunus drew the basic idea of the Grameen Bank through experiences he had with a small credit program during the famine.

[34] See Banerjee *et al.* (2015) and Meager (2019).

Door-to-door health services are provided by NGOs through village-based community health workers, focusing mostly on preventive care and simple curative care for women and children. NGOs have also achieved notable success in promoting behavioural change at community level by providing water and sanitation services. Their community work also includes programmes on child nutrition and tuberculosis treatment, in collaboration with the Government.

BRAC is the pioneer in launching primary education and has become the single largest NGO in the world working in primary education, social enterprises, microfinance, health services, housing, and water and sanitation programmes all over the country and also abroad. Today, BRAC provides primary education to over 1 million children in 22,000 education centres nationwide. It lends half a billion US dollars a year to 7 million people and employs more than 100,000 people for an annual budget of 750 million dollars.[35] Other NGOs are smaller but altogether they may amount to two to three times BRAC's size. Their role is thus far from marginal. Although not quantified, their contribution to poverty reduction, in the multidimensional sense used by UNDP, has been and continues to be crucial.

V ENVIRONMENT AND CLIMATE CHANGE CHALLENGES

Bangladesh is highly vulnerable to climate change impacts because of its vast low-lying areas, large coastal population, high population density, inadequate infrastructure, and high dependence on agriculture. For Bangladesh, climate change is manifested as both changes in the severity of extreme events and in greater climate variability. Climate variability involves haphazard wet and drought years, whereas extreme weather events take the form of violent tropical cyclones which also generate powerful storm surges, and whose effects are amplified by rising sea levels. About 20% of the population lives in the low coastal zone and any increase in sea level will have disastrous effects. Because of the flat topography, even small increments in sea level rise will affect large areas, directly through inundation and salt intrusion. In the Global Climate Risk Index 2019, Bangladesh has been ranked seventh among the countries most affected by extreme weather events in the 20 years since 1998.[36]

Climate change–linked problems are likely to act as a drag on the nation's growth prospects. The Asian Development Bank (ADB, 2014) concluded that climate change poses big economic and development challenges for Bangladesh. The study pointed out that the country will face annual economic costs equivalent to about 2% of its GDP by 2050, widening to 9.4% by 2100. The reasons for these losses include an immense decline in crops, land loss and salinity,

---

[35] BRAC (2018).
[36] https://germanwatch.org/files/Global%20Climate%20Risk%20Index%202019_2.pdf

and internal migration, among other things. Climate-related disasters regularly cause migration movements and changes in poverty patterns. Because of major climate shocks, poor people from the south of the country are migrating to urban areas. Analysis at the district and sub-district levels shows that there is a strong positive correlation between the incidence of poverty and the intensity of natural hazards. On average, districts that are ranked as most exposed to natural disasters also show poverty rates that are higher than the national average. Strikingly, of the 15 most poverty-stricken districts, almost 13 of them belong to high natural hazard risk categories.

VI THE COVID-19 CRISIS

Bangladesh is currently the second most affected country by COVID-19 in South Asia (after India) with 1.5 million confirmed cases and 28,000 confirmed deaths between January 2020 and December 2021. However, excess mortality estimates released by *The Economist* Magazine suggest a much higher death toll, probably above half a million. Despite measures intended to attenuate its impact, the pandemic led to a serious economic and social crisis, and one may wonder whether the growth potential of the country has not been affected. GDP kept growing but its growth rate fell by 3–4% in 2020 and was likely still below trend in 2021. As far as poverty is concerned, on the other hand, it is estimated that at the heart of the crisis, in the spring of 2020, the headcount may have doubled, reaching maybe 40% of the population.[37] It went down, probably close to its initial level since then.

The drop in GDP growth is due to three major causes: (i) the pandemic itself, which has affected the health workers and may have forced some of them to temporarily cease working even outside lockdown periods; (ii) the lockdown episodes, especially the longest one from 23 March to 30 May 2020; and (iii) the fall in global demand. A stimulus package, consisting mostly of subsidised loans to support furlough strategies by firms, and cash/food transfers to needy households, for 3.5% of GDP, was meant to attenuate the shock.

It is difficult to disentangle the role of these various factors. Yet, global demand has undoubtedly played a major role. The quasi-stagnation of manufacturing output for the whole of 2020 is almost entirely due to the RMG sector, despite the fact that it partly defied the lockdown by resuming work a month before it ended. Other sectors are much less exposed to foreign demand. They were much less affected by the lockdown or recovered quickly when it was lifted. Over the whole year, rather than the few months of the lockdown, the main shock on the Bangladeshi economy turns out to be a 20% drop in exports, which mechanically generated a drop of GDP around 3%, a bit less than the observed slowdown of growth. This confirms the dominant role of

---

[37] Raihan *et al.* (2021a); BIGD (2021a).

RMG exports in the economy and the vulnerability of the latter to any kind of shock in that sector.

That GDP kept growing in Bangladesh during the pandemic is quite remarkable when comparing it to India where GDP fell by 8% in 2020. The pandemic has been more severe there, at least by the relative number of estimated casualties with respect to the population, but lockdown, social distance and school closure measures were very much the same. It would be interesting to know whether this divergence is due to differences in the socio-economic structure of the two countries or in their reactivity.[38]

As far as poverty is concerned, a difference must clearly be made between the impact of COVID-19 measured at the time of the lockdown or averaged over the whole year in a way that is consistent with GDP growth measurement. On the spot, it was seen above that the shock was violent, mostly because the lockdown affected more those low-income people whose occupation in the informal sector required some spatial mobility. Unlike formal workers, they could not benefit from the furlough system based on subsidised loans to formal firms, or work from home. Food distribution and cash transfers only moderately attenuated the income shock that they suffered. Estimated over a longer period, or a few months after the end of the 2020 lockdown, the situation is likely to be different. The calculation of the change in poverty, in line with the observed GDP growth and what is known about the growth elasticity of the poverty headcount, indicates that the proportion of poor people may have been between 0.5 and 1 percentage point below trend by December 2020, except if the recovery from the crisis came with a strong increase in income inequality.

Such a calculation does not take into account the potential permanent effects of the crisis on those people who were the most affected at the peak of the pandemic and during the lockdown. Those damages may be related to health, either through the pandemic itself or as a result of undernutrition, on productive economic assets sold to face up to income losses, or on the education of the children. As schools have been closed for more than a year it is expected that a higher proportion of students will drop-out than in normal times, whereas it is not clear that, without an effective remedial programme, others will be able to make-up for the time lost. This deficit of human capital is unlikely to have a major impact on future aggregate growth because it will affect only a few cohorts. However, this may not be the case with poverty and inequality as students from distressed families are likely to bear a higher burden from the disruption.[39]

---

[38] A detailed analysis of the impact of COVID-19 on the economy is still to be performed, as standard economic aggregates look sometimes contradictory. This is the case for instance of the 10% drop in the volume of imports that does not seem consistent with the growth of GDP, unless major changes have been observed in inventories.

[39] As analysed in (Amirapu *et al.*, 2020), there also is a risk that families may look to early marriage as a means of providing security

A final word should be said about what the crisis revealed about the capacity of the government to handle such shocks. From that point of view, the existing evidence is far from satisfactory. The crisis not only exposed a lack of administrative capacity within the health and social protection sectors, but also difficulties in co-ordinating across sectors and public entities. They have been compounded by the under-development of the public health sector, and issues surrounding finance, equity, quality and efficiency. Similarly, underlying weaknesses in the social protection system, such as the inability to quickly and efficiently disburse funds and other forms of support to those most vulnerable, exacerbated the social consequences of the pandemic.[40] On the economic side, on the other hand, the policy response has been uneven, benefiting some groups far more than others.

These shortcomings have deep institutional and political economy roots, since they reflect how certain vested interests benefit from the status quo, and how policy decisions mirror the political and lobbying power of particular groups. Micro, small and medium enterprises have seen little benefit from the stimulus packages. In contrast, larger firms with powerful lobbying and useful political links, despite the fact that many of them may not need the stimulus package, dominated the scenario, as shown in Raihan *et al.* (2021b). As a consequence, the inherent bias towards large firms, especially in the RMG sector, that has been a hallmark of Bangladesh's industrial development in the past, has been replicated in the manner in which the government has sought to respond to the economic harms due to the pandemic.

VII CONCLUSION

This in-depth analysis of the achievements and challenges of the Bangladeshi economy may be summarised in three basic points.

First and foremost, the economy has experienced, and may still be experiencing, a very successful development episode, based on an extremely vigorous export manufacturing sector born in the 1980s out of the opportunities offered by the MFA and then expertly exploited and amplified by a dynamic and influential entrepreneurial class. It can be estimated that, directly and indirectly through backward and forward links, the RMG sector may have been responsible for 30–40% of Bangladesh's very solid growth performance over the last two or three decades. The role played by the remittances of migrant Bangladeshi workers which peaked at 10% of GDP around 2010 must also be mentioned as a powerful factor affecting growth, through their major impact on domestic demand. Together, manufacturing exports and remittances are estimated to explain two-thirds of Bangladesh's growth over the last 20 years.

---

[40] Bangladesh's flagship social protection scheme, the prime minister's cash support scheme, did mobilise quickly and achieved a relatively high level of coverage, but offered low transfer values in the form of one-off payment. For a detailed evaluation of government's cash transfer and food distribution response, see MAINTAINS (2021).

The fact that both RMG exports and remittances have slowed down in the recent past is a source of concern – and makes the GDP growth rate estimates for the last few years a bit of a puzzle.[41]

Second, Bangladesh's strong development performance is all the more surprising given that, except for the forward and backward linkage effects of RMG exports and the multiplier effects of remittances, the diagnostic regarding the rest of the economy is not very favourable. An underdeveloped public sector and public services, an infrastructure deficit, among the worst investment climates in the world, and a rather corrupt banking sector may all explain a lack of dynamism outside the RMG sector. This is more apparent in other manufacturing export activity. Domestic-oriented sectors, including a few import-substitution sectors, benefited directly from the expansion of RMG exports and remittances, through their impact on aggregate demand. All in all, Bangladesh may not be very different from those developing countries exporting a natural resource that feeds the development of domestic-oriented sectors. The difference is that export prices in Bangladesh do not fluctuate as much as those of commodities, and the demand for its exports have grown at a steady and fast rate over time, in part thanks to a comparative advantage and in part based on low-wage labour.

The third point is that, when abstracting from the successful RMG export sector, Bangladesh exhibits most of the features of low-income countries, despite having graduated from the LDC status and accessing the group of lower middle-income countries: extended poverty, a huge traditional farming sector, overwhelming informality, low human capital, and weak public services. With respect to the latter, however, one feature of Bangladesh is the presence of a buoyant NGO sector that partly compensates for the failings of the state. Besides the role of the NGO and RMG sectors, and despite favourable past growth performance, Bangladesh thus faces many of the structural obstacles that hinder the development of countries at the same level of income, except the strong dependence generally observed on foreign financing.

Looking now to the future, the main challenge is whether the RMG sector will continue to be as dynamic as it was before the recent slowdown, or whether the latter has some premonitory meaning. Competition from other low-wage countries; the mechanisation of the industry, which reduces its employment capacity, notably of women, and which may trigger some reshoring policy among some clients of Bangladesh; the loss of trade preferences that comes with graduating from the LDC status – will all affect the main growth driver of the economy. Given the high product concentration of exports, manufacturing export diversification, including the upgrading of RMG production, is the

---

[41] There are, however, debates on the official GDP growth numbers in recent years. While the official statistics show accelerated and increasing growth rates in GDP since 2013, sluggish growth in exports and remittances are not consistent with the official claims. Civil society think tanks and development partners like the World Bank and the IMF have questioned the credibility of the official statistics (see The Daily Star 2018a; The Daily Star 2019; New Age, 2019).

strategy that should be pursued in order to maintain the rate of growth of the economy. This requires not only an adequate investment programme, but also progress in infrastructure, banking, human capital accumulation, and state capacity in general – all areas where Bangladesh is presently under-performing. The present slowdown in RMG exports and in remittances suggests that there may be an urgent need to launch such an ambitious strategy.

It remains to be seen whether Bangladesh's institutional context is conducive to such an inflexion of its economic development strategy. Chapters 4–9 analyse in more detail this crucial aspect of development.

ANNEX 2.1 DECOMPOSITION OF GROWTH IN BANGLADESH

The methodology[42] consists of decomposing output growth into a weighted average of the rate of growth of the factors of production, labour, and capital, and a residual, termed TFP (or 'Solow residual').

A neoclassical production function represents output at time t, Y_t, as a function of the economy's capital stock, K_t, its labour force, L_t, and the economy's TFP, A_t. With a Cobb–Douglas specification, this function is written as:

$$Y_t = A_t K_t L_t^{1-\alpha}$$

where α and $1-\alpha$ are, respectively, the output elasticity of capital and labour. It is well known that at a competitive equilibrium of the economy, α and $1-\alpha$ also are y, the share of capital and labour income in GDP.

Within this framework, output changes can only be caused by changes in the capital stock, the labour force, or in TFP. Taking logarithms and differentiating leads to the identity:

$$Ln\, Y_t - Ln\, Y_{t-1} = Ln\, A_t - Ln\, A_{t-1} + \alpha \left(Ln\, K_t - Ln\, K_{t-1} \right)$$
$$+ \left(1 - \alpha \right) \left(Ln\, L_t - Ln\, L_{t-1} \right)$$

Or:

GDP growth = S_k.Cap growth + (1 – S_k). Lab growth + TFP growth

Observed GDP	↓ Observed Cap growth	↓ Observed Lab growth	Residual
	Observed GDP share of capital income	Observed GDP share of labour income	

However, it should be mentioned that there are some limitations of this exercise. TFP growth factor productivity is calculated as a residual, and therefore any measurement error in the variables that measure labour, capital, or the GDP share of labour and capital income, are mechanically imputed to TFP. Also, growth accounting is a descriptive tool, and it does not provide insights into the nature of TFP growth (technological, structural, and/or institutional change).

---

[42] See, for instance, Vincelette and Koehler (2009).

The above growth accounting identity may be generalised to any production function that exhibits constant returns to scale. A crucial assumption is that the economy is competitive so that the weight of capital and labour growth in the accounting identity are their income shares in GDP. This may be considered to be a rather strong assumption.

ANNEX 2.2 DECOMPOSITIONS OF AGGREGATE LABOUR PRODUCTIVITY

From Avillez (2012): For the aggregate economy in period t define $X_t(Y_t)$ as aggregate real (nominal) output, N_t as labour input, and $A_t := X_t / N_t$ as aggregate labour productivity. Variables with subscript i refer to corresponding variables in sector i, of which there are M, for example $A_{it} := X_{it} / N_{it}$ is productivity in sector i in period t. Define, furthermore, sector i's labour input share as $S_{it} := N_{it} / N_t$ and denote overall (sector i's) productivity growth as follows:

$$G_t := \frac{A_t - A_0}{A_0} \left(G_{it} := \frac{A_{it} - A_{i0}}{A_{i0}} \right).$$

Assume that real output is measured in constant prices – more specifically, using fixed-base Laspeyres quantity and Paasche price indexes – so that aggregate real output corresponds to the sum of sectoral real output:

$$X_t = \sum_{i=1}^{M} X_{it}, i = 1M, \cdots,.$$

Then aggregate labour productivity is equal to the weighted sum of sector labour productivity across all sectors, where the weights are the sectoral labour shares:

$$A_t = \frac{\sum_{i=1}^{M} X_{it}}{N_t} = \frac{\sum_{i=1}^{M} A_{it} N_{it}}{N_t} = \sum_{i=1}^{M} A_{it} S_{it}.$$

Accordingly, for a given year t and base year o, we can decompose Gt as follows:

$$G_t = \frac{\sum_{i=1}^{M} \left(A_{it} S_{it} - A_{i0} S_{i0} \right)}{A_{i0}}$$

$$= \sum_{i=1}^{M} \frac{A_{i0}}{A_0} \left(S_{i0} G_{it} + \left(S_{it} - S_{i0} \right) + \left(S_{it} - S_{i0} \right) G_{it} \right)$$

$$= \underbrace{\sum_{i=1}^{M} \frac{X_{i0}}{X_0} G_{it}}_{\text{WSE}} + \underbrace{\sum_{i=1}^{M} \frac{A_{i0}}{A_0} \Delta S_{it}}_{\text{SRE}} + \underbrace{\sum_{i=1}^{M} \frac{A_{i0}}{A_0} \Delta S_{it} G_{it}}_{\text{DRE}}.$$

Here, $\Delta S_{it} := S_{it} - S_{i0}$ represents the movement of labour across sectors. Labour productivity growth can thus be decomposed into three distinct effects:

WSE – reflects the impact of productivity growth within individual sectors on aggregate productivity;

SRE (Denison effect) – captures the impact of the reallocation of employment from less productive to more productive sectors (i.e. it arises from sectoral differences in productivity *levels*); and

DRE (Baumol effect) – describes the impact of reallocating employment into sectors with growing productivity (i.e. this results from asymmetric productivity growth *rates* across sectors). The Baumol effect detracts from aggregate productivity growth when labour moves towards (away from) a sector with negative (positive) labour productivity growth. Note that the magnitude of the DRE depends not only on the sectoral productivity rates and sectoral employment shifts but also on the ratio between the sector's labour productivity level and the aggregate labour productivity level.

ANNEX 2.3 FACTORS AFFECTING GROWTH IN BANGLADESH

To analyse the sources of growth in the Bangladesh economy, we use a time series econometric model. The model aims to estimate the relationship between economic growth and the potential drivers of growth analysed in the main text, which are exports and remittances. We begin with the Solow model specification with a Cobb–Douglas production function, along the lines employed by Luintel *et al.* (2008) and Rao *et al.* (2008):

$$y_t = a_t k_t^\alpha, \quad 1 > \alpha, \beta > 0 \tag{1}$$

where y = real GDP per worker, a = TFP or accumulated stock of technological knowledge, k = capital stock per worker, and t = time period.

The Solow model assumes that the evolution of technology is exogenous and TFP grows at rate g:

$$a_t = a_0 e^{gT} \tag{2}$$

where a_0 = initial stock on knowledge.

As suggested by Rao *et al.* (2008), it is assumed, in addition, that the growth drivers affect growth essentially through their impact on TFP, for instance, by facilitating technological import. Thus, assuming Cobb–Douglas functional forms, TFP may be specified as:

$$a_t = a_0 e^{gT} EX_t^\delta REM_t^\gamma \tag{3}$$

where EX = real exports of goods and services per worker, REM = real migrants' remittances per worker, and δ and γ are constants.

Substituting into (1) and taking logarithms leads to the following linear equation:

$$Ln\ y_t = Ln\ a_0 + gT + \alpha.Ln\ k_t + \delta.Ln\ EX_t + \gamma.Ln\ REM_t + \varepsilon_t \tag{4}$$

where ε_t stands for random deviations from the theoretical relationship.

As some variables in this model may be non-stationary, a cointegration approach is adopted. The method of estimation is the auto regressive distributed lag (ARDL) framework by Pesaran and Shin (1999).[43] The ARDL approach to cointegration involves estimating the conditional error correction version of equation 5 and allows for combining non-stationary variables – supposedly I(1) – and stationary variables – that is I(0). An F-statistic makes it possible to test the null hypothesis of no cointegration.

Prior to the testing of cointegration, we conducted a test of the order of integration for each variable in the model, using augmented Dickey–Fuller (ADF) and Philip–Perron (PP) techniques. Even though the ARDL framework does not require pretesting of the variables of the model, the unit root test could inform us whether the ARDL model should be used. The results show that there is indeed a mixture of I(1) and I(0), with trends.

The ARDL model was applied to equation (5) using Akaike information criterion (AIC) as information criterion and time trend. The number of lags is selected by the Pesaran and Shin (1999) and Narayan (2004) techniques. Two lags were introduced in the procedure. The calculated F-statistic of 26.47 made it possible to reject the null hypothesis of no-cointegration at the 1% level of significance.

The empirical estimates of the long-run relationship between the variables of equation (4) are shown in Table 2.4-A. The regression results suggest that the long-run elasticity of real GDP per worker with respect to capital stock per worker is 0.64. In addition, a 1% increase in real export per worker leads to a 0.123% increase in real GDP per worker, and a 1% increase in real remittance per worker leads to an increase in real GDP per worker of 0.137%. The short-run coefficients (in first differenced form), not shown here, for capital per worker and export per worker are positive and statistically significant, while that for remittance per worker is not statistically significant.

As explained in the text, exports and remittances may also affect directly the accumulation of capital, by providing the foreign currency needed for importing equipment and by incentivising investment in domestic production through their impact on aggregate demand. There are two ways for estimating these

---

[43] The advantages of using ARDL approach over the conventional Johansen (1991) approach is that while the conventional cointegrating method estimates the long-run relationships within a context of a system of equations, the ARDL method employs only a single reduced form equation. Furthermore, the ARDL approach does not involve pre-testing variables, which means that the test on the existence relationship between variables in levels is applicable irrespective of whether the underlying regressors are purely I(0), purely I(1), or a mixture of both. Furthermore, the ARDL method avoids the larger number of specifications to be made in the standard cointegration test. These include decisions regarding the number of endogenous and exogenous variables (if any) to be included, the treatment of deterministic elements, as well as the optimal number of lags to be specified. With ARDL, it is possible that different variables have different optimal lags, which is impossible with the standard cointegration test. Most importantly the model could be used with limited sample data (30–80 observations) in which the set of critical values were developed originally by Narayan (2004).

TABLE 2.4 *Results of ARDL estimation (long-run model)*

A. Dependent variable: log of real GDP per worker	Coef.	Std. err.	t	*P > t*
Log of capital per worker	0.642	0.076	8.35	0.000
Log of real export per worker	0.123	0.032	4.85	0.000
Log of real remittance per worker	0.137	0.057	2.39	0.024
T (time trend)	0.000034	0.0008	0.04	0.968
Constant	4.15	1.99	2.08	0.047

B. Dependent variable: log of capital per worker	Coef.	Std. err.	t	*P > t*
Log of real export per worker	0.396	0.099	4.02	0.000
Log of real remittance per worker	0.132	0.063	2.59	0.044
T (time trend)	0.0018	0.0011	1.54	0.138
Constant	0.391	0.282	1.39	0.178

C. Dependent variable: log of real GDP per worker	Coef.	Std. err.	t	*P > t*
Log of real export per worker	0.220	0.022	10.18	0.000
Log of real remittance per worker	0.143	0.022	4.46	0.000
T (time trend)	0.00145	0.00078	1.84	0.074
Constant	3.2821	1.222	1.69	0.088

Source: Authors' estimation.

effects. The first one consists of analysing the relation between the stock of capital and the two growth drivers, EX and REM. The second one consists of estimating the reduced form model, where the capital stock is omitted in the output regression. In that case, the estimation should reveal the overall impact of the growth drivers, through both TFP and the accumulation of capital.

These two models are respectively:

$$Ln\ k_t = Ln\ b_0 + hT + \lambda.Ln\ EX_t + \mu.Ln\ REM_t + \eta_t \tag{5}$$

$$Ln\ y_t = Ln\ c_0 + mT + \theta.Ln\ EX_t + \pi.Ln\ REM_t + \omega_t \tag{6}$$

where b_0 and c_0 are constants and η_t and ω_t are random deviations from the corresponding theoretical relationship. The estimation results obtained with the same procedure as before are shown in Table 2.4-B and Table 2.4-C.

Together, models (4) and (5) provide a 'structural view' of the way the growth drivers EX and REM affect output growth. They do it in two ways: through the TFP effect in equation (4), and through their impact on capital accumulation in equation (5). The overall elasticity is obtained by combining the coefficients of the two equations. The EX elasticity is thus: $\delta + \alpha.\lambda$ and is worth: 0.12+0.64*0.40 = 0.37, whereas the REM elasticity is $\gamma + \alpha.\mu$ or 0.14+0.64*0.13 = 0.208.

The problem of the preceding estimation of the overall effect of the growth drivers on GDP growth is that, by not taking into account the dependency of capital accumulation on the growth drivers, the estimated coefficients of the variables Ln EX and Ln REM in (4), already take into account their effect on TFP as well as on the accumulation of capital. There thus is some double-counting in preceding calculation, which over-estimates their effect.

To correct for this, *Ln k* in (4) should be instrumented through equation (5), adding to the later equation an instrumental variable orthogonal to both the growth drivers and to growth itself. In the absence of such a variable, only the reduced form model (6) can be estimated, with the time trend possibly accounting for unobserved output determinants that increase with time. Thus, the estimates of θ and π combine the TFP and the capital accumulation effect.

Based on the estimations in Table 2.4-C, the overall effect of a 1% change in exports results in a 0.22% increase in GDP, the corresponding figure being 0.14% for remittances. Between 2000 and 2018, EX and REM both increased at an annual rate of 12%, thus entailing an annual growth of, respectively, 2.6% and 1.5% of GDP on average, for an overall growth rate of 6%.

3

Critical Institutional Areas for Bangladesh's Development

Selim Raihan, Rafiqua Ferdousi,
and Towhid I. Iqram Mahmood

I INTRODUCTION

This chapter presents analyses using information from a variety of sources in order to identify areas where in-depth research can identify institutional challenges that are most critical to Bangladesh's economic development. Two approaches are employed. The first approach uses a variety of institutional measures available in international databases to examine how a country, in this case Bangladesh, differs from a set of comparators. A questionnaire survey of various types of decision makers and academics is used in the second approach, as well as a set of open-ended interviews with senior policymakers and decision makers.

II BANGLADESH'S POSITION IN THE GLOBAL RANKING OF INSTITUTIONAL INDICES

Since the pioneering work of North (1990), there has been widespread agreement that institutions matter for development. Narratives have described some features of the relationship between institutions and development and theoretical models of that relationship have been proposed that fit some stylised facts, often drawn from history. Numerous authors could be cited, but Acemoglu and Robinson (2012), Khan (2012a, 2018), or more recently Pritchett *et al.* (2018) are prominent examples of the first approach, while Acemoglu and Robinson (2008) are a good example of the second. Going beyond this approach and getting into more detail on the nature and the quality of institutions requires the availability of qualitative or quantitative indicators describing them. Such country-level indicators and indices have been developed over the last two or three decades, which has given rise to an empirical cross-country literature exploring the relationship between institutions (as described by some of these

indicators) and particular characteristic of economic development (primarily
the level and growth rate of gross domestic product (GDP)). Knack and Keefer
(1995), Acemoglu *et al.* (2001), and Rodrik *et al.* (2004) were the first notable
attempts in this direction.

While relying on the same type of data, that is the existing databases of
institution-oriented indicators, the objective of this exercise is somewhat different. Focusing on a single country, Bangladesh, its main objective is to characterise its institutional profile as reflected in available indicators and to see
what its absolute and relative strengths and weaknesses are. This will be done
in three ways. First, relying on the most complete repository of indicators, the
University of Gothenburg's Quality of Government database (Dahlberg *et al.,*
2020), six aggregate indicators will be defined, and countries, both advanced
and developing, will be ranked according to each of them. The quality of
Bangladeshi institutions will then be analysed according to each aggregate indicator taking into account each of the individual indicators that make up that
aggregate indicator. Because all of these indicators are closely related to economic development, as measured for instance by GDP per capita, the second
question that will be asked is how far away Bangladesh is from what could be
considered an international norm: that is, the level of each aggregate indicator
that corresponds to Bangladesh's level of GDP per capita. To some extent, this
is equivalent to comparing Bangladesh to countries with more or less the same
level of income. The same comparison will be made with geographical neighbours or countries that have outperformed Bangladesh over the last two or
three decades, despite being initially at the same level of development. Finally,
the time evolution of the institutional quality of Bangladesh will be analysed
by relying on a database that makes it possible to cover the last three decades.

Analysing the various findings, Bangladesh's institutional profile as indicated
by institutional indicators will be summarised in Section IV. The general diagnostic is that Bangladesh ranks uniformly rather badly in many institutional
dimensions. Given its high-growth performance, the so-called 'Bangladesh paradox' or 'Bangladesh surprise' of this combination of under-performing institutions and over-performing economy underlined by several observers (World
Bank, 2007b, 2007c, 2010; Mahmud *et al.,* 2008; Asadullah *et al.,* 2014) is
worth serious investigation. It should be kept in mind, however, that the institutional part of this paradox relies on indicators that are essentially imprecise
and that can only give a rough description of the nature of institutions in a
given country.

A Constructing Synthetic Institutional Indices

There now are many databases with sets of indicators that seek to describe
the quality of various aspects of a country's political, sociological, and economic institutions. Well-known databases of this type include the Worldwide
Governance Indicators, the Logistics Performance Index, Doing Business, the

Global Competitiveness Index, and the International Country Risk Guide (ICRG), or Polity IV. Several single indicators have also become a key reference, for instance the Transparency International corruption index. The Quality of Government is a repository of institutional indicators present in all these databases. As such, it comprises more than 2,000 indicators over a period that extends from 1949 to 2018 for some indicators and some countries. However, it would not make sense to use every indicator to study the profile of one specific country in comparison to others. Moreover, there are many missing observations. Instead, the technique used here has been to develop a small number of synthetic institutional indices that aggregate individual indicators in the database with similar distributions across countries at a given point of time – the year 2016. A method of clustering a subset of indicators simultaneously available for the largest number of countries into a pre-determined number of groups – that is clusters – was used. The data selection procedure ended up with a set 97 indicators available in 105 countries – both developed and developing. The clustering method is based on the correlation across indicators in the cluster using the country values of indicators as observations. It thus consists of minimising the variance across indicators within clusters and maximising the variance between clusters. A synthetic index is then associated with the cluster by using a linear combination of all indicators in the cluster. The coefficients of the first axis in a principal component analysis (PCA) of all indicators in the cluster were used. They thus maximise the cross-country variance explained by the synthetic index.

The main parameter in the hands of someone using clustering methods is the number of clusters. In the present case, it was decided to stay with six clusters, and thus six synthetic indices, for both practical reasons and to ensure consistency. The practicality requirement refers to the need to be able to visualise and compare observations across a multidimensional space, which requires minimising the number of clusters. Consistency requires differentiating as much as possible the synthetic indices, while making it possible to give some clear indication of their meaning. Indeed, each cluster may include very different indicators, without an obvious common link between them, although the fact that they are correlated suggests that such a link must exist. However, it turns out that if the number of clusters is increased, it makes it increasingly difficult to identify such a link. In the present case, it also turned out that the six synthetic indices were in rough agreement with the main themes of the institutional diagnostic survey undertaken in this research project, the results of which are analysed in the next section.

The six clusters or groups of indicators that are selected by the procedure just described are Democracy, Rule of law, Business environment, Bureaucracy, Land, and Human rights. Number of indicators used by the synthetic indices of Democracy, Rule of law, Business environment, Bureaucracy, Land, and Human rights are 22, 14, 23, 9, 8, and 11, respectively. Furthermore, the variance captured by the first principal component within the group of each synthetic index of Democracy, Rule of law, Business environment, Bureaucracy, Land, and Human rights are 57.21%, 73.46%, 68.47%, 79.30%, 38.72%, and 54.84%, respectively.

Under the heading democracy are found indicators describing the political regime, its effectiveness, pluralism, stability, or transparency. The rule of law heading comprises indicators describing the effectiveness of the legal framework, the judiciary system, the control of corruption, and the quality of economic regulation. Business environment, not surprisingly, includes the quality of business infrastructure and the market context in which firms operate. Bureaucracy describes the quality of the administration and some public services. Land does not cover many indicators because it turns out to be more focused than other synthetic indices. Finally, human rights comprise indicators of a more social nature, that is education, healthcare, and civil liberties, including freedom of expression.

Each individual indicator was linearly normalised for its value to range between 0 and 100, but of course their distribution across countries, including their mean and median, is not the same. It appears that the mean and median of the democracy, land, and human right indices are above those of rule of law, bureaucratic quality, and business environment. To the extent that the value of individual indicators is not necessarily comparable among themselves, this result is not of major importance for our purposes. Instead, we now focus on the relative position of Bangladesh across the six-dimensional space of the synthetic indices.

B How Does Bangladesh Compare to Other Countries According to the Synthetic Institutional Indices?

This section summarises Bangladesh's relative position in the synthetic institutional indices compared to the top and bottom performing countries of the world. According to Figure 3.1, Bangladesh's relative performance in the global ranking, established on the basis of the synthetic institutional indices, is rather uniformly mediocre, as it systematically ranges in the lowest quartile – as a matter of fact, even in the lowest quintile of the global ranking. The situation is even worse for the rule of law, bureaucratic quality, and land synthetic indices, where Bangladesh ranks in the bottom 5% or close to it. Its position on human rights is only slightly less disastrous, as it still lies at the upper limit of the bottom 10%. In short, it is only on democracy and business environment that Bangladesh gets somewhat away from the very bottom of the global ranking. This is an interesting finding since it allows us to differentiate the relative quality of Bangladeshi institutions with respect the nature of these institutions. It will be shown later that this conclusion resonates rather well with other evidence or judgements about Bangladeshi institutions.

Table 3.1 shows the countries that are ranked close to Bangladesh in the various synthetic indices, the idea being to see whether they share some common features besides their institutional ranking. Diversity is clearly the dominant

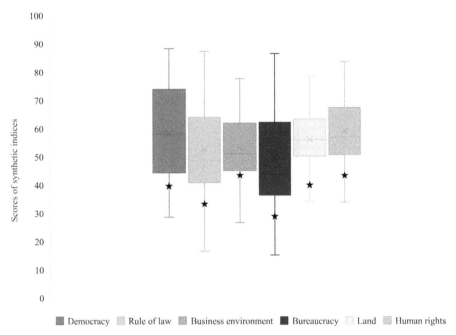

FIGURE 3.1 Distribution of the synthetic indices
Note: The star indicates Bangladesh's position. For each synthetic index, the figure shows the limits of the four quartiles of its distribution among countries, the bottom and top whiskers corresponding to the bottom and top quartiles, and the horizontal segment within the central box, the median, separating the second and third quartiles.
Source: Authors, based on the synthetic institutional index.

factor here. There is little regional alignment, except the presence of Pakistan in democracy and land, something that can be linked to the common past with Bangladesh, first as British colonies and then as two parts of the same political entity. Several Middle Eastern and North African countries appear in the list, with no obvious geographical, historical, or political similarity with Bangladesh. Finally, many low-income sub-Saharan countries are present, but this may perhaps reflect more the relatively large number of countries in that region of the world, their low income, and their absence of efficient institutions.

The most striking feature of Table 3.1 is the absence of countries with a growth record as strong as Bangladesh's over the last few decades: on the contrary, several countries show rather inferior performance. Likewise, only one country (i.e. Thailand) would qualify as a manufacturing exporter (like Bangladesh). All other countries are typical commodity exporters, except Jordan and Lebanon, and four of them are major oil exporters – Algeria, Nigeria, Kuwait, and Iran. These observations reinforce the idea that there is a 'Bangladesh paradox': a fast-growing manufacturing exporter with

TABLE 3.1 *Ranking of the countries around Bangladesh for each summary index in 2016*

Democracy		Rule of law		Business environment		Bureaucracy		Land		Human rights	
84	Kuwait	98	Zimbabwe	82	Zambia	94	Argentina	99	Haiti	93	Zimbabwe
85	Jordan	99	Ukraine	83	Senegal	95	Lebanon	100	Algeria	94	Liberia
86	Nigeria	100	Madagascar	84	Jamaica	96	Dominican Republic	101	Madagascar	95	Tanzania
87	Bangladesh	101	Bangladesh	85	Bangladesh	97	Bangladesh	102	Bangladesh	96	Bangladesh
88	Pakistan	102	Myanmar	86	Guyana	98	Zimbabwe	103	Guinea	97	Algeria
89	Lebanon	103	Haiti	87	Iran	99	Madagascar	104	Nigeria	98	Egypt
90	Algeria	104	Guinea	89	Paraguay	100	Guinea	105	Pakistan	99	Venezuela

Note: This ranking is performed for 105 countries.

Source: Authors' own calculation, based on the synthetic institutional indices.

institutional quality comparable with slow-growing commodity exporters, including oil exporters. It will be seen later in this study that the latter analogy echoes the fact that ready-made goods (RMG) manufacturing exports in Bangladesh may indeed play a role in the economy and the society similar to that played by raw commodity exports in other developing countries.

C Major Institutional Weaknesses of Bangladesh in the Synthetic Institutional Indices

Box 3.1 shows those individual indicators in each synthetic cluster on which Bangladesh performs substantially less well compared to the others, that is the mean of the cluster. For instance, in democracy it performs particularly poorly on the following indicators: the presence of 'fractionalised elites', the lack of 'public trust in politicians', and the strength of the 'political competition'. Likewise, in the rule of the law, it can be seen that the 'corruption perception index' plays an important role in bringing Bangladesh's overall score down, the same being true of the overall evaluation of the 'judicial independence' and the 'inefficiency of the legal framework'.

Given the clustering procedure that was applied in defining the synthetic institution indices, it may be the case that some individual indicators do not fit the label attributed to the cluster very well. For instance, in business environment, some indicators refer more to the behaviour of firms, like 'spending on research and development (R&D)' or 'production sophistication' than their environment, although particularly negative indicators there include 'customs', 'infrastructure', and 'lack of competition'. In the same way, it might be considered that 'irregular payments and bribes' would belong more to the rule of the law than bureaucratic quality – but the fact that it appears in the latter cluster clearly shows that this infringement of the rule of the law is closely linked to unsatisfactory 'public services' and 'favouritism by government officials', and therefore to an under-performing bureaucracy.

Box 3.1 Major areas of weaknesses in each synthetic institutional index

1. **Democracy:** Political stability; Government effectiveness; Public trust in politicians; Transparency of government policymaking; Factionalised elites; State fragility; Political pressures and controls on media content; Political competition
2. **Rule of law:** Efficiency of legal framework in challenging regulations; Efficiency of legal framework in settling disputes; Judicial independence; Strength of auditing and reporting standards; Corruption perception
3. **Business environment:** The efficiency of the clearance process by border control agencies, including customs; Quality of trade and transport-related

infrastructure; Competence and quality of logistics services; Ability to track and trace consignments; Taxation on investment; Financial market development; Labour market efficiency; Production process sophistication; University–industry collaboration in R&D; Capacity for innovation; Company spending on R&D; Venture capital availability; Intellectual property protection

4. **Bureaucracy:** Public services; Favouritism in decisions of government officials; Irregular payments and bribes; Wastefulness of government spending
5. **Land:** Land administration and management; Registering property
6. **Human rights:** Voice and accountability; Freedom of expression; Protection of minority investors' rights; Ethical behaviour of firms

Source: Authors, based on the synthetic institutional Indices.

Box 3.1 could also have shown the individual indicators with scores above the mean of the synthetic indicator. It is worth stressing that, the low government militarisation index and the 'autonomy' of the government do not do as badly as other indicators. However, they do not necessarily do well either. Transparency or press freedom may be above the mean score of 'democracy', but that score is low, and those indicators are simply less low in the global ranking. Yet it may be worth keeping this kind of nuance in mind.

Another interesting point is the relative lack of consistency of various sources on the same topic. For instance, 'rule of law' as evaluated by Freedom House[1] is above the mean in the synthetic rule of law index, whereas 'rule of law' as evaluated by the Quality of Government[2] falls below the mean. Clearly, this kind of discrepancy shows the unavoidable imprecision of these individual estimators – sometimes themselves based on several sources – and underlines the need to be cautious in interpreting these results.

Is Bangladesh an outlier in the institution–development nexus? The preceding comparisons of Bangladesh with other countries were based on *ad hoc* criteria, whereas the analysis of its global ranking is biased because of the presence of so many countries at higher level of development. A relevant comparison may be to match Bangladesh with countries at similar levels of development and to see whether it does so badly, and in what dimension of the

---

[1] Freedom House assesses the condition of political rights and civil liberties around the world. It is composed of numerical ratings and supporting descriptive texts for 195 countries and 15 territories. See https://freedomhouse.org/report/freedom-world.
[2] The 'rule of law', evaluated by the Quality of Governance, is drawn from the Bertelsmann Stiftung's Transformation Index, which analyses and evaluates the quality of democracy, a market economy, and political management in 129 developing and transition countries. It measures successes and setbacks on the path towards a democracy based on the rule of law and a socially responsible market economy. See www.bti-project.org/en/home/.

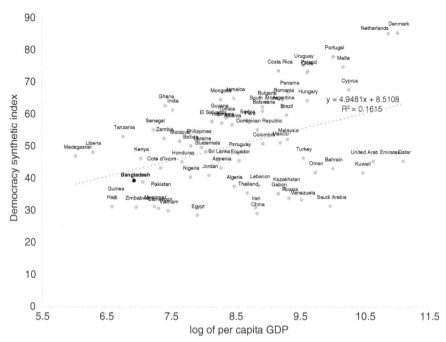

FIGURE 3.2 Scatter plot of the democracy synthetic index against (log) GDP per capita
Note: Democracy synthetic index as a function of (log) GDP per capita (2011 US$).
Source: Authors, based on the synthetic institutional index.

synthetic institutional indices. To do this, a simple approach consists of running a regression of the various institutional indices on a development index of the countries and to test whether Bangladesh is an outlier on the negative side, that is exhibiting a negative gap greater than 2 standard deviations, as usually defined in econometric work. Two definitions of the level of development have been used: GDP per capita – measures in international 2011 dollars – and the Human Development Index (HDI), used by the United Nations, which comprises not only GDP per capita after normalisation but also measures of education and health. To avoid this procedure having to depend too much on the relationship between institutions among advanced countries, or on the difference between developing and advanced countries, the estimation is performed on developing countries only.

Figure 3.2 shows the scatter plot of the democracy synthetic index against the log of GDP per capita for developing and emerging countries, with a trend line that represents the predicted value of the democracy synthetic index on the basis of GDP per capita. It can be seen that Bangladesh lies below the line, which means that, conditionally on its level of GDP per capita, Bangladesh underperforms on that index. Yet the gap with respect to the trend line is not sizeable, which means that Bangladesh cannot be considered an outlier in

TABLE 3.2 *Normalised deviation of Bangladesh from predicted synthetic indices based on GDP per capita and Human Development Index*

	Democracy	Rule of law	Business environment	Bureaucracy	Land	Human rights
Deviation from GDP norm	−0.44	−0.82	0.24	−0.72	−1.19	−0.74
Deviation from HDI norm	−0.53	−0.93	0.04	−0.84	−1.43	−0.91

Note: GDP (HDI) norm = predicted value of the regression of synthetic indices on log GDP per capita (HDI).
Deviations are standardised by standard deviation of residuals.
Source: Authors, based on the synthetic institutional index.

comparison with other observations. In other words, there is nothing exceptional in such a deviation from the trend line. This would not be true, however, of China, Iran, or Egypt, because their gap with respect to the trend line is larger than twice the standard deviation of that gap among all observations.

Table 3.2 summarises the results obtained for the six synthetic indices using GDP per capita or the HDI as normalising device. Because the deviation of Bangladesh from the norm never exceeds 2 standard deviations, it cannot be said that Bangladesh is an outlier in any institutional dimension. What is striking, however, is that, conditionally on its level of development, Bangladesh always underperforms. In other words, it cannot be said that Bangladesh's bad position in the global institutional ranking shown in Table 3.1 is due to its level of development, as measured by GDP per capita or the HDI. Even controlling for this – that is, even comparing it with countries at a comparable level of development – Bangladesh is under-performing. This is true for all institutional indices except one, *business environment*, for which Bangladesh is slightly above the norm. Indeed, it was on this index that it reached the highest position in the global ranking discussed earlier.

D What Have We Learnt from the Cross-Country Comparison?

Bangladesh has gone through several phases of crisis in the past. Despite numerous challenges, most indicators describing the institutional environment and the political and socio-economic conditions have significantly improved over the last three decades, very much in line with the stabilisation of the political scene since the mid-2000s. The overall socio-economic condition has improved. Even an indicator like control of corruption is still gradually improving today.

The situation looks less positive when comparisons are made between the current institutional context in Bangladesh and that in other countries, even when the comparison is restricted to developing countries. The synthetic institutional indices, based on a large number of individual indicators available in databases on governance and the quality of institutions, paint a broad picture of Bangladesh's institutional context that is not positive. Bangladesh is found to be in the bottom 20% of global rankings based on these indices and, in some institutional dimensions, even in the bottom 10%. As a matter of fact, despite its development achievement over the last two decades, Bangladesh is even outperformed on all institutional dimensions by several developing countries, including poorer countries.

This outperforming is not uniform, and much can be learned for an institutional diagnostic from disparities across the various institutional indices. Bangladesh appears as particularly weak in areas like bureaucratic quality, rule of law, land issues, and, to a lesser extent, human rights. However, the situation is noticeably better, though still far from outstanding, when considering the democratic functioning of the country and the business environment it offers. It is interesting that these relative institutional strengths relate to two key features of Bangladesh's development over the last 20 years or so: the relatively stabilisation and pacification of the political game and the surge of manufacturing exports in the RMG sector.

This kind of ranking must nevertheless be treated with caution. On the one hand, Bangladesh does not appear as an outlier when the ranking is made conditional on the level of development of a country. It is still the case that it often underperforms other countries in several areas, though mostly by a narrow margin. It does better with respect to the business environment. On the other hand, it must be kept in mind that individual indicators of governance and institutional quality are necessarily rough and may miss important details that might change the overall judgement to which they lead. Relying only on them to establish a diagnostic would thus be extremely restrictive. Hence the alternative approach of surveying different types of decision makers on their perceptions of the institutional strengths and weaknesses in the context in which they operate, as is discussed in Section III.

III THE COUNTRY INSTITUTIONAL SURVEY (CIS) IN BANGLADESH

Although many thinkers throughout history have thought of societies as organisms with some similarity to the human body, simple diagnostic tools of the kind that are available to detect human diseases do not exist for societies and the institutions that govern them, even when the investigation is restricted to what may weaken their economic development. Economic development per se, and its relationship with institutions, are such complex topics that only in-depth analyses can possibly shed some light on them. Even the 'growth diagnostic' tool proposed by Hausmann *et al.* (2008) identifies 'binding constraints' on growth that are contingent upon the 'economic and institutional environment' of a country and does not say much about the institutional roots of these constraints. This was very much the approach followed in Chapter 2. Yet the complexity of the relationship between institutions and development should not prevent an analysis from relying on simple diagnostic tools, provided that the limitations of these tools is kept well in mind when trying to go deeper in an institutional diagnostic exercise. Simple tools can help us find the way to search for the bigger picture. This was done in the preceding section by trying to extract information from existing cross-country indicators of the quality of governance and institutions. Another simple tool is reported on in the present section: the survey responses of decision makers of various types who were asked about the institutional features that hinder Bangladesh's development.

Two approaches were followed in this survey. The first was a questionnaire survey that was administered among a selected sample of people who regularly confront Bangladesh's institutional context in their activities. This survey was copied from the CIS, which has been used in other countries[3]. The second approach consisted of conducting open-ended interviews with a few key informants in political, business, social, and academic circles.

A The Survey: Background and Design of the Questionnaire

The CIS is a sample survey tool developed as part of the institutional diagnostic activity of the Economic Development and Institutions (EDI) programme. Its aim is to identify institutional challenges as they are perceived by the people in a country who are most likely to confront them on a regular basis. These challenges are then made the subject of deeper scholarly analysis. Being based on a broad sample of respondents, the CIS intends to yield a more diverse view of the country than the numerous institutional indicators that rely most often on the opinion of a few experts.

At the beginning, a pilot for the CIS in Bangladesh was held in late 2018. Those who took part in the pilot occupied top decision-making positions at this time. The reason for choosing respondents from top decision-making positions was to get a lucid idea of the institutions in Bangladesh, since

---

[3] CIS was borrowed from a survey taken regularly among French diplomatic personnel to analyse institutional changes taking place in developing countries – see 'Institutional Profile Database' at www.cepii.fr/institutions/FR/ipd.asp. The questionnaire has been modified to better fit the institutional diagnostic objective of the present research programme. The first editions were run in Tanzania and Benin. As in the preceding editions, the questionnaire used in Bangladesh was designed to fit the local context as closely as possible.

such respondents either interact with the institutions on a regular basis or they work as an active part of the institutions. As decision makers, they have in-depth knowledge of institutions and their weaknesses. Of course, these opinions are quite different than the opinions of the general mass of the people, as they are based on direct experiences with the institutions and/or rigorous analysis of the institutions from their vantage point. The insights gathered from the pilot helped conducting the Bangladesh CIS between December 2018 and February 2019. The remainder of this section will discuss the design of the questionnaire and the execution of the survey, respectively.

The questionnaire had three primary components: a section on the personal characteristics of the respondent; another on the institutional areas seen as most constraining by the respondent; and the last one, a long section on the respondent's perceptions of the institutions and the functioning of institutions in Bangladesh.

The first section was split into two parts. The first part initiated the discussion and asked general questions such as the respondent's name, gender, and sector of affiliation, including political affinity and sub-sectors that the respondent was associated with. The other part compiled more sensitive information on the past and present occupation of the respondent, the location of their work, their family size, and their religion.

The second section of the questionnaire was composed in such a way as to gather information about the most constraining institutional areas in Bangladesh. In this part of the questionnaire, the respondents were provided with the details of institutional areas that we had focused on for the survey. This comprised seven broad institutional areas: 'Political institutions – executive'; 'Political institutions – system'; 'Justice and regulations'; 'Business environment'; 'Civil service'; 'Land'; and 'People' (Box 3.2). Respondents then had to select two institutional areas that, according to them, most constrain development in Bangladesh. The chosen areas were not only important for the analysis but were also important for the subsequent part of the survey since they determined the set of questions presented to the respondent in the third section of the survey.

The core section of the CIS comprised 415 unique questions on the perception of institutions in Bangladesh. The collection of information relied on a Likert scale, ranging from 'not at all' and 'little' to 'moderately so', 'much', and 'very much'. Responses were then converted into discrete numbers, ranging from one to five, for the analysis. The CIS questionnaire was unique in several dimensions, mostly with the aim of making it as close as possible to the specific context of Bangladesh.

There are particular challenges that come with surveying top-tier executives, not only with access but also because their time may be limited. Our survey had a high volume of questions and sought to gather information on a broad spectrum of institutional issues. If we had asked every respondent every

---

Box 3.2 Institutional areas and description

1. **Political institutions – executive:** Effective concentration and use of power; type of governance; relationship with parliament, judiciary, local governments, media, and civil society
2. **Political institutions – system:** Functioning of elections; voice of opposition parties, civil society, and media; checks and balances on the executive
3. **Justice and regulations:** Fairness, independence, and effectiveness of the judicial system; regulation of public and private monopolies
4. **Business environment:** Relationship between the private sector and public administration; protection of property rights and labour contracts; business registration and licensing; taxation; availability of infrastructure
5. **Civil service:** Efficiency, fairness, effectiveness, and transparency in the management of social and economic policy, including customs, taxation, education, health, etc.
6. **Land:** Provision of ownership, protection of tenants and small holdings, promotion of commercial ventures
7. **People:** Sense of solidarity, discrimination practices, security, trade unions

Source: CIS, Bangladesh.

---

question, the survey would be far too long to be of practical use. Keeping these constraints in mind, the survey was conducted in a dynamic way. As mentioned earlier, in the second section of the questionnaire, respondents were asked to identify the most constraining institutional areas according to them, from the list of seven broad institutional areas. Then they were first asked to answer both the primary and secondary questions related to the two institutional areas they had selected, as well as only primary questions related to the other five institutional areas that they did not choose. Notice also that, given the overlap between institutional areas, respondents had to answer about 70–80% of the full set of questions on average.

Changes in institutions are infrequent and most happen over the course of time rather than suddenly and abruptly. Even though there are a few examples of institutional changes which have happened overnight, most institutions persist. At the same time, human psychology works in such a way that people tend to react to the most recent events associated with a certain entity. For that reason, it is quite possible that the perceptions of the respondents were biased towards the present. However, the current de jure institutional authority in Bangladesh has not changed much over the last decade and so it was expected that perceptions about the overall context would be reflected in their responses. In addition, in-depth discussions with top decision makers on the institutional constraints shed light on the changes over time. Second, the enumeration took place right around the time when a general election was taking place in Bangladesh. The election thus had impacts at several levels, in terms of survey responses that commented specifically on recent institutional characteristics. Last but not least, very recent changes in institutions do not explain the past economic trajectory, so the questions about the more stable aspects of institutions were relevant.

The survey covered the views of people who were either affiliated with institutions or in close contact with them. The survey also aimed to capture the view from the top down, where decisions are made or where policies are generated. To do this, it was very important to select respondents from the first- or second-tier position of any institution. These decision makers had experienced the impacts of changes in certain institutions first-hand and were concerned about the functioning of the country's institutions. As a consequence, a pure random sampling in the overall population was not an option. The selection of respondents had to be based on an arbitrary stratification of groups of expert respondents, to make sure various sectors, occupations, and individual profiles would be present in the sample. This implies a strong selection bias with respect to the Bangladesh population, but, of course, this was deliberate.

B Execution of the Survey

The Bangladesh CIS was conducted between December 2018 and February 2019 in a collaborative effort between EDI researchers, Oxford Policy Management (OPM), and South Asian Network on Economic Modeling (SANEM), a think-tank from Bangladesh. A total of 355 individuals were sampled in a purposively stratified sample. The selection process followed two steps. First, researchers listed strata in terms of occupation, position level, geographical constraints, and tentative gender balance. Samples were surveyed in major cities in the country, like Dhaka, Gazipur, Chattogram, Sylhet, Rajshahi, Bogra, Rangpur, Barisal, and Khulna.

SANEM, in cooperation with OPM, determined a list of target respondents who satisfied the occupational, geographical, and gender considerations. Next, these probable respondents were contacted, and if they gave their consent they were interviewed. The sample is divided into five sectors: politicians, bureaucrats, business executives, academics, and civil society members. The respondents included politicians from ruling party and opposition; current and ex bureaucrats; business executives from agriculture, fishing, livestock, manufacturing, construction, Information & communication, wholesale and retail, health, transport, bank; academics from teaching and research professions; and people from non-governmental organisation (NGO). Responses of a total of 48 politicians, 51 bureaucrats, 131 business executives, 76 academics, and 49 civil society members were collected.

Table 3.3 provides details regarding the characteristics of the survey respondents. It is most unfortunate that, though the initial target was for at least 31% of the sample to be female, the enumerators struggled to contact or arrange

TABLE 3.3 *Composition of the sample*

Respondent's main characteristics		Occupation history (number of respondents)	
Number of female respondents	50	Politician	48
Number of respondents: Married	324	Bureaucrat	51
Average family size	4.15	Business executive	131
Average age in years	47	Academic	76
Average education: university degree or above	318	Civil society	49
Average years of experience	21	Total number of respondents	355
Average years of experience at the current institution	15		

Source: CIS, Bangladesh.

interviews with female respondents. This may be linked to the fact that in Bangladesh, only a few of the top-tier positions are held by women. This in fact was observed to be the case when conducting the survey and can be considered a finding of the study. Thus, only 14% of the respondents were female.

The main goal of the CIS in Bangladesh was to capture an amalgamation of viewpoints about the institutions in the country. As mentioned earlier, the survey targeted respondents from the top tier; thus, the mean level of education for these respondents was well above the national average. As we can see in Table 3.3, about 90% of the respondents had a university degree or above. The same argument regarding choosing respondents from the top tier applies to the age distribution of the respondents. Since it takes years of experience to reach a top-tier position, respondents tended to come from older age brackets. The average years of experience of the respondents explains the spectrum of their experiences with institutions in the country, and it also indicates the way in which the survey captures the respondents' perceptions of institutions in a dynamic way: as most of them had worked under varied circumstances, each of them had a unique experience with the institutions in Bangladesh which the survey intends to capture.

It is also important to point out that 23 respondents declared a political affinity with the ruling party and 25 with the opposition, and the rest of the respondents declared no political affinity. This enables us to compare the responses of respondents with ruling party or opposition affiliation with respondents without any declared political affinity, to assess whether party affiliation had any bearing on the responses given. In terms of geographical diversity, most respondents lived in an urban area. It is in fact not surprising to see that most of the respondents resided in urban centres, as the survey targeted the elite in the country, who tend to live in or close to the cities. Since most head offices or main branches of public and private organisations in Bangladesh are located in Dhaka, the region around the capital is overrepresented.

C Results of the CIS in Bangladesh

1 *Critical Institutional Areas for Bangladesh's Development*

According to the respondents, the major constraining institutional areas for the development of Bangladesh are the political institutions and public administration. The ranking of these two areas depends on the measure chosen to aggregate individual opinions. However, it can be seen in Figure 3.3 that they are very close to each other in number of occurrences chosen by respondents. Notice also that, conditionally on being chosen, political institutions were selected by the respondents. Justice- and regulation-related institutions come in third position in the ranking of the most critical institutional areas for development in Bangladesh. On the other side of the spectrum, only 5.1% respondents chose land as one of the two most constraining institutional hurdles in Bangladesh's development, possibly because the respondent assumed that this area needs specific knowledge of land administration. However, due to the design of the questionnaire, most of the respondents had to answer questions related to land, and it has one of the lowest average scores. This will be discussed later in detail.

The probability of framing bias must be considered, with the first areas in the list appearing more frequently than the other choices of respondents. It is possible that the respondents intentionally chose the areas with which they were affiliated as most constraining for Bangladesh's development. However, since all respondents answered most of the questions (through primary and secondary questions), survey responses should be independent of biases and should have provided a robust idea about each of the constraints being discussed.

The choice of the top two constraints to development, according to respondents' opinions, is a piece of information in itself, but it also determined the

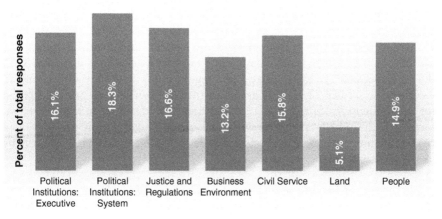

FIGURE 3.3 Choice of institutional areas
Note: For a description of the institutional areas, see Box 3.2.
Source: CIS, Bangladesh.

number of questions asked of each respondent. Given the explicit choices made during the selection of institutional field, the fact that respondents faced detailed questions about their top two choices, and not about other areas, raises a concern. Considering choices of institutional areas by sector of affiliation, it is possible that choices might be biased towards the sector of affiliation of the respondents. Additionally, it is quite possible that some less important areas are left out because there is no information about them. Alternatively, some institutional areas might be left out because of a perception that they were working well, or they could work poorly but be considered unimportant for economic development. For these two reasons, it was important to gather information about all areas. It was thus decided to ask all primary questions in relation to all areas. For this, even the less critical institutional fields were covered by all respondents.

Analysis of the survey results show that choices of institutional areas were somewhat different for male and female respondents. The top choice of male respondents was political institutions, whereas for female respondents, it was mainly public services. This is in line with general norms since women mostly experience discrimination at the public service level. The rest of the institutional areas received an almost equal degree of preference.

Another interesting observation from the CIS results relates to the choices of institutional areas by political affinity. The choices of institutional area of respondents from both the ruling and opposition parties are skewed towards political institutions. Politicians from the ruling party did not consider the business environment as involving any institutional constraints. On the other hand, given the current context and circumstances, it is surprising to see that supporters of the ruling party considered public services as one of the constraints. The institutional choices of respondents with no political affinity are almost equally distributed across institutional areas.

The choices of institutional areas made by respondents from the business sector differed depending on the specific sector they were affiliated with. For respondents affiliated with agriculture and manufacturing, the top choice was 'Business environment'. However, for those affiliated with the service sector, it was 'Justice and regulations'. It is very interesting to see that the choice of 'Land' as an institutional area was more common for respondents from the service sector than for those from the other two sectors. Respondents affiliated with agriculture chose 'Public services' as a constraint more frequently than respondents affiliated with manufacturing or the service sector.

2 The Perceived Functioning of Institutions in Bangladesh

Within and across areas, the CIS aimed to identify, as precisely as possible, which specific institutions were perceived as constraining by respondents. The subsequent analysis evaluates questions by their mean response on a scale ranging from 1, 'very negative', to 5, 'very positive'. For questions asked in

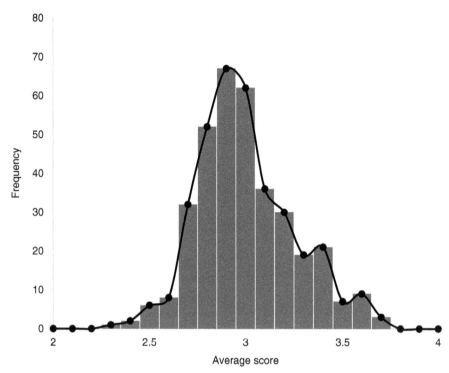

FIGURE 3.4 Distribution of questions by average score – all questions
Note: Total number of questions: 415. Options in the Likert scale: 0 = no opinion; 1 = very negative; 2 = negative; 3 = neither negative nor positive; 4 = positive; 5 = very positive.
Source: CIS, Bangladesh.

a negative way, the Likert scale is inverted to make sure that a higher value always means a better perception. Questions are then divided into clusters and sub-clusters to closely identify the core problems of the institutions in Bangladesh. This section first discusses the state of Institutional areas captured by the CIS and what are the underlying state of each of the institutional areas. Then the underlying problems of the institutions in Bangladesh are discussed. Finally, the choice of institutional constraints is discussed from the perspective of respondents' gender and political affiliation, to identify any differences correlated with respondents' characteristics.

The negative perception of institutions in Bangladesh can be observed if we consider the distribution of the average scores of each of the questions. The mean score is 2.81, slightly below the mid-point of the Likert scale, lying at 3. This is not unusual in opinion surveys and may simply reflect the ways in which respondents answer questions. It is therefore more interesting to look at the tails of the distribution: namely, questions with clearly positive or negative answers. Figure 3.4 plots the distribution of questions by average score. It

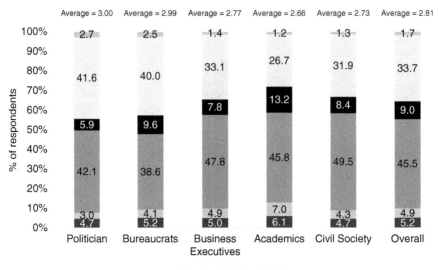

FIGURE 3.5 All questions – analysis by sector of affiliation
Note: Options in the Likert scale: 0 = no opinion; 1 = very negative; 2 = negative;
3 = neither negative nor positive; 4 = positive; 5 = very positive.
Source: CIS, Bangladesh.

shows that the left tail (negative perception) is fatter than the right one (positive perception). A total of 131 questions has an average score below 2.5, while only 39 score above 3.5.

Looking at the perception of the institutions by sector of affiliation, we can see that the average score for each of the sector is either 3.00 or below (Figure 3.5) the threshold level. It is not very surprising to see that politicians and bureaucrats consider institutional quality to be slightly better than do academics and civil society members. Business executives on average gave a score of 2.77 for institutional quality in Bangladesh, a relatively low result. Figure 3.5 suggests that, in general, the no response rate was between 4.7% and 6.1%. While, on average, only 35.4% of respondents expressed positive views (4 and above) about the functioning of the institutions, leaving aside politicians and bureaucrats, all other three categories of respondents held much lower opinions. The dominance of 'negative' views (1 and 2 together) is the highest and is almost the same for business executives (52.7%) and academics (52.8%).

3 Distribution of Average Score by Cluster
Figure 3.6 depicts the percentage distribution of scores by each theme. As the figure shows, on average, the 'no opinion' view had a share of only 5%; the 'very negative' perception had a share of 4.6%; the 'negative' view had a share

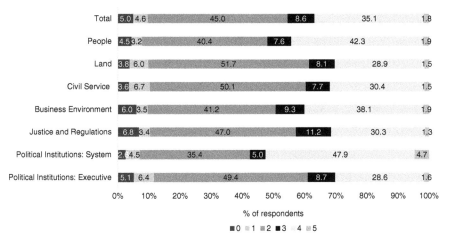

FIGURE 3.6 Percentage distribution of scores by theme
Note: Options in the Likert scale: 0 = no opinion; 1 = very negative; 2 = negative; 3 = neither negative nor positive; 4 = positive; 5 = very positive.
Source: CIS, Bangladesh.

of 45%; the 'indifferent' view had a share of 8.6%; the 'positive' view had a share of 35.1%; and the 'very positive' view had a share of only 1.8%. The worst situation is observed in the case of the theme related to 'Land', where 57.7% of the responses were 'negative' (1 and 2), followed by 'Civil service' with 56.8%. The general picture drawn from these figures offers a pessimistic view of the institutions in Bangladesh. However, in the discussion of each institutional area by cluster and sub-cluster in the previous sub-sections, we identified specific problems associated with the institutions in Bangladesh. This is more useful than generalising perceptions of the institutions in Bangladesh based on these scores.

4 Identification of the Major Areas of Institutional Weaknesses
The previous section discussed the distribution of scores across institutional areas. We saw that, on average, the scores are well below 3. However, generalising these scores can be misleading. In this section, the scores for all the sub-clusters are plotted in Figure 3.7. Although we have previously discussed specific clusters and sub-clusters, a graph like this provides us with the broader viewpoint regarding the institutions in Bangladesh. This also gives us incentives to study further, and concentrate on, those thematic areas that we intend to study for the growth diagnostic for Bangladesh.

It is clear from Figure 3.7 that institutional anomalies in Bangladesh are prevalent in relation to the judiciary, the business environment, the efficiency

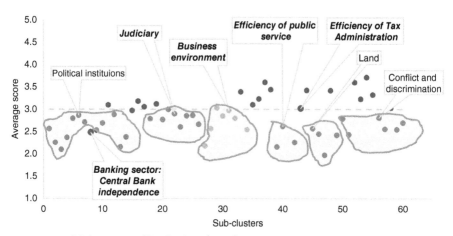

FIGURE 3.7 Major areas of institutional weaknesses
Note: Options in the Likert scale: 0 = no opinion; 1 = very negative; 2 = negative;
3 = neither negative nor positive; 4 = positive; 5 = very positive.
Source: CIS, Bangladesh.

of public services, the efficiency of tax administration, and land. The discussion of each of these areas in the previous sub-sections illustrated that
political institutions and conflict and discrimination are cross-cutting and are
associated with these broader thematic areas, depending on the context of the
discussion.

5 Perceptions of Institutions from a Gender Perspective

An interesting insight of the analysis is that the survey asked some questions related to discrimination based on gender. The majority of the
respondents, regardless of gender, agreed that discrimination on the basis
of gender is prevalent in Bangladesh. As the responses to these questions
show the extent of discrimination spans both public authorities, society,
and the workplace.

Figure 3.8 reports the responses where the largest percentage difference in
responses (in absolute term), related to the sub-clusters, were found between
male and female respondents. The figure shows that the largest difference
in opinion between male and female respondents was in terms of long-term
planning, central bank independence, evaluation of policies, corruption in
electoral process, civil liberties, and quality of public policymaking. For these
sub-clusters, the percentage difference in opinion was at least 10%. However,
it is interesting to see that, though there were vast differences in opinion in
the context of so many sub-clusters, both males and females agreed on the
fact that discrimination exists in the society, especially in the labour market,
as differences in responses were very low for these sub-clusters.

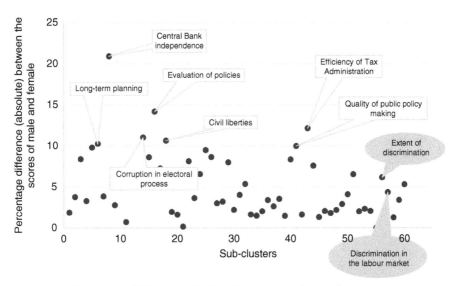

FIGURE 3.8 Percentage difference (absolute) in responses by gender
Source: CIS, Bangladesh.

6 Perceptions of Institutions Based on Political Affinity

The previous sub-sections have discussed in detail the institutional areas based on sector of affiliation. However, as the survey gathered information on the political affinity of the respondents, it is interesting to look at any differences in opinions based on such political affiliation.

First, we plot the differences in opinions between the respondents who were affiliated with the ruling party and those affiliated with the opposition. This is depicted in Figure 3.9-A. The figure shows there was a vast difference of opinions between these two types of respondents. The average percentage of difference in responses lies around 20%.

Next, we plot the percentage difference between the scores of respondents with affiliation to the ruling party and respondents who did not express their affiliation to any political party (Figure 3.9-B). This is almost identical to the previous figure, with a low average percentage difference.

However, the most interesting point to note is that depicted in Figure 3.9-C, where we plot the differences in opinion between respondents with an affiliation to the opposition party and those without any political affiliation. This shows that the average percentage difference in opinions is very low – almost close to zero – showing the similarity between the opinions of affiliates of the opposition parties and the opinions of respondents with no revealed political bias, as regards the institutional areas. Those who stated they had 'No affiliation' are likely to often include opposition people who do not dare say so, or who do not want to be involved in politics.

x

Selim Raihan et al.

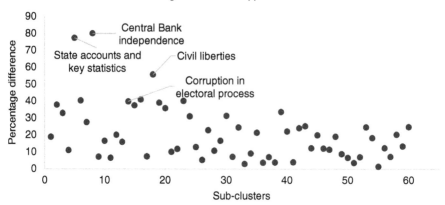

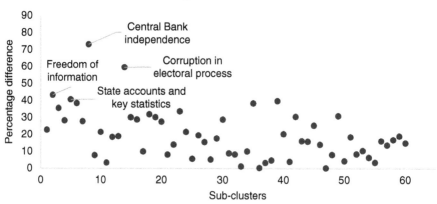

FIGURE 3.9 Percentage difference (absolute) in responses by political affinity. A. Percentage difference (absolute) between the scores of ruling affiliation and opposition affiliation. B. Percentage difference (absolute) between the scores of ruling affiliation and no affiliation. C. Percentage difference (absolute) between the scores of opposition affiliation and no affiliation
Source: CIS, Bangladesh.

7 Open-Ended Interviews with Top Decision Makers and Policymakers

Parallel to the CIS we conducted several open-ended interviews with top decision makers and policymakers in Bangladesh. These decision makers naturally were not interviewed in the same way as the other respondents to the CIS. Nor were they selected based on a stratified sampling technique. These interviewees were chosen simply because they had been working

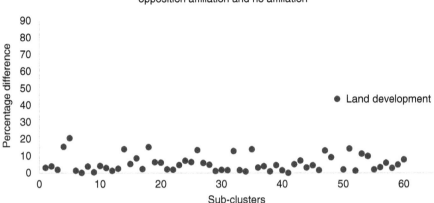

FIGURE 3.9 (Continued)

with the institutions in Bangladesh and/or were closely affiliated to and associated with the functioning of the institutional areas under discussion. These stakeholders (politicians from the ruling and opposition parties, bureaucrats – current and retired, business executives from different sectors, academics – teaching and research, NGO members, and other activities) were carefully chosen to avoid any kind of bias. They were asked several questions about the institutions and institutional diagnostics for Bangladesh. In their responses, they pointed to several sectors it may be useful to concentrate on in order to come up with diagnostic tools for Bangladesh. The anomalies in these sectors were then discussed in detail with these stakeholders. The main aspects of the institutional areas mentioned by these stakeholders are discussed below.

The failure of institutions to diversify markets and exports is causing Bangladesh to lose a huge sum of revenue. The major problems relating to market diversification include: a lack of comparative advantage; the inefficient use of available resources; poor capacity to ensure product diversification; high trade costs; poor physical connectivity; political patronage and bias; and the size of the importing country's economy, etc. In Bangladesh, there are still no proper studies that have been conducted to understand the institutional failures in relation to market diversification. To this end, it is important to understand the dynamics of the vast concentration exports around the RMG sector and the neglect of other potential industries.

The key feature of the fiscal sector is the public revenue and expenditure management, with the aim of reducing infrastructure gaps, promoting private investment, generating employment opportunities, and ensuring the efficient redistribution of wealth through a pro-poor and inclusive fiscal policy. Data show that tax revenue is the major source of income or revenue for the

Government of Bangladesh. Low administrative capacity and strong lobbying by businesses can be seen as the prime institutional failures as regards revenue generation for the Government. The Government should bring the target group under the tax net and make it mandatory to submit income tax returns, whether an entity is taxable or not. However, another important challenge to progress is mismanagement in expenditure in a weak institutional environment. Delayed funds disbursement, delay in land acquisition, and the lack of skilled project directors are also identified by the Implementation Monitoring and Evaluation Division (IMED) of the Ministry of Planning as important reasons behind mismanagement in expenditure.

With a continual wealth transfer from the general public to the corruption-ridden and seemingly incompetent state-owned banks (and ultimately to defaulters), the non-performing loan (NPL) situation has worsened. In Bangladesh, the main source of total NPL is state-owned banks. The experts interviewed identified a few factors behind this situation. Of course, they mentioned systemic corruption, but they also went further and mentioned the appointment of corrupt officials to important positions at the state-owned banks as a fundamental reason for this. A few of the symptoms of political patronage in the sector are: the Finance Ministry's overreach in licensing private banks while exercising political considerations; injecting incentives without the recommendation of the Bangladesh Bank; not complying with the suggestions of the central bank; and influencing the decisions of the autonomous central bank. Though it is an independent regulatory authority, the central bank cannot completely monitor these private banks as they are owned by politically influential people. Historically, there have been many regulations in the banking sector, especially relating to the entry/exit mechanism of banks and their governing bodies. The Bank Company Act, 1991, has been amended six times since its formation. Recent laws have sought to bolster political hold over the governance of these banks. These new laws have brought in changes in directorship positions, triggering a state of panic among depositors and other stakeholders. At the current point in time, from the discussion, we can see that the independence of the central bank is not producing its intended benefits, due to the presence of political pressure. Thus, the institutional efficiency of the banking sector hinges upon diversification of the sector, to control the ongoing political pressure place upon it.

Land litigation procedures and land management in Bangladesh are convoluted. With land being the most valuable asset in the country, the institutions associated with land management are susceptible to bribes. The influence of political patronage has made the transfer of land and land availability for businesses a complex issue. For better and more sustainable economic growth, the availability of land is crucial. However, the current situation in Bangladesh suggests that the problems associated with land are much politicised. Weaknesses in the institutions associated with land are related to the prolonged time required to obtain approval for transfer of land, politicisation in allocating land, and bribery in the transfer or approval of land use. As stake-holders mentioned, the convoluted nature of the problem and the failure of the judicial system to ensure justice in cases related to land may have a long-term impact on Bangladesh's economic system.

The judiciary in Bangladesh is faced with many problems: a low number of judges compared to the number of cases; an unregulated system and laws; and the questionable independence of the system. All of this calls for an elab-orate study on the subject. Complex procedures, case backlogs, and a lack of effective case management are also key constraints to the court system in Bangladesh. An independent judiciary is the sine qua non of democracy and of good governance. However, though the Constitution requires the separation of the judiciary from the executive, no steps whatsoever have been taken by the legislative or executive branch of the government in this regard. The inde-pendence of the judiciary is a must for any democratic country but attempts to influence the judiciary and steer it for political benefit are prevalent in Bangladesh.

D What Have We Learnt from the CIS?

The CIS and the open-ended discussion with top decision makers and policy-makers has provided some interesting insights about the institutional function-ing and mechanisms in Bangladesh. Key findings regarding the institutional strengths and weaknesses, and the recommendations of the stakeholders in the open-ended discussions, are consistent, even though the latter were able to go into more detail than the CIS. The following paragraphs summarises the most salient points that have come out of this double exercise.

In the first place, it should be stressed that the CIS yielded a ranking of problematic institutional areas similar to the one derived from exploiting cross-country institutional indicator databases, as reported on in the preceding section. Namely, the two areas found to be the most favourable (or perhaps the least unfavourable) to Bangladesh's development are the business environ-ment and the political system – an area that roughly fits the 'democracy' syn-thetic index in the preceding section. This convergence between insiders, that is local decision makers, and the experts behind the cross-country indicators, reinforces the view that other institutional areas than the preceding ones are problematic.

Second, it turns out that the general appraisal of institutional areas most likely to hinder development is not very informative, except perhaps in regard to the low weight put on land issues, something that is surprising given the emphasis of key informants on this aspect of Bangladeshi institutions. By con-trast, in the CIS, the detailed evaluations were much more informative. They clearly put the civil service and land issues at the top of the list of poorly functioning institutional areas, closely followed by the state of political and administrative management exercised by the executive.

The sub-cluster analysis, within each institutional area, yielded still more interesting, because more precise, information. Of particular importance are the following weaknesses it pointed to:

- ubiquitous corruption (election, business, and recruitment in civil service);
- executive control of legal bodies, media, judiciary, and the banking sector;
- inadequate coverage of public services;
- the number and intensity of land conflicts; and
- gender discrimination.

A few institutional aspects were also found to be rather satisfactory, though not always without some contradiction as regards other judgements. These include the general development of a middle class, the national feeling, and the quality of public policymaking. Of very special importance for the subsequent analysis in this volume is also the relative satisfaction regarding informal arrangements with the administration and as a way to secure contracts, as an efficient way of avoiding the ineffective formal channels. This may seem a bit paradoxical when evaluating institutions, but this opinion is quite revealing of what may be an important trait of the institutional context in Bangladesh.

Finally, the opinions expressed by the key informants generally confirmed the views of the CIS respondents: as, for instance, when they emphasised the low administrative capacity of the Bangladeshi state, corruption, or the ineffectiveness of the judiciary. But they added to the survey by pointing to sectors of activity where those weaknesses may be more salient. Of special importance from that point of view is their emphasis on industrial policy and the lack of diversification away from the RMG sector, to which this lead, possibly because of the over-influence of the RMG entrepreneurial elite. Key informants' insistence on the severe failings in the regulation of the banking sector, the corruption behind the huge and increasing NPLs, and the lack of regulatory power on the part of the central bank are also deeply revealing of the way several institutional weaknesses generate deep inefficiency in a key sector of the economy.

PART II

SIX CHALLENGING INSTITUTIONAL AREAS

4

Informal Institutions, the RMG Sector, and the Present Challenge of Export Diversification in Bangladesh

Selim Raihan

I INTRODUCTION

The export-oriented ready-made garments (RMG) sector in Bangladesh has registered a remarkable expansion over the past four decades. From a small base of only around US$ 31 million in 1984, RMG exports had grown to around US$ 30.6 billion by 2018,[1] accounting for more than 80% of export earnings. Bangladesh is now the second largest exporter of RMG in the world. The story of growth in the manufacturing sector in Bangladesh over the past three decades has been the story of the success of the RMG sector.

It is argued that the growth in exports of the RMG sector in Bangladesh have contributed to economic growth, macroeconomic stability, employment generation (especially female employment), and poverty alleviation. However, despite the successes, there are a number of challenges which raise concerns over the future of this sector. First, with the expansion of the RMG sector in Bangladesh, the export basket has become more and more concentrated. Though Bangladesh has potential in other export-oriented sectors, industries in those sectors have experienced very weak performance. With a highly concentrated export basket and high dependence on a single sector (RMG), Bangladesh remains in a high-risk situation, should there be any negative shock in that sector. Second, the factors that contributed to the growth of the RMG sector are now under pressure. Historically, the RMG sector in Bangladesh flourished for a number of reasons, including favourable policies, government support, and a number of critical political economy factors, which include the generation of sizeable 'rents' in this sector through the Multifibre Arrangement (MFA) quota[2] (which

---

[1] In real terms, from US$ 41.6 million in 1984 to US$ 22.5 billion in 2018.

[2] The MFA was an international trade agreement on textiles and clothing that was in place from 1974 till 2004. It imposed quotas on the amount of clothing and textile exports from developing

no longer exists) and the Generalized System of Preferences (GSP)[3]; different
forms of subsidies; tax exemptions; the maintenance of a suppressed labour
regime; weak factory compliance; and lawful and unlawful businesses relating
to RMG by-products. However, the RMG sector in Bangladesh is now facing
many challenges with respect to working conditions, labour unrest, technological upgrading and associated employment loss, stiff competition from compet-
itor countries, and pressure from international buyers related to improvement
on compliance issues. Third, Bangladesh will graduate from least developed
country (LDC) status by 2024, whereupon it will face the challenge of the erosion of preferences in major export destinations, and thus the risk of export loss,
especially the loss of RMG exports. Also, the country is seeking to expand its
manufacturing base substantially and aims to become an upper middle-income
country by 2031. Given these challenges, the fundamental question is whether
the 'RMG-centric' export model is sustainable.

Therefore, there are genuine reasons to argue that there is a need for a
major departure from the 'RMG-centric' export model and that the export
basket in Bangladesh needs to be diversified. It is argued that export diversification in developing countries like Bangladesh is a necessary condition
for sustained and long-term growth of the economy, and for job creation
(Ghosh and Ostry, 1994; Bleaney and Greenaway, 2001; Bertinelli *et al.*,
2006; di Giovanni and Levchenko, 2006; Hausmann *et al.*, 2007; Hausmann
and Klinger, 2006; Hwang, 2006). The current 'global value chains' discourse also highlights the importance of export diversification for effective
integration into global value chains. While Bangladesh has been able to
move away from agricultural exports to manufacturing exports, its export
basket still remains highly concentrated around a few low-value manufacturing sector, especially the RMG sector (Mirdha, 2018). For Bangladesh,
it is argued that export diversification will be important for the long-term

countries to developed countries. Under the MFA, the United States and the EU-restricted
imports from developing countries in an effort to protect their domestic textile industries. At the
same time, the MFA also helped spur textile production in certain countries where the quotas
actually gave them access they had not previously had. At the Uruguay Round of the General
Agreement on Tariffs and Trade (GATT), the decision was taken to dismantle quotas on global
clothing and textile trade. The process was completed on 1 January 2005, effectively marking
the end of the MFA (source: www.investopedia.com/terms/m/multi-fiber-arrangement.asp).

[3] The GSP was instituted in 1971 under the aegis of the United Nations Conference on Trade and
Development (UNCTAD). The GSP is a preferential tariff system which provides tariff reduction
on various products. While MFN status provides equal treatment in the case of tariffs being
imposed by a nation, in the case of the GSP differential tariffs can be imposed by a nation on
various countries depending on factors such as whether it is a developed country or a developing
country. Both rules come under the purview of the World Trade Organization (WTO). The GSP
provides tariff reduction for least developed countries but MFN only relates to discrimination
among WTO members. Thirteen countries grant GSP preferences: Australia, Belarus, Canada,
the EU, Iceland, Japan, Kazakhstan, New Zealand, Norway, the Russian Federation, Switzer-
land, Turkey, and the United States.

structural transformation of the economy with respect to shifting from the production of low-value products to high-value products. The long-term structural transformation of the economy requires production to be diversified and complexified, through which transferrable skills and capabilities will be acquired and linkages between sectors will be developed. Such a transformation will help to mitigate the impact of shocks on Bangladesh's economy. However, despite the fact that export diversification has been an important policy agenda in Bangladesh over the past few decades, the country has achieved limited success in this area. In this context, there is a need to evaluate the so-called 'RMG model' of export success.

Against this backdrop, this chapter explores the institutional challenges of export diversification in Bangladesh in the context of the dominant RMG sector. Understanding the reasons behind the lack of success in the diversification of the export basket in Bangladesh requires a better grasp of the critical political economy factors. The major objectives of this chapter are to: (i) evaluate the features of the 'RMG model' of export success, and explore the dynamics of the institutional space around the RMG sector in Bangladesh; (ii) understand the sustainability of the 'RMG-centric' export model as far as the domestic and global scenarios and the bigger development goals of the country are concerned; and (iii) evaluate the challenges of export diversification in Bangladesh in the context of the dominant RMG sector. This chapter uses available data, conducts, and assesses interviews with key stakeholders to gather their views on institutional challenges related to export diversification and applies relevant political economy analytical tools to understand the successes of and the challenges faced by the RMG sector and the institutional challenges of export diversification in Bangladesh.

II REVIEW OF THE LITERATURE ON EXPORT DIVERSIFICATION

While the importance of export-led growth is generally acknowledged in the empirical literature, it is also commonly highlighted that a large number of developing countries are dependent on a relatively small range of export products. Countries that are commodity-dependent or have a narrow export basket usually face export instability, which arises from unstable global demand. Therefore, studies indicate the need for diversification of the export basket. Ghosh and Ostry (1994) and Bleaney and Greenaway (2001) argued that export diversification usually refers to the move from 'traditional' to 'non-traditional' exports and can help to stabilise export earnings in the longer run. A diversified bundle of export products provides a hedge against price variations and shocks in specific product markets (Bertinelli *et al.*, 2006; di Giovanni and Levchenko, 2006). The type of products exported might affect economic growth and the potential for structural change (Hausmann *et al.*, 2007; Hausmann and Klinger, 2006; Hwang, 2006). Diversification provides opportunities to extend investment risks over a wider portfolio of economic sectors, which eventually increases income (Love, 1986; Acemoglu and Zilibotti 1997; Al-Marhubi, 2000; Hausmann and Rodrik, 2003; Hausmann *et al.*, 2007; Hausmann and Klinger, 2006).

There are several channels through which diversification may influence growth. It is therefore essential to make a distinction between horizontal and vertical diversification. Both are positively related to economic growth. Horizontal diversification means the alteration of the primary export mix in order to neutralise the volatility of global commodity prices. Horizontal export diversification benefits an economy by diminishing dependence on a narrow range of commodities that are subject to major price and volume fluctuations. Dawe (1996) and Bleaney and Greenaway (2001) argued that horizontal export diversification may present considerable development benefits as it may lead to well-directed economic planning and also contribute towards investment. Vertical export diversification, on the other hand, refers to finding further uses for existing products or developing new innovations using value-adding activities, such as processing and marketing. By highlighting the role of increasing returns to scale and dynamic spill-over effects, de Piñeres and Ferrantino (2000) argued that export diversification affects long-run growth. Export may benefit economic growth through generating positive externalities on non-exports (Feder, 1983), increased scale economies, improved allocative efficiency and better ability to produce dynamic comparative advantage (Sharma and Panagiotidis, 2004). Studies using regressions on cross-sections of countries (Sachs and Warner, 1995; Gylfason, 2004; Feenstra and Kee, 2004; Agosin, 2007) and panels (de Ferranti *et al.*, 2002) have proposed that export concentration is associated with slow growth.

The review of the aforementioned literature suggests that though many of the aforementioned cross-country papers suffer from endogeneity problems, as growth also implies structural changes, which, in turn, trigger changes in the composition of exports, economic growth, and its long-term sustainability in developing countries are associated with the diversification of the export structure. Bangladesh, with a highly concentrated export basket, needs to align its efforts for export diversification with strategies for accelerating and sustaining economic growth. As Hausmann and Rodrik (2003) argued, there are various uncertainties related to cost in the production of new goods, and therefore, the Government should promote industrial growth and structural transformation by encouraging entrepreneurship, solving information problems to do with innovation, providing infrastructure and other public goods, and providing incentives to motivate entrepreneurs to invest in a new range of activities.

III OVERVIEW OF THE RMG AND OVERALL EXPORT SECTOR IN BANGLADESH

The textile and apparel industry is the gateway for many developing countries to enter into the process of industrialisation. The ease of entry into this field and the high wages in developed countries have created favourable conditions for the manufacturing and exportation of textile- and apparel-derived products (Kim *et al.*, 2006). There are two reasons behind this: firstly, textiles and apparel are basic items of consumption for all people; and secondly, apparel manufacture is labour-intensive and requires relatively little fixed capital, but it can create substantial employment opportunities. The Asia-Pacific region has become one of the most competitive regions in textile and apparel manufacturing; approximately 50% of textile and apparel products are exported from this region (Kim *et al.*, 2006).

RMG exports from Bangladesh have seen a remarkable rise over the past three and half decades. In 1983/84, RMG exports were insignificant, but by 2017/18, they had increased to US$ 30.6 billion. Riding on the growth of RMG exports, the country's total exports of goods and services also saw a significant rise over the same period, from US$ 0.8 billion to US$ 36.7 billion.[4]

The share of RMG in total exports increased from only 3.9% in 1983/84 to as high as 83.5% in 2017/18. Thus, in recent years, the export basket has become more and more concentrated around RMG exports. It also follows that, despite the impressive economic growth record, the export base and export markets have remained rather narrow for Bangladesh, which is a matter of concern. Despite the policy reforms and various incentives offered, it seems that Bangladesh has failed to develop a diversified export structure.

Figure 4.1 presents the evolution of real exports and real GDP considering 1990 as 100. There were two surges: one that followed the end of the MFA in 2004 and one after the global financial crisis in 2008. There has been a rather long stagnation since 2012. There are many reasons for the stagnation in recent years, which include both the demand- and supply-side challenges (which are discussed in Section V). It is also noticeable that the stagnation of export growth since 2012 did not prevent GDP from growing relatively rapidly.[5] However, it should be mentioned that exports represent around 15% of GDP, and less in value-added.

Bangladesh's export concentration[6] is higher than that of any other country groups. The comparable country groups are LDCs, lower middle-income

---

[4] In real terms, total exports increased from US$ 1.1 billion in 1984 to US$ 26.9 billion in 2018.

[5] There are, however, debates on the official GDP growth numbers in recent years. While the official statistics show accelerated and increasing growth rates in GDP since 2013, sluggish growth in exports and remittances are not consistent with the official claims. Civil society think tanks and development partners like the World Bank and the IMF have been questioning the credibility of the official statistics (see The Daily Star 2018a; The Daily Star 2019; New Age, 2019).

[6] Concentration index, also named Herfindahl–Hirschman Index (Product HHI), is a measure of the degree of product concentration. The following normalised HHI is used in order to obtain values between 0 and 1: where H_j = country or country group index; x_{ij} = value of export for country j and product I; and n = number of products (SITC Revision 3 at three-digit group level). An index value closer to 1 indicates a country's exports or imports are highly concentrated on a few products. By contrast, values closer to 0 reflect exports or imports that are more homogeneously distributed among a series of products.

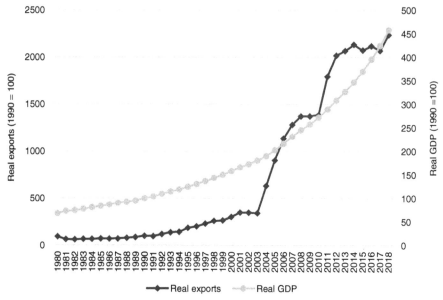

FIGURE 4.1 The evolution of exports and GDP in real terms (1990 = 100)
Source: Computed from the data from the World Development Indicators, World Bank.

countries, upper middle-income countries, high-income countries, and countries in South Asia. UNCTAD's export concentration indices[7] show that the marked differences in export concentration between Bangladesh and those of other country groups are noteworthy. Also, one important point to note here is that while other country groups have, in general, experienced declining export concentration indices, Bangladesh's export concentration indices increased during the period between 1995 and 2016.

   A close examination of the composition of the export baskets of Bangladesh and its major competitors, that is China, India, and Vietnam suggests that while Bangladesh's export basket is highly concentrated around RMG, those of China, India, and Vietnam are fairly diversified.[8] The higher export concentration in Bangladesh is driven not only by the strong performance of RMG exports but also by the very weak performance of non-RMG exports. The performance of RMG exports since the early 1980s, and especially since 2003, has been quite remarkable.

   It is also important to note that Bangladesh appears to be an outlier with respect to the share of textiles and clothing in manufacturing value-added. The data for 109 countries from the World Development Indicators of World Bank

[7] http://unctadstat.unctad.org/EN/Index.html
[8] http://atlas.cid.harvard.edu/

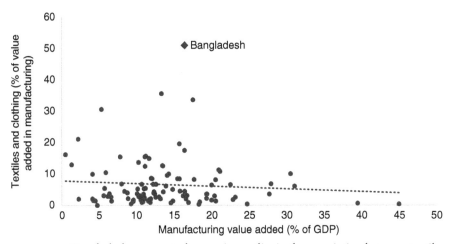

FIGURE 4.2 Bangladesh appears to be a major outlier in the association between textiles and clothing share in manufacturing and manufacturing share in GDP
Note: Average for 2011–2016.
Source: Computed from the data from the World Development Indicators, World Bank.

suggest that Bangladesh has the highest share of textiles and clothing in manufacturing value-added, more than 50%, where the 95th percentile is around 20%. Bangladesh also appears to be a major outlier in the association between textiles and clothing share in manufacturing value-added and manufacturing share in GDP (Figure 4.2).

2011 was an important year due to the change in the double-transformation rule of the European Union (EU) for textiles and apparel (more than 60% of Bangladesh's RMG exports are exported to the EU) to a single Rules of Origin (ROO) for LDCs. The double-transformation for clothing means that at least two substantial stages of production need to be carried out to confer origin status. For textiles, generally spinning and weaving needs to take place. For clothing, the weaving of fabric and making up into clothing needs to take place (European Commission, 2019). In the textiles and clothing sector, single-stage processing (manufacturing from fabric) has been allowed since 2011, in place of the previous two-stage one (manufacturing from yarn). Earlier, RMG exporters from Bangladesh, under the double-transformation rule, faced major difficulties in meeting the ROO criteria in the EU, due to the lack of supply of locally produced fabrics. In particular, a major part of the woven RMG exports from Bangladesh failed to access the duty-free market in the EU as they were unable to meet the double-transformation ROO.

The surge in exports over the past four decades also resulted in a rising export–GDP ratio. The export–GDP ratio was only around 5.7% in 1972 but increased to 15% in 2017. During this period, the import–GDP ratio also rose significantly, from only 13.7% to 20.3%. One important area of concern is that from 2011, both the export–GDP ratio and import–GDP ratio started to decline. Sluggish private investments is one of the major causes of the decline in the export–GDP ratio in Bangladesh.

The number of RMG factories in Bangladesh has increased quite remark-ably since 1984/1985. While in 1984/1985, there were only 384 factories, the number had increased to 5,876 by 2012/2013. After the infamous Rana Plaza incident in 2013,[9] the number of RMG factories then declined sharply to 4,222 in 2013/2014. In 2017/2018, the number rose again to 4,560. Interviews with relevant stakeholders in the RMG industry suggest that the major structural change that is currently occurring in the RMG industry is the introduction of labour-saving machineries for the kind of jobs which were previously done mostly by low-skilled female workers. This has resulted in substantial gains in productivity in the RMG industry in recent years.

The composition of the RMG export products has also seen a major shift over the past decades. In the early years, the RMG exports from Bangladesh were predominantly woven RMG. In 1992/1993, more than 85% of RMG exports was woven RMG. Over the years, the share of knitwear has increased, and by 2017/2018, woven and knitwear had almost equal shares. The main RMG export items from Bangladesh are shirts, trousers, jackets, T-shirts, and sweaters. While in the initial years, shirts dominated, with more than 50% of the RMG export share, in recent years, the share of shirts has declined to less than 10%, while trousers and T-shirts have been major export items.

It is also important to note that Bangladesh's RMG export markets are highly concentrated, with the EU and North America being the major des-tinations. In 2018, around 62.5% of the country's RMG exports went to the EU, while another 21% was destined for North America. In Europe, the major destinations of Bangladesh's RMG exports are Germany, the UK, Spain, and France. The major reason behind the EU becoming the domi-nant destination of RMG exports is the duty-free-quota-free (DFQF) mar-ket access in the EU market under the Everything But Arms (EBA) initiative for LDCs.[10]

---

[9] On 24 April 2013, an eight-story commercial building called Rana Plaza, in the Savar Upa-zila of Dhaka District, Bangladesh, collapsed. The Plaza housed five RMG factories and the collapse killed at least 1,134 people and injured more than 2,500 (see https://cleanclothes.org/campaigns/past/rana-plaza).

[10] The EBA initiative, introduced in 2001 under the EU's GSP scheme, grants LDCs duty- and quota-free access for almost all products (as the programme's name indicates, arms and ammunition are excluded). Access to the scheme is automatic for LDCs as countries do not need to apply to benefit from EBA, they are added to or removed from a relevant list through a delegated regulation. However, EBA preferences can be withdrawn under cer-tain exceptional circumstances, notably in the case of serious and systematic violation of principles of human rights and labour rights conventions (see www.un.org/ldcportal/preferential-market-access-european-union-everything-but-arms-initiative/).

IV THE 'RMG MODEL' OF EXPORT SUCCESS

A The MFA Regime

The development of Bangladesh's RMG sector greatly benefited from the international trade regime in textiles and clothing, which, until 2004, was governed by the MFA quotas. In the global market, the quota system restricted competition, led to allocative inefficiency, and slowed the natural shift in comparative advantage from industrial countries to developing countries (Faini *et al.*, 1993). However, it created opportunities for countries like Bangladesh by providing reserved markets, where textiles and clothing items had not been traditional exports. Bangladesh, being an LDC, benefited from the MFA regime in a number of ways. In the EU, there were quotas on non-LDC exporters, but Bangladesh's RMG items were allowed quota-free access (as well as duty-free treatment under the EU's GSP scheme). In the US market, Bangladesh was allowed significant annual quota enhancement based on growth performance in the preceding year. This gave Bangladesh's RMG exporters a secure market in the United States and also allowed them to gain from the quota-rent.[11]

In 1995, the WTO's Agreement on Textiles and Clothing (ATC) took over from the MFA. By 1 January 2005, the sector was fully integrated into normal GATT rules. In particular, the quotas came to an end, and importing countries were no longer able to discriminate between exporters. The ATC no longer exists: it is the only WTO agreement that had self-destruction built in to it.

B The Genesis of the RMG Industry in Bangladesh

Bangladesh's RMG industry started its journey in the late 1970s, with the launch of the MFA. A handful of foreign companies, particularly the Korean companies Youngone and Daewoo, invested early in Bangladesh, bringing technical experience, marketing expertise, and a willingness to employ women. This was partly because South Korea had reached the limit of its MFA quota. Bangladesh's middle managers and workers gained experience at Youngone and then, hired by other companies, spread their knowledge of operating an RMG business.

The late Nurool Quader Khan was the pioneer of the RMG industry in Bangladesh. In 1978, he sent 130 trainees to South Korea, where they learned how to produce RMG. With those trainees, he set up the first factory, Desh

---

[11] Quota-rent arises due to the fact that the quota is sold at a price that is higher than the competitive price, which more than compensates for the lower quantity being exported. Kathuria *et al.* (2001) estimated that the export tax equivalent of 1999 quotas on Indian RMG exports averaged 40% in the United States and 20% in the EU. That means that the MFA gave a 40% price advantage to those produces exporting within the quota to the United States and 20% for those exporting to the EU.

Garments, to produce garments for export. At the same time, the late Akhter Mohammad Musa of Bond Garments, the late Mohammad Reazuddin of Reaz Garments, Md. Humayun of Paris Garments, the engineer Mohammad Fazlul Azim of Azim Group, Major (Retd) Abdul Mannan of Sunman Group, M. Shamsur Rahman of Stylecraft Limited, and AM Subid Ali of Aristocrat Limited also came forward and established some of the first RMG factories in Bangladesh. Following in their footsteps, other entrepreneurs established RMG factories in the country.[12] These people were able to obtain major advantages from the Government, in the form of back to back letters of credit, bonded warehouses, and different forms of subsidies.

As mentioned before, the RMG sector has experienced an exponential growth since the early 1980s. The RMG sector was heavily promoted by all governments because of its remarkable economic performance, which contributed significantly to changing Bangladesh over the past four decades, from being an aid-dependent economy to being a trade-oriented economy.

C The RMG Industry Has Been the Major Beneficiary of Industry and Trade Policies and Export Incentives

After independence in 1971, the Government of Bangladesh nationalised all heavy industries, banks, and insurance companies. As a result of this mass nationalisation programme, by 1972 nationalised units accounted for 92% of the total fixed assets of the manufacturing sector in Bangladesh (Rahman, 1994). Private sector participation was severely restricted to medium-sized, small, and cottage industries (Sobhan, 1990). After the change in political power in 1975, the Government moved away from the nationalisation programme and revised the industrial policy with a view to facilitating a greater role for the private sector (Rahman, 1994). Together with the denationalisation and privatisation process, these changing industrial policies led to a situation in which the major thrust was to support the growth of the private sector by amending the exclusive authority of the state in the economy (World Bank, 1989).

During the 1980s, the private sector development agenda became more prominent in industrial policies in Bangladesh. The successful outcome of these policies was the rapid growth of the RMG industry. The New Industrial Policy was put in place in 1982 and was further modified by the Revised Industrial Policy in 1986. These policies also aimed at accelerating the process of privatisation of public enterprises. All these policies involved providing substantial incentives and opportunities for private investment (Rahman, 1994). Subsequent industrial policies re-emphasised the leading role of the private sector in the development of industries and clearly stated that the objective

---

[12] www.bgmea.com.bd/home/pages/AboutGarmentsIndustry

was to shift the role of the Government from a 'regulatory' authority to a 'promotional' entity. The industrial policies also encouraged domestic and foreign investment in the overall industrial development and stressed the importance of developing export-oriented industries.

Raihan and Razzaque (2007) highlighted that an important element of trade policy reform in Bangladesh has been the use of a set of generous support and promotional measures for exports. These measures have primarily been directed to the RMG sector. While the import liberalisation was meant to correct the domestic incentive structure, in the form of reduced protection for import-substituting sectors, export promotion schemes were undertaken to provide exporters with an environment in which the previous bias against export-oriented investment could be reduced significantly. Important export incentive schemes available in Bangladesh include, among others: subsidised rates of interest on bank loans; duty-free import of machinery and intermediate inputs; cash subsidy; exemption from paying the value-added tax; and rebate on corporate income taxes. Box 4.1 summarises some of the most important incentive schemes that have been put in place in the country since the early 1980s, alongside the expansion of the RMG sector. With the significant reduction in tariff rates in the early 1990s, and the provision of generous support and promotional measures for exports, the anti-export bias declined

---

Box 4.1 Important export incentive schemes in Bangladesh, especially for RMG

Export Performance Benefit (XPB): This scheme was in operation from the mid-1970s to 1992. It allowed the exporters of non-traditional items to cash a certain proportion of their earnings (known as entitlements) at a higher exchange rate of the wage earner scheme (WES[1]). In 1992, with the unification of the exchange rate system, the XPB scheme ceased.

Bonded warehouses: Exporters of manufactured goods are able to import raw materials and inputs without payment of duties and taxes. The raw materials and inputs are kept in bonded warehouses. On the submission of evidence of production for exports, a required amount of inputs is released from the warehouse. This facility is extended to exporters of RMG, specialised textiles (such as towels and socks), leather, ceramics, printed matter, and packaging materials, who are required to export at least 70% of their products.

Duty drawback: Exporters of manufactured products are given a refund of the customs duties and sales taxes paid on the imported raw materials that are used in the production of the goods exported. Exporters are exempted from paying value-added tax as they can obtain drawbacks on the value-added tax they have paid.

Duty-free import of machinery: Import of machineries without payment of any duties, for production in the export sectors.

Back-to-back letters of credits: Allows exporters to open letters of credit for the required import of raw materials against their export letters of credit in such sectors as RMG and leather goods. The system is considered to be one of the most important incentive schemes for the RMG export. Nurul Kader, the pioneer of the RMG industry in Bangladesh, was the inventor of back to back letters of credit.

Cash subsidy: The scheme was introduced in 1986. This facility is available mainly to exporters of textiles and clothing who choose not to use bonded warehouses or duty drawback facilities. Currently, the cash subsidy is 25% of the free on board export value. In recent times, cash subsidies have been offered to agro-product exporters.

Interest rate subsidy: Allows exporters to borrow from banks at lower bands of interest rates of 8–10%, as against the normal 14–16% charge.

Tax holiday: First introduced under the Industrial Policy of 1991–1993, this incentive allows a tax holiday for exporters, after the commencement of exports, for 5–12 years, depending on various conditions.

Income tax rebate: Exporters are given rebates on corporate income tax. Recently, this benefit has been increased: the advance income tax for exporters has been reduced from 0.50% of export receipts to 0.25%.

Retention of earnings in foreign currency: Exporters are now allowed to retain a portion of their export earnings in foreign currency. The entitlement varies in accordance with the local value addition in exportable. The maximum limit is 40% of total earnings, although for low value-added products such as RMG the current ceiling is only 7.5%.

Export credit guarantee scheme: Introduced in 1978 to insure loans in respect of export finance, it provides pre-shipment and post-shipment (and both) guarantee schemes. The principal risks covered include insolvency of the buyers and political restrictions delaying payment. The scheme was undertaken at the initiative of the Export Promotion Bureau and the ministries of commerce, industry, and finance. The scheme encourages exporters to initiate exports of new products and/ or to enter new markets through covering the risk of insolvency of buyers and political risks inherent in foreign trade. The scheme also provides a guarantee for bank loans taken by the exporters to meet their financial needs during the production period and between exporting of goods and receiving payment from foreign buyers. Bangladeshi exporters can enjoy credit for a maturity of up to 180 days. Risks covered include insolvency and protracted default. Coverage percentages vary from 75% to 80% in the case of commercial risks, and 95% in the case of political risks.

Special facilities for export processing zones (EPZs)[2]: To promote exports, a number of EPZs are currently in operation. The export units located in EPZs enjoy various other incentives, such as a tax holiday for 10 years, duty-free imports of spare parts, and exemption from value-added taxes and other duties. The major exports from EPZs are RMG.

Source: Adapted and updated from Raihan and Razzaque (2007).

---

[1] The Wage Earners' Scheme (WES) was introduced in 1974 to provide incentives to Bangladeshi nationals working abroad to remit their earnings to Bangladesh through official channels (see http://en.banglapedia.org/index.php?title=Wage_Earners%E2%80%99_Scheme).

[2] Romer (1992) argued that the success story of Mauritius was due to the island's policy of supporting an EPZ, which made investment attractive to foreigners. The EPZ was an administrative arrangement: it involved no geographic restrictions and no special investment in infrastructure. The main policies in this arrangement were unrestricted, tariff-free imports of machinery and materials, no restrictions on ownership or repatriation of profits, a 10-year income tax holiday for foreign investors, a policy of centralised government wage-setting, and an implicit assurance that labour unrest would be suppressed and wage increases would be moderate.

---

quite significantly, which helped promote a surge in exports, especially RMG exports, during that period.[13]

A close scrutiny of the performance of sectors, apart from RMG, and consultation with the stakeholders of non-RMG sectors, reveal that many of these sectors, though classified as 'thrust or priority sectors' in the industrial and export policies, were not able to enjoy the incentives provided in these policies, despite having export potential. Instead, the RMG industry has been the major beneficiary of the incentives and facilities specified in these policies.

D Institutional Space, Political Settlement, and Deals Space Favouring RMG

The RMG sector in Bangladesh grew in an environment of very 'weak' institutions (see Chapters 2 and 3). Against the poor quality of institutions, the country became the second largest exporter of RMG in the world. How do we reconcile these two contrasting scenarios? If we look at the well-known institutional indicators (World Governance Indicators (WGI), Doing Business, Transparency International, and Global Competitiveness Index), all refer to the

---

[13] Anti-export bias occurs when EERM > EERX, where EERM is the effective exchange rate for imports (i.e. nominal exchange rate adjusted with protective trade interventions) and EERX is the effective exchange rate for exports (i.e. nominal exchange rate adjusted for such export incentives and subsidies).

quality of formal institutions. However, in countries like Bangladesh, placed at
the lower level of the development spectrum, what governs is a host of informal
institutions, and the formal institutions are weak and fragile. Khan's framework of 'growth-enhancing institutions', in contrast to 'market-enhancing
institutions' (Khan, 2012b), elaborates how the role of informal institutions
can be critical in developing countries. Some developing countries, especially
East and Southeast Asian countries, have been successful in steering unconven-
tional institutions to drive growth. Khan (2012b) further highlights that the
success of the RMG industry in Bangladesh was not replicated in any other
major sectors, as no rent, such as the RMG industry enjoyed, was available
for other sectors. The critical element in the institutional arrangement which
allowed the take-off of this industry was the global institutional mechanism
with the MFA and favourable domestic factors. The MFA facilitated fortuitous
rents on terms that assisted the learning-by-doing that was critical for the RMG
sector. With the high quota-rent, the quota utilisation rate for Bangladesh in
the US market in 2001–2002 was much higher than the rates of other developing countries (Yang and Mlachila, 2007).[14]

Khan (2012b) further points out that the authoritarian clientelism during
the early phases of the sector's take-off allowed the rapid solution of a number
of institutional constraints facing the sector, especially in the form of the poor
quality of formal institutions. Many of these solutions were 'unorthodox' in
nature (e.g. back to back letter of credits), and a 'political settlement'[15] among
the elites in Bangladesh on the RMG industry helped the industry to grow.
This 'political settlement' was initially based on rent-sharing, and later evolved
as the economic interest of RMG business owners coincided with the political
interest of governments in terms of employment generation (especially female
employment) and poverty alleviation.

As discussed in Chapter 1, the deals environment framework, proposed by
Pritchett *et al.* (2018) relates to the idea of 'deals space'. Informal institutions,
which are prevalent in developing economies, may also take the form of 'deals'
among the political and economic elites, in contrast to the formal rules guiding
the relationship between these actors that exist in advanced countries. Deals
can be open (access is open to all) or closed (access is restricted), and they can
also be ordered (deals are respected) or disordered (deals are not respected).
According to this view, countries are likely to exhibit high growth when deals
are open and ordered, and thus deals become closer to formal institutions.

[14] According to Yang and Mlachila (2007), the quota utilisation rates in the US market in 2001–
2002 by developing countries were as follows: Bangladesh (83%), Cambodia (24%), China
(76%), Egypt (10%), Hong Kong (55%), India (68%), Indonesia (33%), Pakistan (31%), Philippines (32%), Sri Lanka (26%), Thailand (56%), and Turkey (23%).
[15] According to Khan (2018), the political settlements framework shows how the distribution of
organisational power determines the institutions and policies that are likely to persist, as well
as the ones most likely to be developmental in that context, and how relative power and the
capabilities of relevant organisations may change over time.

Informal institutions can have two distinct roles with respect to the stages of development. At an early stage of development, if countries can steer informal institutions so that they are 'growth-enhancing', as well as ensuring that the 'deals space' is more ordered (either open or closed), countries can achieve strong economic growth and also some improvements in the social sector. However, for the transition from a lower to a higher stage of development, whether the country can maintain a high growth rate and achieve further development goals depends on the dynamics of how informal institutions evolve, and whether formal institutions become stronger and functional. Not many developing countries have been able to do this. Certainly, the East Asian and most of the Southeast Asian countries are success stories in using informal institutions efficiently at the early stage of development, as well as achieving some notable successes in the transition to functional formal institutions.[16]

In contrast to many other comparable countries in Asia and Africa at a similar stage of development, and especially in comparison to the LDCs, the country group to which Bangladesh belongs, Bangladesh has been successful in creating some efficient pockets of 'growth-enhancing' informal institutions, against an overall distressing picture as regards its formal institutions. The examples of 'pockets of efficient informal institutions' in Bangladesh include the well-functioning privileges and special arrangements for the RMG sector.[17]

However, the next question is how did Bangladesh create such 'pockets of efficient informal institutions' and make the 'best' use of them? The explanations include both historical and political economy perspectives. The 1971 liberation war led to the emergence of an independent Bangladeshi state which for the first time gave unprecedented and enormous independent power to the burgeoning political and economic elites of the Bengali nation. Also, the people, in general, enjoyed some benefits of this power. To a great degree, the entrepreneurial nature of the people of this country is deeply rooted in this feeling of power.[18] Successful entrepreneurship is seen in the case of the RMG sector. As Bangladesh is not rich in natural resources, elites saw in the RMG sector the basis of the generation of substantial rents (the sources of rents in the RMG sector were discussed earlier in this chapter).

---

[16] For a review of formal and informal institutions, see Baland *et al.* (2020).
[17] As Muhammad (2011) argued, the RMG industry enjoyed policy and material support from both the Government and the international financial institutions. The business elites saw the RMG as a sector with high-profit investment opportunities. A huge pool of unemployed young women from poor families, ready to work for rock-bottom wages and longer working hours, made up the new workforce.
[18] Rahman (2018), Alamgir (2019), and Mahmud (2020) highlight the positive role of 'peoples' aspiration' in Bangladesh in economic development. Mahmud (2020) argues that the lack of social barriers of class, caste, or ethnicity, along with the opening up of certain economic opportunities, helped to create aspirations among the poor for upward economic mobility and to promote growth-enhancing entrepreneurship among them.

While Khan (2012b) rightly mentions the institutional perspectives behind the growth of the RMG sector, his narrative of the 'political settlement' is rather narrow and elite-centric. Khan's 'political settlement' is primarily an 'elite agreement', and it overlooks the critical nexus between elites and non-elites within the society. Through large-scale employment generation in the RMG sector and its induced effects of poverty alleviation and female empowerment, the business elites were also able to draw support from both the political elites and non-elites in the society.

Using the lens of the 'deals space' of Pritchett *et al.* (2018), Hassan and Raihan (2018) argue that the RMG sector as a whole has enjoyed closed deals, and parts of the closed deals actually have legal and quasi-legal bases (bonded warehouse schemes, cash incentives, statutory regulatory ordinances, etc.), but these tend to be highly exclusive in nature. The 'state capture' by the RMG lobbies is manifested in the form of ensuring special privileges for them, and a high presence of RMG businesses among members of parliament. *From the perspective of an individual RMG entrepreneur, bypassing the Bangladesh Garments Manufacturing and Exporters Associations (BGMEA) and maintaining bilateral interfaces with the state's regulatory authority, in relation to duty-free import processes, would be prohibitively costly, in terms of the informal transaction costs that would be incurred and the excessive amount of time the process would entail. Therefore, the 'deals environment' became more 'closed' and the system became more 'formal', through voluntary compliance of individual firms with the BGMEA. Also,* the individual firms also saw quite a rapid shift from a relatively disordered deal environment (during the late 1970s and early 1980s)[19] to an ordered deals environment in the subsequent decades. The transition occurred not only because of government prodding in relation to private sector development (through statist policy inducement) but also largely due to market actors' strong incentive to ensure their survival and expand in a globally competitive market. The enactment of various beneficial rules and myriad forms of deals benefitting the RMG sector was mainly the outcome of effective demands and skilful negotiations by a sector that is characterised by strong collective action capability, thanks to the economic and political clout it gradually came to possess.

As was pointed out earlier, the RMG sector as a whole enjoys privileges that are quite extraordinary. For instance, the state has delegated the authority over rule enactments and enforcement of these rules to its collective forum BGMEA, as well as to Bangladesh Knitwear Manufacturing Associations (BKMEA). The most prominent power held by these organisations is the power to issue

---

[19] See Rashid (2008) for the effects of the chaotic policy regime and bureaucratic constraints that RMG firms had to face in the earlier stage of the development of the sector, and how initiatives taken by politically, socially, and administratively well connected entrepreneurs gradually reduced this chaotic environment, which led to a more ordered deals environment.

customs certificates – utilisation declarations (UDs) and utilisation permits (UPs)[20] governing the duty-free importing process. This act by the state tends to blur the distinction between legality and illegality.[21] In this sense, one can legitimately categorise such privileges as *de facto* deals, since they are exclusive to this sector and indicate the RMG sector's ability to generate and preserve a *de facto* closed deal environment that has allowed it to accrue substantial rent for decades, and also to achieve spectacular economic performance.[22]

Over the decades, RMG owners came to be the most powerful and the best organised business group in Bangladesh. The political power of this group derives from its high contribution to economic growth, close political integration with the state (including parliamentary representation) (Rashid 2008), and the class basis of the owners: former military and bureaucratic officials and the white collar managerial class were the pioneers of RMG sector (Rashid, 2008; Kabeer and Mahmud, 2004). The political power of the RMG sector is manifested in the extraordinary tax privileges and subsidies that it has enjoyed during the last three decades. These exemptions and financial incentives have not changed over the decades, despite the fact that the sector has witnessed substantial expansion over time.

E Subcontracting in the RMG Industry in Bangladesh

As the industry grew, the need for subcontracting increased. A large factory has a maximum production capacity (e.g. number of shirts per month), even taking into account some allowed overtime. When orders are larger than what can be produced by the business receiving the order, work is subcontracted. This is necessary to balance production capacity and order size. As buyers moved towards wanting to deal with only a few factories, subcontracting became even more important (Cookson, 2017). In recent years, subcontracting has received a bad name. Buyers believe, usually correctly, that factory compliance is not met by subcontractors. The compulsion to demand compliance leads to a reluctance to allow subcontracting. Demands for compliance have many impacts on RMG costs, but a hidden, very significant cost is the difficulty experienced in using subcontracting (Cookson, 2017). In particular, after the Rana Plaza accident in 2013, and the stringent scrutiny by the Accord and Alliance, the number of subcontracting firms declined drastically.[23]

---

[20] A UD for bonded warehouse facilities is a declaration by the deemed exporters of the duty free imports of raw materials to be used exclusively for 100% exports. A UP for bonded warehouse facilities is given to the deemed exporters if they comply with certain conditions.

[21] As one prominent Bangladeshi lawyer observed: 'BGMEA has no regulatory authority under the laws of the country. It's a clubhouse of the garment industry' (Yardley 2013).

[22] It is worth mentioning that minimum wage negotiations – resulting in a deal with workers – progressively becomes a formal institution.

[23] The Accord (European-based buyers) and the Alliance (North America–based buyers) came into place in Bangladesh after the Rana Plaza factory building collapsed on 24 April 2013, killing 1,133 people and critically injuring thousands more. The Accord is an independent,

F 'Political Settlement' Regarding the Management of the Labour Regime in the RMG Sector

The labour regime in the RMG sector has been managed quite extraordinarily over the past decades. Most workers work in sweatshop conditions. However, the issue only appears in the global media when major fatal accidents occur, like that at the Rana Plaza in 2013. Long working hours, low wages, lack of regular contracts, and systemically hazardous conditions are often reported (Uddin, 2015; Berik and Rodgers, 2010). Trade unions, when allowed, are unable to protect their workers. Not all 'Fundamental' International Labour Organization (ILO) conventions have been ratified, and their concrete application is far from the norm. The UN Guiding Principles on Business and Human Rights, and the OECD Guidelines for Multinational Enterprises fix good standards of corporate social responsibility for Western brands operating in such countries, but they are not binding and do not provide for sanctions if they are not applied. In practice, they have failed to defend workers' rights. While there has been growing unrest from workers, which has led to strikes and protests, their main achievement has been some increases in the minimum wage, which remains far below a living wage[24] (Lu, 2016). Also, subcontracting has been used as a way of escaping constraints.

Trade unions are often suppressed, and union organisers intimidated, including physically. Workers claim that some managers mistreat employees involved in setting up unions, or force them to resign (Bhuiyan, 2012; Parry, 2016). Some claim they have been beaten up, sometimes by local gangsters who attack workers outside the workplace, and even at their homes. The lack of regular contracts means many workers who are injured in factory fires, and the relatives of those who die, do not receive any compensation because they are not registered as formal employees of the companies and the management

---

legally binding agreement between brands and trade unions to work towards a safe and healthy garments and textile industry in Bangladesh. The Accord covers factories producing RMG and, at the option of signatory companies, home textiles and fabric and knit accessories (source: https://bangladeshaccord.org/). The Alliance is committed to conducting factory safety assessments in all RMG factories producing for its members in Bangladesh. These assessments, conducted by independent Qualified Assessment Firms, provide factory owners with a technical understanding of the fire safety and structural concerns related to their facilities and prompt action plans that aim to systematically and sustainably improve safety conditions for garment workers (source: www.bangladeshworkersafety.org/).

[24] A living wage refers to the idea that workers and their families should be able to afford a basic, but decent lifestyle that is considered acceptable by a society at its current level of economic development. Workers and their families need to be able to live above the poverty level and to participate in social and cultural life. According to Anker (2011), a living wage is the remuneration received for a standard working week by a worker that is sufficient to allow them to afford a decent standard of living for the worker and her or his family. Elements of a decent standard of living include food, water, housing, education, healthcare, transport, clothing, and other essential needs, including provision for unexpected events.

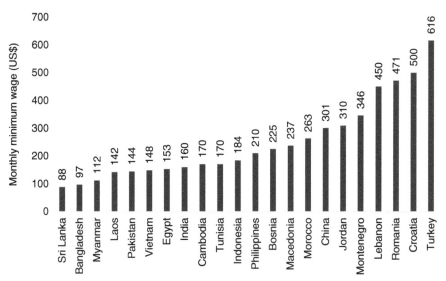

FIGURE 4.3 Minimum monthly wage for garment workers in 2018 (measured in US$)
Source: https://emergingtextiles.com/?q=idx&s=apparel-manufacturing-labor-costs.
The data for Bangladesh take into account the upward minimum wage adjustment that
took place in September 2018.

therefore does not identify them as their workers. The biggest strength that
Bangladesh has over its competitors is its cheap and vast workforce. The mini-
mum wage in Bangladesh in the RMG industry is among the lowest in the top
RMG-producing countries (Figure 4.3).

After the inception of an export-oriented RMG sector in 1978, the first
wage board, formed in 1984, set a minimum wage for the sector's workers at
Bangladeshi Taka (BDT) 560 a month (Figure 4.4). This shows that the country's first wage board for fixing the salaries of workers in the garment sector
was constituted long after Bangladeshi entrepreneurs ventured into the RMG
business, which suggests the weak bargaining power of the workers in this
sector. This low minimum wage continued for the next 10 years, despite the
erosion of purchasing power due to inflation (Figure 4.4).

In the following three and half decades, five more wage boards were constituted, at very irregular intervals. The second (in 1994) and third (in 2006)
wage boards were established at 10-year and 12-year intervals, respectively.
Periodic labour unrest, with the demand for an increase in the minimum wage,
led to relatively more frequent revisions of the minimum wage after 2006, and
a political settlement evolved as workers became more important for political
elites in the political game than in the past. Nevertheless, during the almost
four decades of the RMG industry's existence, the minimum wage in the industry was kept very low. This was done with the support of the state, whoever

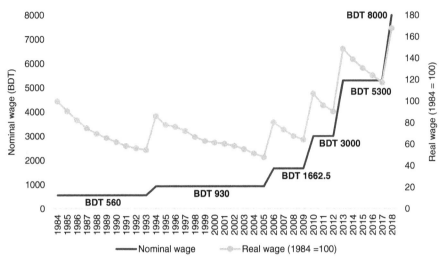

FIGURE 4.4 Minimum wage in the RMG sector in Bangladesh (BDT)
Source: Author's calculation and www.dhakatribune.com/bangladesh/nation/2019/
01/11/a-brief-history-of-the-minimum-wage-in-garment-sector.

was in power. Figure 4.5 also suggests that, in real terms, the value of minimum wages declined over time, even in those years when they were kept fixed in nominal terms. The real increase was 60% between 2010 and 2018. More or less the same evolution is found for 2000–2010, but the increase was only 20% in the decade before. Of course, the loss in real terms is due to the infrequency of the wage adjustments.

The minimum wage is set in Bangladesh's RMG sector[25] through a process that involves the Government forming a new minimum wage board for the RMG sector, to formulate a new wage structure for RMG workers. The board is usually led by a senior district judge, as chairman. In addition to representatives from the owners and workers, the board also consists of three independent members. The representatives of owners and workers separately propose a minimum wage for the workers and propose this to the board. After discussions with stakeholders, the board recommends a new wage structure based on the inflation rate, living costs, the country's economic condition, and strength of the sector as regards paying the settled wage. The wage board then publishes a gazette and gives the workers' and owners' representatives a 14-day period in which to appeal if there have any objection to the recommendations. The board finalises the new wage structure taking into consideration the objections of workers' and owners' representatives, if

[25] www.dhakatribune.com/bangladesh/nation/2019/01/11/a-brief-history-of-the-minimum-wage-in-garment-sector

there are any. The wage board then passes the wage structure to the Ministry of Labour and Employment, which reviews the proposed wage structure and sends it to the Ministry of Law for vetting. After approval is obtained from the Ministry of Law, the Ministry of Labour and Employment publishes a gazette notification and the new wage structure enters the implementation phase. Once the gazette notification is issued, all export-oriented garment manufacturers are bound to implement the new wage structure in their factories. The new wage structure comes into effect from the date set by the Government.[26] However, there are allegations that workers' voices are not heard properly in the wage board as the board includes no 'true' representatives of workers.[27]

There also exists a gender wage gap in the RMG industry in Bangladesh. Menzel and Woodruff (2019), using data from 70 large export-oriented garment manufacturers in Bangladesh, showed that among production workers, women's wages were 8% lower than those of men. A study by ILO-SANEM (2018), using survey data from 111 RMG factories, also found a similar gender wage gap.

G Poor Factory Compliance and a Weak Regulatory and Monitoring Mechanism

The RMG industry started with small factories as it was easy to set up a small garment factory: one could establish a factory by renting space, buying 50–100 sewing machines, wiring up the factory for electricity, hiring and training the workers, getting a contract for a small order of simple garments, and going to work. Sourcing, pricing, and quality control were learned by doing. The profits were high, and therefore small companies could get established. There was no ban on entry (Cookson, 2017).

Systemic hazardous conditions are a common feature of many factories in this sector. The rapid expansion of the industry led to the adaptation of many buildings that were built for other purposes – residential, for instance – into factories, often without the required permits. Other plants have had extra floors added or have increased the workforce and machinery to levels beyond the safe capacity of the building. Lack of appropriate protective equipment, old and outdated wiring that is at risk of short circuiting (a major cause of fires), and non-existent or outdated fire extinguishing facilities are often reported in these overcrowded workplaces. Fire exits are often deliberately blocked by factory owners, and windows even barred, thus increasing the death toll in accidents

---

[26] The Minimum Wage Board, under the Ministry of Labour and Employment, is working on setting minimum wages for workers in tea gardens, security services, printing presses, the plastics industry, the leather and footwear industry, transport services, re-rolling mills, privately owned jute-mills, etc. (see http://mwb.portal.gov.bd/site/view/notices).

[27] See https://rmgbd.net/2018/01/rules-violeted-in-appointing-workers-representative-allege-leaders/.

(D'Ambrogio, 2014).[28] Poor factory compliance persisted for a long time due to a weak regulatory and monitoring mechanism. The Department for Factory Inspection (DIFE), under the Ministry of Labour and Employment, established in 1969, is entrusted with the responsibility for monitoring the compliance of factory conditions. However, due to DIFE's numerous institutional challenges related to weak capacity, corruption, and a lack of interest from the Government in strengthening DIFE, it failed to perform its duties. After the Rana Plaza accident in 2013, there has been an effort to enhance DIFE's capacity.[29]

H Rent Generation and Management through RMG By-products

The business of rent generation and management through the RMG by-product *jhut* (the scrap from clothing items) is an important aspect of the RMG industry. Previously, *jhut* was a waste product produced by RMG factories, but it has now become a by-product of the industry, since it has commercial value. A newspaper report,[30] citing the Bangladesh Garment and Textile Waste Exporters Association (BGTEA), highlights that the market size of RMG by-products is over BDT 2,000 crore (around US$ 2.4 billion, equivalent to 1% of GDP). RMG factories in Bangladesh produce over 400,000 tonnes of by-products annually.[31] The simple scraps of fabric that are a by-product of making RMG generate new jobs, especially for women in the informal sector. Some 150,000 people are currently employed in the informal, small-scale operations of this potentially lucrative sector.[32]

---

[28] Some of Bangladesh's worst industrial accidents since 2005 (source: www.reuters.com/) are:

> *January 2005* – A fire at a garment factory outside Dhaka killed 22 people and injured more than 50.
>
> *April 2005* – At least 64 people were killed and about 100 injured when a garment factory building collapsed in Dhaka.
>
> *February 2006* – A garment factory building collapsed in Dhaka, killing 21 workers and injuring dozens.
>
> *February 2006* – A fire at a textile factory in the port city of Chittagong killed 65 workers and injured dozens.
>
> *February 2010* – A fire at a garment factory in a Dhaka suburb killed 21 workers and injured about 50.
>
> *November 2012* – A fire at the Tazreen Fashions factory in Dhaka, which supplied Western brands, killed 112 workers and injured more than 150. The blaze, believed to have been caused by a short circuit, was the deadliest factory fire in Bangladesh.
>
> *April 2013* – At least 1,136 people were killed and hundreds injured when an eight-storey building housing five garment factories supplying global brands collapsed on the outskirts of Dhaka. The collapse of the Rana Plaza was the worst industrial accident in Bangladesh.

[29] See http://dife.portal.gov.bd/site/page/b2ef53e5-3049-4913-bc29-5ddcc015b712.

[30] www.dhakatribune.com/uncategorized/2014/11/21/rags-to-riches-the-prospects-of-recycled-rmg-by-products

[31] www.thedailystar.net/frontpage/turning-waste-fashion-1496509

[32] www.dhakatribune.com/uncategorized/2014/11/21/rags-to-riches-the-prospects-of-recycled-rmg-by-products

The business of re-using wasted cloth is a three-step process. First, a person, usually a locally influential person, collects the cloth forcibly or via negotiations. Second, it is sold to the re-use or recycling business. Third, the final product is then sold to different consumers and exported. After collection, the process of recycling starts with sorting, which is done by the colour, type, and size of the fabric. Larger scraps of cloth are used to make children's frocks, skirts, shirts, pyjamas, and sometimes pillow covers. Large scraps of fabric are sold to local traders to make garments for children. Most of these children's clothes are sold in Bangladesh but some are exported to India. Dhaka's bedding industry is dependent on *jhut*. Mattresses, pillows, cushions, and seat stuffing and padding in cars, public buses, and rickshaws use recycled cloth and processed cotton.[33]

Because of the lucrative nature of this business, locally influential people seek to obtain more *jhut* through influencing either workers or mid-level management of the factories. Many factories have faced unrest resulting from the politics involved in the *jhut* business.[34] This high rent from the *jhut* business, through legal and illegal means, also makes the RMG industry more attractive than any other export-oriented sectors.

V SUSTAINABILITY CHALLENGES OF THE RMG-CENTRIC EXPORT MODEL

A Increased Competition in the Global Market

In recent years, Bangladesh's share of global RMG exports has increased steadily. In 2012, the share was 4.66%; this had increased to 6.19% by 2017.[35] The increased share of global RMG exports shows that, despite numerous challenges, Bangladesh's RMG industry has been able to strengthen its market share at the global level. With the increased share in the world market, in recent years, Bangladesh has become the second largest exporter of RMG in the world. After China, its closest competitors are Vietnam and India. It can be mentioned that, in 2006, *Bangladesh ranked sixth on the list of top RMG exporting countries, with a share of only 2.8%.*[36]

---

[33] www.dhakatribune.com/uncategorized/2014/11/21/rags-to-riches-the-prospects-of-recycled-rmg-by-products

[34] 'In Bangladesh, regarding "jhut" trading, often news breaks out involving fights, local influential mobs, murders, etc. Few investigation report claims that there are approximately 11,000 organised criminals who have become desperate across the country including capital. Only in Narayanganj, there are 15 groups and each group has minimum 100 criminals.' See www.textiletoday.com.bd/jhuta-processing-bangladeshs-clothing-industry-unique-example-sustainable-solid-waste-management/.

[35] Data source: WTO.

[36] https://medium.com/@stitchdiary/what-makes-bangladesh-a-hub-of-garment-manufacturing-ce83aa37edfc

However, there is also a very high concentration of products in the RMG industry in Bangladesh. An analysis using the Trade Map[37] data suggests that while, products conforming with the six-digit Harmonised System (HS) code level, the top 10 RMG products account for around 68% of total RMG exports in Bangladesh, for China, India, and Vietnam, the figures are 35.5%, 45.6%, and 42.1%, respectively. Moreover, the top five products account for 53.3% of Bangladesh's RMG exports, whereas the figures are only 22.7%, 28.7%, and 25% for China, India, and Vietnam, respectively. Another important concern is that Bangladesh's RMG exports face stiff competition, especially from China and Vietnam. The 16 products conforming with the six-digit HS code level are common among the top 25 RMG products, both in the cases of Bangladesh vs. China and Bangladesh vs. Vietnam. The EU, Bangladesh's largest export destination, has extended duty-free access to Vietnam, under the EU–Vietnam Free Trade Agreement, which eliminates the competitive edge that Bangladesh had held over Vietnam in RMG exports to the EU market.[38]

B Diversification within RMG and Quality Issues

While Bangladesh's export basket remains highly concentrated around RMG exports, diversification within the RMG sector remains a big challenge. According to the data from WTO, products conforming with the six-digit HS code level, just 10 RMG products accounted for 70% of the total RMG exports from Bangladesh in 2017/18. Just two products (T-shirts and men's trousers) accounted for 36% of RMG exports in that year. Most of these are low-value and basic-quality products. According to the Global Sourcing Survey 2018 by AsiaInspection, Bangladesh is still an attractive source of low-cost RMG items.[39]

Attempts within the RMG industry to move up the ladder to high-value and high-quality products have not been very successful. According to IMF (2014), at the four-digit Standard International Trade Classification (SITC) level, only three RMG products have been of higher quality compared to Bangladesh's major competitors, China, India, and Vietnam, and the advantage Bangladesh has in these three products is marginal.[40] However, it should be mentioned that

---

[37] www.trademap.org/
[38] www.newagebd.net/article/99494/eu-vietnam-fta-new-challenge-for-bangladesh-rmg-sector
[39] www.thedailystar.net/business/bangladesh-still-popular-low-cost-apparel-1566334
[40] Note: The methodology for constructing the export quality index is elaborated in IMF (2014). The multi-level export quality database provides quality measures that correct unit values for a number of factors, including production cost differences, firms' pricing strategies, and the fact that shipments to more distant destinations typically consist of higher priced goods. The database covers 178 countries and 851 products over the period 1962–2010. At the most disaggregate SITC four-digit level, it consists of more than 20 million product-exporter-importer-year observations. Quality estimates are also supplied at the (1) SITC 3-, 2-, and 1-digit levels; (2) country level for the Broad Economic Categories (BEC) classification (which makes it possible

while Bangladesh no longer has any duty-free market access or GSP facility in the USA,[41] presently Bangladesh enjoys a 12% 'margin of preference'[42] for its RMG industry under the EU's EBA initiative (United Nations Department for Economic and Social Affairs (UNDESA, 2019).

C The Segmented RMG Value Chain in Bangladesh

Mercer-Blackman (2016) argues that, ideally, successful structural transformation in Bangladesh should consist of two types of processes at this juncture: (i) diversification away from garments into other manufactures by producing goods that entail increasingly more complex manufacturing processes compared to garments, but that are still similar enough that it is easy for workers and managers to master these processes; or (ii) linking to the fashion industry global production chain and providing increasingly more complex and valuable parts of garments: for example, through increasing involvement in the design process of the garment. If the country chose avenue 'ii' – that is, moving up the fashion industry value chain – increasing overall productivity will be very difficult because of the segmented nature of the value chain. It will thus be much easier for Bangladesh to make products that are similar to garments, such as footwear or small appliances, than to begin to understand and master the various aspects of designing and retailing clothes.

Mercer-Blackman (2016) further argues that there are two main reasons why the fashion industry value chain is segmented for Bangladesh. First, the value buyers attribute to clothes – reflected in the price they are actually willing to pay – is the result of a process occurring in a place that is geographically and information-wise very far from Bangladesh, at the retail end, where fashion fads and volatile markets operate in a complicated way. Second, there is a broken link of accountability once the garment is shipped abroad. The sector's production process is completely decoupled informally from the fast-fashion production process. This segmentation also exacerbates the dissociation between the unit cost of production in Bangladesh and its retail price: factories sometimes send the clothes with the price tag – even the sales price – so they are floor-ready. It is possible to send one box to New York

---

to link to national accounts data); and (3) three broad sector levels for the BEC classification (agriculture, manufacture, and non-agricultural commodities). To enable cross-product comparisons, all quality estimates are normalised to the world frontier quality, which is assumed to be the 90th percentile in each product-year combination. The resulting quality values typically range between 0 and 1.2.

[41] Bangladesh was suspended from the GSP in the USA in 2013 as a result of concerns over workers' rights and safety shortly after the Rana Plaza building collapse (see www.dhakatribune.com/bangladesh/foreign-affairs/2018/09/14/bangladesh-denied-duty-free-market-facilities-by-us).

[42] The term 'margin of preference' means the difference between the duty paid on an MFN basis and the duty paid under a preferential system (see wits.worldbank.org/glossary.html).

with shirts price-tagged at US$ 50 each and the identical box to rural New Jersey with shirts price-tagged at US$ 5 each. The price is completely independent of the actual cost. As long as the big buyers maintain price-setting power, garment makers have no incentive to upgrade facilities or enhance workers' skills because race-to-the-bottom, cost-cutting measures will always take precedence, to guarantee a firm's survival. Moreover, because of the focus on meeting orders on time, firms have little leeway to become more proactive in anticipating buyers' needs.

Bangladesh's place at the lower end of the value chain is also related to the fact that RMG factories are predominantly locally owned in Bangladesh. By contrast, in Cambodia, also a large exporter of basic garments, factories are owned mostly by foreign investors. In the case of Bangladesh, local factory owners are economically powerful business persons who have managed to find ways to bypass the institutional weaknesses and inadequate infrastructure, which is difficult for foreign investors. There are also limits on the input side as the industry is dependent on the large-scale import of machinery and raw materials. There is also a lack of sufficient supply of skilled domestic workers to operate sophisticated machinery, let alone maintain it (ADB-ILO, 2016).

D Increased Pressure on Workplace Safety and Compliance

There are concerns with regard to compliance issues and workplace safety in the RMG industry in Bangladesh, and in the last few years, especially after the infamous Rana Plaza accident in 2013, these issues have become critical for the future of this industry (Box 4.2). There is strong international pressure, in the form of the threat of cancelling large preferential treatment in the markets of Western countries, if labour conditions are not improved.[43] Quality competitiveness is being increasingly prioritised over price competitiveness, and, of course, the quality of a product tends to increase the standard of living of labour being used in the production process. These concerns should be addressed in a positive way, by seeing them as an opportunity to build the industry's reputation in the global market. This calls for, among many other things, a more careful engagement with labour issues in the RMG industry. In this context, issues like wages, workplace security, fringe benefits, workplace environment, etc. need to be resolved on a priority basis. Current labour practices prevalent in the RMG industry need to be improved in order to make the sector sustainable. The improvement of labour conditions is closely linked to the enhancement of labour productivity. There is equally a need to invest in training workers to move to high-value garment products (i.e. men's suits, baby garments, lingerie, and sportswear).

[43] Blanchard and Hakobyan (2015) show that the GSP in the US case is very volatile and is completely dominated by the political process.

Box 4.2 Bangladesh after Rana Plaza: from tragedy to action

CUSTOMERS:

The 13 May 2013 Accord on Fire and Building Safety in Bangladesh was signed by the IndustriALL Global Union and UNI Global Union trade unions, and more than 180 enterprises, most of them European. The Accord is to run for five years and is aimed at strengthening safety and fire inspections in the textile industry, and improving workers' health and occupational safety. The Accord provides for the inspection of more than 1,600 factories, the cost of which will be borne by the signatories in proportion to the value of their orders.

North American companies took a separate initiative on 10 July 2013, named the Alliance for Bangladesh Worker Safety. It was launched by a group of 26 North American brands and covers 700 factories. The Alliance is non-binding and less stringent, as regards freedom of association, than the 13 May 2013 Accord.

INTERNATIONAL COMMUNITY:

On 8 July 2013 in Geneva, as a response to the Rana Plaza tragedy, the European Commission, the ILO, and the Government of Bangladesh launched the Compact for Continuous Improvements in Labour Rights and Factory Safety in the Ready-Made Garment and Knitwear Industry in Bangladesh. This Compact seeks to improve labour, health, and safety conditions for workers, as well as to encourage responsible behaviour by businesses in the RMG industry in Bangladesh. In particular, it set out a road map for implementing an action plan, including: reforming Bangladeshi labour laws (in particular regarding freedom of association and the right to collective bargaining); recruiting 200 additional factory inspectors by the end of 2013; and improving building and fire safety, by June 2014.

The ILO launched the Better Work Programme for Bangladesh on 23 October 2013. It covered 500 factories and ran for three years. Factory assessments were due to begin during the second quarter of 2014. The programme had been conceived well before the Rana Plaza tragedy.

BANGLADESHI GOVERNMENT:

A National Tripartite Plan of Action on Fire Safety and Structural Integrity in the Garment Sector of Bangladesh (NTPA) was adopted on 25 July 2013 by the Bangladeshi Government, manufacturers in the sector (BGMEA and BKMEA), and the local unions. It acts as a platform to coordinate the various projects and initiatives to improve working and safety conditions in the textile industry. On this basis, a Ready-Made Garment Programme, in partnership with the ILO, was approved on 22 October 2013 and will run for three and a half years. The NTPA will inspect the 1,500 factories not due to be inspected under either the Accord or the Alliance.

RANA PLAZA COMPENSATION SCHEME:

Following the Rana Plaza tragedy, an arrangement was signed on 20 November 2013 and a Donors' Trust Fund, run by the ILO, was set up. Some US$ 40 million was expected to be collected for distribution among the victims. So far, just less than US$ 18 million has been collected. An advance payment has been made available to injured workers and the families of deceased and missing workers.

Source: D'Ambrogio (2014).

A study by ILO-SANEM (2018) suggests that, despite some improvements after the Rana Plaza accident in 2013, there are still unresolved issues related to occupational safety, hours of work and leave, fixing and execution of minimum wage provisions, workplace training, workplace harassment, and gender equality.

E The Evolving Political Settlement on the Labour Regime

After multiple incidents, including the Tazreen fire and the Rana Plaza collapse, Bangladesh came under international scrutiny for its labour practices and safety standards. However, RMG workers in the country are still being paid one of the world's lowest minimum wages. The success of the fashion industry in the West is built on the 'exploitation' of workers from countries like Bangladesh, who struggle every day to survive above the poverty line. The sector's vision of achieving US$ 50 billion worth of RMG exports by 2021 shows little concern for the well-being of its workers. Oxfam (2017) highlights that for every garment sold in Australia, only 4% of its price goes to the factory workers who made it. Cheap labour is the main factor on which Bangladesh's RMG industry capitalises when it comes to attracting big retail brands. The RMG sector faced severe labour unrest demanding a wage increase in 2006. Since then, labour unrest has taken place in the sector almost every year. This is threatening the political settlement between the political elite and RMG owners, or at least modifying its conditions.

F Crisis in the Deals Environment of the RMG Sector

Hassan and Raihan (2018) argue that despite experiencing massive political and reputational crises (e.g. the Rana Plaza disaster), labour movements for higher wages, intense global pressures for ensuring factory standards, and social compliance and labour's associational rights, the RMG sector has managed to perform reasonably well. During the previous decades, its high performance, notwithstanding the many domestic challenges the industry faced, was possible due to the combination of close and ordered deals that it enjoyed in the economic domain. In the political domain, a robust and resilient anti-labour elite political settlement (between RMG owners and political elites) across political divides has enabled it to cope with the sustained movements and critiques that it faced from labour, media, and human rights actors, both local and global. This settlement has recently become increasingly vulnerable to both domestic and international pressures as the Government might side with labour if pressures do increase.

In the economic domain, the decades-long closed and semi-closed deals are now being questioned by the state and local and global stakeholders. BGMEA has vigorously protested any such policy reform initiatives. Its political capacity to successfully thwart similar policy initiatives many times in the past has proved the robustness of the hitherto elite political settlement. With the crises the sector is now facing, its continuing high performance and its ambition to grow further will largely depend on the nature of the evolving political settlement and the deals that it will be able to renegotiate with political elites, and also on how and to what extent it will be able to neutralise the *de facto* national/global reputation of its actors as greedy entrepreneurs, promoters of economic injustice, and violators of labour/human rights.

G Automation in the RMG Sector and Implications for Job Creation

Technological advances associated with automation raises the concern that new technologies will lead to widespread job losses in manufacturing industries in countries like Bangladesh. What is perhaps different now is that new, interconnected digital technologies will likely have a broader and more far-reaching array of abilities, and so the prospect of new kinds of jobs appearing may well be diminished or limited to increasingly sophisticated domains. In addition, new technologies are now not just replacing jobs, they are also enabling the disruption and restructuring of entire industries (Hamann, 2018).

Between 2013 and 2016/2017, manufacturing jobs in Bangladesh declined by 0.8 million. A major part of this was in the RMG industry (Bangladesh Bureau of Statistics, 2018). Increased use of automation also changed the composition of the labour in the RMG sector. Raihan and Bidisha (2018) show that the RMG factories that were closed down after the Rana Plaza event in 2013 were mostly the ones that were comparatively female labour-intensive. Furthermore, the introduction of labour-saving machinery was speeded up after the Rana Plaza event for the kind of jobs which were previously done mostly by low-skilled female workers, which caused employment loss in respect of female labour. Also, there is a perceived threat of automation to employment, and this affects women disproportionately. Already there is evidence of RMG workers being displaced by automation in Bangladesh.[44] There

---

[44] In December 2019, Faisal Samad, vice president of BGMEA, mentioned that nearly 30% of workers have been displaced from the sweater sub-sector of the RMG sector because of automation. (Source: www.weforum.org/agenda/2020/01/garment-apparel-manufacturing-bangladesh/).

are a few applications of automation in important manufacturing industries related to RMG, a few companies have taken steps to implement automation in their operations, and this automation is increasing.[45]

H The Challenges of LDC Graduation

Bangladesh successfully met all three criteria for graduating out of LDC status in the first review in 2018 and in the second review in 2021 and will finally graduate out of LDC status in 2026. Such a graduation carries with it a risk of preferences for Bangladesh being eroded.

UNDESA (2019) argues that Bangladesh would lose access to DFQF arrangements for LDCs, and to simplified ROO reserved for LDCs, with especially important impacts on the RMG sector. In its main market, the EU, Bangladesh would remain eligible for DFQF market access under the EBA scheme for a period of three years after graduation, given the scheme's 'smooth transition' provision. After that, the terms under which it would have access to the EU market would depend on the new GSP regulation, as the current regulation will expire at the end of 2023 (before Bangladesh's expected graduation date). Under current rules, Bangladesh would in principle have access to the standard GSP, whereby it would face higher but still preferential tariffs. Most of Bangladesh's RMG exports would face tariffs of 9.6% in the EU under the GSP, which would result in increased competition from Bangladesh's competitors. Bangladesh's exports would also have to comply with more stringent ROO to benefit from the GSP than it is required to comply with, as an LDC, to benefit from the EBA. Bangladeshi RMG exports currently benefit from the single transformation rule for LDCs, whereby products qualify for preferential treatment if only one form of product alteration is undertaken in the country, as opposed to the double-transformation rule for non-LDCs, whereby two stages of conversion are required. Despite Bangladesh having had access to the EBA since 2001, it was only after the simplification of the rules in 2011 that the country was able to fully benefit from the preferences, as the country relies significantly on imported inputs, particularly in the case of woven RMG. Woven RMG would be most affected by application of the double-transformation rule.

UNDESA (2019) further argues that no important impacts are expected in the US market, since Bangladesh's most important products are not covered

---

[45] Mohammadi Group has installed automated knitting machines that require human intervention only in the case of programme designs or to clean machines, while Envoy Textiles Ltd (ETL) has employed robotic autoconers. Similarly, DBL Group has made their dyes and chemical dispensing system automated. In addition, Beximco Group is using AI-infused ThreadSol software, offering integrated planning process, which will reduce material wastage by using effective concepts of fabric utilisation (source: https://thefinancialexpress.com.bd/views/seizing-opportunity-of-apparel-40-1575904548).

by an LDC-specific preference scheme. Bangladesh has been suspended from the GSP scheme (including preferential tariffs for LDCs) since 2013 due to labour safety issues. Among other developed country markets, in Canada, Japan, and Australia, the standard GSP does not cover an important part of Bangladesh's exports, which will face MFN tariffs. Moreover, in some countries, such as Canada and Australia, Bangladesh would no longer be able to use dedicated ROO for LDCs, making it more difficult to benefit from preferences for the tariff lines covered by the standard GSP than it is to use the GSP for LDCs. Among major developing country markets, Turkey, Bangladesh's largest importer of jute and jute products, has aligned its GSP scheme to that of the EU. In India and China, still relatively small destinations for Bangladesh's exports but important due to potential and proximity, Bangladesh would no longer benefit from the DFQF treatment reserved for LDCs and would instead export under the Asia-Pacific Trade Agreement (APTA) (for China and India), the South Asian Free Trade Agreement (SAFTA) (in the case of India), and MFN rates.

Raihan (2019a), using a global dynamic general equilibrium model, suggests that due to the loss of preferences after graduation from LDC status, in the markets of the EU, Canada, Australia, Japan, India, and China, Bangladesh might see a sizeable drop in exports of RMG compared to the business-as-usual scenario. The scenario in the model considers the imposition of MFN tariff on imports from Bangladesh in the markets of the EU, Canada, Australia, Japan, India, and China. According to the model simulation, the drop in RMG exports would be US$ 5.4 billion in 2024 (13.5% of RMG exports), which could further fall to US$ 5.8 billion by 2030 (10.8% of RMG exports).

VI CHALLENGES OF THE DIVERSIFICATION OF EXPORTS IN BANGLADESH

A Weak Collective Action of Non-RMG Sectors

Future potential export sectors are leather and footwear, agro-processing, electronics, pharmaceuticals, ICT, light engineering, and ship building.[46] Unlike the RMG sector, these sectors tend to have weak collective action capacity, which is a liability (for a sector as a whole) when operating in a predominantly

---

[46] Raihan *et al.* (2017c) identify a number of sectors based on their capacity to meet three principle criteria: (1) growth drivers – the chosen sectors should help create (higher-paying) inclusive jobs, as well as move productive resources to high-value and high-productivity activities (i.e. structural transformation), helping increase national growth rates; (2) diversification – the sectors should help diversify the Bangladesh economy, in terms of both production structures and export diversification; in practical terms, this means diversification away from two sectors that currently dominate the Bangladesh economy – agriculture and the RMG sector; (3) government buy-in – selected study sectors also need to be in alignment with the Bangladeshi Government's development plans, so there is a solid basis for support for potential sectoral implementation policies.

deals world. This weakness in collective action capacity is perhaps due to the small numbers of firms involved in these sectors. Also, unlike the RMG sector, no 'accidental rent' (in the form of the MFA) has enabled any of these sectors to take off in a robust manner, except for the pharmaceutical sector, which has been enjoying such rent for the last few decades (e.g. through the exemption from patent rights under Trade-Related Aspects of Intellectual Property Rights (TRIPS), which will continue until 2033).

B Inadequate Policies and Strategies That Hurt Non-RMG Sectors

Though Bangladesh's export and import policies are supposed to provide unbiased facilities to all export-oriented sectors, there is an inherent pro-RMG bias in policies and strategies for export diversification in Bangladesh. This is also reflected in a statement by the Md Mosharraf Hossain Bhuiyan, Chairman of the National Board of Revenue, on 3 May 2019: 'In case of diversification, we will give the same facilities that we are giving to the garment sector this year'. At present, the apparel sector enjoys a host of benefits, including a 4% cash incentive on exports to new destinations, lower corporate tax, and a bonded warehouse facility.[47] However, as Box 4.3 suggests, there are inherent biases towards the RMG sector in the bonded warehouse facility, and many of these biases are deals-based.

The new export policy for fiscal year 2018/2019 to fiscal year 2020/2021, like in the past, also highlights the importance of diversification of the export basket. Leather gets a special focus in the new export policy and the benefits enjoyed by the RMG industry are supposed to be extended to the leather industry. Also, in the new export policy, the number of highest-priority sectors has been raised to 15 from the existing 12, and the number of special development sectors has been raised to 19 from the existing 14. Like in past export policies, the new policy also mentions special benefits, including subsidies and tax benefits, for the priority and special development sectors. This new policy also mentions extending easy term loans and other banking facilities from the Export Development Fund (EDF) of the Bangladesh Bank to export-oriented industries.

However, as already mentioned, though export policies identify 'thrust' or 'priority' or 'special development' sectors with a view to promoting the development of potential export items, many of these sectors are probably not in a position to reap the benefits of the incentives reserved for them. For example, although the Government's cash incentive[48] plays a vital positive role in the export of agro-food processing products, exporters complain about difficulties in gaining access to this subsidy as a result of bureaucratic

---

[47] www.thedailystar.net/business/news/other-sectors-get-same-benefits-garment-1737871
[48] The Government of Bangladesh currently provides a 10% cash incentive programme, as well as value-added tax exemptions for agro-food exporters.

Box 4.3 Blessings for RMG are a misfortune for leather: the case of bonded warehouses

RMG sector	Leather goods sector
Audits take place every two or three years	Annual audits
Direct exporters are exempt from annual entitlement process for accessing imported inputs	Annual entitlement process for imported input based on machinery and previous years' production
Utilisation rates used to acquit duty liability set by industry body with industry expertise	Utilisation rates used to acquit duty liability set by customs, with little industry experience
Allowed to use multiple premises of bonded warehouses (within 60 kilometres) on a single licence	Allowed to use single premises only
Goods may be sent to subcontractors as part of the process	Goods cannot be sent to subcontractors as part of the manufacturing process
Not required to house full-time Bond Commissionerate staff on site	Bond Commissionerate station's full-time staff on site, with licensee required to pay towards their salaries

Source: Babi (2020).

---

and other procedural obstacles. Many firms have also complained about the duty drawback system, as the process is cumbersome and bureaucratic in nature and takes a long time to finish (Raihan *et al.*, 2017c). Also, though the Government has set up the EDF to provide pre-shipment financing for imports of raw materials, and support to exporters of new and non-traditional items, many of the non-RMG sectors have been unable to exploit the benefits of the scheme, and so far, the RMG sector has been the prime beneficiary of this facility. Stringent rules and regulations are identified as the major hindrances shutting out many of the non-traditional export-oriented industries from the Government stimulus package meant for export promotion, diversification, and growth (Rahman, 2015). Also, there are allegations that the EDF only benefits big companies.[49] Therefore, it seems that before formulating policies and schemes, it is important to undertake sector-specific diagnostic studies so that structural and policy constraints can be identified, in order to devise the most appropriate incentives.

---

[49] www.dhakatribune.com/business/2019/11/23/only-big-companies-beneficiaries-of-export-dev-fund

Sattar and Shareef (2019) argue that a proper management of the exchange rate is a critical part of a trade policy geared to superior export performance and high economic growth. Between fiscal year 2012 and fiscal year 2017, the real effective exchange rate (REER) appreciated by nearly 45%, serving as a significant damper on exports. Policymakers in Bangladesh have avoided letting the exchange rate slide for fear of fuelling inflation. The policy of keeping a stable nominal exchange rate has gained support from the RMG sector as it is a big importer of raw materials. As Hussain (2020) points out: 'paradoxically, industry leaders (especially the RMG) in Bangladesh have revealed a preference for selective policies time and again. If correcting the overvaluation of the exchange rate through devaluation can produce the same industry specific result as a direct cash subsidy, should they not opt for the former than latter? Do not expect the industry to say yes, because it is in their self-interest to get both. However, when choosing between the two, they insist more on the latter because they do not have to compete with all others to benefit from the devaluation whereas the targeted subsidy is a lock-in for the insiders.' However, a highly appreciated local currency affects exports from the non-RMG sectors, which are not greatly import-dependent for sourcing their raw materials. Also, the growth in RMG exports, with a 'managed overvalued exchange rate regime' leads to a 'Dutch disease' phenomenon which affects non-RMG exports.[50]

Sattar (2019) also shows a systematic anti-export bias in the policy regime affecting export diversification, and which has persisted in recent years. Interestingly, many support measures, such as cash incentives, subsidies on bank interest rates, lower corporate taxes, and bonded warehouse facilities, can offset much of the anti-export bias for the RMG sector. For the non-RMG sectors, such anti-export bias affects their export performance, as these sectors are effectively not the beneficiaries of these support measures, though they should be – as mentioned above.

C An Environment with a High Cost of Doing Business That Disproportionately Affects the Non-RMG Sectors

There are crucial supply-side constraints associated with production and exporting activities faced by business enterprises in Bangladesh. Inefficient

---

[50] The literature on Dutch disease highlights the risk of a negative impact of a high dependence on export earnings from a sector, generally the natural resources sector. Countries that see a rapid influx of income following a natural resource discovery – say, oil or diamonds – are vulnerable to this pattern in a way that could hinder their overall chances of economic growth (Battaile et al., 2014). However, it can be argued that while the conventional Dutch disease literature emphasised an export boom of natural resources, any development that results in a large inflow of foreign currency, including a sharp surge in export earnings from any sector, remittance, foreign aid, and FDI can appreciate the exchange rate and have a depressing effect on the export earnings of other sectors (Battaile et al., 2014).

ports raise the cost of doing business as ports are plagued by labour problems (such as workers' strikes), poor management, and lack of equipment. The state of physical infrastructure is weak. Business enterprises are also subject to invisible costs arising from widespread corruption and malpractices. These activities impose direct costs, thus undermining the competitiveness of trading enterprises. Corruption and a conflicting political situation together make the domestic environment business-unfriendly, discouraging new investment in exporting activities, both from local and foreign sources.

In terms of the components of the Global Competitiveness Index of World Economic Forum and Logistic Performance Index of the World Bank, Bangladesh is seriously lagging behind its major competitors, India, China, and Vietnam. It is important to note that though all business enterprises face the aforementioned challenges, special privileges for the RMG sector and different support measures can compensate for many of the costs arising from the poor business environment. The non-RMG sectors are unable to enjoy these compensations.

VII CONCLUSION

The MFA agreement in 1974 created an opportunity by providing reserved markets for countries like Bangladesh. Despite the absence of proper institutions for the planned development of an RMG-oriented manufacturing sector, a few entrepreneurs moved in. Three key factors explain why the process was self-reinforced over time.

There were *rents* to be obtained from low wages, and the fact that other Asian countries that could compete with Bangladesh were not yet in that game and were essentially closed (e.g. communist China and Vietnam, or closed India). These countries moved in later. At that time, the main player was South Korea. On the other hand, sub-Saharan African countries were not really in the game as wages in their formal sector were much higher than those in Bangladesh.

The sector is labour-intensive, which attracted the interests of the political elite. Because of this, and despite the poor institutional and doing business context, *deals* were possible between innovating RMG entrepreneurs and the elite in power, which facilitated the development of the sector. Informal institutions developed. In other words, circumstances were in favour of cooperation being the sole equilibrium of the game between the RMG sector and the political elite.

Economies of scale are limited in the RMG sector, which means that it was difficult to prevent new entrants when the quotas ceased to be binding. This avoided the syndrome of the 'Big Man' invested with most of the economic power, as is found in many developing countries exporting primary products, and thus this led to more competition. At the same time, as all firms were sharing the same constraints and facing the same administrative weaknesses, collective action was possible. It led to this impressive list of 'incentives' shown in Box 4.1.

As the growth of the RMG sector fed overall growth in the economy (see Annex 2.B of Chapter 2 for a detailed discussion), no need was felt either by the economic or by the political elite to improve formal institutions faster than allowed for by development itself, in the sense of having a well-articulated and implemented industrial policy broader than RMG. It also prevented important aspects of development, such as investment in infrastructure or in education, to take place. It also permitted the exploitation of cheap manpower and the open rejection of formal institutions in defence of labour.

As discussed earlier, despite notable growth in the past decades, the RMG sector in Bangladesh faces a number of challenges, both on the domestic and global fronts. A weak domestic institutional environment also exacerbates these challenges. As the country eyes larger development goals, the sustainability of the 'RMG-centric' export model faces serious questions. The analysis in this chapter suggests that the 'RMG model' is not a sustainable model, and diversification of the export basket should be considered as a top priority given the overarching development goals of the country.

For effective export promotion in Bangladesh, in addition to export policies similar to those used for RMG, a set of other complementary policies and programmes are critically required. It is also essential to keep in mind that comparative advantage does not necessarily translate into competitive advantage. While Bangladesh has a comparative advantage in producing and exporting many labour-intensive manufacturing products, given weak formal institutions and a domestic environment with a high cost of doing business, such comparative advantages may be seized.

In the discourse relating to policy reforms for export diversification, the political economy perspective is generally ignored and the reform of institutions is largely overlooked. Experience from Bangladesh shows that the dominant export sector (RMG) has become the main beneficiary of different export incentives (both formal and informal), while for other sectors, such schemes appear to be less effective, primarily due to various structural bottlenecks (such as weak overall and sector-specific infrastructure, lack of access to finance, and weak collection action). But, as the RMG sector has been, and to a large extent still is, the strength of Bangladesh's development, it might become the country's 'Achilles hell' in the future, if it weakens and prevents other manufacturing exports from developing.

Therefore, there is a need for a well-designed and effective industrial policy targeting the emerging dynamic export sectors. In addition, industrial policy needs to address issues of education and skills development in order to facilitate higher capabilities for export diversification, attracting foreign direct investment (FDI), and integrating with the global value chain. Also, institutional reforms should be considered as a key to overall policy reforms targeting larger export response and export diversification. Examples of such institutional reforms include improving the quality of bureaucracy, ensuring property rights, managing corruption, and ensuring contract viability through reduction of the risk of contract modification or cancellation.

Discussion: Informal Institutions, the RMG Sector, and the Present Challenge of Export Diversification in Bangladesh

Jaime de Melo

This chapter, in the tradition of comparative studies of trade and development (Little, Scott and Scitovsky, Bhagwati and Krueger, and Balassa, among others) is a welcome one for anyone interested in the trade–development–institution nexus. It highlights the difficulty of generalising from the inherent uniqueness brought out in case studies. It also points to the limitations of the lessons to be drawn from cross-country studies. As documented by Ravaillon (2005) in the related trade-and-poverty debate, the case study approach illustrates the necessity to 'look beyond averages'.

Bangladesh is the success story of a single sector, the RMG sector. It is also an old-fashioned story of success: endowments (an ample pool of low-skill, mostly female, labour) matter. This success story is now facing growing challenges. On the domestic front, there is a strengthening real exchange rate appreciation and a capture of the policy process by the RMG company owners. On the foreign front, there is increased competition from low-wage suppliers (Cambodia, Ethiopia, etc.) and stricter compliance requirements in destination markets following multiple incidents that have hampered the use of subcontracting to balance production capacity and order size. To these, one must add the challenge of shifting production towards higher value-added sectors (domestic value addition in RMG is about 40–50%, while it is estimated in the 80% range for leather, a candidate sector for diversification). This chapter also discusses the difficult obstacles to successful upgrading into the fashion industry.

This chapter describes the genesis of this success story, via the acquisition and mastery of technology in the garment industry by the stay of trainees in South Korea in 1978. Policies, including the long list of export-incentive schemes (see Box 4.1) are well documented. The importance of these incentives squares well with the view that an active government was at the origin of the Asian 'miracle', rather than the simple provision of neutral incentives as suggested by the neoclassical recipe.[51] This chapter offers a narrative of the role of institutions in which informality played, and continues to play, a key role in this success story. It is one in which informal institutions were preponderant in a young country (independence occurred in 1971).

This informality is plausible, perhaps even unavoidable, in a young country with low educational levels, where people were – to use Raihan's terminology – operating in a 'deals' rather than in a 'rules' space. In the narrative, deals were initially open (access to all) and ordered (deals are respected), but they then became progressively closed. So, if there is a surprise, it is that the deals space remained open for so long while, as expected, the traditional determinants of comparative advantage (endowments and productivity), accompanied by generous incentives, were the proximate cause of the early surge of the RMG sector.

My remarks seek to place Bangladesh within the landscape of some of the current 'received wisdom' on the role of trade and institutions in successful industrialisation strategies. Where does the RMG success story fit in relation to this received wisdom? I focus on four aspects identified as important ingredients during the take-off stages of a country's industrialisation:

- initial conditions;
- trade and macro policies;
- institutions; and
- supply chain trade.

Initial Conditions

The extensive cross-section of literature on growth, trade, and institutions has been unable to provide convincing evidence to confirm two often-cited anecdotal conjectures: that countries with 'better' institutions and countries that trade more grow faster; and that countries with better institutions also tend to grow faster. Initial conditions shape the paths of countries' development. Here, Bangladesh's high-growth experience has not been accompanied or preceded by the development of formal institutions. To illustrate the importance of initial conditions, contrast the paths of North and South America and those of Bangladesh and Korea.

Taking a long-run view, Engerman and Solokoff (1997) document the diverging paths of the development of institutions in North and South America since the arrival of Europeans. The spread of education and political participation was much slower in the South than in the North, where wealth inequality and rents were lesser, and their subsequent growth paths

---

[51] Pack and Westphal (1986) were the first to document that, while exporters were placed under a virtual free trade regime, the government distinguished between exports and domestic sales. This view that an industry bias – rather than neutral incentives – prevailed throughout the 'East Asian Miracle' was extensively documented in World Bank (1993). In Bangladesh, even though export incentives were in principle open to all, they were only exploited by the RMG sector.

diverged. Bangladesh and Korea, when they started to industrialise, were both resource-poor and in a post-conflict environment with relatively low inequality. In both, industrialisation started from a low base (in Korea, in 1945 manufacturing production was less than a fifth of its level in 1940).[52] But Korea, which had started industrialisation in the colonial period (1910–1945) under the Japanese, had a much higher level of education than Bangladesh, where enrolment rates in schools were still in the lowest quintile of countries in 2007.[53] Ironically, the lower level of education in Bangladesh helped the 'management' of labour in the RMG sector, and hence was conducive to deeper specialisation in RMG.

Conditions for the development of formal institutions were far more favourable in Korea than in Bangladesh. Initial differences in educational levels matter for the growth of formal institutions. Together with the growth of formal institutions, this much higher level of human capital must have contributed to the spectacular transition out of RMG and footwear into heavy manufacturing in Korea, and likewise to the persistence of specialisation in the RMG sector in Bangladesh.

Trade and Macro Policies

The stellar performance of RMG in Bangladesh is an indication of an outward-looking development outcome, yet in the outward-looking vs. inward-looking industrialisation debate, Bangladesh only shares some of the policies of outward-looking successes.

On the micro-trade incentives side, Bangladesh still has relatively high tariff and non-tariff protection. Average applied tariffs went down from 58% in 1992 to 22% in 2000, but still stood at 13.9% in 2015. Non-trade barriers (NTBs) are still pervasive, though Bangladesh not being in the UNCTAD database precludes the estimation of ad-valorem equivalent of NTBs. As for the anti-export bias, in this chapter, it is captured by indicators of effective exchange rates for exports and imports, rather than for sales in the domestic and export markets at the individual product level. This better indicator of the whole array of incentives received by the RMG sector would probably show that producing and exporting apparel was more profitable than producing and exporting other manufactures, whereas in Korea during the early stages of exporting, export incentives were quite uniform across all exporting activities (Westphal, 1990, Table 1).

As in outward-looking East Asian countries, export incentives were widespread. The RMG sector 'enjoyed quite extraordinary privileges' (p. 26). Progressively, the sector captured export incentives that were de jure available for all. Typically, in outward-looking countries, one sector does not capture

---

[52] Pack and Westphal (1986, p. 92).
[53] Devarajan and Johnson (2008).

all export incentives. For example, in Korea's export-led industrialisation, a virtual free-trade regime was established for ALL export activities. Neutral policies were available for all established export activities, whereas for infant industries, 'non-neutral' special incentives were provided (access to preferential credit, exemptions from taxes) (Westphal, 1990). However, Korean policymakers removed these special incentives when they realised that the so-called HCI (High Chemical Industry) drive had given excessive power to firms in the domestic market.

By contrast, In Bangladesh, the RMG sector progressively captured incentives, in principle available to all. This has been, and continues to be, a hurdle to diversification towards higher value-added activities as incumbents in the RMG sector have, in effect, raised barriers to entry into other potential export activities.[54] Raihan describes the process of policy capture as one of moving from an open, ordered deals environment to a closed-deal–ordered environment. This 'raising the cost of rivals', observed elsewhere, is not particular to a 'deals' environment. For example, Djankov *et al.* (2002) display a positive scatter between an index of corruption and the extent of paperwork. This suggests that politically well-represented groups take advantage of their position to protect their rents by raising barriers to entry to newcomers.

Since in their early phases of development, Asian countries' exports of textiles and apparel generated rents (perhaps in the 20–40% range under the MFA), Bangladesh stood out, with higher quota utilisation rates under the MFA than other developing countries outside of East Asia (83% fill rate in the US market in 2001/2002 and no quotas in the European Community). Informal institutions operated smoothly in Bangladesh – perhaps aided by the relative homogeneity of the population – to capture these rents. In Korea, productivity-led rises in wages, and the acquisition and mastery of imported technology in manufacturing, led to a rapid shift out of RMG. By contrast, as an LDC, exporting apparel has continued to be profitable for Bangladesh. In the EU and US markets, LDCs still have a 10–15% preferential margin over competitors exporting under Most Favoured Nation (MFN) tariffs (see Brunelin *et al.* (2019), Tables A2 and A3). Also, the double transformation rule for textiles and apparel was removed for LDCs in their exports to the EU in 2011. All this contributed to maintaining high profits from RMG exports for Bangladesh, acting as a brake on diversification.

On the macro front, Bangladesh had a competitive real exchange rate, at least until recently, a sign of sound macro policies, a key ingredient observed

---

[54] The paper discusses the transaction-costs-reducing activities of two powerful lobbies in the RMG sector, the BGMEA of exporters of garments and the BKMEA of knitwear manufacturers. Notably, BKMEA had the power to issue customs certificates and utilisation certificates governing the duty-free importing process.

across successful outward-looking strategies.[55] Bangladesh also had an 'export surge' over the period 1980–2006. The surge took place relatively early on, in 1986, supporting the hypothesis that a relatively long spell of sustained under-valuation of the exchange rate is necessary for exports to take off, to compensate for the information disadvantage that tradeables face relative to non-tradeables.[56]

In conclusion, looking at the incentive side, exchange rate policies were similar to those of the other successful Asian exporters. Export incentives were also widespread. Policy capture by lobbies was typical of those found in weak institutional environments. However, the distinguishing characteristic here is that rents were obtained from export sales rather than from sales in protected domestic markets. This put a lid on the inefficiency associated with rent-seeking activities on domestic markets. The persistence of these rents over a long period also served as a brake on diversification.

An Institution Puzzle?

Raihan argues that Bangladesh's performance in the RMG sector stands out against its poor ranking on various institutional indicators (Doing Business, Transparency International, and WGI). Doubts are widespread about what is captured by these multi-dimensional institutional indicators, which typically mix policy stances and outcomes.[57] Early on, in their comments on Kaufmann and Kraay, Devarajan and Johnson (2008) use the example of Bangladesh to discuss the downside of indicators like the WGI that allow for intercountry comparisons at the cost of not capturing the multifaceted way in which governance affects development in a particular country – the focus of the country case studies in the EDI project. Devarajan and Johnson note that Bangladesh has a 'vibrant and active civil society that not only delivers services, but provides some accountability to the government' (p. 32). They also note that the Bangladeshi '...people have worked around the country's governance problem to spur development' (p. 32). In their remarks, Devarajan and Johnson (2008) note that '...some countries have managed to sustain rapid growth in spite of weak initial governance because of a strong focus on exports, particularly of

---

[55] In his survey of growth strategies for developing countries, Rodrik (2005) notes that institutions do not travel well and that beyond avoiding a closed-economy development policy, sound macroeconomic policies, including a competitive real exchange rate, are the only common ingredient of successful growth experiences.

[56] Freund and Pierola (2011) show that export surges (defined as export growth above 6% per year lasting at least seven years, and the seven-year average export growth at least a third higher than the previous seven-year average) are preceded by a large exchange rate devaluation of around 25%. Over the period 1980–2006, Bangladesh had one export surge, in 1986.

[57] Rodrik, Subramanian, and Trebbi (2004) gave evidence that indicators of institutional quality trumped geography and policy indicators in cross-country growth regressions, but Svensson (2005) showed that the correlation between growth and indicators of corruption was weak.

manufacturing goods' (p. 35). They conclude that greater efforts should be put into measuring governance more at the local level, both for sectors and for cities.

More recently, in their sample of 10 countries, including Bangladesh, Pritchett *et al.* show that, at the country level, indicators of institutional quality are only correlated with GDP levels. When it comes to GDP growth, they detect only a weak bivariate correlation with GDP growth at the country level. And they fail completely to detect any correlation between improvements in indicator values of institutions and GDP growth (see their Figure 1.8). For Bangladesh, digging in on the measurement of indicators of institutional quality, one only observes weak improvements in rankings of institutional indicators during the growth acceleration episode of 1995–2010, when per capital GDP grew at an average rate of 3.5% per annum. Bangladesh's long sustained period of growth in spite of low and slowly evolving rankings on institutional indicator values evidences the limitations of these indicators as predictors of performance.[58]

However, indicators of the quality of formal institutions could contribute to the explanation of the patterns of comparative advantage in manufacturing. In Bangladesh, concentration of the export basket has been on the rise while the values of indices of complexity have been low and falling (Hassan and Raihan, 2018, Figure 4.4). Nunn and Trefler (2014) report cross-country evidence supporting the overall importance of contracting institutions. They show that their indicators of the contract intensity of sectoral production across markets (product market, labour market, and financial markets), when entered interactively with indicators of governance, as captured by the rule of law of Kaufmann and Kraay (2008), are all significant determinants of the patterns of revealed comparative advantage. Although these results call for careful interpretation, the governance indicators are as important quantitatively as the traditional indicators of comparative advantage (Heckscher–Ohlin and technology indicators).[59]

Supply Chain Trade Under the 'RMG-Centric' Model

In the introduction to this chapter, Raihan points out the importance for success of a diversified export basket, following the adage that 'you get rich by

[58] Kuncic (2014) has built four multi-dimensional indicators of legal, political, and economic quality over the period 1990 to 2010 for a large sample of countries. Bangladesh is in his closed sample of 88 countries that produces rankings of these indicator values, which are comparable across countries and across time (a lower value is a higher rank). For Bangladesh, the beginning- and end-year ranks are the following: legal (80, 71), political (84, 65), and economic (75, 80), indicating mixed progress.

[59] Nunn and Trefler (2014, Table 4) report cross-section results for bilateral trade for two-digit manufacturing sectors for 83 countries. Their measure of product complexity is from the United States.

producing the goods the rich consume'. The argument is that participation in supply chain trade (or global and regional value chains (GVCs and RVCs)) provides new opportunities for developing countries to participate in global trade and to diversify their export baskets (Bangladesh has the most concentrated exports in textiles and apparel among comparators). Without participation in supply chain trade, a country has to be able to produce a complete product before entering a new line of business. The fragmentation of production allows countries to enter a product chain without having to carry out all the stages of production. Supply chain trade can then be a lift for a country to shift rapidly from labour-intensive to capital-intensive, skill-intensive, and information-intensive activities. The World Bank World Development Report of 2020 (World Bank, 2020a) documents the higher growth of countries that have transitioned out of commodities using imported inputs through GVC participation.[60]

When a country's participation in supply chains is high, foreign imports have a high share in a country's gross exports (backward participation or 'upstreamness') and a high share of its gross exports enter into other countries' exports (forward participation or 'downstreamness'). So, to succeed, Bangladesh should strive for a high participation rate in supply chain trade. This has not been the case over the past 25 years, at least relative to comparators. For its level of development, Bangladesh's GVC participation is low, and Figure 4.5 also shows Bangladesh's low GVC participation relative to other RMG exporters. In contrast with Ethiopia and Vietnam, Bangladesh (like Cambodia) has not caught up with the sample average of GVC participation during the 25-year period. By contrast, Ethiopia and Vietnam have caught up with the trend, and now have above-average GVC participation for their income level. Both display a positive correlation between supply chain participation and GDP growth, suggesting that participation in GVC trade could have been growth-enhancing for these countries.[61]

It is also mentioned by Melo and Twun (2020) that compared with Ethiopia and Vietnam, Bangladesh displays vertical industrialisation: a low share of imported intermediates in gross exports and a low share of gross exports entering further processing in destination countries. Also, a low share of Bangladesh exports goes through further processing in the destination countries of Bangladesh exports: a reflection of the RMG-centric model that has delivered final goods (t-shirts, trousers). The domestic vertical specialisation of RMG in Bangladesh has been at the expense of growth in backward integration experienced by competitors, especially Ethiopia.

---

[60] A 1% increase in GVC participation boosts per capita income growth by more than 1% (World Bank, 2020a, p. 3).

[61] The main strength of the EORA Multi-Region Input Output (MRIO) database is it country and sector coverage. Comparisons of measures with those obtained from the more reliable Organisation for Economic Co-operation and Development- (OECD-) WO TiVA database over the period 1995–2010 are reasonably close. See Aslam *et al.* (2017, Tables 7–13).

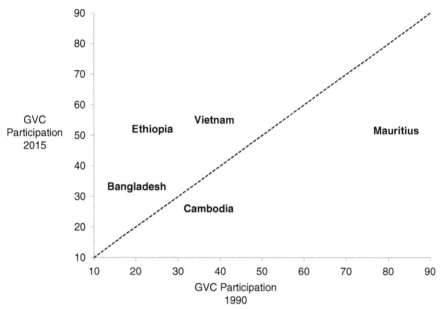

FIGURE 4.5 GVC participation: Bangladesh and comparators
Notes: GVC measures from the EORA MRIO national and global input–output tables
covering the period 1990–2015. GVC participation measures are the sum of the backward and forward participation rates expressed as shares of gross exports (see text),
excluding double counting of exports when intermediates cross borders multiple times.
Points above the 450 indicate an increase in GVC participation over the period.
Source: Author's calculation, from Melo and Twun (2020).

Connectivity is important for both the physical supply chain of goods, but
also effective communication among participants in GVCs, and certainly in
any quest to move up the fashion industry. This low GVC participation in
the aggregate also holds for the RMG sector since, in textiles and apparel,
Bangladesh's GVC participation is the lowest in the group and has not evolved
over the period. GVC participation is also low for wood and paper, a candidate
sector for easy diversification (Melo and Twun, 2020).

Compared with these other successful exporters of RMG, Bangladesh has
a low participation in supply chain trade. In view of the success of RMG, this
low participation seems surprising as most of the literature evidences the productivity gains from a reduction in the tariffs of imported varieties of intermediate inputs (Amiti and Konigs, 2007 for Indonesia and Goldberg *et al.*,
2010 for India), and most recently from participation in supply chain trade.
The incentive system has guaranteed duty-free access to imported inputs for
the RMG sector that has also largely bypassed participation in the slicing
up of the value chain. Kee (2015) shows that the performance of domestic

firms in the RMG sector benefitted from non-pecuniary externalities through contacts with FDI firms. Drawing on a stratified random sample of 10% of domestic firms and 100% of FDI firms in the apparel sector, she shows that firms that shared local suppliers with foreign firms benefitted from significant spillovers. She estimates that from 1999 to 2003, the spillover effects helped explain a quarter of the expanded scope and a third of the productivity gains of domestic firms in the apparel sector. Automation in the RMG sector is increasing. Some factories employ several thousand, mostly unskilled, workers. In the low-end of the garment sector, production runs are long, helping reap economies of scale and economies of scope.

A homogenous population, a stable real exchange rate, incentives that allowed exporters to earn rents on sales abroad rather than on a sheltered domestic market, all contributed to the RMG success. Can Bangladesh replicate this success in other sectors? With a growing number of activities built around networks across several countries, acquiring the necessary mastery of technology will require the competences associated with a functioning education system. As in Korea's industrialisation, a helpful hand from the government will also be required.

5

Political Economy of Private Bank
Governance in Bangladesh

Mirza M. Hassan, Sayema Haque Bidisha, Towhid I.
Mahmood, and Selim Raihan

1 INTRODUCTION

After independence in 1971, the banking industry in Bangladesh started its
journey with six nationalised commercial banks (NCBs), three state-owned
specialised banks, and nine foreign banks. In the 1980s, the industry achieved
significant expansion with the entrance of private banks. Banks in Bangladesh
come under two broad categories: scheduled and non-scheduled banks. Banks
that have a licence to operate under the Bank Company Act, 1991 (amended in
2013 and in 2018) are termed scheduled banks and banks that are established
for specific objectives and operate under the acts that are enacted to meet those
objectives are called non-scheduled banks. As at March 2020, there were 60
scheduled and 5 non-scheduled banks in Bangladesh.[1]

Although the direct contribution of the banking sector to the gross domestic product (GDP) of Bangladesh is only around 3% (Bangladesh Bureau of
Statistics, 2017), there are a number of avenues through which the banking
sector has important implications for economic growth and development in
Bangladesh. Despite issues related to weak institutions and governance (which
are discussed in this chapter), the banking sector has helped move the major
sectors of the economy, that is the ready-made garments (RMG) sector, remittances, and agriculture.[2] As a result, over the past decades, the country has
witnessed a high rate of economic growth, especially in the past decade, when
growth was more than 6.5% per annum. There is a paradox in achieving such

---

[1] www.bb.org.bd/fnansys/bankfi.php

[2] For a discussion on how the RMG sector got special privilege of subsidised interest rates on
loans from the banking sector, see the chapter on RMG and export diversification of this volume. Also, see Khuda (2019) on how the banking sector facilitated remittances inflow and agricultural growth.

a consistently high growth numbers amidst the institutional weaknesses in the financial sector. One explanation of this could be found by looking at the distribution of loans by sectors – the RMG sector, as well as certain big industries (mainly the import substituting industries, e.g. cement, steel, textiles), constitute a significant proportion of the loans being disbursed.[3] With the RMG sector being one of the crucial growth drivers of the economy, weaknesses in the banking sector have not been reflected strongly in terms of growth numbers. It is primarily other export-oriented non-RMG sectors – for example leather, agro-processing, information and communication technology (ICT), and other sectors – which are being affected by such elite capture of loans.[4]

High non-performing loans (NPLs)[5] in the banking sector reduce the capital of the banking sector, creating a fiscal burden and affecting banks' profitability and interest rates, and generating an unfavourable impact on overall private sector investment. All these issues are undermining economic and export diversification prospects, as well as future economic growth prospects. With an almost stagnant private investment to GDP ratio of around 22% over the past decade, the high interest rates prevailing in the banking sector are often argued to be one of the crucial obstacles to boosting private investment. In this context, high NPLs constrain banks' ability to offer loans at lower interest rates, resulting in a high cost of investment.

It is also important to mention that, given the resource constraints, the current trend of significant budgetary allocation for the recapitalisation of inefficient public banks tends to have negative effects on the volume of investment for the development of the country. Also, NPLs have been associated with loan defaulters laundering funds abroad.

The banking sector in Bangladesh suffers from some inherent weaknesses. According to the banking system z-score,[6] in 2017, Bangladesh scored only 6.7 and ranked 147th out of 179 countries. In 2017, Bangladesh had the lowest z-score among the South Asian countries. The institutional and governance-related challenges in the banking sector in Bangladesh include

---

[3] See Monthly Economic Trends of Bangladesh Bank. (www.bb.org.bd/pub/monthly/econtrds/feb20/econtrds.php).

[4] See Raihan *et al.* (2017c) on how access to finance is identified as a major challenge for diversification of the export basket.

[5] Bank NPLs to total gross loans are the value of NPLs divided by the total value of the loan portfolio (including NPLs before the deduction of specific loan-loss provisions). The loan amount recorded as non-performing should be the gross value of the loan as recorded on the balance sheet, not just the amount that is overdue. (see www.theglobaleconomy.com/rankings/Nonperforming_loans/).

[6] A bank z-score is an indicator of the probability of default (mathematically, it is the reverse of the probability of default, thus a higher score expresses lower probability) of the banking system of a country. It compares the buffer, represented by capitalisation and returns of a country's banking system, with the volatility of returns. More specifically, it can be expressed as: $(ROA+(equity/assets))/sd(ROA)$, where $sd(ROA)$ is the standard deviation of return on assets (ROA). (Source: www.theglobaleconomy.com/rankings/bank_z_scores/).

regulatory and policy capture, political patronage-based governance, provision of incentives through monetary injections to the state-owned banks, and lack of autonomy of the central bank. In this context, the rising NPLs are a manifestation of institutional problems that are prevalent in this sector.

Against this backdrop, this chapter provides an overview of the performance and challenges of the banking sector in Bangladesh by looking at: the structure of the banking sector; different performance indicators of the banking sector related to access, stability, efficiency, and depth; the trend in NPLs; efficiency levels of private banks; and the development implications of the status of the banking sector. This chapter also explores the politics of the banking sector and avenues of governance failures in relation to private commercial banks in Bangladesh. This chapter is organised as follows: Section II reviews relevant literature; Section III provides an overview of the key indicators related to the performance and challenges of the banking sector in Bangladesh; Section IV presents a brief history of the politics of the banking sector; Section V provides an analytical narrative of the governance failure in the banking sector; and, finally, Section VI summarises the findings and offers a few recommendations.

II REVIEW OF LITERATURE ON THE BANKING SECTOR OF BANGLADESH

In terms of the quantitative indicators for assessing banks' performance, the existing literature has utilised a number of indicators. For example, one of the important indicators of banks' performance is the CAMELS ratio, which, as the name suggests, encompasses a number of key performance indicators: capital adequacy, asset quality, management, earning, liquidity, and sensitivity to market risks. Based on the assessment of related indicators of CAMELS, Iqbal *et al.* (2012) concluded that development financial institutions (DFIs)[7] are in the most vulnerable position, while foreign commercial banks (FCBs)[8] are in the best situation in Bangladesh.

Nguyen and Ali (2011) highlighted the challenges of the financial sector and commented that the key issue in regard to the financial sector's challenges is lack of competition and a resulting lack of market discipline. In this connection, the

---

[7] DFIs include the Bangladesh House-Building Finance Corporation, Bangladesh Development Bank, Bangladesh Small and Cottage Industries Corporation, Bangladesh Krishi Bank, Rajshahi Krishi Unnayan Bank, Bangladesh Samabaya Bank, Ansar-VDP Unnayan Bank, and Trust Bank. These DFIs are public sector entities (see http://en.banglapedia.org/index.php?title=Development_Finance).

[8] In total, nine FCBs are operating in Bangladesh. These are Bank Al-Falah Limited (Pakistan), Citibank N.A (United States of America), Commercial Bank of Ceylon PLC (Sri Lanka), Habib Bank Limited (Pakistan), HSBC (Hong Kong), National Bank of Pakistan (Pakistan), Standard Chartered Bank (United Kingdom), State Bank of India (India), and Woori Bank (South Korea). See www.bb.org.bd/fnansys/bankfi.php.

authors emphasised the importance of institutional irregularities – for example excessive government intervention, corruption and political intervention, as well as managerial inefficiencies – as the root causes of different problems. Mansur (2015) also emphasised the lack of corporate governance of banks, which are closely related to political connections. Although he expressed concern over the skyrocketing numbers of NPLs, he considered NPLs of public banks to be a greater danger to the economy.

While exploring the factors affecting the profitability of banks, Rahman *et al.* (2015) found that capital strength (both regulatory capital and equity capital) and loan intensity (captured through liquidity – defined as the ratio of total loans to total assets) have a positive and significant impact, whereas cost-efficiency (ratio of cost to income) and off-balance sheet activities have a negative and significant impact on bank profitability. From a technical point of view, Hossain (2012), using data of individual banks, applied the Arellano–Bond panel regression method and attempted to explain a relevant yet slightly different issue of the persistency of high interest rate spread. In addition, he also tried to explain the reason behind different interest rate spreads of different banks, despite the financial reform initiatives during the 1990s. According to Hossain, key determinants of the high interest rate spread are high operating costs, NPLs, market power, and segmented credit and deposit markets.

The status of NPLs in the banking sector of Bangladesh since the adoption of a new loan classification and provisioning system in 1990s has been examined by Adhikary (2006). The analysis indicates that an alarming amount of NPLs, both in NCBs and in DFIs, along with the practice of maintaining deficient loan-loss provisions, have a negative impact on the overall credit quality in Bangladesh. The author concluded that, though Bangladesh has made progress in ratifying international standards of loan classification and provisioning, the overall management of NPLs is ineffective.

Against the backdrop of the privatisation of NCBs, Beck and Rahman (2006) concluded that, to ensure a viable long-term expansion of the financial system, the role of the government is critical and in Bangladesh the Government should play the role of a facilitator, instead of that of an operator. In this context, the authors also recommended that, in addition to divestment from government-owned banks, de-politicisation of the certificating process, and formulation of a market-based bank failure resolution framework, concentrating on intermediation is required for an efficient financial system. Their recommendations also emphasised that the Government should divert from the practice of serving as the implicit guarantee for depositors and owners, and rather start moving towards the practice of involving market participants to monitor and discipline banks. According to the authors, this practice should be extended to other parts of the financial sector, for example micro enterprises and the capital market. However, these suggestions have not been taken into consideration effectively in the financial sector reform process in Bangladesh.

Beck (2008) emphasised the importance of the degree of competition of banks in Bangladesh. According to the author, fragility in the banking sector in Bangladesh in the period reviewed was not related to liberalisation of the sector per se, rather it was connected to regulatory and supervisory issues. Therefore, in order to materialise the benefits of competition, the author saw a need to abide by essential institutional frameworks. Where there is weak institutional framework, according to Beck (2008), unchecked competition can lead to a fragile banking sector. As a remedy, instead of curbing competitive practices, Beck argued that the Government should emphasise improving the institutional environment and opt for an incentive-motivated banking sector. Hossain (2012) also expressed concern over efficiency and competition in the banking sector and concluded that the reform programmes initiated in the 1990s had not been able to generate this in Bangladesh.

Robin *et al.* (2017) applied stochastic frontier analysis to bank-level data of Bangladesh for the period 1983–2012, along with data envelopment analysis (DEA), to understand cost-efficiency in the banking sector of Bangladesh. Their analysis revealed the positive impact of financial deregulation on bank costs. They also found that banks' efficiency could be negatively affected by directors with political connections. Uddin *et al.* (2014) dealt with the wider issue of development and tried to link financial development with performance in poverty reduction and economic growth for Bangladesh in the period 1975–2011. Their Autoregressive Distributed Lag (ARDL) model, with structural break, established the presence of a long-run relationship among the relevant variables.

III BANKING SECTOR IN BANGLADESH: PERFORMANCE AND CHALLENGES

A Structure of the Banking Sector

After its independence in 1971, Bangladesh, as part of its socialist economic strategy, nationalised all banks except a few foreign-owned ones. Following this step, the banking sector did not experience any significant changes until the beginning of the 1980s, when, under the Structural Adjustment Program, the Government liberalised the banking sector and allowed the operation of private banks. Although the speed of privatisation of the banking sector was quite slow during the 1980s and 1990s, there was indeed significant expansion of the branches of NCBs. Privatisation of a few NCBs, and later sanctioning of privately owned commercial banks, which has accelerated over the most recent decades, have resulted in the current operation of 42 domestic private commercial banks (PCBs) in Bangladesh.

Although the number of banks did not change drastically until 2013, the percentage share of PCBs in total industry assets increased quite remarkably. While in 2001, the share of PCBs in total industry assets was around 35%, by

2017 it had increased to 67%.[9] Such an increase in the share of industry assets is not a conundrum as PCBs' share of deposits in the industry also increased over the same period of time. Therefore, in terms of the structure of banks, PCBs can be considered the dominant type of banks, in terms of the aforementioned important indicators.

B Performance of the Banking Sector

This sub-section provides an overview of the performance of the banking sector of Bangladesh in terms of access, stability, efficiency, and depth. An analysis over time, and comparisons with a few comparable countries, is carried out based on the available data.

Table 5.1 summarises the performance of the banking sector of Bangladesh when all types of banks – that is NCBs, DFIs, PCBs, and FCBs – are taken together, according to some standard ratios describing various aspects of banking activity. Ratios are reported for a few points of time over the last 20 years or so, or when they were available. For the most recent year, they are compared to their value in other Asian countries or to averages over groups of countries at the same level of income (least developed countries) or at a higher level (upper middle-income countries (UMICs)).

Looking first at these indicators over time, two opposite evolutions can be observed. On the one hand, accessibility of the banking system to the public has very much increased over the last 15 years, whether in terms of account holders or bank branches. On the other hand, stability and efficiency indicators overall suggest a deterioration over time, except the NPL ratio between 1996 and 2010, an evolution that is discussed in more detail in the next section. On stability, if the liquidity ratio has not changed much, the recent drop in the capital adequacy ratio is worrying as it suggests that the Bangladeshi banking sector would have more difficulty confronting an economic or financial crisis today than was the case in 2010. However, the evolution of the z-score suggests that the probability of the whole banking system defaulting remains low and is even decreasing. On the side of efficiency, however, all indicators show a worsening of the overall performance of Bangladesh's banking system. Over the recent past, it is possible that this deterioration may be due to a drop in the interest rate, as has been observed in most countries in the world.

A final indicator, which is more macroeconomic in nature, appears in Table 5.1. It is the depth of the financial system, as measured by the ratio of total bank credit to GDP. It is generally the case that economic development goes hand in hand with financial development. This is clearly confirmed in the case of Bangladesh.

Comparing Bangladesh to other countries is made difficult because indicators are not always available for countries at levels of development similar to

---

[9] Annual report of Bangladesh Bank.

TABLE 5.1 *Performance of the banking sector*

	1996	2001	2004	2010	Most recent year after 2016	Comparator countries, most recent year after 2016				
						India	Sri Lanka	Thailand	LDCs	UMICs
Access										
Account holders/ 1,000 adults[1]			248		715	726		1271		
Bank branches/0.1 million people[2]			6.9		8.6	14.7		11.9		
Stability										
Liquidity ratio[3]		11.7		9.71	11.8				19.2	21.2
Capital adequacy ratio[4]				6.9	4.7	7.5	8.7	10.8		
NPL ratio	31.5	31.5	17.6	7.3	11	9.5	3.4	3.1		
z-score	11.1	5.8		9.5	6.7	15.9	14.1	7.9		
Efficiency										
ROA[5]	7.02	2.7		4.7	1.4	−0.2	2.1	1.5		
Returns on equity (ROE)[6]	97.1	42.7		54.3	18	−2.5	24.6	11.5		

Bank cost to income ratio[7]	26.7	33.1	37.4	50.3	50.8	54.5	43.7
Depth							
Bank credit/ GDP[8]	18.9	23.9	40.8	46.8	50.1	49.5	112.5

[1] Based on the available data from www.theglobaleconomy.com/rankings/bank_accounts/. Country comparison is also made based on the available data for comparable countries.

[2] www.theglobaleconomy.com/rankings/bank_accounts/

[3] The ratio of bank liquid reserves to bank assets is the ratio of domestic currency holdings and deposits with the monetary authorities to claims on other governments, non-financial public enterprises, the private sector, and other banking institutions.

[4] The capital adequacy ratio or bank capital to assets ratio is the ratio of bank capital and reserves to total assets. Capital and reserves include funds contributed by owners, retained earnings, general and special reserves, provisions, and valuation adjustments. Capital includes Tier 1 capital (paid-up shares and common stock), which is a common feature in all countries' banking systems, and total regulatory capital, which includes several specified types of subordinated debt instruments that need not be repaid if the funds are required to maintain minimum capital levels (these comprise Tier 2 and Tier 3 capital). Total assets include all non-financial and financial assets.

[5] ROA is a profitability ratio that indicates how much profit a company is able to generate from its assets. In other words, ROA measures how efficient a company's management is in generating earnings from the economic resources or assets on its balance sheet. ROA is shown as a percentage: the higher the number, the more efficient a company's management is at managing its balance sheet to generate profits.

[6] ROE is a measure of financial performance calculated by dividing net income by shareholders' equity. Because shareholders' equity is equal to a company's assets minus its debt, ROE can be thought of as the return on net assets.

[7] Operating expenses of a bank as a share of the sum of net interest revenue and other operating income (see www.theglobaleconomy.com/rankings/bank_cost_to_income/).

[8] Domestic credit to private sector by banks refers to financial resources provided to the private sector by other depository corporations (deposit-taking corporations except central banks), such as through loans, purchases of non-equity securities, and trade credits and other accounts receivable that establish a claim for repayment (see www.theglobaleconomy.com/rankings/Bank_credit_to_the_private_sector/).

Source: Data from different sources as mentioned in the footnotes.

or just above Bangladesh. Three countries appear in Table 5.1: India and Sri Lanka in South Asia, and Thailand in Southeast Asia. For liquidity, the comparison is also made for the average LDC or UMIC.

If the comparison is unfavourable to Bangladesh for access – when the benchmark is Thailand – and for the liquidity of banks, the results are more ambiguous for the other indicators. The performance of the Indian banking sector in particular does not look better than Bangladesh's, even with respect to the NPL ratio. It should be emphasised, however, that the inter-comparability of some of these indicators is not granted. For instance, it is well known that the definition of NPL may vary across countries. More important, standard banking indicators are essentially business oriented and may not be good descriptors of the actual economic performance of the banking sector: that is, its contribution to the good functioning of the economy.

The preceding remark applies particularly to the depth indicator in Table 5.1. Bank credit is of a comparable size in Bangladesh as in India or Sri Lanka, but much less than half of what it is in Thailand, which, admittedly, is at a more advanced level of development. Yet, it must be kept in mind that even if two economies extend the same relative volume of bank credit, the overall economic impact of bank lending may be quite different. The quality of loans and their allocation within the economy are of utmost importance. As a matter of fact, it will be seen below that, despite average indicators that are not unduly unfavourable, some aspects of the banking system in Bangladesh are deeply dysfunctional.

A word must be said about the fact that the preceding indicators correspond to very different situations depending on the type of bank that is being considered. Without getting into details, the major difference appears between PCBs and FCBs, with the latter generally performing better than their domestic counterpart, and between private and public commercial banks (and DFIs), with the latter showing a much higher volume of NPLs and a lower capital adequacy ratio than the former.

C Trend in NPLs

NPLs are loans that do not earn any interest income for a certain period of time, and, more importantly, for which there is a lower likelihood of recovery. NPLs are considered to be one of the critical indicators for banks' financial stability, as well as profitability, and high NPLs can seriously affect banks' ability to sustain their operation, including the expansion of credit.

High NPLs are historically considered to be a matter of concern for many Bangladeshi banks and, as shown in Figure 5.1, till the late 1990s the proportion of NPLs was alarmingly high, due mainly to high NPLs of NCBs. Since the late 1990s, with a number of regulatory measures in operation, for the NCBs as well as for many of the PCBs, we observe an immediate decline of NPLs to total loan portfolio. However, that trend has been reversed in recent years as

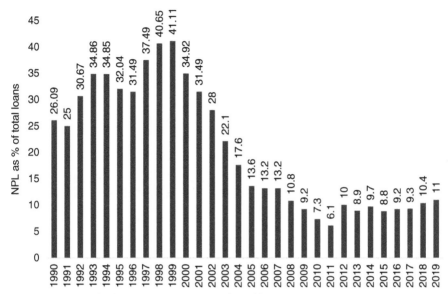

FIGURE 5.1 Trend of NPLs as percentage of total loans
Source: Annual Report, Bangladesh Bank.

the percentage of NPLs to total loans rose to almost 11% by the end of 2019. Whether considering provisions or not, for all four types of banks, sizeable NPLs are observed. In the case of PCBs, although net NPLs on average are quite low, while analysing the loan profile of PCBs we should keep in mind that most of the NPLs in PCBs are held by a few banks, therefore, the average NPLs of PCBs may fail to capture the depth of the issue.

International Monetary Fund (IMF) data show that in September 2019, NPLs as a percentage of the total loans of the banking sector was as high as 12%: the ratios for NCBs and PCBs were around 31.5% and 7.4%, respectively (IMF, 2020). It is therefore evident that, despite the success in reducing the NPLs of NCBs during the 1990s, the problem has returned in recent years. Unlike the 1980s and 1990s, NPLs have turned out to be a problem of PCBs as well, which necessitates further analysis of the issue from a political economy point of view.

A close examination of sector-wise distribution of NPLs reflects that trade and commercial sectors constitute more than 28% of total NPLs in 2018.[10] The RMG sector alone is found to account for more than 12% of the NPLs (and, in fact, around 27% of the NPLs in the manufacturing sector), followed by other large-scale industries (7.63%). This distributional pattern of NPLs is, however, consistent with the distributional pattern of sector-wise shares of

---

[10] Annual report of Bangladesh Bank.

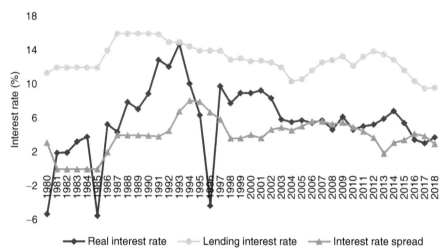

FIGURE 5.2 Trend in the lending interest rate, interest rate spread, and real interest rate
Source: World Bank, World Development Indicators and www.theglobaleconomy
.com/rankings/Lending_interest_rate/.

loans. This highlights that important sectors of the economy constitute a significant proportion of NPLs and that weak institutional discipline of the banking sector has also 'helped' these sectors to grow.

D Trend in Interest Rates

Figure 5.2 presents the trend in the lending interest rate[11] and real interest rate[12] in Bangladesh between 1980 and 2018. In 2018, the interest rate spread in Bangladesh, Sri Lanka, Malaysia, and Thailand was 3%, 2.7%, 1.8%, and 2.9%, respectively. This suggests that the interest rate spread in Bangladesh is not very different from that of other developing countries.

The real interest rate affects financial sector development through its influence on the volume of financial savings and on the cost of capital (McKinnon, 1973; Shaw, 1973; Fry, 1988; Leite and Sundararajan, 1990). As depicted in Figure 5.2, negative or very low interest rates in Bangladesh in the 1980s corresponded typically to a repressed financial system where credit is rationed and allocated in some authoritarian way, or as the result of 'deals' among sectors or firms – which is discussed later in this chapter. The two troughs, in 1985

---

[11] The lending rate is the bank rate that usually meets the short- and medium-term financing needs of the private sector. This rate is normally differentiated according to creditworthiness of borrowers and the objectives of the financing (see www.theglobaleconomy.com/rankings/Lending_interest_rate/).

[12] The real interest rate is the lending interest rate adjusted for inflation as measured by the GDP deflator. This is derived as the bank lending rate minus inflation (see www.theglobaleconomy.com/rankings/Real_interest_rate/).

and 1996, were due to inflation surges. After liberalisation of the financial market and a surge in the real rate, due to decelerating inflation with a lending rate still under control, the real rate followed the same declining trend as the nominal rate, because inflation was stabilised – after the accident of 1996. The declining trend of the lending rate also followed an international trend that started in the early 2000s but accelerated after 2008 – for example the declining trend in the yield on US 10-year bonds or on the German Bund.

It may also be noted in Figure 5.2 that the real deposit rate, which corresponds to the gap between the real rate and the interest spread,[13] has tended towards zero in the recent period. It was high, around 3% on average, throughout the 1990s, shrank in the mid-2000s, and has fluctuated around zero since then.

In 2018, the average real interest rate for Bangladesh, India, Sri Lanka, Malaysia, and Thailand was 3.8%, 5.1%, 6.9%, 4.1%, and 2.7%, respectively. The Bangladesh real interest rate was thus in the lower half of the range defined by these Asian countries.

Despite repeated instructions from the Government (even exhortations by the current, powerful prime minister) to maintain an interest rate spread within 3%, with a 6% deposit rate and 9% lending rate, the banking sector has failed to maintain such a provision.[14] However, following the strict instructions of the Finance Minister to reduce the lending rate to 9% from 1 April 2020, bankers decided not to offer a deposit rate over 6%.[15] However, this announcement has led to concern as deposit interest rates have dropped close to the inflation rate,[16] and also this may decrease banks' profitability (Hasan, 2020).

E Efficiency of Banks in Bangladesh

The trend and pattern of key economic indicators of the banking sector reveal that the performance of the sector as a whole is not satisfactory, and, except for FCBs, neither NCBs nor PCBs can be considered to have exhibited satisfactory performance in terms of relevant indicators. In this section, we attempt to understand whether the chosen banks (PCBs and FCBs) are performing 'optimally' with regard to their assets, income, expenses, and other chosen indicators and to understand the factors behind the 'sub-optimal' performance (if any) of certain banks as opposed to others. In this context, from a methodological point of view, we used the DEA,[17] a statistical tool that is often used

---

[13] This is because the real lending rate – spread = Lending rate – spread – inflation = real deposit rate.
[14] For example, see Islam and Sakib (2019) and Zahid (2020).
[15] See https://thefinancialexpress.com.bd/views/views/should-all-loans-come-under-6-9pc-ceiling-1580913491.
[16] See https://tbsnews.net/economy/banking/uneven-implementation-deposit-interest-rate-risks-chaos-41591.
[17] DEA is a typical non-parametric method that measures relative efficiency by comparing it with the possible production frontiers of decision-making units, with multiple inputs and outputs using linear programming (Farrell, 1957).

to assess the relative efficiency of firms (see Mercan *et al.*, 2003; Debnath and Shankar, 2008). In addition, in order to understand the factors behind the relative efficiency of banks, we estimated a panel logit model where we used the efficiency score with other banking sector indicators: most importantly, the components of the CAMELS[18] rating.

In the analysis of the efficiency of the private banking sector of Bangladesh, we have used the input-oriented[19] DEA analysis using the CCR[20] and BCC[21] models to measure overall technical efficiency (OTE) and pure technical efficiency (PTE), respectively. In the context of the banking sector of Bangladesh, we adopted the intermediation approach for selecting input and output variables, which considers banks as financial intermediaries where banks produce services through the collection of deposits and other liabilities and their application in interest-earning. In this analysis, as input variables we have chosen: (i) total assets; (ii) number of employees; and (iii) sum of deposits and borrowings. As output variables we have included: (i) net interest income; (ii) non-interest income; and (iii) NPLs. Apart from the traditional variables used for the intermediation approach, we have the NPLs variable as a (negative) output variable.[22] In addition, all the input and output variables except labour are measured in Bangladeshi Taka (BDT) in millions, and we have conducted the analysis from 2015 to 2018, on 44 national and foreign PCBs.

Figure 5.3 presents the distribution of the efficiency scores of the banks calculated using the DEA. It is clear that over the years, the percentage share of banks with an efficiency score of 0.9 and above has declined and the percentage shares of very poorly performing banks (efficiency score below 0.25), poorly performing banks (efficiency scores between 0.25 and 0.49), and moderately performing banks (efficiency scores between 0.5 and 0.74) have increased. In

---

[18] CAMELS is a recognised international rating system that bank supervisory authorities use to rate financial institutions according to six factors reflected in its acronym. Supervisory authorities assign each bank a score on a scale. A rating of 1 is considered the best, and a rating of 5 is considered the worst, for each factor.

[19] Coelli and Perelman (1999) show that the choice of orientation does not significantly change efficiency estimation results.

[20] The CCR model of DEA is named after Charnes, Cooper, and Rhodes, who proposed the method.

[21] The BCC model of DEA is named after Banker, Charnes, and Cooper, who proposed the method.

[22] As NPLs are loans that do not earn any profit (i.e. are not performing as a means of obtaining income for an individual bank), they should be considered as a bad output for the bank. The mechanism of DEA is such that it cannot identify a bad output, nor does it take negative values into consideration. Without certain modifications to the NPL variable, the DEA analysis will provide us with a biased outcome, which is unacceptable. In order to deal with this problem, we have used the directional distance function suggested by Barra and Zotti (2014) to modify the variable in such a manner that it captures the true effect of NPL as a bad output. The directional change of the variable will give positive weights to banks with lower value, as if producing lower NPLs is a good sign as regards maintaining their efficiency.

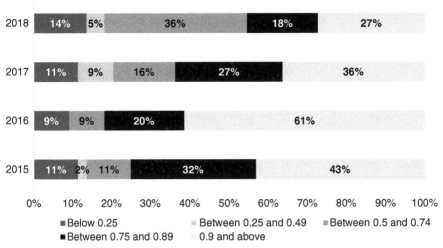

FIGURE 5.3 Distribution of the efficiency score of private banks by year
Note: Total number of private banks = 44.
Source: Authors' calculation from the DEA analysis.

2018, 55% of the banks had efficiency scores below 0.75. In contrast, only 25% of the banks in 2015 had efficiency scores below 0.75. Most of these low-performing banks are PCBs.

F Development Implications of the Status of the Banking Sector in Bangladesh

The linkage between economic development and the banking sector can be multi-faced and often the indirect linkage can be quite strong too. One of the most important ways in which the banking sector might have an impact on the growth and economic development of a country is through channelling the savings of depositors for the purposes of investment. Despite a persistent high growth rate in Bangladesh for the last decade or so, there has not been much progress in terms of private investment as the ratio of private investment to GDP has remained almost stagnant in recent years. There are concerns that poor governance in the banking sector, including the high amount of NPLs, has restricted banks' capacity to maintain a narrow interest rate spread and to reduce the lending rate to borrowers. Such a high cost of borrowing and access to finance is generally considered to be one of the key challenges for entrepreneurs in expanding their businesses (see International Finance Corporation (IFC), 2020).[23]

---

[23] IFC (2020) suggests that more than 24% of the Bangladeshi firms identified access to finance as the most difficult challenge they faced in 2019, while another 18% of businesses ranked corruption as the top constraint to further growth.

One important area of concern is that the Government's borrowing from the banking sector has been on an increasing trend over the past few years, which has also been accompanied by an accelerated selling of National Savings certificates (i.e. 'government bonds'). In FY18, the Government's borrowing from the banking system increased to as high as BDT 1780.9 billion (around US$ 21.34 billion) – equivalent to 8% of GDP. The increase in the Government's borrowing from the banking sector risks crowding out credit to the private sector (Rana and Wahid, 2016; see also the discussion in Chapter 2 of this volume).

It is also important to mention that since the 1980s, the Government has been allocating a significant amount in the annual national budget to subsidising the ailing banking sector, to cover the losses of these banks.[24] After the initiatives to privatise NCBs in the 1990s, a falling trend was observed in the recapitalisation of banks (NCBs) by the Government; this trend has been reversed in recent years. In FY14, there was a massive surge in the recapitalisation process, which, although it has declined in subsequent years, still since FY17 has been annually as high as BDT 10 billion (around US$ 0.12 billion). The national budget for FY20 allocated BDT 15 billion (around US$ 0.18 billion, equivalent to 0.75% of GDP) to the recapitalisation of NCBs. It is not only the direct monetary expense which is at stake here, this recapitalisation expenditure should also be understood from the viewpoint of opportunity costs to the society. With Government education expenditure being around 2% of GDP and health expenditure less than 0.5% of GDP, and also with a very low tax–GDP ratio of around 9%, the consequence of this massive recapitalisation for development cannot be ignored. The 'costs' of poor governance in the banking sector is therefore multi-dimensional and can have long-term implications for the Government's development initiatives.

In addition to the apparently 'visible' macro and fiscal indicators, it is often argued that poor governance of the banking sector is having negative consequences through a number of indirect channels. According to a Washington-based think tank, Global Financial Integrity, the total value gap identified in trade between Bangladesh and all of its trading partners in 2015 was US$ 11.5 billion, which was 19.4% of total trade (Global Financial Integrity, 2020). The gap is between the value of exports reported by Bangladesh exporters and the value of imports reported by importers in importing countries. This estimate puts Bangladesh among the top 30 countries of the world in terms of such trade mis-invoicing data, and third among Asian countries, after Malaysia and India. Though not conclusive, this mis-invoicing is argued to be linked to capital flight from the banking system in the form of NPLs (see Ahmed, 2019; Haider, 2019).

---

[24] See national budget reports of the Ministry of Finance (MOF).

IV POLITICS OF THE BANKING SECTOR: A BRIEF HISTORY

The first Awami League regime (1972–1975) instituted a 'socialistic' economy whereby banks were nationalised. The authoritarian and later dominant party rule (see Hassan and Raihan, 2018 for a definition and analysis of dominant party rule) of General Ziaur Rahman–the Bangladesh Nationalist Party (1975–1981) dismantled the 'socialistic' system of the previous regime and pursued a market-led economic strategy, but banks remained in the public sector. This period witnessed the rise of state-sponsored capitalism that relied heavily on an aggressive and very liberal industrial loan sanctioning policy for the development of private industries. Regulatory weaknesses, bank officials' corruption and collusion (with private entrepreneurs), and the regime's priority to distribute political patronage led to the beginning of the 'loan default culture' (see Sobhan and Mahmood, 1981; Hassan, 2001; Islam and Siddique, 2010 for case studies of loan defaults. Box 5.1 presents two such cases). The loan sanctioning regime during this period can be characterised as based on largely open deals. Closed deals did exist, but marginally.[25]

Box 5.1 Two examples of loan defaults in the 1990s

CASE STUDY I: XYZ PRIVATE LIMITED COMPANY

During early 1990s, XYZ (not its real name) company was owned by close relatives of one of the highest-level political leaders in the country. The company was sanctioned BDT 131.4 million (around US$ 3.32 million) by Sonali Bank, a leading NCB. The bank approved a ratio of debt and equity at 70:30, that is 30% of the total investment would be provided by the borrowing company, which was actually provided through bridge financing by another NCB, Uttara Bank. Interestingly, the company pledged the same property as collateral to Uttara Bank that had already been pledged to Sonali Bank, a typical fraudulent practice. According to the conditions specified in the loan agreement, the borrowing company was supposed to deposit to the bank BDT 38 million (around US$ 0.96 million), as part of the equity for financing construction (factory building) and the purchase of industrial machines, but due to special 'appeal', the board of directors of the bank permitted the borrower to finance the construction and purchase from their own sources. At the borrower's 'request', the bank either relaxed or simply did not enforce various terms and conditions and standard policies related to term lending. For example, the required cash margin to be deposited was lowered from BDT 23.2 million to BDT 10 million (from US$ 0.59 million to 0.25 million); insurance requirements regarding the project in general, and imported machines in particular, were relaxed to provide special benefits to the borrower; special payments by the bank were made to cover the deficit in equity.

---

[25] The deals space analysis is presented in Chapter 1 of this volume.

In the tender process (for importing machines), the bank authority rejected the firm which quoted the lowest price and approved the one which was selected by the borrowing company. Changes in all of these policies and conditions were made on a top-priority basis by the board of directors of the bank. Instead of the minimum requirement of a 90-day duration of a sanctioning project (as determined by the government), this particular project was sanctioned in 74 days. XYZ was registered as an export-oriented industry for which it received substantial duty exemptions, but the company actually produced only for the local market. Commenting on the loan repayment behaviour of the company, the Comptroller and Auditor General (CAG) report observed, 'Although the company is running in full scale, so far the owners have not shown any interest in repaying its bank loans'.

CASE STUDY 2: BANGLADESH MATCH COMPANY

The owner of the company was Ispahani Group, one of the oldest business groups in Bangladesh. The company had been experiencing huge losses and personnel were laid off in 1990. At that time, it owed Rupali Bank (an NCB) BDT 40 million (around US$ 1.16 million). In 1991, the owner decided to close down the company and an arrangement was made with Rupali Bank to pay off the debt in instalments. However, after the 1991 parliamentary election, the Speaker of the fifth parliament wrote a letter to the chairperson of Rupali Bank advising him not to implement the decision to close down the activities or sell them to a third party without receiving clearance from the prime minister. The Speaker apparently intervened on behalf of the trade unions of the particular industry. In 1992, the Speaker wrote another letter to the chairperson of the bank informing him about the prime minister's decision to re-open the industry. The Speaker also advised the bank authority to provide sufficient funds and other assistance deemed necessary to the owner of the industry. The bank management eventually decided to postpone the decision to close down the industry and also to provide BDT 10 million (around US$ 0.26 million) as cash credit. Although the owner continued to default on the total loan (approximately BDT 66.6 million equivalent to US$ 1.66 million by 1994), the bank authority increased the cash credit limit to BDT 15 million (around US$ 0.37 million). This was done by the direct intervention of the Speaker. In 1995, the owner was actually paid more than the authorised limit (BST 17.5 million equivalent to US$ 0.43 million). Since then, the overdue loan of Bangladesh Match Company continued to accumulate and as at 1998 the amount due was approximately BST 80.5 million (around US$ 1.72 million).

Source: Comptroller and Auditor General Report,
Government of Bangladesh, 1998,
reported in Hassan (2001).

The authoritarian regime of General Ershad (Jatiya Party, 1981–1990) nurtured a 'robust' form of crony capitalism through a loan sanctioning process that was largely based on closed deals, in contrast to the previous regime (Hassan, 2001; Hassan and Raihan, 2018; see Kochanek, 2003 for evidence on the rampant crony capitalist practices of the Ershad regime). The regime saw an increasing trend of NPLs and further consolidation of the default culture. Yet such a liberal and aggressive loan sanctioning process (with all the features of mal-governance mentioned above) contributed to significant development of industrial entrepreneurship in the country, particularly in the RMG sector. The critical factor here was the continuation of open deals in terms of accessing loans by the private sector. The period also witnessed trade union-centred militant politics related to de-nationalisation of the banks, and an increasing and aggressive stance of civil society and the media towards the default culture and its consequences (Monem, 2008; Hassan, 2001).

In terms of the policy regime of the banking sector, the period before 1990 can be broadly considered as one of financial repression (see Raquib, 1999 for an analysis of the policy of financial repression followed by different regimes during the pre-1990 decades). This refers to a bundle of government policies characterised by low real interest rates (see Figure 5.2), with the aim of generating cheap funding for government spending. Also, as low or negative real rates generate excess demand, rationing took place. Some sectors were favoured in the rationing scheme: for instance, state-owned companies, at the expense of the private sector. The objective of successive regimes during this period was to supply cheap money to state-owned enterprises and other priority sectors. Given this broader policy objective, the regimes initiated a banking sector reform during 1980–1990, eschewing reforming the broader policy (financial repression)[26] and rather focusing on the policy of promoting the licensing of PCBs and the de-nationalisation of NCBs (three NCBs were privatised in 1983/1984 and four PCBs were granted licences to operate in the early 1980s). The reform agenda during this period essentially reflected the existing elite political settlement/equilibrium among political elites and the burgeoning business class, and influential Western donors (led by the IMF, especially in the domains of privatisation, and fiscal and banking sector reform). Such a political settlement effectively excluded organised labour and white collar staff in the public sector, including NCBs. The latter actors resisted the de-nationalisation of banks, as alluded to earlier, but without any success, indicating the robustness of the elite political settlement. The de-nationalisation of the banks and licensing of PCBs also indicated the IMF's and World Bank's clout over economic policy decisions during the 1980s, when the country was still largely dependent on external aid or support to finance its development expenditures (see Sobhan, 1991; Chowdhury, 2000).

---

[26] Utilising a policy of financial repression meant setting the rate of interest to be charged by private banks and rationing the credit they could deliver. It was expected that private banks would allocate credit in a better way than state-owned banks.

The 'competitive democratic' phase[27] saw a further deepening of the default culture (with some fluctuations). The default culture was rampant during the 1990s, saw some improvements during the 2000s, and then again showed a growing trend during the 2010s. The period also witnessed the rise of private sector banks[28] (numerically as well as a powerful corporate actor), a crisis within private sector banks (weak corporate governance, insiders lending, etc.), and the Government's attempts to rescue problem banks. Also, a significant development during this period was the deeper involvement of the World Bank in prodding the Government to initiate a comprehensive banking sector reform (that eventually led to the establishment of a Commission in 1997). Though the Banking Companies Act (BCA) 1997 was first enacted in 1991[29] as part of the Financial Sector Reform Project (FSRP), one of the core demands of the World Bank was the amendment of this act to bring the prevailing standard of prudential and supervisory regulations up to a par with the Basel Committee guidelines. Due to the World Bank's sustained pressure, the act was finally amended in 1997.

The late 1990s saw a subsequent de facto decline in the power/autonomy of the central bank. Also, there was the emergence of a private sector banking association (Bankers Association of Bangladesh (BAB))[30] as a powerful actor, leading to its ability to capture policies and especially regulatory policies related to banks – a phenomenon termed state capture in the political economy literature. BAB and other prominent business associations successfully lobbied the political authorities to relax, and in some cases completely reverse, the stricter provisions in the BCA (see Box 5.2).

---

[27] The period between 1991 and 2013 when the Bangladesh Nationalist Party and Awami League alternated power every five years based on reasonably free and fair elections supervised by non-partisan Caretaker Governments; for an analysis of the political dynamics of the competitive phase from a political settlement perspective, see Hassan (2013) and Hassan and Nazneen (2017).

[28] Between 1991 and 1996, 7 private sector banks were given licences to operate; between 1996 and 2001, 12 private sector banks were given licences to operate; and in 2013, 9 private sector banks were given licences to operate.

[29] The BCA has extensive provisions to ensure accountability and financial discipline within the banking system. The BCA empowers the central bank to ensure that banks observe: (a) strict internal controls and good governance principle in the management process, which includes clearly defined authorities and responsibilities of the directors and the managers and rules covering conflicts of interest; (b) transparent accounting policies and guidelines, as well as disclosure requirements; (c) standard capital adequacy requirements; and (d) standard loan classification and provisioning rules. It also provides the central bank with necessary sanctioning authorities, which include the power to impose financial penalties, to prohibit activities, to suspend and remove board members and managers, to remove banking licenses, and to proscribe insider and related party lending. The act also specifies standards for licensing banks and financial institutions (BCA, 1997, Government of Bangladesh).

[30] The BAB is an advisory service organisation for private commercial banks. Established under the Companies Act, 1913, the BAB started its activities in 1993 with nine commercial banks, which had increased to 38 as at the end of December 2015. See www.bab-bd.com/.

Box 5.2 State capture by the BAB in the late 1990s

The Government's decisions to standardise rules and regulations for better enforcement of credit discipline evoked strong opposition from influential sections of the business community. Opposition intensified in 1997, when the central bank started implementing new credit regulations and, as a consequence, many big business groups were denied loans. The private sector found the BCA (amended in 1997) detrimental to their interests. Immediately after the amendment of the act, the BAB and other prominent business associations (mainly the Federation of Chambers of Commerce and Industries (FBCCI)) started a systematic campaign to further amend or simply do away with some of the stricter rules and regulations. Organised business successfully lobbied the political authorities to relax and in some cases completely reverse the stricter provisions in the BCA (prudential regulations in the loan repayment process). In other cases (the central bank's supervision over PCBs' internal management), new provisions remained intact, as formal mandatory laws in the book, but were largely ignored in practice by the market actors. Non-compliance with the rules was possible due to collusive linkages of these actors with the supervisory authorities (bureaucratic or political), at the highest levels of the hierarchy.

Source: Hassan (2001).

During 1990–2000, the competitive democratic phase emphasised market-oriented liberalisation, doing away with or limiting the policies of financial repression of the previous decades, and encouraged more private sector participation in the banking sector (Institute of Governance Studies (IGS), 2011). As part of the first objective, the core reform strategies, formulated and implemented under the World Bank–designed FSRP (initiated during the early 1990s), included, among other things, the gradual deregulation of the interest rate structure, and providing market-oriented incentives for priority sector lending. To realise the second objective, a large number of PCBs were given licences. The major beneficiary of the priority sector lending was the RMG sector.[31] The predominantly market incentive–based reform, though it led to the development of a wide range of financial products and services (merchant and investment banking, small and medium-sized enterprise and retail banking, credit card and offshore banking, etc.), failed to tackle some key banking sector problems, such as high ratio of NPLs in both NCBs and PCBs and weak enforcement of capital adequacy and other regulatory policies. Also, in dealing with the policies of financial repression, as mentioned before, the reform ended up with credit rationing, and eventually a deteriorating level of

---

[31] For example, RMG exporters were allowed to borrow from banks at lower bands of interest rates of 8–10%, against the normal 14–16% charge. See Chapter 4. Also, some other sectors, such as agriculture, small and cottage industries, pharmaceuticals, textiles, and ceramics, were in the priority lending category, and some of them are primarily import-substituting.

credit allocation. For instance, the flow of credit declined over the 1990–1999 period to some of the priority sectors, such as agriculture, and small and cottage industries, and a similar decline was also observed in terms of the relative share of the rural banking system (IGS, 2011). In addition, the introduction of the interest rate flexibility failed to create a competitive environment among NCBs and PCBs. The upshot is that the market fundamentalist approach of the FSRP was largely unsuccessful in achieving the desired objectives of the reform programme, since, given its faith in the market per se, it focused heavily on the deregulation dimension and placed less emphasis on the necessity for broadening/deepening prudential regulation aspects (IGS, 2011).

Such lacunae in the regulatory aspects were emphasised by the Bank Reform Committee (BRC), formed after the termination of the FSRP in 1996, which submitted its recommendations in 1999. The BRC blamed supervisory and regulatory forbearance as one of the core issues behind the problems of the banking sector. The phase of reform initiated during the early 2000s essentially premised its policy prescriptions on these issues identified by the BRC and emphasised risk-based regulations and strengthening of the central bank's capacity (both supervisory and technical infrastructure-related) to address the banking sector problems. The Central Bank Strengthening Project, initiated in 2003 (part of the stabilisation programme signed with the IMF for 2003–2006), included strengthening of the legal framework, increased research capacity, capacity building in relation to supervisory and prudential regulations, auditing, and the development of automation-related technology. In terms of addressing the default culture, a series of new laws, regulations, and instruments were enacted. To create a competitive environment for the private sector banking strategy, a staged withdrawal of public ownership from the sector was initiated that involves divestment and corporatisation of substantial shareholdings of three publicly owned banks. Increased private sector participation in the sector continued throughout this phase, with licensing of a dozen PCBs. The reform still failed to achieve what it intended to, due to constraints of meta-level political and governance issues (cronyism, de facto political control of the regulatory authority, a political–business elite collusive nexus, etc.). In the beginning of the 2000s, important improvement was noted in terms reduction in NPLs and the NPL ratio stabilised at an order of magnitude below the 40% level reached in the late 1990s. But this trend fizzled out at the end of that decade, and the NPL ratio started to increase from the beginning of the 2010s. The licensing of the PCBs became largely a political patronage distribution mechanism, and ownership predominantly went to individuals with partisan political identities. Many new PCBs came into being despite the central bank's objections based on an economic rationale (the market saturation of banks being one issue).[32]

---

[32] In 2013, nine PCBs were given licences. All of these banks were backed by politically powerful owners (Khatun, 2018).

Bangladesh's current regime (2014–) can be termed one of 'dominant party rule'. This period has seen an acceleration of NPLs and further marginalisation of the central bank (de facto weakening of its authority). Other relevant features of this period are a continuation of the licensing of private banks based on political considerations, deteriorating governance status of the banking sector, further increases in the capture of the state/central bank by private banks – both individually and collectively (associations) – resulting in regulatory capture (laws, rules, loan classification criteria, etc.), entrenchment of crony capitalistic practices by private bank owners, and the emergence of banking sector oligarchies.

The Finance Ministry's overreach in licensing private banks, under political considerations, without the recommendation of the Bangladesh Bank, not complying with the suggestions of the central bank and influencing the decisions of the autonomous central bank, are a few of the manifestations of policy and regulatory capture and political patronage in the sector.[33] Though it is an independent regulatory authority, the central bank is unable to completely monitor these banks as they are largely owned by politically influential people.[34] Some of these banks have been linked to loan scams, aggressive lending, and violations of banking regulations, among other issues, which tends to pose serious threats to the banking sector, according to the central bank's own assessment.[35] Table 5.2 presents a summary of the scams in the banking sector in Bangladesh in recent years.

Historically, there have been many regulations covering the banking sector, especially regarding the entry/exit mechanism of banks and their governing bodies. The BCA has been amended six times since its formation. Recent regulations tend to be strategically done to bolster political control over the governance of these banks, so they can be used to distribute patronages among loyal political elites. These new laws have made changes in directorship positions, triggering a state of confusion among depositors and other stakeholders.[36]

---

[33] The then Finance Minister, A.M.A. Muhith, in November 2018 acknowledged that new banking licences were granted to entrepreneurs on 'political grounds' in a sector that was already overcrowded, with about 57 banks, of which many had been hit hard by scams (see www.newagebd .net/article/54783/3-more-banking-licences-to-be-granted-on-political-ground-muhith).

[34] See Khatun (2018).

[35] See www.thedailystar.net/supplements/building-modern-economy/banking-sector-and-its-impact-on-bangladesh-economy-1536568.

[36] The changes extended a family's grip on a bank, allowing four members of a family to sit on the bank board at a time. They also paved the way for directors to stay on the board for nine years in a row, up from the previous six years. Opposition lawmakers walked out of the House in protest when the parliament passed amendments to the Bank Company Act in January 2018 saying that the amendment would give more privilege to loan defaulters. See https://tbsnews .net/analysis/will-give-more-leeway-loan-defaulters.

TABLE 5.2 *Scams in the banking sector in Bangladesh in recent years*

Banks	Key irregularity	Measures taken
Sonali, Janata, NCC, Dhaka, Mercantile Bank (2008–2011)	BDT 40.89 million (approximately US$ 0.58 million) bank loan with forged land documents (*Dhaka Tribune*, 28 August 2013)	On 1 August 2013, Anti-Corruption Commission (ACC) filed cases against Sonali Bank, Fahim Attire, and certain individuals; BDT 10 million (US$ 0.13 million) was given back to Sonali Bank (*Dhaka Tribune*, 2 August 2013; *New Age*, 2 August 2013; *The Daily Star*, 2 August 2013)
Basic Bank (2009–2013)	BDT 45,000 million (approximately US$ 604 million) with dubious accounts and companies (*The Daily Star*, 28 June 2013)	In September 2015, ACC filed 56 cases against 120 people (*New Age*, 13 August 2018)
Sonali Bank (2010–2012)	BDT 35,470 million (approximately US$ 472 million) embezzled by Hall Mark and other businesses (*The Daily Star*, 14 August 2012)	In October 2012, ACC filed 11 cases against 27 people (*Dhaka Tribune*, 11 July, 2018)
Janata Bank (2010–2015)	BDT 100,000 million (approximately US$ 1.3 billion) appropriated by Crescent and AnonTex (*Dhaka Tribune*, 3 November 2018)	On 30 October 2018, the Enquiry Committee of Bangladesh Bank submitted a report (*Dhaka Tribune*, 3 November 2018)
Janata Bank, Prime Bank, Jamuna Bank, Shahjalal Islami Bank, Premier Bank (June 2011–July 2012)	BDT 11,750 million (approximately US$ 151 million) by Bismillah group and associates. (*The Daily Star*, 7 October 2016)	On 3 November 2013, ACC filed 12 cases against 54 people (*The Independent*, 11 September 2018)
AB Bank (2013–2014)	BDT 1,650 million (approximately US$ 21.2 million) (*The Daily Star*, 12 June 2018)	On 25 January 2018, ACC filed a case against the former chairman and officials of AB Bank (*The Daily Star*, 12 March 2018)
NRB Commercial Bank (2013–2016)	BDT 7,010 million (approximately US$ 90 million) of loan (*New Age*, 10 December 2017)	On 29 December 2016, the Bangladesh Bank appointed an observer to check irregularities (*Dhaka Tribune*, 7 December 2017)

TABLE 5.2 *(continued)*

Banks	Key irregularity	Measures taken
Janata Bank (2013–2016)	BDT 12,300 million (approximately US$ 158 million) of loan scam (*The New Nation*, 22 October 2018)	In October 2018, Thermax requested to reschedule the loan and Janata Bank's board endorsed it and sent it to the Bangladesh Bank (*The Daily Star*, 21 October 2018)
Farmers Bank (2013–2017)	BDT 5,000 million (approximately US$ 63.7 million) of fund appropriation by 11 companies (*The Daily Star*, 24 March 2018)	On January 2018, the Bangladesh Bank directed that an audit be conducted. In April 2018, ACC arrested four accused persons (*The Independent*, 11 April 2018)
Bangladesh Bank (5 February 2016)	BDT 6,796 million (approximately US$ 86.6 million) by international cyber hacking from the treasury account of Bangladesh Bank (*The Daily Star*, 5 August 2017)	On 19 March 2016, the Government formed a three-member investigation committee (*The Daily Star*, 5 August 2017)

Source: Khatun (2018).

V AN ANALYTICAL NARRATIVE OF THE GOVERNANCE FAILURES IN THE BANKING SECTOR

The governance crisis in the banking sector in Bangladesh is not manifested in frequent collapse of banks but in the serious insolvency of some banks. However, these insolvent banks are typically protected from market competition and not allowed to go bankrupt by recapitalising them through government subsidies. During the last few decades, only one bank has collapsed in Bangladesh.[37] The banking system in Bangladesh is a classic example of what has been known in the banking literature as 'the walking dead bank syndrome', characterised by insolvency and undercapitalisation of an important segment of the system (Burki and Perry, 1998). The implications of such government subsidies and other forms of insurance policies are profound in terms of banking sector governance. Such policies also have serious effects on the incentives of the bank management and depositors to demand governance reforms in the banking system.

---

[37] Managing director, directors, and a section of officers and employees of Oriental Bank, in a nexus with the Orion Group, embezzled funds of BDT 5,950 million (around US$ 86.3 million) of the bank. The scam was exposed during investigations when Oriental Bank came under the control of Bangladesh Bank on 19 June 2006. The bank was renamed ICB Islamic Bank. See www.observerbd.com/2015/10/03/113426.php, www.thedailystar.net/news-detail-16813, and www.thedailystar.net/news-detail-25402.

A Central Bank

Bangladesh Bank, that is the central bank of Bangladesh, tends to be a very weak institution. Due to various formal and informal controls, it actually enjoys only a marginal degree of policy and operational independence. It is de facto subservient to the MOF even in regard to some of the core functions of the central bank, such as regular banking supervision. However, it is not only the formal power that has reduced the independence of the central bank. Governments also tend to act beyond their legal mandates. For instance, existing rules clearly prohibit appointing the Governor or Deputy Governor of the central bank from the government bureaucracy. But these rules have never deterred successive governments (authoritarian and democratic) from appointing members of the civil service to such positions on an ad hoc basis.[38] The Government has also effectively marginalised the role of the Bangladesh Bank in the decision-making processes related to operational matters and banking sector governance. Though the BCA 1991 empowered the Bangladesh Bank to regulate the country's banking sector as an autonomous body, the central bank lost its independence after the MOF established its own banking division. An example of the marginalisation of the Bangladesh Bank can be seen from the following quote of a supernumerary professor at the Bangladesh Institute of Bank Management: 'A few days ago (in November 2017), the central bank turned down proposals for setting up two new private commercial banks. In response, the ministry instructed them to proceed that would allow parties to get licences to set up private banks. How does such an action leave any room for the bank to operate independently?'[39]

In dealing with critical policy issues, such as monetary policy or lending to the Government, and governance issues – for instance, special monitoring of insolvent banks or problems of NPLs of commercial banks – the tendency of the Government has been to bypass the formal approval process of the central bank.[40] In fact when it comes to governance issues, the Government seems to be more inclined to limit central bank's authority. An ex-governor of the Bangladesh Bank mentioned: 'In Bangladesh, there is a "dual" system of

[38] The governors and high officials of the central bank, in most of the occasions, have been from the bureaucracy.
[39] See www.dhakatribune.com/business/banks/2017/11/26/independent-bangladesh-bank.
[40] As an ex-Governor of Bangladesh Bank said: 'Bangladesh Bank may play role in most of the cases, but it is unable to play role in some of the cases as we note from outside. Currently the central bank is issuing some circulars. It seems these decisions are not made on good judgment. It is not taken into consideration what may be the consequence. It seems these circulars are issued after being influenced by a quarter of politicians and bureaucrats for their own interest. It is true that it is not possible for Bangladesh Bank to do anything bypassing the government. But now-a-days various initiatives are being taken outside the central bank to issue circulars. Bangladesh Bank is merely giving the legal recognition.' (See https://en.prothomalo.com/opinion/Financial-sector-crisis-spreads-to-other-sectors).

control of the banking sector. The state-owned commercial banks and special-ised banks, and some statutory banks are controlled by the Bank and Financial Institution Division of the MOF. On the other hand, all private commercial banks, foreign banks, non-bank financial institutions are regulated by the Bangladesh Bank. This "duality" of control has resulted in uncoordinated, often weak, policy measures for the government regulated banks. Bangladesh Bank has serious limitations in enforcing prudential and management norms in these banks, which have made the whole banking sector weak and vulnerable through "domino effect".'[41]

B Corporate Governance in the PCBs

Unlike NCBs, PCBs are characterised by reasonably efficient internal man-agement. The bank authorities have successfully avoided the problems that plagued NCBs, since high priority was given to minimising administrative costs. Also, competitive salaries and various other performance-related incen-tives have contributed to greater management efficiency. However, the cen-tral problem with PCBs lies in the area of corporate governance. For a better understanding of the problem, we need to go beyond the conventional per-spective of corporate governance, which fails to take into consideration the contingent nature of institutions and the political economy settings. The con-ventional perspective, developed essentially in the context of the UK and USA ('Anglo-American model'), assumes the following: the existence of widely held firms (i.e. firms with a fairly large number of dispersed shareholders); firms are subject to effective legal and juridical (civil and criminal) constraints; and firms rely on 'anonymous finance using primarily arm's-length contracts and third-party intervention through the market for corporate control' (Berglof and von Thadden, 1999). The defining characteristic of such corporate governance is 'strong managers, weak owners' (Roe, 1994), and the main governance prob-lem is the conflict between self-interested management and the weak dispersed shareholders.

Such a model of corporate governance cannot explain the realities in the developing world. In the latter context, firms are usually family-owned or closely held (i.e. more or less concentrated ownership), legal and juridical constraints are very weak, and close ties between business interests and gov-ernment is much more common ('crony capitalism'), resulting in large-scale corporate fraud and theft. Also, the stock market is less salient as an external source of finance, and firms typically raise funds from sources such as business groups ('channelling resources between its firms'), family, and friends. In some developing countries like Bangladesh, where the banking sector is characterised

---

[41] See www.thedailystar.net/supplements/strong-institution-good-governance/news/bangladesh-banks-role-independent-regulatory-body-1701913.

by large-scale governance failure, NPLs tend to be another major source for raising funds.[42]

The above features also largely characterise the structure of corporate governance of PCBs in Bangladesh. Concretely, PCBs are closely held firms, that is mainly owned by a few large shareholders,[43] who have strong control over the managers. In that sense, the defining characteristic of the corporate governance of PCBs is (paraphrasing Roe): strong owners, dependent managers (bank management), and very weak outsiders (i.e. stockholders). Consequently, the main corporate governance problem is that there are hardly any effective self-interested countervailing groups to prevent rampant corporate fraud and theft by the bank owners.

In general, the monitoring and supervision of banks are very complex issues involving serious incentive problems and information asymmetry. For instance, depositors may lack necessary incentives to proactively monitor the performance of banks since they have less costly options of withdrawing their deposits if necessary: that is, depositors may vote with their feet if they find the bank is not viable. The incentive problem also arises due to the presence of deposit insurance. For instance, the Deposit Insurance Fund in Bangladesh has largely contributed to depositors' complacency (regarding gross inefficiency and insolvency of the banks) and consequently has hindered the free play of market mechanisms in disciplining banks, that is the depositors may have little incentive to vote with their feet. Such complacency seems to be also an outcome of the presence of the Government's explicit guarantees (bailing out of failing banks) and implicit guarantees (regulatory forbearance).[44] Moreover, depositors tend to lack sufficient information to make a proper evaluation. But even if they have better information, the policy of deposit insurance would reduce the incentive to use that information. There are also collective action problems that severely limit depositors' activism. In contrast to the small and concentrated groups with high stakes in the system – for instance, the bank owners – numerous depositors, each having a small stake in the banks, tend to be less motivated and consequently less effective in realising collective objectives. The costly process of information

---

[42] The United Nations Conference on Trade and Development (UNCTAD) LDC report (UNCTAD, 2019) mentions that Bangladesh lost a significant amount of tax owing to an illicit outflow of funds that accounted for 36% of its total tax in 2015. The report said the ratio of illicit financial flows from Bangladesh was equal to the average for LDCs. Also, at a workshop organised by the Bangladesh Institute of Bank Management on trade service operations on 20 March 2019, speakers identified several factors responsible for the rise of trade-based money laundering in the country. The factors, as they said, include under-qualified bankers, lack of effective communications between customs and banks, an unholy alliance of unscrupulous traders and bankers, a lack of digitisation, and the rise of NPLs (see https://thefinancialexpress.com.bd/views/capital-flight-to-continue-unabated-1577808211).

[43] Discussions with bank officials (current and past) and academics.

[44] Regulatory forbearance refers to the tendency of government to put off disciplinary actions assuming that a bank will recover on its own.

collection and the possibility of other depositors free riding on such information are also strong disincentives facing individual depositors in terms of taking individual initiatives to generate information. The point is this: there are important reasons for depositors to delegate the monitoring and supervision role to specialised agencies that will act on their behalf to mitigate collective action problems and reduce information asymmetry and the transaction costs of monitoring. Two forms of agencies are typically available: the formal regulatory institutions (the central bank, for instance) and varieties of countervailing private actors or 'reputational agents'[45] with strong incentives to monitor corporate firms.

In Bangladesh, reputational agents have largely failed to represent depositors' interest by playing the role of an effective monitor of commercial banks. To begin with, there are very few such agents or institutions in Bangladesh relevant to banking sector corporate governance. For example, credit rating agencies, investment analyst firms, and depositor or stockholders associations have yet to emerge in any significant sense. Organised legal activism tends to focus more on environmental, civil, and human rights issues, rather than financial sector mal-governance. The role of auditing and accounting firms has been very perverse, which in effect reinforces rather than mitigates the information asymmetry between banks and depositors, as well as corporate fraud and other opportunistic behaviour of bank management and owners.[46] An exception, in this regard, has been the print media. In fact, to the extent that a certain degree of transparency and accountability exists in the system, the credit for this can perhaps largely go to actors like the print media. The print media's role as monitor has been very critical. Media trial (naming and shaming of defaulters, exposure of banking sector-related corporate fraud, etc.) has probably played a more important role than formal judicial and law enforcement processes in ensuring some degree of discipline in regard to powerful bank owners, defaulters, and cronies.[47]

---

[45] Reputational agents refers to various private self-regulating bodies, civil society organisations, and media which are able to put pressure on both corporations and government, and that influence public opinion and contribute to increased transparency and reduction of information asymmetry. Their actions also potentially reduce malfeasance and opportunistic behaviour of corporate firms.

[46] According to Afroze *et al.* (2019), the banking sector in Bangladesh has been in a catastrophic situation in recent years. Most of the state-owned banks and some private banks have been operating beyond the regulations and deemed to be in a 'risky' zone. External corporate auditors as trust engendering engines are supposed to protect the trust and confidence of investors and the users of banks. Afroze *et al.* (2019) analysed some distressed state-owned and private banks and revealed that most of the banks received an 'unqualified' audit opinion within the period of financial difficulties, as well as immediately prior to the public declaration of financial difficulties of the banks. But the market did not seem to be assured by the 'unqualified' audit opinions as these financial institutions either collapsed or had to be bailed out within a short period of receiving such an opinion. With public trust and confidence shaken, it raises valid questions regarding the auditors' roles, independence, values, quality, and knowledge.

[47] The BAB, in March 2018, urged the then Finance Minister A.M.A. Muhith to intervene and put a stop to what they claimed was negative reporting on the banking sector. The letter, signed

Discussion with bank officials (current and ex) and academics suggest that auditing and accounting firms in Bangladesh have largely failed to play their role of effective monitors of corporate behaviour of commercial banks.[48] The problem is not a lack of technical competence (although this is low) but mainly bad governance. Whatever formal regulations exist, in practice the auditing and accounting firms do not seem to be subject to any form of accountability. For instance, no legal actions have ever been taken against any auditors by depositors or shareholders. The central bank has never disciplined or disqualified any auditing firms for sloppy work or violations of rules. Given such a weak accountability structure and legal enforcement, a large section of the auditing profession has been involved in blatant violation of corporate rules and ethics, auditing fraud, and collusive corruption with bank management. For instance, auditors collude with bank management to hide irregularities in the records, change loan classification entries and provision for loan losses to conceal loan defaults, and exaggerate the performance of banks by concealing expenses and showing income from interest generated from defaulted loans.[49] Another problem is the distorted accountability structure, that is executive authorities' control over the regulatory agencies. For instance, the central bank does not receive audit reports, instead the MOF does. A collusive nexus is much easier to establish in the executive domain of the state than in the central bank.

by BAB Chairman Nazrul Islam Mazumder, called for establishing an organisation in line with the Financial Information Act to prevent negative publicity in the media. In the views of private bankers, negative news may create panic among people and customers may lose trust in banks. Their call, however, came against the backdrop of media reports that the directors and chairmen of a number of private banks had been involved in some high-profile loan scams in recent years. Economists and banking sector analysts strongly opposed the BAB demand, saying any restrictions on the mass media may further worsen the situation as it was the latter that had brought to light a series of loan scandals (see www.dhakatribune.com/business/banks/2018/04/01/ private-banks-muhith-negative-media-coverage). Furthermore, an editorial of the *Daily Star*, the leading English daily in Bangladesh, on 2 April 2018, asserted that 'we can understand how the boards of some corruption-ridden financial institutions do not like the press. After all, we have been reporting on loan scams since 2009 and it is the inability (or unwillingness) on the part of bank managements and the government to put in checks-and-balances to stop corrupt practices that led to the failure of the Farmers Bank, not because of reports in the press. We in the media stand for transparency and accountability in our banking system and strongly oppose any move to stifle freedom of expression by a coterie of a self-serving interest group that wants the public to remain in the dark about banking irregularities that have destroyed whatever good image the sector had.' (See www.thedailystar.net/editorial/bab-demand-ludicrous-1556620).

[48] Also, the *New York Times*, on 11 April 2016, wrote: 'This is largely because state institutions are underfunded and weak. Technocrats, auditors, courts – all those traditional safeguards don't have enough authority or muscle in Bangladesh to keep the politicians in check.' See www.nytimes.com/2016/04/12/opinion/bangladeshs-other-banking-scam.html.

[49] Mahmud and Ara (2015) explored corporate governance practices in the Bangladesh banking industry through interviews with 54 respondents of 16 randomly selected PCBs and two NCBs. Their analysis shows that most often the external auditors are influenced to give the results desired by the authority. This tendency is seen more in PCBs than NCBs. Incomplete and ineffective audits and disclosure lead to widespread corruption in the banking industry.

The most important public source of external restraint has been the central bank, which has the formal supervisory authority over PCBs.[50] However, experiences in the last two decades (with some variations) suggest that it has largely failed to control such fraudulent practices. The regulatory failure, on the part of the central bank, needs to be explained by relating the corporate governance problem to the larger political–economy settings.

Licences to set up banks in the private sector have mainly been given to politically favoured cronies, most of whom have also been large loan defaulters. The privatisation of Pubali Bank in 1983 is a typical example of this process. The Bank had an estimated value of BDT 3 billion (around US$ 0.12 billion), but during privatisation, it was deliberately undervalued at BDT 160 million (around US$ 6.5 million). The majority of the new owners were already large defaulters (with the same bank), with one of them defaulting in the amount BDT 10 million (around US$ 0.41 million). These bank owners continued to wield political influence over successive democratic regimes. Discussions with senior bankers and recent scanning of print media suggest that the licensing of banks in the private sector (PCBs) over the last decade has also continued to be largely based on corrupt deals and political patronage. For example, several banks that have received licences in past seven to eight years, such as Farmers Bank, NRB Global Bank, and NRB Commercial Bank, suffered a severe liquidity crisis during the 2016/2017 fiscal year. The problem was particularly acute in the case of Farmers Bank, which had to be bailed out by the Government. Prominent economist Wahiduddin Mahmud noted that repeated violations of bank policies led to Farmers Bank's current dilapidated state. He stated: 'The influence of politicians has helped them to establish new banks without extensive scrutiny and obtain huge amounts of loans.'[51]

Given the political clout of the owners of PCBs, and the weak rule of law, the central bank has had very little success in enforcing laws and rules against blatant forms corporate fraud and non-compliance of regulations by the bank directors. Based on scanning of print media and discussions with bankers, including current officials and ex-governors and deputy governors of Bangladesh Bank, the following appears to be the case:

(a) Formal regulations clearly specify the autonomy of the management from the board and the roles of the board, chairperson, and managing director, but such regulations are rarely followed by the bank authorities. In most cases, it is the board that actually runs the bank.

(b) The BCA (section 27) prohibits PCBs from making loans to their directors and affiliated concerns, yet insider lending has been widely practised in the banking sector, especially by insolvent banks, leading to a huge

---

[50] Other important regulators are the MOF and the Public Accounts Committee.
[51] See www.dhakatribune.com/business/banks/2018/12/09/economists-banking-sector-must-steer-clear-of-political-influence.

accumulation of NPLs. Insider lending takes various forms: lending to firms with which bank owners have links, lending to family members of the owners and pure theft (i.e. the adoption of outright fraudulent strategies). The latter includes the transfer of funds by owners to fictitious accounts, taking loans without adequate collateral, and flouting banking rules. Some of these people are well-known business leaders, influential cronies, and benefactors of major political parties, and they have sufficient political capital to circumvent the central bank's disciplinary measures (if they are used against them). Their formidable power also indicates those regulatory bodies like the MOF and Parliamentary Committees are to a large extent beholden to their special interests.

(c) Regulatory forbearance with regard to liquidity requirement, loan classification, accounting standards, or capital adequacy can be ensured by bribing or offering lucrative private sector jobs to the senior officials of the MOF.

(d) By using political connections with the MOF, the Parliamentary Standing Committee, or Prime Minister's Office, one can successfully circumvent regulatory rules and restrictions.

As mentioned earlier, the BCA was first enacted in 1991 as part of the FSRP. The act provided for the licensing, supervision, and regulation of all banks.[52] The BCA also provided the legal basis for the central bank's regulatory and supervisory role in the entire banking system. However, the private sector considers the act against its interests. Right after the Act's amendment, the BAB and other prominent business associations (mainly the FBCCI) began a systematic campaign to further amend or simply end some of the more stringent rules and regulations. Organized business has successfully lobbied the political authorities in recent decades to relax, and in some cases completely reverse, the more stringent provisions in the act (prudential regulations in the process of repaying loans). In other cases (supervision of the central bank over internal management of PCBs), new rules have remained unchanged as compulsory formal laws in the book, but largely ignored by market actors in practice.

Non-compliance with the rules has been possible due to collusive linkages of these actors with the supervisory authorities (bureaucratic or political), at the highest levels of the hierarchy.

VI SUMMARY OF FINDINGS AND CONCLUDING OBSERVATIONS

This chapter, by deploying both quantitative data and qualitative political economy analysis, has attempted to understand the institutional weaknesses of the banking sector in Bangladesh, while primarily focusing on the institutional

---

[52] The Act has extensive provisions to ensure accountability and financial discipline within the banking system. The Act empowers the central bank to ensure that the banks observe: (a) 'strict

loopholes relating to PCBs. Our analysis reveals the following features of the banking sector in this aspect:

- While analysing the trend of key banking sector indicators over the past few decades, it appears that Bangladesh has made some important progress in terms of most of the indicators related to access, stability, efficiency, and depth of the banking system. However, the country in general is lagging behind other comparable developing countries in South Asia and Southeast Asia. Also, there has been a sharp rise in NPLs in recent years. High NPLs are considered a matter of concern for many Bangladeshi banks.

- Our analysis, based on interviews with key informants, reports published in print media, and other research findings, indicates a number of institutional inefficiencies in the banking sector. One such key institutional weaknesses is the lack of autonomy of the central bank and the influence of the MOF in designing/altering key policies and strategies of the sector.

- Our analysis also reveals the weak corporate governance of PCBs, under which PCBs act as closely held firms, that is mainly owned by a few large shareholders, who have strong control over the managers and where there are hardly any effective self-interested countervailing groups to prevent rampant corporate fraud and theft by the bank owners. The symptoms of weak governance have been reflected in frequent cross-lending and insider lending of PCBs based on personal connection/political influence, as well as in the strong influence of board directors in lending decisions. There is a prevalence of political patronage, favouritism and nepotism, crony capitalism, and state capture in the banking sector.

- Interestingly, despite such inefficiencies and institutional weaknesses, except in a few cases, we do not observe any massive case of financial sector crackdown or bankruptcy as the Government either directly intervenes with financial support or instructs the central bank and/or NCBs to do so. Such a practice, though safeguarding the interests of depositors and protecting the sector as a whole, does so through large-scale recapitalisation and at the cost of tax payers money.

- Sector-wide poor governance and institutional weaknesses, therefore, have weakened the financial base of the banking sector, primarily reflected in terms of inefficiency and NPLs. The consequences of this, among other things, are a high interest rate spread, continued fiscal burden, inefficiency

internal controls and good governance principle' in the management process, which include clearly defined authorities and responsibilities of the directors and the managers and 'rules covering conflicts of interests'; (b) transparent accounting policies and guidelines, as well as disclosure requirements; (c) standard capital adequacy requirements; and (d) standard loan classification and provisioning rules. It also provides the central bank with necessary sanctioning authorities, which include, 'power to impose financial penalties, to prohibit activities, to suspend and remove board members and managers, to remove banking licenses and to proscribe "insider and related party lending"'. The Act also specifies 'standards for licensing banks and financial institutions' (The Banking Companies Act, 1997, Government of Bangladesh).

in public spending, and large-scale capital flight, resulting in stagnant private investment, a slow pace of industrialisation, and rising inequality. All such consequences constrain the country's ability to attain the Sustainable Development Goals and act as an obstacle towards growth performance.

Based on the findings, a number of recommendations can be considered for improved governance and greater efficiency of the sector:

Central bank autonomy: As discussed, one of the key institutional weaknesses of the banking sector in Bangladesh is the lack of autonomy of the central bank in governing the sector. As a consequence, we observe the formulation of policies in an ad hoc manner and not taking required actions against different malpractices of commercial banks. The central bank's autonomy is therefore the pre-requisite for establishing good governance in the sector. In this context, it is needless to mention that such autonomy must be backed up with prudent management and an efficient workforce.

Modification of the BCA and strict adherence to it: Any amendment of the BCA must be made on the basis of economic considerations and without any political incentive. In addition, the existing act must be modified carefully to address the institutional weaknesses in terms of loan sanction, appointment of directors, penalty of defaulters, permission regarding establishing new banks, etc. A related policy would be to have supplementary policies for the provision of fresh loans where transparency should be the pre-requisite for granting any loan above a certain threshold.

Political commitment to penalise loan defaulters: Given the very high amount of NPLs, especially in recent years, and the political economy considerations behind this, there is no denying the fact that strong political commitment to penalise defaulters is necessary.

Discussion: Political Economy of Private Bank Governance in Bangladesh

Thorsten Beck

This short note accompanies the excellent chapter by Mirza Hassan, Sayema Haque Badisha, Towid Iqram Mahmood, and Selim Raihan on the performance and governance challenges of banks in Bangladesh. In their chapter, the authors compare the bank performance of Bangladeshi banks with banks in neighbouring countries and across different ownership groups within Bangladesh. They also point to serious regulatory and governance challenges within the banking system. In this note, I will complement their cross-country comparison of financial sector development with a discussion of how to interpret different indicators and a benchmarking model. I will also offer a broader discussion of the factors preventing further financial sector deepening in Bangladesh, and I will conclude with some additional proposals for how to overcome the governance challenge in Bangladesh' financial system.

Financial Sector Development in Bangladesh

An extensive theoretical and empirical literature has pointed to the critical functions of the financial system, including by (i) providing transaction services and thus enabling specialisation of labour; (ii) intermediating funds from savers to entrepreneurs; (iii) assessing investment projects ex-ante and monitoring borrowers ex-post, thus mitigating principal–agent conflicts; (iv) mitigating liquidity risks, allowing savers ready access to funds while enabling long-term investment; and (v) enabling investor cross-sectional and intertemporal risk diversification. An expansive literature has shown a positive relationship between financial development and economic growth, robust to reverse causation and omitted variable bias, and particularly strong in developing countries such as Bangladesh (see Popov, 2018, for a recent overview).

One key challenge when assessing the relationship between financial development and real sector outcomes, as well as when comparing financial sector development across countries and over time, is how to measure the efficiency and development of a country's financial sector. While theory points to specific channels and mechanisms, as discussed above, the empirical literature has not been able to map these different functions onto very specific empirical measures. Critically, several of these functions are complementary to each other: for example, the pooling and intermediating of savings goes hand in hand with the screening and monitoring of borrowers. Similarly, pooling and intermediating savings implies liquidity transformation. By offering payment services, banks learn about potential borrowers and thus get better at screening and monitoring them.

In the absence of variables capturing the individual functions of the financial sector, the literature has used crude proxy variables focusing on the size and activity of financial intermediaries and markets, most prominently private credit to GDP, which is the total claims of financial intermediaries on domestic private enterprises and households in an economy, divided by GDP. By capturing the total amount of financial intermediation by regulated intermediaries in the economy, this variable proxies for the total volume of intermediation. The main advantage of this indicator is that it is available for a large cross-section of countries and over longer time periods, as the underlying data (total credit outstanding and GDP) go back until 1960 for many countries. Confidence in the measure is further increased as it is significantly correlated with other indicators of the efficiency of the financial system, available for fewer countries and over shorter time periods, such as interest rate spreads and margins.

While academics have focused mostly on the facilitating role of the financial sector, which consists of mobilising funds for investment and contributing to an efficient allocation of capital in general, policymakers have often focused on financial services as a growth sector in itself, as captured by the contribution of the financial sector to GDP. However, it is important to distinguish between the importance of the financial system within overall value added in an economy and the support that the financial system provides for the real economy. A larger financial system can both support the real economy but also be a burden on the rest of the economy, by, for example, drawing talent away from the real economy (Kneer, 2013a, 2013b). Based on a sample of 77 countries for the period 1980–2007, Beck Degryse, and Kneer (2014) find that intermediation activities increase growth and reduce volatility in the long run, while an expansion of the financial sector along other dimensions has no long-run effect on real sector outcomes. One specific example is Nigeria, which liberated its financial sector in the late 1980s. Very low entry requirements and the high market premiums that could be earned with arbitrage activities in the foreign exchange markets explained why the number of banks tripled from 40 to nearly 120 in the late 1980s, employment in the financial sector doubled, and the contribution of the financial system to GDP almost tripled. At the same time, however,

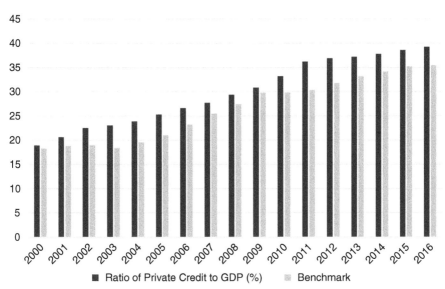

FIGURE 5.4 Benchmarking private credit to GDP in Bangladesh
Source: Author's calculations, based on World Bank data.

deposits in financial institutions and credit to the private sector, both relative to GDP, declined (see discussion in Beck, Cull, and Jerome, 2005).

Comparing financial sector development across countries and over time is made difficult by different and changing socio-demographic structures. One way to address this challenge is to construct a synthetic benchmark based on a panel regression model of many countries over time (see Barajas *et al.*, 2013 for further discussion). Among the explanatory variables included in this model are GDP per capita to proxy for demand-side effects, the young and old dependence ratio to proxy for demographic trends, total population to proxy for scale effects, and also year-fixed effects to control for global trends. This regression model makes it possible to predict financial sector indicators, such as private credit to GDP, for each country and year, and to compare it to the actual value. Figure 5.4 shows the actual and predicted value for private credit to GDP for Bangladesh for the years between 2000 and 2016. Strikingly, for all years, the actual value is above (though not by much) the value predicted by the socio-economic characteristics of Bangladesh.

What Drives Financial Sector Development?

Beyond socio-economic characteristics, financial sector development is critically influenced by the macroeconomic environment and the institutional and regulatory framework (see Beck, 2018 for an in-depth discussion and literature review). I will discuss each in turn.

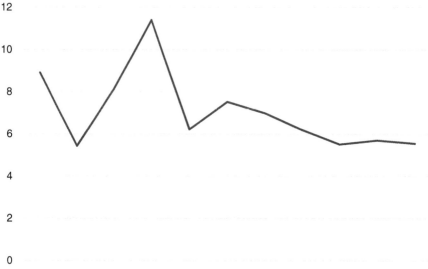

FIGURE 5.5 Inflation in Bangladesh (%)
Source: World Bank data.

Bangladesh has a long history of macroeconomic volatility, as illustrated in Figure 5.5. While the inflation rate has been relatively stable (between 5% and 7%) over the past three years, going back further shows variation between 2% and 16%. Given the intertemporal nature of financial contracts, macroeconomic volatility undermines the appetite and willingness of both lenders and borrowers to commit to long-term contracts.

Given the intertemporal and often abstract nature of financial contracts, the financial system is also among the most sensitive sectors in an economy to the institutions of contract enforcement and property right protection. A second important area is therefore the institutional framework, which encompasses the rights of secured and unsecured creditors, the quality of court systems and efficiency of contract enforcement, and the existence and quality of collateral registries. Table 5.3 presents three indicators from the World Bank's Doing Business database, showing the relative performance of Bangladesh compared to several other countries in the region. In most cases, Bangladesh lags behind the regional comparator countries.

The Governance Challenges in Bangladesh's Financial Sector

The situation as described in this chapter points to a lack of both market and supervisory discipline, and regulatory capture, not only by the state-owned banks but also by domestic private banks. Bank licences seem to be granted for

TABLE 5.3 *The institutional framework in Bangladesh*

	India	Pakistan	Sri Lanka	Bangladesh
Registering Property Score	43.55 (166)	45.63 (161)	51.87 (140)	28.90 (184)
Resolving Insolvency Score	40.84 (108)	59.86 (53)	45.05 (92)	28.20 (154)
Enforcing Contracts Score	41.19 (163)	43.49 (156)	41.16 (164)	22.21 (189)

Note: The figure in parenthesis indicates the ranking out of 190 countries.
Source: World Bank, Doing Business data.

politically connected entrepreneurs. There is a lack of de facto independence of the Bangladesh Bank, in addition to a long-standing 'default culture' (both for borrowers and banks), which explains the high level of NPLs. There is effectively no resolution of failed banks, but rather regulatory forbearance and recapitalisation. Finally, there is a lack of 'reputational agents', that is private institutions that provide information on bank performance and thus enable market discipline – except for the print media.

In 2006, I co-authored a paper assessing the development and stability challenges of the Bangladeshi banking system that painted a very similar picture (Beck and Rahman, 2006). One thing I noticed was that the financial and regulatory regime of high government guarantees and limited supervisory discipline resulted in high bank fragility. Moving to a regime with a stronger emphasis on market forces implies a carefully managed transition towards a more autonomous and powerful supervisory authority, privatisation of state-owned banks, and the establishment of a bank resolution framework, before one could move towards a more market-based banking system (Figure 5.6). In the 2006 paper, I made several policy suggestions, including (i) de jure and de facto autonomy of the Bangladesh Bank supervision from the Government, and (ii) complete divestiture of the Government from nationalised commercial banks. As Hassan, Bidisha, Mahmood, and Raihan eloquently describe, there has been no progress on (ii), and there has been a further deterioration in (i).

What to Do?

The governance challenges in the Bangladeshi banking system call for strong policy responses. But it is important to understand that de jure reforms might not – at least by themselves – address the governance challenges. While privatisation of state-owned banks reduces direct government ownership, it does not address governance and efficiency problems in the private banks. Evidence from other countries (such as Mexico in the 1990s) has shown that privatisation to insiders can create new frictions and fragility. While a strengthening of the de jure autonomy of the Bangladesh Bank is laudable, its de facto autonomy is endogenous to the political structure of the country. And while de jure bank governance can

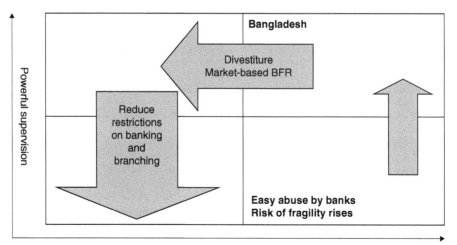

FIGURE 5.6 The interaction of government guarantees and supervisory approach
Source: Beck and Rahman (2006).

be strengthened by legislation, enforcement is again endogenous to the political environment. Finally, a stronger stance against large and politically connected defaulters is necessary, but hard to enforce in the current political state.

I therefore make two suggestions that, though they might not have as strong effects, do take into account political constraints. First, foreign banks are less open to political pressure and can help break the link between politicians, borrowers, and bankers, as the example of Central and Eastern Europe has shown (see, e.g. Gianetti and Ongena, 2009). Foreign banks can certainly have their shortcomings, as they often lack incentives and knowledge to reach out to the most opaque and smallest borrowers; however, evidence from Pakistan has also shown that foreign banks from geographically and culturally closer countries are less subject to such constraints (Mian, 2006). Second, strengthening private monitors (reputational agents) is an important reform item. Such reforms can include: (i) the creation of an FCA-style institution (separate from Bangladesh Bank) that focuses on bank conduct and supervision; (ii) steps to force more disclosure by banks beyond balance sheets and income statements, giving broader insights to depositors, media, and other stakeholders on their ownership structure and business; and (iii) improvements in the quality and governance of the accounting and auditing industry in Bangladesh. The latter can also include a mandatory rotation of auditors for banks.

Bangladesh has developed from 'history's basket case' (as it was referred to by Henry Kissinger) to a rapidly developing and emerging economy, with aspirations of becoming a middle-income country. The banking sector has not yet played the role in this process that it can play. The necessary reforms are clear; what is less clear is how to overcome the political constraints in order to implement them.

6

Institutional Dimensions of Tax Reforms in Bangladesh

Sadiq Ahmed

I DEVELOPMENT CONTEXT

Bangladesh showed strong resilience and dynamism by rising rapidly from the ruins of a war-devasted economy in 1972 that was characterised by a high incidence of poverty (around 80%), low per capita income (less than US$ 100), and badly damaged infrastructure. In 2015, Bangladesh crossed the threshold of the World Bank–defined lower middle-income country category. In financial year (FY) 2018, per capita income stood at US$ 1,767 in current prices, the poverty rate was estimated at around 22%, and GDP growth accelerated to 7.7%.[1] Buoyed by these accomplishments, Bangladesh now aspires to achieve upper middle-income country status and eliminate extreme poverty by FY2031. The target GDP growth rate from FY2019 to FY2031 is around 9% per year (Government of Bangladesh, 2019a).

II THE PUBLIC RESOURCE MOBILISATION CHALLENGE

A macroeconomic framework has been prepared in the context of the Government's perspective plan 2041 (PP2041).[2] The projections are built around major changes in policies and institutions. The public resource mobilisation task is particularly challenging: it seeks to raise total revenues as a share of GDP from 10% in FY2018 to 20% by FY2031 and to raise tax revenues from 8.7% to 17.4% over the same period. This amounts to a near doubling of the tax and total revenue mobilisation efforts over 12 years. The ability to

---

[1] There is a huge literature that looks at Bangladesh's development performance, explains the factors underlying success, and identifies the challenges moving forward. Ahmed (2015, 2017), Ahmed *et al.* (2015), and Mahmud *et al.* (2008) provide useful summaries of these issues. See also Chapter 2.

[2] Government of Bangladesh, 2019.

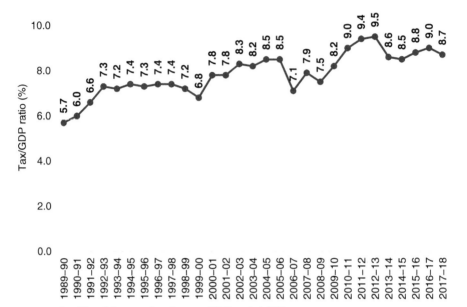

FIGURE 6.1 Trend in taxation (tax to GDP ratio) (%)
Source: Ministry of Finance, Government of Bangladesh.

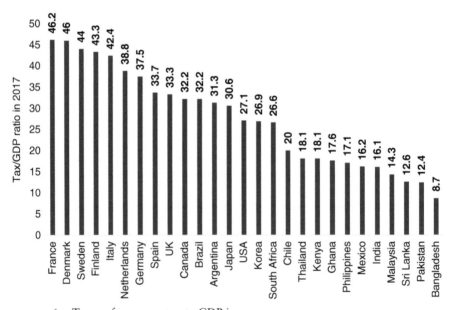

FIGURE 6.2 Tax performance: tax to GDP in 2017
Source: Organisation for Economic Cooperation and Development (OECD) Tax Database for OECD countries; respective ministries of finance for others.

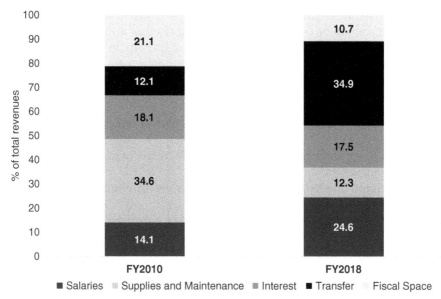

FIGURE 6.3 Declining fiscal space (% of total revenues)
Source: Ministry of Finance, Government of Bangladesh.

achieve the tax effort target will determine the success of the total revenue mobilisation effort.

As against these ambitious tax targets, the tax performance in recent years is summarised in Figure 6.1. The tax to GDP ratio has grown modestly over the past 28 years (3 percentage points on aggregate). In more recent years (FY2010–FY2018), the tax to GDP ratio has basically stagnated, fluctuating around 9% of GDP. This is the lowest tax performance in South Asia and among the lowest in the world (Figure 6.2). Clearly, the PP2041 tax and revenue targets are overwhelmingly large in relation to the actual performance so far and present a huge policy challenge.

One major consequence of this low tax effort is the increasingly constrained fiscal space. Fixed obligations like civil service salaries, defence spending, office supplies and materials, the interest cost of the public debt, and transfers (subsidies, pensions, local government grants, and transfers to state-owned enterprises) are increasingly eating up the low level of available revenue resources (taxes and non-tax revenues), leaving little space for the development spending needed to support GDP growth and human development (Figure 6.3).

III MAIN OBJECTIVES, METHODOLOGY, AND APPROACH OF THE CHAPTER

Main objectives: The main objective of this chapter is to provide a diagnostic analysis of institutional and political economy constraints to tax reforms and tax revenue mobilisation in Bangladesh. It is particularly surprising that tax revenues as a share of GDP have virtually stagnated at a low level of 9% of GDP, at a time when the economy has been most buoyant in terms of the GDP growth rate. This chapter seeks to provide an analysis of this development puzzle, with an emphasis on the institutional dimensions.

Specifically, the objectives are:

- to make a comparative assessment of the tax effort in Bangladesh vis-à-vis other countries;
- to identify and evaluate the institutional constraints to tax revenue generation in Bangladesh;
- to understand how political patronage affects the tax effort and impedes the implementation of tax reforms; and
- to suggest ways to improve tax performance in Bangladesh.

Methodology: The international literature recognises that there are a number of reasons why tax performance on average tends to be lower for low-income countries compared with high-income countries. However, there is no standard theoretical model or approach to the analysis of institutional constraints to tax performance in developing countries.

The commonly adopted approach is to combine standard economic determinants of taxes, such as per capita income, share of non-agricultural income, and easy tax handles like imports and mining, with institutional and governance variables, such as the corruption index and estimates of the role of institutional and governance variables using econometric techniques. This approach has been formalised by Bird *et al.* (2014). They argue that the traditional approach to estimating tax effort that uses per capita income and measures of tax handles is deficient in that it only looks at the supply-side factors, while ignoring the demand-side variables. The demand factors that reflect the society's willingness to pay must be included when carrying out a fuller analysis of the determinants of tax performance. The demand-side factors are essentially a number of institutional variables that impact on the society's willingness to pay and to comply voluntarily with the tax laws. The institutional variables include quality of governance, country risk, regulation of entry, income inequality, and fiscal decentralisation.

This chapter follows this approach and looks at both supply- and demand-side variables in explaining the tax performance in Bangladesh. Given time and resource constraints, a full-fledged model for tax effort along the lines advocated by Bird *et al.*, and its econometric estimation, is not possible. The analysis underlying this chapter is essentially based on a desk review of existing literature and an analysis of the Bangladesh tax database provided by the NBR and the Ministry of Finance, tax administration, and tax reforms. In looking at institutional constraints and implications for tax performance, it reviews the relevant literature and summarises the implications of the findings of relevant econometric studies for Bangladesh tax reforms and tax performance.

Drawing on the findings of international experience, it seeks to relate the various institutional and administrative constraints to explain the failures in tax performance and tax reforms in Bangladesh, and the way forward.

The analysis has benefited from the author's long-standing and deep understanding of the tax mobilisation effort and related institutions in Bangladesh, first while he was Sector Director of the Economic Management Team of the South Asia Region of the World Bank (2001–2006) and subsequently as Vice Chairman of the Policy Research Institute of Bangladesh (2009–present). In both capacities, the author has conducted policy analysis, dialogue, and discussions of tax reforms with officials of the National Board of Revenue (NBR) and the Ministry of Finance. He also has a solid understanding of various governance and institutional challenges of tax reforms in Bangladesh.

IV TAX MOBILISATION ISSUES IN DEVELOPING COUNTRIES: THE LESSONS FROM INTERNATIONAL EXPERIENCES

There is a huge literature on the analysis of tax performance in developing countries. The literature compares tax performance between developed and developing countries, and tax performance over time. It also shows how the tax policy debate and advice for developing countries has shifted over time, including the underlying economic theory and analysis. Importantly, it brings out the political economy and institutional dimensions of tax reforms that have tended to be neglected in early economic analysis and policy advice on tax mobilisation but that now occupy a dominant role in tax analysis and policy advice. Useful summaries include: Besley and Persson (2014); Bird *et al.* (2014); Bird (2012); Bird and Bahl (2008); Bird and Zolt (2003); Gordon and Lie (2005); and Tanzi and Zee (2001).

The main messages and lessons from the tax mobilisation experience of developing countries that have a bearing on the analysis of tax performance in Bangladesh include the following:

• On average, the tax to GDP ratio is substantially lower for developing countries (17–18%) as compared with developed countries (33–34% of GDP).
• There are wide variations in tax performance within each country group for both developing and developed countries.
• While on average the tax to GDP ratio tends to rise with per capita income, this is not a linear relationship. The relationship is statistically significant only for low-income countries.
• The tax structure shows that developed countries on average rely much more on personal income taxes, while developing countries rely substantially more on consumption and international trade taxes.
• Over the past 50 years or so, two major changes have happened to the tax structure globally: many more countries have adopted a value-added tax (VAT), and countries have tended to lower the average tax rates on income (the so-called flattening of statutory income tax rates).

- There is no theoretically determined optimal level of taxation. The size of tax collection depends on the political economy of government services and social preferences.
- All taxes in practice impose a cost on the economy, both in terms of tax collection costs and economic costs generated through the effects of taxation on economic behaviour. A good tax system should seek to reduce these costs to the extent possible.
- There is a growing recognition that the level and composition of taxes in any country is essentially an outcome of tax institutions and political economy, rather than determined by any theoretical model of taxation. Accordingly, tax reforms that ignore political economy and institutional factors are not likely to succeed.

V DETERMINANTS OF TAX PERFORMANCE IN BANGLADESH

A Supply-Side Variables

1 *Level of Development and Tax Handles*

The most fundamental issue is why the tax to GDP ratio has remained stagnant at around 9% of GDP over the past decade or so, despite rapid strides in GDP growth that have led per capita income to accelerate in current prices from US$ 800 in FY2010 to US$ 1,767 in FY2018. In constant 2010 dollars, this amounts to US$ 1,535 in FY2018, a healthy 8.5% annual growth in real per capita income. The very low tax performance of Bangladesh relative to countries at a similar per capita income level is striking (Figure 6.4), suggesting that Bangladesh is a negative outlier in the area of tax performance. This suggests that the low level of development is not the main concern but that there are other factors at play, including the Government's tax reform efforts, tax administration, and willingness to pay.

The tax performance model formalised by Bird *et al.* identifies several supply-side variables: per capita income; share of agriculture in GDP; size of the informal economy; access to natural resources; and share of trade in GDP. The latter two variables reflect the availability of easy tax handles.

The low per capita income relative to developed countries explains a part of the reason for the low tax to GDP ratio in Bangladesh. But, as noted, the low level of per capita income alone cannot explain the poor tax performance in Bangladesh because its tax to GDP ratio is only 50% of the average tax to GDP ratio in developing countries.

Regarding the roles played by the share of agriculture and the size of the informal economy, again they are a part of the factors that account for the low average tax ratio for Bangladesh relative to developed countries, but they do not explain the very low tax to GDP ratio for Bangladesh relative to other developing economies. Moreover, the GDP share of agriculture has fallen sharply over the years and continues to decline, while the share of the industrial

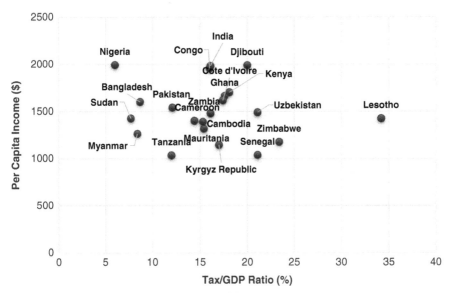

FIGURE 6.4 Tax performance in comparable countries in 2017 (per capita income US$ 1,000–US$ 2,000)
Source: World Bank World Development Indicators.

sector has grown substantially. For example, between FY2013 and FY2018, the GDP share of the industrial sector grew from 29% to 34%, and the share of agriculture fell from 17% to 14%, but the tax to GDP ratio did not pick up, but instead declined from 9.5% of GDP in FY2013 to 8.7% of GDP in FY2018. Indeed, the 2018 industrial sector share in Bangladesh (34%) is substantially higher than the average for low-income countries (25%), yet the tax performance is substantially weaker than the average for low-income economies.

Concerning the role of the informal economy, unfortunately reliable estimates of its size and changes over time are not available. Nevertheless, a priori it is likely to be an important contributor to the low tax performance in general. However, it is not very likely that the share of the informal economy is substantially higher in Bangladesh than the average for low-income economies, and therefore, it is unlikely to be a reason for the very low tax performance relative to countries with similar per capita income.

2 Tax Composition and Structure

The composition of Bangladesh tax revenues is shown in Figure 6.5. The structure of taxation in Bangladesh has improved significantly over the years. The share of income and domestic production/consumption taxation has increased, while the reliance on international trade taxation has declined. The introduction of the VAT in 1991 made a major difference to both improving the tax structure and increasing the tax to GDP ratio. Thus, the increased role of

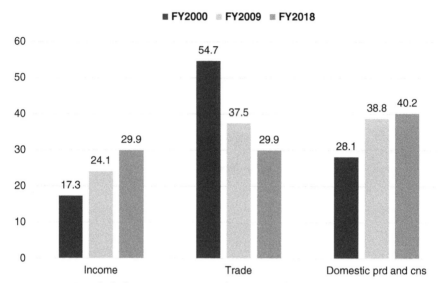

FIGURE 6.5 Bangladesh tax structure (% share in total taxes)
Source: Ministry of Finance, Government of Bangladesh.

domestic production/consumption taxation reflects the growing importance of
the VAT in revenue generation. This is a positive development; yet the revenue
yield of the VAT has been stagnant since FY2011 (Figure 6.6). When compared with the statutory VAT rate of 15%, the low yield is indicative of the
low productivity of the VAT.

A useful way of assessing the quality of the tax structure is to compare the
Bangladesh experience with other countries. Using data from the International
Monetary Fund's (IMF's) International Financial Statistics for the years 1996–
2001, Gordon and Li (2005) summarise the results of the international tax
structure by income groups, as illustrated in Table 6.1. The income groups
were selected from the World Bank classification of low-income (below US$
745); lower middle-income (US$ 746–2,975); upper middle-income (US$
2,979–9,205); and upper-income (greater than US$ 9,206) prevailing during
1996–2001. Although the data in the table are a bit outdated, it illustrates well
the major differences in the observed tax structure by income groups, which is
not likely to change much with updated data. However, the relative weakness
of the Bangladesh tax structure will likely be magnified.

Table 6.1 tells a useful story about the international experience with the
modernisation of the tax structure as income grows and development proceeds. The main messages are set out in the following paragraphs.

First, the survey confirms that the tax to GDP ratio correlates positively
with per capita income on average. Related to this, in order for the tax to GDP
ratio to increase with income growth, the structure of taxation should be such

TABLE 6.1 *Sources of government revenue, 1996–2001*

GDP per capita	Tax revenue (% of GDP)	Income taxes (% of total taxes)	Corporate income taxes (% of total income taxes)	Consumption and production taxes (% of total taxes)	International trade taxes (% of total taxes)
<US$ 745	14.1	35.9	53.7	43.5	16.4
US$ 746–2,975	16.7	31.5	49.1	51.8	9.3
US$ 2,976–9,205	20.2	29.4	30.3	53.1	5.4
All developing	17.6	31.2	42.3	51.2	8.6
>US$ 9,206	25.0	54.3	17.8	32.9	0.7
Bangladesh (FY2018)	8.7	29.9	51.0	40.2	29.9

Source: Gordon and Li (2005).

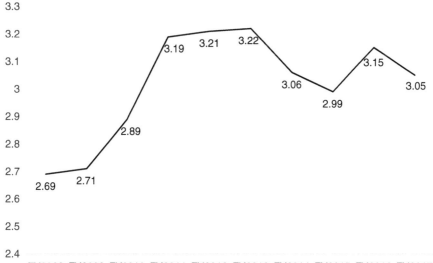

FIGURE 6.6 VAT revenue yield (% of GDP)
Source: Ministry of Finance, Government of Bangladesh.

that it responds well to income growth. In other words, the tax structure must be buoyant with respect to the expansion of economic activities, as reflected by the level of GDP.

Second, as development proceeds, the share of income taxes grows. Indeed, developed countries raise more than 50% of their revenues from income taxes.

The rationale for this is based on the need to have a tax structure that meets three desirable principles of taxation: the ability to pay; equity principles of taxation; and the buoyancy argument.

Third, developed and upper middle-income countries rely much more on personal income taxes relative to corporate taxes. Thus, developed countries obtain as much as 45% of their total tax revenues from personal income taxes; corporate taxes account for less than 10% of total tax collections. The rationale here is that unduly high taxation of the corporate sector would tend to reduce investment incentives and lead to capital flight, which would hurt growth.

Finally, as development proceeds, the revenue role of international trade taxes tends to disappear. Thus, it accounts for less than 1% of total tax revenues for high-income countries and around 5% for upper middle-income countries. Even lower middle-income countries get less than 10% of their tax revenues from international trade taxes. The rationale for this is that trade taxes tend to distort resource allocation, hurting exports, and breeding inefficiency within domestic production.

Against this international evidence, the Bangladesh tax structure has many shortcomings. Bangladesh continues to rely very heavily on international trade taxes (30%), as compared with less than 9% for all developing countries. Even the low-income countries on average get only 16% of their revenues from international trade taxes, which is nearly 60% lower than in Bangladesh. This heavy reliance of Bangladesh on international trade taxes is a seriously negative policy development and indicates the distortionary effect of the tax structure.

The improvement in the performance of income taxes is a positive outcome. It is now roughly comparable with the average for low-income economies. But there are a number of major concerns. Although the share of income taxes from the corporate sector has been falling, it still accounts for more than 50% of income taxes. Corporate tax rates vary considerably by activities, with a heavy load on a few cash cows. Some sectors like mobile phone services, tobacco, and banks are required to pay hefty profit tax rates ranging from 40% to 45%. They account for most of the corporate tax yield. There are many exemptions that lower the average yield of corporate taxes.

A major issue of the tax structure is the very low yield from personal income taxes (Ahmed, 2015). Very few people pay personal income taxes. Bangladesh does not have a universal income tax base, owing to exemptions of many sources of income and the very low taxation of capital gains. In addition, tax compliance is very low. The poor performance of personal income taxation is one of the primary reasons for the low tax buoyancy in Bangladesh, which has constrained the overall tax performance. Sadly, this also speaks volumes about the inequitable nature of the tax structure. Income inequality has grown substantially in Bangladesh, but the collection of personal income taxes has not increased much.

Finally, as noted, the productivity of the VAT has been stagnant, owing to many exemptions and inadequate coverage. This is yet another factor that explains the low buoyancy of the Bangladesh tax structure.

B Willingness to Pay: Demand-Side Issues

Bird *et al.* (2014) have argued convincingly that 'a more legitimate and responsive state appears to be an essential precondition for a more adequate level of tax effort in developing countries'. They capture this effect of social and political institutions on tax performance by developing a fuller model of determinants of tax performance that includes the traditional supply-side variables as well as demand-side variables. Using cross-country data for mean values for 1990–1999 for 110 developing countries, they estimate the tax performance model (tax to GDP ratio) using a various mix of supply- and demand-side variables. The structure of the economy (measured by the GDP share of non-agriculture sectors), representing the supply side, and quality of governance (measured by the World Bank governance indicators and the International Country Risk Guide (ICRG) index), representing the role of institutions or demand-side variables, yield the most robust results. They conclude that institutions are a major determinant of tax performance.

Other econometric studies provide similar supportive evidence about the role of institutions in explaining tax performance (Ghura, 1998; Gupta, 2007; Nguyen, 2015; Ricciuti *et al.*, 2019). Ghura (1998) focuses directly on the role of corruption in explaining tax performance in African countries and finds that corruption is significantly and negatively correlated with tax performance. Using panel data over 25 years for 105 developing countries, Gupta (2007) finds a negative contribution of corruption to tax performance and a positive contribution of political stability. Nguyen (2015) finds evidence that institutional quality has a significant positive impact on tax performance in low-income and lower middle-income countries. Ricciuti *et al.* (2019), in their empirical research focusing on the role of political institutions in building tax capacity, find evidence that the existence of effective constraints on the head of the government makes the tax system more accountable and transparent.

The governance challenges facing Bangladesh are well known. For example, an international ranking of corruption prepared by Transparency International puts Bangladesh at the bottom 15% of the countries ranked (149 out of 175 countries) for 2018. The World Bank governance indicators (2017) rank Bangladesh as follows: voice and accountability (bottom 30th percentile); political stability and absence of violence/terrorism (bottom 10th percentile); government effectiveness (bottom 22nd percentile); regulatory quality (bottom 21st percentile); rule of law (bottom 28th percentile); and control of corruption (bottom 19th percentile). These results suggest that there are major governance issues and challenges in Bangladesh that might serve to constrain tax performance. Drawing from the econometric evidence summarised above, it is most likely that corruption and other elements of weak governance are major factors for the low tax collection in Bangladesh.

The adverse impact of corruption on Bangladesh's economic management is well recognised. It tends to operate through four main channels: land markets; financial markets; public procurement; and taxation. The corruption in tax administration is pervasive. This is a major factor underlying low tax compliance in all areas of taxation, which is a major constraint to tax revenue mobilisation.

The weakness on the demand side raises an important political economy issue. Are Bangladeshis unwilling to pay taxes because they do not feel that resources are used effectively? This is an empirical question that needs further research before an answer can be provided, but some preliminary observations can be made.

There is at least some degree of truth that higher tax collection is possible if citizens can see more and better public service provision in areas related to health, education, water, sanitation, and drainage. In developed countries, these services are typically provided by local government institutions. Bangladesh, on the other hand, is heavily centralised. While there are elected local government institutions, they are highly resource constrained in the absence of fiscal decentralisation (Ahmed, 2017). Local government institutions collectively raise a meagre 0.16% of GDP as tax resources in Bangladesh (Ahmed, 2017), as compared with an average of 6.4% of GDP in industrial countries and 2.3% of GDP in developing countries (Bahl, Linn, and Wetzel, 2013). Better services can also provide greater resource mobilisation through greater use of cost recovery policies (non-tax revenue measures). Strengthening of local government institutions and the associated fiscal decentralisation associated with more and better basic public services can certainly play a major role in increasing tax and non-tax revenues in Bangladesh.

However, there is also evidence that the demand for public services is growing in Bangladesh, and the Government has been making some efforts to respond to them. The budget making process involves considerable public consultation with various citizens groups, including business, non-governmental organisations, research and think tank institutions, and the media. This is conducted at quite a high level, involving the Finance Minister. The budget is also debated in the Parliament. The public consultation process is fairly open and considerable discussions about expenditure priorities and tax reform options are aired in these consultation process. The importance of increasing allocations for health, education, social protection, and infrastructure are raised every year. In response, the Government has done a fairly good job in keeping broad expenditure priorities focused on the development agenda. The Government has also protected total public expenditure as a share of GDP from falling despite shortfalls in revenues by running a budget deficit that is financed by foreign and domestic borrowing. This deficit has grown slightly over the past 10 years but is now capped at around 5% of GDP as a part of the Government's self-imposed fiscal discipline.

The Government's response to the need for tax reforms has also been positive in recent years, with as many as three reform efforts in the past eight years, but implementation has lagged behind due to political economy and administrative capacity considerations. These are discussed in detail in the next section.

The budget debate and discussions in the Parliament are less productive than they could be because the Parliament is usually dominated by the government in power. Tax issues are often raised and discussed but not in a forceful way that could bring about major changes. Additionally, the time when the budget is shared with the Parliament is less than a month before the current fiscal year ends and the new fiscal year begins. The budget is already approved by the cabinet and the prime minister, and the documents are printed. This leaves very little time and opportunity for any substantive budget debate and discussion in the Parliament. This is one area where the budgetary consultation process could be improved. One possible option is to involve the appropriate Parliamentary Committee responsible for oversight on budget and finance issues early in the process of budget making, to get timely inputs into the process. Another possible step would be for the Parliamentary Committee on budget and finance to request national researchers to prepare background papers on tax and expenditure issues and to discuss these with the committee early in the budget process. They could also seek technical assistance on the draft budget as inputs to their own review and discussions.

The Cabinet review of the draft budget could also be made more productive by requiring each Cabinet minister to make a presentation on their development targets and objectives for the year, and how adequate the proposed resource allocations are. Stronger participation by the Cabinet members in the budgetary process could be very useful in bringing out the internal tensions and the challenges posed by the revenue constraints upfront, so as to allow proper policy choices to be made, including the need for meaningfully strengthening revenue mobilisation. The Cabinet could also seek a technical briefing by NBR on the reasons for stagnant tax performance, and possible solutions.

VI TAX REFORM EFFORTS AND IMPLEMENTATION

Governance constraints not only impinge on citizens' willingness to pay and contribute to the low regard for tax compliance, they also adversely affect tax reform efforts and the quality of tax administration. The tax reform experience in Bangladesh provides evidence that weak governance has been a major constraint on tax performance.

A Major Tax Reforms

A large part of the reason for the low tax performance and weak and stagnant revenue structure is the relative absence of tax reforms in Bangladesh.

Tax reforms have generally taken a back seat in Bangladesh. The first and only successful major tax reform was carried out in 1991, when the VAT was introduced. This was the only tax reform that succeeded, despite considerable hiccups. The introduction of the VAT also coincided with a major reduction in trade protection, involving the removal of most quantitative restrictions and a cut in customs duties during the 1990s (Ahmed and Sattar, 2019). Since then, the tax system has been occasionally tweaked, particularly in the area of international trade taxes over the 2000–2010 period, but the underlying motivation was to reform the heavily protected trade regime often as condition for access to international aid. These second-phase reforms of the customs duties did not yield much benefit in terms of a reduction in trade protection. Indeed, once the heavily protected trade regime was brought down to more moderate levels during the first phase of trade and investment deregulation in the 1990s, trade taxes re-emerged as a major tool for revenue mobilisation based on the introduction of a complex system of regulatory and supplementary duties (Ahmed and Sattar, 2019).

The Government sought to re-engage in tax reforms in FY2011, when it announced a major Tax Modernisation Plan (NBR, 2011). This reform was a part of the FY2011 budget, although this was not converted into a law. The Government's Sixth Five-Year Plan incorporated the main features of the Tax Modernisation Plan in articulating its macroeconomic framework and associated policy reforms. This was a fairly ambitious reform effort that sought to modernise the Bangladesh tax system, including reforms of tax laws, tax institutions, tax administration, and capacity building. The record shows little progress in its implementation: some limited progress was achieved in the computerisation of VAT administration, but overall tax administration remains as constrained as before.

A third attempt at tax reform happened in 2012, prodded by the IMF. As a part of its Extended Credit Facility agreement with the IMF, the Government adopted a new VAT reform act, called the 'VAT and Supplementary Duty Act 2012', which aimed at modernising and expanding the scope of the VAT. The reform promised to improve the efficiency of VAT collection and to raise substantial new revenues. However, the 2012 VAT Law remains on paper only and has not been implemented, in view of opposition from politically well-connected vested interest groups.

Finally, the new government elected in 2018 has now announced another round of tax reform in the National Budget FY2020 (Government of Bangladesh, 2019b). It has adopted the PP2041 as the long-term development vision and seeks to initiate implementation of the underlying macroeconomic and fiscal framework. In this regard, it has acknowledged the dismal tax performance in the past and seeks to change this by setting a lofty goal of increasing the tax to GDP ratio by an unprecedented 3% of GDP in one year. This massive tax target is to be achieved by focusing on the implementation of a revised version of the 2012 VAT Law and by strengthening income tax administration. Preliminary assessment of the proposed tax reforms suggests that the proposed tax reforms are inadequate and will not yield the desired revenue outcome (Ahmed, 2019). There may be some marginal improvements in the tax to GDP ratio, but a substantial improvement will not be possible based on the inadequate reform proposals. The budget did not specify what institutional reforms will be undertaken to help mobilise such a massive increase in the tax to GDP ratio. Even the revised VAT 2012 proposal was not well defined in terms of which VAT rate would apply to which activities, and how it would be administered.

B Discretionary and Discriminatory Tax Treatment

Although the only successful major tax reform happened in 1991, in the context of the annual budget cycle, the tax laws/rules/regulations are invariably modified to introduce new measures or to provide exemptions or special tax treatments for activities or entities. This is most prevalent in the area of customs duties and the VAT. These annual interventions are mostly conveyed through the Statutory Regulatory Order (SRO). While it is understandable that budget management needs flexibility and reform measures are needed to increase revenues, the main issue with these annual interventions is that they are not based on proper analysis of the revenue and resource allocation effects of the interventions. More often than not, tax measures are *ad hoc* and based on easy tax handle considerations. For example, the annual changes in income tax measures tend to target easy handles such as tobacco, mobile telephone operators, and the banking sector. The VAT/customs duties tend to target imports. Indeed, to compensate for the revenue and protection loss from tariff reforms, a range of special supplementary duties and regulatory duties have mushroomed, which has offset the positive effects of tariff reforms on resource allocation, seriously distorted trade incentives, and hurt exports (Ahmed and Sattar, 2019). Furthermore, the reduction in the predictability of tax laws is an important constraint on the investment climate for the private sector.

Importantly, the introduction of exemptions and special tax treatment of activities/entities not only dilutes the transparency and predictability of tax policies, it substantially reduces the effectiveness of the tax base and is a major factor for lowering the revenue yields of the tax system. In most instances, these exemptions and special treatments, and often new budget measures, especially those related to trade taxes, are dictated by the political power of the beneficiaries. The potential revenue loss and adverse consequences for resource allocation (especially through the distortion of trade policy) are of no consequence. The large prevalence of discretionary and discriminatory tax interventions also creates room for corrupt practices by the staff of the NBR.

The way SROs reduce the transparency and predictability of the tax system is illustrated dramatically by a review of customs duty–related SROs issued between FY2015 and FY2019. As many as 926 SROs were introduced, each aimed at providing a special benefit to a target group. A sample from this long list of SROs is provided in Annex 6.1, to give a flavour of the kind of negotiated settlements that happen in taxation in Bangladesh. In most cases, these special treatments were allowed as a response to political lobbies by the beneficiary group. There are similar SROs related to income tax, the VAT, and regulatory/supplementary duties. The SROs are also a good illustration of the absence of systematic tax policy analysis. The SROs are mostly introduced to benefit politically well-connected groups: there is almost no concern about what this does to resource allocation or tax collection. This *ad hoc* approach to tax policy and tax administration is a serious problem that must be addressed in order to modernise the tax system in Bangladesh.

C Political Economy of Tax Reforms

The absence of significant tax reforms in Bangladesh despite an overall buoyant economy and the growing fiscal constraint on development is a serious problem that threatens to undermine the long-term sustainability of development progress. The half-hearted attempts with the implementation of the 2011 Tax Modernisation Plan, the inability to implement the 2012 VAT Law, and the inadequacy of the latest attempt to reform the tax system in the FY2020 budget suggest a combination of inadequacy of political will and a lack of readiness to tackle the tax challenge. The transparency and predictability of the tax system is further complicated by the introduction of new budget measures every year on an *ad hoc* basis along, with new exemptions and special tax treatments.

The tax literature recognises the political nature of taxation (John, 2006; Brautigam *et al.*, 2008; Prichard, 2010; Bird *et al.*, 2014; Besley and Persson, 2014; Ricciuti *et al.*, 2019). One important piece of research in the context of Bangladesh that has sought to analyse the tax reform impasse and the frequent use of *ad hoc* tax measures through SROs by applying the political economy lens is that by Hassan and Prichard (2014). Their paper argues that the prevailing tax system in Bangladesh is the outcome of a complex set of negotiations between formal and informal institutions based on micro-level incentives for each of the political actors. As a result, the tax system is highly informal, is administered manually rather than on an automated computerised basis, and involves high levels of discretion. This dysfunctional system is sustained because it serves the interests of powerful political, economic, and administrative actors. Specifically, 'the current system delivers low and predictable tax rates to businesses, provides extensive discretion and opportunities for corruption to the tax administration, and acts as an important vehicle for political elites to raise funds and distribute patronage and economic rents' (Hassan and Prichard, 2014, p. v). Reform efforts are constrained by the need to preserve this 'political settlement'. Reform outcomes are weak or they fail because the resultant negotiations that seeks to reconcile the interests of the various competing groups with the need for reforms cause the reforms to be either abandoned or weakened considerably. In this framework, the SROs are simply instruments for favour distribution through discretionary and discriminatory application of the tax laws and rules and regulations.

The research from Bangladesh and other international experiences support the hypothesis that tax reforms are essentially political in nature and cannot succeed without reform champions at the highest level. They also recognise the strong link between economic and political governance, state tax capacity, and revenue mobilisation. As with any major reform, there are winners and losers from tax reforms. The stakes are particularly high with tax reforms because substantial amounts of money are involved. The beneficiaries of the present tax system in Bangladesh (political elites, big business, and the NBR administration) are happy with the status quo. The influence of these powerful lobbies will need to be offset by reform champions within the political system and in the civil administration.

This political economy lens can help us understand why the 1991 VAT Law was successfully implemented while other tax reform efforts failed. The successful implementation of the 1991 VAT Law and hurdles faced with the implementation of the Tax Modernisation Plan 2011 and the 2012 VAT reform experiences are also consistent with the lessons from international experience that suggest that tax reforms cannot succeed if they are donor-driven or led by international advisers (Dom and Miller, 2018). Tax reforms must be led by the Government, with the Finance Minister in the lead, strong support by the NBR, and solid political backing from the head of the government. It must also have strong technical foundations based on sound background research, and implementation support in terms of suitable administrative infrastructure, including ICT solutions.

The 1991 VAT reform met all of these conditions. The reform was home grown. The technical work was led by senior staff of NBR and supported by technical assistance from the IMF. Overall policy leadership was provided initially by a technocrat Finance Minister and subsequent ministers carried through the work to the implementation stage. An IMF fiscal expert of Bangladeshi origin was procured and stationed in Dhaka on a long-term basis. Most importantly, the reform had the political backing from all heads of the government involved from the design to the implementation phases.

The 2011 Tax Modernisation Plan was grounded in the recognition by the Finance Minister that the tax revenue was inadequate and needed to be increased substantially. Accordingly, the Tax Modernisation Plan targeted an increase in revenue by 4 percentage points of GDP over a four-year period (FY2011–FY2015). The Plan was home grown and developed by a reform-minded Chairman of the NBR. He had the initial support of the Finance Minister, who was enthused by the prospect of substantial gains in tax revenues. But this support was more personal than institutional. The nature of the reforms envisaged required the full support of the prime minister and the cabinet, but a broad-based discussion of the reforms with the prime minister and the cabinet did not happen. Importantly, technical preparations were inadequate. There was also absence of ownership at the NBR staff level. Most unfortunately, the champion of the NBR Modernisation Plan 2011, the NBR chairman, was replaced by a new chairman in 2013. Unlike in the case of the VAT Law 1991, where the reform momentum continued despite the change in government because of a continuity of core NBR staff who were pushing the reform, the change in NBR leadership, combined with the absence of strong support from the political leadership, caused the 2011 reforms to fail.

The VAT 2012 reform was mainly pushed by the IMF under the Extended Structural Adjustment Facility programme. Within NBR, the Member VAT Policy and Member Customs were the main champions. There was also a solid technical assistance programme to help with the design of the new law and its implementation. At the political level, the Finance Minister provided support. The initial delay was caused by the need for adequate preparatory work. Finally, when the NBR was basically ready to launch implementation in the context of the FY2018 budget, it faltered because of strong opposition from the retail-level trading community, represented by the politically powerful and well-organised Federation of Bangladesh Chambers of Commerce and Industry (FBCCI). This opposition was grounded in the reality that except for the large retail units, most retail-level traders are a part of the informal economy and are therefore out of the tax net. The introduction of the new VAT Law would require the exposure of transactions and earnings to NBR through proper record-keeping. In this way, they could be exposed to higher tax obligations and/or rent-seeking intrusions by the tax officials. The prime minister decided to postpone the implementation decision in view of the strong FBCCI opposition and advice from the prime minister's political party about the potential downside risks to the party in the then upcoming 2018 national elections, which were scheduled for the end of December 2018.

The half-hearted attempt to reform the tax system in the FY2020 budget is largely explained by the inadequacy of understanding regarding the complexity of the tax challenge and by an absence of strategic thinking. The installation of a new government elected in 2018 and involving a new Finance Minister provided a major opportunity for Bangladesh to rethink its tax reforms. As noted, there was indeed some positive intent. But the review of the FY2020 budget document shows that this positive political intent is not backed by a well-defined reform strategy and adequate associated specific reforms of tax policies and tax administration. Most unfortunately, instead of implementing the well thought out 2012 VAT Law in its original form, and taking advantage of the administrative progress already made, the new Finance Ministry team developed a hodgepodge variant of the 2012 VAT Law that was not properly studied or analysed in terms of revenue impact and the nature of the administrative preparations that would be required. Additionally, ambitious tax targets for personal income tax yields were set that had no policy or administrative reform content beyond the idea of recruiting additional income tax collectors. This is unfortunately a reflection of the 'policing approach' to tax collection that has proven to be the bane of the income tax system, as further explained below. So, political willingness alone is not enough. It must be backed by sound tax policy analysis and administrative reforms to improve the tax system.

D Tax Administration Issues

1 Taxation of Personal Income

It is well known that weak tax administration can be a serious constraint to tax resource mobilisation in developing countries. An excellent summary of these issues and lessons learnt from country experiences is contained in Bird (2015). A particular challenge is the ability to administer efficient and progressive personal income taxation. Thus, a major difference between developing and developed countries is the much larger share of personal income taxation in total taxation. Bangladesh collects a mere 1.3% of GDP as personal income taxes (FY2018), and this ratio has grown only marginally (it was 1% of GDP in FY2010), even as per capita income more than doubled in nominal dollar terms and increased by 92% in real dollar terms over FY2010–FY2018.

In addition to numerous legal exemptions, at the heart of the personal income taxation problem is the low level of compliance. The estimated compliance rate is a mere 12% (Ahmed, 2019). Owing to exemptions and low tax compliance, actual tax yield from personal income has grown only slowly, from a low yield of 0.41% of GDP in FY2000 to about 1% of GDP in FY2018. As compared to this low revenue yield, depending upon the level of income, the legal tax rates vary from 10% to 30% plus (when the so-called wealth taxes are added). The potential loss of revenue from exemptions and low compliance is illustrated in Table 6.2 under two scenarios. The first scenario considers an effective average tax rate of 10% on the income share of the top 10th percentile. This group has average income much higher than the tax exempted level of Bangladeshi Taka (BDT) 2,50,000. The second scenario is a bit more ambitious and involves an effective average tax rate of 15% on the income share of the top 10th percentile. With proper reforms of the income tax that would not require any increase in tax rates but better implementation, including a move towards the concept of a universal income tax base with minimum exemptions and an effective tax administration mechanism, the yield from personal income tax could reach 3.8% of GDP under Scenario 1 and 5.7% of GDP under Scenario 2. Compared to these personal income tax potential scenarios, the very low actual yield dramatically illustrates the very low productivity of the personal income tax system.[3]

---

[3] Tax productivity is defined as the ratio of actual tax collection to potential tax collection.

TABLE 6.2 *Personal income tax productivity*

HIES	Income share of top 10% (10%)	Effective tax rate (10%)	Potential income tax (% of GDP)	Effective tax rate (15%)	Potential income tax (% of GDP)	Actual income tax (% of GDP	Tax productivity (%) (10% av. effective rate)	Tax productivity (%) (15% av. effective rate)
2000	38.1	10	3.8	15	5.7	0.41	10.8	7.2
2005	37.6	10	3.7	15	5.6	0.60	16.2	10.7
2010	35.9	10	3.6	15	5.4	0.95	26.4	17.6
2016	38.2	10	3.8	15	5.7	1.00	29.0	19.3

Source: Author's estimates, based on income distribution data from Household Income and Expenditure Survey (HIES) and personal income tax data from the Ministry of Finance.

Tax evasion is particularly large at the highest levels of income. A range of factors explain this tax evasion problem, including legal tax exemptions and loopholes, political connections, corrupt practices, complexities of tax assessment and collection, inefficient tax audits, and high marginal rates of taxation. Reform efforts have focused on enlarging the tax base by bringing more taxpayers into the tax base through electronic tax IDs, annual tax fairs, and cross checks on bank accounts, utility bills, home rentals, and import transactions, etc. To improve the productivity of audits, a Large Taxpayer Unit has also been established to monitor the tax returns of large payers. These reform efforts have yielded some results. The number of registered personal income taxpayers has increased noticeably (Table 6.3), but the average nominal yield per taxpayer has been erratic, with no discernible pattern. The average return per taxpayer has fallen when accounting for inflation.

These results suggest two major concerns with the income tax mobilisation drive. First, while the effort to bring more people into the income tax net is laudable, the productivity in terms of impact on revenue yields has been small. Second, the stagnant or declining nominal yield per taxpayer suggests that tax returns are not able to capture the tax benefits of the growth of personal income at a time where the economy is highly buoyant and there is evidence of a growing concentration of personal income from HIES data. The evidence would seem to support the contentions of two populist perceptions: first, that the tax net is focused on capturing low-income taxpayers while many large-income earners remain outside the net; and second, the large-income taxpayers that enter the net end up paying low amounts through collusion with income tax collectors.

Tax evasion is an outcome of three major factors. First, according to the Labor Force Survey of 2017, some 85% of the workforce is in the informal sector and most workers are outside the tax net. Second, most of the rich elites are well connected with the government in power and are able to escape taxes, either by not filing or by sending in low returns that are not subject to

TABLE 6.3 *Personal income tax collection efforts*

	No of tax payers (ml)	Tax collection (BDT, bl)	Average yield (BDT)
FY2011	1.231	99	80,366
FY2012	1.233	125	101,079
FY2013	1.369	167	122,075
FY2014	1.363	119	87,109
FY2015	1.627	126	77,173
FY2016	1.721	173	100,691
FY2017	2.188	209	95,612

Source: NBR.

audits owing to the political connection. Third, it is well known that many taxpayers are able to get away with low returns by making informal deals with tax collectors. The manual approach to tax assessment makes this process so much easier.

A serious problem with tax administration in Bangladesh is the complexity of the tax collection process and the harassment of the tax payer. Tax filing is not user-friendly, simple, or automated. One example of a bad feature of the present tax design that discourages tax filing and leads to harassment and corruption is the requirement to file a wealth statement based on balancing income and expenditure along with the tax return. Many taxpayers find this requirement onerous and it discourages them from filing taxes because of the fear that this will lead them to experience various forms of harassment. It also encroaches on citizens' privacy. While the Government has the right to tax income, it is debatable whether citizens should be required to explain how they spend their money.

The value of this dubious requirement in terms of tax collection is negligible and on a net basis negative because it discourages tax filing. Importantly, there is a common perception that this feature creates incentives for income tax officers to harass taxpayers and extract a bribe. As an example, income tax collections and compliance are very high in the USA, where there is no such requirement to submit a wealth statement based on a matching of income and expenditure. On the negative side, in Bangladesh, the returns from personal income taxes as a share of GDP have hardly grown over the eight years from FY2010 to FY2018, despite a near doubling of real per capita income in dollar terms. It is obvious that the wealth and income expenditure statements have not helped increase revenues but have tended to support revenue leakages through non-filing and collusion between taxpayers and tax collectors.

2 Corporate Taxation
In the case of corporate taxes, similar problems exist as for income taxes. Most small enterprises are not registered and therefore are not a part of the tax net. Even for firms that are registered, the compliance rate is only 21%

(Ahmed, 2019). The low compliance rates reflect a combination of political power of many business houses that are well connected with the Government, and informal settlements between companies and tax officials. The corporate tax rates vary considerably by activities. There is a zero rate for many sectors or activities that are either exempted from taxes or have been given tax holidays for a number of years. Positive rates range from a low of 15% to a high of 45%. The NBR has targeted a few cash cows and slapped them with high tax rates: tobacco (45%); mobile telephone companies (40%); and banks and insurance companies (40–42.5%). Tobacco and mobile telephone companies are already heavily taxed through the excise, customs duties, and VAT instruments. Every year during the formulation of the annual budget, there is extra scrutiny to determine how much additional revenues can be extracted from these companies either through corporate taxation or by taxing their inputs. There is very little analysis to understand the implications of the existing corporate tax structure on incentives, including for foreign direct investments. Tax administration is cumbersome and time-consuming. The burdensome nature of tax filing has been identified as a major factor for the high-cost nature of doing business in Bangladesh, and as a constraint on improving the investment climate (Ahmed, 2017).

An added problem is the large informal economy. Most small and micro enterprises escape the tax net because they operate outside the formal system and are not registered with the Government, either through business licences or through a tax identification number. The fear of taxation in terms of harassment is so large that small firms prefer to stay informal and forgo many benefits of government support programmes, including access to formal credit. In this regard, the tax system may work as an important deterrent to the growth of small enterprises and employment.

3 Implementation of the VAT

Problems of tax administration are also acute in the case of the VAT. The many exemptions and the inability to extend the VAT fully to the retail level, many services and to small and micro enterprises, along with evasion and tax administration inefficiencies, have sharply lowered the productivity of the VAT (Mansur et al., 2011; Ahmed, 2013). Even for firms that are registered, the compliance rate is estimated at 12% (Ahmed, 2019). The present VAT system is very inefficient and is characterised by low productivity. Cross-country comparisons show that this productivity is among the lowest when Bangladesh is compared with Thailand, Vietnam, Sri Lanka, Nepal, India, China, Indonesia, Philippines, and Pakistan (Mansur et al., 2011). The factors that contribute to this low productivity include multiple rates, large exemptions, tax evasion, and inefficiencies in VAT administration. These administrative inefficiencies include: cumbersome tax filing; absence of a centralised registration system leading to multiple registration; a weak and burdensome audit system; and the lack of a modern computerised VAT system (Mansur et al., 2011; Ahmed, 2013).

As noted earlier, in recognition of these difficulties, and prodded by the IMF, in 2012 the Government enacted the new VAT Law. The Law simplified and modernised the VAT, along with provisions for major improvements in VAT administration, including a shift from manual to electronic filing, a voluntary approach to tax compliance, broadening of the tax base, a single registration for each taxpayer, the use of the invoice credit method for tax assessment, and a simplified VAT refund system (Ahmed, 2013). Substantial technical assistance was arranged to prepare for the implementation of the new law. Between 2013 and 2017, good progress was made in preparing for the implementation. The draft budget for FY2017/FY2018 was prepared with a view to implementing the new VAT Law. But, as noted, the implementation was postponed on political grounds.

4 Implementation of Customs Duties
The implementation of taxes on international trade is more organised and better administered. Modernisation of the customs system started in 1994 with the adoption of the Automated System for Customs Data (ASYCUDA) of the United Nations Conference on Trade and Development (UNCTAD). Bangladesh has sought to follow through with the various updates of the ASYCUDA. Progress has also been made on import valuation. Several reforms have been implemented to speed up and simplify the customs clearance process, including rolling out the Authorised Economic Operator programme, initiating implementation of a National Single Window, the establishment of a National Enquiry Point, and the development of the Advance Ruling System. A new Customs Act is also being prepared. Nevertheless, many problems remain. On the revenue mobilisation side, the main problem is tax evasion based on collusive behaviour between importers and the customs staff. This is a governance challenge that permeates the tax administration. Additional issues emerge for private investment in terms of high transaction costs of doing business at ports. Despite progress in simplifying clearance procedures and valuation, the transaction costs remain high, as indicated by the World Bank's Ease of Doling Business indicators.

5 Tax Administration Capacity
A generic problem in tax administration is low tax capacity. The NBR lacks autonomy and is run like any other government department; it is staffed by civil servants. Its primary focus is tax collection through policing and threats: there is no concept of tax service or seeking voluntary compliance through user-friendly approaches.

There is very little capacity to undertake tax policy analysis (PRI, 2013). Tax changes are made in almost all budgets. There is little analysis of the revenue and resource allocation impact of these changes. This lack of separation of tax policy and tax collection, and the absence of capacity of the NBR to implement proper tax policy and analysis, is a severe institutional constraint that has hurt fiscal policy development.

Numerous efforts to upgrade the capacity of the NBR to improve tax collection and tax policy analysis have failed owing to a lack of political and administrative support (PRI, 2013). In situations where a reform-minded NBR chairman has sought to bring about tax administration changes, this has failed because the chairman was replaced before implementation could begin. Frequent changes at the top (chairman NBR) have further reduced the ability to reform NBR.

6 *Summary of Institutional Constraints: Weak State Fiscal Capacity*
The picture that emerges of the taxation system of Bangladesh is of a system that is characterised by informality; negotiated settlements by elites; a highly complex, non-transparent and discretion-based system; a manually run and weak tax administration; low compliance; corrupt practices; and low accountability. The end result is a highly inefficient, corrupt, and low-yield tax system. The political economy tax literature recognises this as an indication of weak state fiscal capacity.[4] The basic argument is that the reason why rich countries have a considerably higher average tax to GDP ratio is because they have invested successively in their fiscal capacities over a long period of time. This higher fiscal capacity is reflected in much greater reliance on modern tax bases like income and VAT, as well as much better ability to enforce tax compliance. By contrast, low-income developing countries have weak state fiscal capacity that sharply reduces VAT and income tax compliance, and therefore their ability to raise adequate fiscal resources. To increase tax revenues, a low-income country will need to invest in institutions that increase the state fiscal capacity. Within developing countries, there are differences in the degree of weakness of state fiscal capacity, some being relatively stronger than others and hence having relatively better ability to mobilise fiscal revenues than others. In this framework, Bangladesh falls into the list of countries that have among the weakest state fiscal capacity.

The specific areas of capacity building required will vary from country to country, but some generic areas that could help build state fiscal capacity include: strengthening the legal framework to enforce contracts; the establishment of property rights; strengthening the rule of law; facilitating the growth of democratic institutions; growth of the financial sector; and strengthening of the tax administration. Thus, state fiscal capacity is a combination of political institutions, economic institutions, and administrative institutions. Progress in any of these three areas will help increase state fiscal capacity and contribute to increasing revenues. The development of political institutions is a tough challenge and will likely evolve over a longer period of time, but investments in economic and administrative institutions hold greater promise for progress in the medium term.

---

[4] See Besley and Persson (2009, 2011) for a useful analysis of state fiscal capacity.

VII THE WAY FORWARD

Summarising his views on the lessons of international experience with tax reforms, noted tax expert Richard Bird writes: 'Fifty years of experience tells us that the right game for tax researchers is not the short-term political game in which policy decisions are made. Academic researchers and outside agencies interested in fostering better sustainable tax systems in developing countries will employ their efforts and resources most usefully if they play in the right game. That game is the long-term one of building up the institutional capacity both within and outside governments to articulate relevant ideas for change, to collect and analyse relevant data, and of course to assess and criticize the effects of such changes as are made. Tax researchers, especially in developing countries themselves, can and should play an active role in all these activities' (Bird, 2015). While tax reforms and tax institutional capacity building are indeed long-term endeavours, the fact that Bangladesh is a negative outlier in terms of the very low tax to GDP ratio when compared with countries at similar per capita income levels suggests that there is scope for progress even in the short term, through some relatively simple tax administration improvements.

A pertinent question to ask is, if tax reforms and administration improvements did not happen in the past why would they happen now? The answer to this question lies in the fact that the awareness at the highest political level of the need for some immediate minimum tax reforms is growing in Bangladesh. This is partly due to the emergence of an increasingly constrained fiscal space that is limiting the capacity of the Government to deliver even basic services at the same time that demand for these services are growing and expectations are building up. The successful implementation of the Government's development strategy has accelerated GDP growth and improved human development and poverty outcomes. To keep the support of the people, the Government is now aspiring to reach greater development heights. It has adopted a new development vision, called the Vision 2041, and has converted this into a new development strategy, PP2041. The vision calls for Bangladesh to secure upper middle-income status (World Bank Atlas method) by FY2031, and high-income status by FY2041. Vision 2041 was an integral part of the Government's 2018 election manifesto.

The Government's own macroeconomic framework for PP2041 shows that the targets to reach upper middle-income status and eliminate extreme poverty by FY2031 require a doubling of the tax to GDP ratio over the next 12 years. Also, as articulated in PP2041, the Government agrees that the main focus of tax reforms should be to raise the revenue base for income and consumption taxes, while reducing reliance on trade taxes, in order to eliminate the anti-export bias of trade protection.

To show its concern about poor revenue performance and signal its intention to follow the PP2041 fiscal path, the Government put forth an ambitious target of raising the tax to GDP ratio by 3 percentage points in the FY2020 budget.

However, as noted, this ambitious tax target was not adequately backed by policy actions. The new Finance Minister was probably not fully aware of the complexities and inherent weaknesses of the tax system. Independent research by fiscal policy experts and associated public debate on the need for credible tax reforms has set the stage for some constructive discussions about what might constitute some helpful and achievable tax administration reforms over the next few years as steps towards achieving the tax targets of PP2041. These reforms are based on the lessons from international experience, as well as experience from Bangladesh. The Government is now open to greater and more meaningful consultation with independent researchers on the type of tax reforms needed to achieve the PP2041 fiscal targets. This is an important development and consistent with Richard Bird's observation noted above concerning the positive role of independent tax research and policy debate in furthering the case for tax reforms.

A Tax Institutional Reforms

Consistent with the analysis of weak state fiscal capacity, some minimum institutional reforms are essential to see any systematic progress with tax revenue effort. These include the following:

1. *Separation of tax policy from tax collection:* An essential institutional reform is to separate tax policy from tax collection. Although the NBR is entrusted with both tax policy and tax collection, it *de facto* serves as a tax collection entity. While it has senior tax policy staff, the overwhelming focus is on tax collection. This single-minded focus on tax collection has come into serious conflict with the design of a broad-based tax policy that is consistent with revenue goals, ensures the efficiency of tax collection, and avoids adverse implications for incentives and national resource allocation. It also explains the *ad hoc* nature of tax policy during the annual budget cycle, where the focus of tax policy is on raising revenues to meet the budget target, without regard to the impact of the tax measure on resource allocation or efficiency. A better arrangement would be to assign the NBR the primary responsibility for collecting taxes and giving tax policy responsibility to either a special unit within the Internal Resource Division or to the Budget Division of the Ministry of Finance. The advantage of assigning this to the Budget Division is that this entity has substantial macroeconomic policy analysis capabilities. It also has the responsibility for developing the medium-term budgetary framework and the annual budgets. These provide the Budget Division with considerable knowledge and stronger capabilities to formulate tax policies than the NBR or the Internal Revenues Division.

2. *Strengthening tax policy and tax collection agencies:* Whatever institutional arrangements the Government may adopt, both tax policy and

tax collection efforts have to be substantially strengthened through the induction of better professional staff. The Government has considerably increased civil service salaries in recent years, which has improved incentives for professional staff to apply for public service positions. The tax departments (the NBR and the tax policy unit) need a much stronger combination of professional staff with civil service staff. If needed, some additional incentives could be provided to attract fixed-term tax professional experts to the Ministry of Finance. This small investment in tax administration capacity would have a high rate of return in terms of better tax policy and revenue performance.

3. *Selection and tenure of the NBR chairman:* The frequency of changes of the NBR chairman has a serious negative impact on tax collection. The Government might want to delink the position from the civil service, select the chairman on a professional basis, and establish a minimum tenure of four to five years. This will strengthen the quality of tax administration leadership, de-politicise this position, and provide stability and an incentive for the chairman to take tough actions against corrupt practices.

4. *Fully digitising the tax administration:* Consistent with the policy of the prime minister to rapidly adopt online technology as the primary mode of transactions with the Government, full digitisation of the tax administration is of the highest priority. Some progress has been made for the customs and VAT administration, but there is a long way to go, especially for income tax administration. Full digitisation of tax administration, especially personal income taxation, will go a long way towards reducing corruption, increasing compliance, and increasing tax revenues.

5. *Strengthening the budget consultation process:* The Government already has a healthy consultation process involving the citizens. This should continue. However, the participation of the Cabinet and the Parliament could be strengthened considerably. The Cabinet review of the draft budget could be made more productive by requiring each Cabinet minister to make a presentation on their development targets and objectives for the year, and to discuss the adequacy of the proposed resource allocation to secure them. This process could be very useful in bringing out the internal tensions and the challenges posed by the revenue constraints upfront, so as to allow proper policy choices to be made, including the need for meaningfully strengthening revenue mobilisation. Regarding the Parliament, one possible option is to involve the appropriate Parliamentary Committee responsible for oversight of budget and finance issues early in the process of budget making, to get timely inputs into the process.

6. *Promote fiscal decentralisation:* Greater fiscal decentralisation could help mobilise revenues by providing a better link between service delivery and accountability. The Government has made some progress with

administrative decentralisation by instituting a system of elected local government institutions. The next step is to assign clear service delivery responsibilities without overlap with competing national entities, build local government institution service delivery capacities, and institute a well thought out fiscal decentralisation system.

B Reform of the VAT

The proposed reform of the VAT leading to the VAT Law of 2012 was sound. Technical assistance to help with implementation had also progressed well. It is most unfortunate that this progress was ignored by the new government and a hodgepodge VAT reform was introduced in the FY2020 budget. As most tax experts familiar with the Bangladesh VAT system agree, the FY2020 VAT reform will likely not work. The Government is hesitant to accept this view and is bent on implementing the modifications to the VAT system it introduced in the FY2020 budget. It is hoped that the implementation experience with the VAT modifications of the FY2020 budget will provide good evidence of its limitations and the need to revert back to the provisions of the 2012 VAT Law. This hopefully can set the stage for the implementation of a solid VAT reform in the FY2021 budget.

C Reform of Income Taxation

Notwithstanding all the caveats associated with political and administrative constraints on income tax collection, it is high time that the Government made a serious effort to reform the income taxation regime, especially as it seeks to achieve upper middle-income tax status.

D Corporate Taxation

Several actions can be taken in regard to corporation taxation, including streamlining the corporate tax rate in a series of steps. As a first step, with the exception of tobacco, the maximum rate of taxation should be lowered, starting with 30% in FY2021 and 25% in FY2022. As rates come down, exemptions and tax holidays for foreign direct investment or specific sectors must be eliminated over a well-defined period, so that by and large all investors are required to pay taxes. Once the tax rates are lowered and made internationally attractive, exemptions will not be needed. Capital flight for taxation purposes will not be an issue because the investor will have to pay taxes in other countries as well.

E Personal Income Taxation

The personal income reform needs a substantial overhaul based on further research and analysis. The reform that is required is to lower the marginal and average tax rates and to increase the tax base through voluntary compliance. Bangladesh can learn the lessons from the positive experience with income taxation from other countries. These lessons include the following:

- The best approach to increasing the tax base is to provide incentives for voluntary compliance. Having large marginal tax rates and putting pressure on those who pay is a recipe for disaster. It is like killing the goose that lays the golden eggs. Many taxpayers will find ways to escape the tax net by entering into collusive behaviour with the tax collectors, as presently.
- The tax system must be based on the principles of universal income, self-assessment, and productive and selective audits. It must be fully digitised wherever possible, with no interface between the taxpayer and tax collector, except when subject to audits.
- The tax system must be simple, with a low compliance cost. Indeed, the simpler the system and the lower the tax rates, the more likely it is that there will be voluntary compliance and the less the scope for tax harassment and corruption.
- The audit system should be highly selective and productive. The objective of the audit system should be to discourage tax avoidance and not serve as an instrument of harassment or to extract a bribe. The audit system should be based on a computer-driven model developed on the basis of well-identified criteria that, if violated, would trigger an audit. The criteria must make the audit productive so that the collection cost is only a fraction of the total taxes raised through audits. It should be highly selective, with no more than 5% of returns audited systematically.
- The attitude of the NBR should change from tax 'policing and harassment' to voluntary tax compliance based on a user-friendly and tax service approach.
- Self-assessment, digitisation, and simplification of personal income tax filing with a user-friendly and service-oriented approach will vastly increase tax compliance and tax collections, as reflected in the experience of countries with good income tax collection records.

F Property Taxation

Most upper middle-income and high-income economies have a well-established system of fiscal decentralisation whereby the property taxes are assigned to local governments as the major source of tax revenues. In Bangladesh, such a political decision on fiscal decentralisation has yet to happen, although it is imminent as Bangladesh aspires to attain upper middle-income status. Indeed, the PP2041 puts considerable emphasis on the need for fiscal decentralisation. The next step is the political debate and buy-in at the top level.

In the interim, the Government should design and implement a modern property tax system that is different from the present fragmented two-part system whereby the NBR collects a wealth tax as a part of the income tax and local governments collect some nominal taxes on properties. A modern property tax that is based on the true market value of properties and evaluated and updated systematically using a computerised property ownership database is an essential element of a modern tax system. There are many models of a well-designed property tax system that can be researched and implemented in the specific political economy context of Bangladesh. Implementation can proceed in a phased manner, starting with the capital city of Dhaka and then extended to other divisional cities and finally to all urban areas.

G Reform of the Customs System

Recognising the continued high cost of customs administration and its adverse effects on trade logistics and private investment, the NBR has recently developed and adopted a new customs reform programme known as the Customs Modernisation Strategic Action Plan 2019–2022 (NBR, 2019). This is a comprehensive and ambitious endeavour that seeks to improve the efficiency of the customs system and reduce the transaction costs related to international trade. Tariff rationalisation is also an objective, although the end game of tariff rationalisation (reduction of trade protection) is less clear. Nevertheless, this is a welcome initiative and its sound implementation should be a high policy priority.

ANNEX 6.1 IMPORT DUTY–RELATED SROs FY2015–FY2019

CPC	Description	Purpose	Beneficiary
135	Car/Micro Bus imported by industrial unit of EPZ	Special exemption for imports of cars/jeeps	EPZ industries
137	Car/Jeep imported by MP's	Special exemption for imports of cars/jeeps	Members of Parliament (MPs)
140	Generator Assembling Plant, SRO 80/2007, CD 0%	LP gas cylinder manufacturers	LP gas manufacturers
148	AIT exempted for warehouse	Special exemption benefit	Special benefit to certain groups
156	Poultry Accessories, SRO-158/2004, CD, SD, & VAT exempted	Special benefit for poultry firms	Poultry sector
157	Textile, SRO-157/2004 (Table-I, CD, SD, VAT exempted & Table-II, CD 7.5%)	Textile machinery and parts	Textile sector
159	Leather, SRO-169/2005, CD 7.5%	Special benefit to raw materials for leather sector	Leather sector

CPC	Description	Purpose	Beneficiary
168	AIT applicable, other duties & taxes exempted in full under Special Order	Special exemption benefit	Special benefit to certain group
170	All Taxes exempted under Authority of NBR	Special exemption benefit	Special benefit to certain group
176	Goods Imported as Defence Stores Memo 246 of 10-04-81	Defence store	Defence forces
189	News Print, SRO-144/2007, CD 10%	News print	Newspaper industry
200	Gas Cylinder, SRO, CD 3%, SD, VAT, & ATV exempted	Gas cylinders	Gas cylinder manufacturers
201	Shipbuilding, SRO-280, CD – 5%	Ship building	Ship manufacturers
205	Tourism, SD, VAT, & ATV exempted	Tourism sector	Tourism sector
208	Fibber SRO, CD & ATV exempted	Textile raw materials	Synthetic textiles sector
209	CNG Conversion, SRO-176/2012	CNG conversion filling station	CNG filling stations
210	SRO 236/2014, Ship Building	Ship building	Ship manufacturers
220	Capital Machinery & ATV exempted	Capital machinery	Industry establishment
222	Toys SRO-145/2015, CD 5%, VAT, ATV 0%	Toys	Toys manufacturing
223	SLK, SRO-146/15, CD 5%, RD, SD, VAT, ATV 0%	Chemicals for handlooms	Handloom manufacturers
227	BEZA Development, AIT applicable	Special exemption for BEZA imports	BEZA
403	Motor Bike, SRO-155/16, SD 20, ATV applicable	Motorcycle assembling	Motorcycle manufacture
407	Amusement Park, SRO 166/2016, CD 10%, ATV exempted	Encouraging tourism sector	Amusement parks, mainly Jamuna Group
409	SRO-148/2016, AC & Freeze manufacturing industry	Special exemption benefit to VAT-registered manufacturers	VAT-registered manufacturers
601	Only CD 7.5% – for Bashundhara City	Special exemption benefit	Bashundhara Group
602	PGC order 17 (1)/98/568, 2001	Special exemption benefit	Power Grid Company
603	Industrial Development Leasing Company Bd Ltd., gets SRO-158 benefit	Special exemption benefit	IDLC

(*continued*)

CPC	Description	Purpose	Beneficiary
604	Shah Cement, gets SRO-158 benefit	Special exemption benefit	Shah Cement
605	Abul Khair Steel Prod. U-2, gets SRO-158 benefit	Special benefit for Abul Khair Group	Abul Khair Group
606	Kycr Coil Industries, gets SRO-158 benefit	Special exemption benefit	Kycr Coil Industries
607	AIT Exempt for Paragon Poultry Ltd.	Special exemption benefit	Special benefit to certain groups
608	SD & AIT exempted for Bd. Lamp & Aluminium Base Cap	Special exemption benefit	Bangladesh lamps
609	Only CD 7.5% for Sarina Inn Ltd.	Special exemption benefit	Hotel Sarina
610	Special exemption for KAFCO, CD + DSC = 6.5%	Special exemption benefit for KAFCO	KAFCO
611	Lafarge Cement, CD 7.5%, AIT & IDSC applicable	Special exemption benefit	Lafarge Cement Industry
612	Asia Energy, CD 2.5%, VAT & IDSC exempted	Special exemption benefit	Asia Energy
615	Unique Hotel and Resort Ltd., CD 6% & AIT applicable	Special exemption benefit	Unique Hotel
618	Saint Martine Seafood Ltd., only CD 3%	Special exemption benefit	Saint Martine Seafood Ltd
622	Walton Freeze & AC parts, VAT, AIT, & ATV 0%	Special benefit to Walton Products raw materials	Walton Group
625	Abul Khair Steel Melting Ltd., only CD 5%	Special benefit to Abul Khair Group	Abul Khair Group
630	Star Ceramics, CD 3%, other tax 0	Special exemption benefit to Star Ceramics	Star Ceramics
631	Kazi Food Industry, CD 3% & other tax exempted	Special exemption benefit to Kazi group	Kazi Group
636	Runner Auto, VAT, AIT, & ATV exempted	Special exemption benefit	Runner Automobiles
637	KSRM, CD 5% & other tax 0	Special exemption benefit	KSRM
639	Rahim Afrooz Battery, AIT 4%, ATV exempted	Batteries	Rahim Afrooz Battery
641	Butterfly Manufacturing Company (BMC) Ltd., AIT 1%, ATV 0% applicable	Special exemption benefit	BMC Ltd.
643	SRO-50, CD 5%, RD, SD, VAT, & ATV 0% for Residential Hotel	Tourism sector	Tourism sector

CPC	Description	Purpose	Beneficiary
644	BSRM Steel Mills, CD only 5%	Special exemption benefit	BSRM Group
652	Abul Khair, AIT 75% exempted	Special benefit to Abul Khair Group	Abul Khair Group
656	Walton Hot rolled sheet, CD 5%	Special Benefit to Walton Products raw materials	Walton Group
904	Dairy/Poultry Farm, CD exempted	Special benefit for dairy/poultry firms	Dairy/poultry sector
907	SD & ATV Exempt for Refined Sugar under HS Code: 1701.99.00 SD SRO-64	Special exemption benefit	Sugar refinery industry
912	CD – 12%, RD & SD exemption for Sealed Lead Acid Bat. <=12 V	Batteries	Battery manufacturers
914	VAT Base 66.67% for CDSO & CPO, also ATV exempted	Edible oils	Edible oils manufacturers
925	SRO 43/2015, AIT 50%	Alloy steel	Alloy steel
926	Poultry feed, ATV exempted	Poultry firms	Poultry sector

Source: NBR.

Discussion: Institutional Dimensions of Tax Reforms in Bangladesh

Christopher Heady

Introduction

The taxation system in Bangladesh is one of the worst in the world. It has a tax to GDP ratio of approximately 9%, as compared to the developing country average of 17–18%, and has been stagnant for the last eight years, reducing the scope for development spending.

The tax system is poorly administered and corrupt, with tax officials harassing taxpayers and extracting bribes to accept low tax payments. Also, politically connected taxpayers are able to reduce their tax payments. Even the government is complicit in reducing tax revenues by the use of SROs that effectively grant extra-statutory tax concessions to favoured entities, with no analysis of their revenue effects.

Also, the compliance rate for VAT-registered businesses is estimated at only 12%, among the lowest in the world. The VAT also has low productivity, of about 3% of GDP, when the statutory rate is 15%. This probably reflects the limited coverage of the VAT, which has not yet been extended to the retail level.

The corporate tax system is very unusual, with as many as nine different tax rates (from 45% to 3%), according to KPMG's Bangladesh Tax Profile (September 2018). Such a complex system must cause considerable administrative difficulties for businesses that produce products in different tax rate categories. As most countries have only one or two corporate tax rates, this structure suggests political favouritism for particular businesses, producing inefficiency and an uneven playing field for businesses.

Difficulties in Raising Tax Revenue

Effective taxation in low-income countries is difficult for a number of reasons:

1. A large proportion of the population is likely to be self-employed, as farmers or individual businesses. This makes them hard to identify. It also means that they are unlikely to keep accurate accounts.
2. For this reason, tax authorities often focus on businesses, which are usually easier to identify as, normally, they need some sort of business licence in order to operate.
3. In some countries (including Bangladesh), corrupt tax officials conspire with taxpayers to reduce their tax payments, with the tax reduction shared between the taxpayer and the official.
4. Some countries (including Bangladesh) have unnecessarily complex tax schedules, especially for corporate income tax, increasing the burden on tax officials and increasing the scope for corruption.
5. As Bird *et al.* (2008) have argued, 'a more legitimate and responsive state appears to be an essential precondition for a more adequate level of tax effort in developing countries'. This argument has particular resonance for Bangladesh because its citizens generally see little in return for the taxes that they pay, with the resulting shortfall in tax revenue. It is therefore not surprising that tax compliance is so low.

Businesses

Businesses generally provide the largest contribution to tax revenue in both high-income and low-income countries. This is partly because they can usually be identified easily, partly because of the requirement for accounts to be kept, and also because they are able to report the incomes of both the employees and of the owner(s) of the business. The accounts also provide information on business purchases and sales, allowing the calculation of liability for VAT or sales taxes.

However, there is a large incentive for businesses to understate their sales and overstate their costs, in order to reduce their tax liabilities. They may reduce their reported income by failing to give receipts to the purchasers of their products, reducing their apparent income. Some countries have tried to reduce this problem by providing purchasers with an incentive for purchasers to demand receipts. For example, in Italy, it is illegal to leave a shop without a receipt for the payment they have made, and the police can demand to see the receipt when the customer leaves the shop.

In addition, there are businesses that are unregistered and that operate outside of any regulatory control.

The Self-employed

Although many self-employed people have low incomes, it is important to make sure that those on higher incomes are subject to tax. It is difficult to identify the wealthy self-employed because they have a strong interest in concealing their incomes. However, this can be done by comparing the lifestyle of the self-employed with their declared incomes. As these investigations can take considerable time and require scarce specialist knowledge, it is best to focus on those self-employed people whose lifestyles are clearly beyond what can be afforded by most rich people.

Many self-employed people attempt to hide their existence from the tax authorities completely, as evidenced by the relatively small proportion of the population that submits tax returns. One way for the tax authorities to reduce this problem is to make use of the Block Management System developed by Tanzania in 2002, and subsequently adopted by Uganda (African Tax Administration Forum, 2014). This works by identifying an area, like a city block, and systematically counting all the people who live in the block and registering them for tax, making sure that all doors are opened to prevent people from hiding. This resulted in a very substantial increase in the number of businesses registering with the tax administration. Once registered, it is much simpler for the tax authorities to follow up businesses in later years.

Corruption

In some countries, corrupt tax officials can be bribed to reduce the taxpayer's assessments, allowing the taxpayer to reduce their tax liability. This form of corruption can be reduced by ensuring that all communications between the taxpayer and tax officials are in written form and in such a way that the taxpayer does not know the identity of the tax official who assesses the taxpayer's liability.

Complex Tax Schedules

Most countries have corporate tax rates that are very simple, with either just one rate that applies to all business profits, or one main rate and a slightly lower rate for small businesses. However, Bangladesh has a large number of different rates of corporate income tax for different products. This makes it very difficult for businesses to calculate their corporate tax liability and provides opportunities for businesses to reduce their tax liability by misrepresenting the type of product, or products, that they produce.

It also increases the burden on tax officials, to check that the correct corporate income tax rates have been applied.

In addition, SROs are used frequently to provide special benefits to particular target groups that are politically well connected, without any concern about the revenue losses.

Improving Tax Revenues

It is very hard to improve tax compliance in a country whose tax system has been as dysfunctional as that of Bangladesh. However, Bangladesh will never progress if important improvements are not made to both tax policy and tax administration.

The main measures that should be applied are the following:

1. Increase the number of tax officials and the level of their training.
2. Prevent tax officials from having personal contact with taxpayers. All communications between the taxpayer and the tax administration should be in writing and should be sent to the tax office for processing without revealing who dealt with the case. This should reduce corruption in the tax administration.
3. Increase the penalties for corrupt tax officials.
4. Ensure all taxpayers submit a completed self-assessment tax form, as the basis for the calculation of the tax due. This includes all government officials and their relatives.
5. Ensure a sample of these self-assessment is audited, in order to verify their accuracy. If the taxpayer's income is found to be higher than shown in the self-assessment form, penalties should be applied. The forms of government officials should be examined particularly carefully, with any irregularities reported to the legal authorities.
6. Remove the requirement for taxpayers to file a wealth statement along with their tax return. This should encourage taxpayers to file tax returns and allow them to become compliant with the tax system.
7. Ensure that SROs are only approved if their purpose is explained and their financial implications are properly calculated. All SROs should be published, including the reason for them and their financial implications. The costs of each one should be clearly stated as part of the annual financial statements of the Government.
8. The VAT administration should be modernised and computerised, to allow easy registration of traders and simple procedures for submitting tax assessments. VAT should be extended to the retail level as soon as possible.
9. The rate structure of the corporate income tax should be simplified to have one main rate. If particular products – such as tobacco products – are judged to require additional taxation, this additional taxation should be in the form of an excise duty rather than part of the corporate tax.
10. Each year, a sample of businesses should have their accounts audited, to ensure that they are reporting accurate VAT and profit figures and to ensure that they are fully reporting the wages that they pay to their employees.
11. A form of the Block Management System should be used to identify those businesses and the self-employed that operate outside the system, earning money without declaring it to the tax authorities.

7

Institutional Challenges in Public Spending

The Case of Primary Education

Selim Raihan, Zubayer Hossen, and Bazlul Haque Khondker

I INTRODUCTION

The provision of public services is one of the most important roles played by the state, and few public services are as important as education. A well-functioning education system is not only an end in itself, as recognised by Sustainable Development Goal 4, but also a means of achieving economic development more generally. Ensuring inclusive, equitable, high-quality education and providing opportunities for lifelong learning is fundamental to generating the skilled labour on which a successful economy depends, as well as to reducing poverty and inequality. Primary education is the foundation on which the education system as a whole is built and has for some time been recognised, both in Bangladesh and internationally, as a key public policy priority.

The provision of primary education is an important institutional issue. It requires effective mechanisms for the recruitment, training, and retention of teachers; the construction and maintenance of schools and other infrastructure; the design and implementation of the curriculum; the monitoring of progress, through inspections and examinations; and the creation of a learning environment. The responsibility for overcoming these institutional challenges lies heavily with the state. An economic rationale is provided by Raihan (2019b), who argues that education, as a *merit* good, creates positive externalities when consumed and has spill-over benefits which have a significant effect on social welfare. Externalities and spill-overs imply that markets would fail if left by themselves, and education would thus remain under-consumed. Private market prices for education services could be so high as to prevent individuals from investing in their human capital. In these contexts, governments have a crucial role in allocating resources to education.

The successful allocation of resources involves far more than merely increasing enrolments, which do not in themselves necessarily guarantee learning (Bold and Svensson, 2016). While Bangladesh has been successful in increasing the enrolment rate in primary schools and in reaching gender parity, a growing literature has documented that a large segment of children in Bangladesh learn little and complete their primary education without the expected reading, writing, and arithmetic skills (see World Bank, 2018; Directorate of Primary Education (DPE), 2017, 2018a; NAPE, 2018). Thus, the remarkable success in enrolment in Bangladesh has meant less progress on quality, and possibly a regress. The education system had to hire more teachers, but could not train them properly and could not pay them satisfactorily, and education infrastructure has remained poor. The point is thus that it was maybe unavoidable that quality today is not at a satisfactory level; this should obviously be the next objective, but there are many obstacles to reaching it. Therefore, rather than focusing on enrolments as an indicator of Bangladesh's educational performance, this chapter provides a detailed investigation of the institutional challenges inherent in the system, which have led to the low-quality result observed.

To this end, this chapter starts with an analysis of the importance of the primary education sector for development in Bangladesh and discusses the trends in major outcome indicators. This chapter explores the challenges related to the coexistence of various actors in the primary education system, the inadequate allocation of resources, the lack of incentives to attract high-quality teachers, the shortage of trained teachers, the low quality of the educational infrastructure, the poor curriculum design, and the flawed examination system. This chapter further describes the institutional processes and challenges for teacher recruitment, promotion, and transfer in government primary schools (GPSs) in Bangladesh.

While delineating institutional challenges that are specific to the primary education sector, this chapter relates some of these challenges to the public sector in general in Bangladesh. Chapter 3 of this volume, using the survey data of the institutional diagnostic, highlights the poor quality of public services in Bangladesh. Faulty recruitment processes have been found to be one of the main reasons behind the poor quality of public service delivery. While the recruitment and transfer processes of teachers in GPSs are not fully representative of the processes followed in the Bangladesh Civil Service (BCS), the analysis in this chapter does illuminate more general institutional public sector challenges in Bangladesh. Finally, this chapter recommends relevant measures to overcome the institutional challenges of public spending in primary education and to improve the quality of services.

II THE IMPORTANCE OF EDUCATION (PRIMARY EDUCATION) FOR DEVELOPMENT IN BANGLADESH

Education important for achieving critical development objectives, that is enhancing productivity, accelerating economic growth, reducing poverty, reducing fertility, and increasing female empowerment. Efficient investment in education can help increase levels of human capital and hence represents one of the most effective ways to reduce poverty and increase economic mobility (Bold and

Svensson, 2016). As well as playing a key role in terms of ensuring that children acquire basic literacy and numeracy, primary education also creates a strong base for acquiring more knowledge and skills, as it gives access to higher levels of education. Using human capital theory, Psacharopoulos and Patrinos (2004) argued that among the types of education, the returns from primary education are higher, especially in developing countries. Education acts as a catalyst in encouraging the development of modern attitudes and aspirations (Psacharopoulos and Woodhall, 1985). Raihan (2019a) highlighted that, as investment in human capital formation is considered a means of improving quality of life and sustaining economic growth, education, together with health, plays a key role in human capital formation. Therefore, maintaining high levels of public spending in these two sectors, as well as ensuring a high quality of services, is very important for achieving the required level of human capital in the economy.

Studies have examined the impact of education on economic growth in Bangladesh. Islam *et al.* (2007), using data for 1976–2003, showed the existence of bi-directional causality between education and economic growth in Bangladesh. A study by Maitra and Mukhopadhyay (2012), with an error correction model, investigated the underlying association between public education spending and economic growth in 12 countries in Asia and the Pacific, including Bangladesh, and revealed a positive association between public education spending and gross domestic product (GDP) growth in Bangladesh. Similarly, Mallick *et al.* (2016) investigated the dynamics of public expenditure on education and economic growth in 14 selected Asian countries, including Bangladesh, by using balanced panel data for 1973–2012. The analysis revealed a positive and statistically significant association between public education expenditure on economic growth in all these countries. The study by Islam (2014), using data for the period 1973–2010, also showed a positive association between public educational expenditure and economic growth in Bangladesh, both in the short and the long term. However, except for Islam *et al.* (2007), it is not clear what causality direction is being captured in these studies.

Education contributes to enhanced productivity; examples from Bangladesh confirm this proposition. Fernandes (2006) explored the determinants of total factor productivity for manufacturing firms in Bangladesh and found that, controlling for industry, location, and year fixed effects, total factor productivity improved with the quality of the firm's human capital.[1] Asadullah and Rahman (2009), using a large dataset on rice-producing households from 141 villages in Bangladesh, showed that household education significantly increased productivity in rice production and boosted potential output. The study found that an additional average year of schooling of adults in the household, and the same for the household head, increased rice production by 6.4% and 3.7%, respectively.

---

[1] Fernandes (2006) measured 'human capital' by the education and experience of the manager, and by using occupation-based as well as education-based measures of workforce skills.

Empirical studies, in the context of Bangladesh, have estimated the return on primary education by reference to 'no education'. Our estimates, using the Labour Force Survey 2016–2017 data of the Bangladesh Bureau of Statistics (2018), suggest that an individual with class 1–5 education earns 6.7% more than an individual with no education. Rahman and Al-Hasan (2018), using the Labour Force Survey 2015–2016 data, showed that one additional year of schooling increases the earnings of males and females by 7.3% and 8.1%, respectively. Sen and Rahman (2016), using the Labour Force Survey 2010 data, showed that the positive impact of primary education on earnings is evident in comparison to no education, and that the average monthly income for individuals with incomplete primary education is estimated to be 10% higher than for individuals with no formal education. The study by Asadullah (2006) estimated the labour market returns to education in Bangladesh using the Household Income and Expenditure Survey data for 1999–2000. The study showed that while an additional year of schooling increased labour market earnings by 7.1%, the overall return on completing primary education compared to no education was 20%. These estimates are consistent with those in Montenegro and Patrinos (2014) for Bangladesh, which, for 2005, were 7% per year of schooling and 24% for primary education, overall. A general conclusion can be drawn from the review of these studies: returns on complete primary education are around 20% or more, and on incomplete primary education are around 10% or slightly less.

Education is also critical for the reduction in poverty in Bangladesh (World Bank, 2018; Majumder and Biswas, 2017; Khudri and Chowdhury, 2013). The higher level of education is associated with a lower level of poverty at the household level. The Household Income and Expenditure Survey 2016 data reveals that, in 2016, the average poverty rate of households if their household heads had no education was higher than the national poverty rate of 24.3%. The poverty rates falls for a household as the household head's level of education rises.

Education helps women's empowerment in Bangladesh. One of the important contributing factors behind this empowerment is declining fertility. It is argued that educational attainment, especially female education, is a prime determinant of the fertility transition in many developing countries (Mahanta, 2016; Islam and Nesa, 2009; Cochrane, 1979). Bangladesh has seen fertility decline over recent decades, from as high as 6.3 in 1974 to 2.03 by 2018 (World Bank, 2020b). Islam and Nesa (2009), with the help of Demographic and Health Survey data, showed that the fertility rate declined considerably with women's education in Bangladesh. Another important factor contributing to women's empowerment is the reduction of the gender wage gap. In Bangladesh, the large participation of girls in education has been instrumental in reducing the gender wage gap. According to Ahmed and McGillivray (2015), between 1999 and 2009, the gap in average wages between men and women in Bangladesh declined by 31%; a key driver of this change was the improvement in female educational qualifications. According to the ILO (2018), in 2017, the gender wage gap in Bangladesh was only 2.2%, which was the lowest in the world (against the world average of 21.2%). It should be mentioned, however, that the figures given by Ahmed and McGillivray (2015) and the ILO (2018) concern only 'wage employees', that is the formal sector, and therefore refer to, at most, only 15% of the labour force. The employment of young women in the readymade garments sector, paid at the minimum wage, has some effect on lowering this gender wage gap, whereas there might be many fewer young men in formal employment and not necessarily covered by a minimum wage.

In the context of this discussion, despite the fact that Bangladesh has made progress over the past decades in the average years of schooling for the 15+ aged population, the country lags behind many other comparable countries. In 2018, among the 15+ aged population, the average years of schooling in Bangladesh was 6.1, which had increased from as low as 2.8 in 1990. However, in 2018, the average years of schooling for the 15+ aged population for Vietnam, Indonesia, India, Kenya, and Ghana were 8.2, 8.0, 6.5, 6.6, and 7.2, respectively (United National Development Programme, 2019). The distribution of the 15+ aged population by level of schooling from the Barro and Lee database[2] suggests that the main reason for the large change in the average years of schooling is the drop in the number of people with no education. Though recent data is not available, the proportion of people without education fell from 55.6% to 31.9% in Bangladesh between 1990 and 2010. However, Vietnam was well ahead of Bangladesh even in 1990; as in 1990, 13.2% people in Vietnam were without education, and by 2010, the proportion remained at around the same percentage. Indonesia experienced a sharp drop in the proportion of people without education between 1990 and 2010 – from 43.6% to 7.5%. Between 1990 and 2010, the average years of primary schooling among the 15+ aged population in Bangladesh increased from 2.2 to 3.4 years. However, Vietnam started with a higher average, of 3.5, in 1990 and increased it further, to 4, by 2010, while Indonesia experienced a rise, from 3 to 5.1, during the same period. Most countries in East Africa (Kenya, Tanzania, Uganda, and Rwanda) also did better than Bangladesh, which in 2010 was at the same level of 'no education' as Kenya or Uganda were in 1990.

All these figures show that Bangladesh suffered from an initial disadvantage in contrast to many comparable countries. But the country has been trying to make up for that gap with huge efforts on school enrolment.

III THE PRIMARY EDUCATION SECTOR IN BANGLADESH: BASIC PERFORMANCE

Primary education in Bangladesh is dominated by the public sector (discussed in detail in Section IV.A). Therefore, the analysis of the performance of primary education sector provides us with some useful insights about the quality

---

[2] See www.barrolee.com/.

of service delivery in other public sector areas in Bangladesh. It is also true that that a significant advantage of the educational sector is that it is relatively easier to measure, at least for some outcomes.

Bangladesh's population is passing through the 'demographic dividend' phase.[3] The concern is that the country is yet to exploit this. The economic benefit of the demographic dividend is that the population has a higher capacity to save – as the old and the young are less of a burden. Investing these extra savings in human capital formation is a good policy. Raihan (2018b) argued that for Bangladesh to make the best use of the demographic dividend, the critical policy areas should include investment in health, education, and skills development. With 9.2% of the population in the 6–10 age group, the investment to be made remains sizeable, however.

Bangladesh saw a large expansion in access to primary education in the 1990s and 2000s. During this period, this expansion was led by non-state providers, and more recently by the Government (Steer *et al.*, 2014). In 1990, just over two-thirds of its primary-aged children were enrolled in primary school, while today there is near-universal education. In 2018, while the gross enrolment rate in primary education was over 100%, the net enrolment rate was around 98% (Figure 7.1).

The gender difference in primary schooling has been in favour of the girls since 1990 (Figure 7.1). Between 1990 and 2018, the net enrolment rate for girls in primary schools increased from 80.7% to 98.2%, while for boys, the rate increased from 69% to 97.6%. Bangladesh has been a frontrunner in increasing girls' enrolment in primary schools. The well-timed conditional cash transfer programme has played an important role in achieving universal enrolment for girls. There are two cash transfer programmes. One was the girls' secondary education stipend,[4] introduced in 1993, but for secondary school only. The other was the primary education stipend,[5] introduced in the early 2000s but with no gender difference. The advantage of girls over boys in primary schools in the 1990s can be linked to the secondary education girls' stipend.

---

[3] According to United Nations Population Fund, the demographic dividend is the economic growth potential that can result from shifts in a population's age structure, mainly when the share of the working-age population (15–64) is larger than the non-working-age share of the population (14 and younger, and 65 and older; see www.unfpa.org/demographic-dividend).

[4] In January 1994, the Bangladesh government launched a nationwide stipend programme for girls in secondary school (Grades 6–10) in all 460 upazilas (subdistricts) of the country with support from the World Bank, the Asian Development Bank, and the Norwegian Agency for Development Cooperation; this programme was known as the Female Stipend Programme. The emphasis of this programme was on closing the gender gap in access to secondary education. See Mahmud (2003) for further details.

[5] Primary Education Stipend Programme started in 2001. Its key objective is to increase educational participation – enrolment, attendance, persistence, and performance – of primary-school-age children from poor families in urban and rural areas. The programme provides a stipend of BDT 100 per month per child to mothers in need of financial support, conditional on their child's school attendance. See DPE (2013) for further details.

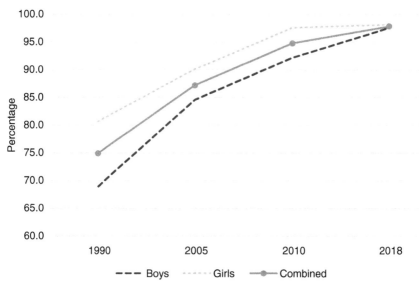

FIGURE 7.1 Net enrolment rate in primary education, 1990–2018
Source: World Bank, World Development Indicators, and Bangladesh Bureau of
Educational Information and Statistics, 2018.

The universal enrolment for girls was in practice achieved 10 years ago, while
for boys, it is only today that full enrolment is close to being achieved.

Despite the progress made in the dropout rate in primary education over
the past decade, in 2018, this rate was still high in Bangladesh. In 2009, the
dropout rate in primary education was 45.1%, which declined to 18.6% in
2018, with boys dropping out slightly more than girls. Along with the dropout
rate, the repetition rate has been another concern for primary education in
Bangladesh. The repetition rate was 5.4% in 2018, which was higher than the
figure for many Asian countries – less than 1% in China, India, and Vietnam
in 2017 (World Bank, 2020b).

Though Bangladesh has achieved remarkable success in bringing nearly all
children into primary school and ensuring gender parity, the quality of education remains a critical concern. The curriculum of its primary education system
does not effectively serve the goals of human development. A significant portion
of students after completing the primary education do not have the expected
skills to read, write, or do basic maths. Though a large numbers of children
do successfully pass the Primary Education Certificate (PEC) examination[6] and
earn a certificate, 35% of students cannot read Bangla comprehensively even

[6] The PEC examination, introduced in 2009, is a public examination in Bangladesh to evaluate the performance of class five students. Under the Ministry of Primary and Mass Education
(MoPME), the Directorate of Primary Education arranges the year-end examination for fifth
graders in public and private schools.

after passing Grade 3 and only 25% of students achieve terminal competencies –
a list of skills a student is expected to attain after completing primary education (World Bank, 2018). According to the National Academy for Primary
Education (2018), only about 49% of Grade 4 students could properly read
sentences from their Bangla textbooks and under 40% of students could read
English textbook sentences with proper and understandable pronunciation.

Even the National Student Assessment (NSA) programme reveals that students of primary schools lack skills in Bengali and mathematics.[7] The NSA
2017 results for the Bangla language suggested that 26% of Grade 3 students
performed to a level below what was expected in Grade 3. The situation was
worse for the Grade 5 students, 89% of whom performed to a level below
what was expected in Grade 5. In the case of mathematics, 59% of Grade 3
students performed to a level below what was expected in Grade 3, and 83%
of Grade 5 students performed to a level below what was expected in Grade 5.

From this analysis, it is evident that although primary education in
Bangladesh has progressed in enrolment and gender parity, performance in
terms of reasonable educational achievement norms has remained unsatisfactory. There are many reasons behind the poor quality of the primary education
system in Bangladesh, and these are discussed in Section IV.

IV INSTITUTIONAL CHALLENGES FACED BY THE PRIMARY EDUCATION SECTOR IN BANGLADESH

A number of institutional challenges that lead to poor service delivery have
beset the primary education sector in Bangladesh and contributed to unsatisfactory outcomes. The major challenges can be categorised as: (i) complex
coexistence of various actors; (ii) challenges related to resources; (iii) challenges related to teachers and teacher management in GPSs; and (iv) challenges
related to the curriculum and teacher training.

A Complex Coexistence of Various Actors

Bangladesh has one of the largest primary education systems in the world.
There are more than 134,000 primary schools; these are run by public, private,
and non-governmental organisations (NGOs), and religious providers, and

---

[7] The NSA programme is an initiative of the MoPME. The objectives of this programme are to
evaluate achievement in primary education and suggest policies to improve student achievement.
The NSA programme assesses the student learning outcomes for the Bangla language and mathematics in Grade 3 and Grade 5 in a nationally representative sample schools selected using a
stratified random method. For the assessment, students are drawn from the eight geographic
divisions of Bangladesh and seven main types of primary schools (government primary school,
kindergarten, ebtedayee madrashah, primary school attached to a high school, Bangladesh Rural
Advancement Committee (BRAC) school, Reaching Out-of-School Children (ROSC) school,
and newly nationalised primary school (NNPS)) from rural and urban regions.

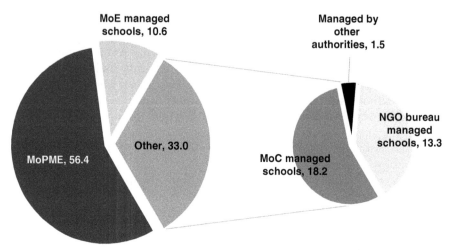

FIGURE 7.2 Share of institutes by type of management authority in 2018 (%)
Source: Education Statistics, Bangladesh Bureau of Educational Information and Statistics.

are overseen by a complex bureaucracy involving multiple ministries (DPE, 2018b). The primary schools in Bangladesh are managed by the MoPME and the DPE, the Ministry of Commerce (MoC), NGOs, the Ministry of Education (MoE), and other authorities (Figure 7.2).

With more than a 56% share in the number of primary schools, MoPME/DPE is the dominant actor in the primary education system in Bangladesh. MoPME/DPE manages eight types of schools, of which GPS and NNPS are considered as the GPSs. The MoE is responsible for three types of formal primary schools and madrasahs. The MoC administers two types of schools and the NGO Bureau oversees two types of school. Other authorities manage non-aligned institutes (DPE, 2018b). A description of these schools is provided in Annex 7.1.

One explanation for the existence of multiple actors in the primary education system in Bangladesh might be that Bangladesh aimed to achieve universal education, reduce dropouts, improve the completion rates, and provide high-quality education in primary schools, but that attaining these targets was a challenge. Shouldering the whole responsibility alone was a difficult task for the Government. The multiplicity of primary schools helped in promoting basic formal and non-formal primary education in the country. It helped to bring more children into primary schools. For example, the engagement of NGOs in providing primary education helped the Government reach the marginalised population of the country.

In this chapter, we focus only on the government primary schools (GPSs and NNPS), run by the MoPME/DPE, which constitute more than 50% of the primary schools. The institutional structure of primary education in Bangladesh, operated by the MoPME/DPE, accommodates three major actors – central, regional, and local (Figure 7.3).

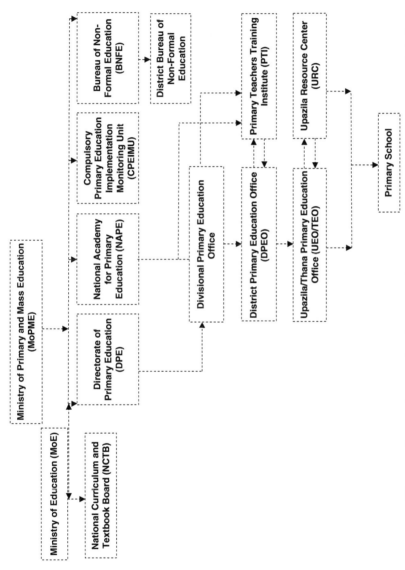

FIGURE 7.3 The complex coexistence of various actors in government primary education in Bangladesh
Note: The figure shows the central, regional, and local actors in the MoPME.
Source: MoPME and DPE.

Teachers' recruitment, salary, and contributions to General Provident Fund[8] and pension are conducted by the central authority. However, transfer, promotion, stipends to pupils, school building construction, reparation and reconstruction, school electricity bills or land development tax, the PEC examination, teacher training, and primary school visits are transferred from MoPME to primary schools through regional actors, that is Upazila (or Thana) Primary Education Office (UEO).[9] Nevertheless, the presence of many actors in the government primary education system in Bangladesh makes the management of the system difficult. For instance, the transfer of teachers in primary schools involves many steps and multiple actors. This makes the whole transfer process complicated and time-consuming. Further, the involvement of many actors reduces transparency and creates opportunities for rent-seeking activities, for example bribes for transferring teachers (see the discussion in Section IV.C.3). The overlapping responsibilities may contribute to the poor-quality services and the failure to attain the expected outcomes in primary education.

B Challenges Related to Resources

1 *Persistent Low Public Expenditure on Primary Education*

Low public expenditure on primary education in Bangladesh is a big concern. The primary education budget as a percentage of GDP has been constantly low in Bangladesh. In 2010–2011, the share of the allocation for primary education in GDP was only 1.05%; the share declined after that, and by 2018–19, stood at 0.81%. Relative to GDP, public expenditure on primary education in Bangladesh is one of the lowest in the world. The most recent data from the World Bank's World Development Indicator shows that the average ratios of public expenditure on primary education for the South Asia, East Asia, and sub-Saharan African regions are 1.3%, 1.2%, and 1.6%, respectively. Except for Pakistan and Sri Lanka, all other South Asian countries spend a higher percentage of their public funds on primary education than Bangladesh. Even many sub-Saharan countries, for example Ethiopia, Chad, and Mali, despite having a lower per capita GDP than Bangladesh, spend a higher share of their GDP on primary education than Bangladesh.

Similarly, public expenditure per primary student as a percentage of GDP per capita in Bangladesh is also one of the lowest in the world. Average government spending per primary student, as per the most recent data from the World Bank's World Development Indicator, was 7.5% of GDP per capita for Bangladesh. The averages for South Asia, East Asia, and sub-Saharan African

---

[8] The General Provident Fund is a fund that is available only for government employees. It allows all the government employees to contribute a certain percentage of their salary to the fund; the total amount that is accumulated throughout the employment term is paid to the employee at the time of retirement.

[9] See www.dpe.gov.bd/site/page/549915d9-b2f5-49c4-8674-e4c94aa22off/Introduction-of-DPE.

regions were 10.5%, 13.8%, and 10.6%, respectively. Here too, many poorer sub-Saharan African countries outperform Bangladesh. As spending on health is also low in Bangladesh, it is the investment in human capital in Bangladesh that is very much below standard.[10]

2 Insufficient Financial Incentives to Attract High-Quality Teachers

A lack of resources leads to low financial incentives, and the primary education sector in Bangladesh fails to attract competent, good-quality teachers. Low salaries and the absence of a career path development discourage young and qualified teachers from continuing their career in the primary education sector. Relative to GDP per capita, teachers in Bangladesh are much less paid than in most other developing countries, and much less even than in Pakistan. Primary school teachers are relatively better paid in Africa – the difference is significant here.[11]

It is, however, somewhat surprising to observe that developed countries pay their teachers less, relative to GDP per capita, than developing countries, even compared to the poorest (Ethiopia).[12] This is not true in absolute terms, of course, and can be explained as follows. In terms of education, teachers in advanced countries do not rank very high – typically, they have the equivalent of two to three years of college. The opposite is true in poor countries, where teachers are relatively high up the education hierarchy and where so many people have no education. Thus, finding Bangladesh between the USA, France, Norway, and Austria is really an oddity.

Failure to keep young and qualified teachers in the primary education sector is considered an important challenge in Bangladesh. Historically, the basic monthly salaries for both an assistant teacher and a headmaster were low.[13] However, in February 2020, a notice was issued by the MoPME about raising the salaries of GPS teachers across the country. According to the new pay scale, the monthly basic salary for an assistant teacher will be BDT 11,000 (roughly equal to GDP per capita), though no changes were made to the pay grades of the headmasters.[14] These salaries are equivalent to salaries in jobs such as junior accountants, client officers in bank, deputy shop managers, store

---

[10] In 2017, according to the data from the World Bank's World Development Indicator, public health expenditure was only 0.4% of GDP for Bangladesh, whereas the averages for South Asia, East Asia, and sub-Saharan African regions were 0.9%, 4.5%, and 1.9%, respectively. Here too, Bangladesh lags behind many poorer sub-Saharan African countries.

[11] See www.cgdev.org/blog/chart-week-teacher-pay-around-world-beyond-disruption-and-deskilling.

[12] See www.cgdev.org/blog/chart-week-teacher-pay-around-world-beyond-disruption-and-deskilling.

[13] See, for example Haq and Islam (2005) and Chaudhury *et al.* (2004). Also, see www.dhakatribune .com/uncategorized/2013/10/04/low-salary-for-teachers-affecting-primary-education.

[14] The government elevated the jobs of primary school assistant teachers to Grade 13 on the national payroll. Teachers with training got a starting salary of BDT 10,200 under Grade 14 as their monthly basic pay, while the amount was BDT 9,700 for those without training under Grade 15. Under Grade 13, their basic pay is now BDT 11,000. See https://bdnews24.com/ bangladesh/2020/02/09/govt-raises-salary-of-primary-school-assistant-teachers.

department managers, and marketing assistants – and these jobs attract barely competent and qualified youths.[15] The fact that a BCS officer gets a basic salary of BDT 22,000 per month, which is twice the salary of a teacher in the GPSs, helps to explain why qualified and talented people refrain from joining the primary education system in Bangladesh.

It is, however, important to note that the minimum qualifications to apply for the jobs of assistant teacher or headmaster in a GPS and those of BCS officer have some differences. Anyone with Bachelor's degree (either a three-year or four-year degree)[16] and minimum second class or equal Cumulative Grade Points Average (CGPA)[17] from any recognised university[18] or any equivalent degree is eligible to apply to become an assistant teacher or headmaster in a GPS. By contrast, to sit for the BCS exam, one needs to have completed at least a Bachelor's Honours degree (a four-year degree) from any recognised university and cannot have more than one-third class equivalent final grade in the undergraduate and graduate degrees. The BCS exam is attended by over 0.2 million candidates every year and only a small fraction of the applicants having a better degree from a reputed university with better skill and knowledge (demonstrated through the selection process) are finally selected.

Looking at the diversity of primary schools (as discussed in Section IV.A), it is important to mention that teachers in the non-private, non-GPSs are paid even less than the teachers in the GPSs and their jobs are not as secure.[19] There is a growing demand for the nationalisation of all non-GPSs so that teachers in those schools also get the benefits of GPSs.[20] These teachers demand permanent jobs and enlistment in the official Monthly Pay Order (MPO) scheme. The MPO is a pay system for teachers in state-controlled public schools and government-approved institutions. In non-MPO educational institutes, teachers and employees depend on student tuition fees and many of the

[15] See www.paylab.com/bd/salaryinfo.
[16] A three-year Bachelor's degree refers to Bachelor's pass course and a four-year degree refers to Bachelor's Honours course.
[17] Second class refers to obtaining marks in the range of 45–59%, and the equal CGPA refers to obtaining a grade point equal to or below 2.75 but above 2 on a 0–4 scale. CGPA is an educational grading system which is used in universities to measure the overall academic performance of a student.
[18] Here 'recognised university' means certified by the University Grants Commission of Bangladesh.
[19] Bangladesh has non-government private schools and government-funded private schools. Non-government private schools include schools run by registered non-government primary schools, unregistered non-governmental primary schools, NGOs, community schools, and Qaumi ebtedayee madrasahs. Government-funded private schools include Aliya ebtedayee madrasahs, schools under the ROSC project, and Shishu Kalyan Trust primary schools (World Bank, 2016). Teachers in the government-funded private schools and registered non-government primary schools, in general, require a similar academic qualification for recruitment as in the case of government primary schools.
[20] For the growing demand for nationalisation of non-government primary schools, see www.thedailystar.net/backpage/nationalisation-demand-pvt-primary-teachers-hunger-strike-7-days-1529107.

non-government school teachers do not receive regular salaries; therefore, the quality of education remains poor.[21]

However, there are a few private schools in Dhaka and other metropolitan cities where admission fees, tuition fees, exam fees, and many other regular and irregular fees are so exorbitant that poor families cannot afford to send their children there. The quality of education in these schools is much better than that of most of the government and non-GPSs. Teachers in these schools are better trained and qualified and better paid (Uddin, 2017).

Teachers in the NGO-run schools are paid much less than teachers in the GPSs. However, the selection process of teachers in the NGO-run schools is very different from that in government or non-GPSs. In the BRAC Primary Schools (BPSs), one of the important criteria for selecting a new BPS site is the presence of at least one adult, preferably a woman, who lives within the community, has completed at least 10 years of education, is willing and able to teach on a part-time basis, accepts wages much lower than those paid to GPS teachers, and agrees to thoroughly follow the BPS system (see USAID, 2006).[22]

Most of the teachers who continue their careers in the GPSs are graduates from sub-standard educational institutions, typically from the affiliated colleges of the National University of Bangladesh (NUB), with a very average record of academic achievement. Studies (BIDS, 2019; World Bank, 2019) found that the quality of the graduates of NUB are not up to the mark and, therefore, a good number of graduates from there are deprived of decent jobs and also face the risk of unemployment. Highlighting employers' views, the BIDS (2019) study mentioned that the NUB graduates lagged far behind their counterparts from other public universities in competence and quality as poor educational quality and lack of practical communication skills were prevalent among NUB graduates. The BIDS study also found that absenteeism among teachers in the NUB-affiliated colleges and student politics hamper academic environment and impose a negative impact on their studies. According to the World Bank (2019), around 2 million students are enrolled in over 2,000 colleges affiliated with the NUB, which is about nine times that of the 34 public universities combined and seven times that of 95 private universities. NUB graduates account for 68% of the total students pursuing higher education in Bangladesh. Given the poor performances of the NUB graduates, the World Bank (2019) study suggested reviewing the system of affiliation of colleges to create a higher education system that is more job market-responsive and addresses the need for multi-tier certification of tertiary education entities.[23]

---

[21] See www.wsws.org/en/articles/2019/08/05/bang-a05.html.

[22] However, the teachers in the NGO-run schools with lower salary levels are observed to be performing better (see Alam, 2000; Asadullah, 2016).

[23] The World Bank (2019) study argued that while it is undoubtedly impressive to see the affiliated colleges provide higher education to a large number of students from the lower socio-economic strata, given the poor graduate employability and low satisfaction over skills acquisition,

Many GPS teachers have no subject or pedagogical training, or are demotivated and busy with private income activities (World Bank, 2013; Hossain *et al.*, 2019). Many teachers leave their job within the first two years, mainly because of working conditions or low pay (ADB, 2017). Focus Group Discussions (FGD) with a group of GPS teachers also confirms that young and good-quality teachers are de-motivated and not interested in continuing teaching in the GPSs; for many of them, it a transitional job. A DPE (2017) report showed that a good number of posts in schools always remain vacant as young teachers leave frequently. In 2017, 8,564 GPSs were facing acute teacher shortages as 79 of them were running with only one teacher, 721 with only two teachers, and 7,764 with just three teachers (DPE, 2017). This has a severe impact on the quality of education in the primary schools. Therefore, a large number of people remain teaching in the primary schools who are not qualified enough or not interested in teaching.

The preceding observations suggest that a rise in teacher wages would attract better qualified candidates. If private employers are assumed to be able to infer from observable characteristics, including degrees and universities where they were obtained, the likely productivity of graduates, then candidates for teaching jobs are those that are judged to be at a lower productivity level by employers. They would even probably be hired at a wage below – or not above – the teachers' wage if they were to stay in the private sector. If the teachers' wage were raised, then more higher-level graduates would be candidates than it is the case today – the issue of training them as teachers remaining open, however.

It might appear that the first discrimination among people takes place in the choice of admission to a good university or the sub-standard one. However, as illustrated by the World Bank (2019) study, sub-standard colleges under the NUB enrol a large number of students from the lower socio-economic strata; therefore, the options for choosing better colleges are limited for these students.

Moreover, career progression opportunities are very limited in the primary education sector. The primary school has two types of post – assistant teacher and headmaster. To get promoted to a headmaster's position from that of an assistant teacher, one requires to have an honours degree (a four-year Bachelor degree), at least seven years of work experience as an assistant teacher, and a Diploma in Education (DPEd) or a Bachelor of Education (BEd) degree. However, since there is no other post between assistant teacher and

policymakers might need to take a close look at a range of system features and question some of the basic premises. The study posed a number of questions concerning whether it would still make sense to affiliate the colleges with varying degree of capacity under a single affiliation rule; whether it would be sustainable and reasonable in the long run to continue to affiliate over 2,000 colleges to a single university; or it would make sense to give a greater share of academic autonomy to the affiliated colleges. They study argued that fundamental questions like these would need to be explored to see how the affiliated college system can be reshaped in the mid to long term towards a more flexible, market-responsive higher education system.

headmaster, many never get promoted in their entire career, and retire as assistant teachers. During the FGD, some of the participants complained that they had not been promoted to a headmaster's position although they were eligible for this promotion. To solve this problem, the Government is considering creating the position of assistant headmaster.[24] But there has not been any progress on this front yet.

Although the salary and career path do not attract high-quality teachers, still a vast number of people apply for the jobs in the GPSs. In 2018, more than 2.4 million candidates took part in the examination for 14,096 posts, which means 170 candidates for one job. There are various reasons behind this scenario. As the economy in recent years has been going through a phase of slow job creation, there is a very high demand for government jobs. Also, these jobs are considered prestigious and secure in society. Furthermore, apart from the monthly salary, there are other incentives: teachers can earn from giving private tuition to students or having a second job. Therefore, the scarcity of jobs and the socio-economic factors mentioned above lead to a huge number of applicants for the jobs in the primary schools.

3 Persistent Poor Quality of Education-Related Infrastructure
Inadequate budget allocation and a low share of capital budget in the education budget over a long and sustained period has resulted in the poor quality of infrastructure in the primary education sector in Bangladesh. Despite the fact that each year there are thousands of requests for schools to be repaired, many of these requests are ignored due to the lack of funds. Moreover, a huge chunk of the allocated funds is wasted because of the lack of transparency.[25]

Another significant challenge is the high level of student–teacher ratio. There are many primary schools where the student–teacher ratio is extremely high, which creates huge challenges for teachers in terms of giving students enough attention and guidance. According to the Primary School Quality Level 14 standard, under the Third Primary Education Development Programme, there should be maximum of 46 students per teacher in primary schools. However, this ratio is still much higher than the international standard of 30 students per teacher. In 2016, 72.3% of the GPS and 50.3% of the Newly Nationalized Primary Schools (NNPS) met the directive of 46 students per teacher, and all the remaining schools had much higher number of students per teacher (DPE, 2017).

Furthermore, the paucity of classrooms, libraries, and playgrounds is responsible for poor-quality education in primary schools. Another related issue pointed out during the FGD is that the majority of schools do not have an adequate security system or personnel, and this is one of the critical reasons for the rise in the non-attendance of students (especially girl students) in primary schools. As mentioned earlier, according to the most recent data, nearly

[24] See www.newagebd.net/article/95665/govt-to-promote-65000-pry-teachers-to-asst-head-teachers.
[25] See www.thedailystar.net/opinion/where-our-education-system-has-failed-1525951.

one-fifth of students drop out from primary education; a report by UNICEF[26] pointed out that lack of safety and the high prevalence of sexual harassment and abuse in public places contributed to the dropout rate among girls from schools in Bangladesh. The same UNICEF report highlighted that schools did not have functional water and sanitation facilities responsive to gender or disability, or accommodating menstrual hygiene, which contributes significantly to the performance and attendance of girls.

The poor infrastructural aspect of the primary schools in Bangladesh can be demonstrated by looking at the average class size (pupils per class). As per the latest data, the average class size in primary school in Bangladesh is 60,[27] whereas the average for Organisation for Economic Co-operation and Development countries is 22, and the corresponding figures for China and Indonesia are 38 and 28, respectively.[28] An ADB (2017) study highlighted that many primary school teachers in Bangladesh do not get appropriate classrooms to teach their subjects (e.g. science classrooms). Teachers sometimes do not even have their own desks to store materials. Classroom facilities are often inadequate to meet students' needs.[29]

C Teacher Management in Government Primary Schools

1 Teacher Recruitment and Related Corruption

I RECRUITMENT. Of the total number of GPS teachers, 89% are assistant teachers and 11% are headmasters. Successful candidates are appointed to the vacant posts as per the guidelines issued by MoPME/DPE. It turns out that 60% of the vacant posts are allocated to female candidates, 20% are kept for dependents,[30] and 20% are given to male candidates.

[26] See www.unicef.org/bangladesh/en/more-opportunities-early-learning/quality-continuity-primary-education.
[27] See ADB (2017).
[28] See www.oecd-ilibrary.org/docserver/eag_highlights-2012-25-en.pdf?expires=1588764472&id=id&accname=guest&checksum=FD6658321IAFF9E3848F4B4A96B64AD7.
[29] This poor infrastructural aspect of the primary schools was aptly delineated by a special feature in a national daily – *The Daily Sun* (see www.daily-sun.com/magazine/details/282920/Poor-Condition-Of-The--Schools-For-The--Poor/2018-01-19). The lack of a sufficient number of classrooms, hygienic toilets, and drinking water facilities are some of the problems in government primary schools in Bangladesh. Usually, the classroom environment in government primary schools is not suitable for the perfect development of young children. Teachers often have to take several classes using a single room at the same time. Most of the classrooms remain dark and have damp walls that smell. Plaster from the walls and the ceiling frequently falls on the students and the children studying there feel scared due to a weak, cracked ceiling. Parents from affluent families often feel ashamed to send their child to government primary schools as these schools are considered the schools of the poor people, which encourages the sense of discrimination among the children from different economic classes. By contrast, though poor people are obliged to send their children to these schools, they feel insecure about this.
[30] If children of teachers apply for an assistant teacher position and pass the written test, they will be recruited.

There are distinct and lengthy procedures to recruit assistant teachers and headmasters. In GPSs, the recruitment of assistant teachers involves four steps – a recruitment circular and application screening, question preparation and a written exam, a viva voce, and final selection.[31] As mentioned earlier, candidates with a Bachelor's degree and minimum second class or equal CGPA from any recognised university (certified by the University Grant Commission) or any equivalent degree are eligible to apply to become assistant teachers in a GPSs. The candidates, however, do not need to have any teaching degree for the recruitment. Headmasters, in contrast, are appointed either through promotion or direct recruitment. Around 65% of the new headmasters come from the promotion of in-service assistant teachers by MoPME/DPE, whereas 35% are recruited directly by the Public Service Commission, representing non-cadres of the BCS.[32]

The teacher recruitment process in GPSs provides some insights into the recruitment process in other government sectors. The recruitment process for an assistant teachers in a GPS comprises a written test followed by a viva voce. Every other public sector, including the BCS, the public commercial banks, the central bank, the autonomous government organisations, etc., follows more or less the same procedure.[33] However, these are jobs at a higher level of salary and qualification and thus attract a different group of people.

II CORRUPTION. As mentioned earlier, the scarcity of jobs and other socio-economic factors (a government job is considered a prestigious and secure job and there is scope for earning extra through private tuition) lead to a large number of applicants for each post. This paves the way for malpractice: corruption appears in diverse forms, such as question-leaking, bribery, nepotism, favouritism, lobbying, and political influence.[34]

Over the past few years, in the government primary teacher recruitment process, the most discernible form of corruption has been the leakage of questions on the written test. The occurrence of question-leaking has achieved a

---

[31] See Annex 7.2 for details.

[32] There is a gap between promoted headmasters and directly recruited headmasters. To get promoted to headmaster from assistant teacher, one has to have an Honour's degree, at least seven years of work experience as an assistant teacher and DPEd or BEd degree. On the other hand, directly recruited headmasters need to have an Honour's degree and be 21–30 years old.

[33] For instance, the Bangladesh Public Service Commission arranges a three-stage recruitment examination to select suitable candidates for BCS cadres. The shortlisted applicants sit a 200-mark multiple choice question (MCQ) preliminary test. The candidates who pass the MCQ test are asked to sit the written test. Finally, to determine the suitability of the candidates who pass the written test, the BCS commission constitutes a board of oral examiners as per the provisions of the BCS examination rules. Based on the marks from written test and the oral test, successful candidates are selected for the announced BCS cadre posts (Bangladesh Public Service Commission, 2019). See www.bpsc.gov.bd/site/page/4bc95017-18d6-412b-8c4f-76d3e1599d8e/%E0%A6%AC%E0%A6%BF%E0%A6%B8%E0%A6%BF%E0%A6%8F%E0%A6%B8-%E0%A6%AA%E0%A6%B0%E0%A7%80%E0%A6%95%E0%A7%8D%E0%A6%B7%E0%A6%BE

[34] See Annex 7.3 for a schematic illustration of the institutional challenges faced in the recruitment of assistant teachers in government primary schools.

new dimension with the advent of the advanced technology, and the government has not been successful in stopping this prejudicial practice.[35]

Another mode of corruption is bribery. The prevalence of bribery is witnessed during and after the written exam. The candidates are entangled with bribery or are deprived of their rightful employment due to their refusal to give bribes. During the FGD, the participants mentioned that there is corruption and bribery in the recruitment process but that the people who benefit usually do not discuss the details. Corrupt circles run the business by contacting all the viva examinees and demanding a bribe, which they return (to some extent) to those who fail to get through the viva.

Nepotism in the recruitment of teachers is also prevalent. According to the FGD participants, sometimes knowing someone influential helps in securing a post. Therefore, nepotism, favouritism, lobbying, and political influence play an important part in the recruitment process.

As in the primary education sector, corruption in recruitment and transfer in other public sectors is extensively visible. For example, the public health sector in Bangladesh faces numerous corrupt practices, such as bribery and political influence in recruitment, transfers and promotions of healthcare professionals (McDevitt, 2015). In 2019, after a long inquiry, the Anti-Corruption Commission of Bangladesh identified 11 areas of corruption in health sector; these included recruitment, promotion, transfer, and posting.[36] Also, Paul (2017) observed that in Bangladesh, quotas[37] and the viva voce are the two main barriers to fair recruitment in the public services. The provision of giving too much importance to the viva voce breeds nepotism, favouritism, and bribery, and ultimately fuels corruption.

---

[35] The incidence of question-leaking is observed at different stages, such as the preparation of the question papers, printing the questions, and delivering the question sets to test centres. There is evidence that the questions are leaking through coaching centres, teachers, police, politicians, government employees, guardians, etc. During the FGD, the participants have also admitted that the corruption related to question leaking happens in various forms; for instance, supplying questions prior the written exam and sitting with a predetermined person who is appearing in the exam in order to help the examinee by showing answers.

[36] See www.dhakatribune.com/bangladesh/nation/2019/01/31/acc-finds-11-areas-of-corruption-in-health-sector.

[37] The quota system was introduced through an executive order in 1972 and has been amended several times since. Under the quota system in the government jobs recruitment process in Bangladesh, 56% of government job entry positions were reserved for specific categories: 30% for the children/grandchildren of 1971 freedom fighters, 10% for women, 10% for districts based on population, 5% for ethnic minorities, and 1% for people with disabilities. As a result, only 44% of the job candidates were able to secure positions on the basis of merit, causing discontent among a large section of general students who held the view that they were being deprived, despite scoring higher than candidates who fell under any quota. During April and August 2018, protests against the quota system erupted at various Bangladeshi universities. Finally, the government, on 4 October 2018, officially issued a circular abolishing the quota system for class I and class II jobs in the civil service. See www.thedailystar.net/country/quota-system-in-bangaldesh-scrapped-officially-1642534.

2 Complex Procedures for Teacher Promotion

The existing teacher promotion structure in GPSs is complex. It promotes discrimination and generates frustration among the teachers. Since only 65% of the vacant headmaster posts are filled by promoted teachers, many assistant teachers never have the opportunity to be promoted to headmaster. Besides, there are many examples where assistant teachers are promoted to headmaster after serving for 25–30 years. Furthermore, when teachers are promoted through departmental exams, the younger cohorts are more successful as they are more acquainted with the new syllabus. Therefore, there is no career progress for the majority of the teachers. Also, the promotion to UEO[38] from headmaster has been stopped since 1996, and UEOs have been recruited from outside. During the FGD, the participants stated that the promotion procedures are so complex in this sector that it is almost impossible for a headmaster to ever get promoted to assistant district or thana teaching officer through the normal process. There are cases of bribery, nepotism, favouritism, lobbying, and political influence in the promotion of teachers and headmasters.

3 Teacher Transfers and Related Corruption

The transfer process of teachers is complicated and involves many intermediate steps.[39] Under the existing system, teachers in primary schools can be transferred during January–March of each year. Given the availability of vacant posts, if a teacher wants to be transferred from one school to another within the same Upazila, the UEO is in charge of that. The District Education Officer does the transfer if it is in the same district. The transfer between districts within a division is done by the Divisional Deputy Director. In addition, the DPE transfers teachers from one division to another and from municipal to metropolitan areas.

This complex transfer process creates rent-seeking opportunities. Bribes are exchanged in majority transfers in metropolitan areas, which disrupts the recruitment rules. In Dhaka, the empty posts are filled via the transfer process instead of via the recruitment process. People want to provide their children with a better education and to help them lead a better life. Therefore, people are keen to be transferred to Dhaka and that is why, in some cases, they are even ready to pay bribes in order to get transferred. The participants in FGD complained that, on average, BDT 0.7 million (around US$ 8,000) needs to be given as a bribe for each transfer. In this process, teachers need to pay at every

---

[38] Each UEO is in charge of administration and management of education at the upazila level. The UEO with support from an assistant UEO performs overall education management of the upazila. The main responsibilities of a UEO include monitoring, supervising, and reporting on education; performing administrative duties; disbursing the government funds as per government rules; implementing the programmes undertaken by government and development partners; and executing the government orders.

[39] The transfer procedure is presented in a schematic diagram in Annex 7.4.

step, starting from the UEO to the office of the deputy director. Otherwise, the vacancy approval file does not move. Moreover, a candidate may have his or her application file lost if he/she refuses to pay a bribe.

Nepotism, favouritism, lobbying, and political influence are prevalent in the teachers' transfer process. According to MoPME/DPE, in 2019, the last date of transfer of assistant teachers of the GPSs was March 31. About 20,000 applications were submitted for the transfer, of which around 12,500 applications were submitted for transfer to Dhaka. However, in 2019, the whole transfer process was heavily condemned due to the presence of unjust practices. Lobbying from many senior ministers, members of parliament, and influential individuals were apparent. In fact, the highest level officials of MoPME/DPE were in an uncomfortable position because of the lobbying from powerful persons.[40]

Similar cases are found in the public health sector, too. For transfer or remaining in a privileged facility for longer period, bribing, nepotism, favouritism, lobbying, and political influence are very common (Transparency International Bangladesh, 2014). The Anti-Corruption Commission of Bangladesh also found wholesale corruption in almost every sector of the Bangladesh Land Port Authority. There was an allegation that irregularities were rife in transfer and promotion and in sending officials abroad for training; nepotism played a key role in allowing such irregularities.[41]

4 Lack of Discipline and Evaluation

In the context of the government primary education sector in Bangladesh, one indicator of a lack of accountability is the frequency of teachers being absent from the school on a school day. A study by Chaudhury *et al.* (2004) mentioned a unique survey in which the researchers made unannounced visits to some government-run primary schools and government-aided but privately run secondary schools in Bangladesh. The visits showed that the average teacher absence rate in primary schools was 15.5%; the absence rate in primary schools was highest among headmasters at 20%. Cross-sectional averages masked the extent of this problem: 23.5% of primary school teachers were absent during at least one of the two visits.

One may argue that this 2004 study is dated and that the situation has improved significantly. However, the situation has not changed and may have even worsened. *The Daily Star*, an English-language daily newspaper in Bangladesh, reported that while visiting a primary school in Chattogram city

[40] See www.banglatribune.com/national/news/443933/%E0%A6%98%E0%A7%81%E0%A6% B7-%E0%A6%93-%E0%A6%9C%E0%A7%8B%E0%A6%B0%E0%A6% BE%E0%A6%B2%E0%A7%8B-%E0%A6%A4%E0%A6%A6%E0%A6%AC%E 0%A6%BF%E0%A6%B0-%E0%A6%A8%E0%A6%BE-%E0%A6%A5%E0%A6 %BE%E0%A6%95%E0%A6%B2%E0%A7%87-%E0%A6%AB%E0%A6%BE% E0%A6%87%E0%A6%B2-%E0%A6%97%E0%A6%BE%E0%A7%9F%E0%A7%87%E0 %A6%AC.
[41] See www.newagebd.net/article/100642/acc-finds-wholesale-corruption-in-bangladesh-land-ports.

at around 9 am on a day in January 2019, the Anti-Corruption Commission chief found that only the acting headmaster was present in the school, while seven other teachers were absent. Due to the absence of teachers, the students were spending idle time on the school premises.[42]

Another English daily newspaper – *The Bangladesh Post* – reported that the teachers in different primary schools in different regions remain busy in other, non-teaching activities. In *haor* (large bodies of water) areas, teachers remain busy harvesting in paddy fields, or in hill regions, the attendance of primary teachers decreases during the cultivation season. Apart from this, the allegation has also been raised against the primary teachers that they come to school late and only sign the attendance sheet. In some schools, it was also found that many teaches have hired teachers (called para-teachers) who provide proxy attendance for the actual teacher. Taking all those issues into consideration, the Government in July 2019 decided to introduce biometric attendance to stop these irregularities.[43] However, little progress has been made on this front so far.

D Curriculum and Teacher Training in Primary Education

1 Poorly Designed Curriculum and Faulty Examination System

The introduction of the PEC examination at the primary level since 2009 has encouraged the students to drill and memorise rather than gain a proper understanding of the material being taught. Students do not get the chance to understand the content or find any scope to create something on their own. Education experts, researchers, teachers, and guardians have questioned the value of this examination. This examination even does not contribute to improving the teaching–learning process. Manzoor Ahmed (an education expert in Bangladesh) argued that, 'The effects of PEC have been to encourage drills and rote memorization, neglect understanding and creativity, disregard basic content of the curriculum, and discourage thinking and reasoning. Formative assessment is needed to evaluate students' learning. In educational terms, this is more important than the summative assessment like PEC. The PEC has taken away time and effort from formative evaluation and regular teaching–learning.'[44]

According to the Ministry of Education (2010), the National Curriculum and Textbook Board is in charge of changing the content of the syllabus as well as the question pattern to assess students' creativity. However, the teachers at primary school level are not capable enough to comply with the plan. The key findings[45] of a survey carried out by Research for Advancement of

---

[42] See www.thedailystar.net/city/acc-chief-iqbal-mahmud-visits-chattogram-schools-finds-most-teachers-absent-1693567.

[43] See www.bangladeshpost.net/posts/biometric-attendance-for-primary-teachers-7609.

[44] For details, see http://m.theindependentbd.com/arcprint/details/43527/2016-05-12.

[45] See www.thedailystar.net/editorial/most-teachers-ignorant-the-creative-education-method-207763.

Complete Education in 2016 showed that around 55% of teachers in primary schools did not understand the creative system; more than half of 100 primary school teachers who took part in a survey were still unclear about the creative education method introduced about five years ago; about half of the teachers surveyed relied on guidebooks[46] to prepare lessons; around 92% of students used guidebooks to understand their lessons; there was a reliance on private tutors and coaching centres among learners; and the PEC exam was perceived to be the root cause of the mushroom growth of coaching centres as well as the publication of guidebooks.[47]

A survey of 216 teachers by Amin and Greenwood (2018) found that teachers felt pressured by headteachers, parents, and particularly by students, to teach in ways that would lead to good marks in the examination. Teachers largely agreed that they actively prepared students for the examination, not only by arranging mock class tests but also by teaching answers to expected questions; interestingly, a majority acknowledged that their teaching style would have been different if there was no examination. Nearly 90% of the teachers agreed that reading and listening tests needed to be included in the national examination process; these are absent in the current system.

2 Shortage of Trained Primary School Teachers

The primary education sector in Bangladesh suffers from the lack of enough qualified and trained teachers; the proportion is roughly the same for man and women. According to DPE (2017), in 2016, 21% of the total GPS teachers had no professional qualification. In addition, most of the teachers are not adequately trained to adopt modern teaching methods, such as computers, in classrooms, which works as a barrier to ensure high-quality primary education (ADB, 2017). There is a serious lack of university-based teacher training programmes. Primary Teachers Training Institutes (PTIs) are the only institutions in the country that train primary school teachers. For untrained teachers serving

---

[46] Guidebooks refer to the books that contain ready-made answers to questions in the textbooks prepared by the National Curriculum and Textbook Board. The heavy dependence by teachers and students on guidebooks to prepare lessons and understand the lessons, respectively, has been a real concern in education, in particular, primary education in Bangladesh. The guidebook culture damages the creativity and innovative ability of students. Students lose their interest to know more about a topic and think differently. Guidebooks encourage students to memorise without understanding the topic. Thus, guidebooks limit the thinking capacity of students as they copy from the guidebooks. Education experts, academicians, researchers, teachers, parents, and officials from education offices have expressed their concern about the rampant use of guidebooks and have asked for immediate action to stop the widespread use of these in the classroom and home. See www.theindependentbd.com/arcprint/details/43527/2016-05-12.

[47] Guidebooks have become the principal instrument for studying for most students, school teachers, private tutors, and coaching centres. The appeal of the guidebook lies in their ready-made answers to likely exam questions. So, the learners have no need to read textbooks, learn the content, or figure out own answers. The schools also prepare the question papers for half-yearly, yearly, and test exams following guidebooks.

in GPSs, NNPS, and Registered Non-GPSs, PTIs provide one-year, in-service training programmes leading to the Certificate in Education. However, there is no pre-service teacher education programme in PTIs in Bangladesh, unlike in other countries. Teachers receive training after their appointment and a placement in a school.

V SUMMARY AND CONCLUSION

Primary education plays an important role in development in Bangladesh. Though Bangladesh has been successful in ensuring a close-to-universal enrolment rate in primary education, poor outcomes in primary education remain a major concern. This chapter has analysed major challenges related to the poor performance of the primary education sector in Bangladesh. Further to this discussion, this chapter suggests some measures to improve the performance of the primary education sector in the country. These include: enhancing the budgetary allocation for the primary education sector; better salary and career paths for primary teachers; improving the recruitment process for primary teachers; initiatives to improve the quality of school infrastructure; initiatives to improve facilities to increase school attendance; improving the curriculum and examination system; ensuring accountability and transparency in evaluation of both teachers and learning achievement; and the harmonisation of the coexistence of various actors.

A Enhancing the Budgetary Allocation for the Primary Education Sector

As discussed earlier, the primary education budget has been historically low in Bangladesh. This budget in Bangladesh has two expenditure components: the recurrent budget and the capital budget – at present around 70% of the budget is spent on teachers' salaries (recurrent expenditure). In proportion to GDP, Bangladesh should significantly increase the allocation to the primary education sector in line with the average allocation observed in many comparable countries. This will result in an increase in the salary of the teachers and will attract qualified and talented graduates to GPSs. Along with enhancing the budget allocation to the primary education sector, attention should also be given to ensure the effective utilisation of the budget. Also, a significant part of the additional budget should be allocated to the capital budget so that infrastructure development, essential maintenance, and repair works can be undertaken.

B Better Salary and Career Paths for Primary Teachers

It has been pointed out that the low salary and the lack of career path do not attract young and qualified teachers and discourage them from continuing their careers in the primary education sector. There was a major pay hike of government job salaries by 91–101% in December 2015, but, by both international and national standards, teacher pay remains largely unsatisfactory. This will remain the case unless further pay hikes are implemented.[48]

The FGD with GPS teachers also confirmed that many talented teachers continued teaching only for 6–12 months before switching to better jobs. Moreover, career progression opportunities are very limited in the primary education sector. In this context, part of the additional budget allocation should be allocated to the higher salary and facilities for the primary school teachers so that the sector attracts qualified teachers.

The lack of promotion or progression to a higher post after some years of service is another adverse factor in the primary education system. The following new posts may be created in the primary education sector to encourage talented teachers to pursue this career: (i) senior assistant teacher (proposed); (ii) senior teacher (proposed); and (iii) assistant headmaster (proposed).[49]

C Improving the Recruitment Process for Primary Teachers

As discussed earlier, the recruitment process for GPS teachers is a huge undertaking in Bangladesh. Further, as we discussed, corruption is prevalent in the recruitment process. It should be re-emphasised that high-quality teaching and effective learning at schools, among others, critically depend on the recruitment of high-quality teachers. In this context, several initiatives may be considered. First, at present, graduate degree holders from any recognised university with a minimum second division/class are allowed to apply for the post of assistant teacher. MoPME/DPE may contemplate modifying this requirement by adding teaching degrees, such as DPEd, BEd, etc. to the prerequisites list. Second, written examinations at centres that are identified with question leaks may be scrapped, which may discourage this type of malpractice. Third, currently, the written examination is the MCQ type, which to some extent is open to question leaks. Thus, the current format may be modified with 30 marks for MCQ and the rest of the marks, 50, on essay-type questions. Finally, districts may not be allowed to take a viva or interview candidates from the same districts. Rather, a different district within the same division may be given the responsibility of taking the viva and interview, or some random allocations, at the last moment, between candidates and recruitment committees can be made. This move may discourage bribes from being paid.

---

[48] See https://thefinancialexpress.com.bd/economy/govt-employees-may-get-25pc-pay-raise-1551497233.

[49] As mentioned before, the government is considering creating this post, but no progress has been made so far. If created, this post may be considered only for schools with a large number of students.

D Initiatives to Improve the Quality of School Infrastructure

The state of infrastructure (i.e. school building, classroom, functional water, sanitation, and security) in most of the primary schools has been reported as poor. Inadequate budget allocation and the low share of capital budget over a long and sustained period has resulted in the poor-quality infrastructure of the primary education sector in Bangladesh. It is alleged that the paucity of classrooms, libraries, and playgrounds are responsible for poor-quality education at primary schools. Therefore, there is a need to allocate part of the additional budget allocation to the improvement of the infrastructural quality of the primary education school system. The MoPME/DPE may undertake a special development project under the annual development programme for the wholesale improvement of the primary school infrastructure, with a special focus on classroom amenities, water and sanitation, and security.

E Initiatives to Improve Facilities to Increase School Attendance

MoPME/DPE is providing more than 33,000 students of 175 primary schools with cooked food. By 2023, DPE aims to provide cooked food to all the schools in the country. An internal assessment by MoPME/DPE shows that school attendance increases by up to 11% if students are provided with cooked food, whereas when supplied with only biscuits, the attendance rate increases only up to 6%.[50] MoPME/DPE also plans to provide each primary level student with BDT 2,000 for their uniform on the understanding that students with new uniforms, and nutritious and delicious food in their schools will feel more attached to their institutions. These initiatives are perhaps policies moving in the right direction. But there is uncertainty about the full implementation and sustainability of these initiatives. Thus, the attempt should be to ensure full implementation and sustainability through the allocation of sufficient resources.

F Improving the Curriculum and Examination System

Given the large gap between acquiring the certificate and actual learning, the emphasis should also be given on reforming the entire primary education system in Bangladesh. In this context, the Government should implement the National Education Policy 2010, which suggested extending primary education to Grade 8. This move will transform the exam-centric education system into a dynamic, learner-centric one. Primary level students should not be assessed through public exams; rather, they should be assessed through

---

[50] See www.thedailystar.net/star-weekend/spotlight/news/primary-education-bangladesh-all-exams-and-no-learning-1798843.

continuous academic performance. The Government needs to improve the classroom environment, the training of teachers, and pay more attention to co-curricular activities.

G Ensuring Accountability and Transparency in the Evaluation of Both Teachers and Learning Achievement

As discussed earlier, institutional challenges in the education system and the resultant corruption are not significantly different from those seen in other public sectors in Bangladesh. Therefore, a more accountable education system needs to be built as part of an overall accountable public service. The ways to achieve effective accountability in the primary education system include hefty penalties for bribery, establishing rules for conflict of interest and codes of conduct, delinking the administration from political influence, merit-based recruitment and career development rules, access to information, and complaint mechanisms for students and parents.

Technology may be used for assessing the accountability of the teachers. Technological advances and improved accessibility of devices such as digital cameras, tablets, and smartphones have facilitated the ability of communities to hold teachers accountable. Most use of technology focuses on reducing teacher absenteeism. However, as mentioned earlier, though the Government has considered introducing biometric attendance to reduce the absenteeism of teachers, so far there has not been any progress in this case.

A UNESCO (2017) report highlighted that in Udaipur, India, students used cameras with tamper-proof dates to photograph their teachers at the start and close of the day. Initial research suggested that this, jointly with the financial incentives provided, helped decrease absenteeism. Also, a Ugandan project to raise teacher attendance in 180 rural public primary schools distributed mobile phones equipped with software to report teacher absence to education officials. The phone monitors were headteachers or parents from the school management committee. In Pakistan, to monitor the attendance of over 210,000 education staff in 26,200 schools, biometrics – fingerprints and photos, coupled with Global Positioning System coordinates – were introduced. As at February 2017, 40,000 absent teachers and 6,000 absconders (employed but long absent) have been disciplined. India's 2016–2017 economic survey recommended the use of biometrics to tackle teacher absenteeism in primary schools. However, overuse or improper use of technology may have negative consequences. UNESCO (2017) report also mentioned that thousands of classrooms in China were livestreamed, allowing parents and the public to monitor and comment on teaching practices and student behaviour. However, critics were concerned that continual surveillance violates teachers' and students' privacy rights and could negatively affect instruction.

A performance pay programme for primary school teachers can also be effective in reducing teacher absenteeism and enhancing learning achievement. Muralidharan and Sundararaman (2011) presented the results from a randomised controlled trial of a programme, which was employed in rural schools in the Indian state of Andhra Pradesh. The programme, administered by an NGO, provided teachers in government-run primary schools in rural India (Grades 1–5) with financial bonus payments of about US$ 14 for each percentage point gain in their students' maths and language test scores. The bonuses were designed to address the interrelated problems of low teacher effort in rural India, such as pervasive absenteeism, minimal teaching activity even among many of those present (as shown in Kremer *et al.*, 2005), and low student achievement, as reflected in the findings from an all-India survey of rural households that approximately half of students enrolled in Grade 5 cannot read at a Grade 2 level (as shown in Annual Status of Education Report Centre, 2014). Muralidharan and Sundararaman (2011) showed that the programme produced gains in all four subjects measured (maths, language, science, and social studies), increasing the average achievement score by between 6 and 13 percentile points in performance pay schools compared to control schools, over a two- to three-year period.

Parents and communities may also be involved in monitoring teachers' presence in the schools. A review of the national education plans of 40 mostly low- and middle-income countries by UNESCO (2017) found an increasing role of parents and communities in teacher accountability. In the absence of clear guidelines, participatory approaches can be organised in a bottom-up manner, relying on community motivation to monitor teaching. Other forms may also be used in this regard. Representatives of local communities can visit classrooms, for instance, to ensure that teachers are present. The UNESCO (2017) study also suggests that community-led surveys concerning teachers have been used in several low-income contexts, especially in rural or disadvantaged regions.

Following these global experiences, Bangladesh may adopt a properly designed technology-powered accountability system in the primary education system. This will enhance accountability and transparency for the evaluation of both teachers and learning achievement in primary schools in Bangladesh.

H Harmonisation of the Coexistence of Various Actors

Finally, in the case of the coexistence of various actors in the primary education system in Bangladesh, there is a need to bring all schools under a single umbrella. The MoPME/DPE can create that umbrella so that many institutional challenges are addressed, and high-quality of education is ensured across all schools.

ANNEX 7.1 TYPES OF PRIMARY SCHOOL IN BANGLADESH

Overseeing authority	Type of school	Description
MoPME/DPE	GPS	Primary school run by the Government.
MoPME/DPE	NNPS	Primary school nationalised recently by the Government and run in the same way as the government schools.
MoPME/DPE	Registered Non-Government Primary School	Private primary school registered under government authority.
MoPME/DPE	Non-Registered Non-Government Primary School	Private primary school not registered under government authority.
MoPME/DPE	Experimental School	School attached to PTI and supposed to be used as a laboratory school.
MoPME/DPE	Community School	Publicly funded school that serves as both an educational institution and a centre of community life.
MoPME/DPE	ROSC School	School under the initiative ROSC, undertaken by the Government of Bangladesh in 2013. These schools aim to provide a second chance to education for disadvantaged children aged 8–14 years who never had the chance to enrol in the primary schools or who had to drop out for other reasons.
MoPME/DPE	Shishu Kalyan School	School run by Shishu Kalyan Trust under the administration of MoPME/DPE to provide education to underprivileged children.
MoE	Ebtedayee	Educational institution that has similar core courses as in the primary schools but has an additional emphasis on religious studies.
MoE	High Madrasah attached Ebtedayee	Attached to high madrasahs. The syllabus and subjects taught in high madrasahs are the same as that of high schools, except for two subjects: Arabic and Introduction to Islam.
MoE	High School attached Primary Section	Primary school attached to high schools.

Overseeing authority	Type of school	Description
MoC	Kindergarten	Pre-primary school for the children aged below six based on playing, singing, practical activities, such as drawing, and social interaction as part of the transition from home to school.
MoC	Tea Garden	School for the children of tea garden workers.
NGO bureau	BRAC school	BRAC primary school offering non-formal education to disadvantaged and school dropout children in Bangladesh, with a particular emphasis on girls.
NGO bureau	NGO Learning Centre	Most NGOs offer three to four years of schooling in a learning centre. This is more on a temporary arrangement for the delivery of basic education to over-aged out of school children.
Other authorities	Non-aligned institute	School for blind, deaf and dumb, jail attached schools, social welfare-based learning centres, mosque and temple-based learning centres, Chattogram Hill Tract schools, etc.

ANNEX 7.2 THE ASSISTANT TEACHER RECRUITMENT PROCESS

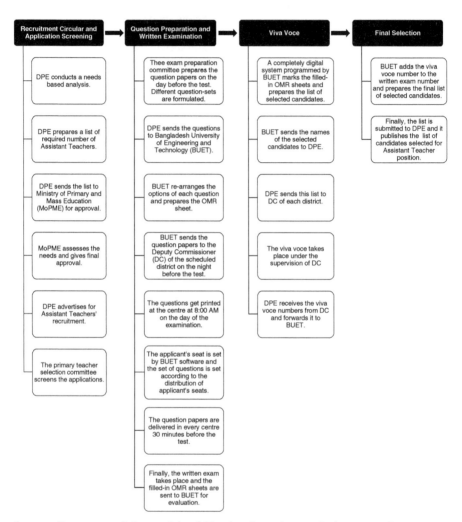

Source: Government Primary School Teacher Recruitment Order 2019; Government Primary School Teacher Recruitment Order 2013; Primary Education Development Programme 3; National Education Policy 2010; and Key Informant Interviews.

ANNEX 7.3 INSTITUTIONAL CHALLENGES IN THE ASSISTANT TEACHER RECRUITMENT PROCESS

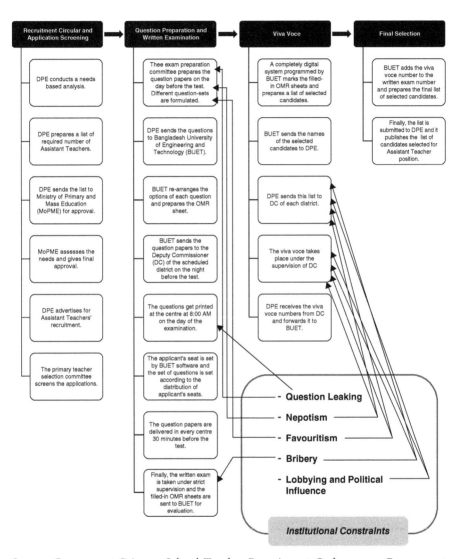

Source: Government Primary School Teacher Recruitment Order 2019; Government Primary School Teacher Recruitment Order 2013; Primary Education Development Programme 3; National Education Policy 2010; and Key Informant Interviews.

ANNEX 7.4 TRANSFER PROCEDURE FOR PRIMARY SCHOOL TEACHERS FROM ONE DIVISION TO ANOTHER, OR TO THE CAPITAL CITY

The teacher submits an application to the District Education Office, recommended by the Headmaster, Upazila Assistant Education Officer, and Upazila Education Officer.
The District Education Officer sends the application file to the divisional office with a recommendation.
The application is then sent from the divisional office to the DPE.
The vacancy is confirmed and the process of authorising the transfer starts for the vacant post.
The Director General goes through the file and sends it to the Director (Policy and Operations).
The file goes to the Deputy Director (School) and is forwarded to the Assistant Director (Policy).
The Assistant Director sends the file to an Education Officer.
The Education Officer despatches the file to the Assistant Director (Policy), seeking approval for whether the vacancy should be sought against the vacant post or not.
The Assistant Director (Policy) redirects the file to the Deputy Director (School).
The Deputy Director sends the file to the Director (Policy and Operations).
The Director (Policy and Operation) approves the vacancy and forwards the file to the Assistant Director (Policy).
The Assistant Director (Policy) sends a letter to the District Education Officer sanctioning the file.
The District Education Officer writes a letter to the concerned upazila seeking approval for the vacant post.
Upazila Education Officer sends a letter to the District Education Officer confirming the vacancy and stating that the teacher can be transferred.
The District Education Officer sends the file directly to the office of the Director General along with the letter received from the Upazila Education Officer.
Finally, the Director (Policy and Operations) issues the order when the transfer order gets approval.

Source: Primary Teachers' Transfer Guidelines 2018, Ministry of Primary and Mass Education, Directorate of Primary Education, and FGD.

Discussion: Institutional Challenges in Public Spending: The Case of Primary Education

Elizabeth M. King

More and More Equal Education

Over the past two decades, Bangladesh achieved an unprecedented expansion in enrolment rates in basic education. As a result, the country's average schooling attainment has exceeded the average attainment in India and Pakistan and is approaching the averages in Sri Lanka, Indonesia, and Malaysia (Figure 7.4). This achievement was a result of effective education programs sustained since the early 1990s and a growing economy.

The most remarkable feature of this achievement is the dramatic increase in girls' enrolment rates and average years of schooling. This is worth noting because the large gains in women's schooling made possible the growth of its garment industry which, in turn, fuelled the country's recent economic growth, as noted in de Melo's comments in this volume. The study by Heath and Mobarak (2015) documents this positive interplay between the progress in women's education and the expansion of the garment industry. They found that young girls were more likely to be enrolled in school after garment jobs arrived, and that older girls were more likely to be employed outside the home in villages closer to garment factories. Although the growth of the garment industry spurred educational development, it was the government's conditional cash transfer program to encourage female enrolment at the secondary level, launched in 1994,[51] that put the country firmly on the steeper path to progress. The stipend program increased girls' years of education by 14–25%, as well as changed several life outcomes for them: girls now marry later, have fewer children, work in the formal sector more than in the agricultural or informal sector, and enjoy greater autonomy in making decisions about household

---

[51] Bangladesh's Female Secondary School Stipend Program made secondary education free for rural girls and gave girls a modest stipend upon enrolment.

TABLE 7.1 *Median number of years of education: both sexes, ages 15–49*

		Residence			Wealth quintile			
Survey	Total	Urban	Rural	Poorest (Q1)	Q2	Q3	Q4	Richest (Q5)
2014 DHS	3.6	4.7	3.1	0.6	2.4	3.8	4.6	7.2
2011 DHS	3.1	4.6	2.5	0	1.7	3.3	4.3	6.8
2007 DHS	2.5	4.2	1.9	0	1.1	2.3	4	6.1
2004 DHS	2.1	3.8	1.7	0	0.6	2.2	3.8	5.7

Source: Demographic & Health Surveys (DHS), 2004–2014.

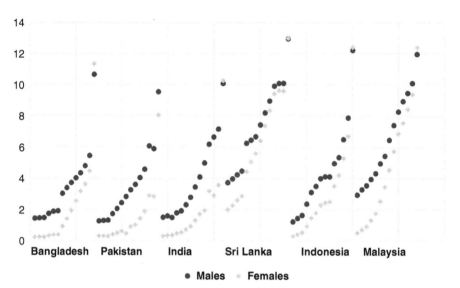

FIGURE 7.4 Estimated average years of schooling, adults 25 and over, males and females, Bangladesh and other Asian countries
Source: Barro-Lee, 1950–2010; HCI, 2018.

purchases (Hahn, *et al.,* 2018). These are long-term impacts that will yield significant spillover benefits in generations to come.

Bangladesh not only closed the gender gap in education but also narrowed the gaps between urban and rural areas and among income groups within a decade (Table 7.1). Innovative non-government and community programs, such as BRAC schools, for which Bangladesh is known, contributed to this progress.[52] In acknowledging its educational successes, the narrowing of these large disparities, especially when comparing wealth quintiles, deserves note. A

---

[52] See, for example, Ahmed and Arends-Kuenning (2006), Ahmad and Haque (2011), and Asadullah, Savoia and Mahmud (2014).

TABLE 7.2 *Learning-adjusted years of schooling in Bangladesh and comparator countries*

	Expected years of school	Harmonized test scores	Learning-adjusted years of school
Pakistan	8.8	339	4.8
India	10.2	355	5.8
Bangladesh	11.3	368	6.5
Indonesia	12.3	403	7.9
Sri Lanka	13.0	400	8.3
Malaysia	12.2	468	9.1

Source: www.worldbank.org/content/dam/worldbank_hci/index.html#years-of-school/PAK& region=SAS.

previous review of the primary education sector concluded that Bangladesh's recurrent public spending in primary education has been largely pro-poor. Public spending per child in the poorest quintile of upazilas was 30% higher than in the wealthiest quintile, although this pro-poor spending has not eliminated large disparities (Steer, Rabbani, and Parker, 2014).

But Schooling Is Not Learning

The importance of learning, not just schooling, has been the focus of recent major education reports because of its critical contribution to economic growth and overall development (Education Commission, 2016; World Bank, 2017). When students go through school without acquiring basic knowledge and skills that they need for life and work, families, communities, and economies do not reap the potential benefits of education. In Bangladesh, as evidence cited in this chapter shows, learning outcomes have not risen apace with years of schooling. According to Asadullah and Chaudhury (2015), about half of the children fail to pass a written numeracy competence test, a finding that also holds for those who had completed primary school. While there is a statistically significant and positive correlation between schooling attained and numeracy competence, this relationship is quite low. Table 7.2 compares Bangladesh with other Asian countries with respect to the quantity and quality of schooling attainment (World Bank, 2020b). Because of deficiencies in the quality of schooling measured by harmonized test scores (Altinok, Angrist, and Patrinos, 2018), the expected schooling attainment in Bangladesh of 11.3 years is equivalent to just 6.5 learning-adjusted years. It performs better than India or Pakistan, but the distance from the other comparator countries is greater.

Improving the quality of primary education is inarguably Bangladesh's next education challenge. This chapter argues that institutional change in four areas are needed to meet this challenge: (1) high fragmentation due to the complex coexistence of multiple actors; (2) inadequate financing resources; (3) low-quality teachers and poor teacher management in GPSs; and (4) lack of a common curriculum and teacher training.

Addressing the Fragmentation of Primary Education System

The high fragmentation of the primary education system in Bangladesh is evident. It consists of several types of primary schools under different central agencies, alongside many types of non-government schools. In addition, the public school system itself is overseen by deconcentrated administrative units, with local subdistricts (upazilas) playing a major administrative role. Nationalization of all schools, as recommended by this chapter, however, is hardly the solution to the problems that arise from high fragmentation. A diverse system of provision may be what the country needs in order to meet the diverse needs of its population, also as suggested by this chapter, and perhaps how Bangladesh was able to achieve the educational development it has today. Nationalization is likely to eliminate an important part of this diversity, in particular, the NGO and private schools that serve rural and poorer areas. Instead of nationalization, what may address the problems of fragmentation is a governance structure that is consistent with decentralized delivery and yet is led by a central agency that sets and oversees common standards of delivery, enforces regulatory guardrails across all schools, and monitors learning outcomes nationwide, all towards achieving shared goals. Even in a decentralized system that assigns responsibilities to local governments and is open to both public and private providers, the central government can – and should – have a critical role for leading a coherent national school system. This view is implied but not elaborated in this chapter's several recommendations, including that on the harmonization of multiple actors.

One important policy and programming tool for the central government is ensuring that timely and reliable information on the whole school system is widely available and that that information is used for decision-making and management. Especially in as large a school system as Bangladesh's, the flow of adequate school data is the key to facilitating decisions and removing implementation blockages, identifying spending gaps, and addressing workforce problems. For example, this chapter is right in calling attention to fraud and corruption in the certification, recruitment, and transfer of teachers and to the significant budgetary resources left on the table and unspent in spite of the low national expenditure allocation for education. These are indicators of the school system's weak management and poor implementation capacity. Without adequate system-wide data, those who formulate policies and manage programs are disadvantaged by not knowing whether their spending decisions and policies are appropriate and whether those decisions affect school performance. When system information is open and shared widely, politics and vested interests are also less likely to drive policy and spending decisions.

Studies have shown that robust accountability and transparency mechanisms help raise the quality of service delivery because the scope and complexity of what governments must do to achieve education goals is nearly impossible without reliable and timely data. This is a lesson that the best performing education systems have learned over time; Bangladesh could use it too in order to transform its primary education system.

Improving the Primary Education Workforce

A large part of this chapter is rightly devoted to institutional issues related to teachers. Teachers are the system's biggest investment and also its most powerful lever for change. How teachers are trained, recruited, inducted into the profession, supported, assessed, and compensated are all relevant to improving teacher performance in any education system. This chapter describes the multi-layered, highly complex mechanism for hiring teachers, that is nonetheless vulnerable to fraud and corruption and hires teachers who do not meet quality standards. This chapter also discusses how this recruitment process can be simplified and be more transparent and efficient. One change that this chapter identifies as a disincentive for improvement in teacher performance is the lack of prospects for promotion and recommends that an additional position of assistant headmaster be created so that teachers can aspire for a promotion. This chapter also argues that teacher salaries are too low and recommends an increase in basic teacher pay. Neither recommendation by itself is likely to obtain better teacher performance, however. What is missing from this chapter is a discussion of teacher reforms that are focused on achieving good teaching and more learning. If the aim is to improve teaching quality and learning, then these lessons, to highlight just a few, from other school systems would be useful:

- In recent reviews of the literature about effective teacher professional development, among the most recommended interventions are changing the pedagogy used in teacher training institutes so that it is more directed to individual levels; provide training with specific subject content rather than general theory since different subjects require different pedagogies; provide follow-up mentoring visits for new teachers and allow new teachers to practice with other teachers; support continuous learning opportunities for current teachers; and involve teachers in curriculum development (Popova, *et al.*, 2018). Many resources are spent on teacher development programs, so a reform of these programs would raise significantly the cost-effectiveness of public spending on education.
- Studies have shown that financial incentives do improve the supply of new teachers and the performance of current teachers (e.g. Duflo, Hanna and Ryan, 2012), but the design of these incentives matter. This chapter recommends increasing teacher pay. Higher salaries do not guarantee better

performance, however. Indonesia's experience with a national unconditional increase in teacher salaries in the early 2000s serves as a cautionary tale. The government was expecting a doubling of teacher salaries to improve teacher morale, motivation, and job satisfaction, thereby increasing teacher effort and ultimately student learning. After the pay increase, teachers were indeed more satisfied with their income and less likely to report financial stress, were less likely to have a second job and worked fewer hours on second jobs, but they did not score better on tests of teacher subject knowledge and did not reduce absenteeism and student learning did not improve (de Ree *et al.*, 2015). Key lessons from other countries about how to make financial incentives more effective are summarized by Imberman (2015): first, the choice of metrics and the incentive structure matters for its effectiveness; poorly designed schemes can make outcomes worse while also more costly. Second, incentives should be based on multiple outcomes, of which better student performance is one of several metrics and at least one of which should be qualitative (e.g. principal evaluation or classroom observations). Third, teachers should be rewarded for reaching certain performance targets, such as for their students performing better relative to a set of comparison students.

- A teacher accountability mechanism is broader than using financial incentives for performance; it should link teacher performance also to promotion and retention outcomes. Its goal is to make teaching an attractive and rewarding profession by recognizing and rewarding high ability and good performance. Effective teacher evaluation systems share a common set of features (Kraft *et al.*, 2018): (1) the use of multiple measures of teacher performance including test-based performance measures such as value-added measures or student growth percentiles, and a qualitative assessment such as classroom observation by school principals or senior teachers; (2) the use of evaluation ratings to inform career ladders and personnel decisions such as promotion and retention. For example, Singapore's teacher performance appraisal process feeds into career ladders by highlighting teachers' abilities to collaborate with each other, their emerging leadership skills, and their teaching skills as part of the regular evaluation system (NCEE, 2016). The model includes three paths that a teacher can follow: a teaching track, a leadership track, and a senior specialist track, and each of these tracks has its own career ladder. Through the teaching track, teachers can aspire first to be Senior Teachers, then they can become Lead Teachers, and then progress further to the level of Master Teachers.

Hossain *et al.* (2017) warn that reforms that are related to teacher performance are difficult because teachers are politically important in Bangladesh, as they are in many other countries, so reforms that are 'more carrot than stick' are more likely to be acceptable, but their success depends on the inherent motivations of teachers. This is a reminder that successful teacher reforms need an astute political leader in the education system.

Increasing Resources for Education

The world of the future will require higher levels of skills and the ability of individuals to acquire new skills throughout life, to know how to adapt to changing social and environmental conditions, and to work flexibly. This is why higher school quality and better academic outcomes is the next education challenge for Bangladesh. Ensuring that the primary education system is equipped to meet that challenge will require greater resources for schools and better management of those resources. This chapter makes a good case for expanding the resources for primary education given the empirical evidence on the returns to economic development and poverty reduction of basic education in Bangladesh, the very low share of education spending to GDP of Bangladesh compared to that of comparator countries, and the poor physical condition of schools and the need for schools to provide more services to low-income students such as meals.

The increase in education expenditures must be accompanied also by a willingness of the education leaders at different levels of government to take bold measures to make those additional resources count. Wastage and leakage of resources due to fraud and corruption must be reduced, and education resources must be allocated to where they can contribute most to higher school quality. Research on other developing countries suggest some useful measures to try, but even better would be for Bangladesh to invest in more program experimentation and evaluations on how to improve quality.

8

Institutional Challenges in Land Administration and Management in Bangladesh

Selim Raihan, Md. Jahid Ebn Jalal, Eshrat Sharmin, and
M. Abu Eusuf

I INTRODUCTION[1]

Bangladesh is one of the most densely populated countries in the world. In 2018, the country had one of the lowest land to man ratios in the world, which was estimated to be 0.08 hectares per person (World Bank, 2020b). While in recent years, the share of agricultural land in total land has been around 70% (World Bank, 2020b), there is a growing demand for land for non-agricultural activities, especially to establish new homes, roads, educational institutions, and industries. This puts immense pressure on land availability and land prices, and thus, land is now the scarcest factor of production in Bangladesh.[2]

The scarcity of land and resulting high prices have important implications for the prospect of industrialisation of the country. The situation is yet more complicated due to the weak land management system, which perpetuates

---

[1] Annex 8.1 provides a glossary of terms used in this chapter.
[2] According to Rahman (2011), for most Dhaka dwellers, the prospect of being able to buy a house appears to be the poorest in South Asian cities as the price to income ratio in Dhaka is 5:1 or more (the neighbouring Indian city of Kolkata has a ratio of 3:1 and normally a ratio of between 2:1 and 3:1 would generally imply that a significant portion of the middle-income population could afford to purchase a house). Also, in areas of Dhaka and its outskirts, land prices increased by more than 350% during 2000s. World Bank (2007d) highlighted that Dhaka's land prices were comparable to those in suburban New York or London, although the median income in Dhaka was 50 to 100 times lower.

An example can be mentioned from Sharif and Esa (2014): Savar municipality, an important satellite town of Dhaka city, saw a great escalation of the land price between 1985 and 2010. The average land price growth rate of Savar municipality during 1985–1995 was 928%, was 225% during 1995–2005, and more than 200% during 2005 and 2010. This was due to a rise in housing, an expansion of settlements, an increase in industrial, commercial, and other non-agricultural uses, and a rise in urban infrastructure services.

land-grabbing, high rent generation, and ineffective property rights. These, in turn, constrain investment opportunities, both from home and abroad. The inadequacy of land is often identified as one of the reasons for the low level of foreign direct investment (FDI) in Bangladesh.[3]

The scarcity of land and consequent high prices exacerbate the challenges related to the dysfunctional land administration and management system in Bangladesh (Hossain, 2017). The land administration and management system in Bangladesh is age-old, inefficient, and involves a considerable degree of inefficient and corrupt practices. Also, the land transfer process is jeopardised by inadequate and flawed land records, and thus, the system fails to keep pace with the growing demand and changing landscape of the economy. Efficient land management has important implications for various development goals, such as food security and ensuring a favourable business environment for private investment, and thus undertaking necessary reform to develop a consistent and functional land administration and management system in Bangladesh will be crucial in the coming years.

All of this justifies government intervention in the land management system. The land issue is discussed extensively in the country's Seventh Five-Year Plan, 2016–2020. The plan identifies many factors as constraints on the functioning of effective land management and administration in Bangladesh: antiquated records, complex and ineffective policies, high transaction costs, and a weak taxation policy. Hence, the plan stresses a range of institutional reforms: digitisation of records, and simplification of transactions and land registration. Additionally, the plan underscores the special economic zones (SEZs) initiative as a medium for providing access to serviced land to investors from home and abroad. However, there are many difficulties regarding land acquisition under the SEZs initiative, as such initiatives rely heavily on the existing dysfunctional land system. Without effective institutional reforms in the land administration and management system, the SEZs initiative is unlikely to realise its full potential.

Against this backdrop, this chapter analyses the importance of a well-functioning land management and administration in Bangladesh; explores the history of the policy reforms and the evolution of rules and regulations related to land administrative and management in Bangladesh; analyses institutional complexities in the current system of land management; explores how the SEZs initiative has emerged as an alternative management system and the complexities related to the acquisition of land for SEZs; and, finally, suggests areas of improvements related to land administration and management. This

---

[3] Economists in Bangladesh have identified a number of reasons behind the poor inflow of FDI to Bangladesh, which include a scarcity of land, infrastructure, gas, and electricity; a delay in giving services; uncertainty in policy continuation; unclear dispute settlement; and unexpected delays in formulating the rules and regulations of the SEZ law (see www.thedailystar.net/business/fdi-still-below-par-90538).

chapter draws on available data, interviews conducted with key informants, focus group discussions (FGDs) conducted with relevant stakeholders, and the use of relevant analytical tools to understand the institutional challenges in the land management and administration system in Bangladesh.

II CONSEQUENCES OF LAND SCARCITY AND INEFFICIENT LAND MANAGEMENT

In recent decades, with a highly dense population, South Asian countries have been experiencing an accelerated rate of land fragmentation. Most of these countries depend on the agriculture sector for a major share of employment. Hence, land fragmentation has forced some farmers to become landless or land-poor and to lean on sharecropping or to take on agricultural day-labour as an occupation. The law of inheritance, lack of a progressive property tax, heterogeneous land quality, and an underdeveloped land market perpetuate the problems in the region (Niroula and Thapa, 2005; Siddiqui, 1997). Greenland *et al.* (1997) also argued that insecure land tenure alters the decision-making process of production in favour of short-term time horizons, which has a detrimental impact on investment decisions.

Like most other South Asian countries, Bangladesh faces many of the land-related institutional challenges mentioned above. Fragmentation of land in Bangladesh perpetuates inefficiency and hurts overall production in the agricultural sector (Rahman and Rahman, 2009). The gravity of the fragmentation of landholding in Bangladesh is that small landholdings (less than 2.5 acres) occupy more than 84% of the total area of farm holding in Bangladesh. It is also found that functional landless[4] households (households in which own no more than 0.5 acres of land) account for more than one-fourth of farming households in Bangladesh.

Fragmentation of landholding also has important implications for private sector investment in non-agricultural activities. Industries require large amounts of land, which is rarely available from a single owner, due to the highly fragmented ownership nature. Therefore, potential investors have to secure land from multiple owners of adjacent land who are will to sell. However, where owners are unwilling to sell, there are cases when the buyers, with the help of politically powerful groups, force them to do so.[5] This is a common practice

---

[4] See Hossain (1986) for further details on the functional landless.
[5] According to LANDac (2016), 'hundreds of housing companies in urban areas have started to demarcate their project area using pillars and signboard before receiving titles. They use local musclemen with guns and occupy local administrations, including the police. Most of the time, land owners feel obliged to sell their productive resources to the companies at a price inferior to market value. Civil servants within the government support these companies and receive some plots of land in exchange.' (See www.landgovernance.org/wp-content/uploads/2019/09/20160608-Factsheet-Bangladesh.pdf.)

among powerful business elites and poses a serious problem to those investors who lack 'effective' connections with powerful political groups.

Rapid urbanisation is a growing phenomenon in Bangladesh. Over the past four decades, the urban population in Bangladesh increased at a rate faster than the South Asian average. The share of the urban population in the total population in Bangladesh in 1980 was only around 15% (the South Asian average in 1980 was 22.3%), which increased to 36.6% in 2018 (the South Asian average in 2018 was 34%) (United Nations, 2019a). Bangladesh is fast losing arable land due to growing industrialisation and rapid encroachment of human habitats on farming areas (Khan, 2019). A consequence of the depletion of farmland is the growing migration of landless people from rural areas to the urban areas, landing mostly in urban slums. Also, as private investors intensify exploration of the availability of land in remote areas of the countryside to set up factories, this leads to a hike in the price of agricultural land (Hossain, 2017).

Apart from land scarcity, administrative complexities and associated institutional challenges also appear to be acute in Bangladesh. The existing policies are inconsistent due to the outdated and complex land laws. The laws are described in such a way that they are hard to implement. Raihan *et al.* (2009) argued that though various reform efforts were undertaken related to land management and administration, in many cases they were not effectively implemented. The way in which land is currently administered remains firmly rooted in practices established during the colonial era: little has changed in the post-independence era.

Raihan *et al.* (2009) also highlighted that though the Pakistan and Bangladesh periods saw attempts at redistributive reforms through the establishment of land ceilings and placing land in the hands of the tiller, and returning water bodies to those who fish them, the reforms were largely circumvented by the wealthy and powerful. This was particularly true in the case of the distribution of *khas*[6] land among poor people. The estimated amount of total identified *khas* land in Bangladesh is 3.3 million acres, with 0.8 million acres of agricultural *khas* land, 1.7 million acres of non-agricultural *khas* land, and 0.8 million acres of *khas* waterbodies. The above-stated amount of *khas* suffers from underestimation (Barkat *et al.*, 2001). A large part of the *khas* lands are grabbed by local elites and powerful forces who have a strong political nexus (Rahman, 2017).

Hossain (2017) emphasised that corruption, administrative problems, and ancient practices of data management are the common features of the land management system in Bangladesh. Hasan (2017) also labelled the land administration system in Bangladesh corrupt, inefficient, and unreliable, and

---

[6] *Khas* land means government-owned fallow land, where nobody has property rights. It is the land that is deemed to be owned by the Government and available for allocation according to government priorities (see www.clcbd.org/lawdictionary/159.html).

emphasised that the problems of land management are acute due to the over-lapping involvement of multiple government bodies in the land management system. The basic functions of land administration (record-keeping, registration, and settlement) are maintained in different offices under different ministries, and there is a lack of coordination among these organisations. Hence, the system enables multiple ownership, leads to duplicate records, creates disputes, and exacerbates land-related corruption.

There are also several institutional challenges related to land acquisition in Bangladesh. According to Atahar (2013) and MJF (2015), the process of determining and implementing compensation for acquired land is arbitrarily determined and lacks transparency. Unequal land valuation, unfair compensation, and corruption are all elements of the acquisition process. The amount of monetary compensation that an individual receives is often less than the land's actual market value. Moreover, the valuation method is not widely credited. Government officials have the monopoly power to decide location, area, and compensation rates, without consulting the owners. Using loopholes in the law, government officials determine compensation that is below the market price. In some cases, some individuals obtain a higher value by means of bribery and nepotism. According to a survey conducted by MJF, Uttaran and CARE Bangladesh, 69.5% of studied households reportedly lost land in the last 10 years, among which one-third reportedly lost land due to land-grabbing (18.9%) and acquisition (13.2%) (MJF, 2015).

Inefficient land management is not specific to Bangladesh. There are problems in all South Asian countries, as can be judged from a quick review of the literature. Wijenayake (2015) discussed land administration in Sri Lanka, which was found to be fragmented and geographically incomplete. Due to complications and fear of failure, the Sri Lankan Government had neglected the parcel-based land information system (where parcel refers to a standard of measurement of land used in the land information system). Perera (2010) argued that Sri Lanka's land registration system should enforce pragmatic strategies rather than relying only on standardised and costly approaches. Similarly, Ali and Ahmad (2016) argued that due to a diverse range of issues, ranging from economic and social, to technical, legal, political and institutional, land administration in Pakistan has huge problems. Non-conducive policies, complex legal framework, unnecessarily restrictive regulations, weak legislation, distinct administrative bodies, differential access to information, lack of standardised data and ICT infrastructure, weak coordination, etc. are barriers to efficient land administration in Pakistan and several policy reforms are needed to enhance the capacity of the institutions involved. Deininger (2008) argued that land administration in India was complex and varied considerably across states at the time (2008). The integrated system, that tried to separate out different administrative bodies (e.g. registry and records or survey etc.), was not helping. Under the existing laws, the transfer of land was maintained by both the revenue department and the stamps and registration department, which increased transaction costs and created the potential for fraud. As rural areas became increasingly urbanised, the survey department's responsibilities in relation to maintaining accurate spatial records of land ownership were often not fulfilled. This resulted in outdated map products of inferior quality, and land-related conflict. Thus, entrusting one single agency with sufficient capacity to maintain spatial records in rural and urban areas was deemed by the authors to be beneficial. Ghatak and Mookherjee (2013) also studied land acquisition and compensation for industrialisation in India. The study found that compensation rules affected the decision-making process of the landowners and tenants. Depending on the amount received, they decided whether to sell to the industrial developers or to invest in specific agricultural activities. Moreover, the process of determining and implementing compensations was arbitrary and lacked transparency. A study by Ghatak *et al.* (2012) in 12 villages in Singur, India, showed that the majority of the people affected by land acquisition were marginal farmers and that an inability to distinguish between land qualities led to under-compensation.

III OVERVIEW OF THE LAND LAWS AND POLICIES IN BANGLADESH

Most South Asian countries share similar kinds of problems regarding land administration and laws, due to the shared history of colonialism. For centuries, this geographical region was ruled by Arya, Hindu, and Muslim rulers who implemented a traditional revenue collection and land management system. Then colonialism provided the country with a predetermined land administration system. The land laws that were enforced by the representatives of a foreign nation had rent-seeking motives from the beginning. Therefore, the laws were seldom written with the marginal population in mind, were unnecessarily complex, and were overlapping. A land ceiling to curtail inequality based on land was imposed for the first time in 1950, after the colonial period ended. The 1950s was a notable decade for land rights in the region because of the Tenancy Act, which ensured the rights of sharecropper following the *Tebhaga* Movement[7] of 1946. However, the 1984 Ordinance Act placed a 21-acre celling on the acquisition or holding of agricultural land and invalidated *benami* transactions[8] so that the land ceiling could be avoided. Table 8.1 shows the key developments in land policy and administration in Bangladesh from the pre-colonial period to the present day.

[7] The *Tebhaga* Movement was a sharecroppers' movement demanding two-thirds of the produce from land for themselves and one-third for the landlords. Under the leadership of the communist cadres of the Bengal provincial *krishak sabha*, the *Tebhaga* Movement spread out to 19 districts of Bengal (Banglapedia, 2014).

[8] A Benami transaction refers to a land sale in which someone purchases the land using someone else as the owner recorded in the deed.

TABLE 8.1 *Key developments in land policy and administration in Bangladesh*

Era	Key developments	*Khas*[1] land	Fiscal policy	Surveys	Civil society	Land ceiling	Administration
Pre-colonial	Indian Hindu rulers introduce first land revenue systems. C16 Sher Shah reforms made a systematic survey and measurement of the entire cultivable land + revenue assessment and collection						
Colonial (1757–1947)	1793: Permanent Settlement Act establishes *Zamindari*[2]	1825: Bengal regulation 11 1868: Bengal Alluvion Act 1919: Government Estates Manual 1932: Bengal Crown Estates Manual	1882: Transfer of Property Act 1908: Registration Act	1888–1940: Cadastral Survey of Undivided Bengal creates first comprehensive record of land rights. Still accepted by contemporary courts	1946: *Tebhaga* Movement		

Pakistani era (1947–1971)	1950: East Bengal State Acquisition and Tenancy Act abolishes *Zamindari*: land should pass to tiller	1950: Remains largely unchanged	1956–1962: State Acquisition Survey using Cadastral Survey as blueprint 1965 Present Revisional Survey settlement begins	1950s to early 1970s: leftists pursue land reform agenda	1950: Ceiling of 33.3 acres imposed for first time 1961: Raised to 125 acres by Ayub Khan	
Bangladesh (1971–...)	1972: Revised State and Tenancy Act 1984: Land Reform Ordinance legally recognises sharecropper rights	1975: President's Order LXI 1987: Land Reform Action Programme 1997: Agric. *Khas* Land Management/ Settlement Policy	1972: Tax exemption for smaller holders 1976: Land Development Tax 1992: Revised Land Development Tax 2000: Stamp duty reform	1984: NGO role in *khas* land distribution	1972: Re-established as 33.3 acres 1984: New acquisitions max. 21 acres. *Benami*[3] transfers outlawed	1972: Travel allowances end 1989: Land Appeals Board 1991: New Land Admin Manual

1 Ibid.

2 A *Zamindar* in the Indian subcontinent was a feudatory under a monarch with aristocratic prerogatives and hereditary titles. The term means land owner. Typically hereditary, *zamindars* held enormous tracts of land and had control over their peasants, from whom they reserved the right to collect tax on behalf of imperial courts or for military purposes.

3 Ibid.

Source: CARE (2003).

After the Independence of Bangladesh in 1971, under several political regimes, attempts were made to reform the land administration, though most of them were not properly implemented. Some of these significant initiatives are described in Box 8.1, which provides a detailed timeline of land policy and administration reforms in Bangladesh. Bangladesh has suffered from archaic colonial law and administration. Although the country has undergone some forms of land reform, efforts have been rather slow-paced and uncoordinated. One example was the re-establishment of the land ceiling in 1972, retracting Ayub Khan's[9] extension of the ceiling to 125 acres in favour of rich and influential elites. Although the ordinance and presidential orders of 1972 attempted to redistribute *khas* land, more specified laws regarding *khas* land were introduced in 1997. The ordinance of 1984 outlawed *benami transfers*[10] and introduced a number of reforms related to sharecropping. However, a survey conducted in 1991 showed that 90% of the rural population were unaware of the 1984 reforms (Hossain, 2017). A Land Administration Manual promulgated in 1991 laid down detailed instructions regarding the inspection and supervision of union[11] and thana[12] land offices. This manual is still in use.

Box 8.1 Land policy and administration timeline of Bangladesh

1972: A land ceiling of 33.3 acres was re-established[1] and various presidential orders provided for the distribution of *khas* land among the landless. It was expected that 2.5 million acres of excess land would be released, but in reality, there was far less. Newly formed land vested in government became a second type of *khas*. Exemption from land tax granted for families owning less than 8.33 acres.

1976: A variety of land-related charges were consolidated into the Land Development Tax, which covered the whole country except Chattogram Hill Tracts (CHT),[2] but deficiencies in the record system mean individual holdings cannot be checked, and switches to more heavily taxed non-agricultural uses frequently go unrecorded.

1982: The Acquisition and Requisition of Immovable Property Ordinance, 1982.

1984: The Land Reform Ordinance 1984 limited future land acquisitions to 21 acres while retaining the existing ceilings. Benami (ceiling-avoiding) transfers to family members were outlawed, but evasion was easy. Legal recognition of the rights of share-coppers was given for the first time and sharecropping was established as the only admissible form of tenancy contract.

---

[9] Field Marshal Mohammad Ayub Khan (1908–1974) was a military ruler and President of Pakistan.
[10] *Ibid.*
[11] The smallest rural administrative and local government unit in Bangladesh (Khan, 2008).
[12] The lowest administrative unit in Bangladesh (Banglapedia, 2014).

1988: The cluster village programme resettled landless people on state land, but only 800 villages, with some 32,000 households, had been formed by 1996.

1989: Muyeed Committee[3] recommended that the functions of land registration (Sub-Registrar) and record (tahsil) be brought together in a single office at field level, but this was ignored.

1989: Board of Land Administration split into Land Appeals Board and Land Reforms Board to deal with the ever-increasing volume of quasi-judicial appeals.

1991: A Land Administration Manual was created for the inspection and supervision of Union and Thana land offices.

1992: Farms of 8.33–10 acres were charged at Bangladeshi Taka (BDT) 0.5 per acre, and larger holdings at BDT 2 per acre.

1997: New Agricultural Khas Land Management and Settlement Policy introduced.

1998: Total *khas* land was found to be 0.75 million acres (or 3% of arable land area), but the actual amount remained unclear as a result of de facto private control arising from informal local settlements.

2001: National Land Use Policy, 2001: stopping the high conversion rate of agricultural land to non-agricultural purposes; utilising agro-ecological zones to determine maximum land use efficiency; adopting measures to discourage the conversion of agricultural land for urban or development purposes; and improving the environmental sustainability of land use practices.

2010: National Economic Zone Act, 2010: Under this act, the Government may establish economic zones. The aim is to encourage rapid economic development in potential areas (including backward and underdeveloped regions of the country) through an increase in and diversification of industry, employment, production, and exports, as well as to fulfil the social and economic commitments of the state.

2017: Acquisition and Requisition of Immovable Property Act 2017.

Source: CARE (2003), Hossain (2017), and authors.

---

[1] The land ceiling was primarily established by Ayub Khan in 1959; there was a 500-acre ceiling at the time in which Bangladesh was Eastern Pakistan.

[2] This region has been kept outside the general rules of the country, as the majority of the people of this region are indigenous people. The forms of land ownership in the CHT region are very different from those in the rest of the country. For centuries, the CHT inhabitants have applied a traditional collective ownership principle, coupled with customary rules and regulations for land management. There have been disputes over land between indigenous people and settlers, which has led to armed conflict in the past. The 1997 Peace Treaty led to the formulation of the Chittagong Hill Tracts Land Dispute Resolution Commission Act 2001 and the setting up of a Land Commission. However, till now this commission has remained dysfunctional (see www .thedailystar.net/law-our-rights/law-vision/news/the-settlement-land-disputes-the-cht-1841356).

[3] In 1989, a retired senior bureaucrat, Mr Abdul Muyeed Chowdhury, was made the chairman of a government committee that came to be known as the Muyeed Committee. The committee recommended major changes to the land management system in Bangladesh.

The Government of Bangladesh has formulated various policies on land use, transfer, acquisition, and rehabilitation. Notable among them is the National Land Use Policy, which was adopted by the Government in 2001, setting guidelines for land use, land improvement, and zoning regulations. The policy was issued by the Ministry of Land, but its implementation faced difficulties as the land administration system is dependent on many ministries. Furthermore, other cross-sectoral policies were not harmonised in the policy, which also created problems in regard to its successful implementation. Though land acquisition by the Government is a regular phenomenon, detailed measures related to the compensation of the affected persons only came in the Acquisition and Requisition of Immovable Property Act 2017. While many policies and reform measures have been undertaken in Bangladesh since Independence in 1971, these measures have often been ineffective due to a lack of proper implementation.

IV CHALLENGES IN LAND ADMINISTRATION AND MANAGEMENT IN BANGLADESH

If we consider the recorded history of land usage in Indian sub-continent, the purpose of the administration system has hardly changed: it remains to secure stability in relation to the division of land between individuals, groups of individuals, or other legal entities; the collection of tax revenue; surveying property; and administration, including record-keeping, land usage planning, and land judiciary (Sida, 2008). Though the administrative system in respect of land has experienced negligible change since the colonial period, the structure of the economy in Bangladesh has changed considerably over the past two centuries. The usage of land has changed from exclusively traditional agricultural and habitual purposes to including industrial and various other non-farm purposes. Despite the structural change in the economy, the importance of allocating land for agricultural usage has not been diminished as the country is also essentially dependent on agriculture for food security and employment. Hence, a well-functioning land administration and management system is critically important for the economy.

A Institutional Structure of Land Administration

The existing structure of land administration in Bangladesh is multi-layered (see Figure 8.1). The system is paper-based and maintenance of record is done mostly manually. These records are kept in different offices, which creates duplication and a lack of coherence. The land administration system in Bangladesh is managed by multiple government authorities simultaneously. These government offices are entrusted with the transfer of land rights from one party to another in sale, lease, loan, gifts, and inheritance; control of land

and property development; land use and preservation; revenue gathering from land through sales, leasing, and taxes; and resolving conflicts regarding ownership and usage of land.

The current institutional structure of land administration in the country comprises four major bodies under two ministries: the Ministry of Land, and the Ministry of Law, Justice and Parliamentary Affairs (MoLJPA). The four major bodies that administer the land management system are the Directorate of Land Records and Surveys, the Land Reform Board, and the Land Appeals Board under the Ministry of Land, and the Department of the Land Registration System (under the MoLJPA).[13] However, the Ministry of Public Administration, formerly known as the Ministry of Establishment, is authorised to appoint an Assistant Commissioner (Land), who is the responsible authority connected to both the Ministry of Land (through the Land Reform Board) and the Ministry of Public Administration (through the Deputy Commissioner's (DC's) office). Other government bodies that play a minor role in administering land management are the Ministry of Forests, the Fisheries Department, the Directorate of Housing and Settlement, and the Department of Roads and Railways.

There are four core stakeholders in the land administration and management system in Bangladesh:

i. **The Settlement Office:** The Settlement Office generally takes on the task of updating the Record of Rights. Moreover, this office is appointed with the task of preparing, printing, and distributing the *mouza*[14] and *thana* maps of every district, defining borders among the *mouzas*, *thanas*, and districts, and providing training to the newly recruited civil service cadres working at the field level of different directorates, as well as ministries, such as the administration, land, and forest. In addition, the determination of ownership of land is done by surveying neighbourhoods every 30 years.

ii. **Assistant Commissioner (Land):** Under the State Acquisition and Tenancy Act 1950, the Assistant Commission of Land authorises the transfers of land rights, except during land survey. The country is administratively differentiated in various levels, starting from unions; with a couple of unions forming a sub-district or *thana* or *upazila*[15]; a couple of *thanas* forming a district; a couple of districts forming a division; and eight divisions forming the whole country. The land administration follows this hierarchy in a broad sense. According to a report published by the Local Government Engineering Department,

---

[13] https://minland.gov.bd/site/page
[14] Lowest level of revenue collection unit (Banglapedia, 2014).
[15] After divisions and districts, the third largest type of administrative division in Bangladesh.

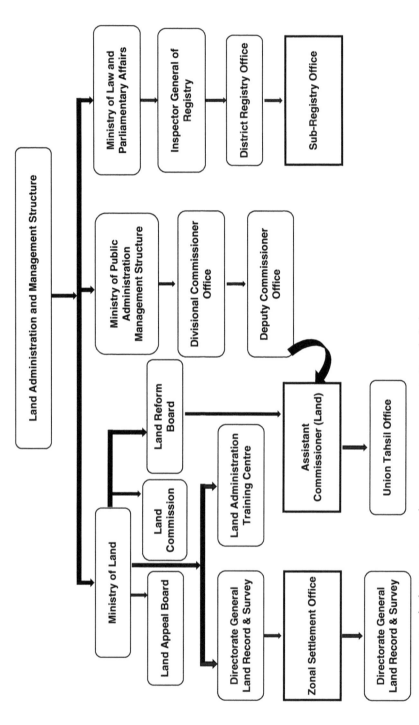

FIGURE 8.1 Land administration and management structure in Bangladesh
Source: Transparency International Bangladesh (TIB) (2015).

United Nations Development Programme (UNDP), and UN-Habitat (Shafi, 2007), land management functions through the Commissioner at the division level, the Deputy Commissioner at the district level, the Assistant Commissioner (Land) at the *thana* level, and the *Tahsildar* at the union level. Assistant Commissioner (Land), the executing authority of the Assistant Commission (Land), discharges all the activities of the *upazila* land office through a detailed structured administrative system comprising various levels of clerical assistants. The Assistant Commissioner (Land) has to perform multiple responsibilities regarding land, including those of Upazila Revenue[16] Officer, *Upazila* Settlement Officer, Circle Inspector, Revenue Circle Officer,[17] and Revenue Circle Inspector.[18]

iii. **Sub-Registry Office:** The Sub-Registry Office is administered under MoLJPA and is appointed with the responsibility for registering lands and other properties under the Registration Act of 1908. The Sub-Registrar is the executive authority of the Registry Office and the representative of the MoLJPA at the *upazila*[19] level. The Sub-Registrar registers the transfer of land through a stamped deed declaring the property value. There are 503 Registry Offices in Bangladesh, including one in every *upazila*, where, on average, 7,000 land transfers occur per year. These offices provide BDT 14 billion (equivalent to US$ 165 million) in tax revenue every year, which is 0.4% of total government tax revenue; this is not managed by the National Board of Revenue (Ministry of Finance, 2019).

iv. **Land Survey Tribunal:** The State Acquisition and Tenancy Act 1950 lays down the provisions for the Land Survey Tribunal and the Land Survey Appellate Tribunal. In case of any disputes, for example fake documents or fake mutations,[20] the affected party files a lawsuit with the Land Survey Tribunal. In consultation with the Supreme Court, the Government appoints the judge of the Land Survey Tribunal from the Joint District Judges.[21] Against a decision of the Land Survey Tribunal, an appeal can be made to the Land Survey Appellate Tribunal, which is constituted with a judge who is or has been a judge in the High Court division of the Supreme Court.

---

[16] Tax revenue at the sub-district level.
[17] The post of Revenue Circle Officer, widely known as Circle Officer (Revenue), was created as a separate post in each *thana* after 1961. Their function was limited to revenue work only, which included general supervision and control over *tahsildars* (Banglapedia, 2014).
[18] State Acquisition Rules, 1951, Rules 20 and 39.
[19] Sub-district.
[20] Mutation refers to the insertion of the names of the new owners in the record of rights, in the place of the former owners, after the transfer of the ownership of land.
[21] State Acquisition and Tenancy Act, 1950 Section 145 A (3).

Upazila administration, which is under the jurisdiction of the Ministry of Public Administration, is primarily concerned with updating the Record of Rights in regard to mutation. Land buying or transfer of rights is directly connected to both the Sub-Registry Office and the Assistant Commission (Land) office. If any interested party enquires about the land that he/she intends to purchase by formally applying to the Sub-Registrar, he/she is granted the aforementioned information. Deeds are maintained by generating both alphabetically and plot number-wise ordered content so that information can be provided. When land transfer occurs, theoretically two parties have to agree on the price of the property and then the buyer will have to arrange the deed preparation. Next, both parties will visit the Sub-Registry Office together so that the Sub-Registrar can establish the money transfer between the two parties and collect the immovable property tax. The Sub-Registrar finally registers the transfer and forwards the record of land transfer to the Assistant Commission (Land) office, where the tahsildar[22] inspects and updates the record. Through this process, the Record of Rights, locally known as Khatiyan, is supposed to be updated. Moreover, buyers can check the Record of Rights from the Assistant Commission (Land) office to confirm the rightful owner of the property he/she intends to buy. Nonetheless, this land transfer has to be notified while the land survey is done by the settlement office. Figure 8.2 illustrates the land transfer procedure that would occur if the system worked properly.

Interviews with two Sub-Registrars and two Assistant Commissioners (Land) from the Northeast and Northwest regions of the county, and FGDs with relevant stakeholders, reveal that the land transfer process often takes a detour in the steps involving the Assistant Commission (Land) office. Inherited lands are not mutated properly in most cases, due to lack of awareness among the landowners. In some cases, land mutation of sold land goes through years of red tape, ultimately reaching the DCs' office from the upazila land office via the local tahsil office (revenue office). Often the process of the Registry Office sending the land transfer record to the Assistant Commission (Land) office takes too long, and sometimes it does not take place at all. The lack of timeliness in the process results in a lack of coherence of information between the stakeholders. Therefore, the possibility of multiple landowners existing in different government records for the same property arises, creating the opportunity for fraudulent activities and litigation. When a potential buyer attempts to check the ownership of the property, the information he/she obtains from Assistant Commission (Land) office might not be synchronised with the information in the Registry Office. The buyer can obtain information from the

---

[22] A *tehsildar* is a tax officer and is in charge of obtaining taxes from an area with regard to land revenue.

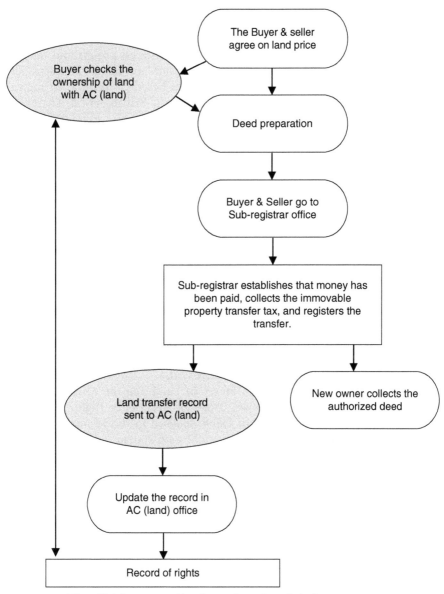

FIGURE 8.2 The official process of land transfer in Bangladesh
Source: Authors.

Assistant Commission (Land) office only, limiting his/her chance of comparing the information regarding ownership of the property. In this way, forgery
and intentional multiple-selling of the same land can take place.

B Challenges Related to Land Administration

The land administration system in Bangladesh is characterised by pervasive corruption, incidents of land-grabbing by vested interest groups and influential politicians, and social tensions emanating from land-related conflicts. The land management system in Bangladesh is still based on traditional regulations, with most of the rulebooks framed during the British period. Therefore, inefficiency in the provision of legal and administrative services related to land intensifies corrupt practices in this sector. Box 8.2 sets out some examples of corruption in the land administration system in Bangladesh that have been discussed in the national media.

Figure 8.3 provides a schematic representation of the complexities of land administration, and the respective consequences in Bangladesh. The land-related challenges occur for two main reasons: internal issues (e.g. a lack of adequate infrastructure, the analogue records system, and inconsistent human resources) and external issues (e.g. lack of coordination among the administrative entities). The subsequent sub-sections provide an analysis of these challenges.

1 *Internal Administrative Issues*

Internal administrative problems relating to the stakeholders, from infrastructure to analogue record-keeping, arise from the inability to modernise the system, which is a hold-over from the inherited colonial system. Key informant interviews (KIIs) with relevant stakeholders, conducted in July 2019, highlighted the following internal administrative issues.

Lack of digitisation: Both the Ministry of Land and the Ministry of Law lack necessary digitisation. However, copies of Records of Rights and mutation of names are in the process of being digitised in the Ministry of Land. The Government initiated an electronic application system for the mutation of names, or e-mutation, in 485 *upazilas* and 3,617 union land offices in 61 districts, barring the three hill districts in the CHT, on 1 July 2019. However, over 40% of the *upazilas* underperformed in the e-mutation process, and three districts from the CHT are yet to be included in the process.[23] The official reason given for this underperformance is that it has been hard for staff to adapt to the new technology. Moreover, a grievance redress system, in the form of a hotline, was initiated in 2019. However, the hotline only aims to accept complaints, it cannot guarantee the resolution of them.[24] People often find themselves paying more than required. Also, corrupt officials at land offices harass service seekers, and threaten to delay mutations by confiscating documents unless a bribe is paid. There is resistance to the digitisation of the system by vested interest groups.[25]

---

[23] www.newagebd.net/article/84835/all-land-management-issues-need-to-go-digital
[24] https://unb.com.bd/category/Bangladesh/land-ministry-launches-complaints-hotline/30259
[25] https://thefinancialexpress.com.bd/views/why-is-automation-of-land-registration-taking-so-much-time-1530721504

Box 8.2 Recent examples of corruption in the land system in Bangladesh published in the media

- **Case 1:** The land surveyor demanded US$ 825.63 for providing a digital Record of Rights to a service seeker, with US$ 236.20 having to be paid in advance. (*The Business Standard*, September 2019)
- **Case 2:** A deputy assistant officer from the union land office was caught red-handed with US$ 176.92 in bribe money. (*The Business Standard*, October 2019)
- **Case 3:** One surveyor was caught with US$ 109,834.51 and documents proving incidents of bribery, with 29 other employees from the same Land Acquisition department involved. (*Dhaka Times, Jugantor, Manab Zamin, Daily Janakantha, Bangla Tribune, Prothom Alo, Ittefaq*, February 2020)
- **Case 4:** A land officer from the union land office demanded five times ($59.05) the original fee ($13.82) as a bribe. (*Jugantor, Dainik Amader Shomoy, Jago News24*, October 2019)
- **Case 5:** A land officer from the union land office took US$ 59 for providing a tax receipt for US$ 2.36. The bribes for the mutation of vested property amounted to US$ 1.771.52; for mutation in general, it was between US$ 240 and US$ 2,400; and for leasing it was US$ 710. The officer allegedly harassed the service seekers, threatening to delay the mutation by confiscating documents unless the bribe was paid. (*Prothom Alo*, June 2019)
- **Case 6:** According to TIB, the amount of the bribe for mutations was 50–60 times the original rate. In one example, a service seeker mutated the name by paying a US$ 300 bribe. The employees, along with the middlemen, solicited bribes, according to the service seeker. 50% of the bribes went to the Sub-Registrar, and the rest was divided among other employees. (*BBC Bangla*, September 2019)
- **Case 7:** A bribe for providing compensation for land acquisition: surveyors took 30% of the compensation as a commission or bribe from the afflicted owners, in exchange for providing the compensation. (*Aparadh Bichitra*, February 2020)
- **Case 8:** In an upazila land office, land-related documents were 'misplaced' unless a bribe was paid. The rate of bribes differed depending on the service seekers' economic situation, profession, influence, and connection to elites. In the Sub-Registry Office, the middlemen had access to the official documents to the same extent that they performed various duties, such as keeping records in the record room. (*Dhaka Times*, September 2019)
- **Case 9:** The Chattogram district administration made a contract with BBC Steel Company and leased 7.1 acres of land of coastal forest despite a court order forbidding this. (*The Business Standard*, January 2020)
- **Case 10:** In a period of two years, one afflicted landowner, a day labourer by profession, was subjected to 70 litigations by a local neighbour, locals with connection to political elites, and business elites. (*Prothom Alo*, May 2019)

Source: Authors' compilation from different media reports.

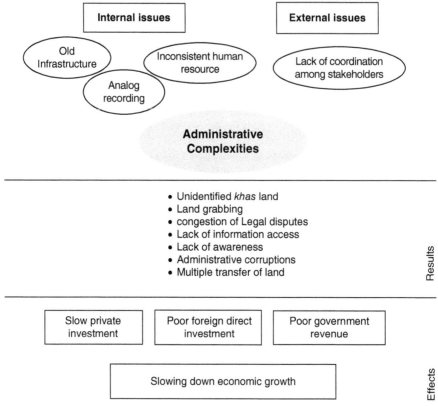

FIGURE 8.3 A schematic presentation of the complexities in land administration, and their consequences
Source: Authors.

Infrastructure: According to the present law, only the deeds from the current year are supposed to be retained in the Sub-Registry Office. Nevertheless, these offices are preserving all deeds from 1987 onwards, due to the unavailability of space in the district offices. The deeds are stored in old and damp record rooms, causing them to deteriorate. The records are vulnerable to fire or other hazards, which will turn the main document held by the owner into the only evidence available. A lack of proper duplicates or backups is causing legal complexities due to lost deeds and record books. Moreover, presently, there is a record book crisis in the Registry Offices. The Registry Offices are constrained to collect deeds without proper records due to the lack of record books. Record books (locally known as *Balaam Boi*) are not provided to the Registry Office for years, even after communicating repeatedly with the MoLJPA. In Dhunat *upazila* of Bogra district, the collection of property tax by union land offices was postponed for more than a month due to a lack of receipt books.[26] This lack of receipts stopped the land transfer process and relevant people getting loans from the banking system, since such receipts were required as legal documents to obtain bank loans secured against any property. Also, in most cases, inadequate logistics and transport facilities restrict the settlement offices from conducting their regular responsibilities, such as monitoring of land record surveys.

Human resources: There exists a lack of manpower within several posts of various departments of the land offices, constraining the required services provided to people. The currently employed manpower also has a wide skills mismatch. The settlement offices lack updated training regarding the land survey methodology (Transparency International Bangladesh, 2015). Though the participation of non-government organisations and academia in land-related policy consultations has been on the rise, the participation of the private sector in technical aspects of land management remains limited. Therefore, the precision and transparency of surveys is widely discredited after land surveys are conducted (Hossain, 2017). Here, the self-interest of various stakeholders prevents the system from working efficiently. For instance, the lack of necessary manpower in the Registry Offices is made up for by unofficially employed human resources, who are employed through nepotism and corruption; the latter harass the service seekers by multiplying official registration fees.[27] The author's interview with a Sub-Register in Dhunat *upazila* of Bogra district suggests that, for that specific Registry Office, there are 87 copyists, with more than 100 assistants, whereas only 20 copyists were required.

2 External Administrative Issues

The second reason behind the administrative complexities can be described as the lack of coordination among the stakeholders. The administrative offices that are bestowed with the responsibility for land management work separately, with little coordination among them. The Sub-Registrar registers the land after checking the record of the settlement office and the mutation of the Assistant Commissioner (Land). Additionally, a land transfer notice is supposed to be sent to the Assistant Commissioner (Land) office If any work is registered in the registration office. However, in reality, the records are hardly ever updated due to the lack of coordination between these two offices. The mutation of land is performed by the Assistant Commissioner (Land) whenever someone submits the registered documents, regardless of whether they receive a copy from the Sub-Registry Office. Therefore, a multiplicity of documents or Records of Rights arises due to the lack of coordination inside the land administration system (Hasan, 2017).

---

[26] www.kalerkantho.com/online/country-news/2019/07/24/795338
[27] https://samakal.com/todays-print-edition/tp-upakhantho/article/1908338/

Evidently, a gap exists between land management by the Ministry of Land and the registration of land by the Ministry of Law. An expert committee suggested to address this gap by developing a database, using appropriate technologies for coordination, and introducing a Certificate of Land Ownership as the sole document for registering land ownership (LANDac, 2016). However, until now, there has not been any progress on this front.

3 The Results of Administrative Complexities

Internal and external administrative complexities lead to unidentified *khas* land, lack of access to information, corruption, congestion of legal disputes, and multiple transfers of land.

Unidentified *khas* land: Since the colonial period, this region has experienced people abandoning their land due to communal riots, war, etc., which has led to the Government being assigned the abandoned land. Many areas of *khas* lands, *khas* water bodies, *khas* ponds, enemy property, abandoned property, as well as unused land under different government offices, are not properly identified and reported by the land administration. Around 70% of the farm households in Bangladesh have less than 1.5 acres of land, which means a large portion of these land-poor households depend on seasonal employment opportunities or sharecropping, including other tenancy arrangements, to access land for their livelihoods (Hossain, 2017). The aforementioned *khas* land, which could be used to maximise social welfare by distributing it among the landless and land-poor population, or investing in development projects, often gets misused, due to administrative complexities, such as a lack of manpower to identify and report it, fake documents submitted fraudulently to the Registry Office or Assistant Commission (Land) office, and simply grabbing of the land by influential people (Barkat, 2005). Obtaining and retaining *khas* land is a complex issue for land-poor and landless people who need it the most and who require assistance to expand their land ownership (Barkat *et al.*, 2001). A lack of manpower, along with a lack of transport facilities, to periodically monitor land and verify the field reports after monitoring exponentially extends the volume and extent of misuse of *khas* land (Transparency International Bangladesh, 2015).

Lack of access to information: As Rahman and Talukder (2016) argued, administrative complexities, such as lack of digitisation, complicates the whole process of accessing the information related to land ownership. Demand to access land tenure records, land information, and land documents often produces very little results. The level of access to land data and related information by the mass of people remains low, hampering the fulfilment of the right to information. The updating and sharing of information among stakeholders is virtually ineffective due to the lack of effective coordination among government agencies. The lack of access to information perpetuates a lack of awareness among the general population. A general population who lack awareness cannot protest or demand their rights. In addition, they cannot demand a modern land administration system. Therefore, government efforts to solve the issues are often not implemented, due to people being unaware of the issues.

Corruption: Red tape in land administration causes corruption. Since citizens are mostly unaware and unable to access services without paying bribes, they end up being part of the corrupt practices. According to a nationwide survey conducted by Transparency International Bangladesh (2015), 16.6% of households resorted to the land administration, and 59% of them were victims of corruption. According to the same survey, 54.9% of the households paid a total of BDT 22.61 billion (around US$ 0.27 billion) as bribes in 2012, 1.6 times higher than the land revenue collected in 2019. According to another survey, conducted by MJF, Uttaran and CARE Bangladesh in 2015, around two-third of households (65%) did not receive the services required from land offices, or were asked for bribes, or received services late.[28] Moreover, agricultural land is often used for unplanned real estate and industrial purposes, by resorting to bribes or political influence (LANDac, 2016). As part of an overall study of the institutional diagnostics of development in Bangladesh, a survey (SANEM-EDI survey in 2019, see Chapter 3) was conducted among 355 respondents covering major stakeholders in Bangladesh. According to the survey results, almost 90% respondents indicated that land-related operations at the local community level were subject to corruption.

Congestion of legal disputes: In the absence of an effective governance system capable of resolving land-related disputes, the reliance on litigation without administrative process leads to legal disputes. The presence of a multiplicity of legal documents perpetuates disputes over land, which comprise almost two-thirds of the total legal disputes in the country, resulting in about 1.7 million pending cases as at 2014 (Transparency International Bangladesh, 2015). On average, 2.5 million new mutation-related cases are created every year.[29] Moreover, land-related disputes are dealt with by the Land Survey Tribunal, which lacks sufficient manpower to deal with the enormous congestion of legal proceedings. The SANEM-EDI Survey in 2019 found that 65% of the respondents held the view that the implementation of land laws was very poor in Bangladesh.

Multiple transfers of land, and land-grabbing: FGDs and KIIs reveal that due to the lack of coordination among the administrative entities involved in the land transfer process, the possibility of selling land multiple times arises. A buyer's failed attempt to update the record manually in the Assistant Commission (Land) office inevitably results in a multiplicity of land-related documents and a multiplicity of ownership, causing disputes in the long run (Hasan, 2017). This phenomenon is common in relation to applications for

---

[28] www.thedailystar.net/rural-land-market-in-bangladesh-a-situation-analysis-61897
[29] www.jugantor.com/todays-paper/sub-editorial/277712/

compensation from the Government during the acquisition of land for development purposes, as various political opportunists and previous owners claim
to be the real owners of the land. Also, wealthy and influential people encroach
on public lands using false documents and obtain court decrees to confirm
their ownership, often with the help of officials in the land administration and
management departments (Feldman and Geisler, 2011).

4 Investors' Opinions about Land Operations

Unavailability of serviced land is a prominent investment hurdle in
Bangladesh (World Bank, 2012). Investors' opinions about land operations in Bangladesh can be ascertained from the Doing Business Index of
the World Bank. Bangladesh ranked 168 out of 190 countries in the World
Bank's Doing Business Index in 2020, while India, Sri Lanka, and Pakistan
ranked 63, 108, and 99, respectively. Among the Doing Business indicators,
the *Registering Property* indicator considers four distinct areas comprising
'number of procedures', 'amount of time (days)', 'the cost required to register a property', and 'quality of the land administration index'. In Bangladesh,
registering property requires eight procedures (around 1.2 times more than
the South Asian average), takes 264 days (more than twice as long as the
South Asian average), costs 7.2% of the property value (around 1.1. times
higher than the South Asian average), and the quality of the land administration index is 6.5 (around 74% of the South Asian region's average). All
of these results suggest that the performance of the land operation system
in Bangladesh, as perceived by investors, is lagging behind that of its neighbouring countries.

C Dynamics of Political Power and Institutional Configurations

The complexities of land administration and management are greatly compounded by the political economy, which prevents problems from being
solved. The more explicit scenario includes land-grabbing and congestion of
litigation, for which politically influential groups and the beneficiary business
elites are directly responsible.[30] Furthermore, in many cases, the same parties
have created internal and external issues related to land administration, as
already discussed.

The recruitment procedures for the land administration are beset by corruption and nepotism.[31] Due to the corrupt recruitment process, including
bribing and enforcing political influence, the recruited manpower in the land

---

[30] Chapter 9 deals with this issue.
[31] In 2019, TIB conducted a study in 41 selected Sub-Registry Offices across the country. The
study revealed that there was corruption at every step in land-related services. Recruitment,
transfer, or promotion were also traded at different levels in those offices (see https://tbsnews
.net/bangladesh/tib-sub-registry-offices-risk-institutionalisation-corruption).

administration system is mostly inefficient, unenthusiastic about the service they are required to provide, and prone to further corruption. KIIs and media reports reveal that there are unnecessary numbers of employees who are overcharging people in the Registry Offices.[32] As discussed before, while digitisation can solve some of the administrative problems, including corruption, the KIIs suggest that digitisation would decrease the number of currently employed people, and there is a resistance to such reforms from vested interests. Also, these vested interests are closely linked to the local politically influential elites, who are also the beneficiaries of the rent being generated from the corrupt practices in the land offices (Chowdhury and Panday, 2018). Due to the substantial benefit from corruption, Sub-Registrars are generally reluctant to be promoted to district-level registrars. The reasoning for this also partially lies in the lack of capacity bestowed upon a District Registrar as well.[33]

The issues related to infrastructure, congestion of legal disputes, access to information, fake documents, and the manpower required to manage the whole chaotic current process can be improved by digitisation. However, despite the overwhelming consensus about the necessity of digitisation, the self-interest of various stakeholders with political influence, who are directly benefitting from the current system, prevents the system changing for the better. These interest groups of politically influential people and business elites with political connections are directly or indirectly involved in the corruption related to land tax submission procedures, land registration procedures, mutation of ownership, changing land type to acquire an unjustified price from potential industrialists and other buyers, selling water bodies to uninformed buyers, and unnecessary bureaucratic complexities.[34] According to the Minister for Land, as reported in a newspaper article, land surveys are entangled with corruption to such a degree that surveys provide millions to the people who are involved in the process, and they are 'ruthless'.[35]

While some business elites are in favour of reforms of land management, the ruling political elites are not very keen as reforms would eliminate sources of rents, including among Assistant Commission (Land) and Sub-Registrar employees, who are likely to be there because of loyalty to the ruling political

---

[32] KII refers to an interview with a Sub-Register conducted in Dhunat *upazilla* of Bogra district, and media reports refer to the examples provided in Box 8.2.

[33] The 2019 TIB study also revealed that a number of officials in all tiers, from deed writers to the Sub-Registrar, accepted bribes while providing land-related services to people. The money was then allegedly distributed among themselves in proportion to their position. 10–50% was fixed for the Sub-Registrar, while the rest went to other officials. A share of the bribe money allegedly went to the District Registrar's office, and even sometimes to the Directorate of Registration (see https://tbsnews.net/bangladesh/tib-sub-registry-offices-risk-institutionalisation-corruption).

[34] FGDs with the stakeholders and KIIs.

[35] https://bangla.bdnews24.com/bangladesh/article1666466.bdnews, published on 18 September 2019.

elites. However, powerful business elites with strong political connections are able to bypass the system.

V ADDRESSING LAND-RELATED PROBLEMS THROUGH SEZS, AND THE INSTITUTIONAL CHALLENGES OF LAND ACQUISITION FOR SEZS

As discussed earlier, registering property is very difficult for new investors, especially if they lack a connection to the political elites. Moreover, the high land price causes high input costs, which bar potential investors. Identifying and acquiring suitable land is also challenging for private investors, and especially for foreign investors. At present, private investors can access land through the existing land system, which is full of institutional weaknesses, as discussed above. To solve these issues and enhance private investment, the Government created Export Processing Zones in 1983, with preferential treatment given to the labour-intensive ready-made garment sector. However, EPZs catered only to export-oriented industries. Hence, the Government initiated SEZs, through the Bangladesh Economic Zone Authority (BEZA). The SEZs offer a prospective solution, among other things, to the challenges faced by new investors in accessing land.

A SEZs in Bangladesh

SEZs are geographically delineated 'enclaves' in which the regulations and practices related to business and trade differ from the rest of the country, and therefore all the units located therein enjoy special privileges (Raihan, 2016). According to Ge (1999), SEZs are characterised, in general terms, '*as a geographical area within the territory of a country where economic activities of certain kinds are promoted by a set of policy instruments that are not generally applicable to the rest of the country*'. Theoretically, SEZs are supposed to accommodate both export-oriented and domestic market-oriented industries.

Under the Bangladesh Economic Zones Act, 2010, BEZA was established as the public regulatory body for implementing SEZs. Till now, BEZA has approved 88 SEZs, through its governing body, which comprises 59 government SEZs and 29 private SEZs.

BEZA has started to work on four types of SEZs: government, private, public–private partnerships, and foreign. Feasibility studies, land acquisition, area-specific social and environmental studies, and other initiatives are underway for these approved SEZs. There are plans to acquire approximately 75,000 acres of land for these SEZs. By 2030, BEZA expects to create employment for about 10 million people and to export US$ 40 billion worth of products annually[36] by establishing 100 economic zones nationwide.

[36] See https://thefinancialexpress.com.bd/.

Although BEZA plans to establish SEZs in 31 districts, most of the projects are situated within Dhaka and Chattogram region. Regardless of the authority given to BEZA, there is a need for concerted effort from all the state stakeholders to implement its plan. The SEZs require a massive amount of land acquisition, which concerns all the stakeholders of land administration. Although BEZA is supposed to ease the complications in respect of accessing land, pace has been slower than expected.[37]

Among the private SEZs, so far success has been seen in the case of the Meghna Industrial Economic Zone, which is located beside the Dhaka–Chattogram highway. Situated on 110 acres of land, in February 2020, this economic zone started its operation with nine new industrial units (related to consumer products and industrial raw materials), at a cost of BDT 40,000 million (around US$ 0.5 billion).[38]

B Challenges in Land Acquisition under SEZs

Land acquisition in a densely populated and land-scarce country like Bangladesh is always a complex task. Therefore, the success of the SEZs policy will depend on the way the institutional challenges in the land administration system are handled. At the same time, the tempting facilities of SEZs present the possibility of relocating firms for rent-seeking reasons (Razzaque *et al.*, 2018).

Land acquisition refers to the process by which the Government forcibly acquires private land for a public purpose with or without the consent of the owner of the land, compensating the owner in exchange for the aforementioned land in an amount which can be different from the market price of the land.[39] Land acquisition is intricately connected to development blueprints envisaged by the Government of Bangladesh, such as its five-year plans, the Delta Plan, and so on. Additionally, appropriate land acquisition procedures assist in the timely execution of development projects. According to the KIIs with land owners and officials of the land office, legal owners are regularly harassed and exploited at the land offices throughout the country. Moreover, the financial compensation related to land acquisition perpetuates an overwhelming amount of corruption around the DC offices of the country. Many development projects are hindered for years due to land acquisitions and the corresponding compensation process.

---

[37] For example, the progress on Jamalpur Economic Zone progress has been stalled in the land acquisition process, and the time period has been extended for the third time so far, from 2017 to 2020. Furthermore, 42.7% of the project's funds have been spent on land acquisition, whereas only 24% of the land development work and 21.5% of the total project has been completed. During this time period, the project director has been changed six times, which underlines the institutional problems in SEZ actualisation (see https://tbsnews.net/).

[38] See www.thedailystar.net/business/news/catkin-field-the-model-economic-zone-1874809.

[39] See www.prsindia.org/theprsblog/faq-why-land-acquisition-so-controversial.

In this context, the land acquisition process for SEZs required clarification in order to resolve the complex issues surrounding compensation. In this context, the Acquisition and Requisition of Immovable Property Act 2017, currently used by BEZA for land acquisition, was developed to replace the Acquisition and Requisition of Immovable Property Ordinance 1982, which in turn was descended from the Land Acquisition Act 1894, established during the colonial period. In the 2017 Act, a detailed clarification is provided of the compensation process. Although the Ordinance of 1982 prohibited the state from evicting people from their homesteads, the vagueness of the law obstructed marginal people from receiving compensation. However, the 2017 Act also needs further amendment to solve complexities at the ground level.

As the success of SEZs depends on effective land acquisition, the land acquisition process for SEZs needs to be different from the usual land acquisition processes applied for any other purposes. However, our FGDs and KIIs confirm that the land acquisition process for SEZs has not been very different from the usual process, and it suffers from several of the corrupt practices related to land administration and management mentioned in Section IV. For example, in the land acquisition process, while the last owner of the deed, whose name has been mutated and who provides revenue receipt, should be treated as the actual owner of the land, corrupt officers in land offices send the land acquisition notice to various previous owners and thereby complicate the situation. In this process, opportunists, in association with corrupt officers in the land offices, file claims for compensation for the acquisition of land. In the end, the actual owner of the land has to bribe the corrupt officers in the land office to provide the compensation.

Our FGDs and KIIs also reveal that the news of a land acquisition causes hasty construction to acquire higher compensation for the hollow land by opportunists, in order to obtain higher compensation.[40] People who do not have any connection with political elites are forced to pay bribes in order to receive compensation. However, a bribe often does not ensure the compensation. Filing for compensation can lead to encounters with influential goons and middlemen who seek to snatch away the money. The presence of intermediaries or middlemen in the land acquisition offices worsens the woes of the actual

---

[40] Such activities are also seen in the Government's other land acquisition cases too. For example, while the Government has decided to convert the two-lane Dhaka–Sylhet highway into a four-lane one (under this widening project, the land on the two sides of the highway will be acquired along a 12-kilometer stretch within the district), in a bid to get fat compensation, local touts, with the help of landowners, have started constructing hundreds of illegal establishments on the land adjacent to the highway. Hundreds of illegal establishments have already been built on both sides of the highway in order to get hefty compensation as a result of the land acquisition for the project. These installations are being constructed for houses, markets, and industrial establishments. See www.theindependentbd.com/arcprint/details/231765/2020-01-12.

owners. Intermediaries distribute bribes to the different levels of employees in the land acquisition office.[41]

One example of the aforementioned difficulties in land acquisition for SEZs is the Sreehatta Economic Zone. The presence of fake landowners, a mismatch in the price of land, and inadequate compensation angered villagers, who filed hundreds of cases in the courts, delaying the zone's development.[42]

C Sreehatta Economic Zone: An Example

Sreehatta Economic Zone is located in Moulavibazar district (Northeast of Bangladesh), which is to the east of Sylhet, west of Habiganj, north of Sunamganj, and south of Moulavibazar district. This SEZ was established on 352 acres of land in Sherpur at Sadar *upazila*, with a view to generating employment for 44,000 people in the Sylhet division. In March 2017, six private entities invested US$ 1.4 billion to establish their industries in this economic zone. Moreover, land development, utility supply, and lake development have already started in this zone under the supervision of BEZA. Figure 8.4 depicts the land acquisition process of SEZs under the Ordinance of 1982. Sreehatta Economic Zone acquired 240 acres of land from approximately 2,000 families and the remaining 112 acres from government *khas* land.

While maintaining the valuation methods described in the Ordinance of 1982, the process takes into account whether the land is used for agriculture, habitat, and so on. The overall value also depends on the details of the usage, that is the type of crop being cultivated on the land. For the Sreehatta Economic Zone, the Sub-Registrar's office determined a market price of BDT 34,600 per decimal of Aman land[43] and BDT 66,700 per decimal of Aus land.[44] Generally, the responsible DC office requires assistance from the Housing and Public

---

[41] According to a report published in a Bangla daily on 26 January 2019, extensive corruption, such as bribes and forced payment of tips, occur in the Land Acquisition offices across the country. In some instances, the owners have to tip 10% to the responsible officer or employee while collecting the check book for the first time. Under article 50 of the Land Acquisition manual, compensation for the acquisition of land cannot be provided while the aforementioned land is subject to legal proceedings. Therefore, in the Land Acquisition offices, refusal to engage in bribery can result in a fraudulent complaint being filed against the claim for compensation. Hundreds of legal complaints relating to compensation have been filed in this way. The lawful landowners are thus forced to spend a large amount of time and money in courts. Furthermore, the employees of the Land Acquisition department provide compensation to fake owners in exchange for bribes. There have been several incidents of land acquisition officers being found guilty of fraudulent activities. However, disciplinary measures against these corrupt employees in Land Acquisition offices are rare (see www.bd-pratidin.com/first-page/2019/01/27/395135).

[42] See https://today.thefinancialexpress.com.bd/first-page/land-disputes-threaten-sreehatta-zone-1526061030.

[43] Land where only Aman rice/Kharif-I crops are being cultivated.

[44] Land where only Aus rice/Kharif-II crops are being cultivated.

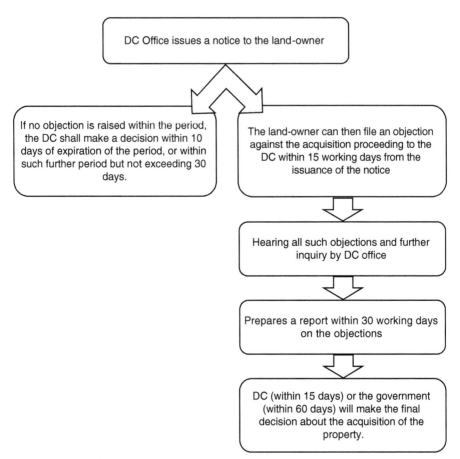

FIGURE 8.4 Land acquisition process
Source: Authors, through review of official documents.

Work Division, Agriculture Division, and Forestry Division to determine the value of infrastructure, food, crops, and trees, respectively. According to the Ordinance of 1982, the affected owners should get 150% of the market price as compensation. Although in Sreehatta Economic Zone, around 85% of total compensation has been paid, it took three to four years for the amount to be paid, revealing the challenges faced by the owners. Thus, closer inspection of marginal landowners' cases reflects the critical situation in the land acquisition process. Also, as mentioned earlier, hundreds of cases were filed in the courts related to confirming the legal ownership of the acquired land.

As mentioned earlier, the Acquisition and Requisition of Immovable Property Act 2017 replaced the Ordinance of 1982. But the late implementation of the new law prevented many people obtaining fair compensation in the case of

Sreehatta Economic Zone. The landowners accused the Assistant Commission (Land) of undervaluing the land price since the then market price of agricultural land was more than the price determined by the Assistant Commission (Land). Moreover, according to the Acquisition and Requisition of Immovable Property Act 2017, if in consequence of the acquisition of the property, the affected person is compelled to change his/her residence, reasonable expenses, if any, incidental to such a change must be considered in determining compensation. However, there are allegations of violations of these provisions in the case of the compensation provided to the landowners in the case of Sreehatta Economic Zone.

We investigated the land acquisition cases of two people: *E* and *T*, who are brothers. They live in Sherpur village at Sadar *upazila* in Moulvibazar District. About 7.66 acres of land were acquired from them for the purpose of Sreehatta Economic Zone. Out of this 7.66 acres, 1.52 acres was agricultural land (Aman) and the remaining 6.14 acres included a homestead, pond, and plantation. The two brothers received BDT 7.81 million (after deducting taxes, including income tax) as compensation for 1.52 acres of agricultural land (Aman type), on the basis of the compensation of per decimal land was BDT 51,000 (150% of the market price determined by the Assistant Commission (land)). They also received around BDT 12.9 million as compensation for infrastructure, trees, food, and crops. However, the compensation for the 6.14 acres of homestead land is still unpaid. Since there was a legal dispute in the High Court regarding these lands, the payment was stalled by the DC's office at the time of payment. During the valuation process, the Assistant Commissioner (Land) categorised the lands (6.14 acres) as agricultural land and accordingly the total unpaid amount was BDT 32.63 million. Since the land from the aforementioned economic zone was acquired under the old law, that is the Ordinance of 1982, the landowners (E and T) were dissatisfied with the valuation process. Therefore, as the aforementioned land was homestead type and located beside the road, they claimed further compensation and rehabilitation support. After formally complaining to BEZA, they received only indifference, and presently the situation is at an impasse.

VI WAY FORWARD

The research underlying this chapter suggests the following measures, both at the policy and institutional levels, for the improvement of land administration and management in Bangladesh.

An efficient land survey: The land management system of Bangladesh still accepts Cadastral Survey, State Acquisition Survey, and Revisional Survey records due to a lack of updated surveys conducted in recent times. The land survey and documentation process need to be efficient and credible. The survey process requires updating in regard to survey methodology and technology, and there is a need to train relevant employees.

Digitisation of record-keeping: The analogue colonial method of record-keeping perpetuates the multiplicity of documents and corruption. The colossal infrastructure necessary to preserve the analogue record creates an array of problems in itself. Therefore, digitising the whole record-keeping documentation process is essential.

Administrative reforms: Rigorous administrative reform is a precondition for mitigating challenges regarding access to land. The current administrative system of colonial descent has to be modified, keeping the context of the country in mind. The Land Administration Manual needs to be updated, and land administration needs to be capable of handling land-related disputes. Administrative reforms can be piloted in specific offices and further extended nationwide if they succeed.

Harmonisation of different stakeholders with overlapping responsibilities: Different stakeholders with overlapping responsibilities need to be harmonised based on their functioning. The recommendation of the Muyeed Committee[45] to combine Land Registration (Sub-Registrar) and record (*tahsil*) offices into a single office at the field level needs to be implemented

Allocation of public lands: A higher degree of coordination should be achieved at the national level to allocate public land to ensure its most productive and essential use. This could be achieved through a coordination institution or body and the establishment of a public land database that would list all plots available for development by location, size, facilities, and other attributes (UNCTAD, 2013; Kathuria and Malouche, 2016).

Reform of the judicial process: The judicial process needs to be reformed to resolve the congestion of litigation. Land survey tribunals need to be reformed to resolve contemporary land–related litigation. Land survey tribunals should be composed of three members involving representation from the judiciary, settlement department, and land administration.

Building awareness: Access to land is difficult to achieve for the general population due to the lack of information regarding the land administration system and the services provided by them. The land laws need to be translated into colloquial Bangla to build awareness. Furthermore, setting up a one-stop service centre to provide information and primary guidance, coupled with digitised administration, can improve the overall land-related problems among the mass of the population.

The present land administration system in Bangladesh has been inherited from the colonial era and fails to meet the needs of the present. The archaic land management system and land laws require modernisation, and there is a need for well-functioning institutions. To increase the effectiveness and credibility of reforms, the Government should also focus on the alignment of cross-sectoral policies (National Agricultural Policy, National Rural Development Policy, National Forest Policy, and Coastal Zone Policy). Entrusting one single agency

---

[45] Ibid.

with sufficient capacity to maintain spatial records in rural and urban areas would be beneficial.

While the Government of Bangladesh has adopted the strategy of establishing SEZs to address the land-related problems facing domestic and foreign investors, the success of SEZs will require an efficient mechanism of land acquisition. While some laws and administrative procedures have already been laid out to provide assistance to SEZs, the progress made so far needs to be critically examined to achieve long-term success.

ANNEX 8.1 GLOSSARY OF TERMS

Alluvion	Accretion of land by movement of water in river or sea.
Aman land	Land where only Aman rice/Kharif-I crops are being cultivated.
Aus land	Land where only Aus rice/Kharif-II crops are being cultivated.
Ayub Khan	Field Marshal Mohammad Ayub Khan (1908–1974) was a military ruler and then the president of Pakistan.
Balaam Boi	Book of land registration records (kept in Registry Office).
Benami transactions	Benami transactions refers to a land sale in which someone purchases the land using someone else as the owner in the deed.
Bigha	Unit of land measurement (0.333 acres).
Cadastral Survey	The Cadastral Survey of Undivided Bengal was the first comprehensive record of land rights in the country. This survey started from Ramu of Cox's Bazar *upazila* in 1888 and ended in 1940. The Cadastral Survey Record of Rights was prepared under the Bengal Tenancy Act 1885. It is still accepted by contemporary courts.
Kanungo	Union Land Assistant Officer.
Khas land	Public property or government-owned land, where nobody has property rights.
Khatian	The Cadastre or Record of Rights; contains the area and character of land (by plot or by owner).
Mouza	The lowest level revenue collection unit.
Mutation	Mutation refers to the insertion of names of new owners in the Record of Rights, in place of former owners, after the transfer of the ownership of land.
Newly formed land	Newly formed land refers to land created from some geographical event, such as sediment accumulated due to changes in river course (char), volcanic eruption, etc.
Parcel-based Land Information System	Cadastre can also be labelled as a parcel-based GIS, which, according to statute/law, records units of immobile property, their identifiers and attributes.

Revenue Circle Officer	After 1961, a separate post of revenue circle officer, popularly known as Circle Office (Revenue), was created at each thana.
Revisional Survey	The Revisional Survey was carried out after 50 years of the Cadastral Survey.
State Acquisition Survey	The Settlement Attestation Survey of 1956–1962.
Sher Shah	Sher Shah was an emperor of north India (1540–1545) who organised a long-lived bureaucracy which was accountable to the ruler and created a carefully calculated revenue system.
Tahsil (Tehsil)	Lowest union-level revenue unit comprising several Mouza.
Tebhaga Movement	Tebhaga Movement was the sharecroppers' movement demanding two-thirds of the produce from land for themselves and one-third for the landlords. Under the leadership of the communist cadres of the Bengal provincial <u>krishak sabha</u>, the *Tebhaga* Movement spread out to 19 districts of Bengal.
Tehsildar	Local revenue collector.
Thana	A unit of police administration.
Union	The smallest rural administrative and local government unit.
Upazila	After divisions and districts, the third largest type of administrative division in Bangladesh.
Upazila Revenue Officer	The Assistant Commissioner of Land also acts as *Upazila* Revenue Officer.
Zamindari	The office or territory held or administered by a *zamindar*. In British India, the system of landholding and tax collection was conducted by *zamindars*.

Discussion of 'Institutional Challenges in Land Administration and Management in Bangladesh'

Dilip Mookherjee

Poorly functioning institutions undermine the functioning of land markets in many developing countries. This chapter provides a rich description of these problems in Bangladesh and offers reform suggestions. Once prominent in traditional academic literature and development policy discussions, these issues have received less attention in recent decades. This is unfortunate, as they continue to be important in low-income countries in South Asia and sub-Saharan Africa. Improper record keeping and lack of transparency undermine security of land rights, as well as transactions facilitating the transfer of land to more efficient farmers and non-agricultural uses in the process of structural transformation. In countries neighbouring Bangladesh, such as India and China, the implementation of land reforms have been shown to have significantly impacted the growth of agricultural productivity, and the evolution of inequality and poverty.

This chapter provides a detailed and informative review of these problems in the context of Bangladesh, including comparisons with other Asian countries.

The set of areas covered are divided into two main topics:

1. land policies (land redistribution, tenancy protection, and land sales) and land administration (land records, sales and transfers, and taxes);
2. land acquisition for non-agricultural purposes by government and private industry, with the related issues of compensation and SEZs.

The former topic is relevant for development within the agricultural sector, while the latter pertains to the non-agricultural sector and structural transformation from agriculture to industry and services. I discuss each of these in turn.

Rural Development

Section III describes the evolution of laws pertaining to land ceilings, redistribution, and tenancy protection in Bangladesh. Section IV focuses on problems in land administration and enforcement, with a detailed explanation of organ-isational structure. Various weaknesses are highlighted: the lack of digitisa-tion of land records; poor infrastructure; human resource problems (such as lack of training and skills, and low motivation); and the overlapping juris-dictions of different divisions, resulting in lack of coordination. The discus-sion clearly illustrates how these weaknesses reduce land security, inhibit land transfers, and promote corruption. Data from household surveys indicate that corruption and lack of transparency are pervasive. Comparisons with neigh-bouring Asian countries on land registration delays and the quality of land administration shows the situation in Bangladesh to be considerably worse than in those countries.

One would like to learn more about these problems, and in particular their consequences for rural development in Bangladesh. For instance, when were the last cadastral surveys completed? For the country as a whole, how much land has been acquired under the land ceiling rules, and distributed? How many sharecroppers were registered? I am not sure if there are any statistics readily available on these, which might be compared with neighbouring coun-tries or regions (such as West Bengal in India, which, in conjunction with Bangladesh, historically constituted a united province until the partition of 1905, engineered by the colonial British authorities). Some facts noted in pass-ing suggest a very low extent of implementation of land reforms. For example, the progress achieved with respect to the distribution of vested land in the 1970s was far lower than expected; only 0.2% of agricultural value added was collected in the form of land taxes during the 1980s. The recommendations of the Muyeed Committee on the rationalisation of land administration were ignored. About 90% of the rural population in 1991 were unaware of their entitlements under the existing legislation.

Additional research is probably needed to create a systematic database on land reforms implemented and to answer important questions relating to the evaluation of land policies in the past as regards rural development in the Bangladeshi context. While these are probably beyond the scope of this chap-ter, I list some questions below, in the hope that future research efforts will be directed towards answering them. I mention in this connection the work of Abhijit Banerjee, Paul Gertler, and Maitreesh Ghatak (*Journal of Political Economy*, 2002), which showed a significantly higher growth of rice yields in West Bengal compared with Bangladesh during 1978–1994, ostensibly owing to substantially greater success in implementing tenancy reform laws.

(a) How did the land distribution change over time, and what role did land reform policies play? How active is the land market? Have land markets equalised or dis-equalised landownership?

(b) It appears that many of the regulations in place are intended to protect small and marginal households in the rural sector, who are poor and comprise a large fraction of the population. In evaluating the implications of existing land regulations, one therefore needs to understand whether these redistributive policies retard or enhance economic growth. Are small farms more or less productive than large farms? How much agricultural tenancy exists? What are the nature of tenancy contracts, the regulations they are subject to (e.g. crop shares or eviction rights of landlords), and the effects of such regulations? Are there increasing returns to scale in farming? To what extent do scale effects depend on differential access of small and large farmers to credit, technology, infrastructure, or marketing? How smoothly does the market for leasing or buying land function? Are there restrictions on outsiders buying land? What are the effects of land policy on migration to the urban sector?

(c) To what extent are landholdings fragmented? What are the productivity effects of fragmentation? If this is a serious problem, is there any scope for the Bangladesh government to coordinate land consolidation efforts?

(d) This chapter indicates many dimensions on which land policies are poorly implemented, owing to lack of transparency, poor land records, and low motivation of land administration officials. As in neighbouring West Bengal, only a small fraction of land collected for redistribution has actually been distributed to the poor. More details of the implementation process would throw more light on the underlying reasons. For instance, who decides on how to select beneficiaries, and on what basis? What happens to the undistributed lands: do they lie fallow or are they used in some way (if so, by whom)? If implementation has been a major problem, to what extent is this a result of weak political will, rather than weak institutions?

(e) Related to the question of political will, what are the political economy effects of land concentration? Do those with large landholdings exercise disproportionate power by virtue of their access to politicians and political parties? If so, what effects does this have on tax evasion and local government revenues, on the allocation of local infrastructure, or the implementation of land regulations? Is there scope for wider reforms of electoral processes and empowerment of local governments in Bangladesh which may improve the implementation of land policies?

(f) How important are water management problems, such as groundwater extraction, irrigation/electricity pricing, or conservation incentives? Are there serious problems of sustainability, for example encroachment on forests, and other common properties? How is the rise of the water level near the coast affecting neighbouring farming and fishing communities? What policies are being considered to help them adapt and possibly to resettle in the future?

(g) What is the potential for the development of modern export-oriented agribusiness? What restrictions currently apply on ownership of land by large firms or foreigners? Can a multinational corporation invest in agribusiness, acquire land, and operate large farms, hiring local labour? Are there restrictions on contract farming? Do land regulations constrain the growth of agribusiness? If there has been any significant agribusiness development in Bangladesh (e.g. in fishing or specific cash crops), what have their growth and distributional impacts been?

Land Acquisition for Industry and SEZs

The remainder of this chapter provides many interesting details about SEZs in Bangladesh and raises a number of important policy questions concerning land acquisition and compensation policy.

I think it is useful to distinguish between two issues here. The first concerns broader aspects of SEZ policy, which do not necessarily have anything to do with land policies *per se*. SEZs typically include the provision of infrastructure and subsidies, the relaxation of labour/environmental regulations, and fast-track approval on a preferential basis for large investors in manufacturing and services. The aim is to attract and stimulate investment by relaxing constraints and regulations that are pervasive in the economy. By its very nature, this creates a dual system. The authors raise concerns about differential access between small and large investors, between those oriented towards the domestic market and those oriented towards the export market, and between regions. This suggests an underlying tension between efficiency/growth objectives and equity/fairness goals that Bangladeshi policy-makers need to confront. Could it be better to focus on growth and to foster special privileges favouring large, export-oriented investors and urban centres, and then expect the resulting benefits to gradually trickle down to the rest of the economy via migration and internal trade?

The second set of issues concerns the specific problems created by poor land administration institutions, which this chapter discusses in detail. Complications owing to poor land records and lack of transparency are illustrated by this chapter's Sreehatta Economic Zone case study. The land authorities deliberately created problems that enhanced corruption and delays, such as informing both the prior and current owners. Problems arose with market price assessment procedures, raising the question whether they should include rehabilitation costs. Some of the problems seem similar to those in West Bengal that I found in my research (in the 2012 article with Maitreesh Ghatak, Sandip Mitra, and Anusha Nath that the authors cite). Those problems arose from failure of land records to verify land quality, thinness of land markets (which makes it difficult to assess the market price for comparable properties), and undervaluation of properties owing to incentives among owners to evade stamp duty on land transfers. However, the West Bengal study did not indicate corruption in the compensation process to be as important as the authors suggest is in the case of Bangladesh. This is broadly consistent with the poorer quality of land administration in Bangladesh reported earlier in this chapter.

Before concluding, let me raise some additional questions regarding land acquisition and compensation policy for academics and policymakers in Bangladesh to consider, in the wake of the West Bengal experience:

i. Should compensation to owners of acquired properties be related to market price? How should market price be assessed? At which point of time (relative to the acquisition date) should market price be assessed? These tend to arise for the following reasons. After land is acquired and makes way for industrial or real estate development, property values tend to rise. Previous owners often claim it is unfair to let all the benefits of property appreciation accrue to the new investors. Moreover, linking the compensation amount to future appreciation would reduce the incentive for previous owners to hold out and litigate, thereby reducing delays.

ii. How should rules and procedures for government acquisition of land and provision of compensation to owners be designed? For instance, should procurement auction–based mechanisms be used to allow existing owners more autonomy? What should be the minimum proportion of owners whose assent is necessary for an acquisition to be authorized? To what extent should local governments, communities, and non-governmental organisations be involved in the acquisition process? Is there scope for flexibility regarding form of compensation (e.g. lump sum payments, shares in property within the SEZ, training/employment in SEZ firms, or indexed annuities)? Such procedures can alleviate the hardship on previous owners who tend to be displaced and lower the political resistance to land acquisition.

iii. How should tenants and workers be compensated? Their livelihoods are disrupted by land acquisition, thereby raising inequality and poverty, and threatening the political viability of the transition process. The design of rehabilitation and resettlement policies is perhaps the most critical, and most difficult, aspect of policy design and implementation. The 2011 Land Acquisition Bill passed in India mandated tribunals to listen to and adjudicate on these concerns, besides mandating high minimum compensation levels. These are widely viewed to have contributed to the post-2010 growth slowdown. This is yet another manifestation of the growth–equity trade off that each society has to confront.

9

Political Economy Analysis of the Role of the Judiciary in Land Dispossession Litigation in Bangladesh

Rafiqua Ferdousi, Kazi Maruful Islam, and Selim Raihan

I INTRODUCTION[1]

Landlessness and the resulting poverty are major development issues in Bangladesh, not only because of the scarcity of land – since Bangladesh is among the most densely populated countries on earth – but also due to the fact that land grabbing or illegal dispossession of land is frequent in Bangladesh and often results in landlessness. The institution of the judiciary has a key role to play in correcting this situation in Bangladesh. There is no denying that access to justice and the rule of law are key elements of sustainable and equitable development. Access to justice is foundational to people's access to public services, curbing corruption, restraining the abuse of power, and establishing a social contract between people and the state (United Nations, 2019b).

In Bangladesh, there are many institutional weaknesses related to land administration and management which exacerbate the problems of illegal dispossession of land and land litigation. As land is one of the most important means of livelihood security in Bangladesh, improper and unfair litigation of land-related issues can exacerbate poverty, as well as affecting prospects for economic growth (Barkat and Roy, 2004).

The judiciary, by definition, has the prime role in solving land litigation issues. However, the judiciary has not been able to perform its due role with respect to land litigation in Bangladesh. A number of issues cause inordinate delay in the litigation procedure and create backlog of cases. In developing nations generally, deficiencies and institutional challenges relating to the judiciary further complicate issues related to land litigation, and thus affect economic growth and poverty (United Nations, 2019b). By contrast, where a judiciary functions effectively it can effectively mitigate irregularities and

---

[1] Annex 9.1 provides a glossary of terms used in this chapter.

300

conflicts, and thus can play a critical role in ensuring economic growth and alleviating poverty.

Against this backdrop, this chapter aims to explore the current state and performance of the judiciary of Bangladesh and its possible impact on poverty and development by considering involuntary land dispossession litigation as an example. This chapter attempts to provide a narrative analysis of the process through which involuntary land dispossession takes place in the particular socio-economic and historical context of Bangladesh. Involuntary dispossession of land results in the economic outcome termed forced asset transfer. This chapter aims to examine how this outcome is influenced by the overall functioning of the judiciary in Bangladesh. Consequently, this chapter aims to scrutinise the interrelation between economic assets, human actions, and state institutions, and its possible impact on the overall trajectory of long-term development. Finally, this chapter aims to identify potential reform measures and agendas in relation to land dispossession litigation in Bangladesh.

II THE EFFECTIVENESS OF THE JUDICIARY IN BANGLADESH: A GENERAL ASSESSMENT

A well-functioning civil justice system protects the rights of all citizens against infringement of the law by others, including by powerful parties and governments. An essential component of the rule of law is an effective and fair judicial system that ensures that the laws are respected and appropriate sanctions are taken when they are violated (Organisation for Economic Co-operation and Development (OECD), 2015). In order to understand the current state of the effectiveness of the judiciary in Bangladesh, the following subsections set out a brief account of the structure of the judiciary and the degree of its fairness, the expeditiousness of judicial procedures, and the degree of independence of the judiciary from the executive branch of government.

A An Overview of the Structure of the Judiciary

The current justice system of Bangladesh has its roots in both the traditional subcontinental justice system which was developed over centuries during the reigns of Hindu and Muslim rulers, including the Mughals, and the common law justice system introduced by the British colonial ruler in the subcontinent (Halim, 2008). Moreover, the Constitution of the Peoples Republic of Bangladesh lays out the structure of the judiciary, and has undergone multiple amendments since independence in 1971. Among these amendments, some have greatly influenced the structure, functions, and jurisdiction of the higher and lower courts. Currently, the judiciary of Bangladesh is composed of three adjudicative bodies: the higher judiciary, the lower judiciary, and specialised tribunals. The structure of the judicial system of Bangladesh is presented in Figure 9.1.

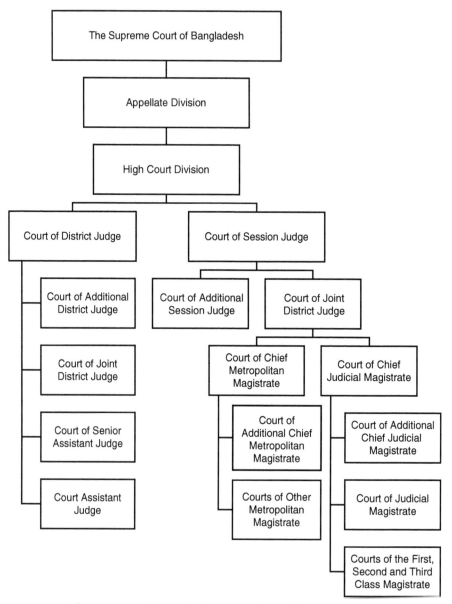

FIGURE 9.1 The structure of the judicial system of Bangladesh
Source: Based on Judicial Portal Bangladesh, www.judiciary.org.bd/en/judiciary/
court-structure (accessed 15 May 2019).

The higher judiciary refers to the Supreme Court, which consists of the Appellate Division and the High Court Division.[2] The Appellate Division is the constitutional court, with no original jurisdiction. It hears appeals against: (a) High Court Division orders, judgements, decrees, or sentences involving constitutional interpretation, capital punishment, life imprisonment, and sentences for contempt; and (b) judgements or orders of specialised tribunals, such as the Administrative Appellate Tribunal and International Crimes. The courts that are subordinate to the Supreme Court – namely, the Appellate Division and the High Court Division – were established under Article 114 of the Constitution. The Civil Courts Act 1887 directs the subordinate civil courts, and the Code of Criminal Procedure guides the courts of magistrates and sessions. In the case of civil courts, there are five grades, including: Courts of Assistant Judge, Senior Assistant Judge, Joint District Judge, Additional District Judge, and the District Judge. The District Judge heads these courts for all districts except for the three Chittagong Hill Tracts districts.[3] There are also five classes of subordinate criminal courts: the Courts of Session, Metropolitan Magistrate, Magistrate of the First Class, Magistrate of the Second Class, and the Magistrate of the Third Class. In the Court of Sessions, the District Judges are empowered to function as Session Judges. In addition, the Government of Bangladesh has enacted the Village Court Act 2006 and has taken the initiative to activate village courts at the union level (UNDP and Government of Bangladesh, 2019). However, village courts have yet to be established throughout the country. When they are, their jurisdiction will be very limited, and they will deal only with civil issues.

The Constitution of Bangladesh guarantees human rights and freedom, equality, and justice and the rule of law for all citizens (Huda, 1997). In agreement with the Constitution, there are three basic requirements of a judicial system: fairness (which includes various dimensions); the effectiveness and the expeditiousness in the procedures; and the independence of the judges. The available evidence on various measures of the effectiveness of the judicial system in Bangladesh is discussed in the following subsections.

B Degree of Fairness of the Judiciary

Access to justice is one of the basic principles of the rule of law. If access to justice is hindered and any form of discrimination or bias persists in the process

---

[2] SC is made of AD and HCD. AD is the appeal entity. There are a number of higher court judges called 'Justices' who manage the cases that comes to these two separate bodies. However, the highest court authority is the Chief Justice. Therefore, issues that are of great importance (i.e. Constitutional matters) are usually supervised by the Chief Justice or special benches.

[3] The Chittagong Hill Tracts (CHT) are an area within the Chattogram division in south-eastern Bangladesh covering 13,295 square kilometres. This area is divided into three administrative districts namely Khagrachari, Rangamati, and Bandarban Hill Districts.

of delivering justice, this can undermine the voice and rights of the people. According to an estimate by the OECD, around 4 billion people around the world live outside the protection of the law, mostly because they are poor or marginalised within their societies. The lack of legal accountability propels local corruption and diverts resources from where they are needed the most. In addition, women are particularly affected by legal exclusion as they often face multiple forms of discrimination, violence, and sexual harassment. Thus, access to justice and fairness of the judiciary are essential to enable the basic protection of human rights (OECD-OSF, 2016).

In Bangladesh, there is a lack of well managed data regarding the various features and functioning of the judiciary. Thus, in order to capture some dimensions of the fairness of the judiciary, in the analysis in this section, three indicators are considered from the World Justice Project (WJP) Rule of Law Index[4] (WJP, 2019): 'people can access and afford civil justice', 'civil justice is free of discrimination', and 'civil justice is free of corruption'. It should be noted that the selected indicators are related to civil justice. This is because the main focus of this chapter is land dispossession litigation, which falls under the jurisdiction of civil courts, and this chapter principally intends to highlight the situation of civil justice when discussing the performance of the judiciary.

It should be noted that the WJP Rule of Law Index contains a number of limitations. First, the index has been constructed based on a significant proportion of subjective information given by both experts and the general public. Second, the opinions and perceptions of the individual respondents may vary to a great extent across time and geographic region. Despite these limitations, the WJP Rule of Law Index 2019 provides an opportunity to examine the relative position of Bangladesh compared to another 125 countries. Out of the total 126 countries in the index, roughly 28 can be broadly categorised as developed countries and the rest as developing countries.

The first indicator 'people can access and afford civil justice' measures the accessibility and affordability of civil courts, including whether people are aware of available remedies and can access and afford legal advice and representation. It also measures whether people can access the court system without incurring unreasonable fees, or facing procedural hurdles or physical and linguistic barriers. The second indicator 'civil justice is free of discrimination'

---

[4] The WJP Rule of Law Index (2019) measures how the rule of law is experienced and perceived by the general public in 126 countries based on more than 120,000 household and 3,800 expert surveys. The index has 8 factors and 47 sub-factors, where 1 signifies the highest score and 0 signifies the lowest score. The conceptual framework for these has been developed in consultation with academics, practitioners, and community leaders from around the world. The data have been subjected to a series of tests to identify possible biases and errors and a sensitivity analysis was conducted by the Econometrics and Applied Statistics Unit of the European Commission's Joint Research Centre, in collaboration with the Index team, to assess the statistical reliability of the results.

measures whether the civil justice system discriminates in practice based on socio-economic status, gender, ethnicity, religion, national origin, sexual orientation, or gender identity. The third indicator 'civil justice is free of corruption' measures whether the civil justice system is free of bribery and improper influence by private interests (WJP, 2019).

Bangladesh ranks 106 among the 126 countries for the 'people can access and afford civil justice' indicator of the WJP 2019, with a score of 0.4498, compared to the median score of 0.5637. Likewise, for the 'civil justice is free of discrimination' indicator Bangladesh's relative position is 115 among the 126 countries. Again, its score is 0.3613, relative to the median score of 0.5623. Finally, Bangladesh ranks 100 among the 126 countries for the 'civil justice is free of corruption' indicator, with a score of 0.3674, in comparison to the median score of 0.5224. The data show that Bangladesh's relative performance in all of the three areas with regard to the fairness of the judiciary is in the bottom quintile or the bottom decile of a set of 126 countries.

C Expeditiousness of the Judicial Procedures

One of the fundamental aspects of the effectiveness of the judiciary is the expeditiousness of the judicial procedures. The well-known legal maxim 'justice delayed is justice denied' is based on the principle that if redress is not available in time and there is little hope of resolution, it may well be regarded as there being no redress at all. This principle forms the basis of the right to a speedy trial and similar rights which are meant to expedite the legal system. Thus, the expeditiousness of the judicial procedures is often considered to be a critical element for ensuring an effective justice system. If the judicial system guarantees the enforcement of rights, creditors are more likely to lend, businesses are dissuaded from opportunistic behaviour, transaction costs are reduced, and innovative businesses are more likely to invest (OECD, 2013; IMF, 2017; World Economic Forum (WEF), 2018; World Bank, 2017). The relative picture regarding the current degree of expeditiousness of the judicial procedures in Bangladesh is discussed here.

The 'civil justice is not subject to unreasonable delay' indicator of the WJP Rule of Law Index measures whether civil justice proceedings are conducted and judgements are produced in a timely manner without unreasonable delay. It can be observed that Bangladesh's performance is again particularly poor for this indicator, ranking 121 out of the 126 countries in 2019, with a score of 0.1917, compared to the median score of 0.4384.

A closer examination of the primary data reveals that the case backlog is especially acute in the subordinate or district courts of the country.[5] The total

---

[5] Any courts below the High Court of Bangladesh are generally known as lower or subordinate courts, which follows the progression of the organigram presented in Figure 9.1. Thus, here we refer to all of the civil courts that are subordinate to the High Court of Bangladesh.

civil case backlog at the end of 2018[6] was 1,321,038, and the number of total cases including new cases was 1,396,350. Among these, only 58,234 cases were resolved, which is about 24 times less than the total cases. A comparatively smaller number of cases (6,001 cases) were transferred or received a stay order from the higher courts, and also a few (1,716 cases) were resolved through Alternative Dispute Resolution (ADR). It can also be observed that the total number of civil and criminal cases has increased overtime in the High Court and Appellate Division.

A number of factors may have propelled the growth of the total number of pending cases in the higher and subordinate lower courts of Bangladesh. One of the main reasons behind the growth of pending cases in the last decade is the lack of capacity and resources in the judiciary. The total number of judges compared to the total population and number of cases is still quite low in Bangladesh. According to the annual report of the Supreme Court of Bangladesh, there were a total number of seven judges (including Chief Justices in the Appellate Division and 95 judges in the high Court) in 2018 (The Supreme Court of Bangladesh, 2019), which shows the lack of capacity of the overall system. Similarly, the total number of approved posts of judges for the lower courts was 1,655, of which 387 remained vacant until 2017 due to delays in the recruitment process (Sarkar, 2017).

In addition, in Bangladesh, civil cases are generally based on documented evidence and oral evidence is only taken as a supplement to documents. The civil courts still follow the Evidence Act of 1872, the Civil Courts Act of 1887, the Code of Civil Procedure of 1908, and some other special laws that are applicable to the operation of civil cases. The common practice of examining witnesses in civil courts involves stating the whole case line by line, with the judge writing every statement out by hand. If this manual recording is not followed, then further clarification is required according to the Code of Civil Procedure 1908.[7] For this reason, the present nature of peremptory hearings consumes a considerable amount of time and the dependence on manual paperwork contributes to increasing case backlog (Tahura, 2015). Likewise, as mentioned earlier, along with a shortage of judges, a number of systematic problems compound the backlog problem, including poor investigation by the police, too many adjournments at courts, an absence of witness, the lack of capacity of legal professionals, a lack of coordination among different government departments, and the unwillingness of some lawyers to settle the case within a short time (Tahura and Kelly, 2015; The Supreme Court of Bangladesh and UNDP, 2015; Transparency International Bangladesh, 2017; Rahman, 2018; The Justice Audit Team, 2018).

Moreover, political turmoil and deterioration of the rule of law over time has caused an increase in the number of cases in recent years (Sarkar, 2015).

---

[6] Based on the data collected from the office of the Registrar of the Supreme Court of Bangladesh.
[7] Rule 5 and 8 Order XVIII of the Code of Civil Procedure 1908.

Besides, according to Bangladesh Bank, the central bank of Bangladesh, more than 55,500 cases involving default loans were pending with the courts as at June 2018 (The Daily Star, 2018b). Furthermore, the Vested Property Return Act of 2013 came as an additional complicating factor as it allowed the Government to confiscate the property of individuals considered to have acted as an enemy of the state during the India–Pakistan war of 1965 (Yasmin, 2016). From 2013 to 2016, the Government of Bangladesh activated special tribunals throughout the country to restore vested property. Since 2016, claims for vested property have been managed by the formal judiciary.

The upshot of the above situation is that the judicial system of Bangladesh is increasingly burdened with a backlog of cases due to various socio-economic, political, and historical factors. A lack of initiative to compel clerks, advocates, litigants, or witnesses to comply with the due codes, rules, and processes leads to inordinate delays at the different stages of the litigation procedure. However, along with the lack of any adequate initiative to improve the performance of the judiciary, institutional failures in other areas – especially with respect to land management, default loans, and the overall deterioration of rule of law – are also producing a significant growth in the backlog and the slower disposal of cases. This growing backlog and slowly disposed cases are seriously hampering the overall performance of the judiciary. This scenario especially holds in the three major business and administrative hubs of Bangladesh, namely Dhaka, Chittagong, and Khulna. As a result, individuals, businesses, and private investors are increasingly facing uncertainties and challenges. Ultimately, the low level of expeditiousness of judicial procedures in Bangladesh is a severe impediment for the overall business climate and competitiveness of the country.

D Independence from the Executive Branch of the Government

Independence of the judiciary is based on the axiom of the separation of powers: the judiciary should remain separate and independent from the executive and legislative branches of government. The independence of the judiciary depends on certain conditions like the mode of appointment of judges, security of their tenure in office, and adequate remuneration and privileges. Such independence enables the judiciary to perform its due role in the society, thus inspiring public confidence in it. The independence of civil justice thus requires a set of detailed rules and procedures to ensure that a dispute will be treated in a neutral way, without biases in favour of any party (OECD, 2015).

In Bangladesh, despite a constitutional mandate for the separation of the judiciary from the executive organs of the state, the recruitment of subordinate court judges used to be conducted by the Bangladesh Public Service Commission (Islam, 2014). However, the government-versus-Masdar-Hossain case in 1999[8] produced a landmark judgement regarding judicial independence. Nevertheless, until 2006, the judgement remained largely unimplemented. In 2007, the caretaker government took initiatives to implement the judgement.[9] This removed the impediment to the separation of the lower judiciary from executive control and the appointment of judicial magistrates (Biswas, 2012). However, the ordinances of the caretaker government have not yet been fully enacted and the judiciary has yet to be completely separated from the influence of the executive branch. The Law and Justice Division of the Ministry of Law, Justice and Parliamentary Affairs has the constitutional authority to manage the appointment, transfer, resignation, and removal of the judicial officers, judges,[10] and additional judges[11] of the Supreme Court of Bangladesh and the Attorney-General.[12] In addition, the appointment of the next senior Judge of the Appellate Division of the Supreme Court as the Chief Justice is also the responsibility of the division[13] (Law and Justice Division, 2019). This leaves the judiciary somewhat vulnerable to political manoeuvring and vested interests (Huda, 2017; Islam, 2017; The Daily Star, 2018c).

The 'civil justice is free of improper government influence' indicator of the WJP Rule of Law Index measures whether the civil justice system is free of improper government or political influence. Bangladesh ranked 76 out of 126 countries in 2019, with a score of 0.4412, compared to the median score of 0.4907. This shows that Bangladesh has an average level of performance in terms of judicial independence. Overall, there is still much room for improvement with regard to the complete separation of powers in Bangladesh.

---

[8] Secretary, Ministry of Finance vs. Md. Masdar Hossain and others, 52 DLR (AD) 82. Masdar Hossain, a lower court judge, lodged a writ petition with the Supreme Court (SC) seeking an order for the separation of the judiciary from the executive as required in Article 22 of the Constitution. The High Court Division (HCD) in May 1999 issued a directive to the government to separate the judiciary, both higher and lower from the executive within eight weeks. This ruling prevailed on appeal in November 2000 and reaffirmed in the revision case in June 2001 in the Appellate Division (AD). The SC ruling worked out 12 directives for the government to implement the separation without any constitutional amendment, which went unheeded. Despite Articles 102 and 112 of the Constitution making all SC rulings binding for all citizens and authorities, the then government sought 26 extensions of time to implement the ruling and eventually left the office in October 2006 without separating the judiciary.

[9] The caretaker government promulgated two ordinances (No II and IV of 2007) and formulated four service rules, namely (a) Bangladesh Judicial Service Commission Rules, 2007, (b) Bangladesh Judicial Service (Pay Commission) Rules 2007, (c) Bangladesh Judicial Service Commission (Constitution of Service, Appointments in the Service and Suspension, Removal & Dismissal from the Service) Rules, 2007, and (d) Bangladesh Judicial Service (Posting, Promotion, Grant of Leave, Control, Discipline and other Condition of Service) Rules, 2007. The caretaker government also amended the Code of Criminal Procedure 1898 by Act No. XXXII of 2009. In addition, there was an initiative to create a separate judicial service examination in 2007.

[10] According to Article 95 (1) and Article 96 (2) of the Constitution.

[11] According to Article 98 of the Constitution.

[12] According to Article 64 (2) & (4) of the Constitution.

[13] According to Article 97 of the Constitution.

An independent and strong judicial system is an essential element of a free, fair, and just society and an efficient economy. If the independence of the judiciary is undermined, it further aggravates many other issues and concerns. For example, when it comes to ensuring the legal accountability of government officials, the judiciary can exercise *suo muto* (by own initiative) power to uphold justice (Mollah, 2010).[14] Again, the judiciary can ensure checks and balances in a society through judicial activism. However, these practices will not be effective in the absence of an independent and well-functioning judiciary.

III THE EFFECTIVENESS OF THE JUDICIARY IN BANGLADESH: THE CASE OF LAND LITIGATION

Understanding the effectiveness of the judiciary encompasses several dimensions. This chapter adopts land litigation in the civil courts of Bangladesh as a case study to explore the effectiveness of the judiciary. This section provides a brief account of the nature of land conflicts, the related litigation process, as well as the methodology and major findings of a qualitative appraisal of effectiveness of the judiciary with respect to land litigation in Bangladesh.

A Land Conflicts and Litigation

It should be noted that the terms land dispossession and land grabbing are sometimes used interchangeably in the Bengali language. In general, land grabbing is synonymous with large-scale land appropriation, usually by large corporations (Rudi *et al.*, 2014; Semedi and Bakker, 2014; Suhardiman *et al.*, 2015; Tura, 2018). As mentioned earlier, Bangladesh is a land-scarce country and due to extreme population pressure, large-scale land appropriation by private companies does not occur on a scale compared to some other countries of the world where land constraints are not as prominent. However, the Government sometimes acquires sizeable quantities of land for special economic zones or other similar economic activities. What appears to be the major land issue is forced or fraudulent takeovers of land of relatively small or moderate size. For this reason, the nature of land grabbing in Bangladesh may best be described as the involuntary dispossession of land. This chapter therefore centres on cases of such dispossession and looks at the effectiveness of the judiciary in resolving them.

1 Land-Related Conflicts

In local dialect, land grabbing reflects the notion of *bhumi dakhal*, which can be literally translated as 'to take control of land'. In the Bangladeshi

---

[14] The judiciary can hold public offices and private bodies accountable on its own if necessary, without the filing of any cases. The exercise of such special judicial authority is called judicial activism.

context, land grabbing means forceful dispossession. In its most basic form, land ownership is defined by the physical act of occupying a piece of land. Essentially, *dakhal* is an outcome of the relations between different sources of power and authority, from large landowners, local strongmen, and goons (*mastaans*) to influential government officials (military and civil service both), elected officials, and national politicians. Thus, grabbing or *dakhal* is the result of continuous negotiations between these different actors (Suykens, 2015).

Land grabbing or involuntary dispossession may occur for many reasons. Adnan (2013) has explained that very often, when peasants are not willing to sell their piece of land due to either emotional attachment to ancestral holdings or its location specificity, involuntary dispossession or *dakahl* involves use of force through extra-economic and non-market mechanisms, including violence and use of state machinery. In recent years, increasing amounts of land have been taken out of agricultural production as a result of fast urbanisation and industrial expansion. These takeovers are mostly done by realtors for housing, by corporate interests for commercial use, and by the state for military or industrial use.

Feldman and Geisler (2012) examined land grabbing in Bangladesh and viewed such seizures through the lens of displacement and land encroachment. Their study examined two different but potentially interacting displacement processes. The first takes place in the *char*, riverine and coastal sediment regions, which are in a constant state of formation and erosion and consequently are ripe sites for contestation and power play. In this region, mainly small producers are uprooted from their rich alluvial soils. The second displacement process is observed in peri-urban areas where elites engage gangs and corrupt public servants to coerce small producers into relinquishing titles to their ever more valuable lands. Thus, there are both *in situ* displacements where people may remain in place or experience a prolonged multi-stage process of removal and *ex situ* displacements where people are brutally expelled from their homes, communities, and livelihoods.

It is evident that where landholdings are small and everyday subsistence is precarious, even a limited amount of land dispossession at the expense of those whose subsistence depends on agriculture is an engine of landlessness and chronic poverty. This situation in Bangladesh therefore highlights the role of the state, especially the role of the judiciary and its sanctions regarding involuntary land dispossession. During the fieldwork for the present study,[15] a number of sources of land-related conflicts in Bangladesh were identified. These conflicts are broadly depicted in Box 9.1.

The major types of land litigation can be divided into a number of categories, including: a declaratory suit, cancellation of a deed, a partition suit,

[15] The detailed information on the fieldwork and primary data collection procedure is outlined in Section III.B.1.

		Box 9.1 Common types of land conflicts in Bangladesh	
Types of land conflicts	Victim	Nature of land	Source of conflict
Conflict with the state/ government	Private owners	Private land	Involuntary dispossession due to land acquisition for state-led development activity
Conflict with large companies	Government, poor individuals, indigenous community	Private land, community land, public property, or *khas* land, hills, rivers	Involuntary dispossession due to land acquisition for commercial activity or private gain
Conflict with smaller companies	Individuals/ indigenous community	Private land, community land	Involuntary dispossession due to land acquisition for commercial activity or private gain
Conflict with elites/ politicians/ goons at the local level	Mostly poor individuals with less economic and socio-political influence/ capital, absentee owners	Private land, community land	Involuntary dispossession due to miscalculations or mistakes in the land survey; elite capture due to loopholes in or undue misinterpretation of the existing laws or regulations
Conflict with neighbours and family members	Individuals	Private land	Involuntary dispossession due to miscalculations or mistakes in land surveys, fraudulent behaviour, ambiguity in inheritance procedures, and informality in inheritance distribution

Note: The type and nature of land, victims, and sources of conflict vary based on different circumstances.

Source: Authors' analysis.

recovery of *khas* possession, eviction of a tenant, a money suit, a pre-emption case, pre-emption under *Mohammedan* law, a vested property release case, a land survey tribunals case, a mandatory injunction, an arbitration suit, succession cases, and other miscellaneous cases. If the suit valuation ranges from

Bangladeshi Taka (BDT) 100,000[16] up to BDT 200,000, the jurisdiction for litigation will fall under the Court of Assistant Judge. Similarly, if the suit valuation ranges from BDT 200,001 up to BDT 400,000, it will fall under the Court of Senior Assistant Judge. Finally, if the suit valuation is BDT 400,001 and higher, the jurisdiction for litigation will fall under the Joint District Judge. Typically, land litigation in Bangladesh follows the workflow of civil litigation (see Figure 9.1 for the detailed hierarchal structure of the judicial system of Bangladesh).

2 Land Litigation in the Formal Judicial System

As suggested by Figure 9.2, the first step of any civil litigation process in Bangladesh begins with the filing of suit to the *sherestadar*, a court officer. The suit is then entered into the register of suits. The defendant is informed about the case and provided with a copy of the plaint, and thus summons is served. Then if the defendant appears at the court with his written statement, the court tries to mediate between the parties. If the mediation fails, the court fixes a date for a first hearing. At the first hearing, the court examines the claims of the parties and frames the issues. After that, the court announces the date for a peremptory hearing and orders the parties to submit a list of witnesses. The peremptory hearing is followed by a further hearing and presentation of the arguments. Subsequently, the court pronounces the judgement on the day of the trial or later at a fixed date. Ultimately, the court may pass an order. However, if the defendant does not appear before the court throughout the overall litigation process, then an *ex-parte* hearing takes place. In this case, the evidence is recorded and an *ex-parte* order is given. Finally, based on the argument and evidence, the court draws up the decree irrespective of the appearance or absence of the defendant at the hearings.

Thus, a plaintiff usually first goes to the *muhuri* to have an appointment with a lawyer. The lawyer then files the case and sends it to the court. The case is then recorded in the *sheresta* by the *sherestadar* and summons is issued through the *nezarat* by the *nazir*. After that the date of the hearing is usually managed by the *peshkar* of the court.

B A Qualitative Appraisal of Judiciary Dysfunction in Land Matters

1 Methodology

The purpose of the qualitative analysis in this chapter is to focus on the inherent political economic issues of the factors and processes underlying land dispossession litigation and their outcomes in terms of poverty and well-being in

---

[16] US$ 1 is equivalent to approximately BDT 85, based on the inter-bank exchange rate set by the Bangladesh Bank, www.bb.org.bd/econdata/exchangerate.php (accessed on 15 December 2019).

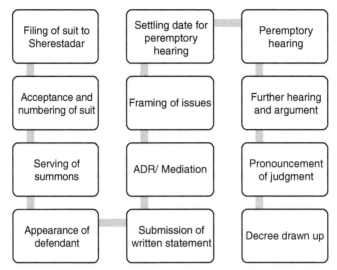

FIGURE 9.2 Procedure of land litigation in Bangladesh
Source: Based on Judicial Portal Bangladesh, www.judiciary.org.bd/en/judiciary/trial-procedure/subordinate-court/civil-court (accessed on 15 May 2019).

the particular social–historical instance of Bangladesh. The analysis is based on a rich variety of primary data collected through a number of detailed case studies, key informant interviews, focus group discussions, and participant observations conducted between April and July 2019. The victims of the case studies were identified with the help of local activists and the District Lawyers' Association. References from the case studies will be made in this chapter with the help of coded names. In order to understand the political economy of land dispossession litigation, two areas of Bangladesh, which display different characteristics, were selected for the study: Anwara and Gazipur upazila. The first study area is a heavily industrialised area located near the major sea port, and the second area is situated near the densely populated capital.

Anwara upazila is located in Chattogram Division of Bangladesh. It has an area of about 164.13 square kilometres. Anwara is one of the most heavily industrialised areas of Bangladesh. It is the location of a number of companies, including: Karnaphuli Fertilizer Company Ltd, Karnaphuli Polyester Products Company Limited, Chattogram Urea Fertilizer Limited, and the Korean Export Processing Zone, which is financed by the Korean Young One Corporation. The Korean Export Processing Zone is the largest private export processing zone in the country, spanning 2,492 acres. Korean Export Processing Zone is located on the south bank of the river Karnaphuli, opposite to Chattogram International Airport and close to the country's major sea port at Chattogram. In addition, the Government of Bangladesh is also building an underwater tunnel under the Karnaphuli River which is going to be connected to a six-lane highway. On the other hand, Gazipur Sadar upazila is located in Dhaka division. It has an area of 446.38 square kilometres. There are also a number of water bodies near Gazipur and the Sadar upazila is home to a number of historical monuments, relics, archaeological heritage sites, and national parks. Moreover, Gazipur is situated right next to the capital and city dwellers can easily plan a day trip to the location. For this reason, the area is a popular destination for tourists and recreation seekers. Furthermore, the proximity to the capital Dhaka has turned Gazipur into a hub of manufacturing and industrialisation. The Bangladesh Small and Cottage Industries Corporation (BSCIC) industrial areas in Tongi and Konabari alone host a plethora of large and medium-sized industries.

Some secondary data related to case statistics have also been collected from a variety of documentary sources and from the office of the Registrar of the Supreme Court of Bangladesh. At the same time, the study draws insights and information from a rigorous review of the relevant literature.

2 *Findings*

There are a number of possible causes of institutional inefficiencies in the judiciary. However, we focus here only on the causes of institutional inefficiencies in relation to involuntary land dispossession litigation. Based on the analysis of primary data, these inefficiencies can be attributed to various factors, including: the ambiguity of procedural laws; poor updating and preservation of land records; a shortage of qualified personnel and misallocation of roles; unequal access to justice; delays in procedures; and influence peddling and power asymmetries. A brief account of the causes of institutional inefficiencies in the judiciary with respect to involuntary land dispossession litigation is presented in the following subsections.

I ACTORS INVOLVED IN THE LAND LITIGATION PROCESS. The analysis of the qualitative data reveals that different actors are involved at each level of involuntary land dispossession litigation, with different interests and degrees of power or influence (Box 9.2). However, it is worth noting that the actors are connected to each other through various degrees of contest and coalition. The identified actors can be grouped in four categories: state actors, non-state actors, internal actors, and external actors.

State actors refers to actors who hold positions in government offices and who have a role in land litigation in one way or other. Many of these actors do not have any direct authority over the litigation process: for example, the union *parishad* chairman has only informal influence over the process. Although the union *parishad* chairman is not directly a part of the formal litigation process, he can influence the legal support-seeking behaviour of common citizens. On the other hand, non-state actors are those who have a stake in the litigation process but have no official authority to influence the outcome of the litigation. For example, as a professional body the lawyers' association plays an

---

Box 9.2 Categories of actors involved in the land litigation process in Bangladesh

	State actors	Non-state actors
Internal actors	Police	Muhuri
	Public prosecutors	Lawyers
	Judges	Plaintiffs
	Sherestadar	Defendants
	Nazir	
	Peshkar	
External actors	Union *parishad* chairmen and members	District Lawyers' Associations
	Tehsil offices	District Bar Associations
	Kanungo	Local brokers
	Sub-registrars	Local influential people
	ACs Land	Local businessmen
	Upazila *Nirbahi* Officer	Politicians of the opposition party
	Deputy Commissioner (DC) offices	
	Politicians of the ruling party (holding public office)	

Note: The above categorisation and the position of the actors in the matrix may sometimes vary based on different contexts.

Source: Authors' analysis.

---

important role in identifying the appropriate lawyer for the litigation. Usually, the leader of the lawyers' association has informal influence over the proceedings of the court as the support of the leaders of the lawyers' association may help to speed up the litigation process.

Similarly, there are brokers active in the court area who can connect a service-seeker to an influential lawyer who might not be known to the service-seeker otherwise. These brokers are people who live on their network with court staff and lawyers. However, while monetary transactions take place between the different actors involved in the litigation process, among these payments only the court fee and lawyer's fees are officially due, while the rest are unofficial fees. In addition, lawyers are also active in national politics and many lawyers aspire to a career in politics. These kinds of intangible interests also play a role in influencing the litigation process. Although the power and influence of the key actors in the land litigation process may vary depending on the context, a general scenario of the interplay between the interests and influence of the main actors is presented in Figure 9.3.

Figure 9.3 shows that the judge and other court officials have a high degree of influence over the proceedings, but they also have a low degree

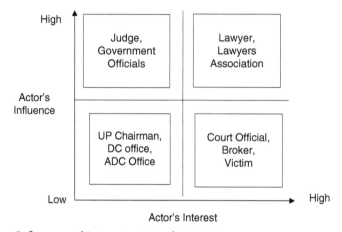

FIGURE 9.3 Influence and interest matrix of actors
Note: The above categorisation and the position of the actors in the matrix may sometimes vary based on different contexts; 'government officials' in this figure refers to the formal state actors from Box 9.1 (i.e. police, prosecutors, *sherestadar*, etc.).
Source: Authors' analysis.

of interest in them because they are overburdened with cases. However, the lawyer and the lawyers' associations have a higher interest and relatively higher influence. If they want, they can increase or decrease the speed and cost of the process. On the other hand, petty court officials like *peshkar* and *serestadar* have a high degree of interest because they are usually paid in an unofficial manner by clients for their support and services. On the other hand, they do not wield a high level of control over the litigation process: they have a facilitating role but cannot determine the outcome of that process.

II THE AMBIGUITY OF PROCEDURAL LAWS. The current structure of the judiciary also bears the historical legacy of the colonial period and is still heavily guided by the institutional traditions of the British era. For this reason, sometimes the laws, rules, and procedures regarding the civil litigation are not clearly articulated in the local language or contain inherent flaws. One senior lawyer explained during an interview that, after a number of amendments, the current law states that a defendant will receive a maximum of three chances to respond to a summons. However, the law does not clarify what will happen after the three opportunities are over. It is unclear whether the case will then become an expert judgement or an unreported right. In sum, the cumulative legacy of the past creates difficulties for the general public to effectively comprehend, access, and use the judicial system.

III POOR UPDATING AND PRESERVATION OF LAND RECORDS. Land management in Bangladesh is done by several government agencies, among which coordination is almost non-existent.[17] Mismatches in historical government records and personal records are a major source of institutional inefficiency as these create inconsistency regarding the identity of the landowner and the size of the landholding at stake. In the case of a land ownership transfer, the sub-registrar office registers the new deed in the book of records (*balam bohi*). In Anwara, there are two separate index books for accessing these *balams*. They are ordered according to the names and the *daag* or plot number. However, as these records are handwritten and manually preserved, they are prone to damages and accidents. Furthermore, the sub-registrar offices do not have access to the *khatian* or Record of Rights (RoR), which is managed by the AC Land office. It is therefore quite difficult for a sub-registrar to verify the information regarding the ownership, and this again contributes to creating further conflicts and backlogs. In addition, when it comes to the transfer of ancestral property, most contracts are informal in nature, which creates fertile terrain for conflicts.

IV A SHORTAGE OF QUALIFIED PERSONNEL AND MISALLOCATION OF ROLES. There is lack of professional and well-trained civil lawyers in Bangladesh. A land litigation process requires a substantial amount of knowledge and expertise as the relevant documents contain sophisticated and complicated information. Nonetheless, the key informant interviews and focus group discussions reveal that most of the time lawyers are not adequately trained to successfully manage land litigation. In addition, the newly recruited judges and workforce in the judiciary may also not be well equipped to deal with complicated cases. As a result, hearings become lengthy, and this ultimately adds to the overall backlog. Moreover, a lack of resources and a lack of proper infrastructure are another major cause behind the huge case backlog in Bangladesh. Finally, during the fieldwork, one of the judges mentioned that people in the different administrative tiers often make wilful mistakes (e.g. misreporting and fraudulent behaviour by local people or rent seekers) and one of the main causes of land disputes in Chattogram is mistakes made during the Bangladesh Survey.[18] This judge also suggested that government officials are not doing their part, thus forcing people to file cases to obtain a correction of the mistakes made in the survey. Consequently, the judges now have to bear the extra workload involved in correcting petty mistakes.

V UNEQUAL ACCESS TO JUSTICE. In recent years, the Government of Bangladesh has been acquiring land for the implementation of a number of large-scale or mega infrastructural projects. In many instances, poor and illiterate people have fallen victim to land dispossession in such cases, due to a lack of proper knowledge regarding their legal rights. On top of this,

---

[17] A detailed analysis is presented in Chapter 8.
[18] The Bangladesh Survey is the most recent land survey to update the information of the RoR. The survey began in 1970 and is still ongoing.

there is also a lack of adequate state-supported legal services for ordinary citizens. One of the respondents from Anwara described how about two years ago, the Government acquired a large amount of land in order to build the Karnaphuli Tunnel. As a result, around 300–400 households may have been evicted from their ancestral land. A good number of these evicted families have filed a case against the Government. However, according to the law of the acquisition of land, if a person files a case against the decision of a government acquisition, he/she cannot receive any compensation until the litigation is over. In the absence of adequate state-supported legal aid facilities, local brokers easily mislead illiterate and helpless people to file such cases and repeatedly seek to obtain various rents from both the victims and lawyers. This is due to the fact that landowners, or the victims in general, lack the proper information, and lawyers and brokers are usually more informed. As a result, lawyers and brokers exploit the lack of knowledge of the owners or victims.

VI DELAYED PROCEDURE. According to one of the senior lawyers of the Chattogram District Bar, there are often undue delays in the issuing of notices. Nevertheless, when the date of the hearing finally arrives, it is quite common for either the plaintiff or the defendant not to be present in the court room. This unnecessarily prolongs the case time. The judge has to set another date for the hearing, and this occurs repeatedly. In this scenario, a judge can declare a one-sided verdict and stop the process. However, some respondents believe that in recent years, as judges usually want a full hearing in the presence of all parties to a case, and as these hearings are often piecemeal in nature, this again is causing a backlog and delays. A number of respondents mentioned the prevalence of numerous such dilatory tactics in the courts.

VII INFLUENCE PEDDLING, FRAUD, AND CORRUPTION. When asked about the main reason for the case backlog and delays in the process of land litigation, each of the key actors in the overall land administration and litigation process claimed that they are doing their part and that the other parties involved are to be blamed for the existing problems. During interviews, the local government authorities largely blamed the judges and lawyers, while one of the local judges blamed the local government authorities and lawyers. The latter mentioned that the executive influences the judiciary in a number of ways. Similarly, during the interviews, the lawyers mainly blamed the judges and also the local government officials. Behind this game of responsibility shifting, there is a complex dynamic of power and influence that affects the overall scenario of land dispossession litigation in Bangladesh.

Corruption and rent sharing is one of the propelling forces behind the overall institutional inefficiency of litigation system of Bangladesh in respect of land dispossession. Sometimes people are forcefully evicted or compelled to sell their land at an unfair price to large companies due to widespread corruption (i.e. bribery, extortion, cronyism, nepotism, patronage, etc.). During the fieldwork, one of the respondents in Anwara explained that large companies first buy small amounts of land in a scattered fashion and then they start pushing the surrounding land owners to sell their lands to them. In most cases, these big companies have established a good understanding with the local government officials and the law enforcement agency. For this reason, the local land owners are often compelled to sell their land off to them at an unfair price, and sometimes are even forcefully evicted. Local small landholders are not strong enough to go up against these big companies. They often do not report malpractices or seek any redress, out of fear.

Moreover, local government officials sometimes exercise their authority to seek undue rent. In one of the case studies,[19] Mr X, a resident of Anwara, explained that a pond that is part of his ancestral property was mistakenly recorded as *khas* land or government-owned land during the time of the Pakistan Survey.[20] Although his father had ownership of this pond according to the Cadastral Survey (CS),[21] he had to file a case and go through the costly litigation process to recover his claim, which took almost three years. Finally, the verdict was in his favour and he went to land office and applied for mutation. However, the upazila office disagreed to act upon the verdict and gave away the lease to another company. Mr X went to the DC and requested him to solve the matter. The DC ordered the Thana *Nirbahi* Officer (TNO) and AC Land to look into the matter. Even after that move, the problem was not solved, and eventually, Mr X had to go to the High Court. Up until the time of interview, he could not obtain a hearing data.

In addition, Anwara upazila is one of the most unique areas in Bangladesh from the viewpoint of social and demographic features. According to the locals, around 72% of the inhabitants are followers of the Hindu religion, while all other upazilas surrounding Anwara are Muslim-dominated. As a result, there is constant tension between the Hindus and Muslims over the ownership of land. It was also observed that women in general face greater challenges in seeking justice or redress. However, no matter which religion one follows, it is usually the poor and underprivileged segment of the society which is the victim of the worst forms of involuntary land dispossession. In one of the case studies,[22] Mr Z mentioned that once his grandfather rented part of his ancestral land to a Muslim farmer for share cropping. Later, when his grandfather became old, that farmer forcefully took over

---

[19] Case study number 1, included in Annex 9.2.
[20] The Pakistan Survey or Settlement Attestation Survey was carried out under the State Acquisition and Tenancy Act of 1950. The RoR of this survey was mainly prepared based on the information provided by the *Zamindars* or landlords. It was held from 1956 until 1962.
[21] The CS of undivided Bengal was the first comprehensive record of land rights. It is still accepted by contemporary courts. The CS RoR was prepared under the Bengal Tenancy Act 1885. This is known as the SC. This survey started from Ramu of Cox's Bazar upazila in 1888 and ended in 1940.
[22] Case study number 3, included in Annex 9.2.

the land. Mr Z's family went to the local authorities but failed to obtain any redress. Mr Z claimed that this is because he belongs to a religious minority in his community. Eventually his family filed a case; the case has been pending in the court for almost 12 years.

In one of the case studies from Gazipur, Mr A reported that his cousin fraudulently sold his land without his consent. When Mr A went to the *shalish* for redress, his cousin's husband, who is a dominant political leader, threatened him and influenced the *shalish* through bribery. There were even instances of intimidation and vandalism. The local police even arrested Mr A instead of the perpetrators. He was in jail for about two months. After getting bail, he filed a case. There was a verdict five years ago which according to Mr A was distorted, and he did not appeal due to his poor economic condition.

VIII THE PROBLEM OF ILLEGAL OCCUPANCY. It is often the case that absentee owners or migrants face special problems regarding their land or property. The absence of the owner creates room for illegal occupancy by others. Moreover, if the owner is absent during land surveys, and if he does not claim possession, other people can provide incorrect information to the surveyor and change the ownership in the government land records. In one of the case studies,[23] Mr D from Gazipur mentioned that his father's uncle had claimed false ownership of his property during his absence as a migrant worker. Mr D came back from abroad and filed a case, which has been pending for around two years now. Most of the time, the defendant, who is a local political leader, has not been present at the hearing. According to Mr D, money plays a vital role throughout the litigation process. From lawyer to *muhuri*, everyone demands money every time there is a hearing date. This scenario was repeated in a number of other case studies. Mr C from Gazipur was also a migrant worker, and in his case,[24] it was his uncle who deprived him of the proper share of his ancestral land. His case has been pending in the courts since 2010. According to Mr C, frequent transfers of judges, excessive bureaucracy in the court room, and political influence hinder a fast disposition of the cases.

Similarly, during the absence of Mr Y, a migrant worker from Anwara, a group of people claimed false possession of his property on the occasion of the Bangladesh Survey.[25] When he learned about this issue, he filed a case at the District Court and the court ordered the correcting of the mistake in the Bangladesh Survey. The opposite party in his case appealed against the verdict at the High Court. According to him, there might be some kind of collusion between the lawyers of both parties as none of them wants to end the case soon. He believes that the *peshkar*, lawyer, and *muhuri* are all informally connected and have conspired to lengthen the duration of the case.

---

[23] Case study number 7, included in Annex 9.2.
[24] Case study number 6, included in Annex 9.2.
[25] Case study number 2, included in Annex 9.2.

3 What Do We Learn from the Qualitative Appraisal?

The above-mentioned institutional inefficiencies with respect to land dispossession litigation are caused by an increasing number of errors and petty issues that are repeated on a regular basis. While many of these petty issues can be resolved through effective collaboration between the actors, in reality, the land administrative bodies, judiciary, and law enforcement agencies tend to delay in resolving the issues, and even reproduce similar scenarios in some instances. This is because these issues and problems regarding land dispossession litigation generate a comparatively small amount of rent. However, this rent increases significantly when it is generated multiple times and over a long period. This creates an incentive for the major actors to reproduce the overall scenario of institutional inefficiency. For this reason, the actors may sometimes have a deliberate or spontaneous understanding among themselves to act together. The higher the number of interactions between different parties the higher the transaction costs, and thus, the accumulation of rent keeps growing. Thus, the major motivation behind keeping this inefficient system alive is the reality of huge rent generation and rent sharing across the major actors, which is the result of an auto-reproducible, strong but lower level of equilibrium. This strong equilibrium persists because none of the actors have the incentive to break it.

In this overall process, there may be rent sharing only among the actors within the judiciary, rent sharing among the actors in the judiciary and different external actors, and also rent sharing only among the external actors themselves. In the specific case of involuntary land dispossession, there can be delays in several steps of the overall litigation process. Although lawyers or defendants may sometimes attempt to create undue delay, the judges can play a major role in speeding up the hearings, and ultimately reaching a verdict within the time specified in the law. However, the proper implementation of the verdict is also important and the land administration authority here has the major influence, because local-level political leaders and law enforcement agencies usually tend to cooperate with the DC office or subsequent local government offices. Thus, it is evident that the state institutions have the major role to play in either promoting justice or prolonging institutional inefficiency in the judiciary in respect of involuntary land dispossession litigation in Bangladesh.

Nevertheless, it is imperative to note that all of these actors act within a context-specific environment and, given the reality, each individual is bound by their own circumstances. As a result, these actors are influenced by the context-specific actions of others and consciously or subconsciously iterate their process of decision-making at each stage of the overall process. Thus, it is not only the issues within the judiciary that slow the performance of the judiciary but also external factors. Since institutional inefficiency and corruption in other areas affect the overall functioning of the judiciary, the judiciary alone cannot solve these issues. A generic focus on upgrading only the capacity of the judiciary will not be sufficient to solve these issues in Bangladesh.

IV CONCLUSION

Institutional norms in a society are often dictated by the overarching socio-political and historic factors. The analysis in this chapter shows that the institutional inefficiency in the judiciary of Bangladesh has been an outcome of a longstanding interplay between social, historical, political, and economic factors which have accumulated over the years. In the particular case of Bangladesh, this accumulation of institutional inefficiency has created a spontaneous and auto-reproducible strong but lower level of 'equilibrium', with an effective mechanism of rent sharing.

Based on the analysis of the data collected during fieldwork, it is evident that the poor, illiterate, and marginalised suffer the most because of a lack of rule of law, and institutional inefficiency. In fact, they suffer twice. First, they suffer because they are the victims of land dispossession, and later they suffer again in the courts during the litigation process. The judiciary as an institution can have a profound impact on the overall well-being of the citizens of a country. As the fundamental institution to protect the principles of fundamental rights and justice, the judiciary can play a critical role in ensuring the rule of law. Nevertheless, in Bangladesh, if institutional inefficiency continues to persist in the judiciary, it can further propel poverty and marginalisation. Thus, the long-term sustainable development of Bangladesh critically depends on a well-functioning judiciary. For this reason, it is imperative to overcome institutional inefficiencies in the judiciary and to promote the rule of law.

Ultimately, overcoming institutional inefficiency in the judiciary of Bangladesh will require a lot more than the usual generic reform agendas. While there is a need for capacity building within the judiciary, a thorough review of and proper amendments to the existing laws in order to update century-long practices, and the establishment of low-cost legal services for the poor and underprivileged, these measures alone will not be enough to meet the challenges and issues in contemporary Bangladesh. The Government must take steps to ensure the separation of powers between the executive and judicial branches, in order to uphold judicial independence. At the same time, it should be kept in mind that ensuring judicial independence alone also may not be a sufficient measure for ensuring the rule of law if institutional inefficiencies persist in other areas in Bangladesh. Thus, with respect to judicial functioning regarding involuntary land dispossession, external interventions are required to break the inefficiency of the existing system. As long as the 'equilibrium' continues to exist, judicial reform alone will not be sufficient. In the past, there have been some failed attempts to digitise the land and court records. Even if the digitisation of court and land records will not necessarily result in the absolute removal of all forms of institutional inefficiencies in the judiciary of Bangladesh, it will surely contribute to improving its performance.

ANNEX 9.1 GLOSSARY OF TERMS

AC Land	Assistant Commissioner (Land)
ADR	Alternative Dispute Resolution
Balam Bohi	Book of land registration records
Bangladesh Survey	The Bangladesh Survey started in 1970 and is still ongoing
Bighas	Unit of land measurement (0.333 acres)
CS or Kistwar	The Cadastral Survey of undivided Bengal was the first comprehensive record of land rights in Bangladesh. It is still accepted by contemporary courts. The CS Record of Rights (RoR) was prepared under the Bengal Tenancy Act 1885. This is known as the CS. The survey started from Ramu of Cox's Bazar upazila in 1888 and ended in 1940
Char	Alluvial land or land thrown up from rivers
Daag	Plot number
DC	Deputy Commissioner
Kanungo	Union Land Assistant Officer
Khas land	Public property or government-owned land, where nobody has property rights.
Khatian	Cadastre or RoR containing the area and character of land (by plot or by owner)
Mastaan	Local goons
Muhuri	Assistant to a lawyer
Namzari	Mutation or actions of Tehsildars and Assistance Commissioners (ACs) (Land) to update records to reflect a change in ownership and physical alterations
Nazir	The chief of staff of the Nezarat
Nezarat	A central administrative office of a court dealing with a service of summons, etc.
Nirbahi	Executive
OECD	Organisation for Economic Co-operation and Development
Peshkar	Bench clerk/bench assistant of a court
Revisional Survey	The Revisional Survey took place 50 years after the CS survey
RoR	Record of Rights (Khatian)
Settlement Attestation Survey or Pakistan Survey	The Settlement Attestation or Pakistan Survey of 1956–1962
Shalish	Local informal adjudication
Sherestadar	An administrative officer assigned to each judge who sits in a separate room called the Sheresta and can receive a plaint/suit on behalf of the court
Tehsil	Lowest union-level revenue unit comprising several Mouza
Tehsildar	Local revenue collector
TNO	Thana Nirbahi Officer
UNDP	United Nations Development Programme
WEF	World Economic Forum
WJP	World Justice Project

ANNEX 9.2 SELECTED CASE STUDIES

Case Study 1: Mr X lives in Raipur, Anwara. He is 76 years old. During the Pakistan Survey, part of his ancestral land, a pond, was mistakenly recorded as *khas* land or government property. Mr X filed a case to reclaim his possession; the case lasted for almost three years. Finally, in 1993, the verdict was in his favour. Mr X then went to the land office and applied for mutation. However, the upazila office refused to act on the verdict. Although Mr X showed them the verdict and requested them to solve the matter, they sanctioned the lease of the pond to another company. Mr X went to the DC and requested him to solve the matter. The DC ordered the TNO and AC Land to look into the matter. Even after that the problem was not solved and Mr X went to the High Court. Up to now he has been unable to obtain a hearing date. Mr X said that this has cost him around BDT 300,000, and he has to visit the court on a regular basis.

Case Study 2: Mr Y lives in Anwara. He is 47 years old. He used to live abroad as a migrant worker. A group of people claimed ownership over his homestead during the Bangladesh Survey. After learning of this, Mr Y filed a case at Patiya Court. However, according to him, the court did not check his documents thoroughly and dismissed the case. He then appealed to the District Court and received a verdict in his favour. The court gave an order regarding correcting the mistake in the Bangladesh Survey. After he completed the mutation, the opposite party in this case appealed against the verdict at the High Court. Nevertheless, once again, the verdict was in favour of Mr Y. Although Mr Y has the proper documents of ownership (land deeds, records from the Revisional Survey), the defendants are unwilling to accept the verdict. His case has been running since 2007 and until the time of the interview, Mr Y had spent around BDT 400,000 to pursue his cases. He said he managed these expenses by selling almost half of his property. The per day rate for a Supreme Court lawyer is BDT 100,000–150,000, which he feels is quite high. Mr Y believes that there is some kind of connection between both of the parties' lawyers. Because of this informal contact, none of them wants to end the case soon: the *peshkar*, lawyer, and *muhuri* all have this informal connection, which is the main reason behind the long suit. The political power of the defendant's lawyer is one of the major problems in his particular case.

Case Study 3: Mr Z lives in Banikpara, Anwara. He is 40 years old. His grandfather rented their ancestral land to a Muslim farmer for share cropping. When his grandfather became old, the farmer came to Mr Z's father and told him that Mr Z's grandfather owed him some amount of money. The farmer tried to force the family to sign a transfer of ownership of the land. Mr Z's father then went to the District Court and filed a case. The court gave a verdict in favour of him. However, the plaintiff then went to the High Court and then to the Supreme Court and appealed against that verdict. As Mr Z's father was very poor at that time, they could not go to the Supreme Court. As a result, the case went on for about 12 years. The current market price of the land is about BDT 600,000–700,000. Mr Z said that they have gone to the local chairman but nothing had happened. There were even incidents involving physical assault. Currently, the land is in the possession of the plaintiff party. Mr Z believes that they are suffering more because they are a religious minority in their community.

Case Study 4: Mr A is a farmer. He lives in Gazipur with his wife and four daughters. The problem started when his paternal cousin sold his land without his consent. The land includes his homestead, and its monetary value is about BDT 2,000,000. Mr A went to the *shalish* to solve the matter. However, according to him, the defendant influenced the *shalish* through a bribe. After being denied justice from the *shalish*, he was very disappointed and decided to file a case against his cousin. Nevertheless, before he could do so, he was threatened by his cousin's husband, who is a dominant political leader in Gazipur. There were even instances of vandalism and although he was the victim, the local police arrested Mr A. He was in jail for about two months. After getting bail, he went to the court and filed a case. The case has been ongoing since then. There was a verdict five years ago which according to Mr A was distorted. As a result, he appealed against it. Mr. A said that from the very beginning, the opponent party influenced the case with money and power. From the local police to the court, he did not get justice anywhere. The defendant party did not only seize Mr A's homestead: they are not even allowing him to utilise his other lands. He tried to build a house adjacent to the disputed land. After working for a few months, his brother-in-law used his political power again and demolished his hut. He is now living in a one-room house with five other members of his family. Mr A and his family have been suffering for a decade due to corruption, a lack of justice, and the effects of political influence.

Case Study 5: Mr B is the second among the six sons and two daughters of his father. He has one uncle who has a son and two daughters. They live in the village of Vanua in Gazipur Sadar. His father and uncle jointly bought 132 decimals (4 bigha) of land in 1978 from their neighbour, Mr E, who died in 2001. Mr E has five sons and a daughter. When the father and uncle of Mr B bought the land, they completed the registration and collected all the deeds associated with the land. After that they occupied the land and started to cultivate it. From that time onwards, the land has been under their possession and they provide the due taxes to the government associated with the land. However, in September 2016, the sons of Mr E filed a case in the court claiming that his father did not sell the land. From the case files, the family of Mr B came to know that before selling the land Mr E registered a portion of the land (13/14 decimals) in his son's name. Thus, his sons filed a case claiming ownership of all of the 132 decimals of land and stated that the registration that Mr B's family holds is not valid. Before filing the case, they did not inform Mr B's family or any local representative. The family of Mr B had no choice but to hire a lawyer and the litigation is still ongoing. In August 2018, due to the request of Mr B's family, the upazila AC Land investigated the land.

When the AC Land came to investigate, the plaintiffs were absent because they thought that he was influenced by the defendants. Mr B thinks that the report of the AC Land will have a great influence in the verdict and hopes that the verdict will come in his favour as he has legal documents. The land associated with the case is agricultural land and the family of Mr B cultivate paddy in the land. Every year they get approximately BDT 240,000 revenue from the land. The cost of producing paddy is approximately BDT 130,000, which implies an approximate profit of BDT 110,000 per year. The current value of the land is approximately BDT 20,000,000 at the current market price. Moreover, as the land is situated in a good location (adjacent to the road), the value of the land is increasing day by day.

Case Study 6: Mr C lives in Bhanua, Gazipur. He is 47 years old and studied until Secondary School Certificate level. His father had four brothers and one step-brother and Mr C has three brothers and five sisters. There are five members in his household, including: his mother, his wife, and his two daughters. Mr C used to live in Saudi Arabia and worked as a day labourer. He came back to Bangladesh in 2010. When his father was young, his uncle convinced him to buy some land from him, around the year 1970. His father bought the land and obtained the deed; however, he did not know how to properly calculate the amount of land that he deserved. During that time, his uncle misinterpreted the total amount of land that he deserved and deprived him of the proper share of the land. However, during 1975, this same uncle demanded that Mr C's father owed him some amount of land, and thus, the conflict between these two parties began. According to Mr C, when the two parties to the local *shalish*, they found out that Mr C's uncle actually owed them around 2 *bighas* of land. Mr C filed a case in the District Court in 2012 and since then the case has been ongoing. Every time he visits the court, he has to pay the lawyer, *peshkar*, and *muhuri*. The fee of the lawyer is around BDT 2,000 and other costs vary from BDT 500 to BDT 1,000. The litigation process has cost him around BDT 80,000 till now. The present value of the land is about BDT 11,000,000. According to Mr C, frequent transfers of judges hinder the path to obtaining a fair verdict. Besides, an insufficient number of judges and excessive bureaucracy prolongs the litigation. He also believes that the local police and *shalish* are heavily influenced by a local political leader who is a patron of the defendant.

Case Study 7: Mr D lives in Vanua, Gazipur. He is 65 years old. He has two sons and a daughter. None of his children received a formal education. He went to Iraq in 1982 and worked there as a day labourer. His father was a farmer, and his grandfather had 24 acres of land. His father's uncle claimed false ownership over his father's property. When he came back from Iraq, he went to the *shalish* to solve the problem. The local chairman and member tried to solve the case. However, the opposing party did not accept the verdict and did not agree to give Mr D his land back. As a result, he went to the District Court and filed a case against them. After filing the case, the opposing party sent the police to threaten Mr D. For the past two years, he had to go to the court every now and then and most of the time the opposing party, who is a local political leader, is not present for the hearing. According to Mr D, money plays a vital role in the court process. The case has already cost him around BDT 200,000, over the last two years. From the lawyer to the *muhuri*, everyone demands money each time there is a date for a hearing.

Discussion: Political Economy Analysis of the Role of the Judiciary in Land Dispossession Litigation in Bangladesh

Jean-Philippe Platteau

There is a general consensus that the judiciary plays a key role in relation to social, political, and economic development. In particular, an effective judicial system is expected to prevent government abuse, protect property rights, and guarantee the proper enforcement of contracts. These functions should not only be performed in an impartial, independent, and consistent manner but also expeditiously enough to avoid creating costly uncertainties for claimants and defendants alike. How these objectives can be best achieved and what are the social costs of ill-performance are therefore critical development issues. Answering these questions involves the thorny question of whether and to what extent a well-functioning judiciary is a precondition of economic growth and development. To put it in another way, is it not the case that the judiciary is an institution that evolves gradually and whose effectiveness improves in the course of development? Finally, there is the important concern that arises from the presence of informal judicial authorities in most developing countries. This raises the question as to how to allocate judicial functions between the informal and the formal spheres, and how this allocation should evolve as development proceeds.

This chapter provides answers to some of the aforementioned questions and is a welcome addition to a scarce literature. It is comprised of two parts. In the first part, the authors examine the effectiveness of the formal sector of the judiciary in Bangladesh, and they use three different criteria to guide their diagnosis: the fairness of this sector, its expeditiousness, and its independence from the executive. As for the second part, it is devoted to a case study of land litigation in the same sector. Let us now look in turn at these different sections of this chapter. To begin with, the authors' assessment of *judicial fairness* is based on three indicators extracted from the Rule of Law Index of the World Justice Project (2019). All of these indicators are subjective as they reflect the perceptions and opinions of the sampled individuals. While the first two measure the extent of inequality in access to the courts and in the treatment of cases, respectively, the third one tries to capture the degree of corruption and bribery of the judges. Essentially, they converge to show that Bangladesh does not fare very well along the three dimensions considered. Where it performs especially poorly (with a rank of 115 among 126 countries) is in regard to the second indicator (measuring the degree of discrimination in case treatment), for which Bangladesh nevertheless does slightly better than its two big South Asian neighbours, India (ranked 117) and Pakistan (ranked 118).

To assess *the expeditiousness of the judicial procedures*, the authors look at an objective measure, the backlog of pending cases. The picture that emerges here is not encouraging, as shown by the following statistics. The proportion of civil court cases resolved during the year 2018 represented less than 80% (77.3%) of the total number of cases received and filed during that year. This implies that the backlog of pending cases increased during that year. This is clearly not a new or transient phenomenon since at the end of the year 2018, about 26.5% of the total backlog of civil cases consisted of cases that had been pending for more than five years. The rise in the backlog of pending cases is confirmed if attention is paid to the total number of civil and criminal cases: apart from a short pause in 2008–2010, this statistic has increased exponentially since the early 2000s. Among the chief reasons behind this worrying situation, the authors mention the shortage of judges but also the ineffectiveness of the judicial procedures, which continue to be based on manual paperwork and even require the judges to write out by hand the statements of witnesses. Finally, it is noteworthy that case backlogs are especially large in the three administrative divisions that are economically the most prosperous.

In contrast to the above two dimensions of judicial dysfunction, no systematic data are proposed by the authors to assess the *lack of independence of the judiciary from the executive*. The mode of appointment of the judges, which is critical for their independence, has apparently improved since this prerogative was taken away from the Public Service Commission and actual implementation of the new mode seems to have occurred in 2007. Yet there is lingering doubt about the extent to which in actual practice the judges are appointed based on their competence and experience, rather than due to their political loyalty. In addition, the Supreme Court remains under the control of the Government since its judges are nominated by the Ministry of Law, Justice and Parliamentary Affairs, thus making them vulnerable to political manoeuvring. In a recent study on Pakistan, Mehmood and Seror (2019) argue that meddling by the executive in judicial matters does not mean that all types of judgements are biased. Decisions most liable to be influenced by such interference concern cases where resources valuable to politicians are directly or indirectly at stake (think of expropriation of private property by government agencies, for example). They thus show that the rise of religious landowning elites in Bangladesh, taken as a proxy of democratic regression, has increased the incidence of court rulings in favour of the Government for cases involving land disputes with the Government, and for cases involving violation of human rights. By contrast, no effect is detected for ordinary criminal cases, such as thefts. Moreover, democratic regression has reduced the quality of judicial decisions as measured by case delay (the difference between the year of the case decision and the filing year) and by merit, as proxied by a dummy indicating whether the decision was based on evidence rather than technical or procedural grounds.

Unfortunately, Mehmood and Seror (2019) do not have the data required to explore the influence of politicians on judicial decisions for civil cases. In a logic of patronage, one would expect civil judgements to be biased towards the clients of local politicians. Thus, Lyon (2019) argues that one important reason why a Pakistani landlord may decide to engage in politics is to get a serious land conflict settled in his favour with the help of powerful politicians at the district level.

In the second part of this chapter, the authors address the issue of land litigation and the possible dysfunction of the competent courts. To this end, they use case study material rather than systematic but hard-to-obtain data. It bears emphasis that this material contains few instances of land expropriation or contested appropriation by the Government. Instead, most cases relate to conflicts between private parties.

That land conflicts are pervasive in Bangladesh is the result of two major characteristics of the country: strong population pressure on land resources and huge migration outflows. These two factors tend to go hand in hand: in the absence of significant land-saving innovations in agriculture, population pressure causes labour productivity and income to be low, thereby inducing members of farming families to seek better employment opportunities outside of the village of origin. In the case of Bangladesh, migration does not only take the form of temporary rural–urban migration inside the country but also of permanent migration to foreign countries (e.g. India, the Gulf countries). When migration is permanent, a landholder is absent for long spells of time, and this creates opportunities for local land-hungry relatives or neighbours to occupy his/her land and lay claim to it. Evidence provided in this chapter points to the importance of land disputes of this type. Inheritance supplies another frequent occasion for conflicts in contexts of acute land scarcity.

The above two types of land conflicts are quite common in countries exhibiting small land–labour ratios. Conflicts around land bequests are inherently difficult to resolve because they are very sensitive and cannot be easily governed by indisputable allocation rules, especially when the land available is short (see André and Platteau, 1998 for an account of land conflicts in pre-genocide Rwanda). But conflicts over land ownership, including fraudulent sales without the owner's consent, are more amenable to settlement if land tenure rights have been well demarcated and certified. The question therefore arises as to why in Bangladesh many of these conflicts arise and frequently end up in formal courts. This chapter provides at least a partial answer to that question by highlighting serious shortcomings not only in the judiciary but also in the land registration system of the country. A critical flaw of the latter thus appears to consist of inadequate surveying and recording of land rights, as well as poor updating of land records. Ambiguous and even contradictory land rights are the unfortunate outcome of this situation, which is also observed in neighbouring India. At the root of it are weak coordination between different public agencies or departments, inappropriate methods of registration, a shortage of skilled personnel, and a lack of financial resources.

From the case study material used in this chapter, yet another reason emerges to explain judicial dysfunction in Bangladesh, namely the corruptibility of the judges and their susceptibility to pressures exerted by powerful claimants or defendants acting through influential politicians. Such unlawful interference in the judicial system harms growth and development not only because it causes uncertainty and inequity but also because it causes delays in obtaining a final decision after all appeal possibilities have been exhausted.

Although the policy implications of the foregoing diagnosis seem rather obvious, they are not necessarily easy to implement. This is not only because hard choices must be made by the Government but also because changes in the country's political economy are required. Regarding the former aspect, the Government's budget priorities must be redefined with a view to earmarking more money for both the Department of Justice and the land administration. Urgent attention must also be paid to the need to streamline both administrations so as to avoid overlapping competencies and to modernise the methods used for recording, processing, and safeguarding data (digitalisation must play an important role here). It is especially important to reduce the backlog of pending cases in the courts, whether civilian or criminal.

The latter aspect (political economy aspect) is even more delicate since it touches on the way politics interacts, or interferes, with various spheres of social and economic life. At the highest level is the desire of the executive to exert control over the highest branches of the judiciary – the Supreme Court in particular. This control aims at keeping political rivals at bay and buttressing the ruling political regime. At lower levels, as numerous examples presented in this chapter testify, judicial dysfunction assumes the form of undue interventions in judicial decisions that favour people with money and strong political connections. Being essentially exploratory, this chapter does not provide enough details for the reader to identify how precisely the mechanism of interferences operates at the level of local and district courts. But if we can go by the experience of Pakistan (see Martin, 2016; Mohmand, 2019), a patronage system anchored at the village level prevails that enables landowners connected to a political machine to secure the recognition of their perceived rights, involving bribing or intimidating judges if needed. Clearly, these institutional realities are hard to change since their transformation would involve attacking vested interests and opening up the political system. A ray of hope may nevertheless come from Pakistan: there, an important reform consisting of the appointment of judges by peers rather than the executive seems to have produced significant effects in the form of more expeditious and less skewed decisions (Mehmood and Seror, 2019).

The question, raised at the start of this discussion, as to whether the effectiveness of the judiciary is mainly an endogenous outcome of development or a precondition for it must therefore receive a nuanced answer. Because a well-functioning judicial system is an important pillar of a modernising country, bold steps must be taken as early as possible to reduce its most blatant failures (think, for example, of budget increases and changes in the mode of appointing judges). This said, it must also be reckoned that some measure of dysfunction will persist until growth spillovers have reached a large number of people. Only then will people feel empowered enough to demand strong accountability of the judiciary and to publicly question the secretive patronage networks that work hard to keep judges under their control.

Finally, there is the question of the informal conflict-settlement mechanisms operating in all of the developing world, particularly in rural areas. This is a critical aspect of any diagnosis of a country's institutional system. Given that this chapter does not contain information about these mechanisms, we are unable to address the issue of the respective roles of the informal and formal sectors of the judiciary in Bangladesh. What we can say, however, with all the necessary caution, is that acute population pressure on land resources and huge outmigration on the scale observed in Bangladesh will generally tend to erode informal land tenure arrangements and dispute settlement mechanisms. As a result, state failures in the domain of land and justice administrations are bound to cause great harm to a country confronted with these conditions (Platteau, 1992, 2000).

PART III

AN INSTITUTIONAL DIAGNOSTIC
OF BANGLADESH

10

The Bangladesh Institutional Diagnostic

The Synthesis

François Bourguignon, Selim Raihan, and Umar Salam

I INTRODUCTION

The time has now come to put together what has been learned from the in-depth review of the economic and institutional aspects of Bangladesh's development in the first part of this volume and from the in-depth study of key thematic areas in the second part. This diagnostic exercise will be presented in two steps. First, in Section II.E, a summary will be offered of each previous chapter, with the idea of stressing their most important messages in terms of the specific economic development constraints and institutional aspects of development to which they point. Second, in Section III, the diagnostic project will be presented. It will consist of three parts. In a first stage, an attempt will be made to identify the development-related institutional features that are common to all, or some subset, of the areas covered by the chapters in this volume. This exercise will allow us to see how a small number of basic institutional factors recur in multiple contexts in Bangladesh, and together condition and shape the development of the country. In a second stage, a reflection will be provided on the proximate and deep causes behind these factors. In a third and final stage of the diagnostic, directions for reforms that would correct weaknesses and/ or enhance strengths will be explored. In this respect, part of the reflection will bear on how the implementation of these reforms may depend on deeper causes including the political economy context.

Four notes of caution are needed before proceeding with this final exercise.

The first note of caution relates to the somewhat exceptional character of Bangladesh, sometimes referred to as the 'Bangladesh paradox'. More than is the case for most low-income or recently graduated low-income countries, Bangladesh's development experience combines authentic successes, as testified by its rapid rate of economic growth over a little more than two decades, and major weaknesses, manifested most notably in key institutional areas. These weaknesses are sufficiently serious to threaten further development. Thus, in contrast with institutional diagnostics of less successful countries, the objective of the present exercise is not only to identify weaknesses that hinder further progress but also to understand how past successes relied upon specific institutional features that might either sustain or undermine future development. Among these features is the ability to circumvent ineffective formal institutions. The objective of the diagnostic is thus to highlight the causes of dysfunction, to uncover the inherent strength of the economic and social apparatus, and, possibly, to suggest ways they could be harnessed to correct dysfunctions and allow a sustainable and rapid pace of development.

The second note of caution relates to the intrinsic complexity of the relationship between institutions and development, and, more precisely, its circularity. The analysis conducted for the present institutional diagnostic focuses on one aspect of the relationship: the way institutional features affect development. Yet the opposite causality direction is equally important: development itself has an impact on the evolution of institutions. This aspect is especially important in the case of Bangladesh, where some of the deep factors plausibly influencing the nature of institutions and their capacity for reform today may precisely be related to the previous performance of the economy, notably in connection with ready-made garment (RMG) exports.

The third word of caution concerns the status of the reforms that may be considered as the natural outcome of an institutional diagnostic. Reforms that could improve the welfare of all actors in society would presumably have already been undertaken. Thus, the reforms that come out of a diagnostic exercise like the present one are unlikely to benefit all social groups. Hence an objection to the reforms suggested by the diagnostic will be that they are unlikely to attract a political consensus. Yet this does not make considering them any less important. On the one hand, identifying those social and political actors favouring a reform and those opposing it helps to clarify the political economy debate by better understanding the sources of resistance and, hopefully, the ways to surmount them. On the other hand, the distribution of political power within society may change in the future and reforms that are difficult today may become easier tomorrow. Therefore, a list of reforms resulting from the institutional diagnostic may usefully feed into the national public debate, even though their implementation may not be straightforward. We offer such a list in the annex to this chapter.

The last note of caution is about the COVID-19 crisis that struck the world and Bangladesh at the time the initial version of this volume was being finalised. There is no doubt that this crisis, above all its global economic consequences, has changed, and will continue to change the overall context of Bangladesh's development. When this original version of this institutional diagnostic was concluded, it was obviously too early to be more precise. In the light of the information available today, we now suggest that the institutional weaknesses identified in this diagnostic will most likely become more significant in the new economic environment Bangladesh will face in the coming years. In fact, we argue further that those same institutional weaknesses have also been and still are critical determinants of the country's limited ability to respond to the pandemic itself.

II IDENTIFYING INSTITUTIONAL CONSTRAINTS IN BANGLADESH'S DEVELOPMENT

As noted above, before presenting the institutional diagnostic, this chapter will provide a summary of the findings of previous chapters in the volume, in terms of the successes and failures of Bangladesh's development, and their institutional roots. This is done in Section II.E. However, before embarking on this task, and to make this chapter self-contained, it will be useful to first briefly recall some key features of the political history of Bangladesh,[1] as several allusions will be made to them in Section II.E.

A A Sketch of Bangladesh's Political History

The history of Bangladesh since the independence war with Pakistan in 1971 can be broken down into three eras, or three types of regime.

Although a democratic constitution, in the Westminster style, was adopted at the time of independence, the first 15 years of the People's Republic of Bangladesh were extremely turbulent. The assassination of the founding leader, Sheikh Mujibur Rahman, occurred within a few years and triggered a long succession of military regimes and coups. Out of this chaotic period came two main parties: on one side, the Awami League (AL), the party of Sheikh Mujib, which had played a leading role in pre-independence resistance against Pakistan; and, on the other side, the Bangladesh National Party (BNP), founded in 1978 by General Ziaur Rahman, then the president of Bangladesh. General Zia, as he was known, was assassinated in 1981 during a failed coup, and he was succeeded by General Ershad. The discontent of the population with respect to the military nature of the regime fed social unrest and eventually led to general elections being held in 1991, which were won by the BNP. A parliamentary constitution was then reinstated.

For the next two decades, the two main parties alternated in power, with the incumbent systematically losing to the opposition in the general elections that took place every fifth year. Throughout that period, the struggle between the two parties, and to some extent between their leaders, Khaleda Zia, the widow of General Zia, and Sheikh Hasina, the daughter of Sheikh Mujib, was intense. Democracy in that period was a kind of long winner-takes-all competition between the Awami League and the BNP, and virtually all means to destroy

---

[1] Key recent references on the political history of Bangladesh include Jahan (2018), Lewis (2011), Riaz (2016), and Hossain (2017). A more complete summary is provided in Chapter 1 of this volume.

the opposition and to stay in power were used by both sides. Elections were so contentious, the temptation of rigging them so strong, and street violence so high in those periods that a non-partisan caretaker government was regularly appointed to ensure fair elections and to handle current affairs in particularly turbulent circumstances.

At some points, even the institution of the caretaker government was unable to comply with this task. In 2006, the BNP government was suspected of weighing in on the appointment of the caretaker government that would have to handle the forthcoming general election. The military had to come in to support a caretaker government, which took two years to organise the election and, in some instances, took initiatives that went far beyond this assignment. The Awami League won the election that finally took place in 2008 and has been in power since then. This was the end of the period of political alternance, often rightly termed 'competitive democracy' on account of the harsh political competition prevailing in those years.

Once returned to power, the Awami League was able to progressively impose full political control over the country. The institution of the caretaker government was made unconstitutional, and the BNP opposition was gradually silenced (this was partly its own fault since its failed attempt to disrupt the 2013 election through general protests and strikes eventually pushed it to boycott the election). As a result, the BNP lost a lot of political leverage, whereas the Awami League gained a 'dominant party' position and was able to weaken its opponent further, notably by having BNP leaders tried for and convicted of corruption. Consequently, the Awami League won the 2018 election with 289 seats – including 30 seats won by allied parties – leaving only 11 seats for the opposition, and six for the BNP. At the present time, the Awami League is thus governing without any real formal opposition, whether external or internal (since power has always been extremely concentrated within the Awami League party, as it is within the BNP).

This is where Bangladesh presently stands in its long quest for full democracy. It is difficult at this moment to predict what the next step will be. On many occasions a vibrant civil society in Bangladesh has shown its determination that the country become a true democracy. It is likely that opposition forces will reappear, based on the old parties or new ones, if the present party proves unable to maintain the fast rates of development that have been observed practically since the early days of the regime of competitive democracy. In this sense, the 'dominant party' era is best seen as a particular stage in the general evolution of democracy in Bangladesh.

B Successes and Challenges of Bangladesh's Economic Development

Bangladesh has been able to maintain a rate of gross domestic product (GDP) per capita growth of between 4% and 7% over the last 20–25 years.

Moreover, it has succeeded in more than halving extreme poverty since the turn of the millennium. Two key drivers are behind a large part of these remarkable achievements: the exports of the RMG sector, which have grown at an average annual rate of 12% since the late 1990s, and the remittances from Bangladeshi workers abroad, which have grown in real terms at a similar pace. It was estimated in Chapter 2 (Annex 2.3) that these two factors are jointly responsible for two-thirds of the country's GDP growth. Increases in agricultural productivity account for most of the remaining growth performance.

The distinction between the two drivers of Bangladesh's growth is important. The surge in RMG exports must be seen as the result of deliberate efforts to develop an internationally competitive manufacturing sector in this line of products. Bangladesh thus fundamentally differs from most countries at a similar stage of development, which have relied on more passive development strategies based on the export of primary commodities and which have therefore been highly vulnerable to strong fluctuations in world prices and demand. It is true that remittances from migrants suffer from the same vulnerability in Bangladesh, yet they have only been a secondary engine of growth. Unlike RMG exports, they contribute to overall growth essentially by boosting aggregate demand and therefore the sectors oriented towards domestic demand.[2] However, that the stock of Bangladeshis working abroad has been continuously increasing over the last 10–15 years is not a positive sign with respect to the capacity of the economy to absorb its labour surplus.

Another favourable aspect of development is the relative autonomy of the country with respect to external financing. Bangladesh's dependence on foreign finance flows, most notably official development assistance, is much less than it was before the mid-1990s.[3] Because this reduced dependence is narrowly linked to the rising importance of foreign remittances, however, vulnerability to shocks in countries that host Bangladeshi migrant workers remains an issue, as illustrated by COVID-19.

Apart from the successful development of manufacturing exports, Bangladesh exhibits many of the characteristics and weaknesses of less dynamic, low-income or low middle-income countries. This is most notable when considering the size and low productivity of the informal economy, as well as the size and role of the public sector. Atrophied by an exceptionally low average tax rate, a restricted fiscal space hampers the delivery of public goods in desirable quantities and of desirable quality, and, in particular, slows down the accumulation of infrastructure and human capital that are required for sustainable development. In addition, the civil service is not working properly

---

[2] This economic diagnostic much resembles the one drawn 10 years ago by Mahmud *et al.* (2008), which suggests a continuity in Bangladesh development that is infrequent in developing countries at a similar stage of development.

[3] The importance of aid in the first two decades after independence was such that it led Hossain (2017) to title her recent book on the 'Bangladesh surprise' *The Aid Lab*.

and is highly corrupt, the business environment is poor, and the regulation of the economy, including taxation and the supervision of the banking sector, is dysfunctional.

Social development appears better, but from the public policy point of view, it also shows weaknesses. Whereas undeniable, and in some respects impressive, progress has been made in primary school enrolment, partly thanks to an early conditional cash transfer programme,[4] levels of learning achievement are unsatisfactory. Public healthcare expenditures are extremely small. In these social areas, the failures of the state have been partly compensated for by an extremely dynamic non-governmental organisation (NGO) sector that has gained global recognition. Yet achieving real social progress that covers the whole population depends on adequate public policies. In brief, there is a real discrepancy between Bangladesh's growth achievements through the RMG sector, on the one hand, and the situation of the rest of the economy, as well as social achievements, on the other.

These weaknesses might soon become of even greater consequence, as Bangladesh confronts major challenges in trying to maintain its development momentum in a global context very much affected by the economic consequences of the COVID-19 pandemic. As a matter of fact, the growth rate of RMG exports – as well as that of remittances – has slowed down over recent years, even before COVID-19. The same is true of agricultural productivity.[5] GDP growth rate in Bangladesh, though still positive, dropped by around 5 percentage points in the 2020 COVID-year. Also, total exports declined by around 17%. Several threats hover over RMG exports, including growing competition between low-wage countries, rising mechanisation that reduces the comparative advantages of developing countries, stricter regulations of labour conditions imposed by foreign clients, and the loss of least developed country (LDC) trade preferential status with advanced countries. It is thus far from certain that Bangladesh will be able to keep on increasing its global market share in RMG. Since there is additional uncertainty about – or at least significant variability of – the volume of foreign remittances, expanding exports through diversification, both within and (most importantly) outside the RMG sector, has become essential for sustaining the country's development momentum. Such a strategy requires adequate measures and a well-articulated industrial policy, which is presently missing. The need for diversification is recognised in several official planning documents, but the strategy for reaching that goal is not well designed or implemented. The reasons for this situation will be analysed later.

---

[4] The Primary Education Stipend programme, which replaced the Food For Education programme, was launched in 1993.
[5] Which raises some doubts about recent estimates of GDP growth rates. See https://bdnews24 .com/economy/2018/04/09/where-is-the-source-of-growth-wb-asks-casting-doubt-on-bangladesh-s-gdp-projection.

C Bangladesh's Institutional Performance in Global Rankings

As discussed above, Bangladesh experienced turbulent political times between independence and the early 2000s. Most indicators describing the institutional environment and the political and socio-economic conditions of the country show a strong overall improvement has taken place since then.[6] Even an indicator measuring the control of corruption has improved. Yet the broad picture is much less encouraging when we compare Bangladesh to other countries today, even when the comparison is restricted to developing countries.

According to most synthetic institutional indicators, Bangladesh is in the bottom 20% of global country rankings for all institutional dimensions, and even in the bottom 10% for some of them. Despite its growth performance, it is behind – on all dimensions – many developing countries with a comparable, or even lower, GDP per capita.

This disappointing performance is not uniform, though. If Bangladesh appears as particularly weak in areas like 'bureaucratic quality', 'rule of law', 'land issues', and, to a lesser extent, 'human rights', its relative performance is less disappointing in regard of the democratic functioning of the country and the business environment it offers to investors. It is interesting that these relative strengths relate to two key features of Bangladesh's development: the maintenance of political stability over the last 10 years or so, and the surge of manufacturing exports in the RMG sector since the turn of this century. This observation may raise some questions about the causality of the relationship between institutions and development. Indeed, relatively better achievement on the business environment are likely to have resulted from the success of the RMG sector, rather than having caused the latter.

These rankings must be viewed with some caution, though. On the one hand, Bangladesh does not appear to be fundamentally different from other countries when the ranking is made conditional on the level of development.[7] If it underperforms relative to other countries in most areas, this is often by a narrow margin. It even does better with respect to the business environment. On the other hand, global indicators are rough measures of governance and institutional quality and may miss important details that might change the overall judgement to which they lead. In any case, it is largely on the basis of these indicators that the idea of a 'Bangladesh paradox' was formed: Bangladesh appears as a country with impressive economic growth performance but weak institutional performance. It is precisely because there can be some doubt about the reliability of institutional indicators in global rankings that we need a more detailed, and probably more nuanced, view, based on the sort of institutional diagnostic that is undertaken here.

---

[6] Although, the performance on some of those indicators, such as Voice and Accountability or Political Stability, has deteriorated slightly following the widely criticised election in 2018, and the outbreak of COVID-19 in 2019.

[7] See, for instance, Asadullah *et al.* (2014) and Chapter 3.

D Bangladesh's Institutional Performance Based on the Views of National Decision Makers

To obtain an idea of how local decision makers assess their country's institutions, a Country Institutional Survey (CIS) was administered to a number of selected decision makers in various areas of activity: business, farming, politics, academia, the judiciary, the army, and civil society.[8] The survey was complemented by interviews with top decision makers and policymakers, so as to provide more detailed insights about Bangladesh's institutional functioning. Fortunately, key opinions on institutional strengths and weaknesses expressed in the survey and the views and recommendations of top stakeholders in open-ended discussions proved to be broadly consistent with each other.

In the first place, it should be stressed that the CIS resulted in a ranking of problematic institutional areas similar to the one derived from exploiting cross-country institutional indicator databases. In broad accordance with the picture emerging from the global indicators describing the democratic functioning of the country, the two areas found by the respondents to be the least unfavourable to Bangladesh's development are the business environment and the political system. This convergence between the views of insiders, that is local decision makers, and those of the international experts behind the cross-country indicators, is rather reassuring as it suggests that both approaches to detecting institutional strengths and weaknesses are credible.

The identification by survey respondents of problematic institutional areas did not prove to be particularly informative, because of rather small differences in their assessment across areas. Detailed evaluations of each area in the survey were much more informative. Respondents clearly put the 'civil service' and the 'treatment of land issues' at the top of the list of ill-functioning institutional areas, closely followed by the 'political and administrative management' by the executive.

Interesting results were obtained from questions related to specific sub-domains. The following weaknesses were especially stressed by our respondents:

- ubiquitous corruption (electoral, business, recruitment to the civil service);
- executive control over legal bodies, the media, the judiciary, and the banking sector;
- inadequate coverage of public services;
- the number and intensity of land conflicts; and
- gender discrimination.

Some institutional aspects were found by the respondents to be rather satisfactory, though not always without some contradiction with other judgements. Among them were the development of a middle class, a feeling of national pride, the quality of public policymaking, and the positive role of informal

---

[8] Similar versions of this CIS were carried out in Tanzania and Benin.

arrangements. The latter's importance was emphasised with special force, particularly in regard to dealings with the administration and the enforcement of contracts. In these two domains, informal channels and procedures were deemed to provide an effective alternative to deficient formal channels. This assessment fits well with the expressed distrust of central institutions, such as the judiciary, and the repeated denunciations of corruption.

Finally, the opinions expressed by key informants generally confirmed those of the CIS respondents. This is particularly evident in the fact that the former emphasised the low administrative capacity of the Bangladeshi state, corruption, and the ineffectiveness of the judiciary. But these informants also enrich our knowledge by pointing to sectors of activity where those weaknesses were considered by them to be most salient. Of special importance here is their emphasis on the weakness of industrial policy and the resulting lack of diversification away from the RMG sector, allegedly because of the disproportionate influence of the RMG's business elite. The weak regulation of the banking sector, as evidenced by the pervasive and growing incidence of non-performing loans (NPLs), and the lack of autonomy of the Central Bank are other severe institutional flaws that negatively affect efficiency in this key sector of the economy. Failures in the way land conflicts are handled by the state and its administration are also revealing of a missing sense of direction on their part, with negative consequences for land allocation from the double standpoint of efficiency and equity.

E Some Critical Areas

Chapters 4–9 consist of thematic studies that focus on specific areas that were found to be critical on the basis of Chapters 2 and 3. For reasons of space, these areas do not cover the whole range of issues that were pointed to by CIS respondents and key informants. They were chosen because they are of direct importance for development per se, or because they provide a focus on the working of specific institutions. These areas are as follows:

- the RMG sector, and the difficulty of diversifying manufacturing exports;
- the failure of the regulation of the banking sector, and the problem of NPLs
- the design and collection of taxes;
- primary education as a major component of public expenditures;
- the management of land issues, including the special economic zone (SEZ) policy; and
- the judiciary and the treatment of land litigation cases.

In Sections II.E.1–II.E.6 for each in-depth study, a brief summary is offered of what they reveal about the functioning of Bangladeshi institutions, the root causes of their inadequacy, or (in some cases) the way their weakness can be bypassed, and their development consequences.

1 The Success of the RMG Sector and the Failure to Diversify Exports

How was Bangladesh able to increase the volume of RMG exports from virtually nothing in the early 1980s to a total value of US$ 30.6 billion in 2017/18 – becoming, in the process, the second largest exporter of RMG in the world? What were the institutional arrangements – both formal and informal – which facilitated this remarkable transformation and which made the RMG sector such a powerful driver of economic growth, and, reciprocally, how has the growth of the RMG sector itself affected Bangladeshi institutions? And, perhaps most importantly of all, what does the future hold for the sector and the economy as a whole?

This concern about the future is fundamentally a question of sustainability. It reflects an awareness that the growth of the RMG sector was driven by a number of opportunities and advantages, each of which is under severe and increasing pressure. These include international trade agreements, Bangladesh's preferential LDC status, a political economy environment that, though clientelist, was nonetheless competitive, a suppressed labour regime, and simple, labour-intensive technology.

But, as emphasised in both the chapters by Selim Raihan and in the comments by Jaime de Melo, there are further concerns about the RMG industrialisation model itself, and in particular the (lack of) export diversification. Indeed, it is argued that the strength of the RMG sector not only reflects the weaknesses of other sectors but is, in fact, also a cause of those weaknesses. It also fundamentally calls into question the pathway of industrial development and structural transformation that Bangladesh has embarked upon. Is Bangladesh's lack of export diversification a symptom of a deeper malaise – a set of institutions which may have generated success in the past and yet may now be acting as powerful constraints on development in the future?

Three main economic outcomes of the surge of the RMG sector are highlighted in the chapter by Raihan. The first of these is the structure and performance of the sector itself, both in terms of the growth of the sector and the nature of its production (e.g. the changing composition of products from woven to knitwear) and the production process (e.g. the adoption of subcontracting, the current trends towards labour-saving automation, and the low-value and basic quality of much of the production). The second is the way in which the sector dominates Bangladesh's export basket, and how weak other sectors have been: it is striking how Bangladesh's export concentration is higher than that of other country groups, and significantly less diversified than developing manufacturing exporters, and, in fact, not more diversified than some low-income commodity exporters. And the third and final observable outcome is the quite extraordinary management of the labour regime in the RMG sector, in which long working hours, low wages, a lack of regular contracts, and systematically hazardous working conditions are commonplace – as dramatically illustrated by the Rana Plaza disaster.[9] Trade unions have been suppressed and union organisers intimidated: wage negotiations, such as those conducted through the Wage Board, do not have proper worker representation.

The institutional issues behind these economic and social consequences are complex. The RMG sector was able to benefit from the presence of certain institutions and to exploit the absence of others. The growth of the sector was, in the first instance, crucially dependent on the international trade regime in textiles and clothing, such as the Multi-Fibre Agreement (MFA) system of quotas. This not only created reserved market opportunities for Bangladesh and other countries but also provided incentives for international collaboration – with South Korean companies, for example. Over time, the sector became extremely competitive and was able to regularly increase its share of the global market. To achieve these results, it was able to obtain a series of favourable *ad hoc* measures from successive governments – these included export performance benefits, the bonded warehouse system,[10] subsidies of various kinds, tax exemptions, export credit guarantee schemes, and export-processing zones. In effect, the RMG sector was, for several decades, the primary focus of Bangladesh's *de facto* industrial policy, thus leading to a remarkably high degree of export concentration. From the outset, the RMG sector also crucially benefited from the absence of vigorous formal institutions that could defend industrial labour rights. This privileged status has continued during the COVID-19 episode, with RMG able to monopolise the benefits of the government's economic stimulus package, and to successfully lobby for the reopening of factories and suspension of lockdown measures so as to minimise the disruption to the industry.

The evidence suggests that the very same institutional features which enabled the growth of the RMG sector are missing in other sectors – that there is not the same organisational capacity for industry leaders to participate in collective bargaining with the state, while key policy instruments are biased in favour of RMG and against other sectors, such as leather: think of the bonded warehouse scheme, or of the exchange rate policy, which has not been used to help industrial diversification, or indeed the policy response to COVID-19, which did very little to help MSMEs, in particular. It may also be the case that rent opportunities comparable to the MFA environment in the development of the RMG sector are not available in other activities, in which case they might have to be provided through a consistent industrial policy. However, in a time when the dominant RMG sector is experiencing several weaknesses and facing serious challenges, its politically powerful business class may not agree with, and may even block, any change in the present informal policy framework.

---

[9] In April 2013, more than 1,000 workers died when the factory building collapsed.

[10] By which exporters are practically exempted from import duties on intermediate products. On the asymmetry between the RMG sector and other manufacturing exporters with respect to that facility, see Babi (2020).

Despite the fragility of the current situation, this diagnosis of Bangladesh's industrial development demonstrates many important points. First, the successes of the RMG sector show that Bangladesh has developed and retained significant organisational and firm capabilities, as well as an entrepreneurial class. However, it must now channel those capabilities into other sectors. Second, it shows that industrial policy within a 'deals environment'[11] can be highly effective at an initial stage of industrial development, but care must be taken not to consolidate existing patterns of rent-seeking within a single sector, but rather to support dynamism and innovation. Third, transparent and non-politicised formal institutional structures responsible for industrial policy are needed to achieve this. They were – and still are – missing in Bangladesh. And fourth, if economic development is possible within a mostly informal institutional environment, such a context is inadequate as regards establishing and maintaining a social contract by which all stakeholders, including workers, commit to well-defined development strategies and are guaranteed to receive their fair share of the benefits. Such a contract is necessary for the long-run social sustainability of development strategies and requires formal institutions rather than an informal set of deals, even if the latter have proven temporarily successful.

2 Governance Failures and the Political Economy of the Banking Sector

At intermediate stages of development, the banking sector is of crucial importance through the role it may play in collecting savings and efficiently allocating investment resources in the economy. Bangladesh is at a stage where the sector, which was initially completely state-owned, has been substantially privatised, and several new banks have recently been licensed. Yet some important banks or financial institutions remain in the hands of the state, leading to a kind of dual structure of the whole sector. If, overall, the sector has been, and still is, effective in supporting the development of the RMG sector, it also shows major weaknesses and exhibits serious failures of regulation, most notably apparent in recurrent excessive NPLs. Often caused by fraudulent behaviour rather than problems of profitability, NPLs exert adverse effects on the efficiency of the economy, reinforce the culture of corruption in the country, and contribute to rising inequality.

The chapter by Hassan, Bidisha, Mahmood, and Raihan provides an overview of the performance and challenges of the banking sector in Bangladesh by looking at its structure, several financial performance indicators (including the NPL ratio), the efficiency of private banks, and the development implications of weak institutions. This chapter also explores the political economy of the whole sector and examines types of governance failures.

---

[11] See the definition of this concept, borrowed from Pritchett *et al.* (2018) in Chapter 1.

The comments by Thorsten Beck emphasise key reforms needed in the governance of the sector, including the full *de jure* and *de facto* autonomy of the central bank – the Bangladesh Bank – and the divestiture of the Government from nationalised commercial banks. He observes that policy suggestions were made in the mid-2000s in that direction, but as confirmed in the chapter by Hassan *et al.*, no progress was made, and the situation even became worse.

If the banking sector apparently provides a volume of credit to the economy that seems comparable in relation to GDP to levels observed in comparator countries, its management performance is mediocre. In 2017, Bangladesh ranked 147th out of 179 countries according to the international Z-score, an indicator of the probability of default of the whole banking system. Its Z-score was also the lowest among the South Asian countries. This bad performance is related to the low quality of the sector's lending operations. Through regulatory and policy capture, political patronage often leads to unproductive loans, or simply loans that bankers know will never be repaid. Also, cases of embezzlement through legal insider lending – i.e. to the bank's owners or their family – have been reported. NPLs, and the frequent need for monetary injection in state-owned banks or bailouts of private banks, are the manifestation of these governance failures of the whole sector, foreign commercial banks aside.

It may seem surprising that, despite these major weaknesses, the banking sector was able to financially support the major driver of the economy, the RMG sector, in the first place. RMG firms, as well as certain big import-substituting industries – for example cement, steel, and textiles – received a significant proportion of the loans disbursed. These loans, most often granted with extremely favourable conditions, are another example of the sort of 'deals' made between powerful entrepreneurs and the banking sector, possibly under the pressure of the political elite. Meanwhile, other export-oriented non-RMG sectors, such as the leather and the agri-processing sectors, faced difficulties in securing bank loans, or obtained them but with much harsher conditions attached.

NPLs have been a major concern in the banking sector ever since independence. They represented 25% of outstanding loans in the early 1990s, but that rate exploded at the end of that decade, reaching 41% in 2000. Effective reform measures were then taken, in part under the pressure of the International Monetary Fund, but also as part of an anti-corruption policy led at that time by the BNP government. The ratio was successfully brought down to around 6% by the late 2000s, but it increased again and has practically doubled since then. Initially, NPLs tended to be concentrated in state-owned banks, but in recent years, they have been on the rise in private commercial banks too. Besides affecting banks' prudential ratios, they contribute to higher interest rates, and reduce private investment, outside the sectors that benefit from favourable deals. Overall, this situation undermines the prospects for export diversification, as well as future economic growth, in a non-negligible way.[12]

A major institutional weaknesses of the banking sector in Bangladesh is the lack of autonomy of the central bank in regulating the sector, because of the clear subordinate position of the governor with respect to the Government and, through political links, private bankers. As a result, regulation is essentially *ad hoc*, implying that most often required action is not taken against malpractices committed by commercial banks. Dual authority in the banking system, by which state-owned banks are governed by the Banking Division of the Ministry of Finance and private banks are under the purview of the central bank, is another factor leading to ineffectiveness in the regulation of the whole system. There are also issues with the rising political influence of the BAB, the Bangladesh Association of (private sector) banks. The recent amendment of the Banking Company Act, which provides for the removal of several constraints governing the boards of private banks, reflects this influence.

With the emergence of COVID-19, a further consequence of the institutional weaknesses in the banking sector has become apparent – namely, the significant problems Bangladesh has experienced in disbursing funds, both to support firms and as social protection for vulnerable households. These issues – and the inequalities they expose, in the sense that smaller firms and the poor are disproportionately affected – continue to skew the recovery.

3 Taxation and the Difficulty of Tax Reforms

At 8.6%, Bangladesh is among the countries with the lowest overall average tax rate – that is the ratio of tax revenue to GDP. It follows that its fiscal space, that is the capacity to spend on public goods and correct rising income inequality, is extremely limited. The low average tax rate results from both low nominal tax rates and a low rate of tax collection, itself due to pervasive tax evasion (often with the paid support of tax collection personnel) or to tax exemptions generously granted by the Government to its supporters. In addition, albeit in a limited way, taxation distorts economic incentives, either directly through non-uniform tax rates that favour some sectors or firms and penalise others, or indirectly through exemptions and evasion.

The chapter by Sadiq Ahmed on taxation identifies and evaluates the institutional causes of these failures of the tax system. It also explores the reasons behind the difficulties that have surrounded previous attempts at tax reforms and the underlying political economy factors. It finally lists the most attractive reforms in terms of increasing tax revenues, the effectiveness of tax collection, and the redistributive impact of the tax system.

---

[12] It is worth stressing that, even a stable moderate NPL ratio may imply a sizeable positive annual flow of new NPLs, depending on the recovery flow of old NPLs and the writing-off of some others. In Bangladesh, a stable 10% NPL ratio and a recovery plus write-off rate as low as 20% implies a new NPL flow equivalent to around 1% of GDP being diverted from investible funds.

Tax revenue represents a little less than 90% of the Government's revenue in Bangladesh. Over the past decade, tax revenue in proportion to GDP has slightly declined and, as just mentioned, has remained well below international norms, that is less than 9% (vs. 17–18% on average in developing countries). Such a low tax rate, and the low level of non-tax revenue, severely constrains public expenditures, which, again by international standards, are extremely low, particularly with respect to education and public health. The gap between total expenditure and total revenue is actually widening, forcing the Government to increasingly borrow from the domestic economy, with the risk of causing a crowding-out of private investment.

With the present tax to GDP ratio, the Government is unable to spend as much as needed on social sectors or on infrastructure – a situation that seems likely to worsen due to COVID-19. For quite some time already, a political consensus seems to have emerged regarding the dire need to increase taxation. The recent Government's long-run plan, the Perspective Plan 2041, even includes doubling the tax to GDP ratio over a 10-year period. However, no progress has been recorded so far. Worse, a well thought out reform of the value-added tax (VAT) was buried several years ago.

Low administrative capacity, limited technical innovation (digitalisation), a high degree of administrative fragmentation, significant human resource constraints, tax evasion, corruption of officials, and strong lobbying by business to obtain exemptions are the main problems responsible for the low level of tax collection in comparison to the revenue that would be obtained with full compliance. The actual revenue of VAT among registered firms is only 12% of its nominal potential. The proportion is only between 20% and 30% for personal income tax, since many potential taxpayers, including many ultra-rich people, remain outside of the tax net or pay very few taxes. Likewise, numerous firms or economic sectors that can well afford to pay the corporate tax are either fully exempted or enjoy substantially reduced tax rates.

If tax collection is one obstacle to higher tax revenues, the structure of taxation is another. This structure distorts economic decisions and the allocation of resources, and, in some cases, discourages compliance. For instance, the multiplicity of corporate tax rates may give wrong incentives to investors – although effective rates may differ substantially from official rates because of special deals between business managers and the state. The income tax return process is unduly complex, with a marginal tax rate that depends on the wealth of the taxpayer. The VAT rate is 15%, but 10 lower rates are in place for specific services.

Tax policies should aim at horizontal and vertical equity: individuals in similar financial circumstances should be taxed at the same rate, and individuals with different abilities to pay should be taxed at a rate that increases with their income. In Bangladesh, the culture of tax avoidance works against horizontal equity, whereas the heavy reliance on indirect taxes and the pervasive incidence of income tax evasion cannot prevent vertical equity from declining or income inequality from rising.

The failure of the attempt at reforming the VAT in 2012 illustrates the strength of political economy constraints on tax reform. The reform was quite advanced, and a law was even passed, to be implemented a few years later. At the last moment, however, the implementation was postponed under the pressure of the Federation of Bangladesh Chambers of Commerce and Industry. The postponement then proved indefinite – although a new reform is apparently being prepared although, according to experts, it is unlikely to be as effective.

The resistance to tax reform does not come only from politically powerful taxpayers: it also comes from civil servants in the National Board of Revenue (NBR), who do not want to lose their sources of rent: for instance, digitalisation and computerisation would prevent them putting pressure on taxpayers or offering them illegal rebates against the payment of bribes. In some cases, there may thus be a coalition of interests on both sides of the tax system against reforming it.

The reforms that are needed are well known. Christopher Heady gives a useful list of them in his comments on the tax chapter – for example, the advice to avoid *in vivo* contacts between taxpayers and tax collectors (!). Yet most of these reforms would likely meet resistance from the sort of coalition mentioned above and would therefore be blocked in the absence of a strong political will at the centre of government.

4 Primary Education

Primary education, which is the foundation on which the education system is built, has long been recognised, both in Bangladesh and internationally, as a key public policy priority. As such, spending on this area in Bangladesh represents a sizeable part of public expenditures. It also raises important institutional issues, some of them common to the delivery of public services in general. It requires effective mechanisms for the recruitment, training, and retention of teachers; the construction and maintenance of schools and other infrastructure; the design and implementation of the curriculum; the monitoring of progress, through inspections and examinations; and the creation of a learning environment.

Taking an institutional view of the education system, as in the chapter by Raihan, Hossen, and Khondker, is important for obtaining a proper understanding of the outcomes it produces and, more specifically, for determining whether the system actually delivers learning beyond immediate goals, such as increased enrolment. In this regard, Bangladesh's impressive record of increasing enrolment and achieving gender parity is tempered by the growing body of evidence showing that learning outcomes for many of its children are very poor indeed, although not poorer than those for children in India or Pakistan, as stressed in Elizabeth King's comments. This underlines the importance of looking in-depth at the components of the system and the way they work together, instead of relying exclusively on basic indicators, including enrolment and indicators measuring the nominal growth of the system. The main systemic challenges identified in the chapter can be categorised as: (i) a complex coexistence of various actors; (ii) challenges related to resources; (iii) challenges related to teachers and teacher management; and (iv) challenges related to the curriculum and teacher training.

Regarding the first of these challenges, there are significant structural problems in the education system, whereby multiple actors are often faced with confusing and sometimes conflicting divisions of responsibility. This applies not only to overall ministerial control, in which three main ministries and several smaller authorities have management roles with respect to primary schools, but also to the devolution of responsibility across central, regional, and local authorities. The presence of multiple actors in this complex system makes it difficult to establish clear chains of accountability. At the level of resources, it is striking that Bangladesh has one of the lowest rates of public expenditure on primary education in the world (at 0.81% of GDP, it is well below the South Asian average of 1.3%) and also one of the lowest rates of teacher pay (the ratio of average teacher salary to GDP per capita is just under 1 in Bangladesh, as compared to over 4 in rural India and slightly under 2 in Pakistan). If we go beyond these headline numbers, we quickly discover that there exist serious problems in teacher quality, qualifications, and motivation, as well as many infrastructural deficiencies, in the form of badly maintained schools and a lack of adequate teaching materials, in particular.

In terms of the mechanisms for teacher training and recruitment, there are numerous institutional problems, as reflected in bribery, nepotism, and widespread corruption, including undue political influence. The recruitment of teachers is often distorted by the selective leakage of written exams, while the payment of bribes often serves to decide which teachers will be transferred to Dhaka. As with other institutional areas in Bangladesh, such practices are enabled by a dysfunctional level of oversight, monitoring, and accountability, which they in turn reinforce. There are such low expectations as regards being held to account that corrupt practices, such as paying bribes to get a transfer, or other sorts of unacceptable behaviour (such as teacher absenteeism), are virtually normalised. Finally, among all the structural problems, there is the curriculum itself and its implementation through examinations such as the Primary Education Certificate (PEC). This exam-oriented focus, it is argued, favours rote-learning and drills and does little to encourage the development of creativity, a sense of criticism, and reasoning.

Although the problems in Bangladesh's education system, and indeed in its public services more generally, are both severe and deep-rooted, there are various reforms which could and should be undertaken. The historically low budgetary allocation towards primary education suggests that an increase in resources to the sector ought to be a major political priority. Improving teachers' pay and career profiles, in particular, should raise the overall level of candidates for teaching positions, even though, as stressed by King, such a measure should come with an adjustment in the structure of base pay, to guarantee efficiency gains. While increased resources as such will not solve all of the problems, the analysis identifies key areas in which they might generate the greatest effects, including ensuring teacher quality and motivation through improved salaries, career progression, and training; addressing the longstanding inadequacies in infrastructure; and investing in curriculum reform to move away from superficial certification towards a more substantive learning-oriented model. As with other areas of reform, the experiences of COVID-19 have only reinforced these conclusions – in trying to mitigate the negative impacts of school disruption experienced by a whole generation of children,[13] there can be few higher priorities than investment in education.

5 Institutional Challenges in Land Administration and Management in Bangladesh

Land markets raise important institutional issues in many developing countries but especially so in Bangladesh, as land is so scarce and the population is so large. Institutional problems may arise in two senses: first, land arrangements may function sub-optimally as a means of allocating land in an equitable manner and of securing property rights; and second, allocation of land between traditional and modern uses, such as agri-business or some other industrial activity, may be distorted. The chapter by Raihan, Jalal, Sharmin, and Eusuf analyses both aspects, making a distinction between the operations of institutions (e.g. politicised land administration) and their outcomes (e.g. inequitable allocation of land, constrained industrial development).

The most immediate institutional land issues are purely administrative: a lack of proper records, an absence of digitisation, poor levels of infrastructure, external administrative issues, such as the lack of coordination between ministries, administrative complexities, such as unidentified *khas*[14] land; lack of transparency and information; congestion of land disputes; and extended corruption in various forms.

In understanding why these institutional issues should be so persistent and difficult to reform, despite being so readily identified, it is necessary to look deeper into the specific historical and political context, in which the tension between equity and efficiency is a recurring theme. The historical context matters because the weaknesses in the current land administration system are, in part, a legacy of the piecemeal way in which the law evolved through the pre-colonial, colonial, Pakistani, and post-independence eras. The political context matters because at each stage in this process, land reforms have been subject to political pressure in their design and have generated political

---

[13] Schools in Bangladesh were closed for almost 18 months between March 2020 and August 2021, one of the longest closures in the world (see www.unicef.org/bangladesh/en/press-releases/future-37-million-children-bangladesh-risk-their-education-severely-affected-covid).
[14] Unallocated publicly owned land.

effects in their operation. Very often what this has meant in practice is that land reform has been intended to promote equity (e.g. awarding land to land-less peasants) but has not been implemented fully or its implementation has been resisted or subverted by local elites. In some cases, land reform may have been used for political purposes (e.g. dispossessing indigenous people in the Chittagong Hill Tracts). The institutional issues regarding land reform are therefore inseparable from the political economy. However, although policy at a national level is important in institutional terms, it is at the local level that the most decisive institutional effects occur. Here we see something similar to the 'deals environment', in the sense that informal deals, involving low-level corruption, nepotism, and the interference of business elites acting through political parties, rather than formal management, underpin land transactions. Consequently, the process of land administration has not only been captured by elites but has also become resistant to change, as political elites have a vested interest in obstructing reform or effective regulation, and the more the system works in their favour, the greater their resistance to reform.

There is an inherent tension between the equity/distribution aspects of land reform and those of efficiency/growth, which can manifest itself in several ways. Although land regulation may be subject to capture by local elites, the main purpose of such regulation is to protect the rural poor through the secur-ing of land rights. The extent to which it might result in smaller farms, and what effects the size of farms might have on productivity – as asked by Dilip Mookherjee in his comments – is one channel through which institutional prob-lems relating to land might constrain economic development. Alternatively, the pursuit of economic objectives might distort the equity-promoting goals of land-allocating institutions. Fragmentation of landholdings also presents industries and investors with information problems in regard to purchasing land, when both the value of land and the identities of those who hold it may be hard to determine because of highly imperfect land operation registers. In some cases, coercion has been used to force unwilling sellers to sell their land – a practice that is not only unfair to the sellers but also biased in favour of those purchasers who possess political connections. The result may be the shutting out of investment by those who are deprived of the right connections.

Another important channel is the use of land itself for economic purposes, such as the promotion of agri-business or industrial development through the designation of SEZs. It is with the latter that the final section of the chapter by Raihan, Jalal, Sharmin, and Eusuf is particularly concerned, illustrating the link between land and industrial strategy. How are Bangladesh's attempts to use SEZs in order to create an attractive investment climate, foster innovation and entrepreneurship, and diversify its economy, enabled or constrained by its land allocation mechanisms? This chapter offers a detailed analysis of these issues, especially through the mechanisms of land acquisition and compen-sation. As with the land management system, the institutional mechanisms of acquisition and compensation are subject to a range of corrupt practices, which in turn create vested interests that resist change and a bias towards politically connected purchasers, or towards those willing and able to pay bribes. Such an environment is inimical to a good business climate and undermines the strategic economic purpose of the SEZs.

In summary, the institutional issues that constrain both the equity and efficiency objectives of land management come, in the first instance, from inadequate and sometimes outdated administrative frameworks. There is little political will or state capacity to reform or effectively regulate these frameworks. In addition, the system is opaque – it is often very difficult to get accurate information, especially for the poor – and there is little transparency or accountability. These are specific political economy problems, often arising at the local level, in which informal deals substitute for efficient institutional practices, and have the effect of entrenching the political status quo. A range of institutional reforms are recommended, from updating and improving the land survey to digitising records, to achieving a higher degree of state coordination, and to improving the mechanisms through which compensation is awarded for land acquisition. Of course, the aforementioned political economy issues themselves constitute barriers to such reforms, as does the resistance of the civil service, which are afraid to lose rent-seeking opportunities. This being said, initiating a dialogue around the value of reform is an important step on the way to building the political will needed to overcome these obstacles.

6 Judiciary and Land Dispossession Litigation

In Bangladesh, as in most developing countries, landlessness is often synonymous with poverty, and often extreme poverty. Landlessness has greatly increased in Bangladesh, with the proportion of landless rural workers or pure tenants surging from 45% to 65% since 2000 (Sen, 2018). Moreover, a survey conducted by the MJF (2015) found that around 70% of households reported losses of land in the last 10 years, with 17% reportedly the victims of land grabbing. How such practices can be curbed and how they can be dealt with in the judicial sector are crucial questions.

The chapter by Ferdousi, Islam, and Raihan provides a narrative analysis of the process through which involuntary land dispossession takes place in the socio-economic context of Bangladesh, and the relative inability of the judiciary to resolve such cases. It also provides information about the way the judiciary works in general – another aspect of 'state capacity' where Bangladesh appears relatively weak, for both logistical and institutional reasons. Logistical reasons relate to a lack of resources, whereas institutional reasons relate to the way the judiciary is influenced by both political and economic interests, as well as the fact that most actors in the judiciary extract rents from the system and act, almost collusively, to maintain its dysfunctionality.

Despite a constitutional mandate for the separation of the judiciary from the executive organs of the state, the judiciary still remains somewhat vulnerable to political manoeuvring and vested interests. As noted by Jean-Philippe Platteau in his comments, this is already true at the highest level of the system, as supreme court judges are nominated by the Ministry of Law, Justice and Parliamentary Affairs, thus making them vulnerable to political strategies. A 1999 Supreme Court ruling that the Government must strictly implement separation of the judiciary and the executive was never fully executed. Political interference is also observed at the local level in instances of land dispossession. In several cases reported in this chapter, the final judgement is directly influenced by political pressure. It may also sometimes happen that political pressure aims at indefinitely postponing a final judgement.

A second general weakness of the judiciary is the increasing backlog of unresolved cases, due mainly to a lack of capacity and resources. In Bangladesh, civil cases still follow century-old procedures which legally require manual recording at each stage of the proceeding of a case. This consumes considerable amounts of time and the dependence on manual paperwork contributes to an increasing backlog. Delays are compounded by the fact that records of previous stages are often lost from the registers, which further impedes cases. Other factors responsible for the slow processing of cases are the shortage of judges, poor investigation by the police, an excessive number of adjournments, an absence of witnesses, a lack of capacity of legal professionals, and failures in coordination among different administrative departments. A lack of authority to compel clerks, advocates, litigants, or witnesses to comply with the due codes, rules, and processes is another source of delay. Institutional failures in other administrative areas matter too, especially in land management, as attested by the frequent difficulty of obtaining appropriate records of land operations.

Another major cause of delay is the collusion between employees in land administrative bodies, the judiciary, and law enforcement agencies, as well as between numerous actors, including lawyers and clerks, which often has the effect of delaying case resolution through multiplication of the procedures. A simple land dispossession litigation generates a comparatively small amount of rent through the bribes to be paid by the plaintiff or the defendants to clerks, advocates, and judges, but the rent increases significantly if the whole process can be slowed down, and the opportunities to extract a bribe are multiplied, allegedly for the purpose of 'accelerating' the resolution of the case. A suspicion then arises among the actors involved in a case that collusion exists that aims to delay its conclusion. The higher the number of interactions between different parties, the higher the amount of transaction cost and rents that can be extracted.

Ultimately, overcoming institutional inefficiencies in the judiciary of Bangladesh will require a lot more than the usual generic reform agendas. While there is a clear need for capacity building within the judiciary, other urgent steps include a thorough review and proper amendments of the existing laws in order to update century-long administrative practices and to establish low-cost legal services for the poor and underprivileged. Most importantly, the Government must strive to ensure a separation of powers between its executive and judicial branches, to uphold judicial independence at the central as well as at the local levels. But ensuring judicial independence alone may not be sufficient for proper enforcement of the rule of law. Forces that have an interest in the status quo will fiercely oppose any reform in that direction, including the actors who benefit from the low capacity of the judiciary system in charge of land litigation. External interventions are required to break the collusion among actors in land dispossession litigation cases, knowing that they will oppose a reform that would threaten their way of generating rents.

III THE INSTITUTIONAL DIAGNOSTIC

Based on the material accumulated so far, the institutional diagnostic presented in this section is organised into the following three parts. First, looking across the summaries of the preceding chapters, a list of three *basic institutional weaknesses* is highlighted. These are common to all or several of the areas covered above and are also consistent with the analysis of institutional challenges based on cross-country indicators, and those based on the responses provided by a number of decision makers in Bangladesh to the CIS. Second, this list is then broadened in a so-called Diagnostic Table where the basic institutional weaknesses appear with their economic and social consequences on one side and their *proximate causes* on the other, the latter being themselves related to several *deep factors*. The reason for this juxtaposition is that the identified weaknesses are often more the symptoms than they are the causes of an institutional problem. A diagnostic must therefore start from the symptoms in order to go to the root of the problems, and then to the possible remedies, which depend themselves on which deep factors are at play. Third, based on that comprehensive view of institutional challenges in Bangladesh, the three basic institutional weaknesses are re-examined in the light of their relationship with the rest of the diagnostic table, and with a view to considering potential reforms, and their political economy context. Some proximate causes are also subjected to the same reflection due to their particular role in affecting the basic weaknesses, and the reforms they call for.

It is important to note that this diagnostic was originally conceived before the emergence of the COVID-19 pandemic, and that it has, therefore, been necessary to reassess the argument in the light of subsequent events. The conclusion of that reassessment, however, is that the essential findings and structure of the diagnostic are unchanged. Indeed, they are strengthened by an analysis of Bangladesh's experience of COVID-19. Not only are the three basic institutional weaknesses and their proximate causes as pertinent as ever in terms of general economic development, but in fact provide a useful means of understanding why the pandemic affected Bangladesh in the way that it has, thus far, and in anticipating the likely future challenges that the country now faces as a result. The rationale for reform remains unchanged as a consequence, but the COVID-19 crisis calls for some specific recommendations that we make explicit.

A Three Overall Basic Institutional Weaknesses of Bangladesh's Development

The general feeling that results from the short summaries of the previous chapters (see Section II.E) is that of a dichotomy in the recent economic history of Bangladesh between remarkable growth achievements very much centred on RMG exports, on the one hand, and deep weaknesses in most other sectors, on the other. These deep weaknesses make the country comparable to many low-income countries that have growth and development performances far below Bangladesh's. It is as though Bangladesh's growth achievement has created few incentives, and possibly even generated disincentives, for the ruling elites to address major sources of inefficiency and inequity that coexist with growth factors. The consequences of this neglect, in terms of the poor functioning of the state, the poor delivery of public goods, the high degree of corruption, and rising income inequality, were and still are politically manageable as long as the growth engines continue to raise living standards and reduce poverty. On the other hand, institutional failures may become a prime obstacle to further development if the slowdown that is presently observed in RMG exports and remittances increases. Unfortunately, there are many reasons to believe that this possibility may materialise, especially so in the present conditions of a global economic crisis caused by the COVID-19 crisis. This makes it all the more urgent to remedy the institutional weaknesses that presently prevent the economy of Bangladesh from achieving better performance and that might hamper necessary adjustments in the future.

The many problems mentioned earlier may be grouped into three overall 'basic institutional weaknesses':

- **Supremacy of 'deals' over formal industrial (or development) policymaking**

  By this it is meant that industrial – or, more generally, development – policies and key investment or resource allocation decisions often result from agreements, that is 'deals', made between the political elite in government and the economic elite. These deals concern particular operations or programmes that are chosen on an *ad hoc* basis, meaning without reference to some well-defined overall strategy. Deals relating to RMG exports yielded positive results. Others did not, or prevented better options, like export diversification, being taken. To be sure, deals are not necessarily incompatible with formal industrial policies as long as they fit a well-defined general strategy and the state keeps full control of the support provided to particular industries. It is not clear, however, that the deals environment observed in Bangladesh meets these requirements.

- **Ineffective regulation**

  This refers to the difficulty the Government faces in regulating certain key activities in order to ensure greater efficiency and equity in the economy. In some cases what is at stake is the legal framework for such regulation, which may be outdated or otherwise unfit for the objective pursued, and in relation to which reform attempts have consistently failed. In other cases, the framework may be in place but there is not sufficient capacity to implement it. Examples in the areas covered in this volume include the dysfunction of the banking system, the failure to regulate labour conditions in a key sector like RMG, or simply the dismal performance of taxation. Regulatory agencies in other areas that are not covered in this volume may be equally ineffective.

• Weak state capacity

This major governance failure in Bangladesh takes different forms. Some are readily apparent, such as the lack of public resources and therefore the limited provision and low quality of public goods, the lack of skills in public service, delays or high costs incurred in the provision of infrastructure, or an inefficient administrative organisation. Others are more obscure, such as the high level of corruption in most administrative clusters, which tends to make the delivery of public services both inefficient and inequitable, reduces revenues, and often discourages economic initiatives. Weak capacity is particularly patent in the judiciary. A lack of resources and a high level of corruption make the judiciary completely ineffective in major areas, especially in the protection of property rights in agriculture.

To be sure, these three 'basic institutional weaknesses' are not independent of each other. The ineffectiveness of regulation or the inability to integrate deals with the business elite within a consistent development framework may be considered as constituting weak state capacity. Deals themselves may be viewed as the consequence of a limited state capacity, that is the lack of a coherent and comprehensive perspective on development, or ineffective regulation. Yet these three headings appear as a convenient grouping of the many deficiencies pointed to in the chapters in this volume. At the same time, they cover different aspects of the malfunctioning of the country's institutions.

It is reassuring that these three basic institutional weaknesses conform well with the general institutional weaknesses revealed by global institutional indicators. It certainly comes as no surprise that global indices have ranked Bangladesh in the lower part of the scale on indicators like 'rule of law' or 'bureaucratic quality'. The basic weaknesses also match the opinions expressed by the respondents to our questionnaire survey, and by the key informants whom we interviewed. In this respect, the emphasis put by our interviewees on the role of informal arrangements, that is 'deals', is worth singling out. Nonetheless, the present institutional diagnostic will go much further than these mechanical diagnostic tools in providing a deeper understanding of the basic weaknesses of the institutional fabric of the country and of the way they interact to impinge on the pace and structural features of national development.

A priori, many aspects of the three basic weaknesses could be corrected by simple reforms. Auditing government policies and evaluating civil servants, enforcing penalties for corruption, changing the rules for appointing the governor of the Central Bank, digitalising land records or judiciary decisions, etc. are all reforms that are rather evident and could drastically improve the institutional environment in Bangladesh and enhance its development. Yet, for these reforms to be enacted, and successfully implemented, other conditions must be met that most often involve political economy mechanisms or more fundamental constraints on the society and the economy. The three basic weaknesses set out above result from 'proximate causes' that need to be identified, and which are themselves linked to 'deep factors' that are rooted in the way the political system and the civil society work, in conjunction with other possible exogenous factors. It is this complex relationship that will now be explored.

B The Diagnostic Table

Table 10.1 offers a general view of the institutional diagnostic that the in-depth analysis in this volume leads to. Starting from the three basic institutional weaknesses defined in Section III.A, the table can be read from left to right, with the right-hand column showing the major economic and social consequences of these weaknesses. It can also be read from right to left, with a column showing the main proximate causes of the weaknesses and then a column displaying the deep factors that ultimately determine the feasibility of reforms that could correct the proximate causes and improving the institutional context. While reading this table, it is important to notice that logical implications go from column to column, not from one item in a column to the item in the same row in another column. In other words, it is generally the case that all items in a column depend on, or jointly determine, the items in another column. It should also be kept in mind that the relationships between the items in different columns, and within a column, may be circular. For instance, one may hold the view that it is the success of the RMG export sector that has made governments less attentive to regulatory issues, which in turn explains the dysfunction of the banking sector and a sub-optimal allocation of funds away from non-RMG potential export sectors.

There is no need to elaborate on the right-hand column of the table, which is only a reminder of the major economic and social implications of the institutional weaknesses discussed in the preceding section. What is new in the table are the first two columns.

1 Proximate Causes for Institutional Weaknesses
Six items appear in the 'proximate causes' column. They are briefly discussed here, while emphasising how they relate to the basic weakness column.

The 'elite capture of the Government' is particularly important for the supremacy of deals over formal industrial policy, and, specifically, the role played by the business class of the RMG manufacturing sector. As the sector

TABLE 10.1 *The institutional diagnostic table*

Deep factors	Proximate causes	Institutional weaknesses	Economic and social consequences
Political settlement (political and industrial elites against labour) Winner-takes-all electoral democracy Vertical structure of political parties Vibrant civil society Population pressure on land Role of donors Contemporaneous deep factors Dominant party politics Dominance of the RMG sector and sustained fast growth	Elite capture of government (e.g. RMG entrepreneurial class) Weakness of labour organisations Lack of resources and skills in the public sector Stable corruption equilibrium - anti-reform coalitions - clientelism Inadequate laws and administrative organisation Opacity and unaccountability	*Supremacy of 'deals' over formal industrial (and development) policymaking* *Ineffective regulation* - banking system - tax system - labour conditions *Weak state capacity* - weak delivery of public goods and services - delays or high costs incurred in the provision of infrastructure - corruption - ineffective and corrupt judiciary	Past successful development based on RMG exports but threats to future growth Excessive export concentration Suppressed labour regime Gender discrimination NPL: leakage of resources Misallocation of investments Unattractive investment climate Abnormally low tax revenues Limited quantity and quality of public goods (education, infrastructure) Rising inequality and slowing down of poverty reduction Compensation for limited public goods by, and poverty reduction role of, NGOs Inefficient shock responsiveness (COVID-19)

Source: Authors.

gained in importance, both through its size in the domestic economy and its dominant role in exports and general economic growth, it quickly acquired considerable leverage over the Government, whichever party was in power at the time. Even the regulation of the sector, which would normally be expected to fall under the responsibility of some entity within the Ministry of Industry, is completely internalised within the sector. Its producer unions, one for woven wear and another for knitwear, are thus able to impose industrial policy choices in their own favour, often at the expense of other export manufacturing sectors, and, possibly, future growth.

The 'weakness of labour organisations' in Bangladesh results from a political settlement between political and industrial elites at the expense of labour (one of the 'deep factors'). Labour union leaders are generally affiliated to political parties whose leaders have strong links with private firms, especially in the RMG sector. As a result, unions are generally disinclined to challenge employers, which may be the reason why over the last 30 years wages lagged GDP per capita by a wide margin and income inequality increased. The weakness of labour unions and low wages are key factors in the global competitiveness of the RMG sector, but, paradoxically, they may also be responsible for the structural inertia of Bangladesh's industrial sector, including within RMG. Faster growing wages would have been an incentive to move towards higher value-added and more 'complex' products, along the line of the Hidalgo *et al.* (2007) theory of industrial development.[15]

The 'lack of resources and skills' within the public sector is a constraining factor that is common to most developing countries. In the case of Bangladesh, however, it is not only an issue of a low level of income but also of a particularly low level of public revenue – and particularly tax revenue. It is a cause of institutional weakness, but also a consequence, since it results largely from a dysfunctional tax authority. This is an example of a circular relationship between the elements of the diagnostic table (Table 10.1).

The existence of a 'stable corruption equilibrium', or a culture of corruption, explains why it is so difficult to control corruption, at least directly though carrots and/or sticks. When every actor expects others to behave in a corrupt way, no incentive exists to deviate from that common behaviour, and even carrot-and-stick approaches may become ineffective. Moving out of that equilibrium requires both a strong political will and the effective use of power.[16]

The presence of 'inadequate laws and administrative organisations' in Bangladesh is a rather direct cause of why some institutions do not function well. It also means that effective reforms of these institutions require the modification of the legal or administrative framework. Examples mentioned earlier include some land laws inherited from the colonial or the pre-independence period, or overlapping administrative responsibilities in land matters, primary education, or the regulation of banking.

---

[15] According to the theory, industrial development proceeds through moving from less to more technologically complex, and presumably less labour-intensive, products, a process that is not observed in Bangladesh, despite initial success in RMG exports.

[16] The existence of multiple corruption equilibria is suggested by observation of the varying degree of corruption across countries. A simple theoretical model showing why this occurs has been proposed by Dixit (2017). The case for multiple equilibria in the presence of 'social norms' was made much earlier in Akerlof (1980). On the empirical side, see Joarder and Munim (2011).

Finally, the 'opacity and unaccountability' of the public sector reflects the fact that a key incentive for a government to effectively reform weak institutions lies in the opinion held by the general public, and mobilised by the political opposition, regarding deficient institutions. Weak institutions may persist because the public information on their limitations is concealed, restricted, or falsified, or because the government does not assume responsibility for them. The high level of corruption in Bangladesh's public sector and regulatory failures that favour government clients are cases in point.

2 Deep Factors for Institutional Weaknesses

Deep factors are those factors constraining reforms that would remedy the proximate causes of basic institutional weaknesses. It bears emphasis that deep factors refer here to institutional factors that may hinder development, and not to development itself. For instance, the geopolitical location of Bangladesh may be considered as a deep factor that influences its development, in particular through outmigration to India or to the Gulf countries, the partial relief of population pressure this permits, and the flow of remittances that it generates. Yet it is not clear that this factor plays a direct role in explaining the basic institutional weaknesses or the proximate causes set out in the diagnostic table (Table 10.1).

Deep factors found to be of institutional relevance in the present framework are reported in the first column of Table 10.1. The first factor is the enduring 'political settlement' between the industrial elite and the political elite, whatever the government in place. This factor echoes the elite capture proximate cause discussed above but is more fundamental. The elite capture might take different forms and work through different channels. The political settlement factor refers to converging interests between whoever is in government and the industrial elite, especially the RMG business leaders and managers. The deal provides that the Government will bring strong support to the rapid development of RMG exports, at the cost of repressing labour, a condition that may be necessary to maintain the global competitiveness of the sector. Overall economic growth is the Government's reward, the growth of their companies is the industrial elite's reward. As long as growth prospects remain favourable, and in the absence of major political change, this settlement can be expected to persist. But the question then is: what would happen if the growth potential of the RMG sector were to go into decline?

The second deep factor refers to the 'winner-takes-all' type of political confrontation between the two main parties in Bangladesh during the so-called competitive democracy regime, as described previously in this chapter, which saw those parties, the Awami League and the BNP, alternating in power since 1990. The competition has indeed been fierce, the party in power essentially trying to annihilate the opposition and the latter responding by mass protests, strikes, and boycotts in electoral periods. This period apparently came to an end when the Awami League won the 2008 election and was then able to considerably weaken the opposition, apparently with the same winner-takes-all approach to politics. The most recent elections are the third time in a row that the Awami League has won the elections, so that one may reasonably question whether a profound change has taken place in Bangladeshi politics. It may be noted, however, that despite the democratic constitution of the country, democratic debate has always played a limited role in Bangladesh. This was true at the time of competitive democracy, when parties were struggling for full control of power, and is even more true today, when the party in power has been able to successfully weaken and repress the opposition.

The 'vertical structure of political parties' means a democratic debate is not taking place within parties either. The two leaders have managed their respective parties in similarly authoritarian styles for the last 30 years, with little space left to dissenting minorities. They are both now ageing, but apparently remain in full control of their succession, making sure that power within the party will continue to be concentrated in the hands of their successors, most likely to be chosen from among close relatives.

The 'vibrant civil society', the next deep factor, includes many different actors, from professional unions to think-tanks, media, religious organisations, and NGOs. The latter are particularly numerous and active in Bangladesh. Their origin is often traced back to the intense solidarity that developed during reconstruction of the country when it was devastated by the independence war, a deadly cyclone, and a terrible famine. Some, like BRAC or the Grameen Bank, have acquired global reputations for installing micro-finance throughout the country. But their involvement in education, healthcare, and women's empowerment are equally remarkable. Overall, the NGOs and civil society are so dynamic that Bangladesh is sometimes described as combining a 'strong society' and a 'weak state' (Lewis, 2011: 103). NGOs are mostly independent from the Government, which may raise problems of coordination in sectors where both actors operate, and from political parties. This is not necessarily the case for other components of the civil society, which have often been considered to be part of the political game discussed earlier.[17]

The next two deep factors in the first column of Table 10.1 do not require much discussion. Natural conditions always play a role in determining the institutional context of a country. In Bangladesh, this is especially obvious in regard to the exceptionally strong population pressure on land availability and the incidence of land litigation. It makes land-related institutions and the judiciary particularly important. The role of donors has also been crucial in the past, and today's economic institutions in Bangladesh have been influenced by the conditionality which donors have imposed in several instances on the

---

[17] See, for instance, Tasmin (2017).

country. This is much less the case today as the country has become more autonomous with respect to foreign financing.[18]

The last two deep factors that appear at the bottom of Table 10.1 try to account for the fact that factors conditioning policies and reforms do change over time, often as a result of the past evolution of society. Under the heading 'contemporaneous' deep factors, the diagnostic table emphasises two such factors. One is the present 'dominant party' regime and the current weakness of the opposition, which make the political economy context distinct from that in the past. One cannot rule out the possibility that the complete control of the Awami League over political power is only a transient stage of the winner-takes-all political game played in Bangladesh since the early 1990s, and that it has lasted longer than it used to. In this view, sooner or later the opposition will wake up and, in turn, try to acquire full control. But it may also be that the party in power is here to stay for a long time, possibly through repressing all types of opposition. Whatever the case, the important point is that, because of this, the political economy of reforms today may differ from the situation in the past.

The second contemporaneous deep factor typically reflects path dependence in development. The surge of RMG exports 20 or 30 years ago must be logically seen as the result of exogenous opportunities and an existing political settlement between the political elite (whatever the party in power) and the business elite of those days. Today, RMG exports have acquired such a prominent role in the development of Bangladesh that the whole sector largely conditions many policy reforms, like, for instance, those related to the diversification of manufacturing exports or to the adoption of labour-friendly measures. Reforms that would have been possible 30 years ago, provided the political will were present, might not be feasible today given the economic importance of the sector and the political power that it entails for its entrepreneurs. The experience of sustained fast growth over the last two or three decades is a similar contemporaneous deep factor, in the sense that it may have generated different attitudes, beliefs, and expectations in the population about how the society and the economy function, or should function.

C Analysing the Basic Institutional Weaknesses and Potential Directions for Reform

To complete the diagnostic, this sub-section analyses in more detail the basic institutional weaknesses identified earlier, focusing on potential directions for reform while taking into account their proximate causes and the deep factors behind them. However, reforms are envisaged at a rather general level; being more explicit would require getting into practical details that are beyond the scope of the present study. A short list of the reforms considered in the next sub-sections is provided in Annex 10.1.

---

[18] It may be noted that donors have also considerably contributed to the development of Bangladeshi NGOs.

• The supremacy of deals over a formal industrial policy

Despite the vast recent literature on industrial policy,[19] it is difficult to define what a 'formal' industrial policy should be, even though a consensus now seems to have formed about the need for, and the utmost importance of, industrial policy. As Rodrik (2008) put it some time ago: 'Industrial policy: don't ask why, ask how'. On the 'how', another view seems to have become consensual, which can be summarised by the simple recommendation 'Don't try to pick winners'. This view is based on the observation of a huge number of complete failures resulting from *a priori* decisions of governments, often pushed by strong private interests, to invest massively in particular ventures or sectors. This does not mean, of course, that in some instances winner-picking has not been successful.

A 'deals environment' where entrepreneurs convince governments of the private and public benefits of a project and obtain advantages on an individual basis is a winner-picking strategy. It may work, and the impressive success over the last decades of the RMG sector in Bangladesh is a clear testament to this. But it may also fail or prevent other and better projects from developing. In Bangladesh, the success of the RMG sector and the leverage it acquired because of its macroeconomic importance now means that some deals struck with the Government may be monopolising resources that other sectors thus miss out on, even though they may be most promising. The fact that non-RMG manufacturing export sectors like leather, agri-business, or simple mechanics have not been able to take advantage of the same facilities as RMG export-ers suggests that industrial policy may not be working properly, or has been skewed in favour of established interests.

In defining what would make industrial policies effective, Rodrik (2008) emphasised three features: embeddedness, carrots and sticks, and accountabil-ity. They all seem particularly relevant in the case of Bangladesh.

Embeddedness means that industrial policy is not a conventional top-down planning exercise, or the resolution of a principal–agent model where the prin-cipal, the Government, indirectly controls agents, the firms, through subsidies, special credit lines, or infrastructure investments. Policies must closely and continuously interact with market reality and be re-evaluated and redesigned depending on the results obtained. This does not mean that they should focus on a few firms or sectors. In the words of Rodrik, industrial policy should be designed according to 'a model of strategic collaboration and coordination between the private sector and the government with the aim of uncovering where the most significant bottlenecks are, designing the most effective inter-ventions, periodically evaluating the outcomes, and learning from the mistakes being made in the process'.[20]

---

[19] On developing countries, see for instance, Rodrik (2004), Altenburg (2011), Stiglitz *et al.* (2013), Chang and Andreoni (2020), and the critical view in Pack and Saggi (2006).
[20] See Rodrik (2008, p. 20). Also, Chang and Andreoni (2020) give a rather extensive list of the ways policymakers must be 'embedded' in industrial development, drawing on examples from both advanced and developing economies.

The nature of the *incentives* provided to individual firms to achieve industrial objectives are well known. They have been successful in some cases,
for instance in East Asia, but less so in others, as witnessed by the failure
of import-substitution policies despite initial success in Latin America or
sub-Saharan Africa. Two features have been singled out in the successful
carrot-and-stick manufacturing export policy in East Asia. One is the use of
the stick through credibly conditioning carrots on export performance and
withdrawing all types of subsidies in cases where results do not materialise.
The other is the reliance on competition, making sure that domestic firms not
only compete, albeit with some advantages, with foreign producers, but also
among themselves. Such a strategy requires embeddedness but also the autonomy of the government with respect to private interests, something that cannot
be taken for granted in Bangladesh today.

The last recommendation of *accountability*, or transparency, is essential in
all policy areas but is even more important in industrial policy because of
the danger of collusive behaviour between private firms and policymakers.
Publicising the objectives and the main instruments of the policy, routinely
reporting on the resources engaged and their use, and regularly and publicly
analysing results, including failures, so as to possibly change orientation, is
a way to make industrial policy more effective and to prevent collusion with
private interests.

The deals environment that seems to stand for industrial policy in Bangladesh
is not necessarily incompatible with the embeddedness and even a carrot-and-
stick recommendation. Because of unaccountability and opacity, however,
there is no way to know whether deals agreed with private interests were good
policy or not. One can only observe that the export diversification objective
repeatedly set by the Government was not attained, which means that deals
were incompatible with this goal. This does not suggest, though, that a clear
reorientation is not required, since the policy has never been openly stated or
debated.

Several proximate causes and deep factors in the diagnostic table make it
harder to reform industrial policy in the directions just mentioned. The elite
capture of the Government by the RMG entrepreneurial class, which results
from the dominant role of that sector in economic growth, has apparently
blocked reforms that would have been in the interests of the non-RMG export
sector in the past, and may make a deeper reform of industrial policy difficult today. The recommendation of an accountable and transparent policy
also goes against the practice of most governments, including the present one,
because they rely on deals that they do not want to publicise, rather than on
an articulated policy.

Two further points should be made about industrial policy. First, it must be
stressed that industrial policy actually connects with all other policy instruments
in the hands of the Government, be it macroeconomic policy – for example the
real exchange rate – public infrastructure or, as seen in the chapter on land,

SEZ management. Transparency and accountability with respect to what these policies imply for industrial development matter too. Second, it bears emphasis that the general business climate is essential for industrial development, particularly for attracting foreign direct investments, which, as experienced by many East Asian countries, play a crucial role in enhancing manufacturing exports. However, the business climate is conspicuously adverse in Bangladesh, and, from that point of view, improving Bangladesh's ranking in business climate indicators is a top priority.[21]

These concerns remain highly relevant in the wake of COVID-19 – in effect, the government's strategy to bring about a recovery is a form of industrial policy, on a grand scale. Thus far, the major policy announced by the government has been stimulus packages amounting to 3.7% of the GDP.[22] But the implementation of any such policy requires robust and rigorous decision-making mechanisms and here, as argued by Raihan (2020), the targeting of firm support has been problematic. While firms may select themselves to apply for benefits, the assessment of their need has been neither formal nor systematic. In the absence of a rigorous assessment process, many eligible firms, and especially smaller firms, have been denied vital support to which they should have been entitled. Even when support was agreed, problems arose with the disbursement of subsidised credit to selected firms through banking channels. These problems, connected to pressures on the banking sector, such as the NPLs and governance issues described in Chapter 5 have affected micro, small, and medium enterprises particularly severely (Raihan *et al*, 2021b). By contrast, powerful firms, with strong lobbying and useful political links, appear to have been able to use the system to their advantage and have captured the greater share of the loans, despite, in some cases, facing significantly less dire needs. In this way, the pandemic seems to have magnified the bias towards the larger, more politically connected firms, especially in the RMG sector, and diminished the possibility for smaller, more entrepreneurial firms to emerge or simply survive in other sectors, thus impeding progress towards diversification into other sectors beyond RMG.

- **Ineffective regulation**

Weak enforcement of regulation is observed in many instances; obvious examples shown in this volume include: non-compliance with legal rules in the banking sector, or with labour protection and minimum wage legislation in manufacturing; capital flight; and numerous tax exemptions (Statutory

---

[21] Recall that Bangladesh ranks 168 out of 190 countries in the World Bank 'doing business' ranking before it was interrupted.

[22] Most of the package consisted of subsidised loans aimed at covering the wage bill when workers were given furlough, cash flow and working capital disruptions at different interest rate depending on the sector. Some support was also provided to returning migrants and some cash transfers were aimed at alleviating poverty.

Regulatory Orders, SROs). But flaws in regulation are also found in many other areas, such as public transport, drug administration, and even the Anti-Corruption Commission. Their consequence is a waste of resources, for example through excessive NPLs in the banking sector or SROs in taxation, their misallocation, social damage, and lost lives in Rana Plaza–like accidents, numerous scam scandals, and rising inequality since breaches of rules generally benefit the rich and hurt the poor. Although it is often difficult to evaluate, the economic cost of these breaches of rules may be sizeable.

There are various causes for this lax compliance with rules in Bangladesh. The capture of regulatory officials through the political links of an unscrupulous economic elite, or sheer corruption, is one. Opacity and unaccountability is another. To be sure, print media cover scam scandals, but it is not clear that this has any impact on the transgressors. Even in cases where an administrative inquiry is conducted, it often ends up being inconclusive or leaves the perpetrators unpunished.

Another, more directly institutional, cause of the weakness of regulations is the inadequate organisation of the regulation system itself. This is particularly evident in the case of the banking system, with its dual governance (the Central Bank for private commercial banks and the Ministry of Finance for national commercial banks). The Central Bank may well try to impose NPL discipline among private banks, but, overall, the impact on the whole banking system will be limited if the Ministry of Finance continues its lax stance towards national banks. Even if this dualism were to stop and the regulation of the banking sector were placed in the sole hands of the Central Bank, another issue would be its autonomy. The latter is presently not granted since the governor and board members are all appointed by the Government and may be dismissed at any moment. It may thus be embarrassing for the governor of the Central Bank to discipline the relationship between private bankers and government members or closely related people.

As another example, the head of the Anti-Corruption Commission is also appointed and may be dismissed by the Government. In addition, the Commission must obtain the Government's permission to investigate or file any charge against bureaucrats or politicians. Even when granted such permission, the Commission may end up declaring suspected Government members innocent.

It tends to be a feature of weak regulatory environments that dysfunctionality, in terms of performing regulatory functions, is intimately related to structural problems – each sustains the other. This is seen in the health system – exposed by the COVID-19 crisis – in which the structure is that of a 'stable anti-reform coalition' (Raihan, 2020) among the dominant actors, and the regulatory functions exhibit a 'policy paralysis'. By this is meant a situation in which critically important and necessary laws and reforms are not undertaken, or, even if undertaken, are not implemented as a result of a lack of commitment from the government or inability of the dominant actors to reach a consensus over the legitimacy or the soundness of the reform. The 'policy paralysis' in the health sector is observed through the continued staggeringly low public spending on health year after year, the high prevalence of mismanagement and corruption, and a general lack of accountability and transparency. This system persists because there are hidden interests not represented among the dominant actors[23] and because there are strong incentives to maintain the status quo, in which the generation and distribution of rents perpetuates the 'stable anti-reform coalition'.

Reforms to correct such ineffective regulation are rather obvious. Rules that govern the appointment of regulatory agencies' heads must be modified to allow the civil society, including opposition parties, to participate in the decision process – or at least to be openly consulted. The same is true for dismissals. Agencies like the Central Bank and the Anti-Corruption Commission must have complete autonomy in fulfilling a clearly defined mission. Auditing of regulatory authorities must take place regularly, with audit results made fully public and detailed inquiries being triggered when malpractices or illicit agreements are suspected.

The biggest impediment to this kind of measure is essentially of a political nature. In a democratic context, it would be difficult to oppose a reform that would add non-government personalities with voting or consultative rights to committees responsible for appointing the managers of key regulatory entities. Whether in the context of the competitive democracy or in the present dominant party regime, things are different in Bangladesh. For good or bad reasons, the executive may prefer to wield total control over such entities, and the opposition may not be strong enough to effectively contest the prevailing practices, or it may even be complicit, in anticipation of a future shift of power.

- **Weak state capacity**

In Bangladesh, weak state capacity takes the form of underperforming public services. In previous chapters of this volume, this under-performance was readily apparent in the areas of taxation, the quality of primary education, land management, or the judiciary. Since the pandemic emerged, under-performance has also manifested in the failure to rapidly and efficiently disburse social protection to the poor and vulnerable. Under-performance occurs in most of the public sector.

---

[23] The main actors can be grouped into four categories, namely state, non-state, direct, and indirect actors. The direct state actors in the health sector are the Ministry of Health and Family Welfare, its Directorate Generals, and in particular, the Directorate General of Health Services (DGHS). The indirect state actor is the Ministry of Finance. The direct non-state actors are Bangladesh Medical Association, private sector hospitals and diagnostics and their associations, and non-governmental organisations led medical service. The indirect non-state actors are the pharmaceutical industry, importers of medicine and medical equipment, civil society, and international organisations.

Primary causes of weak state capacity may be found first in the lack of resources. By international standards, the public sector is abnormally small in Bangladesh, so it is unsurprising that the provision of public goods and services is deficient. Insufficient funding is indeed responsible for a lack of equipment and lagging technology. These limit the productivity of the civil service, for instance through the unavailability of advanced digital technology in key areas. In the case of COVID-19, long-term failures in the Bureau of Statistics and Ministry of Planning also resulted in incomplete and inadequate records being kept as to the identities and locations of the poor, thus hampering efforts to correctly and swiftly allocate funds – a major portion being erroneously given to the wrong recipients with many poor and targeted groups being left out altogether (BIGD, 2021b). A failure to invest in public services also results in limited training and low salaries. These may prevent the recruitment of civil servants possessing the right competences for, and the right commitment to, their job. Bangladeshi primary school teachers, for instance, are among the worst paid compared to those in other developing countries, and they teach packed classes in school buildings that are often dilapidated, dysfunctional, and cramped given the number of attending pupils.

More than anything, generalised corruption through bribery, rent-seeking, and inappropriate use of public funds is responsible for the poor performances of the public sector and the actual cost of public services for users. As Khan (2006) remarked, corruption is endemic in the early stages of development, but the situation in Bangladesh is worse than in most countries at a comparable level of income per capita.[24] A host of laws have been formulated in recent decades to tackle corruption, yet they remain relatively ineffective in a culture of non-compliance.[25]

As far as anti-corruption policies are concerned, two strategies are available. The first one is to tackle corruption directly by using appropriate incentives: that is, attractive carrots and hard sticks. To be effective, both instruments need to be used simultaneously. For instance, the recent pay hike in Bangladesh, which was expected to reduce the need for civil servants to resort to corruption to improve their livelihood, has not actually discouraged bribery. This is because opportunities for bribery are still present, public office holders hardly face any judicial oversight, and controls within public administration are not very effective, even when they are 'reinforced'. Practically, there is no stick, or at best a very weak one. Indeed, the pervasive corruption culture makes controls ineffective: those in charge may themselves be willing to accept bribes

---

[24] For instance, Bangladesh ranks significantly below Cote d'Ivoire, Ghana, Zambia, Honduras, and Nicaragua, which are all in the purchasing power parity US$ 4,200–5,200 GDP per capital range (2018), in Transparency International's corruption perception index, or in the World Governance Indicators control of corruption ranking.

[25] The Anti-Corruption Public Procurement Rules 2008, the Public Finance and Budget Management Act, 2009, the National Human Rights Commission Act, 2009, the Chartered Secretaries Act, 2010, the Prevention of Money Laundering Act, 2012, and The Competition Act, 2012.

or they have themselves a corrupt past that might be used against them by those whom they are supposed to monitor. This may be the main reason why anti-corruption laws and initiatives in Bangladesh have had such little impact.

The second strategy consists of eliminating rent-seeking opportunities and other mechanisms that prompt public officials to collect bribes. A good example is the digitalisation of administrative operations, which would reduce the possibility of falsifying or selling administrative records and eliminate direct contact between the public and civil servants, and thus the opportunity for the latter to collect a bribe from the former. This is true in tax collection, as with the digitalisation of VAT collection, as well as in land litigation or land management in general. Simplifying laws, reducing their opacity, and publicising them should also reduce rent-seeking by curtailing the power of officials. In the field of taxation, for instance, the complexity of the income tax or the multiplicity of VAT rates or corporate tax rates acts as an encouragement to tax evasion or to bribery of tax officers. The strategy of reducing rent-seeking opportunities offers two neat advantages: reducing corruption and improving the efficiency of public services in general.

The second strategy will nonetheless meet two obstacles. First, rent-seeking agents in the bureaucracy will always seek to defend the status quo. Civil servants themselves will resist reforms that suppress opportunities to collect bribes, in one form or another, and in many instances, they will get the support of the people who benefit from bribing them. This is particularly obvious in the case of tax collection since the benefit of tax evasion is typically shared by tax inspectors and taxpayers. The indefinite postponement of the 2012 VAT reform and the low effectiveness expected from the reform in progress are good examples of the power of such coalitions. The second obstacle is the clientelist bias of the Government. Civil service positions in Bangladesh are assigned to members or close allies of the party in power, the situation being apparently the same today as it was at the time of the competitive democracy regime. Reducing the benefit obtained from their position through rent-seeking would be badly received by these supporters, even if it were partly compensated for by a general pay hike.

The strategy aimed at reducing rent-seeking opportunities should also include the strengthening of all auditing and evaluating mechanisms provided by the law or administrative rules. This often requires changes in the mode of appointing the managers of auditing units, who are too often under the sole control of the Government, as is the case with the Anti-Corruption Commission, or the Comptroller and Auditor General (CAG). Here too, allowing reputable external personalities to sit on appointment committees or to participate in auditing missions may guarantee more impartiality in the monitoring of the administrative apparatus, and more transparency in general. Along the same lines, making major auditing and evaluation reports public may be another way of discouraging illicit behaviour by civil servants, provided that the administration fully complies with freedom of information as required by the Constitution (Art. 39).

Other weaknesses that affect state capacity and require a proper corrective strategy have already been mentioned, but in one way or another, their proper implementation is conditional on enlarged resources. Increasing the pay of civil servants to recruit more qualified people, training them better, providing them with a work atmosphere that is conducive to strong motivations and recognition are all well-known means of improving the delivery of public services. In many areas, simple digital technology can make the administrative machinery more efficient, besides reducing bribing opportunities. A huge literature has developed over the last decade or so on the use of information and communication technology (ICT) to fight corruption (Chêne, 2016), but the main benefit from digitalisation is to make information readily available while curtailing personal contacts between public officers and people or firms.

All these reforms aimed at improving state capacity in Bangladesh require strong political will, especially those reforms concerned with the curbing of corruption. The present Government will be missing a golden opportunity if it refrains from taking advantage of its dominant political situation to launch such reforms, especially so because they would be most favourably received by the public. However, political economy considerations and the need to keep 'clients' satisfied may push the Government in the opposite direction.

Although it may not be considered as the state proper, a particular word must be said about the weak capacity of the judiciary system in Bangladesh. As a result of both a lack of skills and resources and the high level of corruption among most professionals – judges, counsels, bailiffs, and police – involved in court cases, this sector is to a large degree ineffective and deeply unfair and inequitable. Such a state of affairs is very unfortunate as it precludes any serious attempt at reining in the general culture of corruption in the country. It also considerably weakens property rights, especially in rural areas where land-grabbing cases are frequent, with potentially negative consequences for production. Reforms that would curtail rent-seeking opportunities in that key sector, for instance the simplification of procedural rules and the digitalisation of court records, are urgently needed. Equally urgently needed is the implementation of a legal act that ensures the full independence of the judiciary from the Government, at both the national and local levels.

D Two General Directions of Reform

The aforementioned reforms cover a broad range of areas. The range would be even broader if the focus was on specific areas of the public sector. Yet two sets of suggestions keep coming back. The first relates to the need to correct inadequacies in the legal and administrative framework that are creating rent-seeking opportunities for some actors in society – the public sector employees and the political elite in power in particular. The second set of suggestions relates to the need to improve accountability and transparency in the Government and public administration, again in order to eliminate rent-seeking opportunities, to improve the information available both to decision makers and the public, and to make policymaking more effective. These two lines of reform, which happen to correspond to two key proximate causes in the diagnostic table above, are now examined in more detail.

• Curtailing inadequate laws and inadequate administrative organisation

Inadequate administrative organisation and inadequate rules and laws are key proximate causes of basic institutional weaknesses, weak state capacity especially. First, they generate simple inefficiency, incurring delays, extra costs, and sub-optimal allocations of resources. Second, they lead to rent-seeking, to the extent that individuals, firms, or other organisations are prompted to seek to bypass these delays, costs, and misallocations by paying bribes or exploiting political connections. And third, in some cases administrative capacity is so ineffective and the administrative organisation so inappropriate that the system may be bypassed altogether. All three phenomena are present in most Bangladeshi institutions, but they are particularly visible in the areas of land management and tax.

Inadequate organisation is observed in land management where the administrative structure is multi-layered, comprising two ministries (of land and law) and multiple sub-units, such as the Settlement Office, Assistant Commission, Sub-Registry Office, and Survey Tribunal. A lack of coherence and coordination between these entities exacerbates the capacity issues, which are particularly acute in land matters. The same complexity is observed in the management of public education, with three different ministries and other authorities managing public primary schools with different status, secular vs. religious, state- vs. NGO-run, experimental schools, etc. In several instances, this complex administrative organisation raises issues regarding the consistency of human resource management and the alignment of curricula. And in the tax system, a key institutional weakness is the lack of separation between tax policy and tax collection: the NBR is notionally responsible for both, although in practice, it devotes far more time and resources to collection.

Transforming the NBR into an independent agency with precise tax collection objectives, in which personnel would receive better incentives but would also be more tightly monitored than in the civil service, as is done in several countries,[26] might be a solution to make tax collection more effective. Providing autonomy for the Central Bank and involving civil society, at least in a consultative way, in the appointment of the governor would make the regulation of the banking sector both more effective and transparent. Likewise, depoliticising the appointment of the heads of major agencies like the

---

[26] This is the route that has been chosen by several countries in sub-Saharan Africa. On these integrated autonomous revenue agencies, see Junquera-Varela *et al.* (2019) and Fjeldstad (2007) for an early evaluation.

Anti-Corruption Commission, the CAG,[27] and the like would have the same effect in their respective areas. Also, in the health sector, ensuring transparency and accountability in public health spending, and reforming and restructuring the institutions through which health policies are implemented could improve public health service delivery. Together with regular evaluation involving reputable independent experts, such reforms would cost-effectively strengthen state capacity in many key institutional areas. It should also be noted that, in almost all areas, the administrative system would benefit from being streamlined so that clear chains of responsibility and accountability are established (avoiding inter-departmental conflicts), as well as from greatly simplifying Bangladesh's arcane and unwieldy administrative procedures.

The inadequacy of the legal framework is in part a historical legacy reflecting difficulties in reforming legislation that dates, in some cases, from the colonial or Pakistani periods. Some important reforms, such as the revision of land ceiling laws in 1972 and 1984, the Land Use Act of 2001, or the National Economic Zone Act of 2010, were never fully implemented, while others, such as the redistribution of *khas* land or the recognition of sharecroppers' rights, suffered from a lack of coordination, with long gaps between co-dependent pieces of legislation. Such political indecision and the resulting ambiguity of the laws are responsible for contemporary sources of corruption and rent-seeking. The lack of precision of the legal framework also characterises several other areas.

Strengthening the legal framework and the administrative organisation to make it simpler, more transparent, and more internally consistent are logical and important areas for reform. However, the most significant challenges facing reformers arise from the rent-seeking opportunities that are opened up by administrative weaknesses and legal loopholes. Probably the most serious obstacle to reform is overcoming the resistance of those who benefit from this situation, including those within the high echelons of land and tax administrations.

• Reducing opacity and unaccountability

As mentioned earlier, the institutional failures of Bangladesh are compounded by a general sense of opacity and a lack of accountability that cut across all areas. Institutions operate in a way that is fundamentally opaque. Although there is a high degree of public awareness of such problems as political patronage, rent-seeking, and corruption, there are few, if any, effective formal mechanisms that can provide detailed scrutiny of such practices and direct accountability for their consequences.

The most egregious form of unaccountability is found at the level of procedural democracy or, at least, democratic elections. In the new era of the

---

[27] It is not only the case that the CAG is appointed by the president of the republic, but also that, according to a constitutional amendment passed in 1983, 'the government can suspend all authorities and power given to the CAG.'

'dominant party regime', the lack of a functioning political opposition and the impotence of parliament as a way of checking the ruling party – the Awami League alliance won 289 of the 300 parliamentary seats in the 2018 Election– mean that the ultimate form of accountability – the ballot box – is null and void. Moreover, because there is no expectation that there will be any change in government for some time, there are even greater incentives for individuals and firms to form clientelist relationships with representatives of the ruling party. This adaptive behaviour only heightens the opacity of the deals environment and further reduces the efficiency of the state apparatus.

Recent reports by the Bangladesh office of Transparency International on the Office of the CAG (Roy, 2015) and the Anti-Corruption Commission, two agencies that should be in the forefront as regards ensuring accountability for, and the transparency of, government operations, confirm their ineffectiveness. The press release of the Transparency International report on the Office of the CAG thus says that it 'found unabated corruption in this constitutional body resulting from legal, institutional and organizational limitations',[28] a conclusion that perfectly illustrates and reinforces the present diagnostic.

Beyond the mechanisms of electoral or constitutional accountability are the organs of civil society – the media, NGOs, public discourse, and the Internet. Here Bangladesh is unusual, even exceptional, in that public debate is lively, well-informed, and critical. The presence of international organisations in the NGO sector adds an extra level of awareness. But such scrutiny does not, of course, translate into formal powers and there are limits to what can be said. Bangladesh does not compare well with other countries in terms of press freedom: it comes only 150th out of 180 countries in the 2018 ranking of the organisation Reporters without Borders, and it has remained close to that rank during at least the last five years.

However, it is within particular sectors that the most enduring forms of opacity may be found. The deals environment, as illustrated in the politics– business nexus through which business interest groups (especially within the RMG sector) secure concessions from politicians, has always been intrinsically opaque. Similarly, the low levels of compliance in the tax system, and the regulatory issues inside the banking sector, such as the lack of autonomy of the central bank and the high levels of NPLs, point to a business culture in which the deliberate avoidance of accountability is an essential feature. Similarly, administrative issues in land management and litigation compound the problems of opacity because inadequate capacities in the processing and recording of land transactions make it impossible to provide proper scrutiny.

This diagnostic about the lack of accountability and its consequences for the dysfunction of Bangladeshi institutions and, beyond this, its negative

---

[28] www.ti-bangladesh.org/beta3/index.php/en/activities/4528-tib-study-finds-corruption-in-the-office-of-comptroller-and-auditor-general

impact on development, is undoubtedly correct. It bears emphasis, however, that this dysfunction may be seen as relatively innocuous by a large part of public opinion. The fast growth enjoyed by the country over the last 30 years or so may have resulted in a kind of loose implicit social contract under which politicians in power are simply supposed to deliver a sufficient pace of growth to the citizenry, while, together with their allies in the economic elite, appropriating a large part of the benefits from growth through opaque and partly illicit operations. The situation is different for those who, in one way or another, are players in the political game. But the opposition is so weak today that public criticisms about governance failures are ineffective when the benefits from growth are not too unequally distributed and there is no perceived risk of a growth slowdown on the horizon. The challenge for the present government may precisely lie in the fact that inequality is rising and growth may be impeded unless substantial policy changes are adopted by the ruling elites.

In this sense, the sustained and rapid growth performance experienced in Bangladesh over the last decades may appear today as one of the deep factors behind the country's institutional weaknesses – as noted in the diagnostic table above. A key conclusion is thus that while unaccountability and opacity may be less immediately problematic in an era of sustained and rapid economic growth, serious concerns over the sustainability of Bangladesh's growth model mean that they cannot go on unchallenged.

IV CONCLUSION: ADDRESSING INSTITUTIONAL CHALLENGES AT A TIME OF AN UNPRECEDENTED SHOCK

At the time of writing, the COVID-19 pandemic and accompanying economic crisis continue to severely affect Bangladesh. In addition to emergency health-care expenditures, and the slowdown of the domestic economy as a result of lockdown measures, the crisis also threatens the global demand for RMG products, as well as the demand for migrant workers, already hurt by the impact of the fall in oil prices in the Gulf countries. If, as appears to be the case, the pandemic continues to disrupt the global economy, then we may expect significant structural changes that affect global trade flows. The risk that the key growth drivers of Bangladesh's development will be damaged, as repeatedly considered in this diagnostic, is thus materialising. The challenge today, rather than being one of maintaining the previous pace of development, is one of coping with a severe adverse shock, minimising its social cost, and triggering an economic rebound as soon as possible.

Indeed, insofar as one can draw any conclusions from Bangladesh's attempts to rise to the challenge of COVID-19, it is that addressing institutional weaknesses and the political economy conditions that constrain them seems a more urgent task than ever. This urgency manifests itself in two ways. First, and more obviously, in that institutional weaknesses, for example the health or social protection systems, limit the effectiveness of the shock response. Second, and in a subtler way, those political economy factors that have conditioned Bangladesh's industrial development in the past, and in particular have obstructed diversification and complexification, continue to influence the shock response in the present, and thus the path to recovery in the future.

Potentially, the consequences of neglecting these institutional issues are severe. It is quite possible – indeed, at the time of writing it seems likely – that Bangladesh will have experienced significant economic and social harm as a result of the pandemic, yet undergone little or no political or institutional reform along the way. Although the government has been widely criticised for a range of failures (see Section VI of Chapter 2), these criticisms have not led to any significant change in direction. The government remains largely unscathed – threatened neither by a resurgent opposition nor by any grassroots political movement. In part, this may simply reflect that the effective suppression of the opposition in previous years means that there is no articulate voice through which to channel such opinions into a genuine political alternative. Or, it may be that the experience of the pandemic – though severe – was less severe than some expectations or is perceived to be less severe than in other countries, especially India. Or, it may be that an acceptance that a crisis of such magnitude can only be addressed by the state generates a reluctance to be too critical, whatever the shortcomings of the response. Whatever the reason, the risk is that a major crisis has led to little institutional change when, in the argument of this diagnostic, it is just such change that is most needed and just those institutional issues which are the greatest impediment to development.

The point is not to reflect here on what should have been, or should be done to cope with the COVID-19 crisis and its economic consequences, but rather to say that the conclusions of our diagnostic exercise may turn out to be even more relevant in such a context than when only smooth changes in Bangladesh's economic environment were considered. Indeed, the manner in which the main institutional challenges uncovered in this chapter will be dealt with is likely to have a profound effect on the capacity of the state to surmount the present crisis, and on the subsequent development path.

The three critical institutional areas detected by our institutional diagnostic are as follows:

1. The supremacy of deals over formal industrial policy, and the risk of the dominant RMG manufacturing sector capturing industrial policy, thus preventing its own upgrading and the necessary diversification of manufactured export products.
2. The ineffectiveness of regulation in various key sectors of the economy, mostly due to damaging and, at times illegal, alliances between private interests and the senior management of regulation agencies.
3. Weak state capacity in practically all areas of public services, from tax collection to education, to land management, to the judiciary. The lack

of capacity is caused by both a lack of resources – partly stemming itself from weak capacity in tax collection – and skills but also by generalised rent-seeking behaviour on the part of civil servants.

For each of these weaknesses, various reforms were suggested earlier in this chapter or in previous chapters in this volume. A common feature of these reforms – summarised in the annex to this chapter – is that they generally require additional resources to rationalise and modernise the functioning of the government sector and regulatory agencies. From that point of view, an absolute priority should be given to making tax collection more effective by drastically modifying the way the government unit that is responsible for it presently works. The lack of resources to improve public services is common to all developing countries, but it is particularly acute in Bangladesh because of an abnormally low level of tax revenues.

The other common feature of the suggested reforms is that they refer either to improving the legal or administrative framework that governs economic operations in several areas, or the need to make economic management and policy more transparent and accountable. These appear as two complementary ways of curtailing the opportunities available to private and public agents to circumvent formal institutions and, often, to engage in corrupt dealings, instead of directly confronting such behaviour – something that is not really feasible today in Bangladesh precisely because of present institutional weaknesses. Streamlining the legal and administrative framework will eliminate many existing rent-seeking opportunities hidden in its frequent complexity and inadequacy. Promoting more transparency and accountability in public economic matters will likewise inflict a reputational cost on all those agents who deviate from formal rules once the latter are appropriately streamlined.

It seems unnecessary to come back to the multiple examples that have been given of such reforms in this volume. They are generally quite simple on paper, but the reality is of course much more complex. Any measure that simplifies the administrative framework to make it more corruption-proof by reducing rent-seeking opportunities in some area will most likely be opposed by all those who share the rent in that area. Digitalisation of records will be opposed by both tax officers and taxpayers, or by judiciary actors and politically influential intermediaries in land operations. Concerning transparency and accountability, on the other hand, members of the executive and top civil servants would probably say that such transparency already exists in Bangladesh, that development or industrial policy are made public and are debated in parliament, and that the auditing of major administrative units and public agencies is more or less regularly done. This is certainly true, yet only up to a point since the credibility of the corresponding statements and reports is in doubt. A development plan that commits to more than doubling the tax to GDP ratio in a decade or so is not credible, and it is still less so when no change is seen after a few years. An industrial policy that considers the promotion of 15 manufacturing export sectors is not more credible. Evidence of rigged auditing commissions abound so that publicised results are often dubious. So big is public defiance today that, even if some truly independent and autonomous commission peopled with experts untainted by corruption were appointed to audit a public agency, it is not even sure that its conclusions would be taken for granted. It would need several experiences of impartial and competent commissions able to release reports condemning the Government or senior civil servants before the credibility of the executive could be bolstered in the eyes of ordinary citizens. Each condemnation would harm the administration, but in the medium run, and assuming some longevity of the government embarked on these daring reforms, credibility would be established and would seriously reinforce state capacity.

In sum, undertaking reforms that diminish rent-seeking opportunities requires both political will and power manifested in clear priorities set by top authorities to improve institutions and governance.

Bangladesh's governments have shown such strength and determination on multiple occasions in the past, such as when they supported the RMG sector at an early stage, when they opted for rigorous macroeconomic policies, when they invested massively in power generation or liberalised imports and opened up the economy. Political power, political will, and policy wisdom were present in many key decisions as, for instance, in the case of the peaceful abolition of food rations on the grounds that they were a costly way of supporting the urban middle class rather than the poor; or in the case of the pioneering introduction of food and, later, conditional cash transfers to accelerate universal primary school enrolment. Are reforms aimed at eliminating notorious rent-seeking opportunities much more difficult to achieve? Is the present Government of Bangladesh in a situation to undertake them, and is it willing to carry them out?

That the Government is in the hands of a strongly dominant party ensures that political leverage for reforms does in principle exist. But at the same time, the weakness of the opposition is a disadvantage because the threat it can issue against a wavering government is weak. Up to now, moreover, the economy has done well, with solid growth benefiting most of the population, though more so those at the top of the income scale. On grounds of pure political strategy, reform incentives may thus seem to be rather weak. This may be the case. But the present diagnostic has emphasised the various risks that bear on the future rate of growth in Bangladesh. They have materialised today with the COVID-19 shock and its possible medium-run impact on growth. That the government's position does not seem insecure as a result of its handling of COVID-19 suggests that it may have been more skilful in political management than in addressing the entrenched and self-perpetuating institutional features which this diagnostic has sought to identify.

These arguments belong to political strategy. Social values in Bangladesh are strong: they are an asset that has often led to major achievements, particularly in relieving poverty. There is a strong demand for doing much more in social areas, especially at a time of a major sanitary and economic shock. This requires that institutions and the economy work better to free more resources and to allocate them where they are most needed. The vibrant civil society and its demand for a higher level of welfare, but also for more solidarity and more democracy, is another asset for Bangladesh's development. Decisive steps have been taken in these directions since the end of military regimes 30 years ago. For the sake of the society, but also for its own sake, it behoves the present government, possibly taking advantage of the COVID-19 shock, to push for further progress through courageous institutional reforms of the type advocated in this volume.

ANNEX 10.1 A LIST OF INSTITUTIONAL REFORMS SUGGESTED IN THE INSTITUTIONAL DIAGNOSTIC, BY THEME

Taxes and Budget

- The NBR as an agency with its own staff regulations and incentives, and with obligations regarding results.
- The appointment (and dismissal) of directors made by a commission comprising reputable independent experts, at least in consultative mode, alongside members of the executive.
- Simplification of the income tax.
- Unifying corporate tax rates and reducing the number of VAT rates.
- Modernisation of the tax collection process: digitalisation of records.
- Regular random auditing of taxpayers and annual reporting on tax-effectiveness (share collected of potential revenue).
- A High Commission on Public Revenues with reputable independent experts and Office of the CAG senior staff reporting annually on the effectiveness and efficiency of revenue collection.
- A ceiling on the number or amount of SROs.

Banking

- The appointment (and dismissal) of the governor and directors by a commission comprising reputable independent experts, at least in consultative mode, alongside members of the executive.
- The Central Bank as single regulatory authority for private and national commercial banks.
- Boards of directors comprising reputable independent experts.

- Full autonomy of the Central Bank in regulating the banking sector (key prudential ratio setting and monitoring, non-compliance penalties, bank licensing, bailout decisions, etc.).
- Re-examination of the Banking Company Act to make it consistent with central bank regulation and to make bank management more transparent.

Industrial Policy

- Full alignment of export incentives across manufacturing sectors.
- Transparency of industrial policy: statement or revision of objectives – including export diversification – and instruments, periodic evaluation of results.
- The creation of a High Commission on Manufacturing Development comprising reputable independent experts reporting annually on industrial policy achievements and challenges.

Sectoral Regulation (Including the Anti-corruption Commission and Comptroller and Auditor General along Transport, Power, Telecoms, Competition, etc.)

- Regulation of private sector activity to be operated by para-regulatory agencies, with derogatory staff rules in comparison with civil service, rather than ministries' directorates.
- Full autonomy of agencies: no restriction of competence in respective fields of activity – for example Anti-Corruption Commission should be free to investigate civil servants in cases of suspected corruption.
- Appointment (and dismissal) of directors of these agencies by commissions comprising reputable independent experts, at least in consultative mode, alongside members of the executive.
- Periodic evaluation of these agencies by *ad hoc* commissions comprising Office of the CAG senior staff and reputable independent experts.

Teacher Management and Other Public Sector Issues

- Upgrading of teacher pay and adjustment of career profiles.
- Rationalising the teacher recruitment process, curtailing corruption opportunities.
- Monitoring of teacher presence (lessons from the huge academic experimental literature).
- Regular assessment of learning achievement in terminal primary school grades on random samples of schools ('primary school pupil assessment').
- Streamlining school system management and supervision, including reducing responsibility overlaps.

Land Management

- Reviewing, amending, and streamlining land laws.
- Updating land survey methodology.
- Full land record digitalisation and a public land database.
- Streamlining administrative responsibilities on land matters.
- Alignment of land-related cross-sectoral policies.

Judiciary

- Separation of powers between the executive and the judiciary – including at local level.
- Digitalisation of court records.

References

Acemoglu, D., Johnson, S. and Robinson, J. (2001) 'The Colonial Origins of Comparative Development', *American Economic Review* 91, pp. 1369–1401.

Acemoglu, D., Johnson, S. and Robinson, J. (2005) 'Institutions as a Fundamental Cause of Long-run Growth', In: Aghion, P. and Durlauf, S. (eds.), *Handbook of Economic Growth*, Elsevier, Amsterdam, pp. 386–472.

Acemoglu, D. and Robinson, J. (2008) 'Persistence of Power, Elites and Institutions', *American Economic Review* 98, pp. 267–273.

Acemoglu, D. and Robinson, J. (2012) *Why Nations Fail: The Origins of Power, Prosperity and Poverty*, Crown Business, New York.

Acemoglu, D. and Zilibotti, F. (1997) 'Was Prometheus Unbound by Chance? Risk, Diversification, and Growth', *Journal of Political Economy* 105(4), pp. 709–751.

ADB (2014) *Assessing the Costs of Climate Change and Adaptation in South Asia*, Asian Development Bank, Mandaluyong City, Philippines.

ADB (2017) *Innovative Strategies for Accelerated Human Resource Development in South Asia: Teacher Professional Development with Special Focus on Bangladesh, Nepal, and Sri Lanka*, Asian Development Bank, Mandaluyong City, Philippines. www.adb.org/sites/default/files/publication/385091/teacher-professional-development-sa.pdf.

ADB-ILO (2016) *Bangladesh: Looking beyond Garments*, Asian Development Bank and ILO, Mandaluyong City, Philippines. www.adb.org/sites/default/files/publication/190589/ban-beyond-garments-eds.pdf.

Adhikary, B. K. (2006) 'Nonperforming Loans in the Banking Sector of Bangladesh: Realities and Challenges', *Bangladesh Institute of Bank Management* 4(26), pp. 75–95.

Adnan, S. (2013) 'Land Grabs and Primitive Accumulation in Deltaic Bangladesh: Interactions between Neoliberal Globalization, State Interventions, Power Relations and Peasant Resistance', *The Journal of Peasant Studies* 40(1), pp. 87–128.

African Tax Administration Forum (2014) *Block Management System for Enhancement of Revenue Collection*, African Tax Administration Forum, Pretoria, South Africa.

Afroze, S., Zohra, F. T. and Akter, S. (2019) 'Financial Crisis in the Banking Sector of Bangladesh and Auditors' Silence', *The Cost and Management* 47(06), pp. 4–11.

Agosin, M. (2007) 'Export Diversification and Growth in Emerging Economies', Working Paper wp233, Department of Economics, University of Chile.

Ahmad, A. and Haque, I. (2011) *Economic and Social Analysis of Primary Education in Bangladesh: A Study of BRAC Interventions and Mainstream Schools* (Vol. 48). BRAC Centre, Dhaka.

Ahmed, A. U. and Arends-Kuenning, M. (2006) 'Do Crowded Classrooms Crowd Out Learning? Evidence from the Food for Education Program in Bangladesh', *World Development* 34(4), pp. 665–684.

Ahmed, N. (2013) 'Improving Tax Compliance in Bangladesh: A Study of Value-Added Tax (VAT)', Working Paper Series No. 11/2013, Institute of Governance Studies, BRAC University.

Ahmed, N. (2019) 'Improving Tax Compliance in Bangladesh', draft policy note, BRAC Institute of Governance and Development (BIGD), BRAC University, Dhaka.

Ahmed, S. (ed.) (2013) *Leading Issues in Bangladesh Development*, University Press Limited, Dhaka.

Ahmed, S. (2015) *Growth with Equity: Contemporary Development Challenges of Bangladesh*, Bangladesh Institute of Bank Management, Dhaka.

Ahmed, S. (2017) *Evidence Based Policy Making in Bangladesh: Selected Case Studies*, Policy Research Institute of Bangladesh, Dhaka.

Ahmed, S. and McGillivray, M. (2015) 'Human Capital, Discrimination, and the Gender Wage Gap in Bangladesh', *World Development* 67, pp. 506–524.

Ahmed, S. and Sattar, Z. (2019) *Bangladesh Trade Policy for Growth and Employment: Collected Essays*, Policy Research Institute of Bangladesh, Dhaka.

Ahmed, S., Alamgir, M., Mujeri, M. and Rahman, A. (eds.) (2015) *Bangladesh Vision 2030: Framework for Economic Policy Making and Strategy in a Pluralistic Democracy*, Bangladesh Institute of Bank Management, Dhaka.

Ahmed, W. (2019) 'Capital Flight to Continue Unabated!', *The Financial Express*, 31 December 2019, https://thefinancialexpress.com.bd/views/capital-flight-to-continue-unabated-1577808211.

Akerlof, G. (1980) 'A Theory of Social Custom, of Which Unemployment May Be One Consequence', *The Quarterly Journal of Economics* 94(4), pp. 749–775.

Alam, M. (2000) 'Development of Primary Education in Bangladesh: The Ways Ahead', *Bangladesh Development Studies* 26(4), pp. 39–68.

Alamgir, M. (2019) 'Human Capital Development for Long Term Prosperity', Paper presented at the Bangladesh Economists' Forum Conference 2019.

Ali, A. and Ahmad, M. (2016) 'Analysis of the Barriers to Land Administration in Pakistan', presented in GSDI 15 World Conference.

Al-Marhubi, F. (2000) 'Export Diversification and Growth: An Empirical Investigation', *Applied Economics Letters* 7, pp. 559–562, http://dx.doi.org/10.1080/13504850050059005.

Altenburg, T. (2011) 'Industrial Policy in Developing Countries, Overview and Lessons from Seven Case Studies', Deutsche Institut für Entwicklungspolitik, Bonn.

Altinok, N., Angrist, N. and Patrinos, H. A. (2018) 'Global Dataset on Education Quality 1965–2015', Working Paper No. 8314, World Bank Policy Research, Washington, DC.

Amin, M. A. and Greenwood, J. (2018) 'The Examination System in Bangladesh and Its Impact on Curriculum, Students, Teachers and Society', *Language Testing in Asia* 8(4), https://doi.org/10.1186/s40468-018-0060-9.

Amirapu, A., Asadullah, N. and Wahhaj, Z. (2020) 'The Threat to Female Adolescent Development from Covid-19' EDI Covid-19 Essay AAW-Covid-19-Policy-Final-14.09.2020.pdf (opml.co.uk).

Amiti, M. and Konigs, J. (2017) 'Trade Liberalization, Intermediate Inputs, and Productivity: Evidence from Indonesia', *American Economic Review* 89(3), pp. 605–618.

André, C. and Platteau, J. P. (1998) 'Land Relations under Unbearable Stress: Rwanda Caught in the Malthusian Trap', *Journal of Economic Behavior and Organization* 34(1), pp. 1–47.

Anker, R. (2011) *Estimating a Living Wage: A Methodological Review*, ILO, Geneva.

Annual Status of Education Report Centre (2014) Annual Status of Education Report (Rural) 2013, Provisional 15 January 2014. Annual Status of Education Report Centre, http://img.asercentre.org/docs/Publications/ASER%20Reports/ASER_2013/ASER2013_report%20sections/aser2013fullreportenglish.pdf.

Asadullah, M. N. (2006) 'Returns to Education in Bangladesh', *Education Economics* 14(4), pp. 453–468.

Asadullah, M. N. (2016) 'Do Pro-Poor Schools Reach Out to the Poor? Location Choice of BRAC and ROSC Schools in Bangladesh', IZA Discussion Paper No. 10326, http://ftp.iza.org/dp10326.pdf.

Asadullah, M. N. and Chaudhury, N. (2015) 'The Dissonance between Schooling and Learning: Evidence from Rural Bangladesh', *Comparative Education Review* 59(3), pp. 447–472.

Asadullah, M. N. and Rahman, S. (2009) 'Farm Productivity and Efficiency in Rural Bangladesh: The Role of Education Revisited', *Applied Economics* 41(1), pp. 17–33.

Asadullah, M. N., Savoia, A. and Mahmud, W. (2014) 'Paths to Development: Is There a Bangladesh Surprise?' *World Development* 62, pp. 138–154.

Aslam, A., Novta, N. and Rodrigues-Bastos, F. (2017) 'Calculating Trade in Value-Added', IMF WP 17/178, Washington, DC.

Atahar, S. A. (2013) 'Development Project, Land Acquisition and Resettlement in Bangladesh: A Quest for Well Formulated National Resettlement and Rehabilitation Policy', *International Journal of Humanities and Social Science* 3(7), www.ijhssnet.com/journals/Vol_3_No_7_April_2013/33.pdf.

Avillez, R. (2012) 'Sectoral Contributions to Labour Productivity Growth: Does the Choice of Decomposition Formula Matter?', *No. 2012–09, CSLS Research Reports*, Centre for the Study of Living Standards.

Babi, N. N. (2020) 'Challenges of Export Growth and Diversification in Bangladesh: The Case of Bonded Warehouse Modernization', presentation made at the Fifth SANEM Annual Economists Conference, 2–3 February 2020, Dhaka.

Bahl, R., Linn, J. and Wetzel, D. (2013) *Financing Metropolitan Governments in Developing Countries*, Lincoln Institute of Land Policy, Cambridge, MA.

Baland, J-M, Bourguignon, F., Platteau, J-P. and Verdier, T. (2020) 'Economic Development and Institutions: An Introduction', In: Baland, J-M, Bourguignon, F., Platteau, J-P. and Verdier, T. (eds.), *Handbook of Development and Institutions*, Princeton University Press, Princeton, pp. 1–20.

Banerjee, A., Karlan, D. and Zinman, J. (2015) 'Six Randomized Evaluations of Microcredit: Introduction and Further Steps', *American Economic Journal: Applied Economics* 7(1), pp. 1–21.

Bangladesh Bureau of Educational Information and Statistics (2018) *Bangladesh Education Statistics 2018*, Bangladesh Bureau of Educational Information and Statistics, Dhaka.

Bangladesh Bureau of Statistics (2017) *Bangladesh Economic Review*, Bangladesh Bureau of Statistics, Government of Bangladesh, Dhaka.

Bangladesh Bureau of Statistics (2018) *The Labour Force Survey 2016–17*, Bangladesh Bureau of Statistics, Ministry of Planning, Government of Bangladesh, Dhaka.

Bangladesh Institute of Development Studies (2019) *Baseline Satisfaction Survey of College Education Development Project*, Bangladesh Institute of Development Studies, Dhaka.

Bangladesh Public Service Commission, (2019) 'BCS Examination'. www.bpsc.gov.bd/site/page/4bc95017-18d6-412b-8c4f-76d3e1599d8e/%E0%A6%AC%E0%A6%BF%E0%A6%B8%E0%A6%BF%E0%A6%8F%E0%A6%B8-%E0%A6%AA%E0%A6%B0%E0%A7%80%E0%A6%95%E0%A7%8D%E0%A6%B7%E0%A6%BE

Banglapedia (2014) *Banglapedia: The National Encyclopedia of Bangladesh* (online ed.), Asiatic Society of Bangladesh, Dhaka, http://en.banglapedia.org/index.php?title=Main_Page.

Barajas, A., Beck, T., Dabla-Norris, E. and Reza Yousefi, S. (2013) 'Too Cold, Too Hot, or Just Right? Assessing Financial Sector Development across the Globe', IMF Working Paper 13/81, International Monetary Fund.

Barkat, A. (2005) 'The Share of the Poor in the Khas Land of Bangladesh; Problems and Proposals for Overcoming Those', In: *Land Rights and Poverty Alleviation*, Bangladesh Legal Aid and Services Trust, Dhaka, pp. 16–28.

Barkat, A. and Roy, P. K. (2004) *Political Economy of Land Litigation in Bangladesh: A Case of Colossal National Wastage* 1(4), Association for Land Reform and Development.

Barkat, A., Zaman, S. and Raihan, S. (2001) 'Political Economy of *Khas* Land in Bangladesh', Association for Land Reform and Development (ALRD), Dhaka.

Barra, C. and Zotti, R. (2014) 'Handling Negative Data Using Data Envelopment Analysis: A Directional Distance Approach Applied to Higher Education', MPRA Paper No. 55570, Munich Personal RePEc Archive.

Barro, R. and Lee, J.-W. (2013) 'A New Data Set of Educational Attainment in the World, 1950–2010', *Journal of Development Economics* 104, 184–198.

Battaile, B., Richard, C. and Harun, O. (2014) 'Services, Inequality, and the Dutch Disease', Policy Research Working Paper No. WPS 6966, World Bank Group, Washington, DC.

Beck, T. (2008) 'Bank Competition and Financial Stability: Friends or Foes?' Policy, Research Working Paper no. WPS 4656, World Bank, Washington, DC, pp. 448–476.

Beck, T. (2018) 'What Drives Financial Sector Development? Policies, Politics and History', In: Beck, T. and Levine, R. (eds.), *Handbook of Finance and Development*, Edward Elgar, Cheltenham, UK, pp. 448–476.

Beck, T. and Rahman, M. H. (2006) 'Creating a More Efficient Financial System: Challenges for Bangladesh', World Bank Policy Research Working Paper 3938, World Bank, Washington, DC.

Beck, T., Cull, R. and Jerome, A. (2005) 'Bank Privatization and Performance: Empirical Evidence from Nigeria', *Journal of Banking and Finance* 29, pp. 2355–2379.

Beck, T., Degryse, H. and Kneer, C. (2014) 'Is More Finance Better? Disentangling Intermediation and Size Effects of Financial Systems', *Journal of Financial Stability* 10, p. 5064.

Berglof, E. and von Thadden, E. (1999) 'The Changing Corporate Governance Paradigm: Implications for Developing and Transition Economies', In: Pleskovic, B. and Stiglitz, J.E. (eds.), *Annual World Bank Conference on Development Economics*, The World Bank, Washington, DC, pp. 135–162.

Berik, G. and Rodgers, M. (2010) 'Options for Enforcing Labour Standards: Lessons from Bangladesh and Cambodia', *Journal of International Development* 22, pp. 56–85.

Bertinelli, L., Salins, V. and Strobl, E. (2006) 'Export Diversification and Price Uncertainty in Sub-Saharan Africa and Other Developing Countries: A Portfolio Theory Approach', mimeo, Universite de Luxembourg, Universite de Paris X, Ecolé Polytechnique.

Bertocci, P. J. (1981) 'The Bangladesh Liberation Movement: Role of Different Parties and Groups', *Dacca University Studies A* 35, pp. 45–60.

Besley, T. and Persson, T. (2009) 'The Origins of State Capacity: Property Rights, Taxation, and Politics', *American Economic Review* 99(4), pp. 1218–1244.

Besley, T. and Persson, T. (2011) 'Public Finance and Development', draft chapter for *Handbook of Public Economics* [Accessed on 15 October 2019].

Besley, T. and Persson, T. (2014) 'Why Do Developing Countries Tax So Little?', *Journal of Economic Perspectives* 28(4), pp. 99–120.

BEZA (2019) 'Annual Report', Bangladesh Economic Zones Authority, Government of Bangladesh, Dhaka.

Bhuiyan, M. (2012) 'Present Status of Garments Workers in Bangladesh: An Analysis', *Journal of Business and Management (IOSRJBM)* 3, pp. 38–44.

Bhuyan, A. R. and Rashid, M.A. (1993) 'Trade Regimes and Industrial Growth: A Case Study of Bangladesh', Bureau of Economic Research, Dhaka University and International Centre for Economic Growth, San Francisco, USA.

BIGD (2021a) 'Livelihoods, Coping and Recovery during COVID-19 Crisis: Evidence from Three Rounds of PPRC-BIGD Survey', Brac Institute of Governance and Development, Dhaka.

BIGD (2021b) 'State of Governance in Bangladesh 2020–2021: Governing COVID-19 in Bangladesh – Realities and Reflections to Build Forward Better', Brac Institute of Governance and Development, Dhaka.

Bird, R. M. (2012) 'Taxation and Development: What Have We Learned from Fifty Years of Research?', International Center for Public Policy Working Paper 12–02, Andrew Young School of Policy Studies, Georgia State University.

Bird, R. M. (2015) 'Improving Tax Administration in Developing Countries', *Journal of Tax Administration* 1(1), pp. 23–45.

Bird, R. M. and Bahl, R. W. (2008) 'Tax Policy in Developing Countries: Looking Back and Forward', Working Paper Series III B Paper No. 13, Institute for International Business.

Bird, R. M. and Zolt, E. M. (2003) 'Introduction to the Tax Policy Design and Development', Draft Prepared for a Course on Practical Issues of Tax Policy in Developing Countries, World Bank, Washington, DC.

Bird, R.M., Martinez-Vazquez, J. and Torgler, B (2008) 'Tax Effort in Developing Countries and High Income Countries: The Impact of Corruption, Voice and Accountability', *Economic Analysis and Policy* 38(1), pp. 55–71.

Bird, R. M., Martinez-Vazquez, J. and Torgler, B. (2014) 'Social Institutions and Tax Effort in Developing Countries', *Annals of Economics and Finance* 15(1), pp. 185–230.

Biswas, Z. I. (2012) 'Do We Have an Independent Judiciary?', *Forum* 6(09), *The Daily Star*.

Blanchard, E. and Hakobyan, S. (2015) 'The US Generalised System of Preferences in Principle and Practice', *The World Economy* 38(3), pp. 399–424.

Bleaney, M. l. and Greenaway, D. (2001) 'The Impact of Terms of Trade and Real Exchange Rate Volatility on Investment and Growth in Sub-Saharan Africa', *Journal of Development Economics* 65(2), pp. 491–500.

Bold, T. and Svensson, J. (2016) 'Education, Institutions and Economic Development', https://edi.opml.co.uk/wpcms/wp-content/uploads/2017/06/EDI-PF-PAPER-8.2-Svensson.pdf.

BRAC (2018) 'Annual Report 2018', BRAC, Dhaka.

Brautigam, D., Fjeldstad, O-H. and Moore, M. (eds.) (2008) *Taxation and State Building in Developing Countries*, Cambridge University Press, Cambridge.

Brunelin, S., de Melo, J. and Portugal-Perez, A. (2019) 'How Much Market Access ? A Case Study of Jordan's Exports to the EU', *World Trade Review* 18(3), pp. 431–449.

Burki, S. and Perry, G. (1998) *Beyond the Washington Consensus: Institutions Matter*, World Bank, Washington, DC.

Cadot, O., Carrère, C. and Strauss-Kahn, V. (2011) 'Export Diversification: What's behind the Hump?', *Review of Economics and Statistics* 93(2).

CARE (2003) 'Land Policy and Administration in Bangladesh: A Literature Review', CARE SDU Reports and Studies, CARE Bangladesh, Dhaka.

Cavallo, E. and Daudé, C. (2008) 'Public Investment in Developing Countries: A Blessing or a Curse?', Econstor Working Paper No. 648.

Chang, H-J. and Andreoni, A. (2020) Industrial Policy in the 21st Century, Development and Change, forthcoming.

Chaudhury, N., Hammer, J., Kremer, M., Mularidharan, K. and Rogers, H. (2004) 'Roll Call: Teacher Absence in Bangladesh', World Bank, Washington, DC, USA.

Chêne, M. (2016) 'Literature Review: The Use of ICTs in the Fight against Corruption', Transparency International, www.u4.no/publications/literature-review-the-use-of-icts-in-the-fight-against-corruption.

Chowdhury, A. (2000) 'Politics, Society and Financial Sector Reform in Bangladesh', Working Paper No. 191, UNU World Institute for Development Economic Research, www.wider.unu.edu/sites/default/files/wp2000-191.pdf.

Chowdhury, S. and Panday, P. K. (2018) *Strengthening Local Governance in Bangladesh: Reforms, Participation and Accountability*, Springer International Publishing, Singapore.

Cochrane, S. H. (1979) 'Fertility and Education: What Do We Really Know?' World Bank staff occasional papers no. OCP 26, The Johns Hopkins University Press, Baltimore, USA.

Coelli, T. and Perelman, S. (1999) 'A Comparison of Parametric and Non-parametric Distance Functions: With Application to European Railways', *European Journal of Operational Research* 117(2), pp. 326–339.

Cookson, F. (2017) 'The Evolution of Bangladesh Readymade Garment Sector', https://thefinancialexpress.com.bd/special-issues/rmg-textile/the-evolution-of-bangladesh-readymade-garment-sector-1506539226.

Dahlberg, S., Holmberg, S., Rothstein, B., Alvarado Pachon, N. and Axelsson, S. (2020) 'The Quality of Government Basic Dataset', version Jan 20, University of Gothenburg: The Quality of Government Institute, www.qog.pol.gu.se. DOI:10.18157/qogbasjan20.

D'Ambrogio, E. (2014) 'Workers' Conditions in the Textile and Clothing Sector: Just an Asian Affair? Issues at Stake after the Rana Plaza Tragedy', European Parliamentary Research Service.

Dawe, D. (1996) 'A New Look at the Effects of Export Instability on Investment and Growth', *World Development* 24(12), pp. 1905–1914.

de Ferranti, D., Perry, G. E., Lederman, D. and Maloney, W. F. (2002) 'From Natural Resources to Knowledge Economy', World Bank Latin American and Caribbean Studies, World Bank, Washington, DC.

de Piñeres, S. and Ferrantino, M. J. (2000) *Export Dynamics and Economic Growth in Latin America: A Comparative Perspective*, Ashgate Publishing Ltd, Farnham.

de Ree, J., Muralidharan, K., Pradhan, M., Rogers, H.F., (2015). Double for Nothing: Experimental Evidence on the Impact of an Unconditional Teacher Salary Increase on Student Performance in Indonesia. National Bureau of Economic Research Working Paper 21806.

Debnath, R. M. and Shankar, R. (2008) 'Measuring Performance of Indian Banks: An Application Data Envelopment Analysis', *International Journal of Business Performance Management* 10(1), pp. 57–85.

Deininger, K. (2008). A Strategy for Improving Land Administration in India. Agricultural and Rural Development Notes; No. 33. World Bank, Washington, DC. © World Bank. https://openknowledge.worldbank.org/handle/10986/9534 License: CC BY 3.0 IGO.

Devarajan, S. and Johnson, S. (2008) 'Two Comments on "Governance Indicators: Where Are We, Where Should We Be Going" by Daniel Kaufmann and Aart Kraay', *World Bank Research Observer* 23, pp. 31–36.

Dey, B. K. (2019) 'Managing Nonperforming Loans in Bangladesh', ADB Briefs No. 116, ADB, Manila.

di Giovanni, J. and Levchenko, A. A. (2006) 'Trade Openness and Volatility', Centro Studi Luca d'Agliano Development Studies Working Paper No. 219, Centro Studi Luca d'Agliano, available at: https://ssrn.com/abstract=927300 or http://dx.doi.org/10.2139/ssrn.927300.

Dixit, A. (2017) 'Fighting Corruption by Altering Equilibrium in an Assurance Game', preliminary draft, www.princeton.edu/~dixitak/home/AssurAntiCorr.pdf.

Djankov, S., La Porta, R., Lopez-de-Silanes, F. and Shleifer, A. (2002) 'The Regulation of Entry', *The Quarterly Journal of Economics* 117(1), pp. 1–37.

Dom, R. and Miller, M. (2018) *Reforming Tax Systems in the Developing World. What Can We Learn from the Past?* Overseas Development Institute, London.

DPE (2013) 'Bangladesh Primary Education Stipends: A Qualitative Assessment', Directorate of Primary Education, Power and Participation Research Centre, and UNICEF Bangladesh, https://reliefweb.int/sites/reliefweb.int/files/resources/Bangladesh_Primary_Education_Stipends_survey.pdf.

DPE (2017) 'Annual Sector Performance Report 2017', Directorate of Primary Education, Dhaka.

DPE (2018a) 'The National Student Assessment Report 2017', Directorate of Primary Education, Dhaka.

DPE (2018b) 'Annual Primary School Census 2018', Directorate of Primary Education, Dhaka.

Duflo, E., Hanna, R. and Ryan, S. (2012) 'Incentives Work: Getting Teachers To Come To School'. *American Economic Review* 102(4), pp. 1241–1278.

EC (2019) 'EU Preferential Rules of Origin', Commission Staff Working Document, European Commission, https://trade.ec.europa.eu/doclib/docs/2019/may/tradoc_157882.pdf.

Education Commission (2016) "The Learning Generation: Investing in Education for a Changing World," A report by International Commission on Financing Global Education Opportunity. https://report.educationcommission.org/wp-content/uploads/2016/09/Learning_Generation_Full_Report.pdf

Engerman, S. L. and Sokoloff, K. L. (1997) 'Factor Endowments, Institutions, and Differential Paths of Growth among New World Economies: A View from Economic Historians of the United States,' In: Haber, S. (eds.), *How Latin America Fell Behind*. Stanford University Press, Stanford, pp. 260–304.

Faini, R., de Melo, J. and Takacs, W. (1992) 'The Effects of EC-92 on the Multi-Fibre Arrangement', *European Economic Review* 36, pp. 527–538.

Faini, R., de Melo, J. and Takacs, W. (1993) 'A Primer on the MFA Maze', Policy, Research Working Paper No. WPS 1088 Trade Policy, World Bank, World Bank, Washington, DC, http://documents.worldbank.org/curated/en/832331468782114101/A-primer-on-the-MFA-maze.

Farrell, M. J. (1957) 'The Measurement of Productive Efficiency', *Journal of the Royal Statistical Society*, 120, pp. 253–290.

Feder, G. (1983) 'On Exports and Economic Growth', *Journal of Developing Economics* 12, pp. 59–73.

Feenstra, R. C. and Kee, H. L. (2004) 'Export Variety and Country Productivity', World Bank Policy Research Working Paper No. 3412, available at: https://ssrn.com/abstract=625289.

Feldman, S. and Geisler, C. (2011) 'Land Grabbing in Bangladesh: In-Situ Displacement of Peasant Holdings', Paper presented at the International Conference on Global Land Grabbing, 6–8 April 2011, www.future-agricultures.org/wp-content/uploads/pdf-archive/Shelley%20Feldman%20and%20Charles%20Geisler.pdf.

Feldman, S. and Geisler, C. (2012) 'Land Expropriation and Displacement in Bangladesh', *The Journal of Peasant Studies* 39, pp. 971–993.

Fernandes, A. M. (2006) 'Firm Productivity in Bangladesh Manufacturing Industries', Policy Research Working Paper Series No. WPS 3988, World Bank, Washington, DC, USA.

Fjeldstad, O.-H. (2007) 'Revenue Authorities: Experiences from Experiences from Sub-Saharan Africa', presentation at Conference on Poverty Policies and Budgetary Processes, Windhoek, 5–6 July 2007, www.cmi.no/publications/file/2725-revenue-authorities.pdf.

Food and Agriculture Organization (2013) *FAOSTAT Statistical Database*, Food and Agriculture Organization of the United Nations.

Freund, C. and Pierola, D. (2011) 'Export Surges', *Journal of Development Economics* 97(2), pp. 387–395.

Fry, M. J. (1988) *Money, Interest and Banking in Economic Development*, Johns Hopkins University Press, Baltimore and London.

Ge, W. (1999) 'Special Economic Zones and the Opening of the Chinese Economy: Some Lessons for Economic Liberalization', *World Development* 27(7), pp. 1267–1285.

General Economics Division of the Planning Commission of Bangladesh (2017) 'SDGs Needs Assessment and Financing Strategy: Bangladesh Perspective', General Economics Division of the Planning Commission of Bangladesh.

Ghatak, M. and Mookherjee, D. (2013) 'Land Acquisition for Industrialization and Compensation of Displaced Farmers', *Journal of Development Economics* 110, pp. 303–312, ISSN 0304-3878, https://doi.org/10.1016/j.jdeveco.2013.01.001.

Ghatak, M., Mitra, S., Mookherjee, D. and Nath, A. (2012) 'Land Acquisition and Compensation in Singur: What Really Happened?' CAGE Online Working Paper Series 121, Competitive Advantage in the Global Economy.

Ghosh, A. and Ostry, J. (1994) 'Export Instability and the External Balance in Developing Countries', *IMF Staff Papers* 41(2), pp. 214–235.

Ghosh, S. (1986) 'Constitutional Changes in Bangladesh: Process of Political Development', *India Quarterly* 42(4), pp. 391–404.

Ghura, D. (1998) 'Tax Revenue in Sub-Saharan Africa: Effects of Economic Policies and Corruption', IMF Working Paper No. 98/135, IMF, Washington, DC.

Gianetti, M. and Ongena, S. (2009) 'Financial Integration and Firm Performance: Evidence from Foreign Bank Entry in Emerging Markets', *Review of Finance* 13, pp. 181–223.

Global Financial Integrity (2020) 'Trade-Related Illicit Financial Flows in 135 Developing Countries: 2008–2017', Global Financial Integrity Report 2020, https://gfintegrity.org/reports/.

Goldberg, P., Khandewal, A., Pavcnik, N. and Topalova, P. (2010) 'Imported Intermediate Inputs, and Domestic Product Growth: Evidence from India', *Quarterly Journal of Economics* 125(4), pp. 1727–1767.

Gordon, R. and Li, W. (2005) 'Tax Structure in Developing Countries: Many Puzzles and a Possible Explanation', NBER Working Paper 11267, National Bureau of Economic Research (NBER), Washington, DC.

Government of Bangladesh (2019a) *Perspective Plan of Bangladesh 2021–2041: Rapid Inclusive and Sustainable Growth for Shared Prosperity*, revised draft, 29 May 2019, General Economics Division, Planning Commission, Government of Bangladesh, Dhaka.

Government of Bangladesh (2019b) *Bangladesh on a Pathway to Prosperity: 'Time Is Ours: Time for Bangladesh'*, Budget Speech 2019-20, 13 June 2019, Ministry of Finance, Government of Bangladesh, Dhaka.

Greenland, D. J., Gregory, P. J., Nye, P. H. and Barbier, E. B. (1997) 'The Economic Determinants of Land Degradation in Developing Countries', *Philosophical Transactions of the Royal Society of London. Series B: Biological Sciences* 352, http://doi.org/10.1098/rstb.1997.0068.

Gupta, A. S. (2007) 'Determinants of Tax Revenue Efforts in Developing Countries', IMF Working Paper No. WP/07/184, IMF, Washington, DC.

Gylfason, T. (2004) 'Natural Resources and Economic Growth: From Dependence to Diversification', CEPR Discussion Paper No. 4804, available at: https://ssrn.com/abstract=697881.

Hahn, Y., Islam, A., Nuzhat, K., Smyth, R. and Yang, H. S. (2018) 'Education, Marriage, and Fertility: Long-Term Evidence from A Female Stipend Program in Bangladesh', *Economic Development and Cultural Change* 66(2), pp. 383–415.

Haider, A. A. (2019) 'Checking Capital Flight before It Is Too Late', *The Daily Star*, 6 February 2019, www.thedailystar.net/opinion/economics/news/checking-capital-flight-it-too-late-1697959.

Halim, M. A. (2008). *Legal System in Bangladesh*, CCB Foundation, Dhaka.

Hamann, R. (2018) 'Developing Countries Need to Wake Up to the Risks of New Technologies', University of Cape Town, https://theconversation.com/developing-countries-need-to-wake-up-to-the-risks-of-new-technologies-87213.

Haq, M. N. and Islam, M. S. (2005) 'Teacher Motivation in Bangladesh: A Situation Analysis', www.tdi-bd.com/aricles_presentations/Teacher%20Motivation%20Study%20report.pdf.

Haque, S. T. (2013) 'Effect of Public and Private Investment on Economic Growth in Bangladesh: An Econometric Analysis', Research Study Series No. FDRS 05/2013, Ministry of Finance, Government of Bangladesh.

Harber, S. (ed.) (1997) *How Latin America Fell Behind: Essays on the Economic Histories of Brazil and Mexico, 1800–1914*, Stanford University Press, Stanford, CA, USA.

Hasan, M. (2020) 'Single Digit Rate on Loans May Decrease Banks' Profitability', Dhaka Tribune, 20 January 2020, www.dhakatribune.com/business/2020/01/20/single-digit-rate-on-loans-may-decrease-banks-profitability.

Hasan, M. I. (2017) 'Land Administration in Bangladesh: Problems and Analytical Approach to Solution', *International Journal of Law* 3(2), pp. 44–49.

Hassan, M. (2001) 'Demand for Second Generation Reform: The Case of Bangladesh', doctoral dissertation, University of London, UK.

Hassan, M. (2013) 'Political Settlement Dynamics in a Limited-Access Order: The Case of Bangladesh', ESID Working Paper No. 23, Manchester University, UK.

Hassan, M. and Nazneen, S. (2017) 'Violence and Breakdown of the Political Settlement: An Uncertain Future for Bangladesh', *Conflict Security and Development* 17(3), pp. 205–223.

Hassan, M. and Prichard, W. (2014) 'The Political Economy of Tax Reform in Bangladesh: Political Settlements, Informal Institutions and the Negotiation of Reform', Working Paper Series No. 21, BRAC Institute of Governance and Development, BRAC University, Dhaka.

Hassan, M. and Raihan, S. (2018) 'Navigating the Deals World: The Politics of Economic Growth in Bangladesh', In: Pritchett, L., Sen, K. and Werker, E. (eds.), *Deals and Development: The Political Dynamics of Growth Episodes*, Oxford University Press, pp. 96–128.

Hausman, R., Hwang, J. and Rodrik, D. (2007) 'What You Export Matters', *Journal of Economic Growth* 12(1), pp. 1–25.

Hausmann, R. and Klinger, B. (2006) 'Structural Transformation and Patterns of Comparative Advantage in the Product Space', KSG Working Paper No. RWP06-041, CID Working Paper No. 128, available at: https://ssrn.com/abstract=939646 or http://dx.doi.org/10.2139/ssrn.939646.

Hausmann, R. and Rodrik, D. (2003) 'Economic Development as Self-discovery', *Journal of Development Economics* 72(2), pp. 603–633.

Hausmann, R., Hwang, J. and Rodrik, D. (2007) 'What You Export Matters', *Journal of Economic Growth* 12(1), pp. 1–25.

Hausmann, R., Rodrik, D. and Velasco, A. (2005) Growth Diagnostics, The Growth Lab, Harvard University, www.tinyurl.com/y3y5zksu.

Hausmann, R., Rodrik, D. and Velascom, A. (2005) *Growth Diagnostics*, The John F. Kennedy School of Government, Harvard University, Massachusetts.

Hausmann, R., Rodrik, D. and Velasco, A. (2008) 'Growth Diagnostics', In: Serra, N. and Stiglitz, J. E. (eds.), *The Washington Consensus Reconsidered: Towards a New Global Governance*, Oxford University Press, Oxford, pp. 324–355.

Heath, R. and Mobarak, A. M. (2015) 'Manufacturing Growth and the Lives of Bangladeshi Women', *Journal of Development Economics* 115, pp. 1–15.

Hidalgo, C. and Hausmann, R. (2009) 'The Building Blocks of Economic Complexity', *Proceedings of the National Academy of Sciences of the United States of America* 106 (26), pp. 10570–10575.

Hidalgo, C., Klinger, B., Barabàsi, A.-L. and Hausmann, R. (2007) 'The Product Space Conditions the Development of Nations', *Science, New Series* 317 (5837), pp. 482–487.

Hoff, K. (2003) 'Paths of Institutional Development: A View from History', *World Bank Research Observer*.

Hossain, M. (1986) 'A Note on the Trend of Landlessness in Bangladesh', *The Bangladesh Development Studies* 14(2), pp. 93–100.

Hossain, M. (2005) 'On the IMF Stabilization Program in Bangladesh', *The Empirical Economics Letters* 4(4), pp. 247–260.

Hossain, M. (2012) 'Financial Reforms and Persistently High Bank Interest Spreads in Bangladesh: Pitfalls in Institutional Development?' *Journal of Asian Economics* 23, pp. 395–408.

Hossain, M. (2017a) 'Improving Land Administration and Management', in *7th Five Year Plan Background Papers Vol. 5, Governance, Gender and Urban Development*, General Economics Division, Ministry of Planning, Bangladesh.

Hossain, N. (2017b) *The Aid Lab: Understanding Bangladesh's Unexpected Success*, Oxford University Press, Oxford.

Hossain, N., Hassan, M. M., Rahman, M. A., Ali, K. S. and Islam, M. S. (2019) 'The Politics of Learning Reforms in Bangladesh', In: Hickey, S. and Hossain, N. (eds.), *The Politics of Education in Developing Countries from Schooling to Learning*, Published by Oxford Scholarship Online. DOI: 10.1093/oso/9780198835684.001.0001.

Hossain, N., Hassan, M., Rahman, M., Ali, K. and Islam, M. (2017). The Problem with Teachers: The Political Settlement and Education Quality Reforms in Bangladesh. ESID Working Paper No. 86. Manchester: Effective States and Inclusive Development Research Centre, The University of Manchester.

Howes, M. (2003) 'Land Policy and Administration in Bangladesh: A Literature Review', CARE Rural Livelihoods Programme, Dhaka, www.carebd.org/Land%20 Policy%20and%20Administration.pdf.

Huda, A. K. M. S. (1997) *The Constitution of Bangladesh*, 1st ed., Vol. II, Rita Court, Chittagong.

Huda, N. (2017) 'Independent Judiciary a Must for Democracy', *The Daily Star*, 27 March 2017, www.thedailystar.net/opinion/straight-line/independent-judiciary-must-democracy-1381690.

Hussain, Z. (2020) 'How Well Founded Are the Devaluation Worries?', *The Daily Star*, 22 March 2020, www.thedailystar.net/business/news/how-well-founded-are-the-devaluation-worries-1850011.

Hwang, J. (2006) *Introduction of New Goods, Convergence and Growth*, mimeo, Department of Economics, Harvard University.

IFC (2020) 'Bangladesh's Journey to Middle Income Status: Role of the Private Sector', IFC, Washington, DC.

IGS (2011) 'The State of Governance in Bangladesh 2010–2011', IGS, BRAC University, Dhaka.

ILO (2018) 'Global Wage Report 2018', International Labour Organization, Geneva.

ILO-SANEM (2018) 'Baseline Study of the Improving Working Conditions in the Bangladesh Ready-Made Garment Sector Programme', ILO, Dhaka.

Imberman, S. A. (2015) 'How Effective Are Financial Incentives for Teachers?' *IZA World of Labor*, https://wol.iza.org/uploads/articles/158/pdfs/how-effective-are-financial-incentives-for-teachers.pdf.

IMF (2014) 'Sustaining Long-Run Growth and Macroeconomic Stability in Low-Income Countries – The Role of Structural Transformation and Diversification – Background Notes', Policy Paper, IMF.

IMF (2017) 'Europe: Europe Hitting Its Stride, Regional Economic Outlook, November 2017', International Monetary Fund, pp. xviii, pp. 40, 70, www.imf.org/~/media/Files/Publications/REO/EUR/2017/November/eur-booked-print.ashx?la=en.

IMF (2020) 'Bangladesh Economic and Financial Indicators', IMF, Washington, DC.

Iqbal, M. J., Vankatesh, S., Jongwanich, J. and Badir, Y. (2012) 'Banking Sector's Performance in Bangladesh – An Application of Selected CAMELS Ratio', Asian Institute of Technology, School of Management, Thailand.

Isham, J., Woolcock, M., Pritchett, L. and Busby, G. (2005) 'The Varieties of Resource Experience: Natural Resource Export Structures and the Political Economy of Economic Growth', *The World Bank Economic Review* 19(2), pp. 141–174.

Islam, F and Sakib, S. (2019) 'Banks Fail to Bring Down Interest Rate to Single Digit', Prothom Alo, 4 December 2019, https://en.prothomalo.com/bangladesh/Banks-fail-to-bring-down-interest-rate-to-single.

Islam, M. and Siddique, M. (2010) 'A Profile of Bank Loan Defaulters in the Private Sector in Bangladesh', UPL, Dhaka.

Islam, M. A. (2019) 'A Comparative Study on Non-Performing Loans of Some Selected State-Owned and Private Commercial Banks in Bangladesh', PhD thesis, University of Dhaka, http://repository.library.du.ac.bd/bitstream/handle/123456789/321/Md.%20Ariful%20Islam.pdf?sequence=1&isAllowed=y.

Islam, M. R. (2014) 'Education and Economic Growth in Bangladesh – An Econometric Study', *IOSR Journal of Humanities and Social Science* 19(2), pp. 102–110.

Islam, R. (2014) 'Independence of the Judiciary – The Masdar Case', *The Daily Star*, 10 March 2014, www.thedailystar.net/independence-of-the-judiciary-the-masdar-case-14760.

Islam, R. (2017) 'Perceived Tension between Judiciary and Executive of Bangladesh', *The Daily Star*, 9 May 2017, www.thedailystar.net/law-our-rights/law-analysis/perceived-tension-between-judiciary-and-executive-bangladesh-1402672.

Islam, S. and Nesa, M. N. (2009) 'Fertility Transition in Bangladesh: The Role of Education', *Proceedings of the Pakistan Academy of Sciences* 46(4), pp. 195–201.

Islam, T. S., Wadud, M. A. and Islam, Q. B. T. (2007) 'Relationship between Education and GDP Growth: A Multivariate Causality Analysis for Bangladesh', *Economics Bulletin* 3(35), pp. 1–7.

Jahan, R. (1997) 'Genocide in Bangladesh', In: Totten, S., Parsons, W.S. and Charny, I.W. (eds.), *Century of Genocide: Eyewitness Accounts and Critical Views*, Garland, New York, pp. 291–316.

Jahan, R. (2018) 'Political Parties, Movements, Elections and Democracy in Bangladesh', Gyantapas Abdur Razzaq Distinguished Lecture.

Jalil, A. (2010) 'War Crimes Trial in Bangladesh: A Real Political Vendetta', *Journal of Politics and Law* 3(2) pp. 110–120.

Joarder, M. and Munim, A. (2011) 'Fiscal Capacity and Multiple-Equilibria of Corruption: Cross-country Evidence', *Journal of International Development* 24(1), pp. 34–60.

Johansen, S. (1991) 'Estimation and Hypothesis Testing of Cointegration Vectors in Gaussian Vector Autoregressive Models'. *Econometrica* 59, pp. 1551.

John, J. J. (2006) 'The Political Economy of Taxation and Tax Reform in Developing Countries', Research Paper No. 2006/74, United Nations University, World Institute for Development University Research.

Judicial Portal Bangladesh (no date) www.judiciary.org.bd/en/judiciary/history-of-judiciary [Accessed on 23 March 2019].

Junquera-Varela, R. F., Awasthi, R., Balabushko, O. and Nurshaikova, A. (2019) 'Thinking Strategically about Revenue Administration Reform: The Creation of Integrated, Autonomous Revenue Authorities', Discussion Paper No. 4, Global Practice, The World Bank.

Kabeer, N. and Mahmud, S. (2004) 'Globalisation, Gender and Poverty: Bangladeshi Women Workers in Export and Local Markets', *Journal of International Development* 16(1), pp. 93–109.

Kathuria, S. and Malouche, M. M. (2016) 'Toward New Sources of Competitiveness in Bangladesh, Key Findings of the Diagnostic Trade Integration Study', the World Bank Group and the Government of the People's Republic of Bangladesh.

Kathuria, S., Martin, W. and Bhardwaj, A. (2001) 'Implications for South Asian Countries of Abolishing the Multifibre Agreement', World Bank Policy Research Working Paper 2721.

Kaufmann, D. and Kraay, A. (2008) 'Governance Indicators: Where Are We, Where Should We Be Going?', *World bank Research Observer* 23(1), pp. 1–30.

Kee, H. (2015) 'Local Intermediate Inputs and the Shared Supplier Spillovers from of Foreign Direct Investment', *Journal of Development Economics* 112, pp. 56–71.

Khan, M. (2006) 'Determinants of Corruption in Developing Countries: The Limits of Conventional Economic Analysis', In: *International Handbook on the Economics of Corruption*, Edward Elgar, Cheltenham, pp. 216–244.

Khan, M. (2010) *Political Settlements and the Governance of Growth-Enhancing Institutions*, School of Oriental and African Studies, University of London.

Khan, M. (2012a) 'Governance and Growth: History, Ideology and Methods of Proof.' In: Noman, A., Botchwey, K., Stein, H. and Stiglitz, J. (eds.), *Good Growth and Governance in Africa: Rethinking Development Strategies*, Oxford University Press, Oxford, pp. 51–79.

Khan, M. (2012b) 'Technological Upgrading in Bangladeshi Manufacturing: Governance Constraints and Policy Responses in the Ready-Made Garments Industry', School of Oriental and African Studies, University of London.

Khan, M. (2018) 'Political Settlements and the Analysis of Institutions', *African Affairs* 117(469), pp. 636–655.

Khan, M. M. (2008) 'Functioning of Local Government (Union Parishad): Legal and Practical Constraints', Democracy Watch, RTI International, USAID.

Khan, S. (2019) 'Strategic Vision for Land Reform', *The Financial Express*, 26 March 2019, https://thefinancialexpress.com.bd/views/strategic-vision-for-land-reform-1553357258.

Khanam, F. A., Hassan, K., Mawla, A. H. M. and Khan, R. S. (2013) 'Management of Non-Performing Loans (NPLs) of Banks in Bangladesh – An Evaluative Study', *Journal of Economics and Finance* 1(3), pp. 1–15.

Khatun, F. (2018) 'Banking Sector in Bangladesh: Moving from Diagnosis to Action', a presentation at the seminar organised by the Centre for Policy Dialogue on 8 December 2018, Dhaka.

Khuda, B. E. (2019) 'Economic Growth in Bangladesh and the Role of Banking Sector', *The Financial Express*, January 2019, https://thefinancialexpress.com.bd/views/views/economic-growth-in-bangladesh-and-the-role-of-banking-sector-1547220114.

Khudri, M. M. and Chowdhury, F. (2013) 'Evaluation of Socio-economic Status of Households and Identifying Key Determinants of Poverty in Bangladesh', *European Journal of Social Sciences* 37(3), pp. 377–387.

Kim, J., Traore, M. K. and Warfield, C. (2006) 'The Textile and Apparel Industry in Developing Countries', *Textile Progress* 38(3), pp. 1–64. DOI: 10.1533/tepr.2006.0003.

Knack, S. and Keefer, P. (1995). 'Institutions and Economic Performance: Cross-Country Tests Using Alternative Institutional Measures', *Economics and Politics, Wiley Blackwell*, 7(3), pp. 207–227.

Kneer, C. (2013a) 'Finance as a Magnet for the Best and Brightest: Implications for the Real Economy', DNB Working Paper 392.

Kneer, C. (2013b) 'The Absorption of Talent into Finance: Evidence from U.S. Banking Deregulation', DNB Working Paper 391.

Kochanek, S (2003) 'The Informal Political Process in Bangladesh', Report Prepared for DFID, UK High Commission, Dhaka, Bangladesh.

Kraft, M.A., Blazar, D., Hogan, D. (2018). The Effect of Teaching Coaching on Instruction and Achievement: A Meta-analysis of the Causal Evidence. *Review of Educational Research* 88(4), pp. 547–588.

Kremer, M., Muralidharan, K., Chaudhury, N., Rogers, F. H. and Hammer, J. (2005) 'Teacher Absence in India: A Snapshot', *Journal of the European Economic Association*, April–May 2005, 3(2–3), pp. 658–667.

Kuncic, A. (2014) 'Institutional Quality Data Set', *Journal of Institutional Economics* 10(1), pp. 135–161.

LANDac (2016) 'Land Governance for Equitable and Sustainable Development: Food Security and Land Governance Factsheet Bangladesh', LANDac, Utrecht University, The Netherlands.

Lata, R. S. (2015) 'Non-Performing Loan and Profitability: The Case of State Owned Commercial Banks in Bangladesh', *World Review of Business Research* 5(3), pp. 171–182.

Law and Justice Division (2019) 'History (About us)', Law and Justice Division, Ministry of Law, Justice and Parliamentary Affairs of the Government of the People's Republic of Bangladesh, www.lawjusticediv.gov.bd/site/page/c99cfd23-8949-4e3d-92da-a8223cfc5045/History [Accessed on 25 December 2019].

Leite, S. R. and Sundararajan, V. (1990) 'Issues in Interest Rate Management and Liberalization', Staff Papers 37, pp. 735–752, IMF.

Lewis, A. (1954) 'Economic Development with Unlimited Supplies of Labour', *The Manchester School* 22(2), pp. 139–191.

Lewis, D. (2011) *Bangladesh: Politics, Economy and Civil Society*, Cambridge University Press, Cambridge.

Love, J. (1986) 'Commodity Concentration and Export Earnings Instability: A Shift from Cross-section to Time Series Analysis', *Journal of Development Economics* 24, pp. 239–248, http://dx.doi.org/10.1016/0304-3878(86)90090-8.

Lu, S. (2016) 'Minimum Wage in the Apparel Industry Continues to Rise in Most Asian Countries in 2016', Blog article. Department of Fashion & Apparel Studies, University of Delaware.

Luintel, K. B., Khan, M, Arestis, P and Theodoridis, K. (2008) 'Financial Structure and Economic Growth'. *Journal of Development Economics* 86, pp. 181–200.

Lyon, S. M. (2019) *Political Kinship in Pakistan*, Lexington Books, London and New York.

Mahanta, A. (2016) 'Impact of Education on Fertility: Evidence from a Tribal Society in Assam, India', *International Journal of Population Research*, vol 2016 (article ID 3153685), https://doi.org/10.1155/2016/3153685.

Mahmud, S. (2003) 'Female Secondary School Stipend Programme in Bangladesh', Paper commissioned for the EFA Global Monitoring Report 2003/4, The Leap to Equality, United Nations Educational, Scientific and Cultural Organization (UNESCO).

Mahmud, S. and Ara, J. (2015) 'Corporate Governance Practices in Bangladesh: An Overview of Its Present Scenario in Banking Industry', *International Journal of Economics, Commerce and Management* III(12), pp. 408–425.

Mahmud, W. (2020) 'The Bangladesh Surprise Explained: Making Progress Amid Poor Governance', The Business Standard, https://tbsnews.net/analysis/bangladesh-surprise-explained-37887.

Mahmud, W., Ahmed, S. and Mahajan, S. (2008) 'Economic Reform, Growth, and Governance: The Political Economy Aspects of Bangladesh Development Surprise', Working Paper No. 22, World Bank.

MAINTAINS (2021) 'Towards Shock-Responsive Social Protection Systems: Lessons from the COVID-19 Response in Bangladesh', kvgkmaintains-bangaldesh-brief-4pp-v2-final.pdf (opml.co.uk).

Maitra, B. and Mukhopadhyay, C. K. (2012) 'Public Spending on Education, Health Care and Economic Growth in Selected Countries of Asia and the Pacific', *Asia-Pacific Development Journal* 19(2), pp. 19–48.

Majumder, S. and Biswas, S. C. (2017) 'The Role of Education in Poverty Alleviation: Evidence from Bangladesh', *Journal of Economics and Sustainable Development* 8(20), pp. 151–160.

Mallick, L., Das, P. K. and Pradhan, K. C. (2016) 'Impact of Educational Expenditure on Economic Growth in Major Asian Countries: Evidence from Econometric Analysis', *Theoretical and Applied Economics* 23(2), pp. 173–186.

Maniruzzaman, T. (1975) 'Bangladesh: An Unfinished Revolution?' *The Journal of Asian Studies* 34(4), p. 891. DOI: 10.2307/2054506.

Mansur, A. (2015) 'Financial Market Developments and Challenges', background paper of the 7th Five Year Plan, Government of Bangladesh, Dhaka.

Mansur, A., Yunus, M. and Nandi, B. K. (2011) 'An Evaluation of the Tax System in Bangladesh', Policy Research Institute of Bangladesh, draft paper.

Martin, N. (2016) *Politics, Landlords and Islam in Pakistan*, Routledge, London.

McDevitt, A. (2015) 'Bangladesh: Overview of Corruption and Anti-corruption with a Focus on the Health Sector', Transparency International, Berlin, Germany.

McKinnon, R. I. (1973) *Money and Capital in Economic Development*, Brookings Institution, Washington, DC.

McMillan, M. and Rodrik, D. (2011) 'Globalization, Structural Change and Productivity Growth', NBER Working Paper No. 17143, The National Bureau of Economic Research, Cambridge.

Meager, R. (2019) 'Understanding the Average Impact of Microcredit Expansions: A Bayesian Hierarchical Analysis of Seven Randomized Experiments', *American Economic Journal: Applied Economics* 11(1), pp. 57–91.

Mehmood, S. and Seror, A. (2019) 'Judicial Independence, Religion, and Politics: Theory and Evidence', Economic Development and Institutions Working Paper, Oxford Policy Management and Paris School of Economics.

Melo, J. de and Olarreaga, M. (2020) 'Trade-Related Institutions and Development', In: Baland, J-M, Bourguignon, F., Platteau, J-P. and Verdier, T. (eds.). *Handbook of Development and Institutions*, Princeton University Press, Princeton, pp. 255–307.

Melo, J. de and Twun, A. (2020) 'Supply Chain Trade in East Africa: Prospects and Challenges', www.theigc.org/wp-content/uploads/2020/02/Melo-and-Twum-Final-Report-2020.pdf.

Menzel, A. and Woodruff, C. (2019) 'Gender Wage Gaps and Worker Mobility: Evidence from the Garment Sector in Bangladesh', Working Paper 25982, National Bureau of Economic Research, www.nber.org/papers/w25982.

Mercan, M. Reisman, A., Yolalan, R. and Emel, A. B. (2003) 'The Effect of Scale and Mode of Ownership on the Financial Performance of the Turkish Banking Sector: Results of a DEA-Based Analysis', *Socio-Economic Planning Sciences* 37(3), September 2003, pp. 185–202.

Mercer-Blackman, V. (2016) 'Why Bangladesh's Garments Won't Go "Haute Couture" (I)', *Asian Development Blog*, https://blogs.adb.org/blog/why-bangladeshs-garments-won-t-go-haute-couture-i.

Mian, A. (2006) 'Distance Constraints: The Limits of Foreign Lending in Poor Economies', *Journal of Finance* 61, pp. 1465–1505.

Ministry of Education (2010) 'National Education Policy 2010', Ministry of Education, Dhaka, Bangladesh.

Ministry of Finance (2019) *Bangladesh Economic Review*, Ministry of Finance, https://mof.portal.gov.bd/sites/default/files/files/mof.portal.gov.bd/page/f2d8fabb_29c1_423a_9d37_cdb500260002/D.%20Appendices%20%28English-2019%29.pdf.

Mirdha, R. U. (2018) 'Bangladesh Still Popular for Low-Cost Apparel', *The Daily Star*, 23 April 2018, www.thedailystar.net/business/bangladesh-still-popular-low-cost-apparel-1566334.

MJF (2015) 'Rural Land Market in Bangladesh: A Situation Analysis', MJF, Uttaran, and CARE Bangladesh, *The Daily Star*, www.thedailystar.net/rural-land-market-in-bangladesh-a-situation-analysis-61897.

Mohmand, S. K. (2019) *Crafty Oligarchs, Savvy Voters: Democracy under Inequality in Rural Pakistan*, Cambridge University Press, Cambridge.

Mollah, A. H. (2019) 'War Crimes Trials in Bangladesh: Justice or Politics?', *Journal of Asian and African Studies* 1(14). DOI: 10.1177/0021909619890117.

Mollah, M. A. H. (2010) 'Does the Judiciary Matter for Accountability of Administration in Bangladesh?', *International Journal of Law and Management* 52(4), pp. 309–331.

Monem, M. (2008) 'The Politics of Privatization in Bangladesh', OSDER, Dhaka, Bangladesh.

Montenegro, C. E. and Patrinos, H. A. (2014) 'Comparable Estimates of Returns to Schooling around the World', World Bank Policy Research Working Paper No. 7020, The World Bank, Washington, DC.

Muhammad, A. (2011) 'Wealth and Deprivation: Ready-Made Garments Industry in Bangladesh', *Economic and Political Weekly* 46(34), pp. 23–27.

Muralidharan, K. and Sundararaman, V. (2011) 'Teacher Performance Pay: Experimental Evidence from India', *Journal of Political Economy* 119(1), pp. 39–77.

NAPE (2018) 'Identifying the Reading Ability of Bangla of Class Four Students in Government Primary Schools in Bangladesh', National Academy for Primary Education, Dhaka.

Narayan, P.K. (2004) 'Reformulating Critical Values for the Bounds F-Statistics Approach to Cointegration: An Application to the Tourism Demand Model for Fiji'. Department of Economics, Discussion Papers, No.02/04, Monash University, Victoria 3800, Australia.

NBR (2011) *Outline of Modernization Plan (2011–2016)*, Ministry of Finance, Government of Bangladesh, Dhaka.

NBR (2019) *Customs Modernization Strategic Action Plan 2019–2022*, Ministry of Finance, Government of Bangladesh, Dhaka.

NCEE (2016). Empowered Educators. National Center for Education and the Economy. Policy Brief, http://ncee.org/wp-content/uploads/2017/02/CareerLadders PolicyBrief.pdf.

New Age (2019) 'GDP Growth Doubted, Quality Questioned', *New Age*, 10 June 2019, www.newagebd.net/article/74842/gdp-growth-doubted-quality-questioned.

Nguyen, C. and Ali, M. M. (2011) 'The Current State of the Financial Sector of Bangladesh: An Analysis', AIUB Business and Economics Working Paper Series, AIUB-BUS-ECON-2011–03.

Nguyen, L. P. (2015) 'The Impact of Institutional Quality on Tax Revenue in Developing Countries', *Asian Journal of Empirical Research* 5(10), pp. 181–195.

Niroula, G. S. and Thapa, G. B. (2005) 'Impacts and Causes of Land Fragmentation, and Lessons Learned from Land Consolidation in South Asia', *Land Use Policy* 22(4), pp. 358–372.

North, D. (1990) *Institutions, Institutional Change and Economic Performance*, Cambridge University Press, Cambridge.

Nunn, N. and Trefler, D. (2014). 'Domestic Institutions as a Source of Comparative Advantage'. In: Gopinath G, Helpman E, Rogoff K. *Handbook of International Economics*. Vol. 4. North Holland. pp. 263–315.

OECD (2013) 'What Makes Civil Justice Effective?', OECD Economics Department Policy Notes, No. 18 June 2013 and 'The Economics of Civil Justice: New Cross-Country Data and Empirics', OECD Economics Department Working Papers No. 1060.

OECD (2015) *Government at a Glance*, OECD Publishing, Paris.

OECD-OSF (2016) 'Leveraging the SDGs for Inclusive Growth: Delivering Access to Justice for All', Organisation for Economic Co-operation and Development (OECD) and Open Society Foundations (OSF), Paris, www.oecd.org/gov/delivering-access-to-justice-for-all.pdf.

Osmani, S. R. and Sen, B. (2011) 'Inequality in Rural Bangladesh in the 2000s: Trends and Causes', *Bangladesh Development Studies* 34(4), pp. 1–36

Oxfam (2017) *What She Makes: Power and Poverty in the Fashion Industry*, Oxfam Australia, Melbourne.

Pack, H. and Saggi, K. (2006) 'Is There a Case for Industrial Policy? A Critical Survey', *The World Bank Research Observer* 21, pp. 267–297.

Pack, H. and Westphal, L. (1986) 'Industrial Strategy and Technological Change', *Journal of Development Economics* 22, pp. 87–128.

Papageorgiou, C. (2003) 'Distinguishing between the Effects of Primary and Post-primary Education on Economic Growth', *Review of Development Economics* 7(4), pp. 622–635.

Parry, S. (2016) 'The True Cost of Your Cheap Clothes: Slave Wages for Bangladesh Factory Workers', *South China Morning Post*, 11 June 2016, www.scmp.com/magazines/post-magazine/article/1970431/true-cost-your-cheap-clothes-slave-wages-bangladesh-factory.

Paul, B. P. (2017) 'A Fair Recruitment Policy for a Stronger Government', *The Daily Star*, www.thedailystar.net/opinion/fair-recruitment-policy-stronger-government-1472953.

Perera, T. (2010) 'Implementing Land Registration Systems in Sri Lanka, Being Pragmatic, Sri Lanka', *Journal of Real Estate*, Department of Estate Management and Valuation, University of Sri Jayewardenepura, pp. 74–96. https://journals.sjp.ac.lk/index.php/SLJRE/article/view/114

Pesaran, M.H. and Shin, Y. (1999) 'An Autoregressive Distributed Lag Modelling Approach to Cointegration Analysis.' In: Strom, S., (ed.), *Chapter 11 in Econometrics and Economic Theory in the 20th Century the Ragnar Frisch Centennial Symposium*, Cambridge University Press, Cambridge, pp. 371–413.

Platteau, J. P. (1992) *Land Reform and Structural Adjustment in SubSaharan Africa: Controversies and Guidelines*, FAO, Rome.

Platteau, J. P. (2000) *Institutions, Social Norms and Economic Development*, Harwood Publishers by Routledge, London.

Popov, A. (2018) 'Evidence on Finance and Economic Growth', In: Beck, T. and Levine, R. (eds.), *Handbook of Finance and Development*, Edward Elgar, Cheltenham, UK, pp. 63–104.

Popova, A., Evans, D. K., Breeding, M. E. and Arancibia, V. (2018) 'Teacher Professional Development around the World: The Gap between Evidence and Practice', Policy Research Working Paper No. 8572, The World Bank.

PRI (2013) *NBR Diagnostic Report: Reforming the Research and Statistics Department*, Policy Research Institute, Dhaka.

PricewaterhouseCoopers (2019) 'Destination Bangladesh', PricewaterhouseCoopers Bangladesh, www.pwc.com/bd/en/assets/pdfs/research-insights/2019/destination-bangladesh.pdf.

Prichard, W. (2010) *Taxation and State Building: Towards a Governance Focused Tax Reform Agenda*, Institute of Development Studies, Sussex.

Pritchett, L., Sen, K. and Werker, E. (2018) 'An Introduction to the Conceptual Framework', In: Pritchett, L., Sen, K. and Werker, E. (eds.), *Deals and Development: The Political Dynamics of Growth Episodes*, Oxford University Press, pp. 1–38.

Psacharopoulos, G. and Patrinos, H. A. (2004) 'Returns to Investment in Education: A Further Update', *Education Economics* 12(2), pp. 111–134.

Psacharopoulos, G. and Woodhall, M. (1985) *Education for Development: An Analysis of Investment Choices*, Oxford University Press, New York, USA.

Rahman, A. (2018a) *From Ashes to Prosperity, A Commentary on the Society and Economy of Bangladesh*, Aloghar Prakashana, Dhaka.

Rahman, A. (2018b) 'State of Lower Court Performance in Bangladesh: Insights from an Empirical Examination', Policy Research Institute of Bangladesh Working Paper, Dhaka.

Rahman, B. (2017) 'Access of the Landless to *Khas* Land in Eradicating Poverty', *The Daily Sun*, 9 October 2017, www.daily-sun.com/post/260407/Access-of-the-Landless-to-Khas-Land-in-Eradicating-Poverty-.

Rahman, H. Z. (2011) 'Urban Bangladesh: Challenges of Transition', Power and Participation Research Centre, Dhaka.

Rahman, M. and Al-Hasan, M. (2018) 'Returns to Schooling in Bangladesh Revisited: An Instrumental Variable Quantile Regression Approach', *Bangladesh Development Studies Journal* 41 (2), pp. 27–42.

Rahman, M., Bhattacharya, D. and Al-Hasan, M. D. (2019) 'Dimensions of Informality in Bangladesh Labour Market and the Consequent Wage Penalty', *South Asia Economic Journal* 20(2), pp. 224–247.

Rahman, M. M., Hamid, M. K. and Khan, M. A. M. (2015) 'Determinants of Bank Profitability: Empirical Evidence from Bangladesh', *International Journal of Business and Management* 10(8), p. 135.

Rahman, S. and Rahman, M. (2009) 'Impact of Land Fragmentation and Resource Ownership on Productivity and Efficiency: The Case of Rice Producers in Bangladesh', *Land Use Policy* 26(1), pp. 95–103.

Rahman, S. H. (1994) 'Trade and Industrialization in Bangladesh', In: Helliner, G. K. (ed.), *Trade and Industrialisation in Turbulent Times*, Routledge, London, pp. 259–291.

Rahman, S. H. and Talukder, S. K. (2016) 'The Costs and Benefits of Digitization of Land Records via Simplified Application Process', Bangladesh Priorities, Copenhagen Consensus Center, www.copenhagenconsensus.com/sites/default/files/rahman_talukder_land_digitization.pdf.

Rahman, Z. (2015) 'Export Development Fund Facility: Some Sectors Allege Bias', *The Financial Express*, 26 August 2015.

Raihan, S. (2007) *Dynamics of Trade Liberalisation in Bangladesh: Analyses of Policies and Practices*, Pathak Samabesh, Dhaka.

Raihan, S. (2015) 'From "Good-Enough" Jobs to "Decent" Jobs", *The Daily Star,* 25 May 2015, www.thedailystar.net/op-ed/economics/good-enough-jobs-decent-jobs-86704.

Raihan, S. (2016) 'How to Make Special Economic Zones Successful', *The Daily Star,* 5 December 2016, www.thedailystar.net/op-ed/economics/how-make-special-economic-zones-successful-1325266.

Raihan, S. (2018a) 'Is LDC Graduation a Panacea?' *The Daily Star,* 5 April 2018, www.thedailystar.net/opinion/economics/ldc-graduation-panacea-1558234.

Raihan, S. (2018b) 'Structural Change in Bangladesh: Challenges for Growth and Employment Creation', In: Raihan, S. (ed.), *Structural Change and Dynamics of Labor Markets in Bangladesh. South Asia Economic and Policy Studies.* Springer, Singapore.

Raihan, S. (2019a) 'Economy-Wide Implications of Bangladesh's Graduation from the LDC Status', Paper prepared for the Planning Commission of Bangladesh.

Raihan, S. (2019b) 'Prioritise Investment in Human Capital', *The Daily Star*, www.thedailystar.net/opinion/economics/news/prioritise-investment-human-capital-1741192.

Raihan, S. (2020) Health Sector Faces 'Policy Paralysis', *The Business Standard*, www.tbsnews.net/analysis/health-sector-faces-policy-paralysis-100708.

Raihan, S. and Ahmed, M. (2016) 'Spatial Divergence of Primary Education Development in Bangladesh through the Lens of Education Development Index (EDI)', Paper prepared for the UK Department For International Development Bangladesh.

Raihan, S. and Bidisha, S. H. (2018) 'Female Employment Stagnation in Bangladesh', EDIG Research Paper, Overseas Development Institute, The Asia Foundation and UKaid, London.

Raihan, S. and Razzaque, A. (2007) 'A Review of the Evolution of Trade and Industrial Policies in Bangladesh', In: *Trade and Industrial Policy Environment in Bangladesh with Special Emphasis on Some Non-Traditional Export Sectors*, Pathak Samabesh, Dhaka, pp. 24–62.

Raihan, S. and Uddin, M. (2018) 'How Do Education and Skill Development Affect the Transition from "Good-Enough" Job to "Decent" Job?' In: Raihan, S. (ed.) *Structural Change and Dynamics of Labor Markets in Bangladesh*, Springer, Singapore, pp. 122–140.

Raihan, S., Fatehin, S. and Haque, I. (2009) 'Access to Land and Other Natural Resources by the Rural Poor: The Case of Bangladesh', Centre on Integrated Rural Development for Asia and the Pacific (CIRDAP).

Raihan, S., Siddiqui, T. and Mahmood, R. (2017a) 'Estimating the Impact of International Remittance on Households Expenditure in Bangladesh', Chapter 7 in *South Asia* Migration Report 2017, Routledge India.

Raihan, S., Lemma, A., Khondker, B. H. and Ferdous, F. (2017c) 'Bangladesh Sectoral Growth Diagnostic: A Research Paper on Economic Dialogue on Inclusive Growth in Bangladesh', UKaid and Overseas Development Institute.

Raihan, S., Osmani, S. R. and Baqui Khalily, M. A. (2017b) 'The Macro Impact of Microfinance in Bangladesh: A CGE Analysis', *Economic Modelling* 62, pp. 1–15.

Raihan, S., Uddin, M., Ahmed, M. T. and Hossain, I. (2021b) *COVID-19 and Business Confidence in Bangladesh: Findings from the 5th Round of Nationwide Firm-level Survey in July 2021.* SANEM Publications, Dhaka.

Raihan, S., Uddin, M., Ahmed, M. T., Nahar, M. A. and Sharmin, E. (2021a) 'COVID-19 Fallout on Poverty and Livelihoods in Bangladesh: Results from SANEM's Nation-wide Household Survey (November–December 2020)', SANEM Publications, Dhaka.

Rana, E. A. and Wahid, A. N. M. (2016) 'Fiscal Deficit and Economic Growth in Bangladesh', *The American Economist* 62(1), pp. 31–42. DOI:10.1177/0569434516672778.

Rao, B. B., Singh, R. and Kumar, S. (2008) 'Do we need time series econometrics?', *Applied Economics Letters.* DOI: 10.1080/13504850802297889.

Raquib, A. (1999) 'Financial Sector Reform in Bangladesh: An Evaluation', Bank Porikroma XXIV (3 and 4).

Rashid, M. (2008) 'Bad Governance and Good Success', In: *Bangladesh Institute of Development A Ship Adrift: Governance and Development in Bangladesh Studies*, Dhaka.

Rashiduzzaman, M. (1977) 'Changing Political Patterns in Bangladesh: Internal Constraints and External Fears', *Asian Survey* 17(9), pp. 793–808.

Ravaillon, M. (2005) 'Looking beyond Averages in the Trade and Poverty Debate, Wider Research Paper #2005/29, Helsinki.

Razzaque, A. and Raihan, S. (2007) 'Anti-Export Bias and Trade Policy Options for Bangladesh', In: *Trade and Industrial Policy Environment in Bangladesh with Special Emphasis on Some Non-Traditional Export Sectors*, Pathak Samabesh, Dhaka, pp. 63–86.

Razzaque, M. A., Khondker, B. H. and Eusuf, A. (2018) 'Promoting Inclusive Growth in Bangladesh through Special Economic Zones', *The Asia Foundation*, http://hdl .handle.net/11540/9324.

Riaz, A. (2016) *Bangladesh: A Political History since Independence*, I.B. Tauris, New York.

Ricciuti, R., Savoia, A. and Sen, K. (2019) 'How Do Political Institutions Affect Fiscal Capacity? Explaining Taxation in Developing Economies', *Journal of Institutional Economics* 15(2), pp. 351–380.

Robin, I., Salim, R. and Bloch, H. (2017) 'Cost Efficiency in Bangladesh Banking: Does Financial Reform Matter?', *Applied Economics* 50(8), pp. 891–904.

Rodrik, D. (2004) 'Industrial Policy for the 21st Century', Discussion Paper No. 4767, Center for Economic Policy Research, London.

Rodrik, D. (2005) 'Growth Strategies', In: Aghion, P. and Durlauf, S.N. (eds.), *Handbook of Economic Growth*, North-Holland, Amsterdam, pp. 967–1014.

Rodrik, D. (2008) 'Industrial Policy: Don't Ask Why, Ask How', *Middle East Development Journal* 1(1), pp. 1–29. http://dx.doi.org/10.2139/ssrn.617544.

Rodrik, D. (2009) 'The Real Exchange Rate and Economic Growth', Brookings Papers on Economic Activity, Spring, pp. 365–439.

Rodrik, D., Subramanian, A. and Trebbi, F. (2004) 'Institutions Rule: The Primacy of Institutions over Geography and Integration in Economic Development', *Journal of Economic Growth* 9(2), pp. 131–165.

Roe, M. (1994) *Strong Managers, Weak Owners: The Political Roots of American Corporate Finance*, Princeton University Press, Princeton.

Romer, P. M. (1992) 'Two Strategies for Economic Development: Using Ideas and Producing Ideas', *The World Bank Economic Review* 6(1), pp. 63–91, https://doi .org/10.1093/wber/6.suppl_1.63.

Roy, D. (2015) 'The Office of the Comptroller and Auditor General: Governance Challenges and Way Forward', Transparency International Bangladesh, Dhaka.

Rudi, L., Azadi, H., Witlox, F. and Lebailly, P. (2014) 'Land Rights as an Engine of Growth? An Analysis of Cambodian Land Grabs in the Context of Development Theory', *Land Use Policy* 38, pp. 564–572.

Sachs, J. and Warner, A. (1995) 'Economic Reform and the Process of Global Integration', *Brookings Papers on Economic Activity* 1, pp. 1–118.

Sarkar, A. (2015) 'Case Backlog Piling Up', *The Daily Star*, 22 March 2015, www .thedailystar.net/case-management-system-to-reduce-case-backlog-58616 [Accessed on 24 December 2019].

Sarkar, A. (2017) 'One Judge, 2,000 Cases', *The Daily Star*, 9 September 2017, www .thedailystar.net/case-management-system-to-reduce-case-backlog-58616 [Accessed on 24 December 2019].

Sarwar, M. R. (2015) 'Bangladesh Health Service Delivery: Innovative NGO and Private Sector Partnerships', *IDS Bulletin* 46(3), Institute of Development Studies, John Wiley & Sons Ltd, Oxford.

Sattar, Z. and Shareef, S. (2019) 'Exchange Rate Undervaluation, Exports and Growth', *The Financial Express*, 24 April 2019, www.thefinancialexpress.com.bd/views/ exchange-rate-undervaluation-exports-and-growth-1556118508.

Sattar, Z. (2019) 'State of Bangladesh Trade Regime and Trade Policy: The Way Forward', presented at the SANEM seminar, Dhaka.

Semedi, P. and Bakker, L. (2014) 'Between Land Grabbing and Farmers' Benefits: Land Transfers in West Kalimantan, Indonesia', *The Asia Pacific Journal of Anthropology* 15(4), pp. 376–390.

Sen, B. (2018) 'The Rise of Landless Tenancy in Rural Bangladesh: Analysis of the Recent Evidence', presentation made at the BIDS Research Almanac 2018, pp. 11–12.

Sen, B. and Rahman, M. (2016) 'Earnings Inequality, Returns to Education and Demand for Schooling: Addressing Human Capital for Accelerated Growth', background paper for the Seventh Five Year Plan of Bangladesh. The Planning Commission of Bangladesh, Dhaka.

Sen, B., Ahmed, M., Yunus, M. and Ali, Z. (2014) 'Regional Inequality in Bangladesh in the 2000s: Revisiting the East-West Divide Debate', BIDS-REF Study Series No. 14-01, Bangladesh Institute of Development Studies.

Shafi, S. A. (2007) 'Land Tenure Security and Land Administration in Bangladesh', final report of the Local Partnerships for Urban Poverty Alleviation Project of LGED, UNDP, and UN-Habitat.

Sharif, S. and Esa, A. J. (2014) 'Dynamics of Land Price and Land Use Change: A Case of Savar Municipality, Bangladesh', *Journal of South Asian Studies* 02(01), pp. 83–89.

Sharma, A. and Panagiotidis, T. (2004) 'An Analysis of Exports and Growth in India: Cointegration and Causality Evidence (1971–2001)', *Review of Development Economics* 9, pp. 232–248.

Shaw, L. (1973) *Financial Deepening in Economic Development*, Oxford University Press, New York.

Sida (2008) 'Land Administration – Why', Swedish National Land Survey, Department for Infrastructure and Economic Cooperation, Swedish International Development Cooperation Agency.

Siddiqui, K. (1997) *Land Management in South Asia: A Comparative Study*, Oxford University Press, Karachi.

Sobhan, R. (1990) 'The Political Economy of South Asian Economic Cooperation', *Bangladesh Journal of Political Economy* 10(1), pp. 26–48.

Sobhan, R. (ed.) (1991) *The Decade of Stagnation: The State of the Bangladesh Economy in the 1980s*, University Press Limited, Dhaka.

Sobhan, R. and Mahmood, S. A. (1981) 'Repayment of Loans to Specialised Financial Institutions in Bangladesh: Issues and Constraints', *The Bangladesh Development Studies* 9(1) (Winter 1981), pp. 35–75.

Steer, L., Rabbani, F. and Parker, A. (2014) 'Primary Education Finance for Equity and Quality: An Analysis of Past Success and Future Options in Bangladesh', Brookings Institution, Washington, DC, USA.

Stiglitz, J. E., Lin, J. Y. and Patel, E. (2013) *The Industrial Policy Revolution II – Africa in the Twenty-First Century*, Palgrave Macmillan, London.

Suhardiman, D., Giordano, M., Keovilignavong, O. and Sotoukee, T. (2015) 'Revealing the Hidden Effects of Land Grabbing through Better Understanding of Farmers' Strategies in Dealing with Land Loss', *Land Use Policy* 49, pp. 195–202.

Suykens, B. (2015) 'The Land that Disappeared: Forceful Occupation, Disputes and the Negotiation of Landlord Power in a Bangladeshi Bastee', *Development and Change* 46(3), pp. 486–507. DOI: 10.1111/dech.12165.

Svensson, J. (2005) 'Eight Questions about Corruption', *Journal of Economic Perspectives* 19(3), pp. 19–42.

Tahura, U. and Kelly, M. R. (2015) 'Procedural Experiences from the Civil Courts of Bangladesh: Case Management as a Potential Means of Reducing Backlogs', *Australian Journal of Asian Law* 16(1), pp. 75–96.

Tahura, U. S. (2015) 'Case Management System to Reduce Case Backlog', *The Daily Star*, 6 January 2015, www.thedailystar.net/case-management-system-to-reduce-case-backlog-58616 [Accessed on 24 December 2019].

Tanzi, V. and Zee, H (2001) 'Tax Policy for Emerging Markets', IMF Staff Working Paper 00/35, IMF, Washington, DC.

Tasmin, F. (2017) 'Politicized Civil Society in Bangladesh: Case Study Analyses', *Cosmopolitan Civil Societies: An Interdisciplinary Journal* 9(1), pp. 98–123.

The Daily Star (2018a) 'WB Doubts 7.65pc GDP Growth Estimate', *The Daily Star*, 10 April 2018, www.thedailystar.net/business/banking/wb-doubts-765pc-gdp-growth-estimate-1560541.

The Daily Star (2018b) 'BB Steps in to Clear Backlog of Cases', *The Daily Star*, 20 December 2018, www.thedailystar.net/case-management-system-to-reduce-case-backlog-58616 [Accessed on 24 December 2019].

The Daily Star (2018c) 'Independence of Judiciary Undermined, Separation of Power Violated by 3 "Cardinal Rules"', *The Daily Star*, 01 January 2018, www.thedailystar.net/country/independence-judiciary-separation-power-undermined-statement-6-eminent-jurists-bangladesh-bd-discipline-conduct-lower-court-judges-law-ministry-151342 [Accessed 25 December 2019].

The Daily Star (2019) 'CPD Doubts 8 Plus Growth this Fiscal', *The Daily Star*, 23 April 2019, www.thedailystar.net/business/cpd-doubts-bangladesh-gdp-growth-8-plus-in-2019-20-1733533.

The Justice Audit Team (2018) *National Justice Audit Bangladesh*, Government of Bangladesh; GIZ; UKAid and Bangladesh Bureau of Statistics, https://bangladesh.justiceaudit.org/library/.

The Supreme Court of Bangladesh (2019) 'Bangladesh Supreme Court – Annual Report 2018', http://supremecourt.gov.bd/resources/contents/Annual_Report_2018.pdf.

The Supreme Court of Bangladesh and UNDP (2015) 'Timely Justice for All in Bangladesh: A Challenge for Change – Court Processes, Problems and Solutions', Judicial Strengthening Project (JUST), UNDP, Bangladesh, www.undp.org/content/dam/bangladesh/docs/Projects/JUST/A%20Challenge%20For%20Change.pdf.

Transparency International (2020) *Corruption Perception Index 2019*, Transparency International, Berlin, Germany.

Transparency International Bangladesh (2014) *Health Sector: Governance Challenges and the Way Forward*, Transparency International Bangladesh, Dhaka, Bangladesh.

Transparency International Bangladesh (2015) *Land Management and Services in Bangladesh: Governance Challenges and Way Forward*, Transparency International Bangladesh, Dhaka, Bangladesh.

Transparency International Bangladesh (2017) *Subordinate Court System of Bangladesh: Governance Challenges and Ways Forward*, Transparency International Bangladesh, Dhaka, Bangladesh.

Tura, H. (2018) 'Land Rights and Land Grabbing in Oromia, Ethiopia', *Land Use Policy* 70, pp. 247–255.

Uddin, A. (2015) 'Politics of Secularism and the State of Religious Pluralism in Bangladesh', *Journal of South Asian and Middle Eastern Studies* 38(3), pp. 42–54.

Uddin, G., Shahbaz, M., Arouri, M. and Teulon, F. (2014) 'Financial Development and Poverty Reduction Nexus: A Cointegration and Causality Analysis in Bangladesh', *Economic Modelling* 36, pp. 405–412.

Uddin, N. (2017) 'Bangladesh: Generation, Education and Nation', In: Letchamanan, H. and Dhar, D. (eds.), *Education in South Asia and the Indian Ocean Islands*, Bloomsbury Academic, London, pp. 13–28.

Uddin, S. S. (2015) 'An Analysis of the Condition of Bangladesh Female RMG Workers', *South Asia Journal* 15(12). http://southasiajournal.net/an-analysis-of-the-condition-of-bangladesh-female-rmg-workers/#:~:text=Findings%20showed%20that%20around%2080,women%20workers%20often%20remain%20unpaid

UNCTAD (2013) 'World Investment Report 2013', UNCTAD, Geneva.

UNCTAD (2019) 'LDCs Report-2019: The Present and Future of External Development – Old Dependence, New Challenges', UNCTAD, Geneva.

UNDESA (2019) 'Ex ante Assessment of the Possible Impacts of the Graduation of Bangladesh from the Category of Least Developed Countries (LDCs)', Secretariat of the Committee for Development Policy, UNDESA.

UNDP (2019) 'Beyond Income, beyond Averages, beyond Today: Inequalities in Human Development in the 21st Century', Human Development Report, United Nations, New York.

UNDP and Government of Bangladesh (2019) *Activating Village Courts in Bangladesh Phase II Project*, www.villagecourts.org/ [Accessed on 04 April 2019].

UNESCO (2017) 'Accountability in Education: Meeting Our Commitments – Global Education Monitoring Report', United Nations Educational, Scientific and Cultural Organization, Paris, France.

United Nations (2019a) *World Urbanization Prospects: 2018 Revision*, United Nations, New York.

United Nations (2019b) UN-*SDGs, Goal 16*, www.un.org/sustainabledevelopment/peace-justice/ [Accessed on 12 December 2019].

USAID (2006) 'Meeting EFA: Bangladesh Rural Advancement Committee (BRAC) Primary Schools', www.epdc.org/sites/default/files/documents/BRAC%20Primary%20Schools.pdf.

Vincelette, G. and Koehler, F. (2009) 'Growth Accounting', World Bank, Kiev, Ukraine, http://siteresources.worldbank.org/INTDEBTDEPT/Resources/468980-1170954447788/3430000-1251993008368/UK20090827_01.pdf.

WEF (2018) 'The Global Competitiveness Report 2018', WEF, www.weforum.org/reports/the-global-competitveness-report-2018.

Westphal, L. (1990) 'Industrial Policy in an Export-Propelled Economy: Lessons from South Korea's Experience', *Journal of Economic Perspectives* 4(3), pp. 41–59.

Wijenayake, N. (2015) 'Corporate-LIS for Effective Land Administration of Sri Lanka, Sri Lanka', Journal of Real Estate, Department of Estate Management and Valuation, University of Sri Jayewardenepura, pp. 54–75.

WJP (2019) *The World Justice Project (WJP) – Rule of Law Index® Current and Historical Data Set*, available at https://worldjusticeproject.org/our-work/research-and-data/wjp-rule-law-index-2019/current-historical-data.

World Bank (1989) 'Bangladesh: Manufacturing Public Enterprise Reform'; Report No. 7654-BD; Asia Country Department 1, World Bank, Dhaka.

World Bank (1993) *The East Asian Miracle: Economic Growth and Public Policy*, Oxford University Press, London and New York.

World Bank (1999) 'Central Bank Technical Assistance Project, Bangladesh', World Bank.

World Bank (2007a) 'Bangladesh Strategy for Sustained Growth', World Bank, Dhaka.

World Bank (2007b) 'Bangladesh Strategy for Sustained Growth', Bangladesh Development Series Paper No. 18, The World Bank Office, Dhaka, Bangladesh.

World Bank (2007c) 'Governance and Growth: The Bangladesh Conundrum', in 'Bangladesh Strategy for Sustained Growth', Bangladesh Development Series, Paper No. 18, The World Bank Office, Dhaka, Bangladesh.

World Bank (2007d) 'Dhaka: Improving Living Conditions for the Urban Poor', World Bank, Sustainable Development Unit, South Asia Region.

World Bank (2010) 'Bangladesh Country Assistance Strategy 2011–2014', World Bank, Dhaka.

World Bank (2012) 'Bangladesh – Towards Accelerated, Inclusive and Sustainable Growth: Opportunities and Challenges. Volume 2. Main Report', World Bank, Washington, DC, https://openknowledge.worldbank.org/handle/10986/12121.

World Bank (2013) 'Seeding Fertile Ground: Education that Works for Bangladesh', Education Sector Review 80613, World Bank, Washington, DC.

World Bank (2016) 'Bangladesh SABER Country Report', World Bank, Washington, DC.

World Bank (2017) 'World Development Report 2017: Governance and the Law', The World Bank, Washington, DC.

World Bank (2018) 'World Development Report 2018: Learning to Realize Education's Promise', World Bank, Washington, DC, USA.

World Bank (2019) 'Graduate Employability of Affiliated Colleges: New Evidence from Bangladesh', Report No: AUS0000633, The World Bank, Washington, DC.

World Bank (2020a) *Trading for Development in the Age of Global Value Chains*, World Bank, Washington, DC.

World Bank (2020b) 'World Development Indicators Database', https://databank.worldbank.org/source/world-development-indicators.

World Health Organization and World Bank (2019) 'Global Monitoring Report on Financial Protection in Health 2019', World Health Organization and the International Bank for Reconstruction and Development/The World Bank.

Yang, Y. and Mlachila, M. (2007) 'The End of Textiles Quotas: A Case Study of the Impact on Bangladesh', *The Journal of Development Studies* 43(4), pp. 675–699. DOI: 10.1080/00220380701259939.

Yardley, J. (2013) 'Garment Trade Wields Power in Bangladesh', *The New York Times*, 24 July 2013, www.nytimes.com/2013/07/25/world/asia/garment-trade-wields-power-in-bangladesh.html.

Yasmin, T. (2016) 'The Illegalities of Enemy Turned Vested Property', *The Daily Star*, 27 September 2016, www.thedailystar.net/law-our-rights/the-illegalities-enemy-turned-vested-property-1290142 [Accessed on 15 October 2019].

Zahid, S. H. (2020) 'The Bank Interest Rate Puzzle', *The Financial Express*, 5 January 2020, https://thefinancialexpress.com.bd/views/the-bank-interest-rate-puzzle-1578240091.

Index

Footnotes are indicated by n. after the page number.